Handbook of Visual Languages for Instructional Design:
Theories and Practices

Luca Botturi
University of Lugano, Switzerland

S. Todd Stubbs
Brigham Young University, USA

INFORMATION SCIENCE REFERENCE

Hershey · New York

Acquisitions Editor:	Kristin Klinger
Development Editor:	Kristin Roth
Senior Managing Editor:	Jennifer Neidig
Managing Editor:	Sara Reed
Copy Editor:	Ashley Fails
Typesetter:	Michael Brehm
Cover Design:	Lisa Tosheff
Printed at:	Yurchak Printing Inc.

Published in the United States of America by
Information Science Reference (an imprint of IGI Global)
701 E. Chocolate Avenue, Suite 200
Hershey PA 17033
Tel: 717-533-8845
Fax: 717-533-8661
E-mail: cust@igi-global.com
Web site: http://www.igi-global.com

and in the United Kingdom by
Information Science Reference (an imprint of IGI Global)
3 Henrietta Street
Covent Garden
London WC2E 8LU
Tel: 44 20 7240 0856
Fax: 44 20 7379 0609
Web site: http://www.eurospanonline.com

Library of Congress Cataloging-in-Publication Data

Handbook of visual languages for instructional design : theories and practices / Luca Botturi & Todd Stubbs, editors.
     p. cm.
  Summary: "This book serves as a practical guide for integration of Instructional Design languages and notation systems into the practice of ID by presenting recent languages and notation systems, exploring the connection between use of ID languages and integration of technologies in education, and assessing the benefits and drawbacks of the use of ID languages in specific project settings"--Provided by publisher.
  Includes bibliographical references and index.
  ISBN-13: 978-1-59904-729-4 (hardcover)
  ISBN-13: 978-1-59904-731-7 (ebook)
 1. Instructional systems--Design--Handbooks, manuals, etc. 2. Visual programming languages (Computer science)--Handbooks, manuals, etc. I. Botturi, Luca. II. Stubbs, Todd.
  LB1028.38.H36 2008
  371.33--dc22
                        2007023444

British Cataloguing in Publication Data
A Cataloguing in Publication record for this book is available from the British Library.

All work contributed to this book set is original material. The views expressed in this book are those of the authors, but not necessarily of the publisher.

Table of Contents

Detailed Table of Contents vi

Preface xiv

Acknowledgment xxii

Section I
Foundations and Theory

Chapter I
Commodity, Firmness, and Delight: *Four* Modes of Instructional Design Practice /
Brad Hokanson, Charles Miller, and Simon Hooper 1

Chapter II
Translate to Communicate: Facilitating Client Understanding of Design Languages /
Jason K. McDonald 18

Chapter III
The Power of Design Drawing in Other Design Fields / *S. Todd Stubbs and Andrew S. Gibbons* 33

Chapter IV
The Culture Based Model: A Framework for Designers and Visual ID Languages /
Patricia A. Young 52

Chapter V
The Virtue of Paper: Drawing as a Means to Innovation in Instructional Design /
Brad Hokanson 76

Section II
Visual Instructional Design Languages

Chapter VI
Plotting a Learning Experience / *Patrick Parrish*.. 91

Chapter VII
E²ML: A Tool for Sketching Instructional Designs / *Luca Botturi*...................................... 112

Chapter VIII
The MOT+ Visual Language for Knowledge-Based Instructional Design /
Gilbert Paquette, Michel Léonard, and Karin Lundgren-Cayrol 133

Chapter IX
coUML: A Visual Language for Modeling Cooperative Environments /
Michael Derntl and Renate Motschnig-Pitrik.. 155

Chapter X
poEML: A Separation-of-Concerns Proposal to Instructional Design /
Manuel Caeiro-Rodríguez.. 185

Chapter XI
Performance Case Modeling / *Ian Douglas*.. 210

Chapter XII
LDL for Collaborative Activities / *Christine Ferraris, Christian Martel,
and Laurence Vignollet* 226

Chapter XIII
Visual Design of Coherent Technology-Enhanced Learning Systems: A Few Lessons
Learned from CPM Language / *Thierry Nodenot, Pierre Laforcade, and Xavier Le Pallec*.............. 254

Chapter XIV
Visual Modeling of Collaborative Learning Processes: Uses, Desired Properties,
and Approaches / *Andreas Harrer and H. Ulrich Hoppe* 281

Chapter XV
Using the IMS Learning Design Notation for the Modeling and Delivery of Education /
Colin Tattersall, Tim Sodhi, Daniel Burgos, and Rob Koper.. 299

Chapter XVI
Comparing Visual Instructional Design Languages: A Case Study / *Luca Botturi, Daniel Burgos,
Manuel Caeiro-Rodríguez, Michael Derntl, Rob Koper, Patrick Parrish, Tim Sodhi,
and Colin Tattersal*... 315

Section III
Research Studies

Chapter XVII
The Pervasiveness of Design Drawing in ID / *S. Todd Stubbs and Andrew S. Gibbons* 345

Chapter XVIII
Lost in Translation: Improving the Transition Between Design and Production
of Instructional Software / *Eddy Boot, Jon Nelson,*
and Daniela De Faveri 366

Chapter XIX
A Visual Learning Design Representation to Facilitate Dissemination and Reuse
of Innovative Pedagogical Strategies in University Teaching / *Shirley Agostinho,*
Barry Harper, Ron Oliver, John Hedberg, and Sandra Wills 380

Chapter XX
Diagrams of Learning Flow Patterns' Solutions as Visual Representations
of Refinable IMS Learning Design Templates / *Davinia Hernández-Leo,*
Eloy D. Villasclaras-Fernández, Juan I. Asensio-Pérez, and Yannis Dimitriadis 394

Chapter XXI
Designing for Change: Visual Design Tools to Support Process Change in Education /
John Casey, Kevin Brosnan, Wolfgang Greller, Alan Masson, Áine MacNeill,
and Colette Murphy 413

Compilation of References 439

About the Contributors 467

Index 475

Detailed Table of Contents

Preface xiv

Acknowledgment xxii

Section I
Foundations and Theory

Chapter I
Commodity, Firmness, and Delight: *Four* Modes of Instructional Design Practice /
Brad Hokanson, Charles Miller, and Simon Hooper.. 1

This chapter is interactive, with surveys and reflective examinations of the reader's own work in instructional design. It examines instructional design using four professional models: manufacturer, engineer, architect and artist to help develop a broader understanding of the process of design. The values of the instructional design are also challenged, with the chapter examining the balance between utility and aesthetics, function and form. It concludes with a call for the instructional designer to work more as an artist, and offers tactics to encourage that change.

Chapter II
Translate to Communicate: Facilitating Client Understanding of Design Languages /
Jason K. McDonald 18

This chapter discusses how principles of natural language translation can help instructional designers communicate instructional design languages in ways more natural to their clients. It argues that instructional designers should focus more on the fundamental meanings they are attempting to communicate through their design languages than on the mechanics and style of those languages. This can lead designers to find representation methods that help their clients better understand design meanings than if designers only used the language conventions with which they were already familiar. The author's hope is that this contribution to the literature on instructional design languages will lead to new language conventions that help designers more easily communicate their intentions and plans to all those who have an interest in a design's overall success.

Chapter III

The Power of Design Drawing in Other Design Fields / *S. Todd Stubbs and Andrew S. Gibbons*....... 33

This chapter is a survey of the literature of design studies, where the various characteristics of a phenomenon called design drawing, are considered. Included in this review is an exploration of the roles and attributes design drawing plays in those design fields outside ID, as an important design language. Its importance to those design fields suggests that design drawing might have much to teach us about visual instructional design languages (VIDLs). In reviewing these attributes of design drawing and how they are implemented in those other fields of design, we hope to inspire a dialogue on how these important characteristics will aid in creating or nurturing VIDLs.

Chapter IV

The Culture Based Model: A Framework for Designers and Visual ID Languages /
Patricia A. Young 52

Globalizing the field of instructional design lies in the building and nurturing of innovative models, frameworks, visual languages, and practices that include culture based considerations. This chapter argues that culture, as a design construct, is integral to educating learners and enhancing the design process. This is supported by a review of theoretical and methodological studies that define culture and an examination of models of culture that are supported by VIDLs. Further, the significance of VIDLs as design tools is offered through the culture based model (CBM) an intercultural instructional design framework that guides designers through the management, design, development and assessment process while taking into account explicit culture based considerations. The chapter provides a description of the origins of CBM, an overview of relevant research, and an outline of the model and its possible applications with VIDLs. This research suggests that VIDLs can serve a broader scope if culture is considered.

Chapter V

The Virtue of Paper: Drawing as a Means to Innovation in Instructional Design /
Brad Hokanson 76

This chapter presents an argument in favor of using paper to conceive, plan, and describe instructional design projects. Such a simple medium has great capability and, as is well known, a tenacious ubiquity; our offices, practices, and lives are filled with paper. We will see how the attributes of paper help us in both social and cognitive ways, particularly as a medium for drawing.

Section II
Visual Instructional Design Languages

Chapter VI

Plotting a Learning Experience / *Patrick Parrish*... 91

This chapter describes an informal visual notation system that can be used by instructional designers in conceptualizing a design for an aesthetic learning experience. It begins by making a case for the importance of aesthetics as a major consideration in designing instruction, distinguishing aesthetic experience from more narrow conceptions of art and aesthetics. Drawing parallels between learning experiences and other narratives, examples of several narrative diagrams used in planning and analyzing fictional narratives are examined. Borrowing strategies from these narrative diagrams, the chapter then proposes the use of engagement curves to help designers more fully consider the aesthetic experience of learners in the design phase of instruction. Several examples of the use of narrative diagrams to analyze existing instructional designs are provided, as well as a demonstration of how an instructional design educator might use a narrative diagram in planning a course on ID models.

Chapter VII

E²ML: A Tool for Sketching Instructional Designs / *Luca Botturi* 112

This chapter introduces E²ML, the educational environment modeling language. E²ML is a lightweight visual language for instructional design; suitable both for complex instructional design processes and simple paper and pencil sketches. E²ML can be used for visualizing the intermediate and final results of design, thus providing documentation in a shared language that can enhance team communication, improve design and contribute to the development of high-quality instruction. The language and its features and applications are presented through a case study, evaluation results are briefly reported, and critical issues are discussed.

Chapter VIII

The MOT+ Visual Language for Knowledge-Based Instructional Design /
Gilbert Paquette, Michel Léonard, and Karin Lundgren-Cayrol 133

This chapter states and explains that a learning design is the result of a knowledge engineering process where knowledge and competencies, learning design, media and delivery models are constructed in an integrated framework. Consequently, we present our MOT+ general graphical language and editor that help construct structured interrelated visual models. The MOT+LD editor is the newly added specialization of this editor for learning designs, producing IMS-LD compliant units of learning. The MOT+OWL editor is another specialization of the general visual language for knowledge and competency models based on the OWL specification. We situate both models within our taxonomy of knowledge models respectively as a multi-actor collaborative process and a domain theory. The association between these "content" models and learning design components is seen as the essential task in an instructional design methodology, to guide the construction of high quality learning environments.

Chapter IX

coUML: A Visual Language for Modeling Cooperative Environments /

Michael Derntl and Renate Motschnig-Pitrik.. 155

This chapter presents coUML, a visual modeling language for cooperative environments. As modern instructional environments have a highly cooperative nature, coUML is proposed as a powerful and effective language for modeling instructional designs in such environments. Being based on UML, it was conceived and refined through application and experience over multiple years, primarily in a cooperative blended learning environment. The chapter presents relevant requirements and applications that contributed to the development of coUML, as well as a detailed specification of model elements, characteristics and features that describe its current state.

Chapter X

poEML: A Separation-of-Concerns Proposal to Instructional Design /

Manuel Caeiro-Rodríguez.. 185

This chapter introduces a new visual educational modeling language (EML) based on a separation-of-concerns approach, PoEML: perspective-oriented EML. EMLs were proposed to support the modeling of educational units. These languages are related to ID, as they are intended to represent models of educational units. This chapter introduces the PoEML separation of concerns and its graphic constructs. The main idea underlying PoEML is to break down the modeling of educational units into separate parts that can be specified independently. PoEML is mainly focused on supporting the computational execution of educational unit models. In addition, the separation of concerns allows us to approach the modeling of educational units in an incremental way, offering advantages in expressiveness, formality, adaptability and flexibility.

Chapter XI

Performance Case Modeling / *Ian Douglas*.. 210

This chapter introduces performance case modeling as a means of conducting a performance analysis. It argues that the design of any instruction focused on practical subjects should be preceded by understanding of the performance requirements for graduates of a course of instruction. This understanding is facilitated by the collaborative creation of diagrams that identify the different roles a performer takes and their associated goals, together with documentation of performance measures for the goals. The measures serve as a baseline for the evaluation of instructional effectiveness. Other approaches to visual languages in instructional design have been more focused on modeling the architecture of the instructional system rather than the performance environment in which its graduates will be expected to perform. The approach described is based on UML use cases and serves to focus thinking on the performance analysis that should occur prior to the design of instruction.

Chapter XII

LDL for Collaborative Activities / *Christine Ferraris, Christian Martel, and Laurence Vignollet ...* 226

LDL (learning design language) is an educational modeling language which was conceived to model collaborative activities. It has roots in social sciences, mainly linguistics, sociology and ethnomethodology. It proposes seven concepts that allow instructional designers to build the model of a collaborative learning activity. It has both a visual and a textual notation, the latter being computer-readable. This means that the produced models can be easily operationalized and executed in an existing virtual learning environment. This chapter introduces LDL, its concepts and the graphical notations associated with each of them. The methodology proposed to facilitate the modeling is also presented. Its use is illustrated by the example of the planet game, which was practically tested with other research teams as a benchmark/competition during the ICALT 2006 conference.

Chapter XIII

Visual Design of Coherent Technology-Enhanced Learning Systems:
A Few Lessons Learned from CPM Language / *Thierry Nodenot,
Pierre Laforcade, and Xavier Le Pallec* 254

Visual instructional design languages currently provide notations for representing the intermediate and final results of a knowledge engineering process. As some languages particularly focus on the formal representation of a learning design that can be transformed into machine interpretable code (i.e., IML-LD players), others have been developed to support the creativity of designers while exploring their problem-spaces and solutions. This chapter introduces CPM (computer problem-based metamodel), a visual language for the instructional design of problem-based learning (PBL) situations. On the one hand, CPM sketches of a PBL situation can improve communication within multidisciplinary ID teams; on the other hand, CPM blueprints can describe the functional components that a technology-enhanced learning (TEL) system should offer to support such a PBL situation. We first present the aims and the fundamentals of CPM language. Then, it analyzes CPM usability using a set of CPM diagrams produced in a case study in a 'real-world' setting.

Chapter XIV

Visual Modeling of Collaborative Learning Processes:
Uses, Desired Properties, and Approaches / *Andreas Harrer and H. Ulrich Hoppe* 281

The modelling of learning processes and its use in computer-supported learning scenarios attracted attention in a wide variety of research fields in the last years, e.g., in Web based education, computer supported collaboration scripts, and intelligent tutoring systems (ITS). Most of the discussion is either focused on the conceptual level of instructional design for exchange between designers or on the automated execution of predefined designs and learning scripts. This chapter elaborates on the whole spectrum of different uses that visual learning models provide for teachers, learners, and researchers. Based on our discussions in an international research project on computer-supported collaboration scripts we identify desired properties for such modeling languages especially considering the needs of the practitioners. Finally it proposes MoCoLADe (model for collaborative learning activity design), an exemplary approach of a visual language for collaborative learning processes that was designed according to the presented principles.

Chapter XV

Using the IMS Learning Design Notation for the Modeling and Delivery of Education /
Colin Tattersall, Tim Sodhi, Daniel Burgos, and Rob Koper.. 299

IMS learning design (IMS-LD) is a notation system for learning and instruction. It supports the description of learning processes using a set of standardised concepts, including roles, activities, acts, objectives and prerequisites. With the availability of such a notation, descriptions of learning processes can be shared, critiqued, modified, rated, compared and evaluated. Moreover, the machine-interpretable nature of the notation means that designs can be executed by software to support the dynamic orchestration of multi-learner, multi-role learning processes. This chapter introduces IMS-LD and describes experience with its use, supported by the first generation of tooling. We then combine these experiences with observations on the tools in the light of new developments in e-learning in order to derive a set of requirements for IMS-LD enabled visual design environments.

Chapter XVI

Comparing Visual Instructional Design Languages: A Case Study / *Luca Botturi, Daniel Burgos, Manuel Caeiro-Rodríguez, Michael Derntl, Rob Koper, Patrick Parrish, Tim Sodhi, and Colin Tattersal*.. 315

This handbook testifies that research on VIDL is lively, and has produced a number of interesting design languages and tools. This chapter wants to support readers in understanding the similarities and differences of some of the VIDL presented in the previous chapters, not in theory, but applying them to a specific instructional design case.

Section III
Research Studies

Chapter XVII

The Pervasiveness of Design Drawing in ID / *S. Todd Stubbs and Andrew S. Gibbons* 345

This chapter is a survey of the literature of ID to look at the breadth and usage of design drawings in this discipline to better understand the emerging use of VIDLs to improve designs. To conduct this research, the authors sampled several ID textbooks, ID journals, software, and case studies looking for examples of design drawing. Design drawings found were then categorized using Gibbons' (2003) seven ID layers as a taxonomy to understand the drawings purposes. The authors did not find the same pervasiveness or level of self-awareness as found in other design fields. Examples of design drawings were found, but were somewhat rare. Furthermore, they discovered that those examples we found tended to document only two of Gibbons' seven layers, indicating narrow application. They believe this gap represents a serious shortcoming in ID, indicating a lack of tradition, skill, and standards for visual representations of design except in limited ways. At present, design drawing is a rare but growing phenomenon in ID, which, when fully understood and implemented, can only benefit the practice of ID.

Chapter XVIII

Lost in Translation: Improving the Transition Between Design and Production
of Instructional Software / *Eddy Boot, Jon Nelson, and Daniela De Faveri*........................... 366

Developing modern instructional software has become very complex. As a result, the communication between instructional designers and other stakeholders in the development process is becoming increasingly important. However, due to differences in background, focus, and tools among ISD stakeholders, instructional designers lack the means to provide reasonably unequivocal design documentation for these stakeholders. These differences in stakeholders create a context where the design documents produced are not sufficiently related to the specific needs of the stakeholders, in terms of meaningful organization and differentiation of level of detail. This problem is complicated by the lack of shared design languages. These problems prevent precise expression of design information. The 3D-model is introduced to support instructional designers to stratify, elaborate, and formalize design documents, even if design languages are hardly shared between designers and other stakeholders. Two validation studies show that the 3D-model contributes to a better information transition between instructional designers and software producers—one of the stakeholders in the development process.

Chapter XIX

A Visual Learning Design Representation to Facilitate Dissemination and Reuse
of Innovative Pedagogical Strategies in University Teaching / *Shirley Agostinho,
Barry Harper, Ron Oliver, John Hedberg, and Sandra Wills* 380

This chapter describes a visual learning design representation devised in an Australian funded project that focused on identifying and describing innovative educational practices employing the use of information and communication technologies (ICT). Referred to as learning designs project (www.learningdesigns. uow.edu.au), the aim was to produce generic learning design resources and tools to help academics in higher education implement innovative ICT-based learning designs in their own teaching contexts. The chapter describes the learning designs project, details how and why the graphical learning design representation was created and provides an example to illustrate the visual formalism. How the authors have built on this work since the completion of the project is also discussed. The purpose of this chapter is to explain how this visual representation works so as to inform teachers and educational researchers of its potential to serve as a common language to describe learning designs.

Chapter XX

Diagrams of Learning Flow Patterns' Solutions as Visual Representations
of Refinable IMS Learning Design Templates / *Davinia Hernández-Leo,
Eloy D. Villasclaras-Fernández, Juan I. Asensio-Pérez, and Yannis Dimitriadis* 394

This chapter introduces the use of diagrammatic representations of learning flow patterns as a means of visualizing refinable IMS learning design (IMS LD) templates. It argues that the incorporation of pattern-based IMS LD templates in authoring tools, which graphically guide users to create their own learning designs, offers a solution to the problem of IMS LD constructs not being familiar to educators because of its technical nature and text-based notation. Furthermore, this solution facilitates the reuse of good practices formulated as patterns, permitting a design process that promotes potentially effective results.

This issue is especially important in collaborative learning designs, in which elicitations of desired social interactions are planned beforehand. Based on these ideas, the chapter also presents Collage, an IMS LD editor which provides templates based on collaborative learning flow patterns (CLFPs), and includes an example drawn from a real scenario that show the feasibility and usefulness of the approach.

Chapter XXI
Designing for Change: Visual Design Tools to Support Process Change in Education /
John Casey, Kevin Brosnan, Wolfgang Greller Alan Masson,
Aine MacNeill, and Colette Murphy 413

This chapter looks at the possible uses of visual forms of instructional design (ID) languages as possible 'change agents' for design practice in the public post-secondary education sector. A lot of work is being done in the technical realm of the standardization and interoperability for educational modeling languages (EMLs), but this is largely restricted to existing ID specialists that use 'dialects' of ID languages and schemes. This is important work but it does not address the vast majority of educators working in the postsecondary public educational sector whose design work is highly individualised and deeply embedded in rich institutional contexts. The challenge for visual ID languages and EMLs in general is how they can move beyond their current specialist niche applications to be useful to mainstream educators. In this chapter we argue that this development needs to happen along two related dimensions: (i) changes in the organization of the educational workplace and related training—what might be termed 'push factors'; and, (ii) the use of tools such as visual ID languages to support that change process at individual and group levels—what might be termed 'pull' factors. We shall be concentrating on this second dimension. Specifically, in this chapter we shall be looking at ideas for how we might apply visual ID languages as a support mechanism in helping educators externalize and share their design models and ideas in order to develop them into semi-formal abstractions that might be developed to feed into the use of EMLs. To ground these ideas, we shall be looking at the experiences of those who have tried these types of approaches in practice. Finally we discuss the effect this type of perspective might have on the future development of visual ID languages and related tools.

Compilation of References 439

About the Contributors 467

Index 475

Preface

LANGUAGES, VISUALS, DESIGN, AND CREATIVITY

Recently, I had the fortune of observing one of the last Italian plasterers (*stuccatore*) that still is a master of the traditional techniques once used for wall decorations in Renaissance and Baroque churches and palaces. The process is rather complex, and requires a good deal of practical ability and expertise. Basically, it all starts from a flat drawing of what will appear on the wall: leaves, fruits, decorations. That drawing can be done on paper and then transposed to the wall surface with a *cartone*, as is done for frescoes, or it can be sketched directly on the wall. It guides the placement of the first layer of matter (*intonaco*) that will then support and give shape to the white plaster, which is made of marble powder. The drawing guides the artist, but it is not a constraint: modeling volumes, he is free to reduce the leaves, or to introduce a new element that will give more balance to the whole piece. It is a project idea, which will acquire concreteness, step by step, and will eventually change, in order to become what it was supposed to be in the artist's mind.

Sitting on a train, drafting this preface, I enjoy taking my eyes off of the laptop screen and contemplating the people in the compartment, what they do, and their environment. We are literally submerged with pictures and visual representations: newspapers and magazines are, more and more, a collection of pictures accompanied by text; signs on the walls of the compartment use color codes and icons to remind passengers that smoking is not allowed, or that the toilet is available, or occupied or, worse, out of order. The same happens with our mobile phones, and even more with computers. We live with pictures, we think in pictures, we often express ourselves in pictures, often complementing or integrating the visuals with verbal language.

This is true of everyday life, but also in many fields of professional life, and especially, as chapter 1.1 will claim, of knowledge work. Visuals support imagination, and therefore also support creative thinking. We imagine things in our minds, we represent them, and this allows us to re-think them, and improve our plans. We are used to that—both those who have a better hand at drawing and those who do not—so used that we are often not aware of it, and do not invest in improving that skill. Some professional fields, especially creative ones, capitalized on the power of visualizations, and developed specific design languages. This is true of course of architecture, but also of electronics or mathematics, or of fashion design and Web design.

A basic tenet of this handbook is that instructional design is a creative profession, and can benefit from the application and use of design languages in a number of ways. The first goal of the handbook is to raise awareness of this opportunity, and to demonstrate the available results of research in this field.

* * *

Imagine an engineer in charge of designing a new bike. It has to be light and durable, and for this reason he will use a new, rather expensive metal. It has also to be aerodynamic, and this means following some constraints in designing its shape. He will sketch it, probably several times, before finding the right gist of a solution, which will be then moved into a CAD program, where the drawing, digitized, will be developed into a detailed plan, taking metal resilience, aesthetics, mechanics, etc., into consideration. As the design progresses, the drawing will be split into parts, and specialists will deal then with details: brakes, gears, etc. After the production, the engineer himself may supervise the final assembly of the prototype bike, guided by an overview diagram.

Within a creative process, we seamlessly move in and out of different design languages and visualizations, according to the needs of the process. Each phase, often each person in a design team, has specific needs, and a specific language to fulfill them. This specific language must be recognized to maximize his/her effectiveness. As in the example of the engineer above, the same happens in instructional design, where interdisciplinary teams are at work. This handbook therefore collects a number of visual instructional design languages, presents them to the reader and, tentatively, provides a comparative view on some of them. The point is not selecting the best one, rather to identify the most adequate to a specific situation, or the mix of them that can support a specific process.

CLASSIFICATION FRAMEWORK

In order to facilitate the understanding and comparison of the different visual design languages presented in the handbook, we asked the authors of chapters in section II to refer to a shared framework, originally published in Botturi, Derntl, Boot, and Figl (2006).

The idea behind that framework is that different design language features address different ways of thinking: a highly formal language like UML fits the way of thinking of a more accurate and technically-oriented person better, while rather sketchy, informal languages are more suitable for creative and intuitive mindsets.

It is comprised of five features, namely:

1. **Stratification:** (nominal: *flat, layered*) A layered language offers a set of tools or representations for describing entities of different types, such as people and roles, activities, or learning materials. On the other hand, a flat language would collect entities of all types into a single representation. For example, UML takes a layered perspective.
2. **Formalization:** (interval: *formal, informal*) A formal language defines a stringent, closed set of concepts and rules for composition of concepts in order to describe designs. For instance, XML or UML are formal languages, while sketches or dialogs are more open and informal. Other design languages may combine formal and informal descriptions.
3. **Elaboration:** (ordinal: *conceptual, specification, implementation*) Each particular design language is able to provide more or less detail of a specific artifact. The three levels of elaboration are taken from Fowler (2003): The conceptual level allows for a general, aggregate view on the design, indicating its rationale and main elements; the specification level provides means for a more comprehensive description, including all elements; the implementation level represents the highest level of detail achieving maximum precision.

4. **Perspective:** (nominal: *single, multiple*) While layered languages foresee the use of multiple representations for different entities, multiple-perspective languages exploit different tools for representing more than one view *on the same entities*. For example, E²ML offers two overview diagrams, one for chronological relationships among learning activities, and one for structural relationships.
5. **Notation System:** (nominal: *none, textual, visual*) If a language exposes a notation system, this can be primarily non-visual (=textual, e.g., IMS/LD) or visual (e.g., UML).

The original paper proposed a tentative classification of some major design languages, which is extended and enriched here. Also, the paper contained a bi-dimensional classification of possible uses of visual instructional design languages, considering that each design language was developed with a specific use framework in mind. The two dimensions are:

1. **Communication:** The first axis in the application framework concerns the main objective of the ID language, with two values: (a) *Reflective* (personal) means that the language is used primarily for personal creative thinking. This is useful for formally-bent or visually-oriented people and for designers in the first conceptual stages of design in which they do not yet collaborate with other designers and stakeholders; (b) *Communicative* (community) indicates that the language is used to communicate with other designers or stakeholders. This is useful for interdisciplinary design teams involving different views/roles.
2. **Creativity:** The second axis describes the relationship between the design language and the generation of design solutions: (a) *Generative* means that the language can be used as a means of exploring the design space and creating and refining design solutions and alternatives, e.g., during redesign. (b) *Finalist* means that it is used to formalize and "freeze" the final design solution, e.g., for creating a final IMS/LD specification of an e-learning module.

We asked authors to describe their languages according to this reference framework, and also to indicate their main type of use. Note that a single design language need not to be located on a single spot, but may occupy a range on an axis or an area in the classification box, respectively. For example, most languages can be used for reflective *and* communicative purposes.

HANDBOOK STRUCTURE

The handbook is structured in three sections. Section I contains foundational chapters and chapters regarding theory behind visual instructional design languages. Section II contains examples of visual languages, and section III contains research regarding the use of VIDLs.

Section I: Foundations and Theory contains chapters that explore the underlying reasons behind visual languages for instructional design. This section will explore their value and importance to the instructional design process—with appropriate reference to design fields which traditionally rely more on visual design languages such as architecture and software design. With this background of design languages for instructional design, we will be able to answer important questions, such as 'Why are they useful?' and 'When do they come into play in the practice of design?' The ideal path moves from the idea that instructional design is a multiform knowledge work, through the idea of communication, visuals, and culture, and then back to the somewhat "old" idea of sketching on paper.

- **Chapter I** proposes a cultural transfer, throwing in ID some potentially explosive elements taken from ancient Roman architectural theory. The authors' goal is to have readers reflect on their practice and on their approach and values as instructional designers. This actually opens up to new perspectives in selecting and applying any kind of design tool—methods, media, software applications and, of course, design languages. Ideally, this chapter pairs with chapter VI, where aesthetics again comes to play a central role.

- **Chapter II** emphasizes the need for clear and effective communication among all stakeholders interested in a design's success, clearly calling for shared, understandable and usable design languages that can enhance communication. This provides an important double perspective to the whole handbook. On the one hand, there are many (visual) ID languages—some are included here, but others are available and being used in the world. On the other hand, such languages live, make sense and must interact with other non-specific languages, and even natural languages, the whole point being achieving more effective communication not only among designers, but also with stakeholders. Several references in the text indicate connections to other chapters in the handbook.

- **Chapter III** is a survey of the literature of design studies (which covers architecture, industrial design and other design fields) regarding the phenomenon called design drawing. In this review, the roles and attributes that design drawing plays in those fields outside of ID suggest important ways in which design drawing might contribute to the practice of ID. Important attributes such as the stages in which designs and their accompanying drawings grow, the value of vagueness in early drawings, and the ways in which drawings focus commitment to designs are covered in this chapter.

- **Chapter IV** adds another, perhaps broader, dimension to the discussion about the use of language and visuals in ID: culture. Indeed, "all designs are based in culture", and also, all languages and visual languages come from and are understandable within a culture. This is highly relevant for designers, who should consider both stakeholders' and learners' cultures. The culture based model presented in the chapter is a practical tool by which to integrate such considerations in the design practice.

- **Chapter V** focuses on paper and pencil as the simplest medium to collect and convey design ideas. While we live in a world of digital images, the author reminds us that the point is not creating visuals, but rather empowering the *human* element of design, and that the choice of media should correspond to that. He suggests that often less technology means more creativity. Also, this chapter explains in detail what we mean by "generative" design languages, which are here called "sketching as visual thinking," emphasising that we do not need (only) closed set of design terms and symbols, but rather the ability to draw to enhance our designs.

Section II: Visual Instructional Design Languages contains a sampling of visual design languages for instructional design, which are presented and illustrated by examples. The goal of this section is to provide exposure and guidance to interested practitioners who personally want to try out new tools for their instructional design projects. These VIDLs are ideally sequenced from less formal to most formal—with the understanding that specific applications may vary greatly in degree of formality.

- **Chapter VI** returns to the idea of aesthetics, broadening the definition and the scope of impact as presented in Chapter I. It draws from the concept of aesthetic experience to offer a novel, narrative-based VIDL, which can provide a new perspective for instructional designers, using narrative briefs and user profiles to develop structured design tools.

- **Chapter VII** presents the educational environments modeling language—E²ML, a simple visual language that supports structured paper-and-pencil sketches to enhance communication within the design team. E²ML was developed to provide documentation of a design and to provide a means of analysis and evaluation of the instruction itself. It, like many of the VIDLs in this book, is based loosely on a few UML representation types. E²ML comes in two versions or levels: a core version which is less formal and more focused on visual representation—more suited to the creative use; and, an advanced version which is more formal. This chapter briefly documents the former.

- **Chapter VIII** first proposes a highly structured ID method, which exploits different kinds of visualizations. Its main emphasis is on representing knowledge, i.e., the learning domain, and couples specific diagrams with specific design phases and documents. The language, MOT+, is also of particular interests as the authors have done an additional effort to make it compliant with IMS-LD specifications, enhancing interoperability. It is also the case in which a large development of a suite of tools supporting VIDL use is observable.

- **Chapter IX** belongs to a triad of chapters (IX, XII, and XIV) whose authors are working on collaborative activities—probably the most tricky and challenging issue in visually modeling learning environments. Interestingly, the three chapters take very different approaches: Chapter XIV is based on language requirements; Chapter XII on pedagogical theory; this chapter moves from the practice, constructing the language on a wide set of collected cases. This is indicative of the various natures of visual instructional design languages in general, and provides the reader with an interesting comparative outlook.

- **Chapter X** proposes a structural enhancement for IMS learning design, by splitting the language into different independent but connected *concerns*. It is an interesting case of formal development of a language along one dimension—layering—in order to respond to the complexity of design situations. It is interesting to follow this track through different chapters, specifically this one and Chapter XVII.

- **Chapter XI** proposes the use of UML use case diagrams as tools for performance analysis to support instructional analysis. It is interesting as it takes a specific tool developed in software engineering and repurposes it in Instructional Design, or better(and this is another merit)in the perspective of performance support, thus broadening the overall scope of the whole handbook. Also, the last part of the chapter reflects on potential pitfalls in which extremist advocates of UML—or of visual design languages in general—might fall. Along the lines of what also other authors argue, Douglas states that, "The success of modeling probably has more to do with the person doing it than with the tool itself."

- **Chapter XII** presents LDL, an alternative instructional design language developed in order to overcome some known limitations of IMS LD in modeling online collaborative activities. As such it develops a number of connections among all chapters dealing with IMS LD, offering an interesting perspective for all of them. Interestingly, LDL is both a language, and a method that structures the design activity in order to best exploit the expressive features of the language.

- **Chapter XIII** presents CPM, a visual instructional design language specifically developed for problem-based learning. While its fundamental language concepts are original, the visual part is borrowed from UML. Also, the author provides interesting insights in the use of a formalized language by non-technically-oriented designers and teachers.

- **Chapter XIV** provides a very in-depth analysis of the continuum moving from visual instructional design languages for designers (people) to that of VIDL for automation ("system perspective").

- **Chapter XV** focuses on IMS learning design, probably the largest effort in design languages ever in the field of distance learning and ICT. Its merit is to provide a picture of the state of the art and also to focus on tools—the link between theoretical discovery and application for many VIDL. The authors also comments on the fact that tools only cover a part of the design process, and cannot substitute, but only support, creativity.
- **Chapter XVI** provides a sort of *in vitro* experiment: we asked several authors to model a specific blended learning scenario with their languages, and to explain what are the advantages and draw-backs, and where they would come into play within the design process

Section III: Research Studies contains the results of the first available studies and experiences about the use of visual instructional design languages in professional contexts.

- **Chapter XVII** viewed a sampling of the literature of ID to better understand the breadth and usage of design drawings in the theory and practice of ID. Several ID textbooks, ID journals, ID software, and case studies were sampled looking for examples of design drawing. Design drawings found were then categorized using Gibbons' (2003) seven ID layers as a taxonomy to understand the drawings purposes. What was discovered was that, though design graphics exist, they are relatively rare and narrowly focused.
- **Chapter XVIII** provides a sort of synthetic point of view and asks a very simple yet powerful question: OK, now we have a lot of VIDLs, what do we do with them? Who should use which, in practical terms? The 3D model is both a way to solve the issue in specific cases, and a way to stimulate reflection in stakeholders' communication.
- **Chapter XIX**. We were not sure where to place this chapter—it both presents an example of a VIDL as well as a research study providing insights about its use and value. To be certain, this chapter has one important story to tell: about a group of designers that did not want to develop a visual instructional design language, but came up with a very neat and expressive one exactly because they needed it to overcome communication barriers. The resulting language moved from "a means to an end" to "an end in itself." This is a very valid demonstration of the opportunities a language can offer to instructional design in practice.
- **Chapter XX**. Visual instructional design languages allow the definition and expression of design patterns—design solutions that can be used over and over again for recurrent design problems (akin to Alexander's, 1979, famed architectural patterns). This chapter is focused on patterns as a solution to the possible intricacies of actual design languages, especially of IMS learning design. Visualizations play a key role in this study, making design constructs accessible to inexperienced users and designers.
- **Chapter XXI**. The authors of this chapter argue that "very few instructional designers exist in the mainstream" of education and this is why present VIDL developments do not currently match needs of the more common users: teachers. Instead they represent where the instructional design research community would *like* mainstream teachers to be. The chapter starts by presenting a systematic analysis of current design practices in the mainstream and then goes on to illustrate this with a set of three case studies that provide a clear and challenging picture of possible research paths for encouraging the understanding and dissemination of visual instructional design languages.

ABOUT THE AUTHORS

Before leaving the floor to the actual chapters, a few words about the authors who contributed to this book.

First of all, a simple run through the biographies shows that this handbook represents a truly international perspective which reflects an added value of the handbook. This work connects research from several European countries, from Canada, the U.S., and Australia, also indicating the relevance of the topic to different research teams scattered around the globe. We regret only not having a chapter about LAMS, a large Australian and international initiative which would have deserved some pages in this handbook. This was unfortunately prevented by copyright problems.

Also, the authors of the chapters contained in the handbook belong to two different scientific communities: one oriented toward instructional design, the other stemming from learning technologies.

These "two souls" of the handbook give birth to a discourse between creativity and machine support, between free form and formalism, between communication and modeling. It is indeed enriching to see how the dialogue between these two communities developed, which will hopefully reach far beyond the pages of this handbook. Interestingly, visuals play a key role in both communities, as a sort of *lingua franca* and meeting point.

GENERAL ACRONYMS

During editing we noticed that many terms and acronyms recurred over and over again in the text. We consequently proposed chapter authors to skip their definitions in order to make chapters more readable. Such acronyms are explained in the following for common reference:

- **ID:** Instructional design
- **IDL:** Instructional design language
- **VIDL:** Visual instructional design language
- **LMS:** Learning management system
- **IMS LD:** IMS learning design (also **IMSLD** and **IML-LD**)

BEFORE THE READING...

As editors, we really wanted this whole handbook to be, first of all, useful to potential innovators in instructional design, learning technologies and e-learning. We really tried to make it something more than a collection of independent chapters, or a "show-off parade" of research. We tried to make it a real handbook, i.e., a book that you want to keep at hand, because it is useful.

This is why we asked authors to try to use the same reference framework, and read each other's chapters to create meaningful connections among them. They responded generously, and we believe the result is outstanding—as a tool that we, as practitioners in the first place, more than as researchers, want to keep at hand for our daily practice. We hope this will also be the experience of other readers.

Finally, this handbook is the result of a dialogue, or better, of more dialogues. Between the editors, between editors and authors, among the authors, between two different research and professional communities—a dialogue which we hope will grow and embrace also our readers, and thus bring new ideas, tools and practices to our professional field.

Luca Botturi & S. Todd Stubbs
August 2007

REFERENCES

Alexander, C. (1979). *The timeless way of building*. New York: Oxford University Press.

Botturi, L., Derntl, M., Boot, E., & Figl, K. (2006). A classification framework for educational modeling languages in instructional design. *Proceedings of IEEE ICALT 2006* (pp. 1216-1220). Kerkrade, The Netherlands.

Fowler, M. (2003). *UML distilled: A brief guide to the standard object modeling language*. Boston, MA,: Addison Wesley.

Acknowledgment

This book is the result of fascinating and challenging research brought about by researchers in different countries—but most of all, it is the result of common work by people that love their jobs as educators and instructional designers and have a strong desire to see it get better.

The editors wish to thank all chapter authors for their outstanding and generous work, and the Association for Educational Communications and Technologies for providing the soil into which the seed idea of this handbook was planted, and where it continues to grow.

We would also like to thank our patient and supportive families, without whom, this work would not have happened: Francesca, Pietro, Chiara, and Emma; Joy, Sam, and Abby.

Section I
Foundations and Theory

Chapter I
Commodity, Firmness, and Delight:
Four Modes of Instructional Design Practice

Brad Hokanson
University of Minnesota, USA

Charles Miller
University of Minnesota, USA

Simon Hooper
Penn State University, USA

This chapter is interactive, with surveys and reflective examinations of the reader's own work in instructional design. It examines instructional design using four professional models: manufacturer, engineer, architect and artist to help develop a broader understanding of the process of design. The values of the instructional design are also challenged, with the chapter examining the balance between utility and aesthetics, function and form. It concludes with a call for the instructional designer to work more as an artist, and offers tactics to encourage that change.

INTRODUCTION

How do *you* solve an instructional design problem? Do you attempt to craft a solution based on the unique demands of each problem and the application of well researched instructional strategies? Or do you build upon an existing model, one that has worked many times before, selecting from solutions developed for a range of previous projects?

Your work is directly connected to your conceptualization of your role within the field of instructional design. And that conception includes assumptions and biases about processes, theories, and products. In the course of this chapter we will ask you to re-conceptualize your professional practice as an instructional designer and to recognize the roles of instructional manufacturer, instructional engineer, instructional architect, and instructional artist. We will describe how the working ethos of each shapes their practice.

What then, would happen if you were an *instructional artist?* As an instructional artist, you might be encouraged to create fundamentally different designs and work in a completely different manner. You might begin from an idea, engaging and desirable, but unconnected with learning, only later to apply it to instruction. It might work; it might not; but the application would be entirely different. We can see that the perspective through which we view ourselves biases how we understand and address problems.

Your Balance in Design

The following survey is intended to stimulate personal reflection and discussion of the ideas included in this chapter. Participating in the survey will help you to engage with the article, to stimulate understanding of the concepts presented, and to reflect on your personal practice as an instructional designer. The survey was built from the characteristics which will be explored in this chapter, and will focus on the Vitruvian

Table 1. Survey

Q1	Are you a teacher or an artist?		Teacher ▫——▫——▫——▫——▫——▫ Artist	
Q2	Which is more important: a functionally useful product or a stable product?		Functionally useful ▫——▫——▫——▫——▫——▫ Stable	
Q3	Should media be used as tools or content providers?		Content providers ▫——▫——▫——▫——▫——▫ Tools	
Q4	Which is more important: pedagogical soundness or innovation?		Pedagogically sound ▫——▫——▫——▫——▫——▫ Innovative	
Q5	Which is more important: software usability or utility?		Usability ▫——▫——▫——▫——▫——▫ Utility	
Q6	Which is more important: software stability or visual richness?		Stability ▫——▫——▫——▫——▫——▫ Visual richness	
Q7	Should designs be easy to use or motivating to the learner?		Easy to use ▫——▫——▫——▫——▫——▫ Motivating	
Q8	Which is more important: functional capability or learner motivation?		Functional capability ▫——▫——▫——▫——▫——▫ Motivation	
Q9	Should people or design experiences be more central in ID?		People ▫——▫——▫——▫——▫——▫ Design Experiences	
Q10	Which is more important: pedagogical soundness or efficiency?		Pedagogical soundness ▫——▫——▫——▫——▫——▫ Efficiency	
Q11	Should products or experiences be more central in ID?		ID Products ▫——▫——▫——▫——▫——▫ ID Experiences	

Continued on following page

Table 1. continued

			Likert Scale	
Q12	Which is more important in media use: content or experience?		Content ▢—▢—▢—▢—▢—▢ Experience	
Q13	Which is more important in media use: usability or aesthetics?		Usability ▢—▢—▢—▢—▢—▢ Aesthetics	
Q14	Are you a teacher or technician?		Teacher ▢—▢—▢—▢—▢—▢ Technician	
Q15	Which is more important: product functionality or visual richness?		Functionality ▢—▢—▢—▢—▢—▢ Visual Richness	
Q16	Do media provide tools for learning or tools to create experiences?		Tools for learning ▢—▢—▢—▢—▢—▢ Tools for experience	
Q17	Which is more important: efficiency or innovation?		Efficiency ▢—▢—▢—▢—▢—▢ Innovation	
Q18	Which is more important in media use: utility or aesthetics?		Utility ▢—▢—▢—▢—▢—▢ Aesthetics	
Q19	Which is more important: ease of use or functional capability?		Ease of use ▢—▢—▢—▢—▢—▢ Functional capability	
Q20	Are you a technician or an artist?		Technician ▢—▢—▢—▢—▢—▢ Artist	
Q21	Should products or people be more central in ID?		People ▢—▢—▢—▢—▢—▢ Products	

values of *commodity*, *firmness* and *delight*. We will pose these questions twice in the course of this writing, the second time at the conclusion of the chapter.

To complete each question, select the point on the Likert scale most aligned with your *current* practice. Note that there is no middle point and there are no right or wrong answers. Questions are intended to create difficult choices, encouraging personal reflection. After completing the survey, score each response according to the directions that follow.

Scoring of Each Item in the Survey

Each question is given two scores which are entered in the boxes to the left and right of the Likert scale. To determine the score for the left box, count the number of blank spaces from the right margin to your entry (each margin is set at 0). For the right box, count the number of blank spaces from the left margin to your entry. In the illustration below (see Figure 1) the sample entry is three steps from the right margin, scoring 3 points for pedagogy. Likewise, the check is two steps from the left margin, scoring 2 points for

Figure 1. How to calculate the survey score

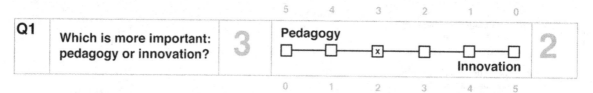

Table 2. Scoring the survey

Q	Commodity		Firmness		Delight	
1CD	Teacher				Artist	
2CF	Functionally useful		Stable			
3CF	Content providers		Tools			
4CD	Pedagogically sound				Innovate	
5CF	Usability		Utility			
6FD			Stability		Visual richness	
7CD	Easy to use				Motivating	
8FD			Functional capability		Motivation	
9CD	People				Design experiences	
10CF	Pedagogical soundness		Efficiency			
11FD			ID products		ID experiences	
12CD	Content				Experience	
13CD	Usability				Aesthetics	
14CF	Teacher		Technician			
15CD	Functionality				Visual richness	
16FD			Tools for learning		Tools for experience	
17FD			Efficiency		Innovation	
18FD			Utility		Aesthetics	
19CF	Ease of use		Functional capability			
20FD			Technician		Artist	
21CF	People		Products			
	Commodity Total		**Firmness Total**		**Delight Total**	

Innovation. Together, the total points awarded for each question must sum to 5. There are 21 questions, with 105 points in total.

Calculating Your Score

After scoring each item, use the table below to assign points to the three categories (i.e., commodity, firmness, and delight). Each question will produce two scores. The short answers for each question are included in the table to help with proper scoring. For example, in the scoring example above, "Pedagogically sound" will be in one box, and "Innovative" in another; the appropriate score should be written in each box. Shaded boxes designate comparisons not included for that question; do not write in scores in those places. Add the points when complete to achieve a total score for commodity, firmness, and delight.

Scores should be interpreted as follows:

- 0-14 points: low
- 20-50 points: medium
- 51 + points: high

We will help you to analyze and interpret your scores later in the chapter.

INSTRUCTIONAL DESIGN

Instructional design is guided by a range of theories and ideas, beliefs and assumptions, not the least of which is a perception of our own practice. Consequently, if we view the process of instructional design as one of production (that is, the manufacture of instructional materials) we will create work limited in conception and execution. Similarly, if we go beyond mere production to engage theories of learning and perception, the scientifically based outcomes are engineered, highly efficient, yet may lack the wholeness needed for the development of knowledge (Wilson, 2005). To be complete, we must extend our self-image and think beyond production or engineering. We must seek a balanced model of professional practice, one which expands our understanding of design itself.

Ultimately, in this chapter, we hope to improve educational practice though the design and development of technology based products and methods. Achieving such a goal requires an understanding of the relationship between instructional design practice and product. To clarify this relationship, we examine instructional design through the architectural dictum of Vitruvius: commodity, firmness and delight. We will identify four modes of design practice; instructional manufacturer, instructional engineer, instructional architect, and instructional artist; and examine how the Vitruvian values are employed. Finally, we offer tactics to promote a balanced approach to instructional design.

Methods

Instructional design specifically addresses learning through products and contexts which facilitate the development of knowledge (Parrish, 2005). The traditional methodology of the instructional design field encompasses the analysis, design, development, implementation, and evaluation of instructional processes and products (Reiser, 2001). Other professional fields of design, such as interface design, systems engineering, information sciences, industrial design, technical communications, and new media design have similarly strong understandings in psychology, community context, implementation, and social value (Wilson, 2005).

To orient the field toward design work that engages learners more meaningfully and effectively, instructional designers must begin to focus on creating *experiences*, as opposed to simply developing products or processes. To engage and involve the learner, instructional designers must shift their practice. Substantial innovation in the field will occur only when designers surpass the technical and pedagogical issues in their work. (Innovation is messy and difficult in most situations, particularly including education). Beyond utility is the affective domain, the engagement of the learner, the beauty within the eye of the beholder; not the steak but the sizzle. This is the aesthetics of design.

For thousands of years, philosophers and designers have used the term aesthetics, often interchangeably with the word beauty, to illustrate the sensual relationship and dynamic perception of art to culture (Lavie & Tractinsky, 2004; Parrish, 2005). For example, Leone Battista Alberti, the Italian 15th century architect, painter, and philosopher, defined aesthetics as "a great and holy matter," essentially the harmony of all design elements in proportional relationship to one another (Johnson, 1994, p. 402).

Formally established as a philosophical means to critique the visual arts, literature, music, performing arts, and even food (Ekuan, 1998), aesthetics is defined by the *American Heritage Dictionary of the English Language* as "an artistically beautiful or pleasing experience" (Tractinsky, 2004, p. 11). However, the influence of aesthetics and its significance to the instructional design community moves beyond illustrating the relationship of art to culture and simply critiquing the surface level elements (e.g., shape, color, texture, etc.) of objects and environments (Parrish, 2005). Parrish (2005) defines aesthetics as "a quality that exists equally in the experiences of everyday life as in the fine arts, and one that certainly applies to the learning experiences we design as instructional designers" (p. 16). Central to human thought and practice (Lavie & Tractinsky, 2004), aesthetic experiences provide a foundation for the intellectual activities associated with learning (Parrish, 2005). For the purposes of this chapter, we define aesthetics as those elements of interactive design which are focused primarily on enhancing and heightening the learner's experience, as opposed to elements that merely satisfy the pedagogical or technological needs of the instructional objectives. In other words, aesthetics is *design beyond done*, the essence of the design process which continues after the completion of operational and technical requirements.

For the most part, aesthetics has been largely overlooked by instructional designers; only a handful of recent articles address the relationship between aesthetics and usability (cf. Aspillagae, 1991; Kirschner, Strijbos, Kreijns, & Beers, 2004; Parizotto-Ribeiro & Hammond, 2004). The instructional design community at present is concerned primarily with performance improvement and systematic instructional design procedures (Reiser, 2001). The field's reluctance to acknowledge aesthetics as an integral facet of instructional design curriculum, practice, and research will suppress the development of engaging learning media and, ultimately, the effectiveness of instruction (Parrish, 2005; Wilson, 2005).

Parrish (2005) posits that instructional designers often view aesthetics as a superficial quality which encourages passivity by creating an illusion of learning, sidetracking the chief responsibilities of instruction. Yet others suggest aesthetics should exist at the core of design, intertwined with utility and usability, to provide pleasant experiences that enhance and extend the way people work and learn with technology (Kirschner et al., 2004). Frequently viewed as superficial, aesthetic design gets overlooked in lieu of utility and efficiency (Tractinsky, 2004) and is traditionally delegated to graphic designers late in the design process (Parrish, 2005).

Although instructional designers often neglect the potential impact of aesthetics on learning and view emotional design as a superficial task, many disciplines (e.g., architecture, automotive engineering, interior design, etc.) view aesthetics as a principal design element in the problem-solving process (Parrish, 2005). For example, automotive engineers often place the aesthetics of their vehicles at the core of the design process, playing a vital role alongside utility and usability in the development of the final design. Instructional designers, "beholden to the dry, yeastless qualities of their work" (p. 5) tend to focus on theoretical strategies and levels of efficiency, rather than discussing how their designs emotionally inspire or motivate learners.

Some in the field of instructional design have begun to address a balanced approach which includes aesthetics in their work. For example, interaction design is a framework anchored in utility, usability, and aesthetics focused on creating pleasurable learning experiences that appeal to and benefit the user (Kirschner et al., 2004). While utility is defined as the array of functionalities and features incorporated by a system (i.e., the tools present in the software that satisfy the outlined pedagogical requirements), usability is concerned with the effectiveness, efficiency, and satisfaction with which learners can accomplish a set of tasks. Together, the utility and usability of a design represent the *usefulness* of the system. For a system to be perceived as useful by its audience, the design of a software environment must balance utility and usability. In addition, interaction design is concerned with aesthetics and emotion, more precisely, how the software may appeal to and benefit learners (Kirschner et al., 2004).

BALANCE

Some design fields have long recognized a value in the balance of the functional, technical, *and* aesthetic aspects of design. It is implicit that no one aspect should dominate, nor should any be neglected. From intercontinental bridges across the Bering strait to the elegant simplicity of an orange juicer (Norman, 2004), delight, beauty, and aesthetics are common in the fields of engineering and product design. Historically, architecture has codified this balance as *commodity, firmness, and delight*.

In the first century B.C., Marcus Vitruvius Pollio, a Roman writer, architect, and engineer, authored a book titled *De architectura*, later known as *The Ten Books of Architecture* (McEwen, 2004). Considered the forefather of systematic architecture theory, Vitruvius advocated that architecture design must satisfy three discrete requirements: *firmitas* (i.e., strength), *utilitas* (i.e., utility), and *venustas* (i.e., beauty) (Tractinsky, 2004). Whereas *firmitas*, or firmness, refers to the construction and physical soundness of a building, *utilitas*, or commodity, deals with the functional use and appropriateness of a design. The phrase "commodity, firmness, and delight" is partially attributed to Henry Wotton, who translated Vitruvius' text in 1624.

The third Vitruvian requirement, *venustas*, or delight, refers to the aesthetic or beauty of architecture. Vitruvius believed architecture was an imitation of nature (McEwen, 2004). Humans, mirroring techniques employed by birds and animals, construct their homes as shields against nature's elements. However, in addition to building strong, durable, and useful homes, Vitruvius believed architects must focus on the aesthetic elements, or beauty, in their designs. Beauty (i.e., delight), is responsible for making design a uniquely human process: "Is it not strange that sheep's guts should hale souls out of men's bodies?" (Shakespeare, W., Much Ado About Nothing, Act 2)

Vitruvius' architectural requirements present an illuminating framework for instructional designers to re-align their design methods. The elements of commodity, firmness, and delight can inspire instructional designers to greater innovation and higher quality, and the three aspects of architecture can be used to inform the work of instructional design.

Within instructional design, the Vitruvian ideal of firmness can be used to describe the technical issues of instructional design, specifically how media are used and how technology is applied in a solution. Technical skill is a requisite for success here. For example, software should not crash; it should run well and be delivered on time. This is the production aspect of instructional design.

Commodity refers to the functional use of a design product. Within the field of instructional design, commodity refers to the application of instructional methods, the use of sound instructional theory, and the structuring of the interface design. Scientifically researched and proven, this is the domain of the engineering aspect of instructional design.

Delight encompasses the affective aspects of the design, from the surface aesthetic to the complete experience of the learning adventure. This is the area that is most difficult in which to succeed, and which will prove most effective and rewarding. As a dominant feature, this would describe the realm of the instructional artist, possibly sacrificing utility for aesthetics and experience.

YOUR VALUES IN THE DESIGN PROCESS

We will now revisit the results of the survey completed at the beginning of the chapter. Your scores will reflect your perception of your own work, illuminating those areas most central to your current instructional designs. Any one aspect rating in the high range (i.e., 50 points and above) indicates a predilection for that area to the detriment of others. Each area scoring in the medium range (i.e., from 20 to 50 points) indicates a balanced approach to design.

Some designers focus on a single design aspect, others successfully integrate two in their work, and many have a goal to balance all three. For example, some architects are known to put buildings together well; others understand the social, functional and programmatic aspects of the field; and some, the rare few, concentrate on the aesthetic domain of the field. (From an old anecdote; Frank Lloyd Wright to a patron with a severely leaking roof: "Enjoy. You live in a Frank Lloyd Wright building.")

Many of the professions that create the designed objects, environments, and experiences we interact with in society can be described through the Vitruvian descriptors of commodity, firmness, and delight. For example, one can imagine the results from various cooks and chefs to the survey. Some would view food as a utilitarian need, as all people need to eat. Sufficient food is provided in many settings. It is warm, it's cooked, and it's safe to eat. A better diet can be provided, however, ensuring some variety and essential nutrients needed for a healthy lifestyle such as fiber, vitamins, and anti-oxidants. It might not taste great, but it's very good for you. Some meals reach the level, however, of *cuisine* where the taste, the smell, the nutrition, the visual sensation, and the experience of the meal combine to make something exceptional. In that case, the chef may have achieved the Vitruvian charges of commodity, firmness, and delight. And so should we in instructional design.

One way to apply the three Vitruvian aspects to instructional design is to use other design professions as models for our work. Although many definitions of instructional design exist, models for professional orientation can provide a means to advance the field.

INSTRUCTIONAL MODES OF PRACTICE

We have identified four modes representing distinct yet common approaches to instructional design practice: the instructional manufacturer, instructional engineer, instructional architect, and instructional artist. The modes were developed from our observations of design practice, and are used as a sorting mechanism, a 'hat' to help understand what is a continuum of practice with varied characteristics (see, for example, Rowling, 1996). Names were chosen to signify various processes in design. Each mode differs on several dimensions (see Table 1). Most importantly, practitioners in each mode differ in how they go about their work; the difference is reflected in the nature of their products. After reading the modes of practice, we ask the reader to identify their personal primary design approach from within the modes.

The *manufacturer* is a developer of instructional materials. The manufacturer is often a technician who applies a pre-defined design model or template to solve an educational problem and delivers a product as efficiently as possible. To a large extent, the solution to an educational problem is presented to the manufacturer whose responsibility becomes one of developmental efficiency. Product consistency and stability are of primary importance, leading to results that are predictable and stable.

The *engineer* is an instructional problem solver. The engineer is generally a highly trained professional who ensures a product achieves its educational goal and is usable by the target audience. The engineer can apply contemporary

Table 3. Focus of the design process for the artist, architect, engineer, and manufacturer

Focus	Artist	Architect	Engineer	Manufacturer
Audience	Self	End users	End users	Irrelevant: Audience has been predetermined
Usability	Irrelevant beyond the artist	Important, but adaptable	Very important	Irrelevant: Usability has been predetermined
Technical robustness	Will vary according to the problem	Important, but adaptable	Very important	Irrelevant: Structure has been predetermined
Aesthetics	Critical	Important, but adaptable	Low	Irrelevant: Aesthetics has been predetermined
Profit	Irrelevant	Less important than for the engineer	Budget driven	Critical
Solution	Internally driven	Externally driven	Externally driven	Template driven

research-based ideas to develop educational materials. Thus, interface design and pedagogical theory are important components of this mode of instructional design. The engineer's principal goal is the functional efficiency of the design.

The *architect* extends the engineer's functional and usable solution and attempts to incorporate aesthetics at the core of the design process. By doing so, the architect explores divergent solutions that extend and cultivate the affordances of a medium. The architect's approach to instructional design attempts to balance utility, usability, and aesthetics.

The *artist* is an instructional explorer. The artist uses instructional problems as stimuli to experiment with media and affordances. The instructional artist may work without client or audience, only later attempting to apply to instructional practice what has been learned through the artistic experience. The artist embraces failure and engages in continuous self-criticism while attempting to understand both the problem and self.

What then is your mode of instructional design practice? One's perception of role indicates one's general orientation; in other words, how you perceive your professional orientation will affect your processes and methods of working. Most designers have one principal orientation for work. In reality of course, most instructional

designers operate in different modes at different times, but for our purposes here, understanding your principal mode of operation will provide a basis for understanding this chapter. The results of your survey can help you locate your own professional practice among these four modes. It is hoped by examining beliefs inherent in the survey questions we can stimulate reflection and encourage balance within the field.

We can examine each of the modes by using hypothetical results from our earlier survey (see Figures 1–4). Although we illustrate the performance of each of the four modes across a range of factors, the illustrations are not presented as quantitatively precise graphs. Instead, they are intended to illustrate the changing values among different professional modes.

Manufacturers would have high scores in the firmness category, indicating a concentration on production, operation, and utility. Instructional engineers would have a high rating in commodity, with interests in usability, the scientific/research basis of education, and a focus on the human aspects of learning; they would also have a medium rating for firmness. Artists would have a high rating in the aesthetic area, possibly ignoring or viewing as less valuable other aspects of the design endeavor. Instructional architects would have a balance in the three areas with no one area having dominance in the design process.

Figure 1. Commodity-firmness-delight:
Instructional architect

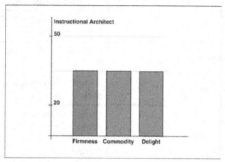

Figure 2. Commodity-firmness-delight:
Instructional artist

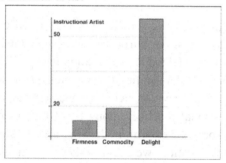

Figure 3. Commodity-firmness-delight:
Instructional engineer

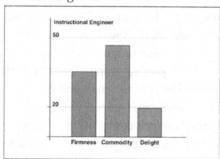

Figure 4. Commodity-firmness-delight:
Instructional manufacturer

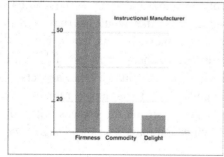

Actual results would vary among modes and even within individuals on a day-to-day basis. We now ask you to return to your initial survey scores to compare and reflect on the illustrated modes in Figures 1–4.

We can compare how each of the four modes of instructional design is differentiated by the Vitruvian aspects (see Figure 5). We believe it is particularly important to understand how different design aspects vary across each mode. Once this pattern has been recognized, we anticipate readers will quickly understand other relationships presented herein and may generate additional relationships of their own.

Artists generally rank highest for aesthetic issues (i.e., delight), but produce correspondingly low ratings for firmness and commodity, reflecting the instructional artist's interest in the experimental, experiential, and visual as opposed to the utilitarian aspects of design. Instructional architects' scores generally reflect a balance across the three areas: no single dimension dominates the design process. Instructional engineers score high in commodity, reflecting interests in usability, the scientific/research basis of education, and a focus on the human aspects of learning. Engineers score medium for firmness. Manufacturers are concerned with the utilitarian aspects of design (i.e., efficiency, robustness, and completion) and score high in the firmness category, reflecting an emphasis on production, operation, and utility. However, they score low in commodity and have little interest in aesthetic design.

These classifications suggest one's attitudes and goals for instructional design. We contend that the field of instructional design emphasizes function and theory, neglecting affective and aesthetic issues to the detriment of education.

INSTRUCTIONAL DESIGN EDUCATION AND INNOVATION

While our observations of the field and subsequent description of modes of practice can shed light

Figure 5. Differences in design approaches for the artist, architect, engineer, and manufacturer

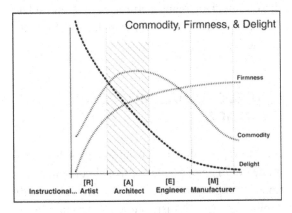

Figure 6. Differences in instructional design education and innovation for the artist, architect, engineer, and manufacturer

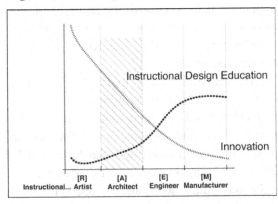

on the field of instructional design, comparisons with other aspects of professional practice can also be valuable. In this graph we illustrate two separate areas, innovation and instructional design education. Each is discussed separately, and in combination below.

Within instructional design education, the focus of learning is principally on the manufacturing and engineering modes. Indeed, we suspect many instructional designers would be happy to complete an instructional design program armed with the ability to select and apply one or more of the most frequently used design models and a foundation in using the most visible software applications in the field (Jonassen, 2006). For those

most interested in manufacturing approaches, the focus on software tools becomes paramount. Many instructional design students learn how to use software to produce instructional materials, which are often based on applying existing models of learning.

More advanced students may approach the engineering mode, employing educational and pedagogical theories in their design work. Few students of instructional design reach the level of instructional architect balancing aesthetic concerns with functional and theoretical concerns. Occasionally, students (and practitioners) assume the mantle of instructional artist, but given the radical and experimental nature of their products, their efforts tend not to be well supported.

Innovation, the ability of the field to develop and implement new methods of instructional design, varies greatly across instructional design modes. Innovation is least evident in manufacturing, where accepted production methods are maintained and applied to instructional design problems, but no new directions are used or sought. Change is incremental and craft based; improvements in efficiency are sought, but are generally modest. Instructional engineers are more likely to innovate through research-based concepts and directions, but change remains moderate. Instructional architects specifically seek new directions for their work, and hence, innovation is increased. Instructional artists, perhaps seeking the "shock of the new" (Hughes, 1991), rate highest in innovation and change.

A hypothetical comparison can be made between the educational system for instructional designers and the value placed on innovation in instructional design. While we often contend creativity and diversity are valuable, in our own students, in instructional design education, those qualities are "messy." Quite often, our goals, like those in mainstream education, are the transmission of content and the development of proper students, graduates, and subsequently instructional designers. We are pleased to produce instructional

Figure 7. Differences in media focus and delight for the artist, architect, engineer, and manufacturer

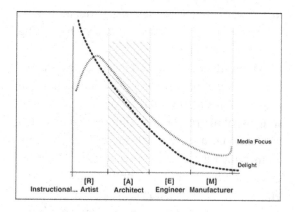

engineers, and often fail to recognize the value of the instructional artist. **A culture of innovation has not developed within instructional design education.**

MEDIA FOCUS

Many instructional design students have an intense engagement with technology; many others develop skills in this area as they practice. Media can be the stepchildren of instructional design: a chore to some, but a pleasure to others. How we emphasize or avoid media is an interesting measure of our instructional design practice (see Figure 3).

Media is an important component of instructional design, and our emphasis or lack thereof is instructive in understanding our modes of instructional design practice. As practitioners vary across the landscape of instructional design, there is a close connection between the focus on the media and our component, delight.

As with practice as an artist, increased skill in media increases the potential for innovation and aesthetic reward. This connection follows with electronic media as well; high levels of skill are often more engaging and more enriching. The instructional architect, however, realizes both the value of a focus on the media and a balanced

approach to function and utility. The artist may overstate the instructional experience, whereas the engineer or manufacturer may overemphasize production and function and undervalue aesthetics.

INSTRUCTIONAL MODES IN PRACTICE

We anticipate the design approaches for each mode could be examined across diverse instructional design problems. To illustrate, we will explore the use of distance learning and how it is addressed by practitioners of each of the four modes of instructional design. Afterwards, we will ask you, the reader to imagine your own hypothetical instructional design problem and to conceive how you could, as an instructional manufacturer, engineer, architect, and artist, address the problem.

Although each solution approach will embody the designer's theoretical conjectures about how people learn and interact with media (i.e. expectations about how designs should function in unique instructional settings) (Sandoval & Bell, 2004), the divergent characteristics of each mode ultimately guide the exploration and solution of the problem.

When asked to develop educational materials for use through distance education, the instructional manufacturer might employ traditional instructional design methods to develop instructional materials emphasizing content presentation and application. Such materials are commonly delivered to learners via the most efficient technologies (e.g., online quizzes, Blackboard/WebCT templates, PowerPoint presentations, etc.). Most of these technologies are stable and, at the core, are based on educational theories such as constructivism, collaboration, or cognitive science, but such theories are remote from the manufacturer. Models for the design process would focus on the functional (i.e. "form follows function"). As with the architecture in the 1960s, an aesthetic could develop based on making the technology work, on utility.

Following a more innovative and media-driven approach than the manufacturer, the instructional engineer could design materials that promote higher-level learning (i.e., both near- and far-transfer) of the content. For example, the engineer could use the linear interactive affordances of a development environment such as Adobe authorware to design animations to highlight key steps in worked examples, simulated models of complex phenomena, and develop interactive exercises adaptive to the prior history of each learner.

The instructional architect, fueled by a balanced approach that includes aesthetics and innovative design, would approach the problem by designing new solutions that promote high-level learning (i.e. generation and challenge), followed by a critical examination of the solution to improve user engagement, motivation, and interaction. By scrutinizing the design and questioning the solution, instructional architects are unique in that they are not satisfied by simply solving the problem. The architect is motivated by extending the boundaries of the available media affordances to explore solutions that enhance the learner experience, moving beyond the pedagogical and technological specifications of the instructional problem (i.e. design beyond done).

The instructional artist, operating with a high expectation of failure, would approach the scenario with little concern for the problem specifications and simply experiment with the available design media and content. For example, the artist could use the graphical capabilities of Adobe Flash to create interactive visualizations or sonic interpretations. Most importantly, although the initial goal may have been pure experimentation with experience, an instructional artist might discover techniques that promote learning. (Note that the term "might" is critical to the nature of the artist; results that are unsuccessful in generating added learning remain valuable.)

We ask now that you, the reader, imagine an instructional design problem of your own. It might be one of your current practice or one that is imaginary. How would this problem be addressed as a manufacturer, as an architect, as an engineer, and as an artist? Which is closer to your own practice or learning? And from which can you draw further inspiration?

It is important to note that most instructional designers are not purists: They do not restrict themselves to a single design mode. Instead, they often shift between modes, borrowing from each mode's approaches and processes. For example, an instructional architect may choose to shift responsibilities toward a manufacturer to construct rapid-prototypes for transient use and experimentation with learners early in the development process. Alternatively, an instructional engineer may shift towards an architectural or artistic practice mode to enhance the aesthetic design and user engagement of their solution, essentially working "beyond done."

The modes are dynamic: any individual designer at times may work in each of the modes. The goal of a balanced approach to instructional design is paramount, encouraging activity across the modes as necessary.

RETAKING THE SURVEY

In reading any article or experiencing any lecture, one measure of success in communication is in changes affected on the reader or audience. We now invite you to revisit the survey from the beginning of the chapter, and this time, answer the questions as to how you would like to perform as an instructional designer. An additional copy is provided after the bibliography.

Reflection on possible changes and alternative directions is valuable for most professionals, including instructional designers. Have your ratings changed? How will this change your outlook on your current position? How should this change the nature of your future design work?

We hope to continue the research surrounding this survey which is available through http://hokanson.cdes.umn.edu/CFD/.

MOVING TO THE LEFT: TACTICS TO INFUSE AESTHETICS IN *YOUR* INSTRUCTIONAL DESIGN

So how should you solve an instructional design problem? We contend that to do it well, you need to step outside of your comfortable answers and ideas. To do it well you need to embrace failure through experimentation. And to do it well, you need to be more of the instructional artist.

How then *will* you become an instructional artist? You might begin by making semantic and conceptual steps, in other words, thinking of yourself *as* an instructional artist and describing your work to others in that way. Extend that to your work procedures: redefine not only your work, but the next project you begin. Assume that the work has hidden meaning, and that you bring to it a completely new vision.

Much of the work in instructional design is done in modes displayed on the right of Table 1, or Figures 5-7 working as an instructional manufacturer or an instructional engineer. Moving to the left (i.e., becoming more balanced in one's approach to instructional design, and working more like an instructional architect or artist) is a philosophy contingent on how *you* value the aesthetic and effectual components of your designs. A number of tactics can be employed to engage and infuse *Delight* in your practice of instructional design; they follow below. Examples of tactics and strategies are described for individuals, professional firms, and schools of instructional design, each encouraging a "move to the left".

Each of these approaches attempts to develop skills of the architect and artist, to help create work that is more engaging, experiential, and delightful. These approaches may be contrary to many aspects of practice in instructional design,

and of course, should not become dominating in one's practice. They are meant to re-orient one's practice. We have based this on a series of observations about those actions which would encourage more innovative and diverse work.

- **Technological immersion leads to insight.** We believe that the instructional medium drives the selection of the method. Limiting design work to a single medium limits the ability to conceptualize those procedures possible with that medium. Similarly, having a range of different media for use allows for a cross-pollination of ideas; what you learn in Flash can help you understand audio software technology. "Intelligence is skill in multiple media" (Hokanson, 2001).

- **Diversity in background leads to innovative practice.** Expertise in a different field provides inspiration and metaphors for novel and innovative work. Pragmatically, alternative expertise stimulates divergent thought, provides varied examples of work, and attracts a wealth of contacts, discussants, and diverse experts to engage.

- **Understanding how to think, communicate, and behave as one's audience, clients, and colleagues is valuable to any practice.** Good instructional design cannot be created in a vacuum; it needs engagement before, after, and during the design process. Understanding one's audience is a constant in the field. We all pay lip service to the idea. However, actively engaging the audience in the design process and seeing their responses is less frequently part of the process.

- **Improve design ideas through learning to criticize and critique the work of others and yourself.** Develop a filtering system that helps you to identify what is valuable, good, and wasteful. Then use it.

- **Finding new ideas and using them is the center of design work.** Develop practices that encourage divergent uses of media.

Creativity, application, and innovation are critical to advancing the field. Creativity, as a skill, can be developed through conscious practice.

- **Strive for continuous innovation and advancement in design; nothing is ever perfect.** The instructional designer should develop dissatisfaction with the status quo, striving to be better with a reach exceeding one's grasp, striving for flow; seeking failure. There needs to be a constant questioning of the ideas, values, assumptions, and procedures of the designer. Self evaluation and critical thinking need to be integrated into the instructional design process.

- **Involvement with others, particularly peers, is valuable to professional work.** Meet, present, publish, engage, and share—discussing and critiquing one's work in a public setting helps people to think divergently.

- **Delaying functional perfection allows aesthetic aspects to evolve.** It is important to experiment with technology and ask questions such as, "What can be done with this medium?" Relevant instructional applications need not be immediately apparent, as the artist creates learning artifacts without consideration for an intended audience or use. Instructional designers, indeed all creative professionals, would be well served by following the model of the 3M Corporation, where it is expected that 15% of budgets will be used for research and experimental development (Kao, 1997).

Table 4 summarizes these topics, and both the table and the listing above are merely beginnings; we ask that you complete the last column in each row, outlining a set of tasks, strategies, or even daily goals to help improve your work as an instructional designer by *moving to the left*.

APPLICATION

How one describes one's work deeply affects the procedures, ideas, and quality of the work itself. We hold that instructional design has long focused on the productive and technical aspects of instructional design, the pedagogical issues or the software delivery system, and has for a long time, ignored the aesthetic and affective domains. Instructional design generally remains a craft based system, with modest theoretical direction. Adherence to traditional procedures, even perfecting the means of production, will continue to produce projects and designs that only have the same capabilities.

Now, as we close, we return to the original questions of the chapter: How *should* you solve an instructional design problem? How could you solve your most common design problem in a different way? How has this changed in reading this chapter?

Instructional designers are not engineers, or artisans, or crafts people, or manufacturers. Their work must go beyond each of these appellations. Instructional design should include all of the aspects reviewed here: commodity, firmness, and delight. Each of these qualities is essential to good design and must be addressed in the design process.

Designers begin each project without knowing the nature or quality of their ultimate solutions. We are not designing if we already know the answer. We are not designing if we follow a cookbook of theories and pedagogy. Yet, we know that the design process, of creating without a net, is engaging, challenging, and leads to superior solutions. To truly design is to extend understanding, to create something new and innovative. To design is a *goal*.

To change education you need to change your perception of your profession. To change your work, you will need to change your mind.

Table 4. Moving to the left: Steps toward becoming an instructional architect or artist

Tactic	Short-hand strategy	Individual tasks/actions	Firm tasks/actions	Curriculum tasks/actions	Outline your tasks/ actions
Technological immersion leads to insight	**Get your hands dirty**	Develop a strong expertise in at least one ID media or technology	Expand divergent skills; encourage cross-team communication of technological advancement	Provide opportunities for technical skills development: include a studio component as part of ID program	
Diversity of background leads to better practice	**Become an expert at something else**	Develop skills in another domain; enrich your 'day job' by expanding your skill set	Support professional development and cultural activity among employees	Provide flexibility and encouragement for non-ID course work	
Understand one's audience, colleagues, and clients	**Understand people**	Ask questions and listen; invite others to use your designs during the design process	Employ active user testing, prototyping, and other public engagement	Include psychology and user-testing courses in curriculum	
Improve design ideas throughout the development process	**Learn to criticize and critique**	Seek feedback on design work; develop a habit/process of self reflection; put your work on display when possible	Celebrate design work with open critiques; publish work through peer review	Model and include active critiques in courses and studios	
Finding and using new ideas is the essence of design	**Learn to be creative**	Choose the other path, the one less taken; destroy your routine; be receptive to new inspirations in any environment	Develop as a creative organization; support and develop creative ideas by all	Add creativity courses; require multiple concepts in problem solving across curriculum	
Strive for continuous innovation and advancement in design	**Never finish**	Integrate self evaluation and critical thinking into the design process; develop dissatisfaction	Always strive for new products; reward exploration and failure; 3M's 15% rule (Kao, 1997)	Develop skills in critical thinking and design critique; encourage and model self-reflection and improvement	
Interaction with peers improves critiquing skills, ideas, and the design process	**Connect**	Talk to someone else; present at conferences in ID and other fields; become active in the design community	Support employees in attending conferences, courses, and community events	Encourage participation, within ID and with other disciplines; encourage projects with other majors	
Delaying functional perfection allows aesthetic aspects to emerge	**Work as an instructional artist**	Create experimental instructional projects; build instructional experiences; do something wrong; value failure	Use competitions and 'what-if' sketches to investigate ideas; become less utilitarian	Reorient priorities of the design process; support "way out" projects; embrace the experimental failures of students	

REFERENCES

Aspillagae, M. (1991). Screen design: A location of information and its effects on learning. *Journal of Computer Based Instruction, 18*(3), 89-92.

Hokanson, B. (2001). Digital image creation and analysis as a means to examine learning and cognition. In M. Beynon, C. Nehaniv, & K. Dautenhahn (Eds.), *Proceedings of the 4th International Conference on Cognitive Technology.* Berlin: Springer.

Hokanson, B., & Hooper, S. (2000). Computers as cognitive media: Examining the potential of computers in education. *Computers in Human Behavior, 16,* 537-552.

Hughes, R. (1991). *The shock of the new.* New York: Knopf.

Johnson, P. (1994). *The theory of architecture: Concepts, themes, and practices.* New York: Van Nostrand Reinhold.

Jonassen, D. H. (2006). A constructivist's perspective on functional contextualism. *Educational Technology: Research and Development, 54*(1), 43-47.

Kao, J. (1997). *Innovation: Breakthrough thinking at 3M, Dupont, GE, Pfizer and Rubbermaid.* New York: Collins.

Kirschner, P., Strijbos, J., Kreijns, K., & Beers, P. J. (2004). Designing electronic collaborative learning environments. *Educational Technology Research and Development, 52*(3), 47-66.

Lavie, T., & Tractinsky, N. (2004). Assessing dimensions of perceived visual aesthetics of web sites. *International Journal of Human-Computer Studies, 60,* 269-298.

McEwen, I. (2004). *Vitruvius: Writing the body of architecture.* Cambridge: MIT Press.

Norman, D. (2004). *Emotional design: Why we love (or hate) everyday things.* New York: Basic Books.

Parizotto-Ribeiro, R., & Hammond, N. (2004). What is aesthetics anyway? Investigating the use of design principles. *Proceedings of the NordCHI 2004 Workshop,* Finland, (pp. 37-40).

Parrish, P. (2005). Embracing the aesthetics of instructional design. *Educational Technology, 45*(2), 16-24.

Reiser, R. (2001). A history of instructional design and technology: Part I: A history of instructional media. *Educational Technology Research and Development, 49*(1), 53-64.

Rowling, J.K. (1998). *Harry Potter and the Sorcerer's Stone.* London: Scholastic.

Sandoval, W. & Bell, P. (2004) Design-based research methods for studying learning in context: Introduction. *Educational Psychologist, 39*(4), 199-201.

Tractinsky, N. (2004). Toward the study of aesthetics in information technology. *Proceedings from the 25th International Conference on Information Systems,* USA, (pp. 11-20).

Wilson, B. (2005). Broadening our foundation for instructional design: Four pillars of practice. *Educational Technology, 45*(2), 10-15.

Chapter II
Translate to Communicate:
Facilitating Client Understanding of Design Languages

Jason K. McDonald
Brigham Young University, USA

ABSTRACT

In this chapter I discuss how principles of natural language translation can help instructional designers communicate instructional design languages in ways more understandable to their clients. I argue that instructional designers should focus more on the fundamental meanings they are attempting to communicate through their design languages than on the mechanics and style of those languages. This can lead designers to find representation methods that help their clients better understand design meanings than if designers only used the language conventions with which they were already familiar. My hope is that this contribution to the literature on instructional design languages will lead to new language conventions that help designers more easily communicate their intentions and plans to all those who have an interest in a design's overall success.

INTRODUCTION

Practitioners in all service fields need to communicate well with clients to be successful. Doctors must communicate with patients to diagnose a physical ailment and then provide a proper treatment. Realtors must communicate with potential customers to show properties and complete a sale. Instructional designers are no different in their need to communicate well with clients. The clients of instructional designers could include university faculty or administrators, classroom teachers, corporate executives, students, or anyone who sponsors, pays for, or uses an instructional product. Instructional designers must communicate with these clients to understand their expectations, explain design concepts, refine designs-in-progress, or evaluate the effectiveness of the final product. And these are only a sample of the countless communication points between instructional designers and their clients. In fact, it may not be overstating the point to say that the business of instructional design cannot be separated from the process of communication. Along this line, the ability to "communicate effectively in visual, oral, and written form" has been deemed "essential" by the International Board of Standards for Training, Performance and Instruction (2006).

Unfortunately, the designer-client communications process sometimes breaks down. Communication problems between consultants and clients are well-researched in the general business literature (Appelbaum & Steed, 2005), and a number of researchers in instructional design have made similar observations (e.g., Keppell, 2001, 2004; Maple, 1994; Miles, 1983). A main theme running through all this research and observation is that communication problems between designers and their clients can lead to frustration at best, or perhaps even more severe consequences such as failure of a project or ultimately a deficiency in students' learning.

Given the topic of this handbook, it seems germane to ask what the emerging perspectives on design languages and notation systems can offer instructional designers to help them solve their client communication breakdowns. The answer is that there is much to learn. The concept of design languages can help instructional designers understand communication and communication problems in new ways. At a very basic level, all communication takes place through the use of language. Instructional designers (and, in fact, designers in general) communicate not only through their natural languages (e.g.,, English, Spanish), but also through one or more design

languages. "A design language is what designers use to communicate designs, plans, and intentions to each other and to the producers of their artifacts" (Gibbons & Brewer, 2005, p. 113). These languages can take the form of such artifacts as "flowcharts, storyboard forms, scripts, diagrams, sketches, and text descriptions" (Waters & Gibbons, 2004, pp. 66-67). Communicating through one of these design languages can be difficult even among those who are skillfully trained in their use. But it becomes much more difficult to communicate when "speaking" in a design language with others who are not fluent in that language. It can sound as foreign as does Italian to the person who only speaks Korean. Additional challenges arise because of the visual nature of many of the languages used to communicate instructional designs. Understanding visual representations is a learned skill (Rose, 2001). One who is attempting to understand an instructional design, then, must not only be familiar with the jargon and terminology of the discipline, but also must understand the conventions of the drawings or other illustrations used to reify the design.

Given the importance of communication in the work of instructional design, it is worthwhile to use the metaphor of instructional designers and their clients speaking different languages to explore possible solutions for when communication breaks down. When people wish to communicate with those who do not speak their natural languages, some process of translation must take place. Natural language translation is typically not as simple as looking up corresponding words in a foreign language dictionary. Translation is described by translation theorists as "an extremely complex phenomenon, comprise[d] of a set of interdependent processes (perceptual, cognitive, pragmatic, interactive, social and communicative) embedded in a matrix of variable temporal, spatial and cultural contexts" (Shreve, 1999). In other words, successful translation can be a difficult and intellectually taxing job. When translators underestimate the number of factors involved to successfully translate a message, the translation will often fail to communicate what the author intended—sometimes with humorous results (for example, see the website http://www. engrish.com).

In this chapter I take the position that translating the design languages used by instructional designers (especially those languages that are visual) into languages more natural to their clients can help improve the communication process between the two groups. My goal in advancing this metaphor is to help instructional designers focus more carefully on the fundamental meanings they are attempting to communicate through their designs, and find representation methods that best help their clients understand that meaning. I first review the concept of natural language translation. Next, I discuss how principles of effective translation can apply to the communication skills of instructional designers. To help make the application of translation principles more concrete, I also describe how advertisers (providers of a service in some ways very similar to instructional design) have successfully used strategies that resemble translation to help ensure their clients understand the messages they intend to send. This will help illustrate how translation principles can be operationalized into processes that can be adopted by instructional designers.

TRANSLATION

In modern translation theory, a text is thought of as the public expression of a given message and meaning, and not the actual message or meaning itself (Newmark, 2003). Effective translation techniques help translators use their knowledge of language, context, and culture to understand the meaning of an original text (called the *source text*), find an equivalent meaning for the text in a new language (called the *target language*), and clearly communicate that meaning to an audience who understands the target language. This is not

a trivial problem. People are often very skilled at using the mechanical and stylistic components of a language to publicly represent their message meanings. Novice translators sometimes assume that these expressions *are* an author's meaning, and translate the mechanics of the source message into a target language while ignoring the underlying meaning the mechanics were intended to signify. Yet it is also possible for translators to ignore the close connection between meaning and style, and produce translations that have no relationship to the mechanics an author may have carefully chosen to evoke specific emotions or thoughts. The skilled translator balances the difficult process of communicating source ideas in ways that are coherent and understandable to fluent speakers of the target language, yet that still approximate as closely as possible the styles of the text in the source language, never losing sight that the goal is to communicate not only words but also the tone and message character the original author intended (Bell, 1991).

Many guides have been developed to help translators balance these sometimes competing concerns. Massoud (1988), for example, developed a guide for preparing successful translations that focused on practical communication techniques. A sampling from her techniques demonstrates some of the critical principles translators follow when conducting their work:

1. Avoiding unnecessary "linguistic subtleties" (p. 37).
2. Identifying the right level of equivalence.
3. Making overt what is implied.
4. Explaining important metaphorical, cultural, or historical factors.
5. Making the translation "fluent and smooth" (p. 19).
6. Using the idioms and grammatical constructions of the target language.

While these techniques are not mutually exclusive, they can be grouped into categories to aid in their analysis. The first two techniques help translators focus on the difference between the meaning of a source text and the mechanics of the source language. The next two help translators concentrate on the bridge between the source and target languages, and making explicit in the target language components of meaning that may be left indefinite or imprecise in the source. The final two help translators attend to the form and style of the translation in the target language, and encourage them to create translations that are intelligible and natural to speakers of the target language. Each of these principles will be discussed in more detail below.

The first principle helps translators focus on the difference between the meaning of a source text and the mechanics of the source language. For example, Massoud's (1988) first technique was to avoid unnecessary "linguistic subtleties" (p. 37) of the source text. Massoud elaborated by stating that sometimes translators:

Are often tempted to sacrifice clarity for the sake of minute formal subtleties that might be pleasing to the reader who knows the original language (in which case he does not really need a translation), but confusing to those who are not acquainted with that language. (p. 37)

In other words, Massoud encouraged translators who are skilled in a source language to not become distracted by the nuances that may make that language pleasing to native speakers, but may not be helpful when communicating the message to others who speak the target language. This is tied closely to Massoud's second technique, which helps further explain how translators can separate a source meaning from the mechanics of a source language. Massoud stated that translators should identify the right level of *conceptual* equivalence for each word or phrase in a text as they are preparing a translation. Baker (1992) expanded on this idea when she stated that each individual word in a source does not have to be literally translated

if the combined effect of the transliterations introduces a potential error of meaning into the full translation. Rather, translators could use a more general word, a more expressive word, or even eliminate a word completely to make the translation's meaning clearer.

Additionally, equivalence between languages is not always at the word level. Translators may also focus on equivalence at the sentence or paragraph level, or even at the level of the full text. In other words, translators could translate a lengthy source phrase into a much smaller number of words, if the overall meaning of the words in the target language was equivalent to the longer passage in the original. Or, a single word in a source language may require a full sentence of translation in the target language to preserve the original meaning. A poem's translation is a good example of the principle of equivalence. Poetry is a complicated art form that depends not only on the words themselves, but also on word order, meter, rhyme, rhythm, stress, and many other stylistic conventions to produce a unique intellectual and emotional effect. To preserve this effect a translator usually cannot just transliterate every word of the poem. The translator must also consider what word order in the new language will evoke the same or similar effect as did the word order in the original language. The same is also true of the poem's meter or rhyme. In fact, in some cases the right level of equivalence for a poem's translation might be at the level of the genre itself. It is possible that the poetic form in some target languages may not evoke the emotional effect an author desired when he or she composed the poem originally. In this case, the skilled translator might choose another genre to stay as true as possible to the meaning and intent of the original author (Massoud, 1988; see also Mbangwana, 1990).

A second principle of effective translation is for translators to make explicit in the target language components of meaning that may be left indefinite or imprecise in the source language. According to Fenner (1989), "converting a text from one language to another often throws up problems that can conveniently be ignored within one language" (p. 52), yet which in another language threaten to make the meaning incomprehensible. Some examples of these problems might include idioms, abbreviations or acronyms, or common cultural practices that do not have a close equivalent in other cultures. Idioms are phrases that have gained meaning beyond the combined effect of the individual words. They may be very rich to a local culture but not be familiar elsewhere, such as the phrase "a bird in the hand is worth two in the bush," meaning to be content with what you have and not pursue risky ventures. Sometimes abbreviations or acronyms become ubiquitous in a language and fully replace the original phrase they signified, such as the English word *scuba*, an acronym formed from the phrase *self-contained underwater breathing apparatus*. And some cultural practices are so widespread as to need no explanation to native speakers of that language. For example, most English-speaking Americans would not need any additional explanation if they find out their restaurant waiter is also an aspiring actor, because of the common stereotype in American society that actors are often out of work and are forced to wait tables to pay their bills.

All of these examples along with my commentary are instantiations of Massoud's (1988) general technique of making overt in the translation what was only implied in the source. Translators solve problems caused by tacit or embedded linguistic components by being more clear and precise in their translations. In particular, they can add a sentence of explanation the first time they introduce an idiom, use the full technical term in conjunction with common abbreviations or acronyms, or include a short phrase to help explain the relevance of a common cultural practice. Without such techniques, the common shortcuts used in every language to make communication more efficient, or the literary conventions that make a language more aesthetically pleasing,

threaten to stall communication with readers in a new language.

As a more extended illustration, consider the case of business communications. When translating a letter with a business purpose from one language into another, translators must often be very willing to modify the text to make it more understandable, linguistically and culturally. For example, good business etiquette in the United States suggests that the writer of a letter will typically state the business purpose of the letter immediately after the salutation, and will close the letter immediately at the conclusion of the business purpose. However, in other cultures readers expect some type of pleasant greeting before beginning the business purpose of the letter, as well as expect some wish of good fortune after the business' conclusion. Even though phrases such as this will most likely not be included in a letter written by an American, a skilled translator will add such phrases because to do so will be true to the letter author's intent of appropriately advancing a business relationship (Massoud, 1988).

A third principle for effective translation is for translators to attend to the form and style of the final translation in the target language. Translators should create translations that are natural to speakers of the target language. Kujamäki (2004) emphasized that is can be a very difficult task, even if translators are fluent in the target language. Sometimes the translator's skill in the target language may lead to translations that sound simplistic or even a little naïve. Native or fluent speakers of a language often can easily identify novice translations because they sound stilted or artificial. Massoud's (1988) two techniques based on this principle can help translators to avoid these problems. First, she encouraged translators to take time to make their translations "fluent and smooth" (p. 19). It is possible for translators to get so caught up in the mechanics of a translation that they neglect to fully examine their final product. Sometimes all that is necessary is for translators to edit their translation, as if they were editing a document they had written themselves, to provide a final touch of elegance to the new mechanics and style.

Massoud's (1988) second technique was for translators to use the idioms and grammatical constructs of the target language in their translations. Skillful use of linguistic conventions is another way of helping a translation sound intelligible and natural. Skilled speakers of a target language will rely on these mechanical and stylistic devices to richly understand messages that they read or hear. For example, an idiom may not only succinctly express a complex idea, but may also express it using a certain tone that helps an audience understand the author's attitude towards that idea, or to them as readers or listeners. Translators, then, can use the mechanics of the target language to express message meanings more expertly. For example, where a message in a source language may emphasize the importance of early problem-solving, and the author used an informal, local idiom, translators may choose to express the idea in English using the idiom "a stitch in time saves nine," even though the source message had nothing to do with stitches or sewing.

While some of the techniques suggested by these principles may appear contradictory, that is often the nature of relying on principles rather than prescriptive rules to accomplish a task. Like other creative endeavors, translation has very few laws that generalize equally well to all situations. Rather, as Chesterman (2004) pointed out, translation is a local, contextual task. It depends as much on situational factors (such as the target audience and purpose of the translation) as much as it depends on the requirements of either the source or target languages. Techniques based on principles tend to apply best to local situations. As a result, one local situation may call for a technique opposite of that required in another situation. Skillful translation is a time-consuming task, then, not only because of the need to fully understand the source text, but also because of the need to fully understand the target situation (Massoud, 1988). Only then can translators be

sure that a particular technique is appropriate, and will lead to a translation that is accurate, natural, and helpful for the target audience to understand the meaning an author intended in an original, source text.

TRANSLATING INSTRUCTIONAL DESIGN LANGUAGES

The preceding discussion provides a foundation for applying the metaphor of translation to communication between instructional designers and their clients. If instructional designers understood the principles of translation and how they applied to the work of design, might they be able to separate their design meanings from the style and mechanics of their design languages? If so, could they also use translation principles to find ways to communicate their meaning in languages more natural and intelligible to their clients? In this section I propose how instructional designers might apply translation principles in their work. As part of this discussion I will draw examples from the field of advertising, a service industry that has adopted communication skills analogous to those described by translation theorists. Similar skills can be added to the repertoire of instructional designers, helping them to successfully translate their plans and intentions into expressions more understandable to those not fluent in the languages of design. Where relevant, I will also reference the literature of instructional design to show how some designers may have already incorporated similar principles into their work. As mentioned earlier, these principles of translation are not mutually exclusive, and are only separated for purposes of convenience in analysis.

First, instructional designers can benefit from a principle for design language translation that focuses them on the differences between the meaning of their designs and the style and mechanics of their design languages. As Bucciarelli (1994) stated:

The design is the shared vision... [While] each participant in the process has a personal collection of sketches, flowcharts, cost estimates, spreadsheets, models... the shared vision, as some synthetic representation of the artifact as a whole, is not in documents or written plans. To the extent that it exists as a whole, it is a social construction—dynamic, plastic, given nuance and new meaning at each informal gathering of two and three in a hallway or at formal meetings such as scheduled design reviews. (p. 159)

This implies that, although the connection between design language and design meaning may be strong, there are some aspects of the design that are independent of any language or notation system used for their development and expression. Instructional designers should be careful not to confuse meaning with mechanics, so that when necessary they can separate the two and express their meaning in other ways.

More specifically, the two techniques Massoud (1988) discussed in connection with this principle, avoiding unnecessary "linguistic subtleties" (p. 37) and focusing on the right level of equivalence, can be applied by instructional designers during the design translation process. One of the exciting promises of new instructional design languages is that they will help designers create more nuanced and complex designs. For example, Botturi's (see Chapter VII in this handbook) E^{2}ML is a design language which allows users to represent the components of an instructional environment through a visual notation system. Botturi's evaluation of the language revealed that trained instructional designers thought it was "potentially powerful, flexible, and adaptable to different strategies and situations" (p. 129). For these designers, E^{2}ML may become a very useful language for expressing their abstract concepts in a public way. Yet other evaluative data also indicated that E^{2}ML's "complexity may make it difficult for instructors and course authors" (Botturi, 2003, p. 222) to learn its conventions. In other words, as do

all good languages, E^{2}ML contains linguistic subtleties that make the language functional and efficient to those trained in its use, but that may make it incomprehensible to those who are not. Instructional designers, in their role as translators, should find the conceptual equivalents for the meanings expressed through these linguistic techniques so they may articulate them in other ways more understandable to those with whom they are communicating.

An example of how this might occur will be instructive. This example is taken from the field of advertising, a service industry with highly developed methods for communicating message ideas to their clients and the public. Advertising campaigns are often created by an advertising agency. Advertising agencies employ account managers to understand their clients' product placement needs, wants, and business constraints. The account managers then plan an advertising campaign, and work with other agency personnel and media producers to create the campaign according to the plan specified (Sandage, Fryburger, & Rotzoll, 1983). The account manager is also primarily responsible to represent the agency to the client. Account managers are expected to know a little of all the languages used by the creative producers they work with, so they can accurately represent the creative plans back to the client (Solomon, 2003). In many ways, this description of an account manager sounds very similar to that of an instructional designer. This may become clearer if one thinks of an advertising campaign as a piece of instruction. As do account managers, instructional designers have the responsibility to understand a client's needs, wants, and constraints, then work with other team members to create an instructional solution that appropriately responds to the situation faced by the client.

Most account managers, when creating the advertising campaign plan, develop what is known as the *strategy* of the campaign to facilitate their communication with clients. The advertising strategy is a short statement of what a successful advertising campaign will accomplish. The strategy is developed by an account manager before any other work on an advertising campaign begins, and both the agency and the client agree in writing that the strategy expresses what the client expects to result from the campaign (Solomon, 2003). The strategy includes general goals for the campaign, for example, "getting existing users to use more, attracting new users, or persuading buyers of rival products to switch brands" (Davis, 1997, p. 30). Additionally, successful strategies will also begin to quantify other important considerations for the campaign. Strategies should consider, "the business goals, the sales goals, and the communication goals. . . . [as well as] the response the client wants from the key constituencies: customers, prospects, employees, company management, shareholders, the press, and the competition" (Solomon, 2003, p. 4).

Typically the strategy is recorded in a document called a *brief*. A brief is intended to be exactly what the name suggests—a concise document that provides all necessary details about the strategy, as well as some of the critical factors that led to its development. Lengthy briefs may contain a wealth of detailed information about the situational factors of a client and the needs of a campaign, but ironically the longer the brief is the less likely it is to be used. There is no set formula for a brief. Lee and Johnson (1999) described the brief as a statement of:

A profile of the target audience; the problem, issue, or opportunity that advertising is expected to address; the advertising objective; the key customer benefit; supportive benefits; and a creative strategy statement (a campaign theme or Big Idea, and advertising appeal, and the creative execution style to be used). (p. 138)

Davis (1997) described an ideal brief as being even shorter—simply a concise description of why the target audience will read, watch, or listen to the advertising, and afterwards what they will think, feel, or believe.

The value of the brief is twofold. First, it helps the creative personnel understand the strategy well enough to develop a campaign that is situationally appropriate and likely to succeed. Additionally, the brief (and the strategy it represents) is used with the client to evaluate design ideas. Each concept is discussed with the client in terms of the brief. If an idea cannot be explained using the brief, it is usually discarded from the design before the client sees it. If the idea seems too valuable to discard, the account manager discusses it with the client to determine whether the brief is incomplete, or whether the concept should be saved for another campaign. The brief becomes a "yardstick" (Solomon, 2003, p. 35), representing what is important to the client, and allowing advertisers to measure how closely their ideas address the client's needs.

An artifact similar to the brief may be a helpful notation system for instructional designers to make explicit the conceptual equivalence between their designs and their clients' concerns. Note that, as described earlier, many of the items typically included in a brief sound similar to those typically included in an instructional design (such as statements of the target audience and the objectives for the campaign). But as opposed to a detailed specification document, a valuable instructional design brief would be much more concise. As in natural language translation, a strict transliteration of terms may not be sufficient to express a message's meaning in a new language. In other words, it may be insufficient to only take the individual expressions from an instructional design and articulate them, in a one-to-one relationship, in other ways. A brief that describes in a simple, jargon-free way the purpose of the instruction, how the students will change having experienced the instruction, and an over-arching theme for the instructional experience may serve as the designer's tool for mapping individual elements of a design to concepts most important to the client. In other words, the designer could use a brief to identify how an individual design element contributes to the realization of the client's most important goals. The brief could then be used by a design team to evaluate ideas before they are brought to the client, potentially eliminating ideas that cannot be mapped to client's needs. It could also help designers be prepared for meetings with the client, by giving them expressions to describe the design not in technical terms, but in clear terms that address what the client is most interested in.

This instructional design brief need not only be verbal, as in the example provided from advertising. A visual notation system for the brief may also be useful, especially if it were able to reduce the complexity of the full design into a proposal easily understood by someone not trained in the complete design language. Although slightly more limited in scope to what I describe as a brief, Keppell's (2001) content production process is an instructional design artifact that seems to meet many of a brief's criteria. Keppell specifically created a process and accompanying visual notation scheme for helping instructional designers work with subject matter experts (SME) to gather content in ways that would be clear to the SME how well the designer understood their business and objectives. Keppell also described how the graphical representation of the content could then be used "as a communication tool for interfacing between the instructional designer, SME, and graphic designer/programmer" (p. 220), helping to ensure that more detailed design specifications as well as the final product were logical derivatives of the information contained in the original, more client-friendly document.

Instructional designers can also benefit from a second principle for design language translation, which is to make explicit in their client's language components of meaning that may appropriately be left indefinite or imprecise in their design language. Examples of imprecise linguistic conventions from natural languages include idioms, commonly-understood abbreviations or acronyms, and the unexplained use of widespread cultural practices. It is simply the nature of communication that there will be manners of expression peculiar to each language used. This makes communication both more efficient as well as more useful to skilled speakers of that language.

Unique linguistic conventions also exist in design languages. Design languages often begin as an individual's personal way of getting their own work done. As Gibbons and Brewer (2005) described, a person originating a design language uses,

Whatever familiar, comfortable, and useful terms the person possesses... As people interact with [each other] in solving design problems, they may see the value of [one person's] personal, idiosyncratic design language or some of its terms and begin to share use of that language. (p. 119)

Over time, these unique conventions not only spread but become natural to users of the language. Large amounts of information become condensed into individual notation elements. For example, as Stubbs and Gibbons (see Chapter III in this handbook) have reviewed, in many fields designers use drawings to initiate design concepts. These drawings are often rough, abstract representations of what the designer envisions will eventually be created, and through successive phases of improvement the design becomes more and more refined until the final product emerges. Applying this notion to instructional design, instructional designers may begin an instructional computer program by sketching a flowchart of each step in the instructional sequence. Eventually the designer begins sketching individual screens, roughly illustrating what elements belong on each screen and their relationship to each other. From these initial drawings the first prototypes of the program could be built and formatively evaluated with students.

The value of the preliminary drawings, according to Stubbs and Gibbons, is precisely because they represent design elements in such vague and ill-defined ways. This, in part, is because designers' thinking about the final design is refined as they commit their initial ideas to paper. In other words, designers' cannot fully develop their early concepts without reifying them in some way. Additionally, vague drawings can allow designers to explore many possible solutions to a design problem without over-committing to ideas that will not be productive to develop more fully.

Yet while designers have the time and interest to explore and become fluent in the conventions of their design languages, the consumers of their designs most likely do not. Designers may not be aware that when they share design concepts with people outside of their immediate group, they may be omitting important information that is compressed by their design language and that are tacitly understood by those fluent in the language but missed by someone who is not (e.g., Maple, 1994). They may be unaware that a non-native speaker of their design language may be expecting very different conventions to understand what is being communicated, as does the American writer of a letter who leaves out phrases of greeting that foreign readers expect to see. Additionally, users of a design language may also believe that their methods of expression are the *only* ways to communicate design constructs, forgetting that their language is only one among many. Although certain design languages may have very efficient or expressive notation elements, regardless of their expressive value to fluent users they can be unintelligible to those not skilled or experienced in their use. For example, it is possible that showing design drawings to those not trained in their conventions may have unanticipated effects. If someone does not know how rough drawings can advance the design process, will that person misunderstand a designer's message if shown an unrefined sketch, and focus more on the lack of polish rather than on the concept being commu-

nicated? An answer to this question can be found in Massoud's (1988) general technique of making overt in the translation what was only implied in the source. Sometimes to translate a design, the instructional designer may need to make design elements more explicit than they would otherwise make if the design were only consumed by them or their production team.

Returning to the case of advertising helps illustrate one way of making overt what is implied, and of how to present design concepts to clients in ways that communicate the message the designer intends. When making advertising concepts public (such as when they are shown to the client for the first time), Solomon (2003) stated that the presentations are carefully managed and in ideal situations are scripted and rehearsed many times. In other words, "client presentations… are about theater" (p. 61). Solomon seems to be stating that, just like in good theater every element of the experience contributes to the overall meaning of the play, every element of a concept presentation should contribute to the overall meaning of the ad campaign being proposed. Any element in the presentation not specifically designed to clearly communicate the concept is an opportunity for the client to become distracted, and lose focus on the idea the advertiser is presenting. Belch and Belch (1995) specifically mentioned how, during presentations, concept storyboards are sometimes "too abstract for most [viewers] to understand" (p. 275). Rather than presenting their rough storyboards one frame at a time, then, some advertisers use an artifact called an "animatic" (p. 275), which is a filmed version of the storyboard with audio narration, which appears closer to the final commercial the storyboards represent. As Roman and Maas (1976) stated in their classic work on advertising, the artifacts used to present concept ideas "must tell the story" (p. 14) of the final campaign. While advertising concepts may originate with a rough sketch or a few words jotted on the back of a napkin, when the time comes to share those ideas with the client advertisers are careful to present them in ways that make explicit the components of meaning that were only tacitly communicated in the original.

The same principle can apply as instructional designers share design concepts with their clients. Design artifacts can contain expressions or visual notations similar to the natural language expressions of idioms, abbreviations, acronyms, or cultural practices so commonly understood they are unnecessary to explain. Instructional designers can make more overt the meanings implied through these conventions in similar ways as do natural language translators. For example, the rough quality of a design drawing is a cultural practice that other designers implicitly understand, and their languages are more useful because of the roughness of early sketches. Yet the rough character of design drawings may need to be elaborated when presented to clients so the meaning they communicate to other designers is not lost. This could take place in a number of ways. In some cases it may be sufficient for designers to provide verbal explanations to their clients of why the drawing is rough and the value communicated by the roughness. On the general topic of designer/client communication, Maple (1994) even suggested instructional designers follow a "script" (p. 38) when discussing technical matters. While Maple did not specifically mention a script for introducing rough drawings to clients the same principle may still be helpful to ensure that designers are not leaving any critical information unexplained.

In other cases the designers may want to refine the drawing before showing it to clients, in a manner similar to that of translators who add phrases to a translation that are not in an original text but that are still true to the original author's intent. This is not to suggest that instructional designers should compromise their design or the overall meaning they are trying to communicate. Designers do need to act with integrity and communicate in ways that maintain the essential qualities of their message. But they also need to remember that they

are not designing only for themselves, and so have an obligation to make sure they present ideas in ways that communicate clearly to others outside of design communities. Just as skilled advertisers carefully prepare their client presentations so the chance of unanticipated distraction is reduced, skilled instructional designers should make their client communications as explicit as they can to avoid turning their clients away from the ideas they are trying to express.

Finally, a third principle for design language translation is for instructional designers to attend to the form and style of client communication in the client's own language. Design languages are not unique to the field of instructional design. Design languages are a common tool in many fields, including engineering, architecture, filmmaking, music, dance, software development, and graphic design (Stubbs & Gibbons, Chapter III; Waters & Gibbons, 2004), and many practitioners of these fields use the services of instructional designers. In fact, enlarging the concept of design languages may also reveal that business leaders, university faculty, or government bureaucrats (other common clients of instructional designers) have methods they "use to communicate designs, plans, and intentions to each other and to the producers of their artifacts" (Gibbons & Brewer, 2005, p. 113). In other words, all of those benefiting from the services of instructional designers already have rich and nuanced ways of communicating their ideas and purposes. To better communicate with any of these clients, instructional designers should become as fluent as possible in the client's own design languages, so they sound intelligible and natural to those with whom they are sharing ideas.

The same techniques Massoud (1988) suggested for natural language translators may help instructional designers accomplish this goal. First, she encouraged translators to make their translations sound "fluent and smooth" (p. 19). Just as translators can sometimes get caught up in the individual procedures of their work and neglect to examine the full effect of their final translation, instructional designers may overlook the overall message they are sending their clients as they perfect the component design elements they want their clients to understand. As with translators, then, instructional designers may benefit simply by reflecting on the whole of their message, in a sense "editing" it so the mechanics and style communicates the design in a manner that is graceful and elegant. Massoud additionally encouraged use of idioms and grammatical structures from the target language to help translations sound more natural to native speakers of that language. Instructional designers can use this technique to help their own client communications become richer and more nuanced. They can use the common expressions or notation systems of their clients to expertly communicate complex ideas in ways that will be more persuasive because they are clearer to the intended audience (O'Keefe, 2006).

As with the other principles discussed in this chapter, the field of advertising also provides examples of how instructional designers might become fluent in their clients' design languages, and so "speak" them expertly during their communications. Solomon (2003) described how effective account managers "lived the client's brand" (p. 9) while they were working with that client's products. In other words, they became familiar with the company's founding and past record, met employees, discovered what consumers and the media thought of the company and its products, and learned about the competition and what threats they posed to the company. Solomon even encouraged account managers to "find a way to use [their] clients' products" (p. 10) in their everyday life, contributing the value of their lived experience to the advertising they created for the products. Solomon believed that this type of research was invaluable. In the words of one of his clients, the company chose Solomon's agency because "you spoke our language. You sounded like one of us. You demonstrated that you knew what we were about" (p. 10).

Implicit in this advice is that, while there may be some generic conventions common to all members of an industry (i.e. all universities probably share some things in common, as do all businesses in a specific market) many other components of a client's design languages may be idiosyncratic. To be fluent in the client's design languages, then, instructional designers should become as familiar as possible with how their clients may use different languages in unique ways. For example, while specific clients may adopt standard methods of expression or communication from their industry, they may also have developed standards of their own. In a more general sense, individual clients may have either formal or informal communication or presentation styles. They may be experienced themselves with the languages of instructional design or be novices to the instructional design process. And, just as Solomon (2003) knew that an account manager could not learn about a company's product in the abstract, instructional designers can also be well-served by richly experiencing the full situation of the local client they are serving. An example of this strategy might be for instructional designers to meet those who will be using the instruction they develop, and not only rely on abstract descriptions of students who are similar. Or, they could spend time working as a temporary employee in a client's business, or using themselves the products or processes for which they are developing training.

These suggestions should not be foreign to those trained in existing processes for need or task analysis. But they do require a different level of commitment from the instructional designer when other methods may seem easier, but would produce less rich information (see Osguthorpe, Osguthorpe, Jacob, & Davies, 2003). And what may be new to some readers is my advise to not only use these rich information sources to produce a high-quality design, but then to use that information to also enrich communication with those sponsoring the design. All of these techniques could potentially be very helpful for instructional designers to communicate their designs to clients in ways that are more meaningful and convincing.

CONCLUSION

In this chapter I have reviewed principles and techniques common to the field of natural language translation, and applied them to the communication processes of instructional designers and their clients. I have also included specific examples from the field of advertising, a service field that has developed methods of communication clients that are analogous to natural language translation, as well as research from instructional designers who have advocated similar principles. Table 1 summarizes these principles and examples.

This discussion was not meant to encourage the use of specific formulas or checklists for designers to apply to their personal communication processes. Chesterman (2004) called natural language translation a local, contextual task. So is the process of translating an instructional design. Each design situation will have embedded in it unique factors that the skilled designer will have to learn to make their translations as successful

as possible. Although one of the values of design languages is the standardization of terms they provide (Gibbons & Brewer, 2005), there has not yet been developed a sure formula for using this standardization to ensure a successful translation. It may be that for the foreseeable future translating designs will remain in the realm of human intervention, as has the translation of natural languages. Yet developers of instructional design languages could take the need to translate into account as they create their languages and notation systems. They can intentionally build interfaces with other languages that at least guide designers towards communicating the essential qualities of a design message, without reducing or eliminating any characteristics that are indispensable to the design's meaning. The ability of instructional designers to communicate with their clients greatly impacts their ability to complete their practice. It is my hope that instructional designers will be able to use the translation principles and techniques explored in this chapter to improve their ability to share the meaning of an instructional design with those who have an interest in the design's overall success.

Table 1. Summarizing translation principles for design languages

Translation Principle	Instructional Design Application	Example
Don't confuse the meaning of a source text with the mechanics of the source language.	A notation system for reducing a complex design into a form easily understood by non-experts.	Keppell's (2001) Content Production Process.
Make explicit in the target language components of meaning that are indefinite or imprecise in the source language.	Present design artifacts in ways that make explicit the components of meaning that are only tacitly communicated through the original.	A script for explaining the rationale of design drawings to clients.
Attend to the form and style of the final translation in the target language.	Become as familiar as possible with how instructional design clients use their own design languages.	Working as a temporary employee in a client's business.

REFERENCES

Appelbaum, S. H., & Steed, A. J. (2005). The critical success factors in the client-consulting relationship. *The Journal of Management Development, 24*(1), 68-93.

Baker, M. (1992). *In other words: A coursebook on translation.* New York: Routledge.

Belch, G. E., & Belch, M. A. (1995). *Introduction to advertising and promotion: An integrated marketing communications perspective* (3rd ed.). Chicago: Irwin.

Bell, R. T. (1991). *Translation and translating: Theory and practice.* New York: Longman, Inc.

Botturi, L. (2003). *E²ML: Educational environment modeling language.* Unpublished doctoral dissertation, University of Lugano, Faculty of Communication Sciences.

Botturi, L. (2008). E²ML: A tool for sketching instructional designs. In L. Botturi & S. T. Stubbs (Eds.), *Handbook of visual languages for instructional design: Theories and practice* (pp. 111-131). Hershey, PA: IGI Global, Inc.

Bucciarelli, L. L. (1994). *Designing engineers.* Cambridge, MA: MIT Press.

Chesterman, A. (2004). Beyond the particular. In A. Mauranen & P. Kujamäki (Eds.), *Translation universals: Do they exist?* (pp. 33-49). Philadelphia: John Benjamins Publishing Company.

Davis, M. P. (1997). *Successful advertising: Key alternative approaches.* London: Cassell.

Gibbons, A. S., & Brewer, E. K. (2005). Elementary principles of design languages and design notation systems for instructional design. In J. M. Spector, C. Ohrazda, A. Van Schaack, & D. A. Wiley (Eds.), *Innovations in instructional technology: Essays in honor of M. David Merrill* (pp. 111-130). Mahwah, NJ: Lawrence Erlbaum Associates.

International Board of Standards for Training Performance and Instruction. (2006). *Instructional design competencies.* Retrieved October 18, 2006, from http://www.ibstpi.org/Competencies/instruct_design_competencies_2000.htm

Keppell, M. (2001). Optimizing instructional designer-subject matter expert communications in the design and development of multimedia projects. *Journal of Interactive Learning Research, 12*(2/3), 205-223.

Keppell, M. (2004). *Legitimate participation? Instructional designer-subject matter expert interactions in communities of practice.* Paper presented at the World Conference on Educational Multimedia, Hypermedia, and Telecommunications.

Kujamäki, P. (2004). What happens to "Unique items" In learners' translations? "Theories" And "Concepts" As a challenge for novices' views on "Good translation". In A. Mauranen & P. Kujamäki (Eds.), *Translation universals: Do they exist?* (pp. 187-204). Philadelphia: John Benjamins Publishing Company.

Lee, M., & Johnson, C. (1999). *Principles of advertising: A global perspective.* Binghamton, NY: The Haworth Press.

Maple, R. J. (1994). "Well, you're the CE... I'm the ID..." Describing your role—and selling your worth—to content experts. *Performance & Instruction, 33*(8), 36-40.

Massoud, M. M. F. (1988). *Translate to communicate: A guide for translators.* Elgin, IL: David C. Cook Foundation.

Mbangwana, P. (1990). Cross cultural communication and miscommunication through connotation usage in translation: The case of two African classics in translation. *Journal of Multilingual and Multicultural Development, 11*(4), 319-335.

Miles, G. D. (1983). Evaluating four years of ID experience. *Journal of Instructional Development, 6*(2), 9-14.

Newmark, P. (2003). No global communication without translation. In G. Anderman & M. Rogers (Eds.), *Translation today: Trends and perspectives* (pp. 55-67). Tonawanda, NY: Ultilingual Matters Ltd.

O'Keefe, D. J. (2006). Persuasion. In O. Hargie (Ed.), *The handbook of communication skills* (6th ed.). New York: Routledge.

Osguthorpe, R. T., Osguthorpe, R. D., Jacob, W. J., & Davies, R. (2003). The moral dimensions of instructional design. *Educational Technology, 43*(2), 19-23.

Roman, K., & Maas, J. (1976). *How to advertise.* New York: St. Martin's Press.

Rose, G. (2001). *Visual methodologies: An introduction to the interpretation of visual materials.* Thousand Oaks, CA: SAGE Publications.

Sandage, C. H., Fryburger, V., & Rotzoll, K. (1983). *Advertising theory and practice* (11th ed.). Homewood, IL: Richard D. Irwin, Inc.

Shreve, G. M. (1999). *Translation at the millennium: Prospects for the evolution of a profession.* Paper presented at the 30th Anniversary Conference of the Monterey Institute for International Studies, Monterey, CA.

Solomon, R. (2003). *The art of client service.* Chicago: Dearborn Trade Publishing.

Stubbs, S. T., & Gibbons, A. S. (2008). The power of design drawing in other design fields. In L. Botturi & S. T. Stubbs (Eds.), *Handbook of visual languages for instructional design: Theories and practice* (pp. 33-51). Hershey, PA: IGI Global, Inc.

Waters, S. H., & Gibbons, A. S. (2004). Design languages, notation systems, and instructional technology: A case study. *Educational Technology Research and Development, 52*(2), 57-68

Chapter III
The Power of Design Drawing in Other Design Fields[1]

S. Todd Stubbs
Brigham Young University, USA

Andrew S. Gibbons
Brigham Young University, USA

ABSTRACT

This chapter is a survey of the literature of design studies, where the various characteristics of a phenomenon called design drawing, *are considered. Included in this review is an exploration of the roles and attributes design drawing plays in those design fields outside ID, as an important design language. Its importance to those design fields suggests that design drawing might have much to teach us about visual instructional design languages (VIDLs). In reviewing these attributes of design drawing and how they are implemented in those other fields of design, we hope to inspire a dialogue on how these important characteristics will aid in creating or nurturing VIDLs.*

INTRODUCTION

In this chapter, we will explore the roles and attributes of design drawing, which serves as an important design language in design fields outside of ID. Its importance to those design fields suggests that design drawing might have much to teach us about VIDLs, if we knew more about it.

We will show that, due to the similarities between ID and other fields of design, we might expect that tools, skills, and methods important in those fields—such as design drawing—might also be valuable to ID. The basis of design drawing's importance in those fields lies in the common characteristic of all design fields' need for models and representations, which design drawing performs capably. In fact, we will show that there are a number of characteristics of design drawing which make it attractive to designers in those fields: its close association with design thinking, its language-like characteristics, the fact that it can adroitly represent all stages of design with a number of expressive forms. Design drawing can also be as concrete or vague as it needs to be to support the design at hand—there being a real advantage to a definable level of vagueness. This characteristic also makes it ideal for working with ill-defined problems, which design is usually characterized to be. Design drawing plays a crucial role in a dialectic (called "the dialectic of sketching"), which some authors (Arnheim, 1995) suggest is essential to design. Drawing, which is often accompanied by some kind of narrative, forms the basis of a shared vision of the design: a catalyst for the social agreement necessary for design to move forward.

In reviewing these attributes and their application in those other fields of design, we hope to expose to ID practitioners to the characteristics of this important design language. This might, in turn, begin an important dialogue on some important characteristics to consider when creating or nurturing a VIDL.

IS ID DESIGN?

Murphy (1992) asks, "Is instructional design truly a design activity?" After comparing ID to the general practice of design (as found in architecture, industrial design, engineering, etc.), he concludes, "…it can be argued strongly that instructional designers are truly involved in design activities" (p. 281). And, further, "…instructional designers need to recognize their links with the wider world of design" (p. 282). Rowland (1993) conducted a similar analysis and similarly concluded, "Designing instances of instruction, or more generally, planning and preparing to instruct, can be considered a subset of designing, and the

defining characteristics…for all types of design appear to hold true for ID" (p. 87). Speaking of the literature on ID, Rowland adds that the results of his study, "…match studies of design processes in other fields, but contradict views in the literature on ID, especially those representing a purely rational perspective" (p. 90). Murphy is emphatic: "Thus far, it appears that not much has been done on the design skills of instructional designers," and warns, "All you instructional designers out there, look and learn from the design world. You ignore it at your peril" (p. 282).

In that larger design world, as in ID, design takes place in the gap between the mind of the designer and how the problem and solution are represented—design is the bridge between the conceptual world within and the physical world without. Simon (1996) puts it this way: because the gap is, "…centered precisely on this interface between the inner and outer environments; [design] is concerned with attaining goals by adapting the former to the latter" (p. 113). Bridging this gap requires a process of externalizing the designer's conceptual world. This externalization may be expressed verbally, visually, or physically—with words, drawings, or models.

For many fields of design, the fundamental bridge is drawing. Archer observes, "It has sometimes been said that drawing is the language of design. There has certainly been an intimate relationship between drawing and design from time immemorial… All the design professions today rely heavily upon drawings of various types for both the development of ideas and the communication of findings." Arnheim reports, "The function and nature of [drawing] is inseparable from that of the design it serves. The creative process of designing, being an activity of the mind, cannot be directly observed. The [drawings], done for the eyes and being directed by them, make some of the design plans visible," which makes drawing the perfect bridge across "Simon's gap" (see also Goldschmidt, 1991).

Robbins (1994) has pointed out, "Because drawing is used to communicate ideas and to instruct others about a design, it is often seen as a language. Architects, when speaking about drawing, assume…that drawing may be construed to be a language or quasi-linguistic order of communication" (pp. 27-28). Design drawing can be considered a language of design.

In ID, visual representations serve two very different purposes. First, visual representations, including drawing, are used during design as part of the design process to represent some aspect of instruction before it has been produced or presented. This may be in the form of storyboards, flowcharts, etc. Because the product of ID is instruction, visual representations may also serve as part of the content being produced. These may take the form of illustrations of the content or diagrams of concepts, etc. (A more complete taxonomy is presented in Chapter XVII).

The latter—visual representation of content—has been studied extensively to determine how it contributes to learning. Unfortunately, the former—visual representations that are used to further the design itself—have not. Schatz (2003) did a small review of the literature of ID where he noted that it is difficult to find literature on design thinking or design methods in ID, much less a specific method like design drawing. It is a paradox that a field that relies so heavily on visualization for the outcome of its designs has not studied its use in its process. In spite of the apparent similarities between ID and other design fields, and the importance of drawing to design in those fields, design drawing as a tool or skill of ID has not been adequately addressed in the ID literature.

DESIGN DRAWING AS AN ESSENTIAL PART OF DESIGN

A large share of the research in design drawing comes from a field of inquiry called *design studies*.

The last decades of the 20th century saw a great deal of research in the study of design methodology as a general field, where the various creative design activities of architecture, engineering, industrial design, graphic design, software engineering, and others were discussed, compared, and analyzed, in an effort to improve methods and process models. This new field of inquiry was called variously design methodology, design theory, design science, and design studies. The importance of this field is evident by the number of research-based journals in design theory and methodology, such as *Design Issues*, *Design Journal*, and *Design Studies*, among others. (Kays, 2003). This literature (in which ID is not generally included) contains a wealth of information on design drawing and its relation to the design process.

In this literature of *design studies*, it has been observed that drawing and design have a long history together. Baynes (1992) identified the development of design drawing in the late 18th century as the principle catalyst to the development of design as a separate discipline, which, in turn, helped to fuel the industrial revolution. However, the use of some kind of drawing to pre-plan work predates the industrial revolution by millennia. Shards of pottery and stone with coarse building directions on them have been found from ancient Egypt (Baynes, 1992).

Press and Cooper (2003) pointed out that "…everyone can draw; however, designers are trained to develop this as an advanced form of communication." Lockard (1977) has observed that, "In…the design process, drawing is still the most flexible and efficient means of representation." This is in part because the speed and ease of production of free-hand sketches support design in important ways. According to Kivett (1998) free-hand sketches allow communication to be almost instantaneous, and drawing facilitates making of changes "on the spot." Referring to sketching, Gedenryd (1998) asserts that:

Sketching is made up of very small and simple incremental steps, which yield to local control and high sensitivity to feedback. This, in turn, makes sketching into a highly fluid and efficient process, which supports the open-ended and conceptual nature of the design work which sketching is typically used for.

Goldschmidt and many of others assert that drawing is a vital part of design (Archer, 1992; Goldschmidt, 1991; Henderson, 1998; Moore, 2000; Ullman, Wood, & Craig, 1990). For example, Ullman, Wood, and Craig say that:

The evidence both from research in cognitive psychology and from the protocol studies of designers points to the importance of drawing in the design process beyond the documentation of final designs. Not only are drawings the preferred form of data representation, for the designer, but they are a necessary part of the design process. Sketching as a form of drawing has been shown to have properties that make its use important in design. (sect. VI, para. I)

Many have speculated on the reasons for the close association between design process and design drawings. Some have investigated the relationship of design drawing to specific design activities of which drawing seems to be a part; others have looked at specific processes and properties of design drawings that support design. Still others have studied the close association between design thinking and drawing. What follows are summaries of these ideas.

THE IMPORTANCE OF REPRESENTATIONS AND MODELS TO DESIGN

Designers rely heavily on representations and models to accomplish their work. According to Goel (1995):

Design, at some very abstract level, is the process of transforming one set of representations (the design brief) into another set of representations (the contract documents). However, not only are the inputs and outputs of the of the design process representations, all intervening transformations are also typically done on representations. (p. 128)

Saddler (2001) observed, "We use sketches, diagrams, specifications, even verbal descriptions throughout the design process to make the concepts in our heads tangible and communicable." These representations are sometime referred to as models. Representations and models are referents (symbols or metaphors) for some other (real-world) thing. Baynes (1992) says:

The term 'model' is used by scientists, mathematicians, technologists, and designers to mean something that stands for something else. In general, models are powerful because they isolate an aspect of reality and allow us to represent, interpret, manipulate, or control it. Models have predictive power because…they can be 'run' to simulate what will happen if proposed changes are carried out. They are indispensable for design activity because they allow designers to develop their designs and understand their likely effects before they are put into practice. (p. 18)

Goel (1995) adds:

This [practice of using models in design] is not an accident…Recall that design typically occurs in situations where it is not possible or desirable to tamper with the world until the full extent and ramifications of the intervention are known in advance. After all, we only get one 'run' on the world. Every action is irrevocable and may have substantive costs associated with it. Thus, it is not surprising to find that designers produce and manipulate representations of the artifact rather than the artifact itself. All the reasoning and deci-

sion making (including performance prediction) is done through the construction and manipulation of models of various sorts, including drawings, mock-ups, mathematical modeling, computer simulations, and so on. (p. 128)

Henderson (1998) observes, "design cultures are intrinsically tied to the way in which their representations are constructed because such representations—sketches, drawings, prototypes—are the heart of design work."

CHARACTERISTICS OF DESIGN DRAWING

Design Drawing and Thinking

Much of the literature about design drawing proclaims the close tie between it and thinking. So much so, that the rest of the topics about drawing that follow in this chapter could be considered, more or less, to be subsidiary to this idea. As Robbins (1994) puts it, "Unless you draw something, you do not understand it" (p. 127).

Design drawing aids the designer by reducing cognitive load during the design process. Because design sketches are an external representation, they augment memory and support information processing. (Tversky, 2002)

It is probably this support of memory that gives design drawings, "…the capacity to transform our understanding of an issue, and, to some extent, free us from the narrowness of words, labels, and classification systems." (Hansen, 1999, p. 203). Laseau (1989), a theorist in design drawing, calls this close affiliation between drawing and thinking *graphic thinking*: "The term *graphic thinking* distinguishes the use of graphics in support of thought from graphics used in presentations. Graphics should play a significant role in design and problem solving, provoking thought and

acting as catalysts for ideas rather than limited representations of products or decisions" (p. 9, italics in original).

Another view of drawing is similar to Vygotsky's description of the relationship of language to thought. Substituting drawings for words, Vygotsky says: "Thought is not merely expressed in [drawings], it comes into existence through them." This seems to be Goel's view, that in his research, design sketching, "played an important role in certain types of open-ended, explorative cognitive processes," different from mere problem-solving. It is also consistent with McKim's (1980) understanding of the role of drawing in design, that "…drawing and thinking are frequently so simultaneous that the graphic image appears almost an organic extension of mental processes" (p. 11).

All this is dependent on the designer's ability to express (or illustrate) an idea in a variety of ways. "In both the exploratory and developmental mode, graphic ideators [e.g., designers] use many graphic idioms. When you are sketching from life or communicating a visual idea to others, you can be content with one graphic idiom. But when you are exploring ideas, you must use graphic language more flexibly…" (McKim, 1980, pp. 134-135) Verstijnen et al. (1998) observed the differences between skilled sketchers and unskilled sketchers, and concluded that the skilled sketchers benefited most from the visual representation in a sketch. When Lockard (1977) compared drawing to a language, he noted that, if the designer has a limited "vocabulary" of drawing skills, he will be plagued by "curious speech stoppages and deadly dull sentence structures…" He goes on to declare, "This vocabulary [of design drawing] needs to be expanded as does the vocabulary of any language that stays alive" (p. 111).

We live in a world, especially in academia, overshadowed by words. Lockard (1977) observed that, "Our cultural heritage is dominated by a linear, verbal, and 'rational' tradition which can inhibit the use of drawing in design." The implication of this tradition is a belief that decisions are made "rationally" (meaning in the mind verbally), and drawing is merely an act of the hand "printing" the decisions out. Instead, he argues for allowing the unconscious mind to contribute to the design process: "We are much older, and perhaps much wiser than our mathematical, verbal, 'rational' left frontal lobes, and drawing is one of the most natural and direct outlets for this rich and mysterious resource."

Design Drawing as Design Language

One reason that design thinking and design drawing seem to be so similar is that drawing is very much like another closely related thinking activity: language. In fact, for most fields of design, we might agree with Archer (1992) who says that drawing is the language of design. Robbins (1994) also noted the similarity between drawing and language: "Because drawing is used to communicate ideas and to instruct others about a design, it is often seen as a language. Architects, when speaking about drawing, assume more often than not…that drawing may be construed to be a language or a quasi-linguistic order of communication" (pp. 27-28). Lockard (1977) says:

It is time we looked at drawing again, or perhaps for the first time, as a conscious activity, and a communicative language having, like any language, a syntactical structure. It is time we realized that the drawings we use, the order in which we choose to draw them, and our free, creative, confident use of, and continual, deliberate expansion of this language of drawing lie at the very base of any design method. (p. 106)

Tversky (2002) has identified several attributes of drawings that are language-like. "[Design drawings] are segmented into elements. They consist of language-like strings of stylized figures, lines, curves, and blobs. These elements can be combined in different ways to create different meanings, again, like language."

Languages facilitate communication. Vygotsky (Vygotski & Kozulin, 1986) proposed that languages also facilitate thought. Simon (1996) identified some of the value of a design language to thought when he noted "By erecting such a hierarchy of concepts for himself, the designer is, after all, able to face the problem all at once. He achieves a powerful economy of thought, and can by this means thread his way through far more difficult problems than he could cope with otherwise." Languages in general provide advantages, particularly useful to design: (1) they allow thought to be communicated so that good ideas do not get lost; (2) they provide a focus of attention which permits higher-power processing and anchoring of thought; and, (3) they provide the ability to question and judge the value of a thought—to construct thoughts about thought (Jackendoff, 1996). Schatz (2003) has suggested that for the field of ID to grow, it needs a design language to communicate what works and what does not, as is the case in engineering. Gibbons and Rogers (2006) have argued for the need for more than one design language in order to express a design: "…many design languages already exist, and new design languages can be created that provide terms appropriate to the solution of sub-problems…"

Stages in Design and Design Drawing

Design takes place in stages, and changes in design drawing shadow these stages. The stages can be traced by observing to whom the drawing is intended to communicate, which is closely paralleled by the purposes for which they were drawn.

Designers in many fields often start their work with rough sketches to "try out" ideas before they commit them to more formal representations. "Engineers are notorious for not being able to think without making 'back-of-the-envelope' sketches of rough ideas. Sometimes these informal sketches serve to communicate a concept to a colleague, but more often, they just help the idea take shape on paper" (Ullman, Wood, & Craig, 1990).

As the design progresses to the latter purposes, the drawings become more formal, more governed by rules and conventions. Bucciarelli (1994) differentiated between the "hastily rendered sketch made to assist in the story telling of the moment" characteristic of early design, and the more formal "graphics, mechanical assembly drawings, circuit topographies, block diagrams, and charts" that exemplify the formal representations used for later purposes of design.

The more formal the drawing, the more commitment on the part of the designer is implied. For obvious reasons, it is better to catch a flaw or make a change at the sketching or drafting stage, or even after a formal design model has been made, than after the product has been produced.

Lockard (1977) organizes the stages of design by identifying the person for whom the communication at each stage is intended, in this manner:

1. Self-communication
2. Inter-professional communication
3. Client communication
4. Builder communication
5. Public communication

Because he is primarily writing for architects, Lockard uses the term "builder communication," but any communication to any production person would fit the described stage. Forms of communication, often design drawings, move through these stages as well.

The creative work of the designer starts with what Lockard (1977) calls "self-communication." McKim (1980) ties self-communication directly to sketching and calls it "graphic ideation": "Graphic ideation is visually talking to oneself; graphic communication is visually talking to others" (p. 135, italics in original). He divides the first, graphic ideation, into two kinds of activity:

Graphic ideation has two basic modes: exploratory and developmental... In the exploratory mode of graphic ideation, thinking and sketching are adventurous...Each sketch captures general features only, not details; it is a kind of rough map that allows you to return later to the concept, if you choose to develop it further.In the developmental mode of graphic ideation, you...develop a more thorough understanding of a promising concept.

This division meshes with Lockard's (1977) original idea of self-communication, where the first, exploratory drawings are analytical in nature to help the designer see broad patterns. Later, developmental drawings are held up for comparison to design determinants to become tentative detailed solutions to the problem (p. 107). These two types of sketches are reflected in the two types of design cognition noted by Ulric Neisser, whom McKim (1980) quotes: "...all cognition consists of a two-stage act of construction: 'the first is fast, crude, wholistic, [sic] and parallel, while the second is deliberate, attentive, detailed, and sequential'" (pp. 147-148).

The earlier, exploratory stage is most closely associated with Simon's (1996) gap, mentioned above, in which design drawing serves as one bridge between the mind of the designer and the real world. McKim (1980) defines exploratory drawing as "a means of probing [the designer's own] imagination, seeking to touch and record the vague and elusive imagery that usually accompanies the conception of a new idea" (p. 134). Verstijnen et al. (1998, p. 520) point out that these exploratory idea-sketches have an important role in the creative process so often associated with design. It is to the exploratory process that McKim alludes when he says, "...drawing and thinking are frequently so simultaneous that the graphic image appears almost an organic extension of mental processes...Drawing not only helps to bring vague inner images into focus; it also provides a record of the advancing thought stream" (p. 11). Hanks and Belliston (1977) seem to be referring to exploratory design drawing when they say, "Since ideas and mental images are foggy, fleeting, and incomplete, it is imperative that they be captured and studied. Drawing is one way this can be done. Drawing allows you to bring the idea to life. It allows you to change, judge, and evaluate your thoughts."

In the later, developmental drawing of the first stage, by contrast, the idea evolves through its embryonic concept into a mature form by repetition and refinement. McKim (1980) says "Developmental sketching is less schematic and more concerned with concrete details." The developmental phase is described by Arnheim (1995) as "a series of approximations, each one incorporating more relevant information and evolving until the final form emerges." McKim notes the memory-supporting facility of design drawing in his description of the developmental stage: "Drawing provides a capability that memory cannot: the most brilliant imager cannot compare a number of images, side by side in memory, as one can compare a wall of tacked-up idea-sketches." In fact, this developmental stage is where design may begin to be shared with other designers as per Lockard's second recipient-based stage: inter-professional communication.

As these drawings progress, they become less free and more formal, less vague and more concrete. At some point the drawings cease to be clarifications, and become proposals: attempts to convince or persuade others of their value. It is at this point that they move to the third stage of communication and beyond: client communication, builder communication, and public communication. "[A]ll further drawings become a persuasive device, 'commercials,' to inform and persuade [the designer's] professional associates, his client, builder and the general public that his design is the correct, reasonable, and beautiful solution to the problem" (Lockard, 1977). Once the client has been convinced (which Lockard says comes by

compromise and negotiation) the design is "set" and the drawing "finished." The design drawings are used to communicate with builders (Robbins & Cullinan, 1994). The design has crystallized or "hardened" where it is unlikely to see major change. Finally, it may be used to communicate directly with the public. Robbins (1994) says that, for an architect, this form of design drawing often takes place after the building is built!

Later forms serve as the long-term memory of the design. Unfortunately, the earlier rough sketches "rarely survive for future generations to inspect" (Bucciarelli, 1994, p. 118). This is unfortunate because, as Lockard (1977) observes, that the importance of design drawings to the creative aspect of design dwindles as the drawing becomes more refined. In a book for aiding architects and designers he laments:

In surveying the drawings I have used to illustrate my ideas I find that they are all rather stiff, studied works… I have never habitually saved the first rough sketches precisely because they are only a means—their only value being an interim visual statement toward a final real building… Except for the need to communicate the architectural idea more formally to other people, the purpose of drawing the space is fulfilled with these little sketches. (p. 36)

Up to this point, we have used Lockard's stages to discuss stages in design and design drawing. These stages use the recipient of communication to identify the stages of design and design drawing. It will be our approach that the progression from stage one to two, from two to three, and so forth, are often indicated by a change in purpose, as much as a change in recipient. These changes in purpose do not map perfectly onto the changes in recipient, but clearly show the same progression:

1. Ideation
2. Negotiation
3. Persuasion

4. Crystallization
5. Dissemination

Both design and design drawing occur in stages that represent the recipients of communications, and also the purposes of communication. Lockard points out that the movement among these is not strictly linear. More often than not, the designer will cycle through previous stages as the design takes form and shape. Earlier stages are gradually abandoned in these cycles as negotiation and persuasion are accomplished; the design crystallizes and the sketches become means of dissemination. The sketches become increasingly formal and set, more useful as communication than ideation.

CATEGORIZING DESIGN DRAWINGS BY FORM

Design drawings may be categorized by their form, that is, by their shape, as well as the purposes for which they are drawn. Four examinations of form are reviewed and the list of groupings described by the chapters in a book by Laseau's (1986) serve as the best characterization of a taxonomy of design drawings in the early, abstract stages of design. To this is added a category for representational graphics (after Massironi, 2002) to serve as a taxonomy of design graphics by form.

Simon (1996) observed that "An early step toward understanding any set of phenomena is to learn what kinds of things there are in the set—to develop a taxonomy. This step has not yet been taken with respect to representations. We have

Figure 1. A taxonomy of graphic productions (Massironi, 2002, p. 3) (Used with permission of Taylor & Francis Group, LLC)

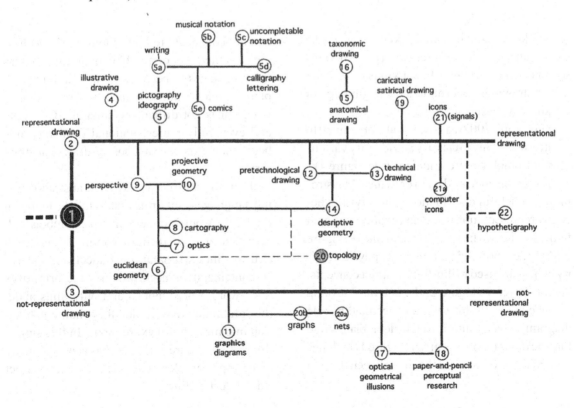

Figure 2. Progression from a bubble diagram (A) to architectural plan (D). (Laseau, 1975, pp. 28-29) (Used with permission of the author)

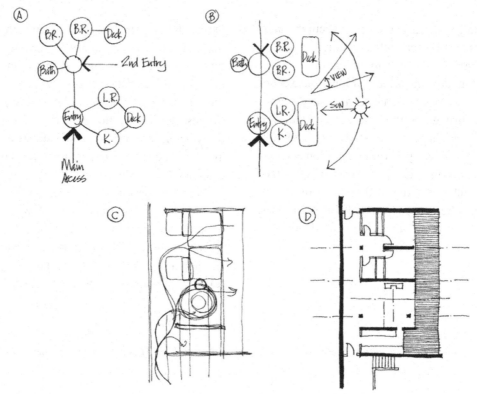

only a sketchy and incomplete knowledge of the significance of the differences" (p. 133). This section will examine different kinds of abstract design drawings to formulate the beginnings of a taxonomy, based on form.

Massironi (2002) has specifically attempted to create a taxonomy to classify and identify various kinds of graphic representations (see Figure 1).

When considering design drawings, Massironi's most helpful contribution is his division between representational and non-representational figures—the two heavy horizontal lines in Figure 1. Many design drawings represent a physical reality, others are used to illustrate abstract concepts. As illustrated in Figure 2, the one may develop into the other. In this case, a conceptual bubble diagram evolves into a rough floor plan. Note that the diagram of Massironi (Figure 1) includes several types of drawing that lie between the two

and are connected to both. Figure 2 shows how ideas in the form of a bubble diagram progress through stages to become a rough architectural plan. Development from that stage to a complete blueprint is not difficult to imagine. Concrete, and even fully representational drawings may begin their existence as loosely-drawn, abstract forms.

Hansen (1999) proposes a basic abstract drawing language built from the symbols found in Figure 3. A quick review of these symbols will reveal that many of them are common sense (such as using lines to separate or connect, and squares as containers). Hansen provides the primitives (the "words" or symbols) and only hints about the "grammar" that would allow their combination into meaningful expressions. In this simple illustration, Figure 3, Hansen has captured many of the important elements and ideas of the abstract side of design drawing.

Figure 3. Hansen's "graphic tools"(Hansen, 1999, pp. 193-220) (Used with permission of MIT Press)

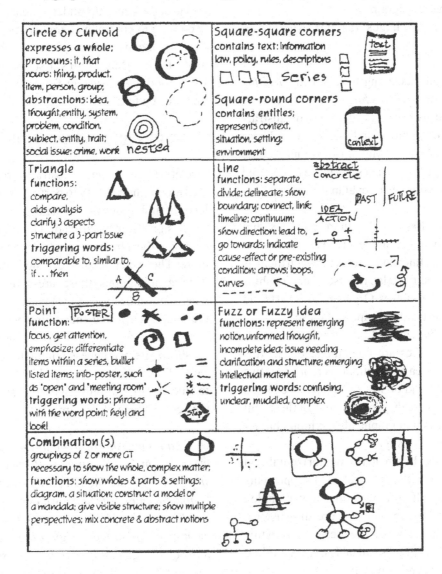

In chapter 21 of his book *Thinking Visually*, McKim (1980) provides common examples of what he terms abstract graphic languages. While McKim did not set out to build a taxonomy, his set of examples is valuable because the types of diagrams he includes specifically serve design and planning, at the same time giving designers ideas of where and how to use them. Though the types identified are very specific, his treatment of them is liberal enough to include instances that may lie on the periphery of each type. He does not imply that the list is in any way complete; on the contrary, you get the idea that this is just a sampler. His list includes the following types of abstract graphic languages:

1. Venn diagrams
2. Organization charts
3. Flow charts
4. Link-node diagrams

5. Bar charts and graphs
6. Schematic diagrams
7. Pattern languages (as per Alexander, 1979)

In a similar, book-length treatment, *Graphic problem solving for architects and designers*, Laseau (1986) condenses all types of abstract design graphics into four basic groups. These groups are inclusive of McKim's abstract graphic languages. Each of Laseau's categories is covered by a chapter, with lots of examples:

1. **Bubble diagrams:** Squares, circles and other shapes ("bubbles") are containers for concepts; lines and arrows between them as well as their overlap represent relationships among the bubbles. Organization charts and flow charts are examples of these.
2. **Area diagrams:** Like bubble diagrams, drawn shapes are containers, but in this case the area of the bubble is representative of some kind of size or importance. Venn diagrams are the most obvious of these, but bar charts and graphs also exhibit characteristics of this type.
3. **Matrices:** In a matrix, the horizontal and vertical positioning of elements represents meaning. It is a way to show complex relationships in two or more dimensions. Schematic diagrams are occasionally of this type, as are graphs and tables. A text outline may be a type of matrix.
4. **Networks:** Networks are essentially bubble diagrams where the arrows and lines take on more importance than the bubbles, forming complex maps of lines showing relationships. Link-node diagrams are clearly of this type, though organization charts and flow charts may also be.

The value of the list of Laseau's chapters, as summarized above, is that it includes the various forms of abstract representation (such as all of McKim's abstract graphic languages) and groups them into understandable categories according to common characteristics. If we add an item for concrete or representational graphics as well, (from Massironi's first division) Laseau list a good, basic system for organizing design graphics by form.

Value of Vagueness in Sketching

One of the advantages to abstract forms of representation is their ability to portray an appropriate level of ambiguity or vagueness—at least until the design has crystallized. The drawing must represent the current level of refinement, but not more. The sketch notates decisions made, while leaving ambiguous those areas of the design where decisions have not yet been made, leaving the door open for further refinement. Arnheim (1995) goes so far as to say that such a sketch, "...shows [its] vagueness with a desirable precision." This vagueness and ambiguity, according to Bucciarelli, not only enables design, but it is the very essence of design:

... a healthy measure of ambiguity and uncertainty makes room for designing... Participants envision and construe the uncertain as options, but behind the mask, the unknown lies waiting—and that too, is valued by participants. Uncertainty is what gives life to the design process and makes it the challenge that it is. If the process lacks uncertainty, then you can be sure it is not designing but copying. (Bucciarelli, 1994, p. 177)

Tang and Vero (2001) empirically confirmed the importance of vagueness in design representations. They observed that:

...a depiction has more than one meaning graphically and semantically after being created. It carries groups of meanings and relationships. Designers utilize this characteristic to generate different concepts and to reason about functional

issues through sketches. Consequently, sketches become affordances of meanings in the design process. (p. 279)

These "affordances of meaning" make it possible that, even though sketches are made with certain ideas and goals in mind, designers may fortuitously "...see new objects and configurations in their sketches. These encounters produce welcome but unintended discoveries, and may be a fruitful source of new design ideas" (Tversky, 2002).

Arnheim believes the vagueness of the sketch accurately reflects the ambiguity in the related mental image. He casts this vagueness as a plus, because, "...it has the positive quality of a topological shape. As distinguished from geometrical shapes, a topological shape stands for a whole range of possibilities without being tangibly committed to any one of them. Being undefined in its specifics, it admits distortions and deviations... This same vagueness is frequently apparent in the designer's sketches" (pp. 71-72).

Design as Ill-Defined Problems.

This ambiguousness in both the sketch and the mental image reflects the way designers tend to think about design problems in general. From the earliest cognitive studies of design (Eastman, 1969), to the present, design has been thought of as a process of solving of ill-defined problems. Cross (2001) declares, "It is widely accepted that design 'problems' can only be regarded as a version of ill-defined problems." (Design has also been called a wicked problem [Rittel & Webber, 1973], which is an expansion of the term *ill-defined*.)

Though the term ill-defined is described in various ways (Newell & Simon, 1972; Reitman, 1965; Zimring & Craig, 2001), what most definitions have in common is that ill-defined problems have "variable problem spaces" (Zimring & Craig, 2001), meaning that these problems require constant restructuring to arrive at a solution. Un-

like well-defined problems, where the solutions can be obtained by reduction, transformation, or optimization of the data in the requirements (Archer & Roberts, 1992), ill-defined problems resist these systematic approaches to being solved, or are at least approached as though that were the case. In ill-defined problems, both the problem and the solution are moving targets, and solution and problem co-evolve in relation to each other (Dorst & Cross, 1996).

This is interesting in light of what Simon (1996) says about solutions to problems being found in their representations of whatever form:

All mathematics exhibits in its conclusions only what is already implicit in its premises...Hence all mathematical derivation can be viewed simply as change in representation, making evident what was previously true but obscure. This view can be extended to all problem solving—solving a problem simply means representing it so as to make the solution transparent. If the problem solving could actually be organized in these terms, the issue of representation would indeed become central. But even if it cannot—if this is too exaggerated a view—a deeper understanding of how representations are created and how they contribute to the solution of problems will be come an essential component in the future theory of design. (p. 132)

Simon's speculation certainly seems to hold true for well-defined problems like those of mathematics, but what if the problems are ill-defined, like design problems are characterized to be? What would then appear to be needed is a mode of representation that is capable of leaving undefined those portions of the design concept that have yet to crystallize while at the same time representing clearly what has crystallized. Sketching in the hands of a skilled designer would seem to meet this requirement.

Another aspect of ill-defined problems and design is that designers, especially expert ones, tend to treat all problems as though they were ill-defined, even when those problems are well enough defined that they might reasonably respond to analysis. Cross (2001) observed that "designers will be designers, even when they could be problem solvers": they tend to approach all problems as though they were ill-defined, as though the problem was as negotiable as the solution. More specifically, designers tend to start off quickly with proposed solutions, however rough they may be, and refine them as they proceed, rather than analyzing the data thoroughly in order to formulate a solution:

Many studies suggest that designers move rapidly to early solution conjectures, and use these conjectures as a way of exploring and defining problem-and-solution together. This is not a strategy employed by all problem-solvers, many of whom attempt to define or understand the problem fully before making solution attempts. This difference was observed by Lawson (1979), in his experiments on problem solving behavior in which he compared scientists with architects: '...[The scientists] operated what might be called a problem-focusing strategy... architects by contrast adopted a solution-focusing strategy.' (Cross, 2001, p. 83)

In many cases design representations—usually sketches and drawings—fill the role Simon suggests, to make the solution transparent. According to Lockard (1977):

In the design process, we need to display tentative design proposals which we can continually compare to the restated design problem. These graphic representations will suggest restatements of the problem, and those restatements will in turn suggest more drawings. (p. 10)

Then, it is back to the drawing board (literally!) to modify the proposed sketch to reflect a new understanding of the problem and the solution—in a repeating cycle that results in constantly more refined drawings, and problems. This cycle between what is and what should or could be, as it applies to the representations, has been referred to as "the dialectic of sketching" (Goldschmidt, 1991).

THE DIALECTIC OF SKETCHING

In her much-cited study about the dialectic of sketching, Goldschmidt (1991) first breaks down design thinking into observable units which she calls *movements*. She observed that progress in the design alternated between one type of seeing to another and back again through these movements. These two types of seeing each support a different type of thinking. One type is analog or metaphorical thought which deals with seeing new meanings in the sketch. She calls this *seeing as*. Creativity is provoked in this reinterpreting of the sketch. The other type of thinking deals with the consequences of the newly perceived meanings—of judgment—which Goldschmidt called *seeing that*.

The importance of Goldschmidt's study is that she observed empirically a phenomenon which has been proposed by others in theory or self-reporting (See, for example, Lockard, 1977; and McKim, 1980). Verstijnen et al. (1998), also observed a dialog, between combining and restructuring of concepts which could be viewed as virtually the same dialectic from a different perspective.

It is Arnheim's (1995) opinion that without drawing, the dialectic that Goldschmidt observed does not happen; and without the dialectic, design does not happen; ergo, drawing is essential to design.

Drawing and Narrative

As important as drawing may be to the design process, it rarely stands alone. Design drawings are nearly always accompanied by narrative, which supplements and adds meaning to the image. Bruner (2003) has stated, "We organize our experience and our memory of human happenings mainly in the form of narrative—stories, excuses, myths, reasons for doing and not doing, and so on" (p. 44). Visual representations, on the other hand, "…can render phenomena, relationships, and ideas visible, allowing patterns to emerge from apparent disorder to become detectable, and available, to our senses and intellect" (Hansen, 1999, p. 198). The two, together, are better at communicating than either is alone.

McCloud (1993) has observed that while, historically, pictures and words have become separate entities in modern culture, they are actually exist together in a larger continuum. He argues that it is their natural state to be mixed together (as indicated in the name of the Kindergarten activity, "Show and Tell.") He elaborates, "Words and pictures are like partners in a dance and each one takes turns leading…. When these partners each know their roles and support each other strengths…" they are powerful.

Bucciarelli observed the important relationship between narrative and drawing:

Drawings…show the characteristics displayed in narratives and, indeed, are themselves essential to narrative. They show hierarchy, are abstract, bounded, measured, and so on. These are not just characteristics of the formal drawings stored and saved for posterity…but they also structure the hastily rendered sketch made to assist in the story telling of the moment. (p. 118)

Schön's (1987) protocol studies of architectural students makes visible the kind of dialogue that occurs between designers and their designs (as well as among designers). These dialogues show that neither the narratives nor the design drawings would be completely comprehensible without the other. Another example can be found in motion pictures' use of narrative and the storyboard. A storyboard is nearly always accompanied (at a minimum) by snippets of the script written under the drawings, or in some cases, full impromptu performances used to complete the conveyance of the information in the drawing (see Hart, 1999).

The narrative associated with design drawing may be text found in the diagram itself (such as labels in boxes, etc.), it may be written nearby (as captions or explanations) or in may be from spoken words (in performance). Regardless of their relative location, words and stories—narrative—often accompany design sketches. These narratives complete and supplement the design drawings, and are, in fact, essential parts of fulfilling the purposes of design drawings.

Drawing as a Catalyst for Social Agreement/Commitment

One thing that makes the combination of words and graphics powerful is their ability to engage others in the act of design. Some have romanticized design in to a solitary act, shared only after it is perfected by the designer (Lockard, 1977). But, as already noted, design and design sketches go through stages of negotiation and persuasion with others: other designers, clients, patrons, builders, collaborators, etc. If they are focused on common goals and outcomes, drawing serves as an important catalyst to draw these people together, or at least give them a common focus of discussion.

Bucciarelli's (1994) ethnographic study of design engineering situations observed that, "Despite differences among individual interpretations and constructions…participants do communicate, negotiate, and compromise; in short, they design" (p. 81). Later, he concludes:

Shared vision' is the key phrase: The design is the shared vision, and the shared vision is the design. Some of this shared vision is made explicit in documents, texts, and artifacts—informal assembly and detail drawings, operation and service manuals, contractual disclaimers, production schedules, marketing copy, test plans, parts lists, procurement orders, mock-ups, and prototypes....The shared vision, as some synthetic representation of the artifact as a whole, is not in the documents or written plans. To the extend that it exists as a whole, it is a social construction—dynamic, plastic, given nuance and new meaning at each information gathering of two and three in a hallway or at formal meetings such as scheduled design reviews. (p. 159)

As he notes in another place, "The final chart is hardly interesting, and rarely referred to, unless it later shows a bug or is challenged by further developments. But if that happens, the negotiation process starts anew" (p. 189). This view is reflected by Robbins (1994, p. 29) where he says, "Drawing and the worlds it represents are a product of social and cultural agreements among architects and others."

Final design drawings and documentation serve as the long-term memory of the design and show commitment. These documents are required to stand on their own in spite of the fact that only those who participated in the negotiation that resulted in this design will be able to derive the full context and meaning from them. They become reference works to which the designers and producers refer. Formalization and crystallization are intended to strengthen and solidify the documents as tools of communication, but it requires careful skill to weave the meaning into these reductions in order for them to convey that meaning through the artifact.

SUMMARY OF RESEARCH ON DESIGN DRAWING IN DESIGN STUDIES

In summary, we have observed that designers in most design fields accomplish their work by means of design representations, of which design drawing is an important type. As noted, the basis of design drawing's importance in those fields lies in its flexibility and power for creating design representations. This flexibility and power is due to a number of characteristics of which make it appealing to designers, including its ability to represent design thinking, its language-like characteristics, and the fact that it can represent all stages of design with a number of expressive forms. Design drawing also has the advantage of being appropriately vague when a vague representation is needed to further the design, or concrete when a concrete representation is needed. This flexibility makes it well suited for working with ill-defined problems—like design. Without "the dialectic of sketching," some authors believe that design itself is in jeopardy. Drawing is often accompanied by some kind of narrative, to act as an artifact for a shared vision of the design—which identifies the true locus of design, in the minds of the creators.

CONCLUSION

This brief review of the many uses and roles of design drawing in fields outside of ID as demonstrated in the literature of design studies. It illustrates the depth of interest that this topic has in that literature. With both a long history and deep connections to practice, design drawing is a staple of most design fields. Unfortunately, that is not the case with ID. As we have shown elsewhere (see Chapter XVII) design drawing in ID lags behind most other fields in exploiting the value of design drawing for designing.

We began this chapter by discussing the similarities between ID and other fields of design. Given these similarities, and the reliance of these other fields on this basic method, ID practitioners would be wise to consider the characteristics of design drawing as they develop and use VIDLs. These characteristics go to the very heart of what makes a VIDL useful to the design process.

REFERENCES

Alexander, C. (1979). *The timeless way of building.* New York: Oxford University Press.

Archer, B. (1992). As complex as ABC. In P. Roberts, B. Archer, & K. Baynes (Eds.), *Modelling: The language of design.* Loughborough University of Technology, Department of Design and Technology.

Archer, B., & Roberts, P. (1992). Design and technological awareness in education. In P. Roberts, B. Archer, & K. Baynes (Eds.), *Modelling : The language of design.* Loughborough University of Technology, Department of Design and Technology.

Arnheim, R. (1995). Sketching and the psychology of design. In V. Margolin & R. Buchanan (Eds.), *The idea of design* (pp. xxii, 285 p.). Cambridge, MA: MIT Press.

Baynes, K. (1992). The role of modelling in the industrial revolution. In P. Roberts, B. Archer, & K. Baynes (Eds.), *Modelling: The language of design.* Loughborough University of Technology, Department of Design and Technology.

Brunner, J. (2003). The narrative construction of reality. In M. Mateas & P. Sengers (Eds.), *Narrative intelligence* (pp. vii, 340). Amsterdam: John Benjamins Publishing.

Bucciarelli, L. L. (1994). *Designing engineers.* Cambridge, MA: MIT Press.

Cross, N. (2001). Design cognition: Results from protocol and other empirical studies of design activity. In C. M. Eastman, W. M. McCracken, & W. C. Newstetter (Eds.), *Design knowing and learning: cognition in design education* (pp. 79-103). Amsterdam: Elsevier.

Dorst, K., & Cross, N. (1996). Creativity in the design process: Co-evolution of problem—solution. *Studies, 17*(4), 341-361.

Eastman, C. M. (1969). Cognitive processes and ill-defined problems: A case study from design. *In The Proceedings of the First Joint International Conference on IA,* Washington, DC, pp. 669-690.

Eisner, E. W. (1998). *The enlightened eye: Qualitative inquiry and the enhancement of educational practice* (2nd ed.). Upper Saddle River, NJ: Merrill.

Gedenryd, H. (1998). *How designers work—Making sense of authentic cognitive activities.* Unpublished Dissertation, Lund University, Lund, UK.

Gibbons, A. S., & Rogers, P. C. (2006). *Coming at design from a different angle: Functional design.* Brigham Young University.

Goel, V. (1995). *Sketches of thought.* Cambridge, MA: MIT Press.

Goldschmidt, G. (1991). The dialectics of sketching. *Creativity Research Journal, 4*(2), 123-143.

Hanks, K., & Belliston, L. (1977). *Draw : A visual approach to thinking, learning, and communicating.* Los Altos, CA: W. Kaufmann.

Hansen, Y. (1999). Visualization for thinking, planning, and problem solving. *Information Design*, 193-220.

Hart, J. (1999). *The art of the storyboard : Storyboarding for film, TV, and animation.* Boston: Focal Press.

Henderson, K. (1998). The role of material objects in the design process: A comparison of two design cultures and how they contend with automation. *Science, Technology, & Human Values, 23*(2), 139-174.

Jackendoff, R. (1996). *The architecture of the language faculty.* Cambridge, MA: MIT Press.

Kays, E. J. (2003). *Architecture and instructional design: A conceptual model for e-learning.* Unpublished Dissertation, Capella University.

Kivett, H. A. (1998). Free-hand sketching: A lost art? *Art, Architecture and Design, 12*(1).

Laseau, P. (1975). *Graphic problem solving for architects & builders.* Boston: Cahners Books.

Laseau, P. (1986). *Graphic problem solving for architects and designers* (2nd ed.). New York: Van Nostrand Reinhold.

Laseau, P. (1989). *Graphic thinking for architects and designers* (2nd ed.). New York: Van Nostrand Reinhold.

Lockard, W. K. (1977). *Drawing as a means to architecture.* Tucson, AZ: Pepper Pub.

Massironi, M. (2002). *The psychology of graphic image: Seeing, drawing, communicating.* Mahwah, NJ: L. Erlbaum.

McCloud, S. (1993). *Understanding comics.* Northampton, MA: Kitchen Sink Press.

McKim, R. H. (1980). *Thinking visually: A strategy manual for problem solving.* Belmont, CA: Lifetime Learning Publications.

Moore, K. (2000). Between the lines: The role of drawing in design. *Environments by Design.*

Murphy, D. (1992). Is instructional design truly a design activity? *Educational and Training Technology International, 29*(4), 279-282.

Newell, A., & Simon, H. A. (1972). *Human problem solving.* Englewood Cliffs, NJ: Prentice-Hall.

Press, M., & Cooper, R. (2003). *The design experience: The role of design and designers in the twenty-first century.* Burlington, VT: Ashgate.

Reitman, W. R. (1965). *Cognition and thought; An information-processing approach.* New York: Wiley.

Rittel, H., & Webber, M. M. V. (1973). Dilemmas in a general theory of planning. *Policy Sciences, 4*(2), 155-169.

Robbins, E., & Cullinan, E. (1994). *Why architects draw.* Cambridge, MA: MIT Press.

Rowland, G. H. (1993). Designing and instructional design. *Educational Technology Research and Development, 41*(1), 79-91.

Saddler, H. J. (2001). Understanding design representations. *Interactions, 8*(4), 17-24.

Schatz, S. (2003). A matter of design: A proposal to encourage the evolution of design in instructional design. *Performance Improvement Quarterly, 16*(4).

Schön, D. A. (1987). *Educating the reflective practitioner: Toward a new design for teaching and learning in the professions* (1st ed.). San Francisco: Jossey-Bass.

Simon, H. A. (1996). *The sciences of the artificial* (3rd ed.). Cambridge, MA: MIT Press.

Tang, H. H., & Gero, J. S. (2001). Sketches as affordances of meanings in the design process. *Visual and Spatial Reasoning in Design II, Key Centre of Design Computing and Cognition,* University of Sydney, Sydney, (pp. 271-282).

Thomas, F., & Johnston, O. (1981). *Disney animation: The illusion of life.* New York: Abbeville Press.

Tversky, B. (2002). *What do sketches say about thinking?* (AAAI Technical Report SS-02-08). Stanford University.

Ullman, D. G., Wood, S., & Craig, D. L. (1990). The importance of drawing in the mechanical design process. *Computers & Graphics, 14*(2), 263-274.

Verstijnen, I. M., Hennessey, J. M., van Leeuwen, C., Hamel, R., & Goldschmidt, G. (1998). Sketching and creative discovery. *Design Studies, 19*(4).

Vygotsky, L. S., & Kozulin, A. (1986). *Thought and language.* Cambridge, MA: MIT Press.

Zimring, C., & Craig, D. L. (2001). Defining design between domains: An argument for design research á la carte. In C. M. Eastman, W. M. McCracken, & W. C. Newstetter (Eds.), *Design knowing and learning: Cognition in design education* (pp. 79-103). Amsterdam: Elsevier.

ENDNOTE

[1]   This chapter was adapted from parts of Stubbs (2006, unpublished dissertation)

Chapter IV
The Culture Based Model:
A Framework for Designers and Visual ID Languages

Patricia A. Young
University of Maryland, Baltimore County, USA

ABSTRACT

Globalizing the field of instructional design lies in the building and nurturing of innovative models, frameworks, visual languages, and practices that include culture-based considerations. This chapter argues that culture, as a design construct, is integral to educating learners and enhancing the design process. This is supported by a review of theoretical and methodological studies that define culture and an examination of models of culture that are supported by VIDLs. Further, the significance of VIDLs as design tools is offered through the culture based model (CBM) an intercultural instructional design framework that guides designers through the management, design, development and assessment process while taking into account explicit culture-based considerations. The chapter provides a description of the origins of CBM, an overview of relevant research, and an outline of the model and its possible applications with VIDLs. This research suggests that VIDLs can serve a broader scope if culture is considered.

INTRODUCTION

The **globalization** of instructional design is the direction for the 21st century and beyond.

Future designs of instruction, like the emerging VIDL, must consider **culture** as an integral component to the **design process**. Culture is a core construct of all design decisions; however its potential to improve the design process has been mostly ignored in the field of instructional design (Subramony 2004; Young, in press-a). This lack of interest in culture as a design construct

may be prevalent for various reasons. First, **designers** are not sure how to represent culture in the design process, what to look for, nor what to include. Second, there may be conflicts between the culture of the target audience and the technology; and many designers are grappling with how to bridge these communication connections (Chu & Reeves, 2000). Third, a comprehensive framework in which to integrate culture into the analysis, design, development, implementation and evaluation (ADDIE) process has not been available. Finally, the inclusion of "cultural frames of reference" may not have been seriously considered (Gay, 2000, p. xix).

Instructional design (ID), over the last 20 years, has seen more of a focus on improving and understanding learning and instruction (Jonassen, 1996, 2004; Reigeluth, 1983; Tennyson & Schott, 1997) and less of a focus on how culture influences learning and instruction (Subramony, 2004; Thomas, Mitchell, Joseph, 2002; Young, 1999, 2008). The literature in ID examines culture through the application of theories and methods such as cultural diversity, cultural pluralism, and cultural sensitivity (Scheel & Branch, 1993); thereby aligning itself with educational trends that promote multiculturalism (Banks & Banks, 2003). Culture is broadly conceived in ID; and its importance in the design process has not been fully considered because there has not been a model or framework that is fully driven by a **cultural context** until the **culture based model** (CBM). CBM is an intercultural instructional design framework that guides designers through the management, design, development and assessment process while taking into account explicit culture-based considerations. The model and its relation to visual languages will be further elaborated on in this chapter.

The designer operates in a larger context in the design process (Kelley & Hartfield, 1996; Winograd, 1996). Therefore, the role of the designer and their tools, such as VIDLs, are part of this context. Botturi, Derntl, Boot and Figl (2006) define a VIDL as a "set of concepts that support structuring a design task and conceiving solutions" (p. 1216). As an example of the designer's role, the architect must learn about the land, laws, people, property rights and other aspects of a culture before creating a blueprint. Given the data about the target audiences' culture, the architect may add an alcove for a religious sculpture, adjust the physical layout (e.g., wheelchair accessible pews), or accommodate language inscriptions to be carved in the concrete pavement upon entrance into a building. Similarly, the designer must learn about the people, learning styles, histories, etc. that will influence the VIDL and the creation of the product.

Taylor (1992) argues that a cultural context does exist between design and designer; therefore the design process must be viewed from the perspective of the culture or society. Visual languages, according to Kress and van Leeuwen (2006), are not "transparent and universally understood; [they are] culturally specific" (p. 4). Given this, designers should be cognizant of their target audience's culture and how culture influences the design, designing and the designer.

This research positions the designer in that larger context, proposes opportunities in CBM in which to use VIDLs and provides a comprehensive portrait of the designer in the design process. The overall argument proposes that culture is integral to educating learners and to enhancing the design process. Further, CBM aids designers in considering culture, and visual languages provide **support structures** for **models of culture**.

This chapter reviews theory and methods that support research on culture, ID, models of culture, visual languages and CBM as an ID framework. First, multiple perceptions of cultures are offered through a review of traditional definitions, a definition specific to ID, and an alternative perspective on the nature of culture in design. Specific to the goals of this handbook, the remainder of this chapter presents relevant examples of visual languages across disciplines that have developed "models of culture" and the application of these models. The chapter further provides a culture-based framework in which visual languages can operate. The chapter concludes with some final thoughts.

CULTURE AND INSTRUCTIONAL DESIGN

Culture means many things. Geertz (1973) interpreted culture as a "historically transmitted pattern of meanings embodied in symbols, a system of inherited conceptions expressed in symbolic forms by means of which men communicate, perpetuate, and develop their knowledge about and attitudes toward life" (p. 89). Hofstede (1991) proposes that culture is learned; it is not part of ones genetic makeup. In the area of cultural studies, culture is concerned with how meanings are interpreted and created in a society (Gray & McGuigan, 1997; Hall, 1997). Williams (1958), a cultural theorist, believes that "culture is ordinary" (p. 74). It is made in the human mind making possible effort, examination and explication. That is, culture is what is known (tradition) and what comes to be known through investigation and invention (creativity). These meanings of culture demonstrate its importance as a theoretical construct to explain the meaning of human kind but also its malleability as a design construct to redefine the design process.

In ID definitions of culture are broadly based to include sociological, anthropological and educational perspectives (Chen, Mashhadi, Ang, & Harkrider, 1999; Powell, 1997; Williams-Green, Holmes, & Sherman, 1997); thus, culture is pervasive (Scheel & Branch, 1993; Williams et al., 1997). Scheel and Branch (1993) offer a comprehensive definition that encompasses the interdisciplinary perspectives of culture:

...the patterns of behavior and thinking by which members of groups recognize and interact with one another. These patterns are shaped by a group's values, norms, traditions, beliefs, and artifacts. Culture is the manifestation of a group's adaptation to its environment, which includes other cultural groups and as such, is continually changing. Culture is interpreted very broadly here so as to encompass the patterns shaped by ethnicity, religion, socio-economic status, geography, profession, ideology, gender, and lifestyle. Individuals are members of more than one culture, and they embody a subset rather than the totality of cultures identifiable characteristics. (p. 7)

This definition of culture in ID helps designers to consider the many facets of culture while building information and communication technologies (ICTs). However, these beliefs, definitions and theories about culture do not address the nature of culture in design.

QUALIFYING THE NATURE OF CULTURE IN DESIGN

The nature of culture in design moves beyond static definitions and interpretations in that culture is dynamic, malleable, fluid, and always in motion. Culture is created and recreated by man's production. (This definition and the ideas in this section have been informed by the following researchers: Giles & Middleton, 1999; Hall, 1996; Kroeber & Kluckhohn, 1966; Scheel & Branch 1993; Williams, 1958.)

A simple question answer scenario about culture might proceed as follows:

- **Who is culture?** Culture is everything human-made and nature-made.
- **What is the purpose of culture?** The purpose of culture is to serve humans.
- **How does culture function?** Culture functions as humans direct it to.
- **When will culture end?** When humankind ends, culture will end.
- **Where is culture?** Culture is everywhere.
- **Why do we need culture?** We need culture to tell our history.

"Culture is not a fixed construct" (Powell, 1997, p. 15). It is not tied to a discipline, theory or controversy. It exists freely in the space of design. This emulsion is the space in which design should exist and designers should work. In the design of ICTs, the goal is to recreate culture or represent culture. Culture does not have physical or virtual properties in design until the designer assigns those properties. Culture is not real until designers make it real.

The nature of culture in design is creative. Creativity is derived through the implementation of the design process. However, some innate creative ability is required of designers and the design. Is creativity a prerequisite for designers? Or can anyone be a designer? An inventive spirit requires the ability to see beyond the obvious and to design new ways to envision one's physical or virtual reality. Kelley & Hartfield (1996) argue that the creative potential is something everyone possesses.

Because culture has to be recreated, simulated, virtualized in the space of design it must contain dynamic—free flowing properties. These properties are assigned by designers, programmers and other members of the design team. The assignment of property gives functionality—purpose. The nature of culture in design maintains fluid properties that are managed by designers.

MODELS OF CULTURE

Models of culture have been designed, developed or discovered to explain humankind and our existence in the world, explore diverse learning and learners, and provide a framework for cross cultural research and analysis. These models of culture can be found across disciplines and conceptualized in a variety of forms and formats. In psychology, models of culture focus on explaining processes of the mind (D'Andrade, 1990; Quinn, 1987; Schank & Abelson, 1977). D'Andrade's (1990) American folk model of the mind, for example, contains six elements related to cognitive states or processes. The six elements include: (1) perceptions, (2) belief/thought; (3) feelings/emotion; (4) desires/wishes; (5) intention; (6) resolution and will. The research of Triandis (1995), in the area of social psychology, focused on the cultural dimension of individualism and collectivism to further explain human behavior.

Triandis continued to build on the individualism and collectivism dimension by defining other attributes such as self, independent or interdependent, horizontal or vertical, in-group goals, and norms/attitudes (Triandis, 1989; Triandis & Gelfand, 1998). Anthropological models of culture examine the whole culture looking at the shared behavior and knowledge of an entire culture (Hall, 1976). Hall (1966, 1976, 1983) theorizes that there are several dimensions of culture—time, context and space. Further, time, context, and space, as models of culture, are perceived and experienced differently by individuals, groups and societies around the world. In the area of intercultural communication, researchers have focused on value systems and orientations and how they differ across cultures (Condon & Yousef, 1975; Hofstede, 1980). Hofstede (1980), by example, identified five dimensions of culture-based on the value systems of respondents in 72 countries/regions, and these values were consistent with human acting, thinking and feeling. The dimensions include: power distance, uncertainty avoidance, individualism versus collectivism, masculinity versus femininity, and long-term versus short-term orientation. In the field of business, researchers have developed dimensions of culture that assist business personnel in understanding the effects of culture on management and how cultural values and practices are similar or different (Javidan & House, 2001; Trompenaar & Hampden-Turner, 1998). A widely used model is the Trompenaar and Hampden-Turner (1998) seven dimensions of culture that seek to help individuals and groups understand cultural differences between and within cultures. The dimensions include: (a) relationships with people; (b) universalism versus particularism; (c) individualism versus communitarianism; (d) neutral versus emotional; (e) specific versus diffuse; (f) achievement versus ascription and (g) attitudes of time & environment. In the field of ID, models of culture focus on the integration of culture in the design process and enhancing learning through the incorporation of culture based **design specifications** (Edmundson, 2007; Henderson, 1996, 2007; Lee, 2003; Thomas et al., 2002). The cultural adaptation process (CAP) Model, designed by Edmundson (2007), is a guide for pre-existing e-learning courses as it connects designers to the "cultural profiles" of learners (p. 267). The model provides a matrix consisting of four levels designating courses that are **generic** (level 1) to more **specialized** (level 4) and Steps 1-5 contain the course characteristics from the most generic to more specialized. The model seeks to aid in the development of culturally appropriate e-learning courses. Henderson's (1996, 2007) multiple cultures model (MCM) is an instructional design model for e-learning and e-teaching that helps instructors to offer culturally specific knowledge to learners and balance academic, industry and global cultures. MCM consists of "various cultural logics" that include: global academic cultures; societies dominant culture; indigenous and ethnic minorities cultures; gender, religion, class cultures; and workplace cultures and pedagogies (p. 136). Thomas et al.'s (2002) third dimension model is an extension of the ADDIE (analyze, design, develop, implement, evaluate) model in that it is iterative, multi-directional and three-dimensional. The Third Dimension seeks to provide instructional designers with design parameters that focus on culture and foster **culturally sensitive** products. The three parameters added to the existing ADDIE model include: intention, interaction and introspection. This multi-disciplinary inquiry of models of culture suggests that there is a need for frameworks grounded in culture that can best help to deconstruct the complexity of cultures and provide guidance in cross-cultural designs, relations, meanings, communications, etc.

VISUAL LANGUAGES AND MODELS OF CULTURE

Visual languages, in an interdisciplinary sense, serve multiple roles. The first is to communicate a message through a visual or functional language (Winograd, 1996). Second, visual languages provide a synthetic idea, image or metaphor of complex ideas (Botturi, 2006). Third, visual languages create a grammar or produce meanings for its use (Kress & van Leeuwen, 2006). An examination of models of culture reveals that most are guided by visual languages or a graphic representation of the researcher's ideologies about culture (Hall, 1966, 1976, 1983; Henderson, 2007; Hofstede, 1980; Thomas et al., 2002; Trompenaar & Hampden-Turner, 1998). Specifically, some graphic representations display the functioning of the model of culture and others the researcher's perception of culture. Overall, this visual language is usually simplistic but some take on more complex forms. The goal of the visuals has been to convey ideas, beliefs, values, meanings and understandings about culture. Edward Hall (1983) for example, used the visual representation of a mandala, a classification device that shows relationships, to convey the cultural dimension of time. Figure 1 represents Hall's "map of time" as perceived in high context and low context cultures. (High context cultures provide little information in communicated messages. Low context cultures offer more explicit information in communicated messages.) Hall (1983) argued that time should not be perceived in a linear fashion but as a "cluster of concepts, events and rhythms" (p. 13). Ultimately, Hall demonstrated how cultures and historical time periods could be categorized and applied to cultures. By example, the Hopi Indians of North America live by sacred time and Americans by profane or micro time. For designers, this suggests that target audiences perception of time and how they use time may need to be considered in the design process.

Trompenaar and Hampden-Turner (1998) used a graphic representation to describe the meanings inherent in the multiple layers of culture. Figure 2 exemplifies "a model of culture." On the explicit layer of culture are those things that can be observed; they are tangible. This includes artifacts and products such as clothing, food, language,

Figure 1. Adapted from Edward T. Hall (1983): A map of time

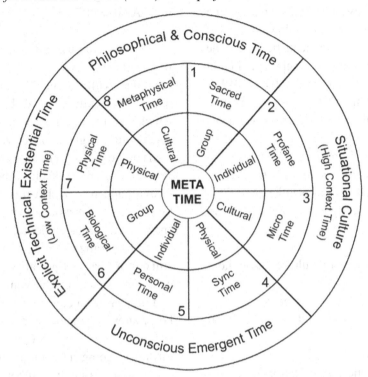

buildings, and agriculture. The middle layer reflects the norms and values of groups. Norms refer to a group's sense of right and wrong.Values refer to shared ideas of a group. At the core are the implicit but basic assumptions of human existence. Assumptions refer to how groups organize themselves to survive in their society and with nature. For designers, this suggests that designs should consider the multiple layers that comprise their target audience's perspective on the world and themselves. Further, there is great depth to our human existence and that can be reflected in our designs decisions.

Visual languages serve to represent processes, applications, methodologies and theories. Researchers and theorists have used visual languages to simplify or deconstruct complex compound ideas about culture. These two examples demonstrate that culture is a core component in articulating humankind. Therefore, it should be central to designer's recreation of human processes (i.e., learning, thinking, doing).

Figure 2. Adapted from Trompenaar and Hampden-Turner (1998): A model of culture

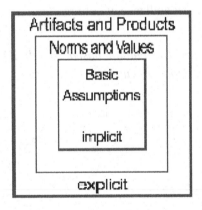

CBM AS A MODEL OF CULTURE

CBM represents a contemporary example of a model of culture (Figure 3). It is symbolized by the graphic representation of a circle encased by other circles to demonstrate its iterative functioning and self-selection process. The functioning symbolizes how the model continues to work like a machine each active component responding to the next. The self-selection allows designers to choose which area components best meet the needs of the project. CBM is comprised of eight areas consistent with the acronym: ID-TABLET. These areas include: **i**nquiry, **d**evelopment, **t**eam, **a**ssessments, **b**rainstorming, **l**earners, **e**lements and **t**raining.

As a model, CBM provides a framework to enhance the design process through the integration of culture-based design specifications. This framework enables designers or researchers to do the following:

- Integrate features of culture throughout ICTs
- Understand people and societies
- Communicate across and within cultural contexts
- Screen for bias
- Design authentic culture-based technologies
- Research the culture-based qualities of a target audience or culture

- Create generic or specialized designs
- Analyze ICTs

This research argues that all designs are based in culture; however some are **culture neutral** and others **culture specific**. This means that all designs are culture-based, but the measure to which one is more neutral and the other more specific to a target audience varies based on the goals of the project. The **culture-based circumference** (Figure 4) displays the space in which design happens and that this space is occupied by design specifications that meet generic and specialized target audiences. Generic features can be generalized across cultures but they are still culture-based. Specialized features focus on meeting the needs of a particular target audience, and they are also culture-based (Horton, 2005). For example, graphic symbols can be generic or specialized. Figure 5 is a generic symbol for turning or going right. Figure 6 is specialized; it is the Hamsa, a Judaic symbol regarded as a sign of protection warding off evil and leading to good fortune and personal well-being.

Figure 3. The culture based model: ID-TAB-LET—A model of culture

Figure 4. Culture-based circumference for use when designing ICTs (Young, in press-a)

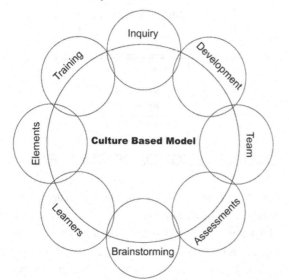

Figure 5. Go right

Figure 6. Hamsa, a Judaic symbol for protection

If the goal of the project is to internationalize, then the design specifications are generic and culture neutral (Figure 4). If the goal of the project is to localize, then the design specifications are specialized and culture specific. Internationalization seeks to eliminate culture making the product one that can be used by all or a universal design. Localization tailors products to the needs of a target audience. For designers, this means that culture-based design specifications exist within a circumference of the generic to specialized; therefore there is a much broader palette in which to design (Young, in press-a).

What is CBM?

CBM is an intercultural instructional design framework that guides designers through the management, design, development and assessment process while taking into account explicit culture-based considerations. The framework provides design guidance from the inception of an idea to beyond its completion. Guidance is approached from the target audience's or learner's perspective.

CBM is adaptive in that the designer prescribes methods based on the pre-production analysis and research, the on-going production, and post production (Reigeluth, 1983). The model, as with any instructional design model, should be modified based on the context of the processes (Gustafson & Branch, 2002; Tessmer & Wedman, 1995). Traditional instructional design models are "blueprint[s] of the instruction itself" and they focus on "what the instruction should be like" (Reigeluth, 1983, p. 24). However, CBM focuses much more broadly. It is a blueprint of the management and design processes and it focuses on what the content should be like. CBM brings the human element into design related disciplines (Douglas, 2006).

Traditionally, instructional design models have been based on learning theories. However, CBM evolved from an empirical study of instructional products designed by and for African-Americans. A treasure of themes and concepts related to culture were found in these materials and were classified as cultural remnants. Cultural remnants are the racial, ethnic, cultural, linguistic, political, social, historical, educational and economic artifacts embedded in discourses. The cultural remnants found in these instructional products were generalized to meet the design needs of cross cultural audiences and this translation resulted in CBM (Young, 1999, 2001, in press-b).

CBM builds a framework that begins with identifying the goal of the design. These goals can be classified in one of the following categories:

C   Custom development
A   Add-ons
R   Re-engineered
D   Diagnostic evaluations

Custom development is for the construction of a project from scratch. Add-Ons refer to making additions to an existing product. A pre-existing off-the-shelf product or on-line environment can be re-engineered. Diagnostic evaluations can be performed on products in any form of ICT.

CBM can be used by instructional designers, e-learning designers, web designers, usability practitioners, researchers, curriculum developers, students, and other practitioners. The model meets the needs of a broad audience by allowing for the selection of components based on the project goals, design specifications, technological requirements and content area needs.

VIDLs AS SUPPORT STRUCTURES

Designers operate in a larger context in the design process (Kelley & Hartfield, 1996; Winograd, 1996); this may include participating broadly in functions or on assignments specific to the implementation of visual languages. VIDLs focus on the "object being designed" (Botturi, 2005, p. 330; Rheinfrank & Evenson, 1996). This perspective and the subsequent notation system complements CBM as this framework focuses on the target audience, process, and content. CBM works on the larger functioning of the production machine, and VIDLs operate the nuts and bolts that make the machine work.

CBM supports designers broadly in all of its components and the modeling of visual languages in the areas of development, elements, assessments, and learners. As a comprehensive tool, CBM is integrated throughout the production process to enable the accurate representation of the target audience and their needs. Therefore, preparing designers for this task is as important as the process and product.

In turn, VIDLs support the structure of CBM. For example, Botturi (2005) found that VIDLs can bring consistency to design decisions. Consistency can bring efficiency to the design process

and enable quicker design decisions. VIDLs can "improve precision and productivity" (Gibbons & Brewer, 2005, p. 111) and allow for the easy replication of minute tasks. The design process can be improved and made more efficient through VIDLs (Gibbons & Brewer, 2005).

CBM AS A FRAMEWORK FOR VIDLs

The following narrative provides an overview of the areas and design factors in CBM. There are eight areas consistent with the acronym: ID-TABLET (Figure 3). These areas include inquiry, development, team, assessments, brainstorming, learners, elements and training. Each area is further defined through design factors; design factors are design related features that assist in the management, design, development and assessment of products and/or services. In total, there are 70 design factors.

ID-TABLET

CBM's ID-TABLET focuses on project management and design. The project management entails problem solving, planning, evaluation, decision making and creativity. The areas under project management include: brainstorming (B1-B10), team (T1-T3), development (D1-D10), learners (L1-L10), assessments (A1-A4), and training (Tr1-Tr2). The project design focuses on monitoring and content development. The areas under project design include: inquiry (I1-I6) and elements (E1-E25) (See template in Appendix A). The template gives a brief outline of the ID-TABLET. If electronically accessible, the template would act as a database for the collection of information gathered about the target audience, the society or culture.

Below each area of the ID-TABLET is described and the corresponding design factors listed. This is followed by explanations of how to use this part of CBM and how this area connects to VIDLs and/or the designer.

Inquiry

Inquiry (I1-I6) monitors development, automates the internal flow of the design process and functions as internal sensors. This monitoring checks and rechecks that the process is executing properly. It is interactive and always operational. Specifically, Inquiry provides a series of questions to be asked and answered during pre-production, production and post-production. These questions outline the design of the product and allow for a review of the product before, during and after production. The list of questions is not exhaustive; but they provide a broad selection of questions meant to focus on the needs of the target audience, enable the design process, and screen for bias. These questions are reviewed and reiterated throughout the design process to keep the design process active.

Inquiry is divided into six design factors:

I1. Genre
I2. Framing
I3. Omission
I4. Backgrounding
I5. Foregrounding
I6. Visual representations

The designer uses the Inquiry area by reviewing with the team the appropriate questions during points in the production process. These questions are reiterated throughout several meetings to bring the project back into alignment with its overall goal and limit bias. As the production evolves the design changes and many times the needs of the target audience gets lost in the process. These questions aid in keeping the team on track by assessing and reassessing the design process.

For the designer, using Inquiry provides a type of qualitative assessment in that the questions covered are those that an outside interviewer might ask. Taken from this perspective, the questions are meant to provide an objective review of the design process.

Development

Development (D1-D10) considers those features that are important in the overall development of the product. This area supports both new and existing products. Design specifications focus on determining features of a design that are technical, aesthetic, content, culture-based and/or target audience (TACCT) related. Then, the ICT format of the product is determined based on the design of the project; format options could include: Web-based, print, audio, software, video, etc. Other development considerations are to build a product that promotes efficiency, accessibility, and versatility. Multiple representations of culture are considered in particular environmental and individual/group cultures. Development focuses on creating a quality design that authentically represents the target audience and limits interference in the form of bias and misrepresentations. Throughout, the production process is supported by models.

The design factors include:

D1. Consider technical, aesthetic, content, culture-based and target audience (TACCT) design specifications
D2. Mass distribution formats
D3. Effective technology
D4. Diversify ICT format
D5. Understand target audience
D6. Explore environmental & individual/group cultures
D7. Quality design
D8. Authenticate product
D9. Control for interference
D10. Model the product or process

In using these factors, the designer determines the type of product they are creating using CARD.

For existing products, TACCT is used to determine the degree that the ICT is technical, aesthetic, etc. For new products, the other factors (D2-D10) of Development are considered. The designer methodically goes through each factor and gathers data, engages discussions, offers considerations, and makes the implementation of the product happen. Product validation and authentication are supported here.

Given that Development is an area where design specifications are strengthened, VIDLs could aid in supporting these areas. For example, Motschnig-Pitrik and Derntl (2005) developed person-centered e-learning (PceL; further developed as coUML, see Chapter IX) templates to help instructors with customizing web support in their online courses. This type of "user-centered customization process" seems a prudent path for VIDLs in education and e-learning (Motschnig-Pitrik & Derntl, 2005, p. 53) as the customization of technologies, personalized computers and individualized computer software are now common place (Kersten, Matwin, Noronha, & Kersten, 2000). The user-centered customization process complements CBM's focus on the needs of a target audience because learning and instruction is culture- based and tailor made.

Team

Team (T1-T3) focuses on the recruitment of a culturally sensitive design team that includes a cultural expert, an educator and other culturally informed members. These experts become a united team that seeks to fulfill the needs of the target audience as the most important goal.

The design factors include:

T1.   Cultural expert
T2.   Enlist educators
T3.   Culturally informed team

The designer uses the Team area to guide the hiring of the design team members and to further educate the existing team about the target audience. These are non-traditional actions; as the design team engages in a somewhat comprehensive education of the target audience as specified under Training.

Fostering a team of highly skilled individuals (Gustafson & Branch, 2002) is extremely beneficial to the design process. The designer and design team prepares for the production process by recruiting an eclectic team of educators, designers and cultural informants. The selection of the appropriate team is key to the successful management, development and implementation of the project. Finding people who can work together in a culturally diverse work environment is important to culture-based designs. It is easy to gather a team of people to whom one is familiar. However, it may seem an imposition to let outsiders into ones circle. Designing for ethnically diverse learners requires designers to step outside of their normal comfort zone and challenge themselves to hear from others and listen to others outside their social circle. The input from the cultural expert, community representative and data from CBM elements is critical to educating the team and authenticating the product. All team members must have strong interests in meeting the needs of the target audience and a belief in the effectiveness of the product being developed.

Assessments

The area of *Assessments* (A1-A4) covers several assessment options. *Multiple evaluation options* means that assessments can include internal and external evaluations that measure the learner's acquisition of knowledge or the effectiveness of a products design. *Assess the assessment* examines the extent of bias and determines the best assessment to support the target audience. *External review* focuses on the hiring of an outside agency. *Culture specific assessments* advises on the building of culture specific evaluations and measurements.

The design factors include:

A1. Multiple evaluation opportunities
A2. Assess the assessment
A3. External review.
A4. Culture specific assessments

The designer uses the assessments area to strengthen the validity of the design, provide evidence of the products effectiveness and to evaluate the goals set for the target audience. This area is a tool to check and balance design specifications.

Applying VIDLs to the area of assessments brings the type of visualization needed to determine learner feedback, product effectiveness and project improvements. Botturi's (2006; see also Chapter VII) educational environment modeling language (E²ML) is a VIDL used to create educational environments; E²ML proposes that visualizing aids in improving designs and communication between team members. E²ML blueprints the plan for instruction through document sets labeled as: goal definition, action diagrams and overview diagrams; this documentation could also detail a broader plan for assessment only. Given that E²ML supports project management by enabling quality checks it could be a useful tool in mapping evaluative processes.

Brainstorming

Brainstorming (B1-B10) is conducted to align the project with its design team, assess the financial status of the project from conception and beyond its completion, discuss the overall design, implement preliminary assessments, and determine learning outcomes. This preproduction period can determine what parts of the project receive more or less emphasis given the financial situation and project due date. The design factors associated with brainstorming determine the direction to proceed and serves as an initial review of the design process.

The design factors include:

B1. Financial support
B2. Pilot studies/field tests of product
B3. Assess community's response
B4. Community representative on the team
B5. Investigate target audience to authenticate product
B6. Reflect and assess learning goals
B7. Affordable design
B8. Meet needs of target audience
B9. Discuss & consider cultural context
B10. Present & consider outcomes

The designer and the design team prepares for the production process by reviewing the design factors specified under Brainstorming. These areas are thoroughly discussed and actions taken to make sure that they are in place. Several brainstorming sessions may be needed. The collection of this information is important in meeting the needs of the target audience, limiting revisions and mistakes in the design process, and creating culture-based technological artifacts. According to Kelley and Hartfield (1996), brainstorming sessions offer the design team an opportunity to come up with ideas about the client's problem and most find these sessions interesting. The Brainstorming sessions with CBM should be more extensive as the needs of people will be the core of the discussion. Engaging in discussions that cover a breath of information, states Kelley and Hartfield (1996), takes more time in the preproduction stage but it saves time in the final stages of production.

Learners

Learners (L1-L10) centers on the needs of learners and learning. These design factors assist in providing a dynamic learning environment that is supportive of the learner's cultural frames of reference and seeks to meet the instructional goals of the project. The design factors are adaptive to learners on multiple levels including intellectual, motivational and educational; thereby providing opportunities for individualized instruction. Other design factors in this area focus on a variety of instructional strategies that focus on multiple points of learning such as: extending and differentiating learning, empowering and engaging learners, instilling proactive learning, identifying educational objectives, enculturating the learner, and incorporating culture based instructional strategies.

The design factors include:

L1. Extend learning
L2. Differentiate opportunities to learn
L3. Empower & engage learners
L4. Teach proactive learning
L5. Identify educational objectives
L6. Culture-specific instructional strategies
L7. Enrich instructional content
L8. Adapt instruction to learner
L9. Plan for instruction
L10 Enculturate the learner

In using Learners, the designer and the design team determines the type of learning environment they want to create. Then they decide which design factors would aid them the most in achieving these goals. The team again meticulously reviews the design factors and descriptions working through each one and returning to others as needed.

VIDLs aid in designs that adapt to learners needs (Gibbons & Brewer, 2005); this is the main goal of CBM learners. The design of instruction is tailored to adapt to the individual needs of the learner. Therefore, the learner is operating at an independent versus frustration level. The designer relies on constructivist theories of learning to guide the construction or improvement of the VIDL. VIDLs that seek to meet the needs of learners initially will require multiple avenues to complete the learning task. Because the path to learning is unique to each individual; however the conclusion could be the same. (That is, one learner may see the path to $4 \times 4 = 16$ as one of

memorization. Another learner may have to visualize 4 objects 4 times is 16. Another learner uses their fingers as a counting tool to get the answer 16.) Therefore, CBM suggests extending learning, differentiating instruction, etc. to address the multiple modalities, cultural uniqueness (Gay, 2000), multiple intelligences (Gardner, 1999), and the diversity of learners. VIDLs can aid in creating these paths to learning because they allow for the replication and visualization of minute tasks (Gibbons & Brewer, 2005).

In addition, Gibbons and Brewer (2003, 2005) argue that layering VIDLs provides the designer with flexibility in the organization of design choices and economizes design processes. CBM is already multi-leveled therefore providing layered VIDLs to expedite instructional processes makes for a more efficient process, saves time and money on the project, and eases tasks for the designer.

Elements

Elements (E1-E25) facilitate content development. These elements seek to be comprehensive in providing the fundamental total of which all culture is composed. The list of elements can be used to understand, define, or evaluate the target audience. The data developed around these elements provides authentic information about societies, cultures and peoples.

There are 25 design factors that include.

The Anthropology of Culture:
E1. Cultural aesthetics
E2. Cultural artifacts
E3. Cultural capital
E4. Cultural classification
E5. Cultural communications
E6. Cultural demographics
E7. Cultural environment
E8. Cultural history
E9. Cultural knowledge
E10. Cultural language

E11. Cultural physiology
E12. Cultural relations
E13 Cultural resources

The Psychology of Culture:
E14. Cultural beliefs & values
E15. Cultural experiences
E16. Cultural ideas
E17. Cultural identity
E18. Cultural interests
E19. Cultural misconceptions
E20. Cultural ways

The Science of Culture:
E21. Cultural anomalies
E22. Cultural cultures
E23. Cultural futures
E24. Cultural infinities
E25 Cultural nature

Van Patten (1989) argues that instructional designs must have two things "(1) a set of elements that require designing and (2) a principle with which to organize them" (p 27). The elements meets the first specification through its set of design factors. In this case, the second principle is to focus on the needs of the target audience. In using the elements area, the designer and design team decides on the goals of the project and what information will be needed to understand the target audience and produce the product. The selection of Elements depends on time, money and the client's goals.

An ethnographic study of a society would require an evaluation of their cultural elements. Who are the people we seek to study? What do they know? How did they come to be? From the 25 design factors, members of the design team engage in a collection of written and graphic data about the target group. This information is housed in a database or CBM guide accessible to all team members. The information gathered is not stereotypic but authentic representations of the target audience. Foucault, Russell, and Bell (2004), with the goal of creating products, successfully implemented ethnographic methods in finding out about their target audience, Chinese consumers. This type of ethnographic data gathering is time consuming, as the inclusion of culture is not a simple task. There will be more initial preparation and education that will save time and costs later in the production process. However, consider the loss of creating a product that does not fulfill the needs of the target audience (Young, in press-b).

Applying VIDLs to the area of Elements can provide visual clarification to what could be a massive amount of data in terms of content development. The unified modeling language (UML) is a language used for designing and describing software systems. Designers using UML are encouraged to model before building. Therefore the sketching mode of UML could prove useful in visualizing the content development path needed in a culture-based design. In particular, the use of forward engineering involves drawing a UML diagram before writing code (Fowler, 2001). Some variation on this could prove useful in VIDLs focused on education.

Training

Depending on whether it is an educational institution or business, the education of employees falls under the area of *Training* (Tr1-Tr2). Specifically, the people (e.g., instructors, employees, etc.) who will be using the product should receive Product Training as needed. These training sessions include culture-based training that provides instructors and employees with knowledge about the target audience based on elements and input from and interactions with the cultural expert.

The design factors include:

Tr1. Product training
Tr2. Culture-based training

The designer and/or design team uses the Training area to plan for the post-production handling of the product and educating the design team members about the target audience. If training materials have been prepared, their proper implementation would be followed up in this area. The design team engages in discussions and maintains a progress report of the product for future reference. The planning and implementation of training for the design team happens in this area. The designer and design team may not be involved in product training. However, this is an opportunity to learn about the product from the perspective of the instructor or practitioner who may be training learners to use the product. In addition to content, the organization and management of materials can be a part of this product training. The designer and design team participate in Culture-Based Training in order to receive a comprehensive knowledge of the target audience.

CONCLUSION

Research in ID has explored improving and understanding learning and instruction (Jonassen, 1996, 2004; Reigeluth, 1983; Tennyson & Schott, 1997); however, there has been little focus on how culture is an integral component to learning and learners (Subramony 2004; Young, 2008, in press-a). This chapter has offered an alternative perspective to understanding culture and the nature of culture in design to give designers a creative position in which to address design and culture. The chapter proposed culture as an integral component to educating learners and to enhancing the design process. It further offered CBM as a culture-based ID framework for the design of ICTs and proposed VIDLs as support structures for ID frameworks. Culture in the design of ICTs is a complex task that is multi-leveled and multi-layered; and it is guided by designers ingenuity in creating or a researchers desire to discover. Manifesting culture is an explicit act.

There were several limitations in this chapter. First, CBM needs to be implemented by designers to validate its effectiveness as an ID framework. Although traditionally, ID frameworks have not been tested in terms of evaluations of their functionality or instructional outcomes, credibility and acceptance is gained through designers who choose to adapt and implement models (Gustafson & Branch, 2002). Second, given space limitations the comprehensive descriptions and explanations of CBMs ID-TABLET could not be covered; only an overview was provided in this chapter and some description in the CBM template.

ID Futures

The future of ID will depend on innovators producing ideas. The inclusion of culture-based designs and VIDLs might engender such innovation. These concepts leave the door open for creative designers and researchers to seek original and imaginative designs to move the field of ID forward. The promotion of ID as a field of creators and builders can be the new future of ID.

Similarly this future of ID is dependent upon globalized learning and globalized thinking. Cheng (2002) argues that "globalized learning" means that learning is provided through many avenues including national and international resources. This type of learning provides access to instructional materials, educators, peers, and experts around the world (p. 14). Globalized thinking requires national and international researchers and designers to validate each others work, see connections in ideas, and collaborate across waters.

Integrating culture into the design of ICTs is not easy, but it is also not impossible. A commitment to a culture-based design means that designers are interested in creating a multitude of products from the generic or culture-neutral to the specialized or culture-specific. This commitment to the needs of the target audience is a move to globalize learning and thinking.

Future questions might ask: How can designers begin to see culture as an integral part in the design of ICTs? If designers of VIDLs consider culture, how will this influence notation systems? Can the integration of culture change the way we see design? Ultimately, there may need to be changes in mindset to truly implement globalized learning. This book begins a new dialogue for ID futures and an avenue for international discourse.

REFERENCES

Banks, J. & Banks, C. (Eds.). (2003). *Handbook of research on multicultural education.* San Francisco: Jossey-Bass Publishers.

Botturi, L. (2005). A framework for the evaluation of visual languages for instructional design: The case of E²ML. *Journal of Interactive Learning Research, 16*(4), 329-351.

Botturi, L. (2006). E²ML: A visual language for the design of instruction. *Educational Technology Research & Development, 54*(3), 265-293.

Botturi, L., Derntl, M., Boot, E., & Figl, K. (2006). *A classification framework for educational modeling languages in instructional design.* Paper presented at the Proceedings of The 6ᵗʰ IEEE International Conference on Advanced Learning Technologies, Kerkrade, The Netherlands (pp. 1216-1220).

Chen, A., Mashhadi, A., Ang, D., & Harkrider, N. (1999). Cultural issues in the design of technology-enhanced learning systems. *British Journal of Educational Technology, 30*(3), 217-230.

Cheng, Y. C. (2002). *New paradigm of borderless education: Challenges, strategies, and implications for effective education through localization and internationalization.* Paper presented at the International conference on learning & teaching: Challenge of learning and teaching in a Brave New World: Issues and opportunities in borderless education, Hatyai, Thailand.

Chu, G., & Reeves, T. C. (2000). *The relationship between cultural differences among American and Chinese university students and the design of personal pages on the World Wide Web.* New Orleans, LA: Paper presented at the annual meeting of the American Educational Research Association.

Condon, J. C., & Yousef, F. S. (1975). *An introduction to intercultural communication.* Indianapolis, IN: Bobbs-Merrill Educational Publishing.

D'Andrade, R. (1990). Some propositions about the relations between culture and human cognition. In J. W. Stigler, R. A. Shweder, & G. Herdt (Eds.), *Cultural psychology: Essays on comparative human development* (pp. 65-129). New York, NY: Cambridge University Press.

Douglas, I. (2006). Issues in software engineering of relevance to instructional design. *Tech Trends, 50*(5), 28-35.

Edumundson, A. (2007). The Cultural Adaptation Process (CAP) Model: Designing e-learning for another culture. In A. Edumundson (Ed.), *Globalized e-learning cultural challenges* (pp. 267-290). Hershey, PA: Information Science Publishing.

Foucault, B. E., Russell, R. S., & Bell, G. (2004, April 24-29). *Techniques for research and designing global products in an unstable world: A case study.* Paper presented at the Computer Human Interaction, Vienna, Austria.

Fowler, M. (2001, June 29). *Put your process on a diet.* Retrieved April 1, 2007, from http://www.ddj.com/dept/architect/184414675

Gardner, H. (2000). *Intelligence reframed: Multiple Intelligences for the 21ˢᵗ Century.* New York: Basic Books.

Gay, G. (2000). *Culturally responsive teaching.* New York: Teachers College Press.

Geertz, C. (1973). *The interpretation of cultures.* New York: Basic Books.

Gibbons, A. S. (2003). What and how do designers design?: A theory of design structure. *TechTrends, 47*(5), 22-27.

Gibbons, A. S., & Brewer, E. K. (2005). Elementary principles of design languages and design notation systems for instructional design. In J. M. Spector, C. Ohrazda, A. VanSchaack, & D. A. Wiley (Eds.), *Innovations in instructional technology* (pp. 111-129). Mahwah, NJ: Lawrence Erlbaum Associates.

Gray, A., & McGuigan, J. (1997). Introduction. In A. Gray & J. McGuigan (Eds.), *Studying culture: An introductory reader* (pp. xi-xv). New York: Arnold, A member of the Hodder Headline Group.

Gustafson, K. L., & Branch, R. M. (2002). *Survey of instructional development models.* Syracuse, NY: ERIC Clearinghouse On Information & Technology.

Hall, E. T. (1966). *The hidden dimension.* Garden City, NY: Doubleday.

Hall, E. T. (1976). *Beyond culture.* New York: Double Day.

Hall, E. T. (1983). *The dance of life: The other dimension of time.* Garden City, NY: Anchor Press/Doubleday.

Hall, S. (1996). Cultural studies and its theoretical legacies. In D. Morley & K.-H. Chen (Eds.), *Critical dialogues in cultural studies* (pp. 262-275). London: Routledge.

Hall, S. (1997). Minimal selves. In A. Gray & J. McGuigan (Eds.), *Studying culture.* London: Arnold, a member of the Hodder Headline Group.

Hall, P., & Hudson, R. (1997). *Software without frontiers: A multi-platform, multi-cultural, multi-nation approach.* New York: John Wiley & Sons, Ltd.

Henderson, L. (2007). Theorizing a multiple cultures instructional design model for e-learning and e-teaching. In A. Edmundson (Ed.), *Globalized e-learning cultural challenges* (pp. 130-153). Hershey, PA: Information Science Publishing.

Henderson, L. (1996). Instructional design of interactive multimedia: A cultural critique. *Education Technology Research and Development, 44*(4), 85-104.

Hofstede, G. (1980). *Cultures consequences: International differences in work related values.* Beverly Hills, CA: Sage Publications.

Hofstede, G. (1991). *Cultures and organizations: Software of the mind.* London: McGraw Hill Book Company.

Horton, W. (2005). Graphics: The not quite universal language. In N. Aykin (Ed.), *Usability and internationalization of Information Technology* (pp. 157-188). Mahwah, NJ: Lawrence Erlbaum & Associates Publishers.

Javidan, M., & House, R. J. (2001). Cultural acumen for the global manager: Lessons from Project GLOBE. *Organizational Dynamics, 29*(4), 289-305.

Jonassen, D. H. (Ed.). (1996). *Handbook of research for educational communications and technology.* New York: Macmillian Library Reference USA.

Jonassen, D. H. (Ed.). (2004). *Handbook of research on educational communications and technology.* Mahwah, NJ: Lawrence Erlbaum Associates, Inc.

Kelley, D., & Hartfield, B. (1996). The designer's stance. In T. Winograd (Ed.), *Bringing design to software* (pp. 151-164). New York: ACM Press.

Kersten, G. E., Matwin, S., Noronha, S. J., & Kersten, M. A. (2000). *The software for cultures and the cultures in software.* Paper presented at the European Conference on Information System ECI2000, Vienna, Austria.

Kress, G., & VanLeeuwen, T. (2006). *Reading images: The grammar of visual design* (2nd ed.). London: Routledge.

Kroeber, A. L., & Kluckhohn, C. (1966). *Culture: A critical review of concepts and definitions.* New York: Vintage Books.

Lee, C. D. (2003). Toward a framework for culturally responsive design in multimedia computer environments: Cultural modeling as a case. *Mind, Culture and Activity, 10*(1), 42-61.

Motschnig-Pitrik, R., & Derntl, M. (2005). Can the web improve the effectiveness of person-centered learning?: Case study in web engineering and beyond. *IASIS International Journal of WWW/Internet, 2*(1), 49-62.

Powell, G. C. (March/April 1997). Understanding the language of diversity. *Educational Technology, 37*(2), 15-18.

Quinn, N. (1987). Convergent evidence for a cultural model of American marriage. In D. Holland & N. Quinn (Eds.), *Cultural models in language & thought* (pp. 173-192). New York: Cambridge University Press.

Reigeluth, C. M. (Ed.). (1983). *Instructional-design theories and models: An overview of their current status.* Hillsdale, NJ: Lawrence Erlbaum Associates, Publishers.

Rheinfrank, J., & Evenson, S. (1996). Design languages. In T. Winograd (Ed.), *Bringing design to software* (pp. 63-80). New York: ACM Press.

Schank, R., & Abelson, R. (1977). *Scripts, plans, goals, and understanding: An inquiry into human knowledge structures.* Hillsdale, NJ: Lawrence Erlbaum Associates.

Scheel, N. P., & Branch, R. C. (August 1993). The role of conversation and culture in the systematic design of instruction. *Educational Technology, 33*, 7-18.

Subramony, D. P. (July/August 2004). Instructional technologists' inattention to issues of cultural diversity among learners. *Educational Technology*, 19-24.

Taylor, D. (1992). *Global software: Developing applications for the international market.* New York, NY: Springer.

Tennyson, R. D., & Schott, F. (1997). Instructional design theory, research, and models. In R. D. Tennyson, F. Schott, N. M. Seel, & S. Dijkstra (Eds.), *Instructional design international perspectives* (Vol. 1, pp. 1-16). Mahwah: Lawrence Erlbaum Associates, Publishers.

Tessmer, M. & Wedman, J. (1995). Context-sensitive instructional design models: A response to design research, studies and criticism. *Performance Improvement Quarterly, 8*(3) 38-54.

Thomas, M., Mitchell, M., & Joseph, R. (2002). The third dimension of ADDIE: A cultural experience. *Tech Trends, 46*(2), 40-45.

Triandis, H. C. (1989). The self and social behavior in differing cultural contexts. *Psychological review, 96*(3), 506-520.

Triandis, H. C. (1995). *Individualism and collectivism.* Boulder, CO: Westview Press.

Triandis, H. C., & Gelfand, M. J. (1998). Converging measurement of horizontal and vertical individualism and collectivism. *Journal of Personality and Social Psychology, 74*(1), 118-128.

Trompenaars, F., & Hampden-Turner, C. (1998). *Riding the waves of culture.* New York: McGraw-Hill Companies, Inc.

Van Patten, J. (1989). What is instructional design? In K. A. Johnson & L. J. Foa (Eds.), *Instructional design: New alternatives for effective education and training* (pp. 16-31). New York: National University Continuing Education Association.

Williams, R. (1958). Culture is ordinary. In N. McKenzie (Ed.), *Convictions* (pp. 74-92). London: MacGibbon and Kee.

Williams-Green, J., Holmes, G., & Sherman, T. (1997-1998). Culture as a decision variable for designing computer software. *Journal of Educational Technology, 26*(1), 3-18.

Winograd, T. (1996). Introduction. In T. Winograd (Ed.), *Bringing design to software* (pp. xiii-xxv). New York: ACM Press.

Young, P.A. (in press-a). Integrating culture in the design of ICTs. *British Journal of Educational Technology*.

Young, P. A. (in press-b). The culture based model: constructing a model of culture. *Education, Technology & Society Journal*.

Young, P.A. (1999). *Roads To Travel: A historical look at African American contributions to instructional technology*. Unpublished Dissertation, University of California Berkeley, Berkeley, CA.

Young, P. A. (2001). Roads to travel: A historical look at The Freedman's Torchlight—An African American contribution to 19th century instructional technologies. *Journal of Black Studies, 31*(5), 671-698.

Young, P. A. (2008). Exploring culture in the design of new technologies of literacy. In J. Coiro, M. Knobel, C. Lankshear & D. J. Leu (Eds.), *Handbook of research on new literacies*. London: Routledge.

APPENDIX: CULTURE BASED MODEL, ID-TABLET TEMPLATE

The following template should be used as the shell structure of a database to input information into each category. CBM's ID-TABLET consists of 70 design factors focused on project management and design. The project management entails problem solving, planning, educating, evaluating, learning, and decision making. The areas under project management include: *brainstorming* (B1-B10), *team* (T1-T3), *development* (D1-D10), *learners* (L1-L10), *assessments* (A1-A4), and *training* (Tr1-Tr2). The project design focuses on monitoring and content development. The areas under project design include: *inquiry* (I1-I6) and *elements* (E1-E25). These areas operate simultaneously; they maintain an interactive relation in that certain steps are repeated or referred back to throughout the design process. Thus, the process is always in motion—something is always happening.

Inquiry

Inquiry (I1-I6) monitors development, automates the internal flow of the design process and functions as internal sensors. It provides a series of questions to be asked and answered during pre-production, production and post production.

I1.   **Genre:** Aids in the selection of ICTs.
    I1a.   *What ICTs are being used and why?*
    I1b.   *Which ICTs are more effective given the content?*
    I1c.   *Is the project affordable to the target audience, given the ICTs used?*
    I1d.   *How have ICTs influenced the design of the product?*
I2.   **Framing:** Assists in maintaining the target audiences perspective.
    I2a.   *Who is the target audience?*
    I2b.   *How is the content presented to the target audience?*
    I2c.   *What is the content presented?*
    I2d.   *Is the content appropriate for the target audience and why?*
    I2e.   *Where, within the products design, is this content most appropriate?*
    I2f.   *Why is this content appropriate?*
I3.   **Omission:** Helps in assessing a design.
    I3a.   *What has been intentionally omitted and why?*
    I3b.   *What has been unintentionally omitted and why?*
    I3c.   *What has not been considered?*
    I3d.   *Will these omissions be detrimental to the project and why?*
I4.   **Backgrounding:** Helps in providing a balanced design.
    I4a.   *What has been backgrounded?*
    I4b.   *Is the backgrounding intentional or unintentional and why?*
    I4c.   *Will this backgrounding be detrimental to the project?*
I5.   **Foregrounding:** Helps in providing an objective design.
    I5a.   *What is emphasized and why?*
    I5b.   *Is this what should be emphasized?*
    I5c.   *How does this emphasis influence the overall design?*

I6.   **Visual representations:** Assists in conveying meaning.

   I6a. *How do the visual representations frame the product?*
   I6b. *How do visual representations assist in the instructional process?*
   I6c. *Who is portrayed in these visual representations?*
   I6d. *What is portrayed in these visual representations?*
   I6e. *What purpose do the visual representations serve?*
   I6f. *Are inappropriate visual representations in the design?*
   I6g. *Where are these visual representations placed in the product?*
   I6h. *Why were these visual representations selected?*

Development

Development (D1-D10) provides the management structure for problem solving. It considers those features that are important in the overall development of the product.

D1.   **Consider technical, aesthetic, content, culture-based and target audience (TACCT) design specifications:** Technical design specifications focus on technical (functional), aesthetic (visual), content (subject matter), culture-based (generic or specialized), and target audience (people).

D2.   **Mass distribution formats:** Produce in formats for mass distribution that allow access and equity.

D3.   **Effective technology:** Use the most efficient and effective technology available to produce the product.

D4.   **Diversify ICT format:** Provide multiple forms of information and communication technologies or manipulatives to meet the needs of the target audience.

D5.   **Understand target audience:** Know your audience. Focus on that audience throughout the design.

D6.   **Explore environmental & individual/group cultures:** Environmental cultures explore societies and cultures ways of life (e.g., workplace). Individual/group cultures explore people (e.g., Japanese culture).

D7.   **Quality design:** Create a good product for other people who desire to create similar products

D8.   **Authenticate product:** Authentic representations of target audiences are needed to validate the product.

D9.   **Control for interference:** Provide products that limit bias, attitudes and prejudices. Try to control for human, machine and environmental interference.

D10. **Model the product or process:** Create prototypes, sketches, storyboards or visual languages.

Team

Team (T1-T3) focuses on the recruitment of a culturally sensitive design team that includes a cultural expert, an educator and other culturally informed members. This is where much of the decision making happens.

T1.   **Cultural expert:** The cultural expert is the insider who acts as a liaison with the target audience and community representative.

T2.   **Enlisted educators:** Educators with expertise in subject matter and/or educating the target audience must enlisted on the team (e.g., professors, teacher educators, etc.).

T3. **Culturally-informed team:** Have an educated creative team with valid interests in the target audience.

Assessments

The area of assessments (A1-A4) covers assessment options. These assessments provide evidence of the products effectiveness and evaluate the goals set for the target audience.

A1. **Multiple evaluation opportunities:** Provide internal and external evaluation opportunities.
A2. **Assess the assessment:** Evaluate the evaluation tools.
A3. **External review:** Implement other evaluations of the product.
A4. **Culture specific assessments:** Create specialized evaluations.

Brainstorming

Brainstorming (B1-B10) determines the direction to proceed and serves as an initial review of the design process. It is the first step in planning.

B1. **Financial support:** Obtain comprehensive funding for the project.
B2. **Pilot studies/field tests of product:** Engage in assessments throughout project.
B3. **Assess community's response:** Get the public's response to the product.
B4. **Community representative on team:** The Community Representative is a person versed in the cultural nuances of the target audience, and they have been designated as an integral part of the design team.
B5. **Investigate target audience to authenticate product:** Provide the team with an ethnographic portrait of the target audience.
B6. **Reflect and assess learning goals:** Engage in ongoing reflections and assessments of the product.
B7. **Affordable design:** Provide an affordable design and ICTs that are financially accessible to the target audience.
B8. **Meet needs of target audience:** Determine how the product meets the instructional and/or cultural needs of the target audience.
B9. **Discuss & consider cultural context:** Discuss and consider historical, social, political, economic and educational reasons for implementing this project.
B10. **Present & consider outcomes:** Throughout the design process, present and consider learner outcomes or the user goals.

Learners

Learners (L1-L10) centers on the needs of learners and learning. These design factors assist in providing a dynamic learning environment that is supportive of the learner's cultural frame of reference.

L1. **Extend learning:** Provide opportunities for extended learning.
L2. **Differentiate opportunities to learn:** Provide a variety of learning options.
L3. **Empower & engage learners:** Provide opportunities for empowering learners and engaging instruction.

L4. **Teach proactive learning:** Help learners to be proactive in improving their own learning

L5. **Identify educational objectives:** Have an underlying educational and/or learning objective

L6. **Culture-specific instructional strategies:** Consider instructional strategies that are individual or group specific

L7. **Enrich instructional content:** Expand instructional content beyond subject matter.

L8. **Adapt instruction to learner:** Provide adaptable instruction that is <u>not</u> too grade level or age level specific.

L9. **Plan for instruction:** Focus on the short and long term instructional needs of the target audience.

L10. **Enculturate the learner:** Use the product to enculturate the learner into the culture.

Elements

Elements (E1-E25) facilitate content development. These elements seek to be comprehensive in providing the fundamental total of which all culture is composed.

The Anthropology of Culture:

E1. **Cultural aesthetics:** That which is considered beautiful

E2. **Cultural artifacts:** Products that exist or remain

E3. **Cultural capital:** Economics and material wealth

E4. **Cultural classification:** Divisions in a culture or society

E5. **Cultural communications:** The exchange or transmission of information

E6. **Cultural demographics:** Characteristics of a population

E7. **Cultural environment:** Physical and social conditions in which human beings, other species or entities live and develop

E8. **Cultural history:** Narrative representation of historical events

E9. **Cultural knowledge:** What is known and what one comes to know

E10. **Cultural language:** Language form, content, use and meaning

E11. **Cultural physiology:** The physiological characteristics of a human being, other species or entity

E12. **Cultural relations:** The relationship of one being to another being

E13. **Cultural resources:** The use and cultivation of resources

The Psychology of Culture:

E14. **Cultural beliefs & values:** Beliefs (shared truths); values (shared ideas)

E15. **Cultural experiences:** The interpretation of the world from inside and out

E16. **Cultural ideas:** The use and meaning of ideas and perceptions

E17. **Cultural identity:** Distinguishing qualities of a human being, other species or entity

E18. **Cultural interests:** Deeply personal desires, wants, wishes

E19. **Cultural misconceptions:** Untruths, myths, stereotypes

E20. **Cultural ways:** Behaviors, norms, feelings

The Science of Culture:

E21. **Cultural anomalies:** Happenings that promote, initiate, or force cultural change
E22. **Cultural cultures:** The scientific identification of cultures, worlds, ecosystems
E23. **Cultural futures:** That which is to come
E24. **Cultural infinities:** Those things without limits: time, space, distance
E25. **Cultural nature:** Intrinsic characteristics of a human being, other species or entity

Training

Training (Tr1-Tr2) is the education of individuals. This is another phase in providing full management of a project.

Tr1. **Product training:** Provide training of the product as needed.
Tr2. **Culture-based training:** Provide training that is culture-based incorporating CBM Elements and interactions with cultural expert and target audience.

Chapter V
The Virtue of Paper:
Drawing as a Means to Innovation in Instructional Design

Brad Hokanson
University of Minnesota, USA

ABSTRACT

This chapter presents an argument in favor of using paper to conceive, plan, and describe instructional design projects. Such a simple medium has great capability and, as is well known, a tenacious ubiquity; our offices, practices, and lives are filled with paper. We will see how the attributes of paper help us in both social and cognitive ways, particularly as a medium for drawing.

PROLOGUE

It was a peculiarly beautiful book. Its smooth creamy paper, a little yellowed by age, was of a kind that had not been manufactured for at least forty years past. He could guess, however, that the book was much older than that. He had seen it lying in the window of a frowsy little junk-shop in a slummy quarter of the town (just what quarter he did not now remember) and had been stricken immediately by an overwhelming desire to possess it.... Winston fitted a nib into the penholder and sucked it to get the grease off. The pen was an archaic instrument, seldom used even for signatures, and he had procured one, furtively and with some difficulty, simply because of a feeling that the beautiful creamy paper deserved to be written on with a real nib instead of being scratched with an ink-pencil. Actually he was not used to writing by hand.... He dipped the pen into the ink and then faltered for just a second. A tremor had gone through his bowels. To mark the paper was the decisive act (Orwell, 1948, p. 23).

In this passage, Winston is about to engage the simplest, most immediate medium—pen and paper. His creative process will be unencumbered by layers of technology involving complex skill sets, which, even when mastered, place their own restrictions on their user and become to some extent autonomous. Central to this act is his own intellect, and he recognizes the danger and importance, the intent of the mark, and its ability to connect with others.

INTRODUCTION

However we use a notation system, a visible language must build on our human experiences. We choose the media and which technologies we work with, and we make those choices based on our social and cognitive practices. Winston Smith's use of paper embodies human attributes that are politically rebellious: the capacities for private notation and independent thought.

Our current challenges are not so much in the technological systems we use, but in how people conceive, develop, and disseminate ideas through media. The choice is not how to use a new technology or software to visually notate our process of instructional design, but rather how to use visual notation to innovate and improve instructional design and education. Communication, creative thought, and interaction in complex processes must be addressed by meeting the needs of the human element of design.

KNOWLEDGE WORK AND VISUAL NOTATION

The focus of our effort is instructional design, the creation of materials for and the structuring of instruction itself. For our purposes here, instructional design is the knowing use of technology for the assistance of learning, and more recently, specifically the use of computer- and Internet-based technologies in the service of learning.

Instructional design can be described as "knowledge work" as described by Peter Drucker (1999) and others, and this description may help us understand the use of paper in the field by comparison with other professions. Knowledge work is a classification of work that involves the generation, development, and implementation of ideas. It can be described as work where the true means of production is the knowledge of the worker. Other fields engaged in knowledge work include the law, surgery, and architecture. Knowledge work is generally complex, quite often socially grounded, and involves complicated technical issues. Knowledge work often requires significant education or training, and the work is generally done in organizations and/or teams. Designing, including instructional design, is knowledge work.

Many of the activities of knowledge work are verbal and visual. They involve sharing, recording, notating, and creating ideas—most supported by some technology, the most ubiquitous being paper. There remains, as we shall see later, a continued use of paper in this electronic age. Knowledge work, particularly design, is tied to the use of paper because paper allows visual notations more easily than other media. It is faster, simpler, more immediate, and less separated (or mediated) from our thoughts.

Later in this chapter, architecture will provide a good comparison to instructional design for its use of notation systems: it has similarly complex technical issues (of building and construction); it is socially based, often practiced within a firm and with clients; and it addresses theoretical and philosophical issues in application. While architecture may result in visual form more than most instructional design, it still provides a strong analogy for an examination of design methods and tools as applied to instructional design.

The general field of design can be said to have evolved from craft when need arose to separate the work of creation from the work of production. Within design, visual notation is needed to create, direct, and communicate. "It is, above all else, the separation of designing from making and the increased importance of the drawing which characterizes the modern design process" (Lawson, 2000, p. 241). Drawing, what first developed as a means to direct others in the making of the end product, has also evolved other purposes, notably to support the imagination. The word design, of course, derives from a Latin word meaning "to mark" or draw.

Design as a profession and as a practice is methodological, purposeful, and goal oriented. It examines the entire problem, seeking a broader understanding, rather than small improvements addressing known problems, as does craft. Both craft and design seek applied solutions; the crafts person creates the result, while the designer directs others in doing so generally through visual means. Advances through craft will be incremental, i.e. minor continued improvements in efficiency or detail; advances in design work may be significant changes or substantial improvements. Currently, much instructional design is craft based, seeking detailed changes in the end product, and often building from existing models of instruction. For greater innovation and invention to occur, however, changes in the design process are necessary.

PAPER

Throughout history, visual notation systems for information recording, conveyance, and investigation have been tied to various media, most frequently paper. Since its broad production and use, paper has helped fuel the development and communication of the world's knowledge.

Over the past twenty years, electronic communications methods and media have rapidly developed—newspapers, books, and whole libraries are now accessible online, and many people work using computers, particularly in knowledge and information fields, while management, communication, and production in instructional design is done principally on computers.

THE GOAL OF THE PAPERLESS OFFICE

The computer and information revolution have significantly changed our work habits and our understanding of information. The concept of "atoms vs. bits" (Negroponte, 1999), of analog vs. digital, and advanced vs. appropriate technology all pressed us forward to embrace computer technology. Not using the latest technology in the workplace is considered laggard or Luddite. As knowledge workers, we are centered in the use of computers, and paper is *passé*. The conversion, quasi-religious, is not complete:

Yes, I've been to the crossroads and I've met the devil, and he's sleek and confident, ever so much more "with it" than the nearest archangel. He is casual and irreverent, wears jeans and running shoes and maybe even an earring, and the pointing prong of his tail is artfully concealed. He is the sorcerer of binary order, jacking in and out of terminals, booting up, flaming, commanding vast systems and networks with an ease that steals my breath away. ... Do we know what we're doing? Do people understand that there might be consequences, possibly dire, to our embrace of these technologies, and that the myth of the Faustian bargain has not become irrelevant just because we studied it in school? (Birkerts, 1994, p. 211)

The "paperless office" remains as a broadly held belief; however, in real life, the use of paper remains important in the workplace.

Computer technology was supposed to replace paper. But that hasn't happened. Every country in the Western world uses more paper today, on a per-capita basis, than it did ten years ago. The consumption of uncoated free-sheet paper, for instance—the most common kind of office paper— rose almost fifteen per cent in the United States between 1995 and 2000. (Gladwell, 2002)

If we examine our own work experience through reflection and the work habits of others through research, we can see the continuing use of paper for knowledge work and the reasons for its persistence. For example, while we use e-mail constantly, the promise of paperless communication has not been achieved. In truth, as organizations install e-mail systems, paper use increases on average by 40% (Sellen & Harper, 1997). With e-mail, we use *more* paper. Why?

WE KNOW HOW PAPER IS USED IN OUR OWN EXPERIENCES

Our own work experience can provide a base for understanding the role of paper in the knowledge workplace. We understand first hand the use, ubiquity, and commonality of paper. The management of "paper" is considered a hallmark of modern professional travail; the clutter of our homes comes significantly from paper; organizations seek to decrease the use of paper and encourage its recycling. We print documents to read and edit, guilty about our use of the world's resources, and about our failure to fully achieve digital literacy.

In general, knowledge workers make a series of choices that take advantage of how to use media. More often than not, we make rational and understandable choices to use paper. For example, we print out e-mail to have a handy record of a communication. We write numbers, names or ideas on available pieces of paper. The grocery list is put on the back of an envelope, a phone number on a sticky note, and contact information is embellished on the back of a business card. We print out documents to read and annotate; our well-read books are marked up and personalized, the notations becoming part of the cognitive record of reading.

Some of these choices are due to the simple physical attributes of paper that are easily recognized. Paper is (among other characteristics) generally inexpensive, lightweight, light in color, translucent, durable in most situations, easy to use, easy to mark, and readily available. These physical attributes help determine for what it can be used, i.e. its capabilities or *affordances*.

Affordances, per Gibson, are those capabilities, properties, and attributes of a tool or medium that "…make possible different functions for the person perceiving or using that object" (Gibson, 1979, p. 24). We often make choices about media use by weighing various affordances, choosing media with a perceived relative advantage for our own use.

For example, we chose to write the grocery list by hand on a used envelope instead of on the laptop because it is lighter and more transportable, more easily carried to the grocery store. While it is possible to carry the laptop to the store, we quickly understand that it would be easier to use a lighter weight scrap of paper to help remember grocery items. We mentally and often unconsciously weigh these attributes when we pick up a piece of paper.

Imagine the process of writing the list on one's laptop to illustrate an alternative choice: go to the laptop, start the laptop, start the word processing program, write the list, visit the refrigerator to check current supplies, start the printer, print the list, close the program and laptop. One could chose to carry the laptop to the grocery store in lieu of printing the list, but that would raise additional difficulties.

We often know it is much easier to use paper without going through a conscious decision making process. We use paper because it has the capabilities we need for the tasks we are performing. It does what we need it to do simply.

AFFORDANCES OF PAPER FOR KNOWLEDGE WORK/DESIGN

Within the scope of simpler tasks, we understand what works well, knowing needed skills and effort. We use what is easy and cheap, paper, the affordances of which stand well apart from our digital tools. There also are more complex or sophisticated affordances of paper that are tied to knowledge work, particularly is how we use paper as individuals and within groups to understand and think.

- **Navigation:** The tangibility, the physicality, of paper helps one navigate and understand a document. Through spatial understanding, through representation of (textual) location, and through a physical gauging of location, we understand the structure of a document. One can understand, visually and haptically, progress in reading a large document or the ease with which one could read a thin children's book. We can find summarizing arguments in many books at the end, and the initial challenge of the author at the beginning. We know the main body of the book contains supporting information in greater detail.
- **Cross referencing:** Spatial flexibility allows the easy comparison of multiple documents, cross referencing between multiple pieces of paper. Multiple documents can be arrayed on a surface and easily cross-referenced, even between paper and electronic sources.
- **Annotation:** Paper based documents can easily be annotated using textual or symbolic notation, using pen or pencil. These marks vary from structural reorganizations to textual comments to visual representations, often all within the same document and using the same marking system.
- **Manipulation:** Paper allows for the multi-dimensional display and reorganization of documents. For example, paragraph five can be physically put at the end of the report, or an image can be located for connection to the text. The manipulation of paper materials is grounded and first hand. For example, we can examine the difference between paper

collage and digital collage. There are real limits to a paper collage. One must budget unique resources, and creation is tied to real constraints of paper, cutting, shaping, and gluing. This is contrasted to the weightless world of the digital creation, which is unlimited and, in the end, without gravity. The paper collage is, however, immediate, personal, and unique.
- **Placeholding:** Paper documents serve as cognitive aids to memory; they remain as left until addressed. They are a constant reminder of tasks undone.
- **Portability:** Paper is portable and can be carried to various locations untethered to one's workplace, e.g. away from one's computer. It can be read in the park, handed to an airline ticket agent, or presented to a flight attendant when "all electronic devices must be turned off". Is it not place bound, tied, at the least to an Ethernet wire or a battery pack.

These capabilities of paper do not mean that other digital systems are not useful; these observations mean that the use of paper is often part of the complete process of idea and document development: a document may be initialized and finalized on the computer, but in the process, it may be converted back and forth to paper many times.

Yet, if the computer is the canvas on which documents are created, the top of the desk is the palette on which bits of paper are spread in preparation for the job of writing. Without these bits of paper ready to hand, it is as if the writing, and more especially the thinking [italics in original], could not take place in earnest. (Sellen & Harper, 2002, p.1)

These affordances can be contrasted to computer-based electronic systems; all of the tasks could be accomplished using a computer. But all would require substantial investment in technology, skills, and cognitive effort. The tasks would be divorced from direct human intervention and not grounded in the real world. Computers and most software packages separate users—through interfacia such as keyboards, mice, screens, and requirements to learn and often extensively develop skills—from the act of creation.

While paper has substantial value for text-based communication and notation, it is also well suited to use to convey visual images or notation. Paper, broadly defined, is a surface for making marks that require little experience; a separate program or marking tool is not required. Most people have sufficient skill in non-textual visual representation, i.e. drawing, to accomplish rudimentary representations and to decode visual images (Goldschmidt, 1999). This is often more efficient than text alone. The hand, unlike computer programs, has never had a significant division between writing and drawing, between textual notation and visual notation. While skills may vary, the medium is not forcing the use of word or image on the page; a mark is a mark, whether text or image, or visual notation.

EMPIRICAL EVIDENCE OF PAPER SUPPORTED KNOWLEDGE WORK

Sellen and Harper (2002) found that knowledge workers employed paper in ways that were complex and sophisticated, and which also illustrated some of the nature of knowledge work. Their research involved observing work in air traffic control, financial management, and policing. Authoring, reviewing, collaborating, and interacting socially were all supported through the use of paper, even when electronic media for communication were available and well understood.

Authoring, an important component of knowledge work, is well supported by paper. As noted, digital technologies may be used for the finished product, but the actual composition of ideas is done through a combination of paper and digital technologies. We write, compose, draw, and create on paper. We may implement those ideas through other media—digital software, oil paint, buildings, and sculpture—but we make our initial authoring choices generally on paper. Even authors who extensively used word processing software move back and forth between print and electronic versions of their work.

Knowledge workers also tend to review the work of others on paper, both for approval and for their own understanding. We understand information through the formation of our own knowledge, and part of the formation of our knowledge often occurs by marking written text.

Similarly, knowledge workers often plan their work using paper, where a lack of imposed structure affords ease and flexibility in jotting down notations, making diagrams, marking emphasis, or connecting ideas. Word processing, by comparison, focuses one type of information and is structured for written documents on a page. The diagram sketched by hand into the paper document is easy; that same diagram in an electronic document requires many additional steps and substantially more skill in software use.

Collaborative activities are also often more easily undertaken through the use of paper. Paper allows the sharing of a common document and making of multiple and diverse marks on it. Knowledge workers can pass around a draft, or even copies of a draft, for annotation and review. Paper often provides the media to record ideas, plans and discussion for working groups. Examples of collaborative paper or paper-based activity in the workplace include the large paper easel pads used to record and archive ideas in team brainstorming sessions, or sticky notes used to plan staffing or procedures.

Finally, paper is often used as a reason for added, informal interpersonal meetings, greasing the wheels for further creativity. Written documents, such as a report or a memo, are often delivered in person. This provides an opportunity to review the materials with the intended audience and to increase creative social interaction in the workplace. Such documents could often be sent by other means, such as e-mail, but the personal meeting is valued more highly than electronic expediency

One of the most developed paper-based collaborative systems is the A3 Report used by Toyota. "These single page data-dense reports are used as part of a process to gather information, share information, make comments, track progress and graphically represent the improvement process" (Liker and Meier, 2006, p. 201). The A3 Report method involves using one side of an A3 sized piece of paper. "It allows only the most critical information to be shared with others for careful evaluation of the thought process used, as a means of requesting support or advice, and for arriving at a consensus."

Initially, A3 Reports were developed as a standardization choice allowing worldwide communication through a single, simple format: "…this was the largest size paper that could fit in a fax machine: 11 × 17 inches" (Liker & Meier, 2006, p. 203). While the documents could be done in electronic form, the use of paper allows for easy distribution, broadly distributed use, and allows input from all. They are dynamic and collaborative documents, not frozen and uni-directional PowerPoint presentations (Sobek & Jimmerson, 2004).

A3 reports are a hallmark of the "lean" management movement. These single pages of A3 sized paper are used for planning, communicating, generating new ideas, and resolving problems. Use of the single sheet for planning reports forces conciseness, summarization, and organization of thought. The reports, consistent with Toyota management principles, are highly structured, yet created to encourage ongoing input, including editing and marking, by others.

The value of the A3 report is that it ensures communication, either formalized or incidental. Reports are duplicated and presented to others for input. The development of the A3 document

is often done in teams or collaboratively; reports can be printed or posted for review, and are easily folded for inclusion in a notebook. Informal annotation of the A3 reports by others, including on the factory or shop floor is encouraged as part of the ongoing process.

DRAWING AS A MEANS TO DESIGN

Much of our understanding and use of paper is for text; most of our communications efforts are centered around words and writing. However, beyond the linear use of one symbol system, writing is an entire array of ways to communicate more effectively and expressively. Drawing, a visual notation system, is central… and common to all design fields. Historically, humans have relied on drawing to communicate.

Drawing is a kind of Universal Language, understood by all Nations. A Man may often express his Ideas, even to his own Countrymen, more clearly with a Lead Pencil, or Bit of Chalk, than with his Tongue. And many can understand a Figure, that do not comprehend a Description in Words, tho' ever so properly chosen. (Benjamin Franklin, 1749)

Central to the use of paper is the ability to generate graphic images or diagrams easily. For the architect or artist, these images are essential to their creation: Drawing, or "making marks," is an act of decision and exploration. Designers make marks, adjust symbols, manipulate forms, and from that manipulation and iterative design process develop new and better ideas (see for example, Waters & Gibbons, 2004).

How we view visual notation, drawing, is an important key to advancing instructional design. If we use it solely to communicate, we will limit its effective use. Communication with colleagues and clients is an important use of visual notation, to be sure, but more importantly, drawing can serve other functions in our design process. It is where we can generate ideas, its principle role in many other design fields.

Why is drawing effective in the development of ideas? Visual form is instantly recognizable, and at the same time encourages interpretation. The generation of visual forms allows the abstraction of ideas and the summarization of complex concepts. One can scribble a drawing, change it, and reinforce one's thoughts. It is "media-as-environment," a place for the development of ideas (Meyrowitz, 1999, p. 45).

REASONS FOR DRAWING

In the design fields, drawing or visual notation is central to the design process and is used for a variety of purposes, ranging from the presentations to the public and reviewers, to the cognitive efforts of individual practitioners.

A drawing is like a theatrical scrim, a gauzelike screen whose properties change dependent on lighting conditions. Like a scrim, a drawing is both opaque and translucent, a filter between the drawer and viewer, drawer and object, between ideas conceived and their two-dimensional manifestation. A scrim and a drawing both prevent as well as allow view, asserting their presence with varying authority and in different ways. When the back light turns on, the scrim disappears. In a similar way, drawings dissolve and open a world of rich possibilities. (Fraser & Hemni, 2000, p.18)

Both Lawson (2004) and Fraser and Hemni (2000) describe multiple functions for drawing in the architectural design process; drawing is used to plan, to communicate, to convince, and most importantly, to ideate (See Figures 1-4). Each of these modes of drawing can be applied to use in the field of instructional design. These types of drawings include:

- **Public communication:** Most design work in architecture is very public; public reviews are common. Many drawings in the design fields are used to present work and communicate intent to outside parties. In architecture, plans are reviewed by government agencies, clients, and communities. These drawings can be described as presenting a positive and finished image to the public (Lawson, 2004). Drawings may be used to support marketing of buildings, securing public approvals, or in convincing a client of the project's value.

  Within instructional design, there currently is less use for representation of design work, as often the preference is to have non-working digital models for presentation of early stages. In architecture though, the economics of physical construction compared to the cost of producing a digital prototype encourages visual and often animated representations. One other comparison for the field of instructional design would be movie production. The development of movies is based on an extensive series of drawn visual representations, story boards, and iterative representations as the cost of final production is quite high. Most animated movies such as Disney/Pixar's *The Incredibles* (Walker, 2005) are extensively developed on paper in hand drawn form prior to the computer-based rendering of the final product.

- **Work communication:** Drawings are extensively used to communicate within the field of architecture. These may take the form of diagrams, representations of data, or representations of ideas. The value of this type of drawing or visual notation is beginning to be well understood in the field of instructional design (cf. Botturi, 2006). Design teams in all areas need to communicate structure, sequence, and organization of their work; visual representation and notation can provide a better understanding than by text alone.

- **Vendor communication:** Drawings are commonly used to communicate directly with those providing services or products; within architecture, some drawings have the legal force of contract and are literally called "Contract Documents." As more of the actual production work in instruction design is done by outside vendors, communication will become a higher priority. Much of this communication will be verbal, but visual notation and communication will also be increasingly valuable.

- **Development testing:** Many ideas cannot be fully understood unless represented visually and those ideas are often explored through drawings. Understanding complex and intricate technologies can be assisted through the use of drawing. For example, the efficient layout of clothing patterns on milled fabric is important for cost effective production; developing hypothetical layouts of furniture in visual form by interior designers helps to understand room use; and urban designers use visual models to understand the ramifications of zoning laws. If verbal annotation is helpful, diagrams, visual representations, or mapping is more so.

In the virtual world of technology-rich instructional design, the real world limits of room layout, fabric width, and neighborhood density are not immediate concerns. However, early development of screen designs could benefit from rapid visualization through hand-based drawings, and hand drawn maps are a good starting method for Web site design.

- **Research drawing:** Architects and others also use drawing as a means to understand observed phenomena. The "grand tour" of Europe, undertaken as part of formal studies in architecture, is often documented with drawings in a sketchbook. Not mere drawing practice, this custom helps the architecture

students cognitively engage and internalize what they see.

Most travelers today carry a camera and forsake the personal time and engagement of drawing what they see, yet for most the cognitive residue of taking a photograph is minimal while the understanding gained by drawing one's observation is long lasting. In Japan, hikers still climb Mount Fuji to paint the sunrise. Again, the reflective experience is of considerably greater value.

Drawing as a tool to research and understanding is not limited to architects and tourists. Early scientists, including Sigmund Freud, used drawing as a means to understand and develop ideas.

In the latter part of the 19th century, German researchers considered drawing to be instrumental to scientific discovery, both as a way to capture the microscopic detail of nerve cells, for example, and to illustrate theories of how the brain might work. (Gamwell, in Carey, 2006)

For example, Darwin's drawings were essential to his seminal work in *The Origin of Species*. And the recorded anatomical observations of Leonardo da Vinci are early examples of the use of drawings for research. Mechanical or electronic reproduction of visual images does not require the same cognitive effect as the engaged and personal representation.

- **Sketching as visual thinking:** The most important aspect of drawing is its ability to help create and develop new ideas. This type of drawing, called "study sketching" by Goldschmidt (1999), and "design drawings" by Fraser and Hemni (2000), occurs in many fields. It is finding answers to complex problems through visual representation, and is "…practiced by individuals who attempt to conceive of a new entity, be it a work of art, a building, a technically-oriented invention or novel artifact, or a scientific concept"

(Goldschmidt, 1999, unnumbered). Many design fields such as architecture, graphic design, and industrial design have active histories of design sketching. This process is drawing to invent, to generate the new, drawing to create.

This type of drawing is often intensely personal. It is a one-to-one visual conversation with oneself through the medium of drawing, and it is generally not meant for extensive communication. Such sketches can be decoded, understood, and valued by knowledgeable others, but their primary purpose is one of supporting thought.

The imperfect feedback (or "backtalk" per Goldschmidt, 1999) of media is an important component of the design process. Representing an idea through drawing is not always an exact science; through the vagaries of the media, the roughness of the paper or bleed of ink, or even through the inaccuracy of the hand, differences and changes occur. This can be a conversation as challenging as an engaging argument with a peer, and it is where ideas develop. Lawson (2004) calls these drawings "proposition drawings." "These are drawings where a designer makes a 'move,' or proposes a possible design outcome" (p. 45).

Designing, particularly within architecture, is often iterative, making a series of choices within a larger conceptual goal. This type of drawing becomes game-like, combative, an interactive argument, and, as often described, conversational. It is an interaction with a sheet of paper, akin to "thinking out loud," helping ideas and decisions emerge from the page, away from the brain, in a two dimensional use of symbols comparable to the leap to writing envisioned by Ong: Thought requires some sort of continuity. Writing establishes in the text a 'line' of continuity outside the mind" (Ong, 1982, p. 39). Drawing expands this capability in multiple dimensions.

This method of drawing is closely related to the concept of cognitive tools developed by Jonassen and others to describe the use of computer-based tools to investigate various hypotheses and directions. A spreadsheet, for example, can be used as a cognitive tool to define, structure quantitative relationships, and to iteratively advance various numerical scenarios. The use of drawing in design can easily fit within Jonassen's (1996) description of cognitive tools as "…readily available, generic applications; they are affordable; they are used to represent knowledge in content domains; they are applicable across different subject domains; they engage critical thinking in learners; they facilitate

Figure 1. Thinking drawings by the author

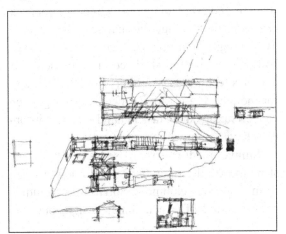

Figure 2. Thinking drawings by the author

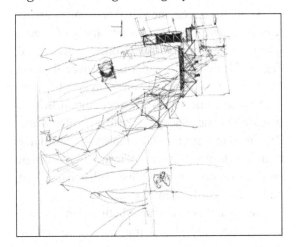

Figure 3. Preliminary site concept drawing for Cambridge Community College, Minnesota, USA. Courtesy Hokanson/Lunning Associates, Inc., architects.

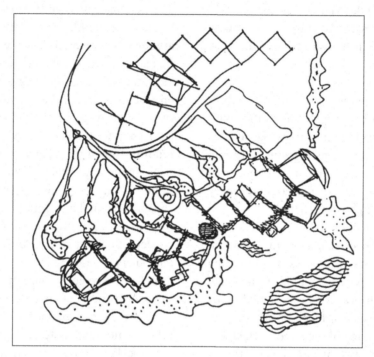

transfer of learning; they are simple, powerful formalisms; and they are reasonably easy to learn" (p. 709). How parallel is Goldschmidt's description of the cognitive mechanism of drawing: "…this is a 'front edge' process in which partial and rudimentary representations are produced, evaluated, replaced by others if need be, transformed, modified and refined, until their maker is satisfied with the result" (1999).

As we have seen, the visual notation of architecture, drawing, serves a wide variety of needs, which can be compared to the work in instructional design. Drawing, i.e. paper-based, free flowing visual notation, has value on many levels, from public communication to private cognition. In both fields, ideas and concepts need to be explored and described in ways beyond simple text. Similarly to architecture, the drawing of instructional design must be free flowing, inventive, both personal and public, and easily used.

Visual notation must have both a cognitive and practitioner base in drawing, a basis gained by making marks *by hand* on surfaces, which occurs most easily and commonly on paper.

DRAWING ON PAPER

Media, of course, are needed to communicate and to support thought. The use of some technology is necessary to extend our thoughts to others. But the type and extent of media technology imposes change on the message and change on the process. Two things stand out: first, the cognitive load and communication skill required to use more complex technologies detracts from the capacity for thought. Using simple media allows greater concentration on the task at hand – design, information, communication, or invention.

Simpler media also impose less of their own structure on the interchange and allow a freer form of idea development. Software is an indispensable tool of instructional design, but any software, as a medium, structures the results, "perfecting" ill-formed ideas in its own likeness (Drucker, 1999). For example, a word processor often completes or re-spells words; presentation programs such as PowerPoint utilize wizards to summarize presentations, limiting expression and communication (Tufte, 2003), and desktop publishing programs make some layouts easier to use than others, encouraging their use.

If the meaning of Goethe's Faust, of Van Gogh's Landscapes, or Bach's Art of the Fugue could be transmitted in discursive terms, their authors should and would not have bothered to write poems, paint, or compose, but rather have written scientific treatises. (Von Bertalanffy, 1965, p.44)

Media biases communication, whether the media is computer-based software or oral speech (Innis, 1951). The clearest, easiest, and least biased use of visual notation (for the foreseeable future) will occur through the use of drawing directly on paper.

CONCLUSION

We have seen, through both our own experiences and through research, that paper continues to be an important component in knowledge work, the work of thinking, invention, design, and innovation. This will be the important work of the coming century, and it also includes instructional design. Paper will continue to be used for a number of reasons, both common and complex. In modern society, it is always present, inexpensive, light weight, flexible, and relatively stable. We note things on scraps of paper or in more developed notebooks, on agendas, on programs, and on napkins and note cards. It also has value in more complex ways; it remains less mediated than computer-based communication as fewer processes are needed to use and understand it. Further, paper

provides abilities in the areas of editing, annotation, collaboration, and manipulation that remain more difficult on the computer; and it supports close interpersonal contact in meetings, conveyance, and personal delivery, i.e. it encourages face-to-face social interaction.

Our ideas come from our use of media. While the other tasks of visual notation or drawing that are primarily representational are important to the process, the generational aspects of any notation, whether drawing or writing are paramount; drawing is a cognitive tool, unmediated through a computer.

Perhaps the most critical element in the use of drawing or visual notation is the ability to generate ideas, to create within this simple medium. Ideas are created through various processes, through thinking, working, communicating, and experimenting. They are not birthed fully formed. Highly developed programs and media short-circuit the process and pre-structure the results. Ideas need an environment, a medium that allows their formation like a cloud of matter coalesces into a planet; an environment for the growth of ideas.

While Einstein was able to mentally generate images, most mortals require some sort of cognitive assistance and some exploration with an external medium. Few humans can completely envision the results of their ideas, whether that is quantum physics, mathematical examples, or designing a new bathroom. This envisioning must occur with ease, with the tools at hand, with the least mediation. That is why Sellen and Harper (2003, p. 185) have written that "the reality [is] that the workplace of the future [is] full of paper." And it's marked with the results of our thinking.

As we develop a common symbolic language for instructional design, we may learn from the work of Christopher Alexander, architect, and author of *Pattern Language* (1971). The book extensively explores hundreds of architectural elements in diagrammatic and photographic form. Ideas for houses, cities, rooms, and spaces are examined and diagrammed as a means to understand the richness of architecture. Far from a template for design, it can be better used as a descriptive observation of the built environment, an artifact from Alexander's own observations. What was most important was the making, not as a product for codified reuse

While there are a number of computer-based notational systems in use, there remains no common system for instructional design. The development of any notational system must be more than a one-off program; it must be based in the human process of design and development, and its use must be easy, inexpensive, shared, and widespread to be of value. Designers will need to use the system on an informal and unmediated manner. They have to be able to use it without a computer, anytime, anywhere, and at a moment's notice.

Such a system will evolve bottom up, through usage by drawing, much as the rules of writing have evolved from informal oral speech: "The rules of grammar in natural human languages are used first and can be abstracted from usage and stated explicitly in words only with difficulty and never completely" (Ong, 1982, p. 7).

Visual notation in design must encompass many tasks. It will be used for communicating with other team members, but will also be used to plan out tactics and set goals as a decision recording method, to define components created by others, to present ideas and progress to clients, or to develop ideas for the invention of new forms of instructional design. What is not needed is a canned set of symbols, like logos, icons, templates, or emoticons, but a broad-based development of representational or generational skills: skills at conceptualizing, summarizing, editing, communicating, organizing, ordering, and structuring for instructional designers. In simpler terms, instructional designers need to draw to plan, to conceive, and to communicate.

REFERENCES

Alexander, C. (1977). *Pattern language: Towns, buildings, construction.* New York: Oxford University Press.

Birkerts, S. (1994). *The Gutenberg elegies: The fate of reading in an electronic age.* New York: Ballentine.

Botturi, L. (2006). E^{2}ML: A visual language for the design of instruction. *Educational Technology Research and Development, 54*(3).

Brown, J.S., & Duguid, P. (2002). *The social life of information.* Boston: Harvard Business School Press.

Carey, B. (2006, April 26). Analyze these. *New York Times.* Retrieved 05.06.06 from http://www.nyam.org/news/2657.html

Drucker, P.F. (1994). *Knowledge work and knowledge society: The social transformations of this century.* [transcript of a lecture]. Retrieved August 11, 2006 from http://www.ksg.harvard.edu/ifactory/ksgpress/www/ksg_news/transcripts/drucklec.htm

Drucker, P.F. (1999, April). Beyond the information revolution. *The Atlantic Monthly, 284*(4) p.47-57.

Franklin, B. (1749). *Proposals relating to the education of youth in Pensilvania*, B. Franklin, Printer, Philadelphia. Retrieved online 7/29/06 from http://www.archives.upenn.edu/primdocs/1749proposals.html

Fraser, I. & Henmi, R., (1994). *Envisioning architecture: An analysis of drawing.* New York: Van Nostrant-Reinhold.

Gladwell, M. (2005, March 25). The social life of paper. *The New Yorker.* Retrieved 5/7/06 from http://www.gladwell.com/pdf/paper.pdf

Gibson, J.J. (1979). *The ecological approach to visual perception.* Hillsdale, NJ: Lawrence Earlbaum.

Goldschmidt, G. (1999). *The backtalk of self-generated sketches.* retrieved online from http://www.arch.usyd.edu.au/kcdc/books/VR99/Gold.html June 7, 2005.

Goldschmidt, G. (1991). The dialectics of sketching. *Creativity Research Journal, 4*(2), 123-143.

Innis, H. (1951). *The bias of communication.* Toronto: University of Toronto Press.

Jonassen, D. H. (1996). Learning with technology: Using computers as cognitive tools. In D.H. Jonassen (Ed.), *The handbook of research for educational communication and technology* (pp. 112-142). New York: Macmillan.

Lawson, B. (2000). *How designers think: The design process demystified.* Oxford: Elsevier/Architectural.

Liker, J.K., & Meier, D. (2006). *The Toyota way fieldbook: A practical guide for implementing Toyota's 4Ps.* New York: McGraw-Hill.

Meyrowitz, J. (1998). Multiple media literacies, *Journal of communication, 48*(1), 96-108.

Negroponte, N. (1995). *Being digital.* New York: Knopf.

Orwell, G. (1948). *1984.* Retrieved April 9, 2006 from http://www.online-literature.com/orwell/1984/1/

Rogers, E. (1995). *Diffusion of innovations* (4th ed.). New York: The Free Press.

Sellen, A. & Harper, R. (1997). Paper as an analytic resource for the design of new technologies. In *the Proceedings of CHI '97.* Atlanta: ACM-SIGCHI.

Sellen, A., & Harper, R. (2003). *The myth of the paperless office.* Cambridge: MIT Press.

Sobek, D. & Jimmerson, C. (2004). A3 Reports: Tool for process improvement. In *The Proceedings of the 2004 Industrial Engineering Research Conference*, Houston, TX.

Tufte, E. (2003). *The cognitive style of PowerPoint.* Cheshire, CT: Graphics Press.

Von Bertalanffy, L. (1965). On the definition of the symbol. In J. R. Royce (Ed.), *Psychology and the symbol* (pp. 26-72). New York: Random House.

Walker, J. (Producer) (2005). *The Incredibles* (DVD). Buena Vista Home Entertainment.

Waters, S., & Gibbons, A. (2004). Design languages: Notation systems and instructional technology: A case study. *Educational Technology Research and Development, 52*(2), 57-68.

Section II
Visual Instructional Design Languages

Chapter VI
Plotting a Learning Experience

Patrick Parrish
The COMET® Program/University Corporation for Atmospheric Research, USA

ABSTRACT

This chapter describes an informal visual notation system that can be used by instructional designers in conceptualizing a design for an aesthetic learning experience. It begins by making a case for the importance of aesthetics as a major consideration in designing instruction, distinguishing aesthetic experience from more narrow conceptions of art and aesthetics. Drawing parallels between learning experiences and other narratives, examples of several narrative diagrams used in planning and analyzing fictional narratives are examined. Borrowing strategies from these narrative diagrams, the chapter then proposes the use of engagement curves to help designers more fully consider the aesthetic experience of learners in the design phase of instruction. Several examples of the use of narrative diagrams to analyze existing instructional designs are provided, as well as a demonstration of how an instructional design educator might use a narrative diagram in planning a course on ID models.

BEYOND TECHNICAL INSTRUCTIONAL DESIGN

Instructional design (ID) is always a complex task. Underlying any ID project are multiple goals and contributing factors that must be considered in making the myriad decisions that lead to a final design. Facing this complexity, instructional designers may feel pressed to conceive of their task in a way that narrows their concerns and allows more control and clear definition. For example, they may place their emphasis on modeling the performance of experts to help clarify instructional goals, on developing a sequence of instructional content designed to build toward better understanding, or on the effective implementation of instructional strategies meant to stimulate the cognitive conditions and processes in which learning can be expected to occur. Each of these focuses provides a framework to help ensure that learning outcomes are appropriate and achievable, and constrains the ID process to a series of problems with clear possibilities for solutions.

Yet, even though these technical qualities of an ID project are essential to care for, in narrowly conceiving instruction to possess only these qualities or assuming that all the other qualities are handled when these critical technical issues are well addressed, instructional designers may not adequately consider the complete nature of learning experiences. Learning experiences are always much more than the cognitive processing of well planned subject matter and structured learning activities. They also encompass how the learner feels about, values, and, ultimately, establishes a level of engagement with the instructional environment. They include the affective qualities that determine how engagement develops in a learning situation, which, while not ignored by ID, are frequently considered secondarily to or separately from the privileged cognitive qualities (for further exploration of the limitations of this dichotomy, see Parrish, 2006b). Beyond being a cognitive activity, learning experience (and therefore ID) is also political, ethical, emotional, and, perhaps most important in consideration of engagement, aesthetic in nature (O'Regan, 2003; Parrish, 2005; Schwier, Campbell & Kenny, 2004; Wilson, 2005). Beyond problem solving, instructional design is also the process of composing an experience that will stimulate the engagement that leads to learning.

In fact, learner engagement is likely the most critical factor in any learning experience. Whether learning is viewed as individual or system change, it will occur only when a learner desires the change or is shown the necessity of embracing it. Engagement describes a relationship to an instructional situation in which the learner willingly makes a contribution that is active and constitutive. Beyond task persistence, it involves investment of effort and emotion, willingness to risk, and concern about both outcomes and means. While IDs work to tame instruction into a manageable, replicable process that begins by predetermining outcomes to be measured through properly aligned assessments, engagement describes that wild aspect of the process in which the learner is as much or more in control of the activities and outcomes as the ID. Natural learning in everyday situations

occurs as people willingly invest themselves in tasks, either alone or with others, with immediately meaningful goals. In formal learning situations like those offered in schools and much of professional training, that meaning, which is both a necessary precondition for and result of learner engagement, is often more difficult for learners to see. Yet the need for engagement remains high if deep and lasting learning is desired. Only when learners invest attention, effort, and emotional commitment is there a chance that they will learn deeply in the situations crafted by instructors and instructional designers.

Aesthetic Instructional Design

The aesthetic, or artistic, qualities of instructional design have received increasing discussion in recent years (Parrish, 2005; Visscher-Voerman & Gustafson, 2004; Wilson, 2005; Hokanson, Hooper, & Miller, Chapter I). This broadening beyond the technical qualities of ID is likely to lead to many innovative approaches to the task of creating engaging instruction. However, aesthetics is a slippery construct, carrying with it many misleading, over-generalized ideas about art and artists, and some conceptions of it have less to offer IDs. This section first examines some of the less promising ideas surrounding art and aesthetics before introducing the concept of *aesthetic experience*, which is not only more successful in explaining the wide variety of artistic expression that exists, but has more to say about learning.

One of these limited conceptions is that aesthetics describes those qualities of an object or event that are attractive, pleasurable, or aimed at creating feelings of delight—qualities to which artists are deemed especially attuned. While they are not without purpose, limiting our conception of aesthetics to these qualities makes it merely a motivator layered onto (or into) more substantive qualities. For instructional designers, these more substantive qualities are of course the instructional strategies that have a scientific basis, and perhaps qualities such as usability and functionality. If art is a model for the application of aesthetics, this conception seems to ignore the fact that many works of art are quite disturbing (consider *King Lear*, Picasso's *Guernica*, or Stravinsky's *Rite of Spring*, for example) and do their work by challenging our expectations and desire for immediate pleasure. These works force us to grow rather than entertain or delight, as would artful works of instruction.

When art is seen as exalting the primacy of the individual, it also has little room in the work of IDs. Examples of this conception include justifying the emotional outpouring of artists, or assuming that artists are always self-referential and unconcerned with the impact of their work on others. It can also be seen in the assumption that artists tolerate no source of judgment other than their own. But of course, like all activity, art is a social phenomenon embedded in a complex activity system, and artists serve an important role or they would not be as valued as they indeed are. Artists, even popular artists, are often harbingers of social change who ask us to perceive the world in new ways, but they function within society, and have obligations to it just like the rest of us. Even though large parts of society may not immediately see the value of some works of art, or may at first be upset by the change in perception they are being asked to undertake, in the end society does not tolerate insular artists that do not attempt a connection, and their works fade away from notice. Nor would learners or clients tolerate an instructional designer that used only his or her own judgment as final arbiter of instructional decisions.

Finally, art is at times linked to an irrepressible urge to innovate with little concern for productive outcomes. While a quick review of twentieth century art, especially the visual arts, might lead one to this conclusion, I suspect this aspect of recent art is more a reflection of the cultural upheaval caused by rapid technological and social change that pervades the times, and is not the nature of art itself. Viewing art in the longer term, or keeping the popular arts in mind, one can see more emphasis on convention than on innovation. Every artist is concerned with productive outcomes—namely the aesthetic experience of those who appreciate his or her work. Innovation in technique, material, or subject matter, or choosing to investigate cultural changes not yet visible to most people, is one tool for achieving this. But extravagant innovation for its own sake is the strategy of minor artists who are missing the point, or perhaps brief a flirtation with the muse for the better ones. Even great artists never quite live down their technical failures. Stories about Frank Lloyd Wright's leaky roof, or Bernini's sinking foundation are often told as parables to self-indulgent, young artists and designers (Schama, 2006: Hokanson, Hooper, & Miller, Chapter I). IDs bent on innovation for its own sake may amuse learners for a time, but this approach has the potential to become a self-indulgent distraction to learning.

Certainly, creating pleasurable experiences, using one's connoisseurship to judge instructional quality, and seeking creative solutions are all valuable attributes of a successful instructional design practice, and in balance with the other important qualities of good design, can lead to well rounded products (see Hokanson, Hooper, & Miller, Chapter I). But limiting aesthetics to any or even all of the three senses described above places it in a distant position in the minds of IDs, who are primarily concerned with qualities of their work that can directly impact learning and serve their clients in appropriate and affordable ways. In other words, an instructional artist, if described as exhibiting the above predilections to the detriment of serving learning, would not last long in practice.

However, the concept of *aesthetic experience* has a more fundamental contribution to make to instructional design (Dewey, 1934/1989; Jackson, 1998; Parrish, 2005). Aesthetic experience describes a type of experience in which our awareness is heightened and a sense of meaning or unity becomes pervasive—clearly a condition that is ripe for learning. This type of experience can emerge during any meaningful activity, but it is particularly characteristic of and more frequently acknowledged to exist in our experiences with works of art, simply because art is expressly created to evoke it. For this reason, works of art can provide models for approaches to the design of aesthetic experiences in other life activities, including learning and instruction, and the lessons they can teach go far beyond the over-generalizations described above.

Whether the work of art takes the form of painting, sculpture, architecture, drama, dance, fiction, or film, our experience of it has narrative qualities. This narrative follows a pattern of inquiry, similar to the pattern of disciplined inquiry, in which we perceive the object or situation and over time, through engagement with it, come to sense its meaning or unity. This general pattern of experience, as described by Dewey (1934/1989), unfolds in the following way when applied to learning situations:

- A felt need, tension, or puzzlement that impels a learner to resolve an indeterminate situation
- A sustained anticipation of outcomes that helps to maintain the initial engagement
- Intent action or observation on the part of the learner, including a concern for immediate qualities and things (not merely a focus on goals or instruction as a means to an end)
- Consideration of how these observations bear on the anticipated end
- A consummation that unifies the experience (not merely terminates it) and makes it significant.

In other words, an aesthetic experience is not just one that causes pleasure or shocks us with creative vision, except to the extent the finding meaning is always pleasurable and renewing. It is one that causes meaning to be realized in a deeply felt way. In such powerful experiences, learning may be deepened and learners made better prepared and enticed to learn further. Rather than serving only immediate needs, such experiences may create learning that continues to grow by making us more responsive to new learning opportunities (Osguthorpe, 2006).

Aesthetic experiences are those in which engagement is sustained by virtue of this recognizable pattern and the unity of experience it brings (Dewey, 1934/1989). This form of experience is played out in our engagement with any art form, either explicitly in the stories we read or see performed in plays or movies, or more subtly when we enter the world of a painting or listen to a musical composition (Berleant, 1991). But it is also indicative of all our inevitable struggles to learn about and interact with the world around us. In fact, as Dewey proposes, it is from these everyday struggles and their empowering effect that the urge for aesthetic experience arises. Aesthetic experiences are unified in intent and purpose, and include following through toward a conclusion that satisfies the initial felt need. This narrative unity is precisely the meaning missing from many formal learning situations, which may be more episodic than unified in treating learning objectives unconnected to a driving goal or question.

As a pattern of inquiry, the concept of aesthetic experience isn't foreign to instructional designers at all (Parrish, 2006b). Many instructional design models stress meaning-making as a central condition of learning. Inquiry-based (Collins & Stevens, 1983), goal-based (Schank, Berman, & Macpherson, 1999), case-based (Kolodner & Guzdial, 2000), problem-based (Savery & Duffy, 1996), and problem-centered (Jonassen, 2004) learning, as well as similar generative approaches to ID, each offer strategies for creating learning experiences with the potential to become aesthetic. However, when these ID models become rigid templates or merely new technical solutions, applications of them may nonetheless miss out on addressing the full range of qualities inherent in a learning experience and, in doing so, slight the need to care for learning engagement. Seen in this way, aesthetic instructional design involves a particular stance toward the design task, the tools for accomplishing that task (including ID models), the instructional goals, and the learner. It suggests approaches compatible with many ID models, and is supportive of those models as a way to enhance their application. On the other hand, it is much more than simply a layer of pleasantness or excitement added to the otherwise technically competent models. It is as much about what is important for learners to experience as how they might experience it (Parrish, in press).

DESIGNING FOR AESTHETIC EXPERIENCE

One way for instructional designers to better plan for aesthetic learning experiences is to pay particular attention to the narrative that unfolds as a learner engages in learning. Viewing learning as a narrative in no way trivializes it or reduces it to a form of entertainment. As the pattern of experience described above demonstrates, narrative is a fundamental way of knowing about the world—perhaps our most fundamental way of deriving its meaning (Bruner, 1990, 2002; Polkinghorne, 1988). Narrative is the story-logic we find in, or impose upon, any experience we consider meaningful. Any narrative, and any meaningful experience, possesses five necessary components—an Agent, an Action, a Goal, a Setting, and a Means (Burke, 1945, as cited in Bruner, 2002). The fact that these fundamental components are also present in the pattern of inquiry, or any intentional act for that matter, reveals the powerful role narrative plays in our interpretation of the world.

Using narrative as a guiding force for instruction, as is done implicitly in each of the ID models mentioned above, can be a powerful way to stimulate learning engagement. Like a narrative, effective learning situations will have well established beginnings, middles, and endings that follow the pattern of aesthetic experience and contain the narrative components described above, revealing a necessary struggle to resolve a problematic situation that leads to learning. Whether the problematic situation is a true problem, a stimulating question or issue, or merely puzzlement or new experience that throws current knowledge into doubt, it is a call to seek out the information that allows one to test possible answers. Any of these situations initiate a sequence of events similar to the dramatic arc found in nearly all narratives, but which also comprise aesthetic experiences of whatever kind (Dewey, 1934/1989).

Caring for and assessing the potential for the aesthetic or narrative qualities of instruction can be accomplished by writing fictional design stories, or scenarios of learner experience, during the design phase of an ID project (Parrish, 2006a). Design stories are short first-person narratives written by designers from the imagined point of view of a user. They explore either an episode of use of a key or problematic design feature or a complete, coherent experience with the designed product, using the process of story writing to allow designers to exercise empathy toward users and make better design decisions. For instructional designers, they explore learning experiences, taking into account the expected qualities of instructional settings and of learners, including their motivations, ambitions, desires, and potential frustrations in learning.

The act of creating design stories can help designers build empathy with learners as they imagine learning experience to a degree of detail not possible through traditional analysis processes, and not possible in the frequently constrained conditions of formative evaluation either. Writing design stories, which stimulates a thought process that exhibits a blend of analysis and synthesis, also makes the compositional nature of design more explicit, avoiding an artificial division of analysis and synthesis in design deliberations (Lawson, 1997; Nelson & Stolterman, 2003).

Written or imagined stories of learner experience can be of use particularly in the early stages of design in which one is trying out potential ideas or communicating those ideas to others, but they can also serve in the formative evaluation stage of projects already in development to help assess the potential success of design decisions. Imagined stories of user experience likely arise in the minds of all designers when they are considering possible designs or design features, but written design stories can help make learning experiences more tangible and detailed, allowing designers to catch qualities of potential user experience that might be missed in analysis or in those brief, imagined episodes of experience. In addition, written stories also have the advantage of becoming a document for creating shared vision within the design team, reminding subject matter experts about instructional goals, and communicating the rationale and value of a design to clients. However, verbal stories are not the only way to focus on narrative qualities in composing or evaluating an instructional design. Visual notation in the form of narrative diagrams can play an important role as well.

Diagramming Narratives

While written stories of learner experience might best capture the details of that experience, narrative diagrams also can be highly useful tools in planning or revealing the dramatic arc of learning. Writers of fiction often find visual tools useful for plotting the essential events of planned narratives or analyzing successful stories to learn how they function. For example, Ray (1994) describes the use of "Aristotle's Incline," a visual depiction of the rising action of a narrative, as a tool to aid in plotting stories (see Figure 1). Both a diagram of causality within the story, as well as a two-axis graph of the rising action of narrative events over time, Aristotle's Incline can help reveal or guide the development of a plot according to Aristotle's dictum that it should have a distinct beginning, middle, and end, with a developing *complication* and subsequent *denouement* (literally, an untying). The three parts are set off by key plot points that redirect the action based on the protagonist gaining new knowledge or on events that propel the story in a new or more clearly defined direction (in some cases this involves a *peripeteia,* or reversal of fortune or revelation of false assumptions) (Aristotle, 1984).

In Aristotle's Incline, the Y-axis depicts level of action, which typically rises in a narrative until the closing, and the X-axis is narrative time. In complex narratives, narrative time may not be chronological time, but instead the sequence in which events are revealed and the story is developed—story-logical time versus chronological time. What is meant by "rising action" is the protagonist's deepening involvement or engagement in events of the story, and the increasing seriousness of the potential repercussions of those

Figure 1. Aristotle's Incline, depicting rising action, the three key divisions of a dramatic narrative, and the relationship of key dramatic plot points

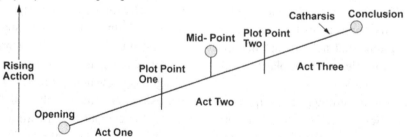

events. One way to view rising action might be to consider how difficult it would be for the protagonist to step out of the course of events. As the action rises, the protagonist becomes more deeply bound to those events and the possibility of extraction decreases. Typically, in the closing scenes of a narrative, extraction is impossible because real or symbolic life and death outcomes are at stake.

Teachers of fiction writing like Ray (1994) advise writers to position their key plot elements along the incline to ensure that each of the prescribed plot structures are defined by those elements, and that the beginning, middle, and end are well delineated by plot points. A well plotted diagram whose elements fit logically together in a cause and effect relationship will be more likely to engage an audience and provide a satisfying dramatic or reading experience. (Narratives can be developed with symbolic or lyric relationships of plot elements as well, but these are not as common, and are often more challenging and less satisfying for some.)

The use of the incline can be explained best by example. Figure 2 shows how it can be applied to a recent work of fiction familiar to millions of international readers, the *The DaVinci Code* (Brown, 2003). As a novel, Brown's book prob- ably does not rate as highly sophisticated, yet its skillfully conceived plot structure creates such a high degree of engagement in its readers that the book has reached record-breaking bestseller status—one not completely attributable to its controversial subject matter.

Other readers of The DaVinci Code may have considered other plot elements as the key components along the incline, but most readings would still reveal strong obedience to Aristotle's poetics. There is a clear, rising complication and the hint of an early beginning of the denouement in Act One as Langdon becomes the key suspect in a mysterious murder and he and Sophie begin following puzzling clues to get at the truth. In Act Two, the complication deepens and the denouement continues as the purpose and machinations of a conspiracy become apparent. In this act, the protagonists must work to protect themselves and find proof of the supposed true story of the Holy Grail. In Act Three, an even deeper conspiracy is revealed, and the protagonists find they have a critical role to play in resolving the situation, one beyond just self-protection. The plot of The DaVinci Code is carried forward by a series of revelations—the supposed truth of the Holy Grail, the existence of the conspiracy (at two levels), the truth of Sophie's identity. In other words, increasing knowledge drives the action as much as outward events.

Figure 2. Aristotle's Incline applied to the plot of The DaVinci Code (Brown, 2003)

Figure 3. Freytag's Triangle, depicting increasing and falling complication

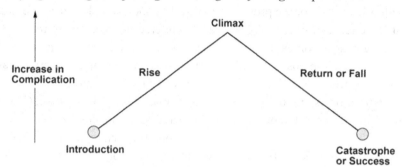

While the pattern of rising action in many fictional narratives may be much more subtle, it usually exists nonetheless. For example, in another popular, recent novel, *Never Let Me Go* (Ishiguro, 2005), the author employs a first-person narrator whose naiveté allows a satisfactory understanding of the situation to be only slowly revealed. There are no dramatic moments of truth as there are in *The DaVinci Code*, but only a growing and never complete understanding of the truth of her life in an unusual boarding school. Of course, this is probably a more realistic depiction of how we come to answers for the big questions of life, and it is what gives the novel its surprising power and narrative sophistication. Even though the plot points reveal the narrator in an understated way, a reader can still identify them as key contributions to his or her growing knowledge. The plot, divided into three parts separated chronologically by several years, is also given a well defined three-act structure befitting Aristotle's poetics.

Many variations on Aristotle's Incline exist, including a version developed by German playwright Gustav Freytag to describe dramatic tragedies, which has been used by Laurel (1993) to explore how users experience interactive software applications. In Freytag's Triangle, shown in Figure 3, rather than level of action, the Y-axis instead depicts the level of complication. In most narratives, but particularly in tragedies, the resulting diagram appears as rising and falling lines, as complications are developed and the denouement brings resolution. In some tragedies, the rising and falling can also be seen as the state of the protagonist's fortune, seemingly improving then dramatically reversing in a fall to ruin. But just as knowledge drives the rise in action in *The DaVinci Code*, the rise and fall in Freytag's Triangle can also be knowledge driven, where complications arise and are irresolvable until knowledge gained at the climax works to unravel those complications. In tragedy, this knowledge might mark the beginning of an inevitable fall, as Oedipus Rex falls in discovering the unwitting fulfillment of his prophecy. But in other forms of drama, the knowledge may help the protagonist achieve a more positive resolution played out in the remaining action.

Another depiction of a common narrative form is the Hero's Adventure as conceived by Campbell in his study of commonalities across world mythologies, *The Hero with a Thousand Faces* (1968). In this case, the rising and falling refer to the protagonist's degree of challenge (similar to complication, as above, but with the Y-axis reversed), and the narrative arc takes the form of a circle. Hero myths are prevalent in probably all cultures, telling the story of those who bring hope to a society by defeating its symbolic enemies and/or bringing knowledge and other boons to share. Symbolically, the hero myth depicts the rite of passage we all go through in becoming adults able to contribute to our society—a passage that is always difficult and dangerous, and not always successful. In this myth, the hero is often called to descend into a dark world of strife or chal-

Figure 4. The Hero's Adventure, depicting a passage into an underworld of challenge and the return to prosperity (Campbell, 1968)

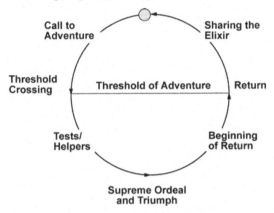

lenge that holds significant rewards if successfully traversed. For example, Prometheus steals fire and knowledge of many other technologies from the gods for the benefit of mankind (in this case, ascending, rather than descending, into the dangerous place). Prometheus is rightly heralded for sharing this knowledge, even though he also faces the punishment of the gods.

Even though Campbell depicted them as a circle to help reveal the cyclical and universally repeated nature of the hero's journey, hero myths can also be plotted as a standard graph (see Figure 5). To remain true to the metaphor of descent, instead of rising action the Y-axis becomes degree of challenge, which increases toward to the origin of the graph. In many ways, it is Freytag's triangle inverted.

Diagramming Instructional Designs

The onus we put on stories to "hang together" is one we should also place on formal learning experiences. In good stories, knowledge gained by the characters (and by the audience) always has repercussions that lead toward a meaningful resolution of the complication. This is what unifies the story and makes it an effective aesthetic experience. Similarly, knowledge gained in formal learning experiences should make a difference within the big picture of the instructional event. It should be given an explicit opportunity to propel new learning or activity involving application of learning and not be merely another check off in a list of objectives. Concern for designing instruction that "hangs together" such that a clear a complication and denouement can be found will lead to more meaningful learning experiences. Narrative diagrams, used in combination with other design tools, can help designers achieve such designs.

Like playwrights and novelists, instructors and instructional designers can use narrative diagrams as tools to help them plot the narrative of a planned learning experience. They can plot the sequence of topics and learning activities along the curve of the incline or triangle or around a circle (depending on their preference), helping to plan for a learning experience that will have the necessary structure to develop deep engagement and a fulfilling outcome. In creating such

Figure 5. The Hero's Adventure plotted as a graph

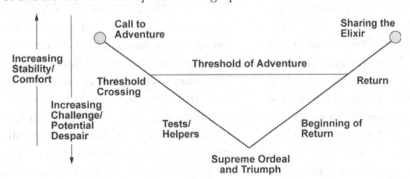

Figure 6. The engagement curve of a typical formal learning experience

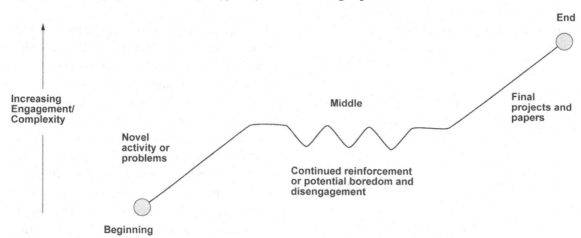

diagrams, instructional designers can also better attend to the holistic nature of the experience, and avoid exclusive focus on creating a conceptually logical content sequence or mechanical treatment of a list of objectives.

While the Y-axis in diagrams used for fictional narratives typically describes the level of action or complication, in plotting learning narratives it can be used more appropriately to depict the changing level of learner engagement and complexity of the learning task (however, the correspondence of these to action and complication should be apparent). In this case, the diagram created can be called the *engagement curve*, depicting the story of a developing interest, or the waxing and, at times, inevitable waning of engagement during the learner's journey into the unknown on a quest for knowledge.

While we would like the experience of all learners to exhibit an engagement curve similar to Aristotle's Incline (Figure 1), in practice, learning experiences rarely follow a steady rise in action or engagement. As suggested in research on aesthetic instructional design decisions (Parrish, 2004), IDs may often find that the practical constraints of formal learning situations lead to more flattened engagement curves. The rapid pace and lengthy courses of study necessary to cover content, as well as conflicting demands on

attention and varied student interests and learning styles, all make sustained engagement, let alone a continuous rise, nearly impossible. Realistic engagement curves may show an initial rise in engagement if the instruction is designed to achieve it or if learners possess native interest. The middle is more likely to be relatively steady, but only if we are sufficiently clever to introduce activities that sustain or reinvigorate interest, or lucky enough to have learners with perseverance. Otherwise, the middle will likely see declines in engagement, as the initial novelty wears off and the arduous work of learning begins to test learners. Endings, with the potential consummation of unifying activities like final reports and projects and their promise of impending relief, may reveal a sharp rise in engagement corresponding to a fluster of closing activities. Figure 6 depicts an engagement curve of this sort.

Because the large amount of work and long-term commitment required by nearly all formal learning situations is unlikely to lead to a steady rise in engagement, instructional designers may find it more useful to depict learning experiences as challenging adventures similar to the Hero's Adventure depicted in Figures 4 and 5, with the learner fulfilling the role of epic hero rather than tragic or comedic protagonist. In such diagrams, the Y-axis depicts level of challenge rather than

Figure 7. The student's adventure as a cycle

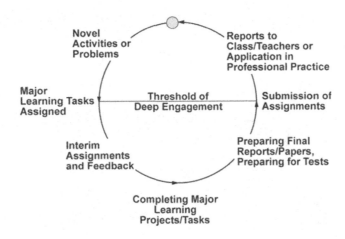

Figure 8. The student's adventure as graph

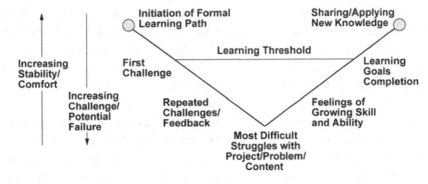

engagement. Depicted in this way, the middle doldrums are instead conceived of as the supreme ordeal or dark challenge of the quest. This adventure or *challenge cycle* depiction may be more motivating to students, especially at the middle phase of instruction when they may be eager to see themselves as about to follow the curve back upward toward the light of completion. Figures 7 and 8 are examples of this form of learning experience diagram depicted as a cycle and challenge graph, respectively. Figure 8 applies a slightly different use of terminology.

PLOTTING ENGAGEMENT CURVES

In this section let us take the generic engagement curve depicted in Figure 6 and use it to help understand the designs of two specific instructional products. Neither of these projects used engagement curves explicitly in the design phase, but the use of similar sketches and frequent discussion about learner engagement, and in the case of the second example, a written design story, led to designs that reveal good adherence to the desired qualities of an engagement curve. So in these examples, the narrative diagrams are used as validation and evaluation tools.

Figure 9. The Hurricane Strike! online module

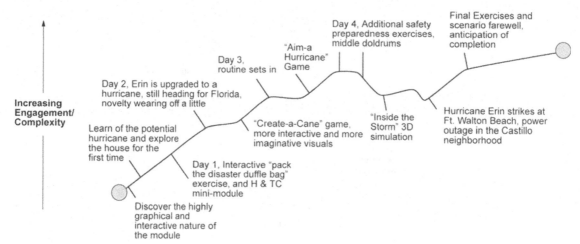

Hurricane Strike! (The COMET Program, 2002) is an online learning module for middle school students about hurricane science and safety. From the beginning of the project, learning engagement was viewed as a central challenge, and for this reason a scenario-based approached was used to strengthen the narrative qualities of the learning experience. This did not, of course, negate the need to clearly identify the required learning objectives and to structure the scenario using a traditional content matrix, nor even to map activities according to U.S. National Science Education Standards (See Appendices A and B). Yet these alone are not enough to fully appreciate the experience of learning made possible by the module.

However, we can turn to an engagement curve to identify how a typical learner might experience the module. Figure 10 depicts how one can apply the diagram to plot key instructional events that may lead to significant changes in level of engagement. Creating this plot may reassure us that the design will hang together and maintain sufficient engagement. On the other hand, it may demonstrate flawed or incomplete story-logic. For example, we might anticipate the following:

- Initial engagement is stimulated at the beginning through the use of a highly graphical and interactive design, as well as by embedding the content in the context of the story. The learner, in fact, is treated as a character within the story of a family preparing for a potential hurricane strike.

- Plot Point 1 occurs when learners find the "Create-A-Cane" game during Day 2 of the scenario, which presents a game-within-a-story that not only enriches the context, but also creates anticipation for more fun interactions and increasing knowledge about this interesting and dangerous weather phenomenon.

- The middle is highly informative, and uses a series of quality interactions to help maintain engagement while learners delve deeper into the topic, but some engagement inevitably wanes.

- Plot Point 2 marks the end of the middle and beginning of the ending as Hurricane Erin strikes and learner concerns move from learning about the science of hurricanes and safety preparations to helping friends and family survive the event. These activities consolidate what has been learned and reveal why it has been important to do so.

In contrast to the engagement curve, Appendix C shows the use of an E^{2}ML diagram (Botturi, 2006; see also Chapter VII) to describe all factors and considerations for a single interaction within the module. While the detail in this diagram helps to ensure that many important considerations have been made, the accumulated E^{2}ML diagrams it would take to describe Hurricane Strike! will never describe the learning experience in the way the narrative diagram can achieve. The fact that these two such different notation systems can usefully complement one another demonstrates the complexity of instructional systems design and the range of considerations that designers might make.

A second example (The COMET Program, 2006), the design of a module for weather forecasters on using a new numerical weather prediction model (the WRF model) as a tool in the forecast process, demonstrates the use of the engagement curve to analyze the instructional design for much more technical subject matter. In this design project, it might have been tempting to forego a concern about learner experience and engagement and focus on the accuracy and scope of the technical content. While an engagement curve was not an early step in the design process, a design story was used in the project plan to clarify the experience goals of the module

and understand its narrative nature. The story was also used to communicate these goals to the client and subject matter experts who would develop the script drafts. The engagement curve depicted in Figure 10 is a summary of the story told in the project plan. A portion of this story can found in Parrish (2006a).

In examining this engagement curve, we see the following structural elements:

- The opening introduction of a forecast problem is left unresolved to create a problematic situation and stimulate engagement. It is couched as a typical problem a forecaster might find in the field, and is told in first person.

- Further along in the beginning act of the module, the problem is more deeply explored and the WRF is shown to be a beneficial tool in resolving the problem.

- The first plot point is the resolution of this first problem, setting the stage to explore further benefits of the WRF model for forecasters.

- The middle includes the introduction of several more forecast problems and demonstration of how the WRF model can provide useful guidance. This section becomes more problematic in terms of sustaining

Figure 10. The using the WRF model online module

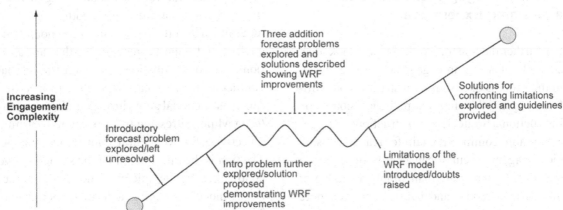

action and engagement, but it introduces necessary content and follows a repeated problem-centered pattern to ensure a degree of engagement.

- The final act is initiated by the second plot point, a section discussing the model's limitations and caveats for using the model. The build up of model benefits is reversed and the task for learners becomes more complex.
- The ending consummation includes presentation and demonstration of systematic guidelines for overcoming the model limitations and recommendations for incorporating WRF model guidance in a suite of forecast tools for the best outcome.

Obviously, there is no guarantee that any individual student is going to experience engagement in the way we have hoped and planned for. An engagement plot is something of a best case scenario—the one we are striving for by arranging the learning activities and introducing content according to narrative principles. There are many potential factors (poor instructional delivery, troublesome interpersonal relationships, and technical difficulties, for example) that can cause a student's engagement to come crashing to near zero. The goal of instructional designers is to make a strong case for engagement that might overcome such factors, should they arise.

Using an Engagement Curve to Plan a Learning Experience

For further demonstration, let us now look at an example of using an engagement curve earlier in the process of designing instruction on a different topic—this time a hypothetical course on Instructional Strategies for Instructional Designers (a more common domain for readers). Using the engagement curve can help remind you to make the course more than simply a catalog of instructional models and theories, and even more than a practical exercise in applying instructional theory.

Let us assume you have several goals for the course based on your personal beliefs about the role of theory in design:

- Design is situated, and theory has to be applied with respect to the situation, not rigidly followed.
- Instructional models demonstrate differing values and assumptions that should be explicitly acknowledged and considered before applying them.
- Whenever possible, theories should be learned through application, not merely as abstract constructs.

However, you also know that many students are looking for an easy-to-learn, cookbook approach to design, and may become bored or frustrated if you do not work to engage them in a demonstration of the value of taking a more open-minded viewpoint. Taking these goals in hand, you decide you want to develop better student engagement in the course than you have seen in the past, so you decide to employ the aesthetic qualities of conflict and anticipation to gain the buy-in you need, all while working toward a meaningful consummation that will remind students how much they have learned. To help, you use a narrative diagram to create an engagement curve to aid your planning (see Figure 11).

You look for a conflict inherent in the subject matter—the wide variety of competing theories that seem to contradict one another seems to naturally fit the bill. You decide to compound this conflict and hope to generate further anticipation for a consummation by demonstrating that conflicting theories can be applied to meet the same instructional goal, through different means (even while addressing the same stated learning objectives). So two natural "plot points" emerge. The first is the introduction of the second of two contrasting, but completely functional, instructional models (creating a form of peripeteia). This demonstrates that choosing an instructional model is not just a matter of picking it off the shelf

Figure 11. An engagement curve used for planning a course on instructional models for instructional designers

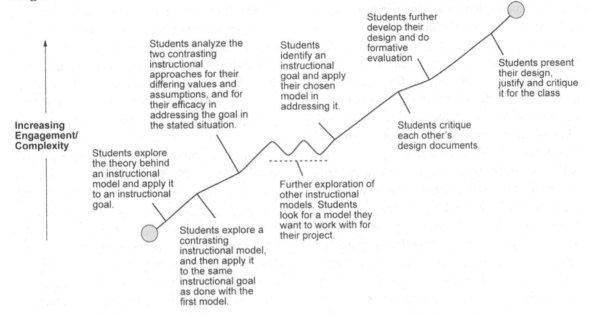

based on well defined criteria. The second plot point, depending on your point of view, might be either the choice of the model that the learner will apply in their own project or the activity in which students critique each other's initial designs. The first establishes the parameters for all the remaining learning activities in the course, but the second establishes the next level of conflict to be resolved. In my diagram, I made the choice of models the mid-point, and the critiquing activity the second plot point. Catharsis is achieved when students present their designs, but perhaps more importantly in the process of watching each of the other students present their own designs. In this case, Act One is the activity of contrasting two divergent instructional models, Act Two is learning about additional models and choosing one to work with, and Act Three has students creating a design plan, critiquing each other's plans, and reacting to the critique of their own plan. However one conceives it, the learning experience is more likely to become aesthetic as a result of including this diagramming activity in the design process.

CONCLUSION AND CAVEATS

Unlike most visual design notation systems, narrative diagrams provide a very broad depiction of the instructional design, rather than attempting to combine lots of details about the design in a single picture. They can be important as a tool for ensuring that the big picture of learning engagement is not lost among the numerous other details that vie for a designer's attention. While notation systems that capture the technical details of an instructional design may lead to diagrams that appear elegant and complete, they may in fact show little care for learner experience. Like architectural blueprints, they can serve a critical need in the design and development processes, but they may also miss the exploration of final user impact that broader sketches and models can provide.

As a visual notation system, narrative diagrams might be classified as *informal* (limited rules are imposed about how to use them), and falling at the conceptual level of *elaboration*

(Botturi, Derntl, Boot, & Figl, 2006). They are primarily meant to help the instructional designer visualize and evaluate the design in a very general way during the early design phase. In other words, they are unlikely to be useful for relaying design specifications to a developer (although they might communicate useful information to a subject matter expert or graphic artist, for example, about emotional or thematic intent). Plotting the experience early and at a high level will help to ensure that the learning experience will be an engaging one, before too many details are imposed that might constrain the goal of having a coherent, over arching learning narrative. In this way, when additional layers of detail are added it can be done in a way that supports the aesthetic experience, rather than attempting to impose an aesthetic surface onto a predetermined, non-aesthetic base. So narrative diagrams, like narratives themselves at times, are primarily *reflective*—they are a mode of creative thinking that aids in the generative processes of design. But they are also secondarily *communicative*—they can help other design team members, such as subject matter experts or artists, understand the experiential goal of the instruction to aid in the process of making their own contributions. This places them high on the creative scale, but spread

Figure 12. Classifying narrative diagrams as a notation system (Botturi et al., 2006)

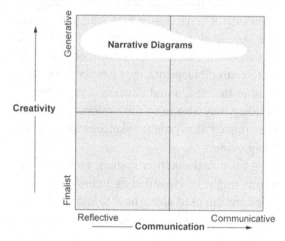

along the communicative scale, clustering toward reflective thinking (see Figure 12).

Narrative diagrams fall on the low end of sophistication in visual representations, but their simplicity is deceptive, having an advantage in increasing their capability to represent fuzzy, difficult to conceptualize qualities. They would formally be classified as non-representational and as graphs (meaning they show values along two indices), although they are also diagrammatic in showing the chronological relationship of instructional events (Stubbs & Gibbons, Chapter III). The indices used (time and, in most examples provided, engagement) have some unique characteristics that make them difficult to quantify. In fact, it is interesting to note that the graph in a narrative diagram is indexical only in metaphorical terms. We think of engagement (or experience) as being at a particular "level" and potentially "heightened," and so it is befitting that we plot it on the vertical or y-axis. Because we speak of time as an "arrow" or as "moving forward," it is plotted logically on the horizontal or x-axis, but it is not a scalar value in this case. While it could be drawn with equal lengths representing equal increments of time, this might interfere with depicting changes in the engagement axis in sufficient detail. For this reason, the time axis is depicted in terms of the learners' subjective experience of time in regards to the learning events (narrative time). In other words, it may be useful to give some short duration events (such as a single class meeting) a length along the axis equal to entire weeks or more of other activities. The engagement (or complexity, rising action, etc.) axis (y-axis) shows a relative value and is of necessity speculative, incorporating many feelings, attitudes, and behaviors. It is plotted according to the intended relative level of engagement, which of course is also relative to each learner and each situation. Where you start the engagement curve on the y-axis would also be relative, and even though the diagrams depicted here assume an origin of near zero engagement for each curve, in objective terms this would likely not be the case for most students. Some may enter the experience full of anticipation and ready to act, and quickly reduce their engagement to more modest levels in finding the experience not so unique. If the instructor or ID is unable to maintain that initial engagement, the low point of the resulting ebbing becomes a point of challenge to raise it back to desired levels, and therefore the bottom value of the Y-axis.

In using any notation system, even narrative diagrams, one should be concerned about generating a false sense of completeness to the design. Because diagrams may appear visually captivating in and of themselves, a designer might be lured into thinking the final user is sure to experience the same captivation. This of course may never happen due to factors not considered in creating the diagram or due to learner characteristics beyond the control of the designer. However, this is no argument to avoid the use of a tool that can help designers grasp critical aspects of learner experience that might otherwise be ignored. Combined with other notation systems, as well as traditional tools such as design documents, storyboards, and content matrices, narrative diagrams of learning experience can provide a designer a powerful method of planning for the aesthetic experience of learning.

An additional caveat exists regarding the use of notation systems. One can not forget that the final learning experience is the result of how the immediate qualities of instruction are executed, including responding to changing conditions and student responses that are difficult to plan for. Engagement or challenge curves are only a starting point in planning for the aesthetic experience of learning. They are akin to an artist's quick sketch that is meant to guide the creation of a painted canvas or sculpted stone. Execution can make the difference between success and failure. Instructional design also requires craftsmanship in writing effective text, producing attractive and intuitive screen designs, creating instructive illustrations, and, perhaps most importantly, anticipating and reacting to student responses to the instruction in ways that reinforce learning—even when this means diverging from well-intentioned plans.

REFERENCES

Aristotle. (1984). Poetics. In J. Barnes (Tran.), *The complete works of Aristotle* (Vol. 2, pp. 2316-2340). Princeton, NJ: Princeton University Press.

Berleant, A. (1991). *Art and engagement.* Philadelphia: Temple University Press.

Botturi, L. (2006). E²ml: A visual language for the design of instruction. *Educational Technology Research & Development, 54*(3), 265-293.

Botturi, L., Derntl, M., Boot, E., & Figl, K. (2006). *A classification framework for educational modeling languages in instructional design.* Paper presented at the IEEE ICALT, Kerkrade, The Netherlands.

Brown, D. (2003). *The Da Vinci code.* New York: Random House.

Bruner, J. (1990). *Acts of meaning.* Cambridge: Harvard University Press.

Bruner, J. (2002). *Making stories: Law, literature, and life.* New York: Farrar, Straus, and Giroux.

Campbell, J. (1968). *The hero with a thousand faces* (2nd ed.). Princeton, NJ: Princeton University Press.

Collins, A., & Stevens, A. L. (1983). A cognitive theory of inquiry teaching. In C. M. Reigeluth (Ed.), *Instructional-design theories and models: An overview of their current status* (pp. 247-278). Hillsdale, NJ: Lawrence Erlbaum Associates.

The COMET® Program (2002). Hurricane Strike! Retrieved from http://meted.ucar.edu/hurrican/strike/index.htm

The COMET® Program (2006). *Using the AFWA WRF mesoscale model.* Retrieved from http://meted.ucar.edu/nwp/afwa_wrf/index.htm

Dewey, J. (1934/1989). *Art as experience* (Vol. 10). Carbondale: Southern Illinois University Press.

Ishiguro, K. (2005). *Never let me go.* New York: Vintage Books.

Jackson, P. W. (1998). *John Dewey and the lessons of art.* New Haven: Yale University Press.

Jonassen, D. H. (2004). *Learning to solve problems: An instructional design guide.* San Francisco: Pfeiffer.

Kolodner, J. L., & Guzdial, M. (2000). Theory and practice of case-based learning aids. In D. H. Jonassen & S. M. Land (Eds.), *Theoretical foundations of learning environments* (pp. 215-242). Mahwah, NJ: Lawrence Erlbaum Associates.

Laurel, B. (1993). *Computers as theatre.* Reading, MA: Addison-Wesley.

Lawson, B. (1997). *How designers think: The design process demystified* (3rd ed.). Amsterdam: Architectural Press.

Nelson, H. G., & Stolterman, E. (2003). *The design way.* Englewood Cliffs, NJ: Educational Technology Publications.

O'Regan, K. (2003). Emotion and e-learning. *Journal of Asynchronous Learning Networks, 7*(3), 78-92.

Osguthorpe, R. T. (2006). *Learning that grows.* Paper presented at the Fourth International Conference on Multimedia and Information and Communication Technologies in Education (MICTE), Seville, Spain.

Parrish, P. E. (2004). *Investigating the aesthetic decisions of teachers and instructional designers.* Paper presented at the Annual Meeting of the American Educational Research Association, San Diego, CA. Retrieved from http://www.comet.ucar.edu/~pparrish/

Parrish, P. E. (2005). Embracing the aesthetics of instructional design. *Educational Technology, 45*(2), 16-25.

Parrish, P. E. (in press). Aesthetic principles for instructional design. *Educational Technology Research & Development.*

Parrish, P. E. (2006a). Design as storytelling. *TechTrends, 50*(4), 72-82.

Parrish, P. E. (2006b). *Learning as aesthetic experience: John Dewey's integration of art, inquiry, and education.* Unpublished manuscript. Retrieved from http://www.comet.ucar.edu/~pparrish

Polkinghorne, D. E. (1988). *Narrative knowing and the human sciences.* Albany, NY: State University of New York Press.

Ray, R. J. (1994). *The weekend novelist.* New York: Dell Publishing.

Savery, J. R., & Duffy, T. M. (1996). Problem based learning: An instructional model and its constructivist framework. In B.G. Wilson (Ed.), *Constructivist learning environments* (pp. 135-148). Englewood Cliffs, NJ: Educational Technology Publications.

Schama, S. (2006). *The power of art.* Great Britain: BBC Books.

Schank, R. C., Berman, T. R., & Macpherson, K. A. (1999). Learning by doing. In C. M. Reigeluth (Ed.), *Instructional-design theories and models: A new paradigm of instructional theory* (Vol. II, pp. 161-181). Mahwah, NJ: Lawrence Erlbaum Associates.

Schwier, R. A., Campbell, K., & Kenny, R. (2004). Instructional designer's observations about identity, communities of practice and change agency. *Australasian Journal of Educational Technology, 20*(4), 69-100.

Visscher-Voerman, I., & Gustafson, K. L. (2004). Paradigms in the theory and practice of education and training design. *Educational Technology Research & Development, 52*(2), 69-89.

Wilson, B. G. (2005). Broadening our foundation for instructional design: Four pillars of practice. *Educational Technology, 45*(2), 10-16.

APPENDIX A: HURRICANE STRIKE! CONTENT MATRIX

(module available at http://www.meted.ucar.edu/hurrican/strike)

	Scenario Elements	Safety Activities and Content	Science Activities and Content
Intro	• Begin your visit with the Castillo family living in Ft. Walton Beach, Florida and learn about potential hurricane approaching Florida		
Day 1	• Tropical Storm Erin is heading toward the Bahamas and southern Florida, where a tropical storm watch is issued • Family prepares their emergency kit for hurricane season	• Pack the "disaster duffle bag"	• "Hurricanes and Tropical Cyclones": Learn when and how hurricanes form
Day 2	• Tropical Storm Erin has just been upgraded to a hurricane of category 1 and heading for Florida's east coast • Family begins to prepare for low probability hurricane strike	• Review the safety list over dinner	• "Create-a-Cane" game: Discover the ingredients needed for forming hurricanes
Day 3	• Hurricane Erin is still at category 1, heading toward the east coast of central Florida • Ft. Walton beach is now near the western edge of a tropical storm watch area	• Go shopping for emergency supplies • Preparing the yard and home for hurricane weather	• "Aim-a-Hurricane" game: Experiment with winds that change a hurricane's path
Day 4	• Hurricane Erin has swept across central Florida and is now in the Gulf of Mexico. Four deaths have occurred. It is expected to gain strength and make landfall once again along the Gulf Coast. • Ft. Walton beach is now within a tropical storm warning area • Mandatory evacuation of some areas is issued, including the home of Aunt Betsy	• Give Aunt Betsy evacuation advice	• "Inside the Storm" simulation: explore a 3-D model of a hurricane
Day 5	• Hurricane Erin, now a strong category 1, is making landfall at Ft. Walton beach • The family is not in an evacuation zone, but has lost power and facing severe winds and rain	• "Danger Zone": Learn about the hazards associated with hurricanes • Advise Camille and her friend Floyd about safety during the storm	
Day 6	• The storm has moved inland and, while no longer a hurricane, poses substantial flooding threats • People begin to return from evacuation shelters to their homes	• "Safety Zone": Learn about hurricane safety • Help Aunt Betsy return home safely	
Day 7	• Farewell and visual summary		

Notes:

- Worksheets for days 1-6 reinforce safety and science activities and content
- Weather Updates are provide for days 1-6 via the Television Weather Report available in the living room, and via office laptop Internet connection to storm tracking, satellite, radar, and text weather reports

APPENDIX B: PARTIAL MATRIX OF HURRICANE STRIKE!

Content as Related to Middle School U.S. National Science Education Standards

Relevant Standards	Where Addressed in Hurricane Strike!

Science as Inquiry
 	
• Abilities necessary to do scientific inquiry
   o Use tools and techniques to gather, analyze, and interpret data
   o Think critically and logically to make relationships between evidence and explanations
   o Use mathematics in all aspects of scientific inquiry
• Understandings about scientific inquiry
   o Mathematics is important in all aspects of scientific inquiry
   o Technology used to gather data enhances accuracy and allows scientists to analyze and quantify results of investigations
	Aim a Hurricane: this exploratory game, with its accompanying questions (6-8) on *Worksheet 3*, engages students in an inquiry process to learn about the effects of wind belts and pressure systems on hurricane movement.
	Create-a-Cane: this game also engages students in an inquiry process that allows them to "create" a hurricane by manipulating key conditions. Question 7 on *Worksheet 2* relates to this activity.
	Storm Track: this condensed collection of weather data depicting the life and times of Hurricane Erin supports the technology and data analysis aspects of this science standard.
	Worksheets: all six of the worksheets include questions that require students to analyze geographic and weather data. These questions support NSES category A.

Physical Science • Motions and forces • Transfer of energy	**Hurricanes and Tropical Cyclones:** a basic introduction to the science, climate, and geography of hurricanes. Numerous pages in this "mini-module" relate to this NSES category. **Aim a Hurricane:** this exploratory game helps students learn about the forces, such as wind belts and pressure systems, that control hurricane movement.

Science in Personal and Social Perspectives
 	
•   Natural hazards
   o   landslides, floods, storms
   o   hazard mitigation
•   Risks and benefits
   o   risk analysis
   o   risks associated with natural hazards
   o   personal and social decision making
	Danger Zone and **Safety Zone:** all of the content in these "mini-modules" relates to important topics in NSES category F.
	Safety and Preparedness Exercises: all 7 safety and preparedness exercises in **Hurricane Strike!** (and their corresponding questions on the **worksheets**) are directly related to risk analysis and safety decision-making.

APPENDIX C: E²ML ACTION DIAGRAM FOR "AIM-A-CANE" EXERCISE FROM HURRICANE STRIKE!

"Aim-a-Hurricane" Game		Day 3, Science 1
Individual Students, Groups, or Entire Class (using projector)		Learning
"Hurricanes and Tropical Cyclones" mini-module (available on the office laptop after day 1)	Ability to predict the path of a hurricane in a highly simplified environment. This includes stable, latitude-specific general flows of equatorial easterly winds and extratropical westerlies, as well as one dominant high and one dominant low pressure system creating anticyclonic and cyclonic rotating flow, respectively, which can have variable, but static positions. Appreciation of the difficulty of predicting hurricane paths.	
5th Grade reading level, Basic computer skills	Understanding of the relationship of atmospheric flow pattern to high and low pressure centers. Knowledge of general atmospheric steering flows based on latitude. A developing interest in scientific problem solving.	
Embedded Introduction and Instructions	Various animated hurricane trajectories based on student input to initial conditions. Selection of predicted trajectories and summary conclusions in the Day 3 Worksheet.	
In this online game, the learner drags a pressure center icon (H or L) to one of four preset locations, drags an image of a hurricane to its starting tropical latitude in the eastern Atlantic, and then observes the resulting hurricane trajectory. Students are asked to retry the simulation to have the hurricane follow as many unique trajectories as they can. Duration: 20-40 minutes		
Within the online module, or downloaded to a local computer, either at a personal workstation or shared computer.		
Computer, mouse, and display. The Hurricane Strike! multimedia module, teacher guidance, optional links and resources listed in the module.		

Key

Action Name		Tag
Roles		Type
Requirements	Expected Outcomes	
Preconditions	Side-Effects	
Input	Output	
Procedures + Duration		
Locations		
Tools		

Chapter VII
E²ML:
A Tool for Sketching Instructional Designs

Luca Botturi
University of Lugano, Switzerland

ABSTRACT

This chapter introduces E²ML, the educational environment modeling language. E²ML is a lightweight visual language for instructional design; suitable both for complex instructional design processes and simple paper and pencil sketches. E²ML can be used for visualizing the intermediate and final results of design, thus providing documentation in a shared language that can enhance team communication, improve design and contribute to the development of high-quality instruction. The language and its features and applications are presented through a case study, evaluation results are briefly reported, and critical issues are discussed.

INTRODUCTION

This handbook includes the presentation of a number of visual languages for ID, each with its specific features, sometimes with striking differences. Even a quick run through the chapters is enough to notice that they can be classified into two main groups.

Some languages were developed for creating a formal and unambiguous representation of instructional activities, eventually to be transformed into some sort of machine-readable code to auto-mate part of the delivery thanks to technologies such as a LMS. Each with its peculiar flavor, to this group belong IMS LD (Chapter XV), poEML (Chapter X), coUML (Chapter IX) and LDL (Chapter XII). The goal of these languages is *modeling*, i.e., describing an educational environment according to well-defined formal primitives—the vocabulary and grammar of the language—in order to generate unambiguous descriptions. In the framework presented by Botturi, Derntl, Boot and Figl (2006), they would be described as *finalist communicative* languages, i.e., they serve the purpose of representing a complete instructional design for communicating it to others for implementation, reuse, or simply archival.

On the other hand, other languages were developed to let designers, instructors, tutors and other stakeholders think about the instruction they are designing, and to support its creation. The main idea behind them is that being able to express an idea, especially through a diagram or other sort of visualization, allows interested people to better analyze and understand it, and consequently to make better design decisions. What these kinds of diagrams allow is *representing*, i.e., they allow designers to *give shape* to their ideas, understandings, insights and design solutions so that they can externalize them, reflect on them, and eventually share them. In the terms of (Botturi, Derntl, Boot & Figl, 2006) these are generative reflective languages.

The educational environment modeling language (E²ML) presented in this chapter falls within the latter class: its emphasis is not on formal descriptions, but rather on the possibility of representing, expressing and sharing design ideas (an analysis of some of its features is also presented in Chapter XVII, using its first appearance in 2003 as reference point).

The best way to understand E²ML and to locate it within the wider current context of VIDL is to tell its story, why and how it was developed, which is the goal of the first section of this chapter. The second section presents a case study, which provides an applied presentation of the language and its use, for those who are interested in learning it. The third section goes over the language elements from a more analytical perspective, providing a sort of summary of the features that were before "scattered" all over the example. Section four provides a focus on flexibility, the main feature of E²ML. Finally, the fifth section introduces some elements for the evaluation of E²ML along with some critical considerations about costs.

THE ROOTS OF E²ML

This first section will briefly summarize the development history of E²ML. This short introduction about the author's research activity is not intended to be celebratory; rather, it is simply the best way to help readers understand the reasons behind E²ML's development, and its relationships with the other VIDL presented in this handbook.

The Need for E²ML

For my PhD research I was working on adaptive hypermedia systems, and I had the feeling that it would have been impossible to set up a sound study of their impact on teaching and learning without a clear understanding of the main features of the whole course or educational environment in which they were used. The same adaptive hypermedia system might be used with different content for example, for a course in programming languages and another in art history, representing two different stories, as the two instructors were likely to select different instructional strategies, and exploit adaptivity in different ways. In the end, because they are *very* different teachers, teaching very different courses, the results would show very different ways to use the same hypermedia technology.

E²ML was originally developed as a tentative visual language to represent the distinctive features of a single educational environment in a more coherent and comprehensible way than was possible with a textual narrative. After it was developed, it was natural to think that it could have been used the other way around: as a language to represent educational environment *before* it was implemented, i.e., for design.

As my native field of research is communication technologies, I labeled this a *modeling* language. At this time, in 2001, the educational modeling language (EML; De Vries, n.d.) was catalyzing the attention in the field. EML was a formal, XML-oriented language for the representation of courses and educational activities, with the goal of creating machine-readable metadata to feed online learning environments. A year later, when E²ML was almost fully developed, I came across IMS LD, which inherited and further developed the structure of EML. This changed my perspective: IMS LD is a fully-fledged, formal *modeling* language. It has an unambiguous concept model, a formal XML-binding, and is supported by a growing set of tools. By contrast, E²ML has a much narrower scope: it is a simple, semi-formal and flexible *representation* tool.

Since then, and with an astonishing speed, the landscape of VIDL has evolved. This handbook testifies that the need for, and the interest in languages for ID brought to the development of a number of new and promising languages and tools.

Specific Features of E²ML

The main assumption behind E²ML is that the ID process, especially in situations where technologies play a central role, is basically a team effort and is interwoven with communication (Botturi, 2006). E²ML was developed as a reflective design tool: a way to quickly jot down design ideas in order share them with the design team and to let them evolve into complete designs. In short, it could be labeled as *lightweight* and *visual*.

Lightweight means that it requires neither (a) a great investment of time or effort in order to be used; nor (b) a deep revision of the design and development process. Bolchini and Paolini (2006) try to formalize the idea of "lightweight" in four basic features, all of which fit E²ML (and which will be illustrated in the case study presented in the next section, and discussed in the last section of this chapter).

1. It must be easy to teach the language to anyone (from students to practitioners), i.e., the

learning curve should not be steep. Professional instructional designers in particular do not have time and resources to invest in learning new tools and methodologies. One of the success factors of "Entity Relationship" (probably the most successful visual design model in computer science) stems from the fact that it is very easy to teach and learn its basic concepts, both in academic and professional environments.

2. It must be possible to use the design language for brainstorming, i.e., for generating, sharing and discussing quickly evolving ideas among developers, with clients and stakeholders, and with potential learners or testers. This is in contrast with design languages capable of representing only fully developed solutions in formal models.

3. It must require little time and effort to jot down design ideas: developers do not like to spend too many resources in preliminary activities.

4. It must be possible to move smoothly from general design ideas to more detailed designs, without the need for excessive reworking and without the need for completeness; in other words, even an incomplete design document must be useful and understandable.

The visual aspect of E²ML means that it relies on graphical representations to support communication in the design team. This idea was developed as an answer the fact that the ID process has become a more and more challenging and interdisciplinary process (Szabo, 2002), which requires interactions way beyond what Bates (1999) calls the "lone ranger approach." ID is more and more a matter of design *teams* than of isolated instructional designers (Greer, 1991; Botturi, 2006 b). E²ML was developed and tested as a tool that allows a design team to (a) enhance team communication; (b) improve the overall consistency of designs; (c) support design process management activities; (d) enable evaluation already at design time, i.e., before testing; and, (e) allow a standard document format for archival and reuse. These features will be discussed through the case study presented below.

According to the framework presented by Botturi, Derntl, Boot, and Figl (2006), E²ML is:

1. **Flat:** It only includes actions as main representation primitives for educational environments.
2. **Conceptual:** It supports conceptual design, without offering means for development or implementation.
3. **Semi-formal:** It has no strictly formal definitions, nor any native XML or other code binding.
4. **Multiple perspective:** It allows—and fosters—the definition of two main perspectives on actions: a temporal one (the activity flow) and a logical one (the dependencies diagram).
5. **Visual.**

While this chapter is definitely applied in nature, a more academic presentation of E²ML is available in Botturi (2006). In that paper, the language is presented more analytically, and its cultural references are put forward. Also in Botturi (2003), is presented an extended version, which is more formal and sophisticated, and is compliant with the conceptual model of IMS LD 1.2 (IMS, n.d.).

THE GAMES AND EDUCATION WORKSHOP

In order to let the readers get a glimpse E²ML in the practice, this section presents the design of a short face-to-face workshop about *Games and Education* in which E²ML was used.

Setting

Each year, the Italian Association for Media Education organizes a summer school in Media Education. During the third week of July, scholars and students in Media Education from all over Italy meet in Corvara, in the Dolomite Mountains to work together in workshops on various topics. The *Games and Education* workshop was developed in summer 2006 as part of the summer school. It addressed a class of 15 students, either master students in Media Education, Education or Educational Technologies, or in-service teachers pursuing a certificate in Media Education. As a standard workshop in that setting, it required six seat hours and was repeated twice during the summer school. Two instructional designers carried out the design, and one of them was also the instructor.

The main ideas behind the workshop were (a) to introduce videogames as a new digital medium within the framework of Media Education, and (b) to do this focusing not only on "video", but to emphasize the tight relationship between game playing and learning. This was translated into the learning goals presented in Figure 1.

The setting in Corvara is both challenging and stimulating. Corvara is located among some of the most beautiful peaks in the Dolomites, in an open and sunny valley, away from the main transportation routes. The spectacular character of nature generates a relaxed and positive environment, which fosters learning. At the same time, the secluded position of the village makes it impossible to have a computer lab or a broadband Internet connection, and only a few rooms are equipped with video projectors—facts that, in the case study presented here, raised some design issues.

The following paragraphs describe how E²ML was used during the design and delivery of the workshop; their perspective is "applied," and

*Figure 1. Learning goals for the **Games and Education** workshop*

After the instruction the workshop participants will be able to:
1. Describe the main elements that make a game as such, i.e., "engaging" and "fun"
2. Describe the relationship between learning and playing
3. Recall three examples of instructional videogames
4. Recall and describe different types of relationships between game content and game structure
5. Distinguish different types of games and videogames
6. Recall the names of the main authors in the field of games and videogames in education

they are not intended to present the language in an analytical way, which will be done in the following section.

JOTTING DOWN IDEAS WITH OVERVIEW DIAGRAMS

Because E²ML is a lightweight visual tool for creative design, it can be handy from the early stages of design for jotting down still-unformed design ideas. In particular E²ML provides two *overview diagrams* that can be useful for a coarse-grained representation of the main ideas behind an instructional unit. During the design of the *Games and Education* workshop, the two types of overview diagrams were used from the very start as a structure for quick jot-down and later progressive refinement of design ideas.

The idea behind overview diagrams is that any instructional activity can be represented from two different perspectives: (a) chronological, i.e., more or less as it would appear in a course schedule; and (b) logical or structural, i.e., evidencing meaningful connections other than temporal sequences among its different parts. The two together provide "the big picture", a synthetic but complete view of the whole instruction.

Overview diagrams are composed by *actions*, i.e., the bricks of the instruction. More precisely, an action can be defined as the performance of a set

of acts with a unity of purpose by defined acting subjects (Botturi, 2006). Unity of purpose means that the action is aiming at one thing, e.g., producing a report, completing an exercise, achieving the understanding of a concept, etc. The acting subjects can be a single learner, a whole class with the instructor, a tutor, etc. An action can be split in several sub-actions according to the time and/or space unity criterion in the specific setting, e.g., a single lecture or a videoconference.

In the following overview, diagrams are presented one after the other. Actually, they are created together and should be read simultaneously, as they actually only make sense when viewed together. Each of them alone is only a part of the complete information.

The Activity Flow

The first overview diagram implements the chronological view of the instruction. It is a sort of flowchart representing the learner's path through the instruction by sequencing actions. For the Games and Education workshop, the first version of the activity flow was developed for giving a shape to the main design ideas. It was used to control time allocations to the different learning activities that the instructor had in mind, represented as actions (Figure 2). Time requirements for each action are annotated beside each action.

The diagram indicates the overall schedule for the workshop. It starts with an engaging interaction game, called *Mafia*. Playing is followed by a debriefing, which evidences the main elements that "make the game", not elicited at this stage of design. The idea is to have the participants play a game together, win or lose and possibly have fun, and then start critically reflecting on their own experience. After that, a more formal presentation of the workshop, its goals and schedule takes place, followed by a presentation of the key conceptual points, which ends the first part of the workshop. The second part includes ACTIVITY 1, a group

Figure 2. Activity flow sketch (1)

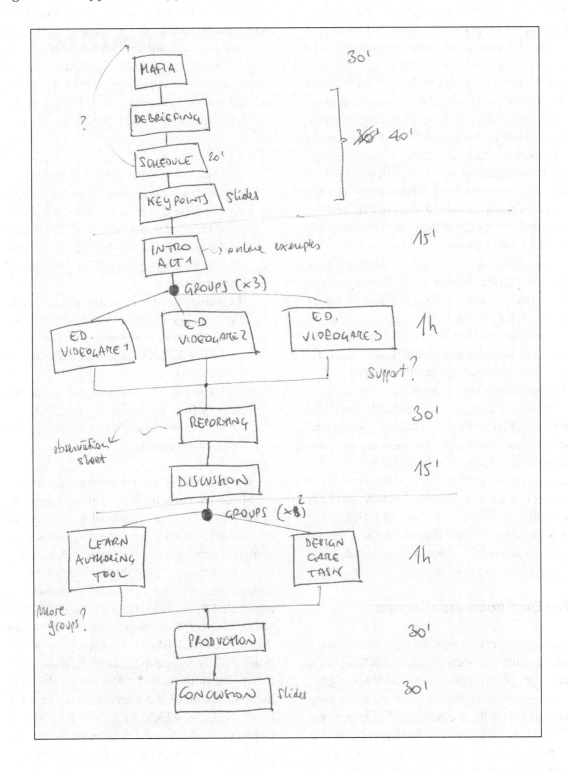

activity, in which each group has time to play with an educational videogame and record its activities on a report sheet. The activities of each group—there are three of them—are concluded with an oral report to the rest of the class, followed by a discussion. The discussion of ACTIVITY 1 closes the second part of the workshop and opens the last one, which is basically a design activity. The first half of the class works on the design of a small instructional videogame, while the second half experiments with a 3D instructional games development environment. They then put together their results and produce a short demonstration. The whole workshop is then concluded with the CONCLUSION action.

The design at this stage is coarse-grained, and actually the diagram is far from complete: it is closer to a structured set of notes, useful for keeping track of ideas or for discussion, than to a full description—and actually, this is how it was used. The whole point is that it is more synthetic and effective in sharing ideas than the page of text that would have been required to "explain" it.

Figure 2 already includes a simple branching device (called *split*) for indicating the parallel activities of groups. Annotations to splits can be used for indicating split conditions (e.g., "if the learner's grade from the previous activity is at least 6"), options ("choose 1 activity out of N possible") or selections ("chose M activities out of N possible"). Notice that, for sound notation, after the parallel activities are completed, a *join* sign (a small dot) is used.

The Dependencies Diagram

The second overview diagram represents the logical, or structural, view of the instruction, i.e., it tries to emphasize the reasons why it is designed that way, and the meaningful connections among its parts that make it consistent. The idea is that like the human body has a hidden skeleton that supports it, each educational environment has a deep structure that connects its activities in a

meaningful way, and that this is not necessarily mimicked in the streamlined disposition of the activities on the calendar.

While the diagram must include the same actions of the activity flow, its overall shape can be completely different, as it is the case for the *Games and Education* workshop reported in Figure 3.

The relationships represented in the diagram are:

1. Product (simple arrow): the first action produces some artifact that is required as input for the second action (e.g., PRODUCTION requires input from LEARN AUTHORING TOOL and DESIGN GAME TASK). Product arrows may be tagged with an indicator of the product.
2. Learning prerequisite (arrow with dot head): the first action provides a learning outcome that is the prerequisite for the second action (e.g., DISCUSSION requires KEY POINTS in Figure 3).
3. Aggregation: an activity is part of another activity (it is a sub-activity; e.g., MAFIA, DEBRIEFING and KEY POINTS are part of macroaction A).

The dependencies diagram provides a different but complementary view with respect to the activity flow. Once the relationships arrows that connect activities are clear, the diagram is quite straightforward. Some remarks may help focusing on critical details. First of all, the three main parts (or macroactions) are given more emphasis, and are labeled A, B and C. They represent the three logical elements that compose the workshop; for the same reason, the SCHEDULE activity, which is not directly related to the content, is set aside; notice that in the activity flow it was placed in the mainstream of the activity. Also, the KEY POINTS action, which is a presentation, has the largest number of incoming prerequisite arrows, one from each macroaction: this indicates that its success is critical for the whole workshop,

Figure 3. Dependencies diagram sketch (1)

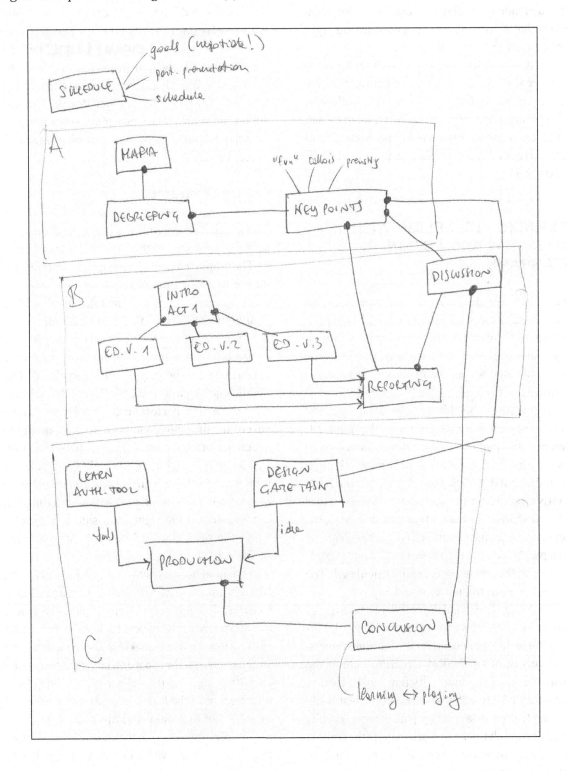

much more than less "central" actions. Finally, the dependencies diagram has place for some notes that clarify, always in a note-taking style, the content of some actions.

At this stage the two overview diagrams were used mainly to collect and structure the first design ideas in a standard way. The following design steps can rely on the two visualizations to leverage creativity, focusing on some details and further refining the plan, as presented in the next section.

REFINING THE DESIGN WITH OVERVIEW AND ACTION DIAGRAMS

Moving on with the design, the overview diagrams were used as basis for discussion, and as experimental field for suggesting possible alternatives, e.g., moving one action forward, or extending the time allocated for it. The result is a progressive refinement that leads to the final version.

In this case—but this is of course not a general rule—they did not change much: the main difference was that the activity flow was displayed over a time grid. For the rest, only minor changes or additional details appeared, e.g., that the KEY POINTS action will exploit some online examples of instructional games and some slides. Also, the reporting and discussion activities that close the first part of the workshop were merged into a single action, as they were not actually articulated. The result is shown in Figures 4 and 5.

At this level of detail the activity flow diagram works as a sort of workshop schedule for the instructor, while the dependencies diagram remains as a record of the logical structure behind the instruction. Also, the activity flow can be further transformed into a text-based schedule that could be handed out to workshop participants, even if the informal character of workshops in the context of the Summer School and its limited duration suggested not doing it in this case.

The next step in the design is to break down each action and work on the details: how should the MAFIA game be introduced? What are the main key points to be made in the KEY POINTS presentation? How will the instructor lead the discussion? What happens in the conclusion? For this task E²ML offers another device, namely, action diagrams. They provide a sort of "zoom in" on the action box of overview diagrams with space for details.

Action Diagrams

The general schema for the representation of an action is presented in the left-hand side of Figure 6. The upper part of the diagram contains the proper identification for the action, i.e., its identifier tag, name, type and the roles involved (the acting subject). The middle-left area describes the initial state, i.e., the necessary and sufficient conditions for learning to be achieved, or for the performance to be successfully completed. The middle-right area describes the (desired) final state after the action performance. Finally, the lower part of the diagram contains a description of the action performance, including locations and tools. The squares hanging on the right-hand side are references to the learning goals associated with this action. The complete E²ML action diagram is presented in the right-hand side of Figure 6, while the definitions of elements are provided in Table 1.

Learning actions are directly concerned with learners' progress with the instruction, and include lectures, discussions, exercises, personal study, etc. Support actions concern the staff's work for the instruction, such as correcting and evaluating the submissions, setting up materials, solving logistical issues, etc. Clearly, support actions may have no reference to the learning goals, and a minimal definition of the initial and final states.

The definition of the initial and final state may appear somewhat complicated, but it was conceived to be as flexible as possible and at the

Figure 4. Activity flow sketch (2)

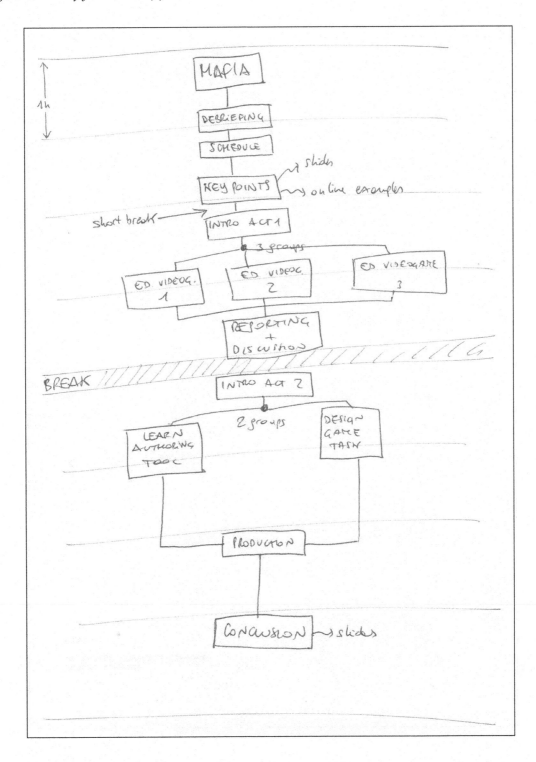

Figure 5. Dependencies diagram sketch (2)

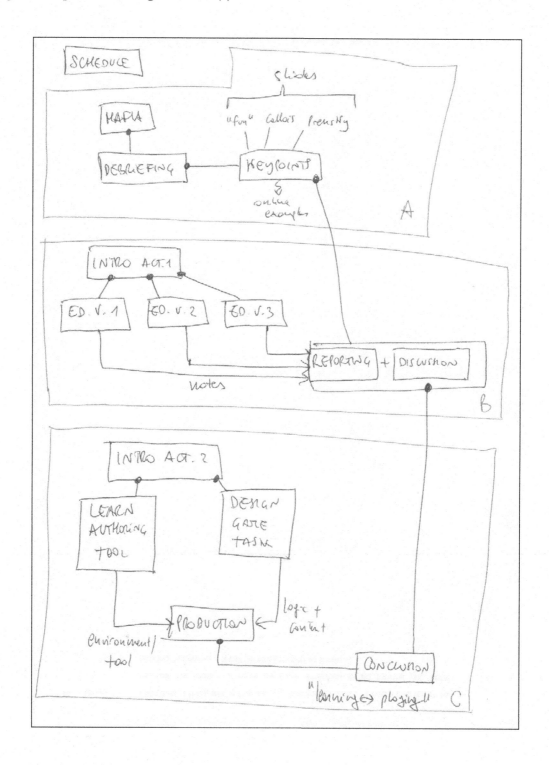

Figure 6. Action diagram schema: simple (left) and detailed (right)

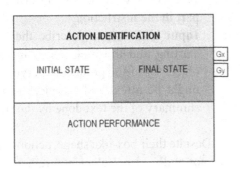

Table 1. Action diagram definition table

Element	Description	Example
Tag	A unique identifier (used for reference)	PS4
Name	The action name	Practice session 4
Type	The type of action (LEARNING/SUPPORT)	Learning
Roles	The roles involved in the action, eventually the names of the people	Students (all), Tutor (Mark)
Prerequisites	Competencies or prior knowledge that should have been acquired within the learning environment in order to successfully perform the action	Assessing the difference between internal and external corporate communication; naming at least three types of messages for internal and external communication.
Preconditions	Competencies or prior knowledge necessary to the action but that do not belong to the goals	Proficient use of MS Word (or other text editor)
Input	Object or materials that are provided for the action, but not listed as tools	Acme Web site www.acme.com
Expected Outcomes	The expected learning outcome related to the learning goals, in terms of goal or sub-goal achieved	Understand, analyze and evaluate efficiency and viability in a corporate communication policy statement
Side-Effects	Competencies or knowledge acquired through the action but not directly addressed by the action (or course) goals	Advanced skills with MS Word.
Output	The material product or object designed, developed or realized during the action	A report of 20 pages submitted via e-mail.
Procedure	A description of how the action is to be performed, including specific tasks for each role	Present the case study ("ACME corporate policy") with the related question sheet. Divide students in groups of three and ...
Location	The location(s) in which the action takes place or ANYWHERE	Classroom A34
Tools	The tools and materials exploited in the action	ACME case study, ACME question sheet
Goal Reference	The goal(s) towards which the action moves the learners.	G1, G7

same time, fine-grained. The three rows crossing the initial state and the final state areas describe different types of conditions:

1. **Prerequisites and expected outcomes** describe the learner's starting and arrival points in terms of knowledge and learning in relation with the course goals. Prerequisites are essential and necessary conditions for the learner to achieve learning.

2. **Preconditions and side effects** describe the learner's starting and arrival points in terms of knowledge that is not related to the instruction. Fluent English may be a precondition for entering a course in Game Theory, and a side effect of that course would be improved English fluency—yet language skills are not directly bound to Game Theory as such, and will not probably be a topic in the evaluation. Preconditions are accessory yet necessary conditions for learners to take part in the instruction.

3. **Input and output** describe the learner's starting and finishing points in terms of objects used and produced. A typical input might be a text and a typical output is a summary of the text done by the students.

Despite their box-like shape, action diagrams are not really visual elements, rather a sort of structured template that guides the designer in filling in the details and move on to the next stage of design without losing the big picture. Detailed action diagrams have a threefold goal:

1. They can support the development of instructional materials offering a detailed account of the context of use, be it a simple report

Figure 7. Example of action diagram

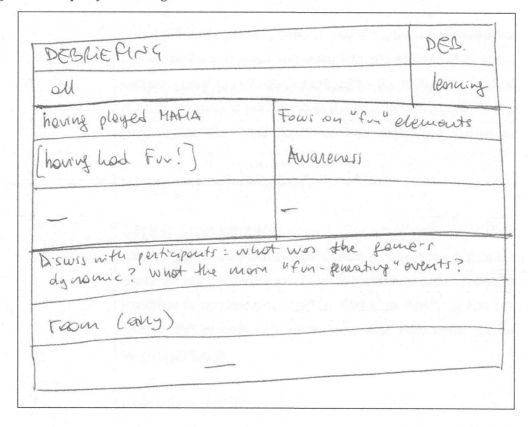

sheet or an online self-learning activity.

2. They provide a structured and detailed record for archival and reuse (see Figure 7).

3. The very act of filling in an action diagram helps the designer not to overlook relevant details.

As any detailed design activity, completing action diagrams for a whole course or set of activities might require a large investment of time, and its return should be calculated in advance according to each specific project. For example, detailed design might be paramount in an online distance instruction setting in which courses are designed once and then assigned to distance tutors for multiple editions—actually, the template for the description of instructional activities in some open universities looks very similar to this. Yet this is often not the case with short face-to-face courses. For the *Games and Education* workshop full activity diagrams were developed only for critical activities. As example, Figure 7 reports the action diagram for the DEBRIEFING activity.

So far E²ML has been used to support creativity: capturing design ideas, giving them initial shape, providing basis for discussion, offering a structure for plugging in details. Basically, E²ML comes into play after the instructional analysis, supporting design and development. The next two paragraphs will briefly presents two other ways in which E²ML diagrams can be useful during and after the delivery of the instruction.

Redesigning On-The-Fly

After careful design, the *Games and Education* workshop was ready to go. But of course, teaching is the art of managing unknown situations, and so, the very morning the first session of the workshop was about to start, the organizers communicated to the instructor that, contrary to what was expected, the room to which he was assigned was small, and had no video projector and no Internet connection. This clearly made

it difficult to perform the workshop as planned, in particular for two critical issues that required immediate redesign:

1. It was impossible to display the slides that should support the KEY POINTS action.

2. It was impossible to show the planned examples of online games for the KEY POINTS action.

The two issues are not marginal, as they impact the central action in the whole design, as shown in the dependencies diagram. How do you replace these elements? On the other hand, sunny weather offered an opportunity to exploit the outdoor facilities of the center that hosted the summer school, also introducing a novelty to which participants could be expected to react positively. These two conditions prompted the instructor to revise the plan following two principles:

1. Reinforce the idea of making the instruction fun by playing part of it outside—therefore, without technologies.

2. Introduce more face-to-face playing and less videogaming, taking out the examples of online games.

The most rapid way to see how the new principles affected the instruction was altering the two overview diagrams according to the new needs. The results are shown in Figure 8, which presents the first part of the activity flow, and Figure 9, which presents the first group of actions in the dependencies diagram. Notice that in the latter, a new articulation is introduced with the *outdoor* and *indoor* labels.

Archival and Reuse

E²ML diagrams can be also useful for the archival and reuse of instructional designs. Storing textual narratives can be useful as they allow keyword searching. But storing visuals along with them (or

Figure 8. Revised activity flow

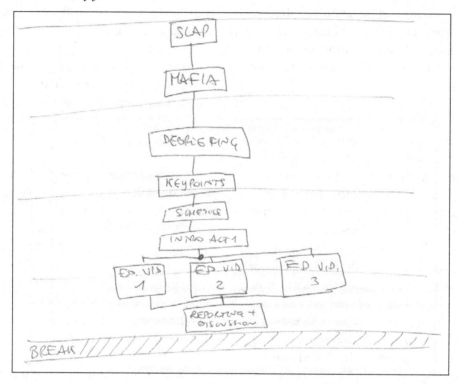

Figure 9. Revised dependencies diagram

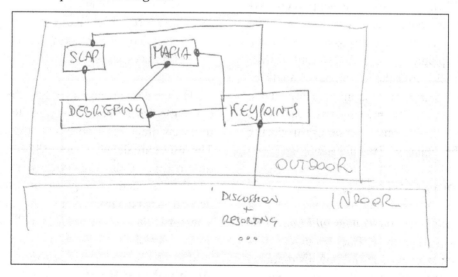

along with shorter summaries) provides a chance to skim through them and get a rapid glimpse of each design. From this perspective, E²ML is a possible framework.

This would be useful for the next editions of the *Games and Education* workshop, both in the case it was to be repeated "as is" and in the case it was to be revised. In order to do that, any simple digital version of the diagrams (e.g., a scan or a MS PowerPoint slide), along with a short narrative reporting the learning context and goals might work.

E²ML only records a sketchy version of the instructional design, and is far from unambiguous. For this reason when archiving a design for further reuse, it is paramount to place extreme attention on a clear formulation of learning goals: they are the key that can make the whole design understandable. Botturi (2006) suggests completing the basic E²ML documentation with a structured goal statement and possibly a visualization of learning goals, e.g., using Merrill's content-performance matrix (1983), the revised Bloom's taxonomy (Anderson & Krathwohl, 2001), or the QUAIL model (Botturi, 2004).

E²ML AT A GLANCE

On the one hand, the case study developed in the previous section provided the readers with an opportunity to see E²ML applied to a real instructional design, but on the other it did not allow a logically ordered view of the language as a whole. The goal of this section is to complement the case study with a short analytical reference.

The E²ML representation of an instructional design is based on two sets of diagrams, as follows:

1. Overview diagrams: provide "the big picture"
   a. The activity flow (chronological view)
   b. The dependencies diagram (logical/ structural view)
2. Action diagrams: provide details
   a. A collection of single action diagrams

The activity flow is a sequence of actions represented as boxes that can be articulated with *split* and *join* devices, basically, a large dot for splits and a smaller one to illustrate joining. For enhancing legibility, the boxes can be placed on

Figure 10. Summary of visual notation for overview diagrams

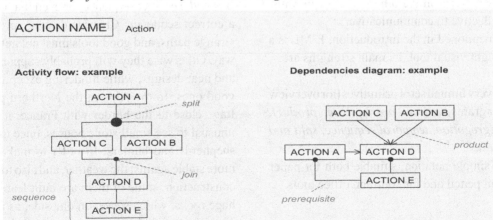

a time grid. The dependencies diagram is a network of action, represented as boxes that can be connected by two types of connections, namely, (a) prerequisites, and (b) products. Prerequisites are shown with lines ending in a dot; products are illustrated using lines that end in an arrowhead. Actions can also be grouped with larger boxes which enclose them. Figure 10 provides a summary of their visual notations.

Action diagrams on the other hand are more templates for collection details of the instructional activities than real visual devices. Their structure, organized in details, initial and final conditions and description, can be found above in Figure 6.

A FOCUS ON FLEXIBILITY

The case study presented in the previous section has illustrated four ways to take advantage of E²ML in a simple ID situation: (a) capturing design ideas; (b) refining design ideas; (c) adding details to activities; and (d) archiving and reusing. While the first three are related to creativity and communication in the design team, the last one concerns the organizational life of instructional designs. For this reason, referring to the framework presented in Botturi, Boot, Derntl & Figl (2006), E²ML can be classified as a mainly generative language, although it can also be used as finalist. Also, on the other axis, it can range from reflective to communicative.

As mentioned in the introduction, E²ML is a lightweight visual tool. Its main strengths are:

1. A very limited set of primitives (for overview diagrams, *action*, *prerequisite*, *product*, *aggregation*, *temporal sequence*, *split and join*).
2. A simple notation, suitable both for paper and pencil and for common office tools.

Extensibility, Integration, and Design Phases

These features make it a flexible tool in at least three ways, namely, from the point of view of (a) extensibility; (b) integration; and (c) relationship with design phases.

Concerning *extensibility*, E²ML was conceived to be a *scaffold*, more than a complete and fully-fledged language. In the hectic reality of the ID practice, any real design process and each real instructional situation has its own unique features: the role of E²ML is not to be prescriptive of the design, but to be flexible, allowing continuous adaptation, simplified or detailed, as needed to respond to each specific context or design team. An example of this flexibility is the ability to introduce new terms, such as creating a sort of template action for "course introduction" or "round disclosure"—whatever it might mean in the jargon of a specific ID team. Another interesting outlook is the ability to notate pedagogical patterns (cf. Belfer & Botturi, 2003; Belfer & Botturi, 2004; Derntl & Botturi, 2006), to be reused as the gist of a standard solution over and over in multiple designs.

Integration is concerned with how E²ML diagrams are sequenced during the production of a single design. It should be noticed beforehand that the order of presentation of diagrams followed in this chapter should not suggest that this is *the* correct sequence, or even that there *is* a correct sequence. Creative design can follow strange paths, and good tools must not get in the way. Otherwise they will probably support good and neat designs, while hindering exceptionally good ones. In the Alps in the Northern part of Italy, close to the border with France, it is not unusual to see small stone houses, once used by shepherds and hunters. In order to make them more stable against the weather, and also to speed construction, some of them are built leaning on huge rocks, which serve, on one side, as a wall. The same might happen in instructional design.

Imagine a course on team communication for corporate training. In this setting it is paramount to design warm-up activities that free the participants from formalities and stress, and let them positively engage with the learning experience. Such activities should be fun, but at the same time, should be related to the subject matter. While any experienced instructor has many ready-made activities of that kind, not all are effective in every setting. In this case, an instructor might conceive a whole session of the course *around* a specific activity, i.e., starting from (leaning on, if it were a rock) an action diagram and building the rest around it. Also, in reusing a course, an instructor might start from the dependencies diagram and then adapt it to the peculiar schedule for the new edition in the activity flow, and so forth.

Finally, concerning the *relationship with design phases*, E²ML design documents—overview diagrams and action diagrams—might be produced at different moments in the design process, and do not have a tight correspondence with specific phases.

Language Systems

Flexibility is also at stake if we consider the fact that a design language actually lives and is used within a system of languages. When architects design buildings, choreographers shows, or fashion designers dresses, they all mix up several languages that help them work on the different *layers of design* that concern the object of design. For example, an architect will use different languages and styles of drawing to think out the house (e.g., sketching on paper), to communicate with the clients (e.g., a 3D rendering), and with the construction crew (e.g., printed AutoCAD executive plans).

As Gibbons and Stubbs pointed out (see Chapter XVII; see also Gibbons, 2003), ID has layers too, and ID teams need different design languages for handling them. For example, each specific media has its own design language(s) that can be used for development: storyboards for animations and video clips, hypermedia design diagrams for Web applications, graphical layouts for printed materials, etc. No single design language alone can cover such complexity.

Teaching E²ML

Flexibility also positively affects the teaching of E²ML, which can follow different paths and can be smoothly integrated in project assignments or on-the-job training. Experience indicates that students (undergraduate or master students) usually need a half-a-day tutorial for being able to correctly read and interpret E²ML design diagrams. With another day of practice in producing designs, they become fluent enough to start using the language not only for producing the assignment to be submitted, but also to conceive design solutions.

Apart from teaching a useful tool for their future professional life, introducing E²ML in a class engaged in ID courses, or even in an ID curriculum, has the advantage of creating a shared language that allows students to communicate their solutions more effectively, and also to compare their designs and start learning from each other.

EVALUATION AND COSTS

Evaluating E²ML

A first evaluation of the perception of usefulness of E²ML is reported in (Botturi, 2005), and its results clearly indicate that professional instructional designers see it as a potentially useful tool for their practice.

That study involved a sample of 12 designers employed as course designers or course developers at universities in Canada and the United States, and was focused on the very first introduction of the language in the design practice. Data were collected through focus groups and interviews after a presentation of the language and the discussion of some cases. The overall impression that all designers expressed during focus group sessions is that E²ML looks potentially powerful, flexible and adaptable to different strategies and situations. They confirmed that they developed a mental image of the course, and that if it can be visualized with E²ML, it can provide "an interesting focus for the discussion" and it can "speed up collaboration", as it "works well in organizing people's thinking"—this echoes what is expressed in Chapter II about the translation of designs to stakeholders and team members. According to their perception, E²ML is mostly useful for keeping the overall consistency of a course, and in particular to discuss the consistency of goals and instructional activities with the instructors or course authors. Personal interviews with designers reinforced those results: all designers agreed that the language enhances team communication, supports the comparison of different designs, and helps maintain the overall consistency of the instruction.

That study represents a first step in the evaluation of E²ML, and also, thanks to the evaluation framework it proposes, in the evaluation of design languages in general. This track is positively followed by Boot, Nelson & De Faveri in this handbook (Chapter XVIII). On this point much is yet to be done not only by researchers, but also by practitioners: if "the proof of the pudding is in the eating," the proof of a language is in the happiness of its users.

Costs

Adopting a new design language is an investment: the resources spent to learn it and to deploy it in the design practice should be balanced by a measurable return in terms of quality or revenue. Determining the overall costs derived from the adoption of a design language is a though challenge (Botturi, 2004), as languages are not tools

in the same sense as software applications are, as their cognitive impact is much broader. As anyone who has learned more than one foreign language knows, each language has a different learning curve, depending on its relationship with the speaker's native language, her or his predisposition, willingness to learn it, etc.

These issues would deserve a whole book, but to the purposes of this chapter, some figures about the case study reported above might do the work and provide concrete and useful indications, along with what has already been said about teaching E²ML, to interested readers.

The road taken by E²ML is simplicity: it is an essential language, studied in order to flatten the learning curve as much as possible, and to reduce the overhead costs for the production of documentation. The design of the Games and Education workshop was based on a previous experience that was condensed in a short (one page) textual instructional plan. Its development to its final form, when all E²ML documents were finalized, took a whole day of work, excluding the production of teaching materials. How much of that time was devoted to creating E²ML diagrams? The production of the sketches reported in this chapter took about 1 hour, but it would be incorrect to say that the overhead of using E²ML is 1/8 of the design time. Without the language, it would have simply been *another* design, another game with different rules. A design language is not a tool that can merely be applied over a design process, but can act as a catalyst that, in a favorable environment, engenders a new way of doing design.

CONCLUSION

E²ML was conceived as a flexible visual language suitable for pencil-and-paper design with the goal of fostering creativity and smoothen team communication. The chapter presented the structure of the language, articulated in overview diagrams and action diagrams through a case study, and then reprised its main elements in a more analytical way. The idea of flexibility behind the language was discussed, and some issues concerning its integration in the design process and its evaluation and costs were presented.

The quality of a tool is its adequacy to a problem-solving activity for its users. While design languages are an acquired tool and a sort of natural habit in several disciplines, in ID they are now in the first part of the diffusion curve that could be on the verge of growing. Future data about the use of E²ML, or of other languages, both for doing instructional design and for teaching novice instructional designers, will tell what will happen next.

The main assumption behind E²ML is that a visual language may foster creativity and enhance communication. Creativity and communication are two important keys for the quality of designs, and better designs mean increased instructional quality, thus allowing more people to learn better.

REFERENCES

Anderson, L. W., & Krathwohl, D. R. (2001). *A taxonomy for learning, teaching and assessing. A revision of Bloom's taxonomy of educational objectives*. New York: Addison Wesley Longman.

Bates, T. W. (1999). *Managing technological change*. San Francisco: Jossey-Bass.

Belfer, K., & Botturi, L. (2003). Pedagogical patterns for online learning. *Proceedings of the World Conference on E-Learning in Corporate, Government, Healthcare and Higher Education ELEARN,* Phoenix, Arizona, (pp.881-884).

Belfer, K., & Botturi, L. (2004). *Online learning design with pedagogical patterns*. Paper presented at the SALT Orlando Conference 2004, Orlando, Florida, USA.

Bolchini, D., & Paolini, P. (2006). Interactive dialogue model: A design technique for multichannel applications. *IEEE Transactions on Moltumedia, 8*(3), 529-542.

Botturi, L. (2003). *E²ML: Educational Environments Modeling Language*. Unpublished doctoral dissertation. Lugano, Switzerland: University of Lugano. Retrieved online on January 15th, 2007 from http://www.rero.ch

Botturi, L. (2004). Visualizing learning goals with the quail model. *Australasian Journal of Educational Technologies—AJET, 20*(2), 248-273.

Botturi, L. (2005). Visual languages for instructional design: An evaluation of the perception of E²ML. *Journal of Interactive Learning Research, 16*(4), 329-351

Botturi, L. (2006). E²ML. A visual language for the design of instruction. *Educational Technologies Research & Development, 54*(3), 265-293.

Botturi, L. (2006 b). Design models as emergent features: An empirical study in communication and shared mental models in instructional design. *Canadian Journal of Learning Technologies, 31*(2), 119-148.

Botturi, L., Derntl, M., Boot, E., & Figl, K. (2006). A classification framework for educational modeling languages in instructional design. *Proceedings of IEEE ICALT 2006*, Kerkrade, the Netherlands, (pp. 1216-1220).

De Vries, F. (n.d.). EML 1.0. Retrieved on October 4, 2006 from http://dspace.learningnetworks.org/handle/1820/81

Derntl, M., & Botturi, L. (2006). Essential use cases for pedagogical patterns. *Computer Science Education, 16*(2) 137-156 [special issue on pedagogical patterns].

Gibbons, A. S. (2003). What and how designers design? A theory of design structure. *TechTrends, 47*(5), 22-27.

Greer, M. (1991). Organizing and managing the instructional design process. In L.J. Briggs, K.L. Gustafson, & M.H. Tillman (Eds.), *Instructional design: Principles and applications* (2nd ed., pp. 315-343). Englewood Cliffs, NJ: Educational Technology.

IMS (n.d.). Learning design specification. Retrieved online on October 4, 2006, from http://www.imsproject.org/learningdesign/index.html

Merrill, M.D. (1983). Component display theory. In C.M. Reigeluth (Ed.), *Instructional-Design Theories and Models: An Overview of Their Current Status* (vol. 1, pp. 279-333). Hillsdale, NJ: Lawrence Erlbaum Associates.

Szabo, M. (2002). Competencies for educators. In H .H. Adelsberger, B. Collis, & J. M. Pawlowsky (Eds.), *Handbook on information technologies for education and training* (pp. 381-397). Berlin, Germany: Springer.

Chapter VIII
The MOT+Visual Language for Knowledge–Based Instructional Design

Gilbert Paquette
Télé-université Université du Quebec à Montréal, Canada

Michel Léonard
Télé-université Université du Quebec à Montréal, Canada

Karin Lundgren-Cayrol
Télé-université Université du Quebec à Montréal, Canada

ABSTRACT

This chapter states and explains that a learning design is the result of a knowledge engineering process where knowledge and competencies, learning design, media and delivery models are constructed in an integrated framework. Consequently, we present our MOT+ general graphical language and editor that help construct structured interrelated visual models. The MOT+LD editor is the newly added specialization of this editor for learning designs, producing IMS-LD compliant Units of Learning. The MOT+OWL editor is another specialization of the general visual language for knowledge and competency models based on the OWL specification. We situate both models within our taxonomy of knowledge models respectively as a multi-actor collaborative process and a domain theory. The association between these "content" models and learning design components is seen as the essential task in an instructional design methodology, to guide the construction of high quality learning environments.

INTRODUCTION

Building high quality learning designs is a very important and demanding task. It is also a difficult task that we started to address already a decade ago by progressively building an instructional engineering method (Paquette et al., 1994, 2005a; Paquette, 2003), a delivery system (Paquette et al., 2005b) and a graphical knowledge modeling editor (Paquette, 1996, 2002).

In this on-going work and for the present discussion, the point of view is taken that a learning design is the result of a knowledge engineering process, where knowledge and competencies, learning design, media and delivery models are constructed in an integrated framework. In the first section of this chapter, we present the MISA[1] instructional design method based on these four models and their relationships to each other. The second section presents the MOT (modeling with object types) visual language and the specialized editing tools that have been used in numerous applications. We summarize the theoretical basis of the language, its syntax and semantic. Moreover examples within the MISA instructional design method will be presented.

The third and fourth sections address the standardization issues and how the MOT+ software is adapted to provide visual aid to designers building knowledge and/or pedagogical models. The third section focuses on the learning design models, the IMS-LD specification and the specialized MOT+LD editor that helps designers build IMS-LD compliant and interoperable units of learning. The fourth section presents the ontology web language (OWL) and the specialized MOT+OWL visual editor. We use it to represent domain knowledge models and target competency that can be used to plan, support staff roles and evaluate the quality of learning designs. In the fifth section we discuss the association between LD models and OWL models to support what we believe is the central task for knowledge-based instructional design aiming to support learning environments within the Semantic Web.

Finally, the concluding section will summarize the properties of representation languages that we have found most useful while designing and using the various specializations of the MOT+ software through its evolution from a general knowledge modeling tool to a standardized tool at the heart of the instructional design methodology.

INSTRUCTIONAL DESIGN BASED ON VISUAL MODELING

In this section, we present a synthesis of the MISA 4.0 instructional engineering method main

components and concepts. A knowledge modeling approach using the MOT editor was used to define the instructional engineering method itself, its concepts, processes and principles. And thus, this method can also be seen as a visual modeling application.

This R&D initiative, started in 1992, has led to the MISA 4.0 version (Paquette, 2001a, 2002a) and to its support tool, called ADISA[2] (Paquette et al., 2001). The editor MOT+ is embedded in the ADISA system and accessible through a Web browser from workstations linked to the Internet. It can also be used without ADISA together with forms provided by the MISA documentation. Since 2001, the method has been adapted to the huge standardization work that has occurred in the e-learning sector; we will address this aspect in later sections of this chapter.

Overview of the Method

The MISA learning engineering process produces specifications of learning environment grouped in documents called documentation elements (DE). Table 1 presents these DEs.

Each DE results from tasks distributed into six phases. Within phase 2, 3, 4 and 6, these DE can also be viewed according to four axes or dimensions of an e-learning environment: knowledge, pedagogy, media and delivery. Presently, MISA 4.0 comprises 35 basic sub-tasks, each producing one DE, numbered, as shown in table 1, from 100 to 640. The first digit denotes the phase, the second, the axis, and the third, the sequence number within the axis. A DE is either a visual model, identified in bold italic in table 1, or a text-based form describing guidelines for a model or properties of objects in the model.

MISA proposes a a problem solving approach in 6 phases. Each MISA phase is subdivided into a number of steps where parts of a learning environment or system are constructed. These phases are sequential, but spiral, with frequent returns to modify the result or previous tasks:

Table 1. MISA 4.0 documentation elements: Phases and axes

Phase 1: Definition	100 Organization's Training System 102 Training Objectives 104 Learners' properties 106 Present Situation 108 Reference Documents			
	Knowledge Axis	Pedagogy Axis	Media Axis	Delivery Axis
Phase 2: Initial solution	210 Knowledge Model Orientation Principles *212 Knowledge Model* 214 Target Competencies	220 Instructional Principles *222 Learning Events Network* 224 Learning Unit Properties	230 Media Principles	240 Delivery Principles 242 Cost-Benefit Analysis
Phase 3: LE architecture	*310 Learning Unit Content*	*320 Learning Scenarios* 322 Activity Properties	330 Development Infrastructure	340 Delivery Planning
Phase 4: LE detailed Design	410 Learning Resource Content	420 Learning Resource Properties	430 Learning Resource List *432 Learning Resource Models* 434 Media Elements 436 Source Doc.	*440 Delivery Models* 442 Actors and their resources 444 Tools and Telecommunication 446 Delivery Services
Phase 5: Validation	540 Test Planning	542 Revision Decision Log		
Phase 6: Delivery Plan	610 Knowledge/Competency Management	620 Actors and Group Management	630 Learning System/Resource Management	640 Maintenance/Quality Management

- **Phase 1:** Designers build a description of the training problem, its context and constraints. The general goal that the solution must fulfill and the main characteristics of the target population are the most important aspects to address at this point.
- **Phase 2:** Designers define a preliminary training solution, centered on a knowledge model for the learning domain. Prerequisite and target competencies are associated to the most important knowledge entities in the model. In this phase, designers also build a first pedagogical visual model called "the learning event network" grouping the main modules or learning units, their sequencing and the resources needed to perform them or to be produced by learners and facilitators.
- **Phase 3:** Designers construct a detailed learning design and specify the infrastructure necessary. Visual learning scenarios are built for each learning unit defined in phase 2, describing the learning and facilitating activities, the actors that perform them and the resources needed or produced by

these actors. At the same time, a sub-model of the phase 2 knowledge model is associated with each learning unit thus defining "the learning unit content." According to the evolution of the design, media and delivery principles are refined to prepare the next phase.
- **Phase 4:** Centered on the learning resources and delivery models and the properties of objects in these models several professionals may work on the initial design of a learning environment (LE). Another important concurrent task is the description of the properties of resources in learning scenarios and the association of a sub-model of the knowledge model to provide a specification of the "learning resource content."
- **Phase 5:** The project manager plans the validation of the learning environment and produces a list of possible revisions and decisions about how to improve the specifications created in the previous phases.
- **Phase 6:** Designers and project manager prepare elements necessary to the delivery of the learning environment. They produce a

synthetic and global description of the learning environment for its maintenance and quality management by various actors.

A Visual Modeling Approach

In each of phases 2, 3, 4 and 6, MISA also proposes the development of the learning environment along four axes: knowledge and competency (content model), instructional, resources and delivery. The central product of each axis is one or more visual models.

The *knowledge model* centers on a graphical representation of the learning environment content domain. In this model, the domain's facts, concepts, procedures and principles are displayed and interrelated with precise links. Then, target and prerequisite competencies are linked to knowledge elements in the model, thus identifying prerequisites and learning objectives for the pedagogical model. Subsequently, knowledge units and competencies are also associated to learning units and to the resources present in the learning units' scenario models.

The *instructional model* is essentially a visual network of learning events and units, to which knowledge and target competencies are associated. Each learning unit is also described by a visual learning scenario specifying learning and support activities linked to resources in the environment. Resources holding content (as opposed to tools and services) are associated with a subset in the knowledge model.

The *learning resource models* are useful to describe materials (or learning objects) to be adapted and produced, their media components, source documents and presentation principles as well as other properties aimed at graphical designers and learning material producers.

Finally, *delivery models* are produced to show how and where actors use or provide learning materials and resources such as tools, communication means, services and locations, used in the learning environment. Each delivery model is a multi-user workflow, where actors use or produce

resources, while assuming different roles. These processes address organizational issues, such as group organization, staff assignments, technical help, resource delivery, and so on, which must be prepared to ensure smooth deployment of a network-based or a distance learning environment.

Each and every one of these models is built using the MOT+ knowledge representation technique and tool (Paquette, 1999, 2002b). Graphical visual models are the basic DEs in each axis, the backbone of the MISA method. Most of the other tasks, in MISA, describe properties of objects in these models (e.g., competencies, learning units, resources, roles) as well as their relationships.

MOT+: A GENERIC VISUAL LANGUAGE AND TOOL

When designers start building a learning environment, two basic questions arise: "Which knowledge must be acquired, what are the target competencies or educational objectives for that knowledge?" and "How should the activities and the resources be organized to best achieve knowledge and competency acquisition?" To help designers solve this type of questions, we have developed a graphical knowledge modeling method and tools, which help visualizing activity sequences, actors and tools. In this section, we present the MOT modeling language that serves that purpose and the MOT+ visual modeling editor.

The graphic or visual representation formalism that we present here (Paquette, 1996; Paquette, 2002) has been tested for the past 10 years in a vast array of modeling applications and in many various contexts. It is used by trainers for corporate training, and designers or professors use it to prepare university courses or to propose modeling exercises to their students. It has served to model processes for the implementation of a computer-supported high school, or to model instructional methods or research projects processes.

Basis for a Graphical Knowledge Representation Language

It is often said that a picture is worth a thousand words. That is true of sketches, diagrams, and graphs used in various fields of knowledge. *Conceptual maps* are widely used in education to represent and clarify complex relationships between concepts. *Flowcharts* are graphical representations of procedural knowledge or algorithms. *Decision trees* are another form of representation used in various fields, particularly in decision-making expert systems.

All these representation methods are useful at an informal level, as thinking aids and tools for the communication of ideas, but they also have their limitations. One is the imprecise meaning of the links in a model. Another issue is the ambiguity around the type of entities or symbol system that is used. Objects, actions on objects and statements of properties about them are all mixed-up, which make graph interpretation a fuzzy and risky business. Another difficulty is to combine more than one representation in the same model. For example, concepts used in procedural flowcharts as entry, intermediate or terminal objects could be given a more precise meaning by developing them in conceptual sub-models of the procedure. The same is true of procedures present in conceptual models that could be developed as procedural sub-models described by flowcharts, combined or not with decision trees.

In software engineering, many graphic representation formalisms have been or are used such as entity-relationship models (Chen, 1976), conceptual graphs (Sowa, 1964), the object modeling technique (OMT) (Rumbaugh, Blaha, Premerlani, Eddy, & Lorensen, 1991), KADS (Schreiber, Wielinga, & Breuker, 1993) or the unified modeling language (UML) (Booch, Jacobson, & Rumbaugh, 1999). These representation systems have been built for the analysis and architectural design of complex information systems. The most recent ones require the use of up to eight different kinds of model, which rapidly become hard to follow without considerable expertise.

Our initial goals were different. We needed a graphic representation system that was both simple enough to be used by educational specialists, such as teachers, professors and tutors, who are not, in general, computer scientists, still general and powerful enough to represent the components and their relationships of computer-based educational environments.

There is a consensus in educational science to distinguish four basic types of knowledge entities (facts, concepts, procedure and principles), despite some diversity in terminology and definitions. See for example, the work of Merrill (1994), Romiszowski (1981), Tennyson and Rash (1988), and West, Farmer, and Wolf (1991). This categorization is retained as the basis for the MOT graphic representation language.

All four types of knowledge are also considered in the framework of schema theory. The concept of schema is the essential idea behind the shift from behaviourism to cognitivism, the now dominant theory in psychology and other cognitive sciences, based on the pioneering ideas of Inhelder and Piaget (1958) as well as Bruner (1973). In the early seventies, Newell and Simon (1972) developed, on the same basis, a rule-based representation of the human problem solving procedural activity, while Minski (1975) defined the concept of "frame" as the essential element to understand perception, and also to reconcile the declarative and procedural views of knowledge.

Schemas play a central role in knowledge construction and learning (Holoyak, 1991; Anderson et al., 1995). They defined perception as an active, constructive and selective process. They support memorization skills seen as processes to search, retrieve or create appropriate schemas to store new knowledge. They describe understanding as a comparison of existing schema with new information. Globally, through all these processes, learning is seen as a schema transformation enacted by higher order processes, aiming at schema construction and reconstruction through interaction with the physical, personal or social world, instead of a simple transfer of information from one individual to another.

The distinction between conceptual and procedural schema has been accepted for a long time in cognitive science. More recently, a third category called "conditional or strategic schema" has been proposed (Paris, Lipson, & Wixson, 1983). These schemas have a component that specifies the context and the conditions to trigger a set of actions or procedures, or to assign values to the attributes of a concept. These categories map very well on the existing consensus in educational science.

The MOT Visual Modeling Language

We will now present briefly the syntax and semantic of the MOT visual modeling language, based on the notion of schema. Here, we could use graphs similar to UML object models to represent the attributes that describe a schema with different formats according to their type. In the MOT graphic language (Paquette, 1996, Paquette, 1999, Paquette, 2003), we have improved the readability and the user-friendliness of graphs by externalizing the internal attributes of a schema into other objects, with proper links to the original schema or object. For example, the link between the schemas "Triangle" and the "Rectangle Triangle" is shown explicitly on Figure 1 using a specialization (S) link from the later to the former concept. Links between the "Triangle" concept and its sides or angles attributes is externalized using a composition (C) link. The links from an input concept to a procedure and from a procedure to one of its products are both shown by an input/product (IP) link. The sequencing between actions (procedures) and/or conditions (principles) in a procedure is represented by a precedence (P) link. Finally, the relation between a principle and a concept that it constrains, or between a principle and a procedure that it controls, are represented by a regulation link (R).

Figure 1. A simple MOT model

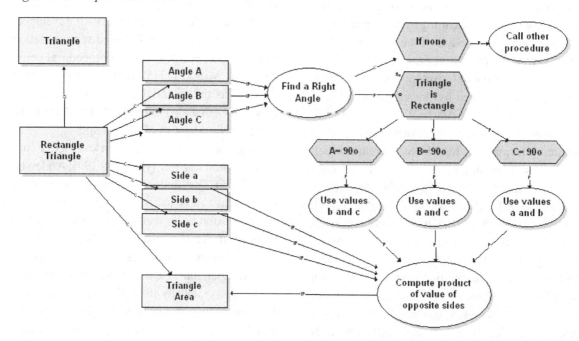

Using these links, the triangle concepts are arranged in the MOT model of Figure 1 where relations between knowledge entities are transparent, mixing the types of entities and links.

Concepts (or classes of objects), *procedures* (or classes of actions) and *principles* (or classes of statements, properties or rules) are the primitive objects of the MOT graphical language. The type of the objects are represented by geometrical figures as shown on Figure 2, where each class or individual is represented by a name within the Figure.

These objects are different types of schema whose attributes are all explicitly externalized and related to other schemas using six kinds of typed links constrained by the following grammar rules:

1. All abstract knowledge units (concepts, procedures, principles) can be related by an instantiation **I** link to a set of facts representing individuals called respectively examples, traces and statements.

2. All abstract knowledge units can be specialized or generalized to other abstract knowledge using specialization **S** links.

3. All abstract knowledge units can be decomposed, using **C** links into other entities, generally of the same type.

4. Procedures and principles can be sequenced together using **P** links.

5. Concepts can be inputs to a procedure using an **IP** link to the procedure, or products of a procedure using an IP link from the procedure.

6. Principles can regulate, using **R** links, any procedure to provide an "external" control structure, to constrain a concept or a set of concepts by a relation between them, or to regulate a set of other principles, for example to decide on conditions of their application.

Figure 3 summarizes these grammar rules of the MOT graphic language in the form of an abstracted graph where the entities represent types of MOT objects.

There are various possible semantic interpretations of these graphic symbols.

*   **Concepts** can be object classes (countries, clothes, vehicles, etc.), types of documents (forms, booklets, images, etc.), tool categories: (text editors, televisions, etc.), groups of people (doctors, Europeans, etc.), or event classes (floods, conferences, etc.).
*   **Procedures** can be generic operations (add numbers, assemble an engine, etc.), tasks categories (complete a report, supervise a production, etc.), activities (take an exam, teach a course, etc.), instructions (follow a recipe, assemble a device, etc.) or scenarios (of a film, of a meeting, of a learning module).
*   **Principles** can state properties of objects (cars have four wheels), constraints on procedures (the tasks must be completed within 20 days), cause/effect relationships (if it rains more than 25 days, the crop will be in jeopardy), laws (any metal sufficiently

Figure 2. Types of knowledge units in MOT

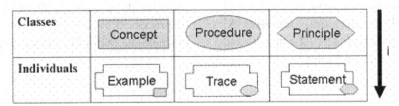

Figure 3. The MOT metamodel

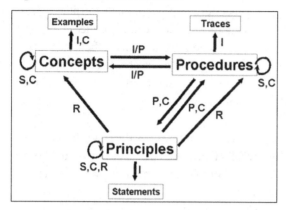

heated will stretch out), theories (the laws of the market economy); rules of decision (advising on an investment), prescriptions (medicinal treatment, instructional design principles), etc.

The MOT+ Graphic Editor

With this set of primitive graphic symbols, it has been possible to build graphic models, from simple to complex representations of structured knowledge. For example, we can build representations equivalent to conceptual maps, flowcharts (iterative procedures) and decision trees, and also other types of models useful for educational modeling such as processes, methods and theories. All these types of models have been used in a number of projects since the first publication of the MOT editor in 1998, and also in the last 5 years with its extension to MOT+. Figure 4 presents examples of the main MISA visual models constructed with the MOT editor.

Figure 4a presents an example of a knowledge model that describes part of the knowledge in the domain of artificial intelligence (AI) for an introductory Web-based course on that subject designed with MISA. Here ovals represent AI processes, rectangles represent AI concepts and hexagons represent AI principles.

Figure 4b presents a example of a *Pedagogical model* representing a learning scenario model for one the course modules where learning activities are represented as procedures (ovals) and learning resources as concept/object (rectangles).

Figure 4c presents an example of a *Media model* representing the structure of a Web site for the course. Concepts represent Web pages or page elements, ovals or circles represent hyperlinks, as possible actions or procedures. Templates are represented by principles. Facts represent concrete object such as page elements with their actual texts, pictures or other resources.

Figure 4d presents an example of a *Delivery model* representing the course delivery process where actors are represented as control principles, acting on tasks represented as procedures, each having input and output resources.

This first version of the MOT editor has been extended to the MOT+ editor, a mature editor with advanced graphic editing capabilities (fonts, color, disposition on a page, etc.). Sub-models can be embedded at any depth and knowledge objects in each one can be displayed in a multi-layer mode. Models may be filtered in order to display only some types of knowledge objects or links. Sub-models from one model can be associated to objects in another model called a co-domain, which is very useful for example to assign knowledge to activities in a pedagogical model. Graphic objects can be associated to any type of document (using the OLE standard) such as a text document, slide presentation, Web page, spreadsheet or database file, which can be displayed by clicking on the graphic symbol. MOT+ has extensive export facilities to XML, HTML, Excel and other commonly used formats. In particular, the "export to XML" command provides the possibility for graphic models to be processed by software agents respecting for example the IMS LD or OWL schemas.

Figure 4a. A knowledge model

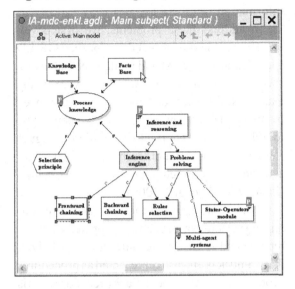

Figure 4b. A pedagogical model

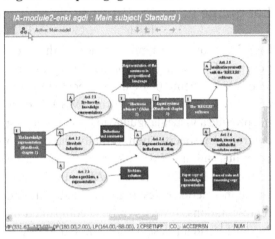

Figure 4c. A media model

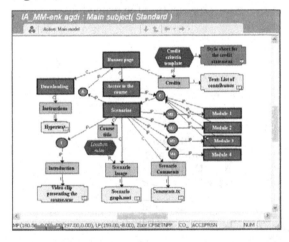

Figure 4d. A delivery model

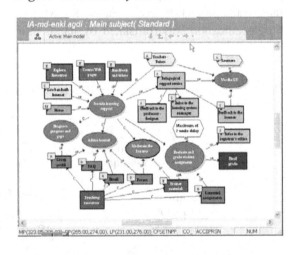

REPRESENTING MULTI-ACTOR WORKFLOWS AND LEARNING DESIGNS

In the two following sections, we address the issues of the standardization of visual modeling languages, to promote the reusability of educational models and the interoperability between systems delivering learning environments. With the advent of an educational modeling standard specification like IMS-LD, we decided to develop a specialization of MOT+ to represent the IMS-LD concepts. During the eduSource and LORNET (www.lornnet.org) projects, we found that this specification was closely related to the MISA pedagogical model including some aspects of the MISA delivery model. This R&D and the extension to a Web-based graphical editor are presented in the following sections.

The MOT+LD Special Visual Language

IMS-LD provides a representation of the components of a learning environment in a standardized XML schema that can be executed by any compliant e-Learning platform. IMS-LD does not provide a visual language to build a learning environment specification. Initially, these had to be built using an XML editor or a form-based editor like RELOAD (2005). Also, IMS-LD is not an instructional design method to build such representations. It needs to be accompanied by any instructional design method, and MISA is more closely related than many other methods. Unfortunately, the MOT+ pedagogical models built in MISA are not executable on a variety of platforms because they are not standardized. In fact, in the projects where we have used MISA, the specification was translated by hand, into the platform's activity editor, with some loss of information.

To address these problems, we first developed a graphic modeling editor for the IMS-LD specification (level A) and made it available as a specialized editor in the MOT+ software. Many examples of learning designs have been produced by different groups using this editor. They can be found at the IDLD portal (www.idld.org). Figure 5 shows part of a unit of learning (UoL) on solar astronomy presented recently at a workshop (Paquette & Léonard, 2006).

It shows an act and its activity structure containing various learning and support activities, all represented as MOT procedures (ovals). Method, plays, and acts are also represented as procedures in other parts of the model. Each procedure type is indicated by a little label at the right lower corner of the ovals representing the procedures.

Figure 5. An example of a MOT+LD learning design

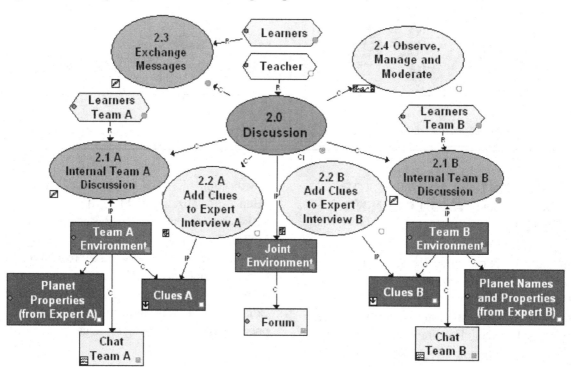

Similarly, roles are represented by different kinds of MOT principles (hexagons). Environments, learning objects, services and outcomes are represented by different kinds of MOT concepts (rectangles). Standard MOT links are used between these objects. C (is composed of), P (precede), R (regulate or govern) and I/P (input / product) links are sufficient to cover all the components of a standard IMS-LD level A learning design.

The MOT+LD editor is presented with some detail in (Paquette, Léonard, Lundgren-Cayrol, Mihaila & Gareau, 2006). It enables a designer to build graphically a compliant IMS-LD model. Afterwards, the graph is automatically validated and exported as an instance of the IMS-LD XML schema. This XML file can be read in form-based IMS-LD editors such as RELOAD (2005), if level B conditions and or level C notifications need to be specified. The XML can then be run by IMS-LD compliant players or platforms to deliver online learning sessions to their users.

Paquette and Marino (2005) briefly discuss the strengths and weaknesses of the IMS-LD educational modeling specification. One weakness is the absence of knowledge representation, which is central to learning and knowledge management that we seek to support by the TELOS[3] system. We have proposed to improve that by the semantic annotation of the activities, resources and roles included in a learning design. A *semantic annotation* is a mapping from a subject matter ontology to the learning design that associates knowledge elements to the components of the design. This aspect will be developed in the following sections.

Extending the MOT+LD Editor

Another aspect of IMS-LD we need to improve is the control structure of the workflow that is actually covered by level B and C specifications, where properties and conditions can be included in the design to alter the flow of activities, notify an actor or present a resource depending on previous actions or results stored in a user and group file or model. This aspect may not be that important in open learning environments where a total or large degree of liberty is left to the learner and facilitators, but for a business workflow in an organization, or to aggregate software components into larger resources, it is an important dimension.

To address that and provide a basis to build a function editor for the TELOS system, conceptual work on function maps has been defined as a central piece of the TELOS architecture (Rosca, 2005; Paquette, Rosca, Mihaila, & Masmoudi, 2006). Moreover, a comparative analysis has been made between business workflows, IMS-LD learning designs and function maps (Marino et al., 2006), leading to the identification of 21 control situations for workflows encountered in software engineering literature (Correal & Marino, 2006). It was found that IMS-LD covers only some of these control situations, but probably the most useful ones for pedagogical design.

Based on this work and the actual MOT+LD editor, we are in the process of designing a new visual editor. The *scenario Editor* aims both to generalize IMS-LD and to capture the main aspects of business workflows. The graphs produced by this editor will be executable, providing interfaces for concrete actors to enact the activities and use the resources during delivery. It will also serve to orchestrate actors, activities and other resources, a fundamental principle built in to the TELOS system. A specialization of the scenario editor is being defined to cover all three levels of the IMS-LD specification.

The scenario editor uses four kinds of MOT objects with subtypes taken from the TELOS technical ontology (Magnan & Paquette, 2006). These are shown on Figure 6. *Concept* symbols represent all kinds of resources: documents, tools, semantic resources, environments, resource-actors, resource-activities and datatypes. *Procedure* symbols represent function models composed of

Figure 6. Scenario editor symbols

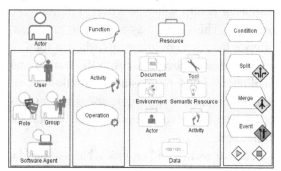

activities and commonly used operation templates. Finally, *principles* are used both to represent different types of actors (as control agents) and control conditions. These two kinds of control entities are represented here by different symbols. The actor's symbols are active agents representing users, groups, roles or software agents that enact the activities using and producing resources as planned by the scenario model. Conditions are control element inserted within the basic flow to decide on the following activities that can be activated.

In Figure 7, we see a combination of some of these symbols where a coordinator writes the plan of a document in a first activity, after which the Figure shows a general split condition. After that,

these activities are executed in parallel, controlled by the properties of the split condition object. Later on, the flow of activities merges through the merge condition object the assemble activity takes control. This activity will wait for some or all of the incoming flows to be activated before it is executed, again based on the properties of the merge condition object.

Figure 8 shows another kind of condition that alters the flow of execution. In activity-2, if the time-event condition is met, the flow of control will change. Depending on the type of the condition, the activity-4 will be shown or hidden. Activity-3 is still available. If activity-4 is shown and completed, then activity-5 can be performed.

Properties of the event condition symbol will provide the details on the condition and action parts of the control principle to provide the execution engine with a clear formal definition of the processing to take place.

In the scenario editor, we see a combination of a control flow and a data flow. The control flow is modeled using the MOT basic P and R links. P links indicates the basic sequence or flow of activities. R linked conditions identify which activities an event will trigger, thus altering the basic flow.

Figure 7. A simple scenario model

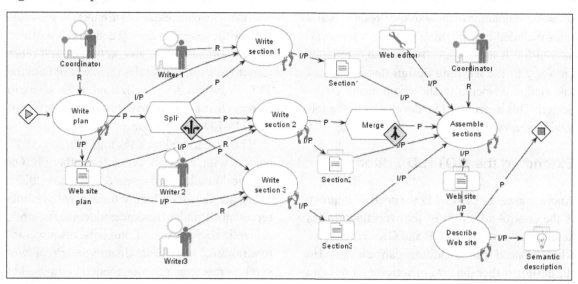

IP links from MOT serve to model the data flow, either from resources to activities where they are consulted, used or processed , or from activities to the resources they help produce. This is why we need to distinguish between actors as active control entities and resource-actors that will serve as data providers or be products of an activity (e.g. a new person of software agent added in a system). A similar distinction is made for resource-activities that can be seen as resources to be transformed, for example by other activities creating or modifying their description.

C links from MOT may also be used to show the composition of an entity into other entities. A new unification, U link, is also necessary to guide the execution engine, when components are aggregated and outputs from one need to be connected with the inputs of another.

In TELOS, the scenario editor will enable engineers to combine resources into larger aggregates, technologist to built platform workflows for designers of learning or knowledge management environments, designers to build courses, work flows or learning /teaching scenarios.

MOT+OWL: A STANDARDIZED ONTOLOGY EDITOR

In the first section we identified the pedagogical and the knowledge models as the most important

Figure 8. Event-based control

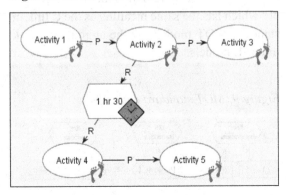

ones. We now proceed with a second standardization task, that of the knowledge model. Any type of knowledge representation, including text-based narratives or informal graphic models, can be used to describe a domain of study. At the initial stage of design, the informal nature of an ontology representation is useful. The user's mind must be free to choose any representation that seems best suited for the educational project to be considered. Still, this very freedom does not facilitate the software processing of the representation.

Semi-formal modeling languages like MOT go part of the way to address this. Unlike informal graphs built with any graphic editor, such as PowerPoint, the MOT graphic syntax is structured and has a general unambiguous semantic. Using the MOT editor, models can be exported in many formats, including a native XML schema. Using this schema, software agents can perform different kinds of processing. Still, some ambiguity remains. In instructional engineering applications, we had to constrain the MOT graphic language even more to enable the delivery of learning scenarios in a digitized platform like Explor@-2 (Paquette, 2001). Even then, part of the transfer of the design to the delivery platform had to be done manually, to prevent enforcing unnatural graphic representations on the designers.

The Ontology Web Language

To deliver computer-based learning environments, after a phase where informal graphic design has cleared up ideas, we need to move from informal or semi-formal graphs to formal computable graphic representations. Knowledge in a subject domain can be represented in many ways: taxonomies, thesauri, topic maps, conceptual graphs and ontologies.

We have selected to use OWL-DL ontologies (see W3C, 2004) for a number or reasons. It is one of the three ontology Web languages that are part of the growing stack of World Wide Web consortium recommendations related to the

Semantic Web. Of these three languages, OWL-DL has a wide expressivity and its foundation in descriptive logic guarantees its computational completeness and decidability. *Descriptive Logic* (Baader, Calvanese, Nardi, Patel-Schneider, 2003), is an important knowledge representation formalism unifying and giving a logical basis to the well known traditions of frame-based systems, semantic networks, object-oriented representations, semantic data models, and formal specification systems. It thus provides an interesting framework to represent knowledge for which a growing number of processing agents are built throughout the world.

OWL-DL provides a precise XML schema but no graphic representation per se. Some ontology editors like PROTÉGÉ (2006), provide some graphical views of the ontology, but the construction of an ontology is essentially form-based. Our goal was to provide a complete formal graphic representation of the OWL-DL that could combine the virtues of interactive construction with the computational capabilities of a formal graphic representation.

The MOT+OWL Visual Language

In the context of the MOT representation system, ontologies, in particular OWL-DL constructs, correspond to a category of models called theories. Ontologies can thus theoretically be modeled graphically using the MOT syntax. While doing this, we found out that while the MOT primitive objects and links were sufficient to represent ontologies expressed in OWL-DL, the graphs would become cumbersome unless new symbols were added. We have thus specialized the MOT language and graphic editor by adding sub-types for concepts, principles and facts and by adding new links.

Table 2 gives a few examples of the MOT+OWL graphic elements with their interpretation in descriptive logic and their correspondence to standard OWL-DL XML schema fragments. See Paquette and Rogozan (2006) for a complete de-

scription of the MOT+OWL graphic language.

Three types of MOT entities are sufficient to represent OWL-DL models. Concepts represent classes, principles represent properties and facts represent individuals. On these graphic entities, icons are added corresponding to axioms or principles stating a property of the class. We also added some new special links to express things like equivalent "equi" or disjoint "disj" classes stating properties of two classes or two properties.

In the standard MOT syntax, these icons or special links would be expressed by principles with "R" links to classes or properties. For example, in the second and the two last examples of Table 2, the following standard graphs (Figure 9) are equivalent, with the same precise OWL-DL interpretation as XML schema components. These would of course make the graphs more difficult to read.

Using a limited set of graphic symbols, we can formally describe any semi-formal MOT model that is amenable to a representation in descriptive logic. This is obviously the case for most conceptual models, laws and theory models. However, this is less evident in the case of procedural models, sometimes called task ontologies. Procedural and process/methods models are important for our purpose because learning environments are built around multi-actor processes.

Figure 10 presents a MOT+OWL visual graph that translates the conceptual structure of a learning design presented in the IMS-LD information model (2003). In the Figure, "C" properties (green hexagons) are an abbreviation for "is-composed-of" which has the same meaning as the C link in standard MOT models, or the aggregation link in UML models.

Figure 9. MOT standard equivalents

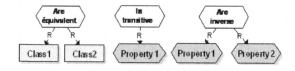

Table 2. OWL-DL equivalents

MOT+OWL graphic symbol	Description logic statements	OWL-DL XML-Schema fragment
Class1 / Class 3 / Class2 (S, S)	Class intersection $\forall x: Class3(x) \leftrightarrow Class1(x) \wedge Class2(x)$	owl:Class> <owl:intersectionOf rdf:parseType="Collection"> *List of class descriptions* </owl:intersectionOf> </owl:Class>
Class1 ←Equi→ Class2	**Equivalent classes** $\forall x: Class1(x) \leftrightarrow Class2(x)$	<owl:Class rdf:about="#name_class1"> <equivalentClass rdf:resource="#name_class2"/> </owl:Class>
Class1 ●—Disj—■ Class2	**Disjoint classes** $\forall x: Class1(x) \leftrightarrow \neg Class2(x)$	<owl:Class rdf:about="#name_classe1"> <owl:disjointWith rdf:resource="#name_classe2"/> </owl:Class>
Individual 1 / Class1 / Individual N (C, C)	Extension of a class $\forall x: Class(x) \leftrightarrow (x = Ind\ 1)$ $\vee...\vee (x = Ind\ N)$	<owl:Class> <owl:oneOf rdf:parseType="Collection"> <owl:Thing rdf:about="#name_individual1"/> <owl:Thing rdf:about="#name_individual2"/> ... <owl:Thing rdf:about="#nom_individualN"/> </owl:oneOf> </owl:Class>
Property1	Functional property $\forall x, \forall y, \forall z: Prop(x,y) \wedge Prop(x,z)) \rightarrow y=z$	<owl:FunctionalProperty rdf:about="#name_property" />
Property1	Transitive property $\forall x, \forall y, \forall z: Prop1(x,y) \wedge Prop1(y,z) \rightarrow Prop1(x,z)$	<owl:TransitiveProperty rdf:about="#name_property" />
Property1 ●INV■ Property2	**Inverse properties** $\forall x, \forall y: Prop1(x,y) \leftrightarrow Prop2(y,x)$	<owl:ObjectProperty rdf:ID="name_Property1"> <owl:inverseOf rdf:resource="#name_property2"/> </owl:ObjectProperty>

This example illustrates the fact that functional relations between components of multi-actor processes such as a learning design can be represented by ontologies. Such ontologies have been used to test, for example, the conformance of particular learning designs to the IMS-LD XML schema (Amorim, Lama, & Sanchez, 2006), and to execute them in the context of an ontology-driven system.

Associating Knowledge and Competencies to Learning Designs

We have pointed out earlier the importance of associating knowledge and competencies to the components of a learning design. This is a key element of the MISA method. Actually, in IMS-LD, the only way to describe the knowledge needed to achieve the activities or that is present in the resources is to assign optional educational objectives and prerequisites, to the unit of learning as a whole and/or to all or some of the learning activities. These can not be added to express the level of competency for a support activity carried out by a teacher or tutor. Objectives and prerequisites correspond to entry and target competencies as used in the MISA method. They are essentially unstructured pieces of text composed according to the IMS RDCEO specification (IMS 2002).

Unstructured texts are difficult to compare.

Figure 10. A simple task ontology for multi-actor scenarios[4]

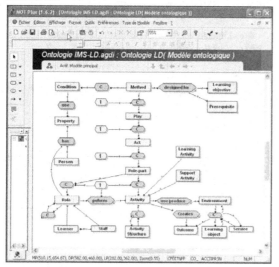

Consistency checking between different levels of the LD structure cannot be supported computationally. Even at the same level of a learning design, for example within an act, no relations exist between the content of learning activities and of the input or outcome resources, and from these to the actors' competencies. In fact, in IMS-LD the knowledge represented in learning resources is not described at all, and the actor's knowledge and competencies are only indirectly defined by their participation in learning units or activities, if, and only if, educational objectives have been associated to the activities.

What we need first is a qualitative structural representation of knowledge and competencies associated to activities, resources and roles. This can be done using domain ontologies. As a first step, the MOT+ editor allows to show side by side a learning design, using the MOT+LD editor, and a domain knowledge ontology using the MOT+OWL editor. An example is shown in Figure 4. The left hand window is the learning design presented earlier in Figure 5. The right hand window presents part of domain ontology of the solar system (that was built before Pluto was declared a quasi-planet).

A *semantic annotation* is simply a mapping from the domain ontology to the learning design that associates knowledge elements (classes, properties and individuals of the ontology) to components of the learning design.

In Figure 11, we see that data on the orbital period of planets in the solar system has been associated to a learning object in the design, which is a PowerPoint presenting this data to team A. This resource is an input to learning activity 2.1.A, but it is not the only input to this activity. There is also another resource (clues A) that gives additional information to team A, plus the chat between team members that will bring other more information to each participant. As a result, the sub-model of the ontology associated to activity 2.1A would logically correspond to the union of the sub-models of all input resources to the activity.

Finally, the Figure shows that most of the ontology model should be the subject of the discussion, since there is another team, team B that has more information to bring to the discussion using also information from input resources and in a team B chat. The larger sub-model is thus associated to the 2.0 activity structure.

This example shows how semantic annotation can help guide the construction of learning designs and to evaluate their coherence. By associating the right amount of knowledge to the different resources and activities, a designer can build a coherent design that will trigger collaboration between learners, or help a trainer decide on its intervention, or guide the actions of an intelligent tutoring system, and, in general support the evolution of the learners' competencies.

Desirable Properties in a Visual Educational Modeling Language

This chapter concludes with a discussion of the most important features and characteristics of a visual educational modeling language, which we think are the most useful and beneficial to the user.

Figure 11. An example of ontology annotation of a learning design

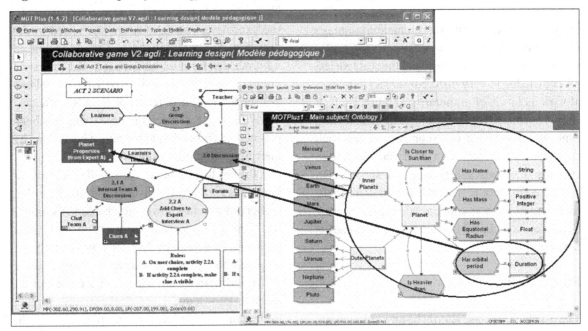

Visual

The benefits of graphical cognitive modeling have been eloquently summarized by Ausubel (1968), Dansereau (1978), Novak (1993) and Jonassen, Beissner and Yacci (1993). Graphs illustrate relationships among components of complex phenomena. They uncover the complexity of actors' interactions and make the most important parts stand out. They facilitate the communication about the reality studied. They favor the global comprehension of the phenomena under study. They help grasp the structure of related ideas by minimizing the use of ambiguous natural language texts. As an example, entity-relation graphs reduce ambiguity compared to a natural language description, but some remain on the interpretation of the terms written on the links or on the nodes. Ambiguity can be reduced further by the use of standardized typed objects and typed links.

User-Friendliness

Not all graphic modeling languages are user-friendly. A good counter-example is UML. The large number of models and symbols require considerable expertise and a steep learning time for the interpretation and for the construction of models. Furthermore, each type of model captures a different viewpoint of the information and it is impossible to mix them in the same graph to provide a global view of a subject domain. The representational system must be easy to use without technical or scientific mastery after a short period of initiation. Dansereau and Holley (1982), have studied experimentally the use of different sets of graphic symbols by learners. Their results show that typed links are preferred by the majority of learners, as long as there are not two few nor two many links and they express sufficiently different meanings.

Generality

Generality means that the representation language should have the capacity to represent, with a relatively small number of object and link categories, all knowledge in very different subject domains, at various levels of granularity and precision. It should enable, to represent simple models such as a multiplication table, up to complex models such as multi-actor workflows, rule-based knowledge systems, methods and theories. It should also embed equivalent representations to commonly used graphs such as conceptual maps, semantic networks, flowcharts, decision trees or cause/effect diagrams.

Formalizable

The graphic language should be upward compatible from informal graphs, up to semi-formal and totally unambiguous formal models. At the informal level, an integrated representation framework facilitates the organization of thought and communication between humans about the knowledge which is exchanged, all along the evolution of the graphic representation model. Here the process is more important than the result. On the other end, the graphic language makes it possible to use more constrained elements to produce totally unambiguous descriptions that can be exported to a set of symbols, such as an XML file, to be processed by computer agents. Here the model is more important than the process.

Declarative

Graphic language can be procedural or declarative. Procedural graphic languages have been built in the past; essentially extending flowcharts to promote graphical programming that would produce code directly. Our proposal is to use, as much as possible, a declarative graphic language, for a number of reasons. Firstly, it is easier for a person to declare the components of his/her

knowledge than to describe the way it should be processed. In expert systems for example, the executive instructions are not wired-in the program, but externalized and made visible in a knowledge base on which a general inference engine proceeds. Secondly, the same model can be used for many different applications, not necessarily the one for which the processing has been planned in a procedural program. This is done by querying the model using an inference engine, in a Prolog-like manner. Thirdly, the processing knowledge itself can be given declaratively, so that higher order meta-knowledge, also can be singled-out. This idea is similar to structural analysis as proposed by Scandura (1973) and it is exactly the way we should see the relation between generic skills and domain knowledge in a competency, as meta-knowledge given declaratively, applied to domain knowledge, for example, rules for diagnosing a component-based system applied to different models describing a car, a software or a learning environment.

Standardized

Standardization is an important property to support knowledge communication and use between persons or software agents. At the informal level, each model constructed by a person must be interpretable by another person. At the formal level, the communication capabilities extend to software agents. The move towards graphic versions of standards like IMS-LD for learning designs and OWL for ontologies adds wider communication capabilities between researchers and educators while at the same time adding formal non-ambiguous interpretation for machine processing.

Computability

Computability is a step beyond standardization. Not only can the graphic model receive a non-ambiguous formal representation that can be processed by computer agents, but this formal representation is complete (all conclusions are guaranteed to be computable) and decidable (all computations will finish in finite time). These considerations have motivated the construction of the MOT+OWL graphic language that is equivalent to the OWL-DL XML schema based on descriptive logic.

CONCLUSION

This chapter has presented a 10-year effort to provide an educational visual language for applications that can span form informal support to idea generation, up to structured semi-formal graphs based on typed objects and links, and finally to graphic design on the formal conceptual and specification levels (MOT+LD, MOT+OWL).

In Botturi et al. (2006), the reader can find a classification of other visual languages, some of them being presented in other chapters of this handbook. According to this classification, MOT+ has the same properties as those of UML. It qualifies as a visual, layered, formal, conceptual and specification elaboration language, with multiple perspectives.

This corresponds to our initial goal of building a virtual language that is both user-friendly for designers (compared to UML) and still general and powerful enough to enable the design of the main components of a learning system, according to standard specifications. With the development of the new scenario editor based on MOT+ concepts, we can now go a step further and provide a visual scenario programming language that can be executed by an ontology-based engine to deliver usable learning environments to its users.

REFERENCES

Amorim R., Lama, M., & Sanchez, E. (2006). Using Ontologies to model and execute IMS Learning Design Documents. In *The 6th IEE International Conference on Advanced Learning Technologies (ICALT-06)* (pp.115-116). Kerkrade: The Netherlands.

Andersson, J.R. Corbett, A.T., Koeudinger, K.R., & Pelletier, R. (1995). Cognitive tutors: Lessons learned. *The Journal of Learning Sciences, 4*(2), 167-207.

Ausubel, D.P. (1968). *Educational Psychology; A cognitive view.* New York: Rhinehart & Winston.

Baader, F., Calvanese, D., McGuinness, D., Nardi, D., & Patel-Schneider, P. (Eds.). (2003). *The description logic handbook.* Cambridge University Press.

Booch., G., Jacobson, J. & Rumbaugh, I. (1999). *The unified modeling language user guide.* Addison-Wesley.

Botturi, L., Derntl, M., Boot, E., & Figl, K. (2006) A classification framework for educational modeling languages in instructional design. In *The 6th IEEE International Conference on Advanced Learning Technologies (ICALT-06)* (pp. 1216-1220). Kerkrade: The Netherlands.

Bruner, J.S. (1973). *Beyond the information given.* New York: Norton.

Chen, P.P.S (1976).The entity-relationship model —Toward a unified view of data. *ACM Transactions on Database Systems I, 1*(1), 9-36.

Correal. D., & Marino O. (2006). *Software requirements specification document for general purpose function's editor* (Technical Report V0.4), Montréal, Canada: Télé-université LICEF Research Centre, Montreal.

Dalziel, J.R. (2005). LAMS: *Learning activity management system 2.0.* Retrieved January 22, 2007, from http://wiki.oamsfoundation.org/display/lams/Home

Dansereau, D.F., & Holley, C.D. (1982).Development and evaluation of a text mapping strategy.

In A. Flammer & W. Kintsch (Eds.), *Discourse processing*. The Netherlands: North Holland.

Dansereau D.F. (1978).The development of a learning strategies curriculum. In H. F. O'Neil Jr. (Ed.), *Learning strategies*. New York: Academic Press.

Holoyak, K.J. (1991). Symbolic connectionism: Toward third generation-theories of expertise. In K.A. Ericsson & J. Smith (Eds.), *Toward a general theory of expertise: Prospects and limits*. New York: Cambridge University Press.

IDLD (2006). *Implementation and deployment of the learning design specification portal*. Retrieved from http://www.idld.org

IMS-LD (2003). Information model, best practice and implementation guide, binding document, schemas. *IMS Learning Design*. Retrieved October 3, 2003, from http://www.imsglobal.org/learningdesign/index.cfm

Inhelder, B., & Piaget, J. (1958).*The growth of logical thinking from childhood to adolescence*. New York: Basic Books.

Jonassen D.H., Beissner K., & Yacci M. (1993). *Structural knowledge—Techniques for representing, conveying and acquiring structural knowledge*. NJ: Laurence Earlbaum Associates.

Magnan, F., & Paquette, G. (2006). TELOS: An ontology driven e-learning OS. In S. Weibelzahl & A. Cristea (Eds.), *Proceedings of the Fourth International Conference on Adaptive Hypermedia and Adaptative Web-Based Systems 2006* (pp. 131-139). Dublin, Ireland: National College of Ireland.

Marino, O., Casallas, R., Villalobos, J., Correal, D. & Contamines, J. (2006).Bridging the gap between e-learning modeling and delivery through the transformation of learnflows into workflows. In S. Pierre (Ed.) *E-Learning networked environments and architectures: A knowledge processing perspective*. Springer-Verlag.

Merrill, M.D. (1994). *Principles of instructional Design*. Englewood Cliffs, NJ: Educational Technology Publications.

Minski, M. (1975). A framework for representing knowledge. In P. H. Winston (Ed.), *The psychology of computer vision*. New York: McGraw-Hill.

Newell, A., & Simon, H. (1972). *Human problem solving*. Englewood Cliffs: NF.

Novak, J. D. (1993). How do we learn our lesson? Taking students through the process. *The Science Teacher, 60*(3), 50-55.

OMG (2006). *Business process modeling notation (BPMM)*. Retrieved on July 24, 2006, from http://www.bpmn.org/

Paquette, G. (1996). La modélisation par objets typés: une méthode de représentation pour les systèmes d'apprentissage et d'aide à la tâche. *Sciences et techniques éducatives, (4)*, 9-42

Paquette, G. (1999). Meta-knowledge Representation for learning scenarios engineering. In S. Lajoie & M. Vivet (Eds.), *Proceedings of AI-Ed'99 in AI and Education—Open learning environments*. IOS.

Paquette, G. (2001). Designing virtual learning centers. In H. Adelsberger, B. Collis, & J. Pawlowski (Eds.), *Handbook on information technologies for education & training* (pp. 249-272). Springer-Verlag.

Paquette, G. (2002). *Modélisation des connaissances et des compétences, un langage graphique pour concevoir et apprendre*. Québec, Canada: Presses de l'Université du Québec.

Paquette, G. (2002). TeleLearning systems engineering—Towards a new ISD model. *Journal of Structural Learning, 14*, 1-35.

Paquette, G. (2004). *Instructional engineering for network-based learning*. Pfeiffer/Wiley Publishing Co.

Paquette, G., Crevier F. & Aubin, C. (1994). ID knowledge in a course design workbench. *Educational Technology, 34*(9), 50-57.

Paquette, G., De la Teja, I., Léonard, M., Lundgren-Cayrol, K., & Marino, O. (2005). How to use an instructional engineering method and a modelling tool. In R. Koper & C. Tattersall (Eds.). *Learning design—A handbook on modeling and delivering networked education and training* (pp. 161-184). Springer-Verlag.

Paquette, G., & Léonard, M. (2006). The educational modeling of a collaborative game using MOT+LD. In *Proceedings of the 6th IEEE International Conference on Advanced Learning Technologies* (pp.115-116). Kerkrade, The Netherlands.

Paquette, G., Léonard, M., Lundgren-Cayrol, K., Mihaila, S. & Gareau, D. (2006, January). Learning design based on graphical knowledge-modeling. *Journal of Educational technology and Society ET&S, Special issue on Learning Design.*

Paquette, G., & Marino, O. (2005). Learning objects, collaborative learning designs and knowledge representation. *Technology, Instruction, Cognition and Learning, 3*, 85-108.

Paquette,G., Marino, O., De la Teja, I., Léonard, M., & Lundgren-Cayrol, K., (2005). Delivery of learning design: the Explor@ system's case. In R. Koper & C. Tattersall (Eds.). *Learning Design—A handbook on modelling and delivering networked education and training* (pp. 311-326). Springer Verlag.

Paquette G., Marino, O., De la Teja, I., Lundgren-Cayrol, K., Léonard, M., & Contamines (2005). Implementation and deployment of the IMS learning design specification. *Canadian Journal of Learning Technologies* (CJLT), *31*(2). Retrieved from http://www.cjlt.ca/

Paquette, G., & Rogozan, D. (2006). *Primitives de représentation OWL-DL—Correspondance avec le langage graphique MOT+OWL et le langage des prédicats du premier ordre.* TELOS documentation. Montreal, Québec: LICEF Research Center.

Paquette, G., & Rosca, I. (2004). *An ontology-based referencing of actors, operations and resources in elearning systems.* SW-EL/2004 Workshop. The Netherlands: Eindhoven.

Paquette, G., Rosca, I., Mihaila, S., & Masmoudi, A. (2007). TELOS, a service-oriented framework to support learning and knowledge management. In S. Pierre (Ed).*E-Learning networked environments and architectures: A knowledge processing perspective.* Springer-Verlag

Paris, S., Lipson, M.Y., & Wixson, K.K. (1983). Becoming a strategic reader. *Contemporary Educational Psychology, 8,* 293-311.

PROTÉGÉ, (2006). *Protégé Homepage.* Retrieved July 24, 2006 from http://protege.stanford.edu/

RELOAD (2005).*RELOAD homepage editor and player.* Retrieved July 24, 2006, from http://www.reload.ac.uk/

Romiszowski, A. J. (1981). *Designing instructional systems.* New York: Kogan Page.

Rosca, I. (2005). *TELOS conceptual architecture.* (LORNET Technical Report: 0.5.).Canada: LICEF Research Centre, Télé-université.

Rumbaugh, J., Blaha, M., Premerlani, W., Eddy, F., & Lorensen, W. (1991). *Object-oriented modelling and design.* USA: Prentice Hall.

Scandura, J.M. (1973). *Structural learning I: Theory and research.* New York: Gordon & Breach Science Publishers.

Schreiber, G., Wielinga, B., & Breuker, J. (1993). *KADS—A principled approach to knowledge-based system development.* San Diego, USA: Academic Press.

Sowa, J. F. (1984). *Conceptual structures, information processing in mind and machine.* Addison-Wesley Publishing Co.

Tennyson, R., & Rasch, M. (1988). Linking cognitive learning theory to instructional prescriptions. *Instructional Science, 17,* 369-385.

W3C (2004). *OWL overview document.* Retrieved February 10, 2004, from http://www.w3.org/TR/2004/REC-owl-features-20040210/

West, C. K., Farmer, J. A., & Wolff, P. M. (1991). *Instructional design: Implications from cognitive science.* Englewood Cliffs, NJ: Prentice Hall.

ENDNOTES

[1] **MISA:** *Méthode d'ingénierie des systèmes d'apprentissage* is a French acronym meaning, "method for instructional systems engineering"

[2] **ADISA:** *Atelier distribué d'ingénierie des systèmes d'apprentissage* is a French acronym meaning "distributed workbench for learning systems engineering"

[3] **TELOS:** (TEleLearning Operating System) is a new system built within the LORNET project (www.lornet.org) to enable engineer and technologists to assemble eLearning and knowledge management platforms and environments.

[4] On Figure 10, principles with 1 express OWL cardinality axioms here meaning "at least one".

Chapter IX
coUML:
A Visual Language for Modeling Cooperative Environments

Michael Derntl
University of Vienna, Austria

Renate Motschnig-Pitrik
University of Vienna, Austria

ABSTRACT

In this chapter we present coUML, a visual modeling language for cooperative environments. As modern instructional environments have a highly cooperative nature, coUML is proposed as a powerful and effective language for modeling instructional designs in such environments. Being based on UML, it was conceived and refined through application and experience over multiple years, primarily in a cooperative blended learning environment. We present relevant requirements and applications that contributed to the development of coUML, as well as a detailed specification of model elements, characteristics and features that describe its current state.

INTRODUCTION

This chapter presents the coUML approach to modeling of cooperative learning designs and environments. coUML stands for "cooperative UML." Its notation is based on UML, and it extends UML with a modeling profile specifically designed to enable the modeling of complex, cooperative learning environments. While coUML clearly focuses on process modeling in cooperative environments, it also allows modeling and

integrating relevant structural information such as goals, documents, and involved roles.

While the name "coUML" was coined during the preparation of this chapter, initial ideas and uses of the coUML language date back to 2002, when we were starting an initiative to discover and document the e-learning practices at our department. During this project the coUML modeling approach proved to be a valuable aid in creating visual models of our teaching and learning activities for documentation, communication, research, and dissemination purposes. The complete and user-friendly specification of coUML in this chapter along with illustrations and examples, is provided to make this approach available to interested readers and practitioners.

The chapter is structured as follows: In the next section we provide some background information on the roots and requirements of the coUML approach. In the third section a detailed specification of the coUML language is provided, illustrated with examples. In the fourth section we present three application scenarios of coUML. This is followed by a discussion on the coUML features and the presentation of a survey on visual instructional design modeling languages among blended learning experts. In the final section we present a conclusion and an outlook on further coUML-related activities.

THE coUML APPROACH

Background

The coUML approach emerged from practice (cf. Derntl & Motschnig-Pitrik, 2005). About 4 years ago, we were searching for a way to capture our teaching and learning designs. Our primary approach to designing the instructional processes for our courses was based on the principles of blended learning (Garrison & Kanuka, 2004). As a traditional university we build on face-to-face meetings in the courses, and we have gradually started introducing online and distant means of collaboration, evaluation, and delivery into our teaching and learning activities. The goal then was to build a comprehensive library of blended course designs or patterns including verbal descriptions and semi-formal models of scenarios that were already in use at our department. As no visual modeling language was particularly suited for such a task, we started to employ the following simple procedure: First, we write down a verbal description of a course and its activities,

including an outline of relevant teaching and learning goals, and the primary teaching approach employed (e.g., project-based learning). The second step is to visualize the course scenario as one or more threads of activities according to the course description. Initially, we used simple symbols for drawing activities and arrows as connectors between activities. Gradually the notation system evolved from requirements drawn from practice and experience, and was finally based on a more formal, standardized notation system. Additionally it was apparent that the current wave of Web-based tools and enhancements not only penetrated educational environments, but any environment where people cooperate to achieve personal and organizational goals, e.g., in projects or communities. Therefore we present coUML as a language that is rooted in, yet not constrained to educational environments.

Requirements and Need

It was clear that a course was, conceptually, not just a sequential thread of activities; we would need additional control-flow structures such as decisions, concurrent flows, and composite activities. We were also interested in a number of additional, instructionally relevant information to be included in the visual models of teaching and learning activities, which are outlined in the following list of requirements:

R1: *Support for logical/temporal arrangement of activities, as well as decisions and concurrent activities.*

R2: *It should be possible to model activities at different levels of detail, which requires a means of refining composite activities. This should allow multiple views on complex activities and help to keep the models clear and understandable, even though this introduces layers of abstraction which might be difficult to grasp for many people.*

R3: *It should be possible to attach roles to activities, for example that online chat support for urgent questions is provided by a student tutor and consumed by course participants.*

R4: *Most learning activities "consume" and/or "produce" documents (Web sites, reports, slides, evaluations, data, etc.); modeling and visualizing that information would help in document management efforts mostly on the side of the instructors and administrators.*

R5: *It should be possible to model the learning goals planned for a course, in order to show which activities in the learning process are "responsible" for supporting and achieving certain goals.*

R6: *As we are interested primarily in modeling blended learning course designs, we need to tag activities as proceeding in a present (i.e., face-to-face), Web-based, or blended mode. The rationale behind this distinction is explained later in the language specification.*

Language Choice

An existing modeling language that immediately supported all our requirements was not readily available. While there were a number of languages available which would support the basic control flow requirements (R1 and R2), only UML provided additional built-in support for R3 and R4. Additionally, UML offers extension mechanisms to define custom model elements, e.g., based on the modes of presence defined in R6, or learning goals according to R5; for this purpose it was necessary to define a UML extension for modeling blended activities, as specified in the following section.

coUML LANGUAGE SPECIFICATION

In this section, the coUML language and its usage is specified in detail. First, we outline and describe modeling artifacts created with coUML, and then, building on basic UML prerequisites, we define the model types and elements used by coUML.

coUML Modeling Artifacts

Using coUML to model a course design produces a number of artifacts, i.e., models and additional information. These are separated into *primary*, *secondary*, and *auxiliary* artifacts, as described below. The procedures taken and the modeling "toolkit" to understand and create these artifacts are described in detail in subsequent sections.

Primary Artifacts

Course activity model (CAM): The primary modeling artifact of coUML is the *course activity model (CAM)*. It comprises a number of activity diagrams showing the course's activities from any desired viewpoint. The CAM aims to provide expressive diagrams showing the chronological order as well as the intent of activities (usually both teaching and learning activities) of the course. coUML allows modeling the CAM diagrams at different, arbitrary levels of detail, which might be helpful with complex course designs.

The CAM is the core of the coUML course model—it can be used to model complete and planned course designs, but it can as well be used to model specific course phases during the course design stage. As such, it can be used as a communication and documentation medium among course designers; by instructors as a handy guide to the conduct of the course; and also by researchers as a conceptual model of the course, e.g., for evaluation or analysis purposes.

Course structure model (CSM): Particularly for modeling complex course designs, another primary artifact is needed, which is the *course structure model (CSM)*. The CSM is created and maintained concurrently with the CAM, as it shows structurally which activity diagrams are used in the CAM to provide a comprehensive course model.

Readers might notice that the CSM—as a complement to the CAM—is not necessarily a mandatory artifact of a coUML course model, as CAM diagrams are still valid without the CSM. However, the CSM acts as an overview or entry point to the CAM, and is therefore also considered a primary artifact, especially from the reader's or viewer's points of view.

Secondary Artifacts

The secondary coUML artifacts as listed below are used to complement the primary artifacts. These complements can optionally be created to provide additional, more detailed information regarding the following:

Roles: Activities in the CAM are performed by persons taking over specific roles in the course. Typical roles would be instructor, student, or tutor. The role model displays the roles involved, and optionally how they are related with each other. Additional textual information regarding the roles can be provided in structured form as well.

Goals: From an instructional point of view, course activities are designed to achieve specific learning goals. coUML offers the option of creating goal models, which explicitly depict learning goals and, if desired, their relationships with each other. This allows systematically breaking down overall course goals into more tangible, readily achievable learning goals; these in turn can be attached to activities in the CAM to show which

activities are intended to support or achieve a goal.

Documents: Instructors typically provide documents and resources as input to learning and teaching activities, and during these activities additional documents and resources might be created or contributed by course participants. To account for this fact, and to provide an overview of which documents and resources are to be provided and created, coUML enables modeling of all relevant documents. These models can be used to structure and describe the documents and to connect roles with documents, showing the document providers and consumers.

Auxiliary Artifacts

Course package model (CPM). The CPM is intended to provide condensed information regarding the course, so to say its "fact sheet." It includes a tabular overview of relevant course parameters, and a model comprising a view of all model packages used for modeling the course. This can be used as an "entry point" to the detail models provided for the course, i.e., roles, documents, goals, CAM, and CSM. It is recommended to create the CPM, as it supports easier usage of and navigation in the course models. However, the fact sheet and model overview are auxiliary and thus optional artifacts.

coUML Modeling Procedures

The coUML modeling procedure to be employed heavily depends on the planned intent of the models and on the concrete ID process for a course, particularly on the current course design status and the desired level of modeling detail. coUML offers a number of features and artifacts for which there may be no use in certain stages of the course design process. For instance, for some courses there might be no explicit information available or needed regarding documents. coUML is flexible enough to separate concerns and allow for detached as well as integrated modeling of such course design artifacts.

There is no particular default procedure for creating a comprehensive coUML model of a course. In the following, we discuss two common usage examples and respective procedures.

Modeling a completed course design: The most straightforward use of coUML is for completed course designs. For example, these models could be used as a "contract" between course administration and instructors; or as a structured course documentation by instructors and instructional designers. In such cases, there exists a verbal or textual description, or at least a consensus, on the design of a course. It could as well happen that the course to be modeled was finished already. Hence, all available coUML modeling features can be exploited in a chronological procedure, which could look like the following:

1. Create the CAM as the primary artifact.
2. Create role-, goal-, and document models according to available information. Leave out or complement missing information.
3. If desired, refine or complement the CAM to include the secondary artifacts defined in step 2.
4. Create a CSM for the final CAM.
5. Create the CPM by identifying relevant course parameters and providing an overview model.

Modeling design-in-progress: coUML can also be used as a tool during the course design stage, e.g., as a more formal communication "language" among instructional designers, or as a personal aid for instructors during course planning and design. In such cases, the steps outlined in the above procedure can typically not be taken in strict chronological order, as working on a later step may require the refinement of artifacts created during an earlier step. Also, optimal and complete information is usually only available for complete (finished) course designs. If coUML is used dur-

ing the course design process the procedure taken could look like the following: modeling roles, then CAM, CSM, documents, goals, revision of the CAM and CSM, and finally creating the CPM. As we see, there is no use for a standard procedure in the design-in-progress case, even though the primary artifacts such as the CAM and CSM would likely be the first to be created. For a given design task it might even be sufficient to experiment with the CAM only.

As an example of the design-in-progress case, we want to show how coUML could support the ADDIE process model. ADDIE defines a simple and frequently used ID process comprising the phases: analyis—design—development—implementation—evaluation. The following list shows how coUML could be used as a "generative" tool for supporting the five phases of the ADDIE model:

1. **Analysis:** In this phase, an initial "map" of the course is created by addressing issues such as characteristics of the learners (e.g., their previous knowledge), desired learning outcomes, delivery options and tools available, suitable pedagogies and strategies, and course objectives (e.g., curricular requirements). With coUML, the analysis results can be written down in the fact sheet provided by the CPM. Initial sketches of involved roles, learning goals, and course/activity structure in the CSM and CAM can be created as well.

2. **Design:** During the design stage the course and learning objectives are elaborated in detail, the course structure and activities are designed in detail, relevant course material is collected and structured, instructional strategies are developed, and the evaluation/ assessment strategy is specified. coUML can help in this phase with the learning goal models for course and learning objectives, the document model for specifying and structuring course content, and the CSM

and CAM for modeling course structure and activities. Integrating coUML secondary artifacts (goals, documents, roles) into the CAM may further facilitate course design.

3. **Development:** For the development of the course content and support systems the coUML models created in the previous model represent a comprehensive documentation of the design; they can be used as a "contract" among developers and instructional designers.

4. **Implementation:** In this phase, a training and delivery plan is developed. The coUML models, in particular the CAM and also the document model, show the crucial points in the instruction to be considered for training and preparing instructors and students, as well as for provision of required tools and learning material.

5. **Evaluation:** coUML models can be used as visual documentation of the whole ADDIE process and thus inform formative evaluation procedures. Summative evaluation procedures can, for example, be supported by the CAM and learning goal models (e.g., for matching actual learning outcomes with learning goals).

UML Prerequisites

Before approaching the specification of coUML model types and elements, we first introduce the relevant model types and elements of UML, upon which all coUML modeling artifacts are based.

UML is a conceptual modeling language that was primarily conceived for modeling static and dynamic aspects of software systems. It was standardized by the Object Management Group (OMG; http://www.omg.org) in 1997 and its current version is 2.0. In the past decade it has been established as the "lingua franca" in computer science. It does not explicitly rely on any particular software design process, nor is it restricted to

modeling computer systems and software systems. It also offers extension mechanisms that allow modelers to define their own model types and modeling elements, both formally and visually. Hence, UML allows modeling static and dynamic aspects of any system or concept.

UML in its current specification offers about a dozen different model types, of which we only need two, namely activity diagrams and static structure diagrams (commonly referred to as "class diagrams"). These two model types and their respective elements provide the basic syntax and semantics of all coUML models. Therefore the following sub-sections briefly introduce these model types and their uses for creating coUML modeling artifacts. Understanding these basic UML model types is required for understanding coUML modeling artifacts, which are specified in detail in the coUML specification section below.

All readers who are already familiar with or interested in UML please note that we do not define a full, formally correct UML extension profile in this chapter. This would require including lots of technical background on and references to UML meta-model and semantics, which would contradict the intended practical nature of this chapter. Therefore all relevant coUML model elements and extensions are introduced and described first and only when needed, that is at the point where the respective coUML model types and elements are explained. Also, UML elements and features not needed by coUML are ignored in the following introduction.

Static Structure Diagrams

A static structure diagram, commonly referred to as "class diagram," is a model type used to build the static structure of a system's analysis or design model by primarily modeling *classes* and their *relationships* (Eriksson & Penker, 1998). A class is a structural element that represents a concept of the application area as it models a set of objects

Figure 1. Class "Student"

Figure 2. Association relationship

Figure 3. Aggregation relationship

Figure 4. Generalization relationship

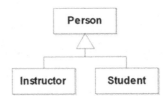

with shared properties and behavior. For instance, all students share some common properties like postal address, date of birth, attended courses, etc., as well as some common behavior like moving to a new address, attending courses, taking exams, and so on. The class representing these properties and the behavior of persons would be "Student". Each student would be an *instance* of this class, with concrete values for each property. In UML a class is visually represented by a solid-outline rectangle carrying the name of the class (see Figure 1).

Classes, or the concepts that they represent, may maintain relationships with other classes. The most important relationships, which are also relevant for coUML, are:

- **Association:** Describes a shared relationship among instances of classes connected through the association. Visually, an association is drawn as a solid-line path between two classes. For example, students can be related to courses they attend; this would require an association relationship between classes "Student" and "Course" (see Figure 2).

- **Aggregation:** An aggregation is a special kind of association representing a part-whole relationship. Thereby, one participating class acts as the aggregate and the other class represents the parts. For example, when each course consists of multiple course units, class "Course" would be the aggregate and class "Course unit" would represent the parts of the aggregate. Visually, an aggregation is drawn like an association adding a hollow

diamond at the end of the aggregate class (see Figure 3). On the other end of the aggregation (i.e., at the class representing the parts) the modeler may note the number of parts constituting each instance of the aggregate class, either as a range or as a fixed number. So Figure 3 models that a course consists of five course units.

- **Generalization:** A generalization relationship connects a more specific concept with a more general concept. Thereby, the more specific concept "inherits" all features of the more general concept and may add new features. Generalizations are used to (hierarchically) refine concepts. For example, a student is a person and an instructor is a person as well, because both have a date of birth, address, etc., but both may also have special properties which are not common to all persons. Visually, a generalization is drawn as a solid line with a hollow triangle at one end pointing to the more general concept (see Figure 4). The generalization arrow can be verbalized as an "*is a*" relationship; Figure 4 therefore states that an "instructor is a person" and that a "student is a person."

- **Dependency:** A dependency constitutes a "weak" association among classes that is usually not structurally relevant to any of the participating classes. For example, a dependency might show that a tutor supports the instructor during a course, which

Figure 5. Dependency relationship

Figure 6. Package

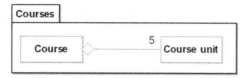

is structurally irrelevant, but still valuable information. Visually, this is depicted by a dashed arrow between involved classes (see Figure 5).

Finally, it is possible to group related model elements together in *packages*. Thereby, a package symbol is drawn around the respective model elements belonging to the package. Visually, a package is drawn as a rectangle with a tab on top of its top-left corner carrying the name of the package (see Figure 6).

Activity Diagrams

Activity diagrams are used to model the behavior of a system, demonstrating how the objects modeled in the structural model interact dynamically. Mapping this general definition to ID modeling, the target "system" would be the course or instruction to be modeled. In coUML, activity diagrams are used for modeling the course activity model (CAM).

Put simply, activity diagrams mainly consist of *activities*, i.e., states in the process where some action is performed, and directed *transitions* among activities. After an activity is completed, the outgoing transition moves the current process state to the activity at which the transition is directed. This is to say that activity diagrams arrange activities performed in a process in chronological order. Visually, an activity is drawn as a rectangle with round edges, and a transition is drawn as an arrow (see Figure 7).

Figure 7. Activities and transitions

Figure 8. Subactivity linking to a set of activities

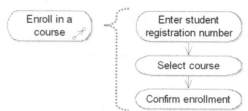

There is a special kind of activity which can be used in much the same way as a normal activity; yet it acts as a placeholder for a number of more specific activities. This is called a "*subactivity*". Subactivities are used to decompose complex activity diagrams into different layers, each with different levels of detail. For example, the subactivity "enroll in a course" would link to a more detailed diagram showing the concrete activities performed by students enrolling in a course, which could be "enter student registration number" followed by "select course" and finished by "confirm enrollment." Visually, subactivities carry a small icon connecting two circles in the lower right corner (see the example in Figure 8).

There might be points in a process, where the next step has to be chosen among a number of alternative steps. Activity diagrams account for such cases by offering *decision* nodes that can have multiple outgoing transitions, of which exactly one transition will become active depending on conditions defined by the modeler. Therefore, decision nodes split up the flow of an activity diagram into multiple alternative flows. For example, "write project report" is succeeded by a decision offering as alternatives "revise project report" and "present project report" as next steps (see Figure 9). The decision would depend on the quality of

Figure 9. Decision among alternative activities

Figure 10. Synchronization of concurrent activities

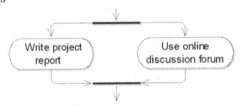

Figure 11. Start node (left) and end node (right)

the project report. Good reports are approved for presentation, while bad reports need to be rewritten first. Visually, decision nodes are drawn as hollow diamonds. Often, alternative flows offered through decisions need to be joined back together at a certain (later) point in the diagram. This is done by drawing another decision node at that point, this time acting as a *join* node with multiple incoming transitions. In Figure 9, the decision symbol is used both as a decision and a join node at the same time.

Additionally, there might be phases in a process, where various activities need to be done concurrently. For example, students would "work on projects," and concurrently "use the online discussion forum." In activity diagrams this is possible by splitting up a transition into multiple concurrent (or synchronized) transitions through a *synchronization bar*. Visually this is drawn as a thick, solid horizontal line. The end of concurrent activities is indicated through another synchronization bar, which continues the process only when all its incoming transitions are active. This means that all concurrent activities have to be completed before the process can continue (see Figure 10).

Finally, each activity diagram has exactly one *start node*, which may carry outgoing transitions only, and at least one *end node*, which may have ingoing transitions only. Visually, a start node is drawn as a filled circle carrying the title or name of the activity diagram, and an end node is drawn as a hollow circle comprising a smaller, filled circle inside (see Figure 11).

Extending UML Elements

Each existing model element in UML can be *stereotyped* to represent a more specific concept. The stereotype is named after the specific concept to be introduced. Such new modeling elements can be introduced and readily used without much effort. Visually, the modeler can define his/her own graphical representation of the new model element, or he/se can just attach the stereotype name as text within matched guillemets («») to the element. This extension mechanism is powerful and highly relevant to our purpose, as coUML derives all special elements from built-in UML elements by adding stereotypes, such as «goal» to classes in the goal model, or «web-based» to activities in the Course Activity Model. For examples of using stereotypes see the following coUML specification section.

Specification of coUML Model Types and Elements

The following sub-sections specify the model types and elements used for creating the coUML course design artifacts as described earlier. All modeling artifacts are specified using a template consisting of five sections: semantics, syntax, example, modeling procedure, and textual information. Regarding examples we try to illustrate the specified models and elements by using a (simplified) course on Web engineering.

The Web Engineering Course

The Web engineering course (hereafter simply "WE course") is an undergraduate course in computer science. It consists of seven consecutive course blocks including project-based learning in teams and face-to-face lectures. The lectures are held by an instructor who also coaches the team projects (where he/she is assisted by a tutor). All documents for projects and lectures are managed on a Web-based learning platform.

The seven blocks are organized as follows: After an introductory block, five blocks are dedicated to advancing knowledge and experience in Web engineering through applying techniques and theories presented in the lectures on team projects. This includes Web technology basics, requirements engineering, conceptual modeling, Web data management, and Web programming. The arrangement of these topics allows for completing the projects in an incremental development process. The final course block concludes the course with a grading procedure and a course quality assessment.

More details on the course are introduced as required for the specification of new elements. Note that in this section we only model those aspects of the WE course required for the introduction of the coUML language elements. A

more complete case study on modeling a whole course using coUML is provided in Chapter XVI of this handbook.

Course Package Model (CPM)

Semantics
The CPM shows which primary and secondary coUML modeling artifacts are provided for a specific course design. As such, the CPM acts both as an overview and entry point to all coUML artifacts provided for a course design.

Syntax
The CPM is modeled as a class diagram with one super-ordinate package carrying the course title. This package includes other packages, each representing (a group of) a primary or secondary coUML artifact. No relationships are used in the CPM.

Example
The WE course is modeled using coUML including examples of the CAM, the CSM, and the secondary artifacts. The CAM and CSM are contained in dedicated packages, and each secondary artifact (i.e., roles, goals, and documents) is also contained in a dedicated package. The CPM for this course would look like Figure 12.

Modeling Procedure
It is easier to model the CPM when all artifacts are already known and available. However, the CPM

Figure 12. CPM for the Web engineering (WE) course

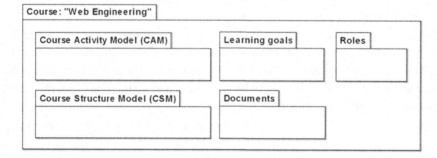

Table 1. Fact sheet of the WE course

"Web Engineering"	
Summary	Integrated lecture and lab course in computer science, held in a blended mode. Relevant Web engineering theory and techniques are presented by the instructor and applied hands-on by the students their team projects.
Structure	The course comprises seven consecutive blocks; each block is conducted in a blended mode integrating face-to-face and online activities.
Presence mode	Blended face-to-face and online
Online support	A Web-based learning platform is available; any required tools for projects are available in the laboratory.
Participants	Twenty undergraduate computer science students with basic knowledge in computers, Internet technologies, and computer programming
Teaching staff	One instructor, one tutor
Instructional strategy	Lectures and project-based learning using a blended learning approach. Projects and subject matter are elaborated in a stepwise, incremental fashion (synchronized with theory input during the lectures).
coUML models	CPM, CSM, CAM, roles, learning goals, documents

may also represent the planned or in-progress state of artifacts. In this case, the CPM would have to be updated if any artifact is added, removed, or renamed.

Textual Information

The CPM is complemented by the course's "fact sheet" including relevant course parameters. This can be used as a quick overview of course facts by course designers, teaching staff, and even students. The fact sheet is presented as a table comprising two columns: parameter and description. The head row of the table shows the course name, and all subsequent rows include relevant parameters in the left column and their respective values in the right column. We propose the following set of parameters, which may be reduced or extended according to specific needs:

- **Summary:** A short summary of the course content and intent.
- **Structure:** A description of the structural organization of the course, e.g., division into multiple blocks with dedicated topics, or weekly lectures, etc.
- **Mode of presence:** Indicates whether the primary mode of presence in the course is face-to-face, online, or blended.

- **Online support:** Lists available online tools and resources, such as course Web sites, learning management systems, etc.
- **Participants:** How many and who are the participants?
- **Teaching staff:** Teaching staff involved in the course, such as instructor, supervisor, tutor, external guest, etc.
- **Instructional strategy:** Description of main instructional strategy employed in the course, such as project-based learning, case-based lab practice, etc.
- **coUML models:** A list of coUML models or artifacts provided for the course design.

Table 1 shows a brief fact sheet of the WE course.

Models for Roles

Semantics

The model for roles is intended to depict roles involved in a course. As a secondary artifact, the role model is created only if deemed to be of significant use to the design team. There are considerable benefits of modeling roles: First, each role must carry a clear and unique name, which facilitates communication and understanding.

Figure 13. The "Instructor" role

Figure 14. Role aggregation

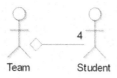

Figure 15. Role generalization

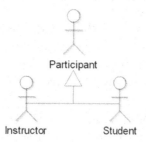

Second, they can be used as additional information in the document model and the CAM. In the document model, roles are represented as providers and consumers of documents, while in the CAM the roles are used to show areas of responsibility in the course phases and activities. On the other hand, if roles are used in the document model or the CAM, the model of the role must be provided to maintain the internal consistency of the models. In either case, modeling roles requires additional effort and also adds to the complexity of the overall coUML model.

Syntax

Roles are modeled in class diagrams. Technically, a role is represented by a class with stereotype «role». We define our own custom visual representation for this, which is a stick-figure with the role name written below it (see Figure 13; UML experts may note that we reuse the built-in UML actor symbol). Packages may be used to group related roles together.

Figure 16. "Support dependency" between two roles

The following relationships are possible between roles:

- **Aggregation:** Means that each instance of the aggregate role consists of a number of instances of the other role. A typical example would be the "team" role that aggregates the "student" role in the sense that each student team consists of a number of students (see Figure 14 showing that each team comprises four students).

- **Generalization:** This means that a more general role is refined by more specific roles. The more general role provides structural and/or behavioral elements for each specialized role. For example, there might be activities in a course where both instructor and student roles actively participate; these two roles could then be generalized through a "participant" role (see Figure 15). Consequently, if the participant role is partaking in any course activity in the CAM we implicitly know that both instructor and student roles can be involved.

- **Dependency:** A dependency relationship between two roles indicates that one role supports the other role in course activities. For instance, the tutor role typically supports the instructor role, which is modeled as a dependency carrying the stereotype «support» (see Figure 16). While coUML only specifies the «support» stereotype, the modeler may introduce additional stereotypes as needed. Modeling dependencies among roles is optional; usage of this feature might increase the informational content of the role model, but it also tends to overload the model.

Figure 17. Role model of the WE course

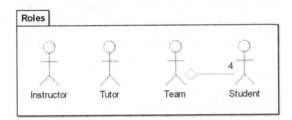

Optionally, roles and role hierarchies can be divided into multiple packages in one or more class diagrams. For example in a more complex role hierarchy it might be useful to separate teaching roles from learner roles. The decision on this is left to the modeler (see the remarks for "modeling procedure" below).

Example

In the WE course, active roles include the instructor, the tutor, and students. Additionally, we identify the "team" role: In the first session, students are organized into teams of four to work on their web engineering projects for the rest of the course. Therefore, the team role is modeled as an aggregation of the student role. At the student role end of the aggregation, the number "4" indicates that each team consists of four students. Activities performed by the team role for one of the WE course blocks can be seen in the CAM example (see Figure 42).

Modeling Procedure

Identifying the roles for a course is straightforward. Most courses involve at least the instructor, student, and tutor roles. It might be easier to identify roles after the first attempts to model the CAM diagrams, as it makes little sense to conceptually define a role which does not partake in any course activity. Also, with most or all course activities available, identification of participating roles is easier.

As coUML makes no assumptions on role granularity, it would also be possible to refine the role hierarchy into greater detail according to the

activities in which they partake. For example the student role could be split up into more specific roles that students take on in different activities. Consider the peer evaluation of student projects: the "student" role could be divided into a "project-contributor" role and a "peer-reviewer" role. The final decision on the granularity of the role model is left to the modeler, however with the advice that fewer roles are clearly easier to handle.

Textual Information

The role model is complemented by a tabular description of the roles. The two columns of the table expose the role name and a short description for each role. For example the role description for the tutor in the WE course would be, "Supports the students and the instructor during various activities, e.g., facilitating/helping project teams, collecting documents from students, maintaining the online content, seeing through online activity, etc."

Goal Model

Semantics

The goal model can optionally be used to explicitly model and describe learning goals as well as their relationships with each other. Like the role model, the goal model is considered as a secondary modeling artifact that can be omitted if not needed. However, this model is useful as a tool to explicitly name and relate goals with each other. The modeler is free in setting the focus for the goal model, which means that coUML does not suggest any underlying taxonomy (e.g., Bloom's taxonomy of learning goals—cf. Bloom, 1956), nor any other assumptions about the learning goals. Nevertheless, coUML allows assigning priorities to learning goals.

If the modeler decides to create this model, the learning goals can subsequently be used as additional content in the CAM, where activities can be connected to learning goals. This is useful for showing which activities support or achieve which learning goals.

Syntax

Goals are modeled in class diagrams. Each goal is drawn as a class with stereotype «goal» above the learning goal name. Additionally a goal identifier (ID) can be placed in the top-left corner of the class symbol, allowing referring to a goal by its ID (can be a number, an acronym, etc.), which is typically shorter than its name. To avoid introducing yet another icon, we reuse the already known class symbol and restrain from defining our own icon for goals (see Figure 18).

Note that some existing goal modeling approaches use the UML use-case symbol for modeling goals, while others use stereotyped class symbols. For coUML we preferred to use the latter option as we consider goals as being structural elements; use cases on the other hand are behavioral elements typically used to represent interactions (or events) preformed by users and the system to achieve some goal. With coUML the achievement of goals can be modeled in the CAM.

Goals are modeled in packages and it is also possible to group related goals together. This is achieved by placing the respective goals inside a grouping box, which is drawn as a rectangle with an attached name for the goal group (see Figure 19).

It is possible to assign priorities to goals, if desired. There are several options of doing so: we could attach a text note to the goal that defines its priority (e.g., "Priority 1"); we could group together learning goals belonging to the same priority by using a grouping element like the one in Figure 19; or we could create a diagram consisting of vertical layers, where each layer represents one priority level. The choice is left to the modeler.

The following relationships are possible between goals:

- **Aggregation:** Means that the aggregate goal is decomposed into a number of smaller, typically more concrete goals. Thereby, the aggregate goal is considered as achieved after all its sub-goals have been achieved. Figure 20 shows an example of goal aggregation in the context of the WE course. Goal 1 can be achieved by achieving all of its sub-goals 2, 3, and 6.
- **Dependency:** A dependency relationship between two goals indicates that one goal plays a role in achieving or supporting the other goal. Dependencies may be stereotyped to

Figure 20. Goal aggregation

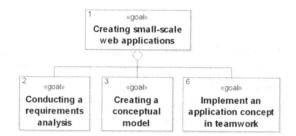

Figure 18. Learning goal "Understand basic Web technology" having ID "7"

Figure 19. Grouping of cognitive learning goals in the WE course

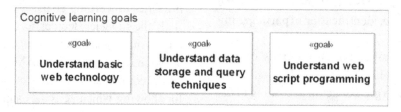

express the particular type of dependency between two goals. The following two stereotypes are defined by coUML (note that this list can be extended according to the modeler's needs):

1. **«require»**, meaning that a goal requires another goal to be achieved first. For example to achieve the learning goal "Implement an application concept in teamwork" in the WE course requires the goal "Understand Web script programming" to be achieved first, as one cannot reasonably implement a Web application without being familiar with Web programming (see Figure 21).

2. **«support»**, meaning that working towards a goal supports the achievement of another goal. This could be interpreted as a weak, inverse form of «require». We could modify the example above to state that Web script programming supports implementation of application concepts, which could also be argued in certain cases (see Figure 22). We see that the choice of dependency relies on the modeler's estimation of the real relationship among two goals, so multiple interpretations are possible.

*   **Generalization:** This means that a goal is refined by more specific goals. This is an advanced feature which can lead to more confusion than to better understanding among novices. However, generalizing goals is also a powerful concept, as the general goal can be used to provide shared properties for multiple sub-goals: If, for example in a course on writing research papers, learning goal *A* ("Writing research papers") is a generalization of learning goals *B* ("Writing case-study papers") and *C* ("Writing empirical papers"), then each relationship that *A* maintains with other learning goals (e.g., with learning goal *D* – "Structuring

Figure 21. "Require dependency" between two learning goals

Figure 22. "Support dependency" among two learning goals

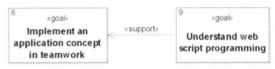

Figure 23. Generalization of goals

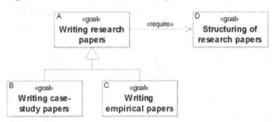

of research papers") is inherited by both *B* and *C*. So if *A* requires *D* to be achieved, then *B* and *C* require *D* as well (see Figure 23).

Like the role model, the goal model can be divided into multiple packages in one or more class diagrams.

Example

Figure 24 shows the goal model for the learning goals of the WE course. Consider a list of learning goals specified textually by the instructor: To create our goal model, we provide a short name and attach a numerical ID for each relevant. Additionally we include the information that goal 1 is an aggregation of goals 2, 3, and 6, and that goals 4 and 5 are generalized by goal 3. While these relationships might not explicitly be stated in the textual description of the learning goals, the modeler should try to identify the most appropriate representation for goal relationships.

Figure 24. Learning goal model for the WE course

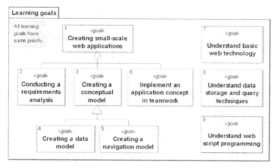

Modeling Procedure

If learning goals are available in structured text form, they can be modeled by identifying relevant learning goals, assigning a short name and an optional ID, and finally – if considered useful—by modeling relationships among goals.

There might be no explicit textual description available for many courses, especially in early design stages. In such cases it would be reasonable to think about and specify learning goals textually and proceed with modeling. If it is not intended to explicitly write down learning goals, it is valid to omit the goal model altogether, or to try to extract the goals from the course activities or other available course information.

Textual Information

The goal model can be complemented by a tabular description of the goals. The two columns of the table expose the ID or the name of the goal and a more detailed description, respectively. See the case study in Chapter XVI for an example.

Document Model

Semantics

The document model shows a structured overview of all documents that are created, provided, and/or used in a course. Moreover, it is possible to show for each document: who are the providers and who are the consumers. This is achieved by con-

necting roles from the role model to documents in the document model.

The obvious benefit of creating this modeling artifact is that it is easy to identify, for example, which documents have to be created prior to the course, which documents have to be provided by teaching staff throughout the course, which documents are produced by students, or which resources are generally available. Creating a document model can provide substantial support in the tedious, yet indispensable task of document management in a course.

As we will show in the specification of the CAM, modeling a document model subsequently allows connecting documents with activities in the CAM, to show which documents are input to and output from activities.

Syntax

The document model is provided in class diagrams. Each document is drawn as a class with stereotype «document» above the document name. No special visual icon is defined for documents. Similar to the goal model, a document ID can be placed in the top-left corner of the class symbol, allowing referral to a document by its ID (see Figure 25).

Documents are modeled in packages and it is possible to group related documents together, for example document resources for student projects.

Figure 25. A case study document on requirements engineering carrying ID "RE 2"

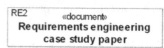

Figure 26. Grouping of project resources

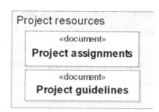

This is achieved by placing the respective documents inside a grouping box (see Figure 26) in the same way as in the goal model.

The following relationships are possible between documents:

- **Aggregation:** Means that the aggregate document consists of a number of sub-documents. Figure 27 shows an example of document aggregation in the context the WE projects. The final project report consists of the sub-documents: project assignment, project plan, and project results. The project report is created at the end of the course, after all sub-documents have been written.

- **Dependency:** A dependency relationship between two documents indicates that one document plays a role in the provision or usage of the other document. Dependencies among documents may be stereotyped to convey the particular type of dependency. Only one stereotype is suggested by coUML (note that the modeler may introduce additional stereotypes as needed): **«require»**, meaning that a document requires another document to be available before it can be provided or used. A typical example would be written feedback: One can only provide feedback on a project report when the project report is already available (see Figure 28).

  It is possible to use a dependency to connect a role defined in the role model with a document and vice versa. This would indicate the *"document flow"* among roles. Note that this is modeled without assigning a stereotype to the dependency. Depending on the direction of the dependency, the following intents are served:

1. A unidirectional dependency pointing from a role to a document means that the document is provided or created by a person embodying that role (see Figure 29).

Figure 27. Document aggregation

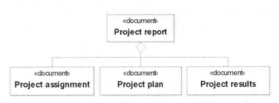

Figure 28. "Require dependency" between two documents

Figure 29. "Document flow" unidirectional dependencies among roles and documents

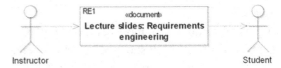

Figure 30. A bidirectional dependency between the instructor role and a document

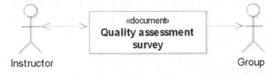

2. A unidirectional dependency pointing from a document to a role means that the role uses this document for some purpose. So, persons embodying that role are addressees or consumers of the document (see Figure 29).

3. A bidirectional dependency between a document and a role means that the role acts as both provider and consumer of the document (see Figure 30). This constitutes an integration of the two unidirectional cases above.

Like the role model and the goal model, the document model can be divided into multiple packages in one or more class diagrams.

Figure 31. Document model for the third WE course block on requirements engineering

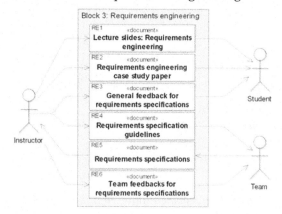

Example

A part of the document model of the WE course is given in Figure 31. It shows which documents are used and created in the third course block ("Block 3: Requirements engineering"): It is apparent that the instructor provides most of the documents, except the requirements specifications which are created by the project teams and submitted to the instructor.

Modeling Procedure

Documents can be identified by studying the textual course description and particularly by analyzing course activities with respect to their input and output documents. Therefore it might be advisable to defer the creation of the document model until after the CAM is modeled. In this case the document model would have to be refined each time the CAM changes its use of documents.

Textual Information

A tabular overview of documents is provided as a complement to the document model. Thereby each document can be specified in great detail according to specific needs. coUML suggests at least providing information on the following properties for each document: ID, name, type (e.g.,

paper, report, Web site, animation, spreadsheet, etc.), description (more detailed information on the content or use of the document), provider (who is responsible for providing/creating the document?), and deadline (a point of time in the course where the document must be available). See the case study in Chapter XVI for an example of a document table. Additional parameters could include: public (is a document available to other roles?), location, online availability, size, already available, and so forth.

Course Activity Model (CAM)

Semantics

The CAM is the primary artifact of a coUML course model. It is used to model the teaching and learning process of a course or instruction. The CAM may provide any number of activity diagrams showing the course activities from any point of view, in any desired level of detail. Its enormous flexibility makes the CAM a very powerful and versatile resource for course analysis, design, and documentation. Moreover, the modeler may reuse secondary artifacts defined in other models and link them to activities in the CAM, e.g., to show which documents of the document model are needed for which activities.

The most basic use of the CAM is for modeling the arrangement of course activities from an organizational point of view, i.e., aligning activities performed by multiple roles in activity diagrams.

Syntax

The CAM comprises a number of activity diagrams. Each activity diagram depicts a phase of a course, or the whole course at a certain level of detail and from a certain point of view. The level of detail and the point of view are determined by the modeler according to the course activities to be modeled. The following elements are used to model basic activity diagrams:

Figure 32. Start node of the WE course activity diagram

Web Engineering
●

Figure 33. Start node of the activity diagram for block 3 of the WE course

Web Engineering
Block 3: Requirements engineering
●

Figure 34. A course activity

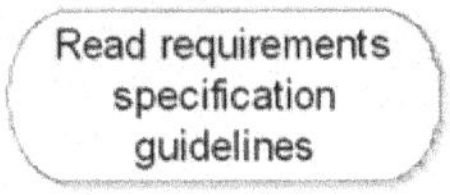

Read requirements
specification
guidelines

- **Start Node:** Each activity diagram must have exactly one start node, which acts as the entry point to the "execution" of the diagram. It carries the name of the current diagram, which is usually the course name (if the activity diagram represents the whole course—see Figure 32) or the name of a particular phase or activity in the course (if the activity diagram models only one part of the course). The latter case may be complemented by placing the course name in smaller letters above the name of the current activity diagram (see Figure 33).

- **End Node:** Each activity diagram contains at least one end node, which represents the end of execution of the current activity diagram. This means that each final activity of an activity diagram must be connected to an end node via a transition.

- **Activity:** An activity symbol in an activity diagram represents a state of the execution of the diagram where a specific activity is performed by some role involved in the course. For example, at one point of the course the students have to read a document containing information on the task of creating the requirements specification for their projects. This activity could be modeled as "Read requirements specification guidelines" (see Figure 34). The name chosen for the activity should be meaningful to potential viewers, while keeping in mind that the name should not be too long.

An activity symbol may also be used to represent more than one concrete course activity, which is possible when modeling a diagram at a lower level of detail. Note that, unlike in many other educational modeling languages, in coUML the size of an activity symbol is not related to its estimated or planned execution time. The symbol should just be drawn large enough to accommodate its name. Also, an activity diagram is usually easier to read when all its activities have about the same size.

The modeler may explicitly denote the mode of presence in which the activity is performed, which is either Web-based, face-to-face (present), or blended. This is particularly useful in blended learning environments. With coUML it can be achieved by assigning a *mode-of-presence* stereotype to the activity. The following three stereotypes are defined:

1. **«web-based»:** This stereotype means that the activity is primarily performed online, using the Web. It is visualized by filling the activity with light-blue color and by placing the letter "W" (standing for "web-based") surrounded by a circle in the activity's right-hand corner. Figure 35 shows an example of the Web-based activity, where requirements specifications for the team projects are submitted online via the Web.

2. **«present»:** This stereotype means that the activity is primarily performed in face-to-face or present mode. It is visualized by filling the activity with

Figure 35. Web-based activity

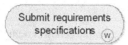

Figure 36. Presence activity

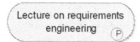

light-green color and by placing the letter "P" (standing for "present") surrounded by a circle in the activity's right-hand corner. Figure 36 shows an example of a face-to-face lecture activity on requirements engineering.

3. **«blended»**: This stereotype means that the activity is performed in a mixed, blended mode using the Web and face-to-face meetings. This stereotype is visualized by filling the activity with light-red color and by placing the letter "B" (standing for "blended") surrounded by a circle in the activity's right-hand corner. Figure 37 shows an example of an activity modeling the blended elaboration of project reports.

Note that for blended activities the level of detail used in the diagram plays a significant role: At the highest level of detail, blended activities can not be modeled, as each single activity will proceed either Web-based or present. At lower levels of detail, an activity may represent more than one single activity, where presence and face-to-face modes can be mixed. This would make the activity a blended activity like the one in Figure 37. Project reports are elaborated in personal meetings and via the Web by exchanging electronic documents, e-mails, etc., making it a truly blended activity with a low level of modeling detail.

- **Subactivity:** A subactivity is a special kind of activity, which links to another activity diagram. This means that the subactivity represents a number of course activities, which are modeled in more detail in a sub-diagram. Logically, subactivities are only needed when modeling at a relatively low level of detail. The sub-diagram to which the subactivity points, is consequently modeled at a higher level of detail. This means that subactivities are a powerful tool to model course activities at different levels of detail, while providing links between these levels. This supports both the modelers and the viewers, because for example overloaded diagrams can be avoided this way.

Note that for easier recognition the start node of the sub-diagram should carry the name of its parent subactivity. Also note that the modeler can assign a mode of presence to each subactivity in the same way as it is done for normal activities. For example, if we want to refine the blended activity in Figure 37 with a sub-diagram showing the

Figure 37. Blended activity

Figure 38. Subactivity (on left side) and its sub-diagram (on right side) showing the elaboration of project reports

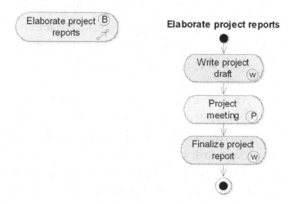

concrete activities performed in elaborating project reports, the resulting subactivity and its sub-diagram would look like those in Figure 38.

- **Transition:** As already defined, a transition is a directed connection (drawn as a solid-line arrow) between two nodes in an activity diagram. It can be used to connect activities, subactivities, decisions, concurrencies, and start- and end nodes. A transition maintains the "control flow" in an activity diagram; it becomes active when its source node has completed its actions, and it immediately passes control on to its target node. This allows temporal and logical arrangement of activities and other nodes. For example, the activity diagram on the right-hand side of Figure 38 starts with the activity "Write project draft." After this activity is completed, the transition becomes active and moves the state of execution to its target activity, which is "Project meeting." After this, the "Finalize project report" activity becomes active. The last transition is directed at the end node. Through transitions the three activities are arranged in chronological order.

- **Decision:** A decision node (drawn as a hollow diamond) denotes a point in a course where the flow of activities is split up into multiple alternative flows. Exactly one of these alternative flows becomes active. To help decide which of the alternative "routes" to take, each outgoing transition of a decision node carries a so-called *guard condition*. If the guard condition of a transition is satisfied, that transition will become active. A flow split up by decisions can be rejoined later in the diagram by another node which is then called a *join* node that is visually identical to the decision node. Consider Figure 39 for example: The instructor lets students choose whether they want the next course unit on data modeling to be delivered as a lecture by the instructor, or as self-study via

Figure 39. Decision and join nodes

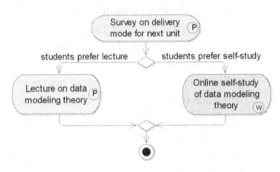

the Web. Depending on the preference of students, two alternative activities need to be modeled, i.e., a face-to-face lecture and an online self-study. The following join node reconnects the split flow of activities.

- **Concurrency:** A concurrency is used to model separate activity flows which proceed concurrently with each other. Concurrencies have a dedicated start and end. At the start a single transition is split up into multiple concurrent transitions with a synchronization bar symbol (thick, solid line), and at the end these multiple concurrent transitions are rejoined again with the same symbol. During execution of the activity diagram, at the end of a concurrency the flow can

Figure 40. Concurrent (synchronized) activities

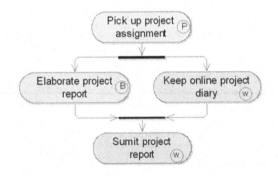

Figure 41. "Support dependency" between an activity and a learning goal

continue only after all incoming concurrent flows are finished. Consider Figure 40 for example. After the "Pick up project assignment" activity is completed, the two activities "Elaborate project reports" and "Keep online project diary" take place concurrently with each other. The end of the concurrency can be seen as a synchronization point: If both concurrent activities are completed, the process can continue with "Submit project report."

- **Temporal constraints:** It might be necessary or useful to explicitly model time slots or constraints such as deadlines for activi-

ties. The modeler is relatively free in the way of adding this information. However, the following is propsed for coUML: Points in time are visualized in activity diagrams by drawing a dotted line with a deadline or other date near the activities to which the deadline is relevant. This feature is used in Figure 42; for example, we can see that the submission of requirements specifications by the project teams has to be completed until Sunday in the third week.

Activity diagrams can optionally be extended with elements from secondary artifacts:

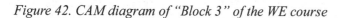

Figure 42. CAM diagram of "Block 3" of the WE course

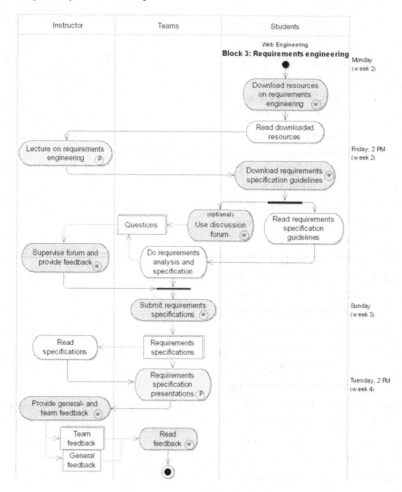

- **Roles:** There is a feature for activity diagrams that allows modeling which role is the primary actor in an activity. An area, in which a particular role acts as the primary actor in activities, is surrounded by a so-called "swimlane," which carries the name of the respective role name. For example, in Figure 42 there are swimlanes for three roles: instructor, teams, and students. Therefore we know that the first activity after the start node (i.e., "Download resources on requirements engineering") is performed by students. In cases where an activity is performed by multiple roles, the activity can be resized to span or touch multiple swimlanes.

- **Documents:** coUML allows modeling the "document flow" in an activity diagram. To achieve this, simple transitions can be replaced by dashed arrows and an object symbol, which is a rectangle carrying the document name as defined in the document model (if the object represents multiple documents a symbol with two stacked objects is used). The document flow feature is especially useful when a document is direct output of one activity and subsequently direct input to the next activity. For example, in Figure 42, the "Requirements specifications" documents are output of the "Submit requirements specifications" activity and input to the following "Read specifications" activity performed by the instructor. If swimlanes are used for roles, it is a service to viewers to model documents in the swimlanes of the role or activity that produces the document.

- **Goals:** (Learning) goals can be connected to activities through dependency relationships. In the CAM, learning goals are modeled as objects, just like documents. The name of the object must match the name and/or ID of the goal in the goal model. To explicitly show the specific type of goal dependency, the following stereotypes are suggested:

  - «achieve»: States that the activity achieves a goal.
  - «support»: States that the activity supports the achievement of a goal. This can be considered as a weak form of the «achieve» dependency. See for example Figure 41, where the "Do requirements analysis and specification" activity supports the achievement of the "Conducting a requirements analysis" learning goal.

Interpreting Activity Diagrams

When viewing and trying to interpret an activity diagram, the best approach for novices is to "walk through" the diagram by placing an imaginary execution token at the start node of the diagram. Then, you continue to follow the outgoing transition of the current node, by moving the imaginary token along the transition arrow to the next node:

1. If you reach an *activity* you are at a point of the course where an activity is performed by some role, which can be identified by the containing swimlane of that activity. The token remains stationary at this activity until the activity is completed.

2. If you reach a *subactivity*, you follow the (imaginary) link to the activity diagram to which the current subactivity points. The execution token is transferred to the start node of this sub-diagram. After execution of the sub-diagram is finished (i.e., the token reaches an end node), you return the token to the originating subactivity and follow its outgoing transition.

3. If you reach a *decision*, you will notice the multiple outgoing transitions leaving the decision node. It is important that the execution token can only proceed along exactly one of the outgoing transitions. To help decide which outgoing transition to follow, the decision may carry a question to be

answered or a condition to be satisfied. Each of the transitions then carries one answer or one possible condition value. You follow the transition carrying the answer or value that is true/correct for the current token. If you reach a decision node with only one outgoing transition, which represents a join for the most recent decision, you just continue to pass the token along the single outgoing transition.

4. If you reach the start of a *concurrency*, you will also see multiple outgoing transitions. Contrary to decisions, *each one* of the outgoing transitions will become active after the synchronization bar. This can be achieved by splitting the execution token up into a number of concurrent execution tokens matching the number of outgoing transitions. Now place one of the tokens on each transition and concurrently proceed with each token. This concurrent flow of activities is ended by another synchronization bar, which can be recognized by its multiple incoming transitions and only one single outgoing transition. At this point, you wait until each part token of the previously split-up execution token arrives at the synchronization bar. After the last token has arrived you rejoin the tokens and continue with one single token along the path of the synchronization bar's outgoing transition.

5. If the current transition you follow represents a *document flow* (i.e., a dashed arrow) you pass the token along the document flow, move it past the document node (at this point you know that the current document was produced by the previous activity), and finally on to the following activity or activities.

6. If the current activity node carries an outgoing *dependency* to a learning activity, you know that this activity supports or achieves the respective learning goal. For the execution token, these dependencies can be ignored, i.e., they just provide additional information to the viewer.

Example
Figure 42 shows the activity diagram of the CAM for block 3 of the WE course. Three roles are involved (the *instructor*, the project *teams*, and the *students*) in this blended course block. The temporal constraints also show important points in time during the two weeks covered by the diagram.

Modeling Procedure
Initial attempts at the CAM can be made while ignoring secondary artifacts like documents or learning goals. As an initial step, relevant activities should be modeled at a low level of detail. Each low-detail activity can subsequently be refined in sub-diagrams to achieve a higher level of detail. During modeling it might become apparent that a diagram becomes too complex or bloated, which might require rearrangement or refinement of activities. This process can be iterated until a satisfying and consistent degree of elaboration of the CAM is achieved. If the modeler decides to add more information, additional elements from secondary artifacts can be included. Typically, roles (swimlanes) are introduced first, followed by the document flow with activities, and finally, if desired, learning goals. Also during modeling, it might be useful to create alternative diagrams for the same course activities, representing a different point of view, a different level of detail, or just to experiment with activity arrangement or available secondary artifacts.

A concrete, effective procedure for a particular modeling/design team and task is best discovered and optimized during modeling practice.

Textual Information
A table should be provided for each activity diagram to describe each activity in more detail. Two columns (name of activity and description) should be sufficient, but additional information can be provided like scheduled start and end time of activities, role responsibility, tool support, etc.

Course Structure Model (CSM)

Semantics

The CSM provides an overview of all activity diagrams modeled in the CAM. As such it acts as a visual aid for users and modelers of a course. Viewers can use it as a guide to "browsing" the CAM.

Syntax

The CSM consists of one or more class diagrams comprising a class symbol for each activity diagram in the CAM. The class symbol carries the name of the respective diagram. There is only one specified relationship between diagrams, which is drawn as a dependency, meaning that the source diagram links to the target diagram through a sub-activity. Packages can be used to group diagrams together. See the following example.

Example

Figure 43 shows the CSM for the WE course. The main activity diagram (indicated with light-gray fill) would be the "Web Engineering" diagram. The CSM shows that this diagram links to seven sub-diagrams detailing each of the seven blocks of this course.

Modeling Procedure

The creation of the CSM follows a straightforward procedure. Start with the main activity diagram representing the whole course, and draw the symbol in the CSM with light-gray fill or pattern. For each subactivity in this diagram, draw a diagram symbol in the CSM and connect the main diagram symbol to it via a dependency. This step is repeated for the whole "tree" of sub-diagrams, sub-sub-diagrams, and so on.

If there are alternative models for certain course activities or phases, another CSM package can be created with links to these diagrams.

Figure 43. Course structure model (CSM) for the WE course

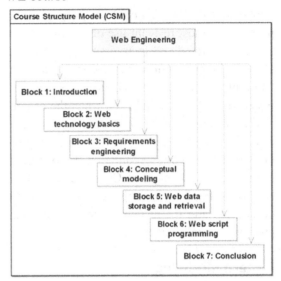

Textual Information

The CSM can optionally be complemented with a tabular overview giving a textual description for each diagram.

coUML APPLICATIONS

This section briefly presents three applications for the coUML approach: first, in its original application area for instructional designs. Second, we expose the coUML language as a means of modeling generic blended learning processes, also referred to as "blended learning patterns," to enable the reuse of blended learning design experience. And finally, we present a more technology-oriented application for modeling and using the learner context in a course.

Instructional Design

Supporting the instructional design process is perhaps the most relevant use of coUML. As it allows integrated and incremental modeling of structural and dynamic aspects of an educational environment, it can be used in different stages of instructional design, and even when the design process is already completed. A comprehensive example for applying coUML in this respect is provided as a case study on a course on "Introduction to Instructional Design" in Chapter XVI of this handbook. Please refer to the textual case-study description and the respective coUML models provided in that chapter.

Pattern Modeling

The primary objective of the pattern approach (Alexander et al., 1977) is to capture generic scenarios in a way that makes them amenable to reuse. With

Figure 44. Excerpt of the Web-based "Diary" pattern

Intent: Make participants' efforts transparent by making them keep track of their work in diaries, especially in collaborative and/or iterative learning processes.

Motivation: Keeping a diary during learning activities has some positive aspects: First, diaries help memorizing and reflecting on experiences, problems, and achievements encountered during problem-solving processes. So diaries are valuable assets to initiate self-reflective thinking. Second, diaries provide the instructor with valuable insight on working progress, activity, and thoughts of participants. Finally, in teamwork scenarios diaries allow for monitoring the (equal) distribution of activities among team members. All of the above points only hold when participants do not treat diaries as annoying appendages but take a stake in keeping their diaries. To facilitate this, it may be worthwhile to provide writing guidelines for participants (e.g., providing a set of questions and points to be considered) and to transparently disclose the intentions of making them keep diaries.

Scenario:

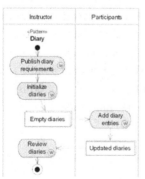

coUML this can be achieved by providing models of useful and effective courses and scenarios with a higher level of abstraction. The resulting pattern of a scenario can be used as a template or model for instantiating or deriving concrete scenarios in different, but similar contexts. To support this, each pattern is provided with detailed descriptions of intent, motivation, coUML scenario model, parameters, and application examples (Derntl, 2005). Consider for instance the Web-based "Diary" pattern described and modeled in Figure 44 (note that the pattern description in the figure is not given in full detail). The scenario is modeled at a high level of abstraction, featuring only the most essential steps in using Web-based diaries in educational environments. Consequently, the scenario can be applied by adapting it to specific needs, requirements, and available technology- and Web support.

Context-Aware Scenario Modeling

In a recent project (Derntl & Hummel, 2005) coUML was extended by introducing learner context information as an additional secondary modeling artifact. Thereby a learner context model was developed to allow modeling of the learner's personal context (e.g., name, expertise, etc.), physical context (e.g., location), digital context, and other more technology- and device-related context structures. The learner's context can subsequently be attached to activities modeled in the CAM. This extension was used to model a laboratory course that employed wireless devices in an RFID-tagged laboratory environment (RFID stands for Radio Frequency Identification; it allows attaching tags to objects which can be wirelessly scanned by RFID-enabled computers such as laptops or PDA's). Based on the context-enhanced CAM models a software system was developed that was, for instance, able to display available books and papers on the current course topic if the student entered the laboratory library. This way it was possible to automatically consider and update each learner's context (e.g., location, learning progress, learning resources, available devices, etc.) during a learning activity.

DISCUSSION

Language Features

coUML is basically an extension of UML. We consider this as an advantage as UML's semantics are formally specified and well documented. Meanwhile UML has a tradition of being used in several fields such as Web design, business processes and workflows, organizational modeling, context modeling, and many more. For example, there are many commercial and open-source UML modeling toolkits available which could be used for modeling basic coUML diagrams. Additionally, transformation procedures for UML-based modeling (e.g., to XML) are already well-researched and tested, and can be applied to coUML models without "reinventing the wheel."

The language-related features of coUML can be characterized as follows: coUML is pedagogically neutral; there are no modeling elements, restrictions, terms or assumptions included which would restrict the user in modeling any particular scenario. It is designed to be simple to learn and use, even for non technically-oriented people. This has turned out to be a tough goal to achieve, as many people are reluctant to use UML, which generally seems to be considered as a tool for pure computer science use. Despite its (debatable) notational simplicity, coUML can be used for modeling processes at almost any degree of complexity and detail; it includes all necessary control-flow structures, and the composite subactivities allow structural aggregation and hierarchical composition of cooperative scenarios through links between activity diagrams. Finally, it can be used for creating new learning designs, analyzing and redesigning existing learning designs, and as a visual toolkit to documenting learning designs. Another aspect, which is presented as an application is its use as a modeling tool for blended learning patterns.

coUML's features particularly related to its artifacts (i.e., models) are:

- Visual presentation of didactical knowledge, in particular of learning strategies such as problem-based learning, inductive derivation of knowledge, deductive learning, knowledge creation, etc.
- Specification of goals, social settings, and roles of learning activities.
- Presentation of learning processes at various levels of detail and arbitrary switching between levels, if that leads to better understanding.
- Knowledge communication between educational scientists and between educators as well as communication between educational scientists and learning-technology developers.
- Supporting the specification of functional requirements on a supporting learning platform.
- Explicitly captured didactic elements such as course phases, threads, and activities can be analyzed and researched in a targeted way, considering different stakeholders' perspectives.
- Specification of the interdependence between process and content flow. This allows for the subsequent derivation of learning activity models and for example the integration of e-content modules.
- Specification, identification, and explicit integration of various means of quality assurance activities into learning scenarios to improve learning processes.
- Specification of different roles as well as modes of presence and interaction involved in cooperative environments. While this is a central feature of coUML, we add that the language is not restricted to modeling

Table 2. coUML feature and application classification

Classification of features	
Stratification	**Layered**, as it allows modeling entities of different types and at different levels of detail.
Formalization	**Semi-formal**; it inherits formal elements and semantics of UML, yet it allows the modeler to be creative in providing additional visual and textual information.
Elaboration	The primary intent of coUML is mostly **conceptual**, but it is also possible to model at the levels of specification and implementation.
Perspective	**Multiple**, as it is possible to model structural (i.e., goals, roles, and documents) and dynamic (i.e., activities) concepts from different perspectives and at different levels of abstraction.
Notation system	**Visual**, based on UML, with extensions and additional textual descriptions.
Classification of application	
Communication	Can be used as a **reflective** and **communicative** tool, depending on involved stakeholders' skills and preferences.
Creativity	Can be used for both **generative** (design-in-progress) and **finalist** (documentation) purposes. However, Its origin lies in finalist use.

of cooperative activities. In fact, it could as well be used to model non-cooperative learning environments.

Language Classification

Using the visual instructional design language (VIDL) classification scheme introduced by Botturi, Derntl, Boot and Figl (2006), coUML's feature and application classification is presented in Table 2.

Expert Survey on Modeling Support

In order to find out whether there is a broader need among researchers and practitioners for visual modeling support in designing blended course environments, we conducted a survey during a business meeting of the "Forum New Media Austria" in November 2005, which was attended by e-learning experts (both researchers and practitioners) from diverse fields such as psychology, pedagogy, mathematics, educational technology, or computer science. During a workshop on blended-learning modeling, we distributed a questionnaire among the participants (N = 27) aiming to survey general perceptions and estimations on modeling support for blended learning. Analysis of questionnaire data indicates that researchers and practitioners are in need of a visual modeling language to support them in their efforts. While the survey was not specifically focused on coUML, the following general results seem noteworthy:

1. The use of visual modeling techniques (e.g., sketches of processes, overview diagrams) in supporting the design or reorganization of a blended learning course is considered highly useful; $M = 6.88$, $SD = 1.51$, on a scale ranging from 1 ("not at all") to 8 ("very much").

2. More than two-thirds of the participants were aware of existing visual modeling techniques and almost as many are using them in their daily practice: 40% use informal modeling notations like sketches or block diagrams; another 22% use "real" modeling languages like UML or IMS Learning Design (IMS Global, 2003).

Figure 45. Experts' estimate of relevant uses of visual modeling languages for learning design

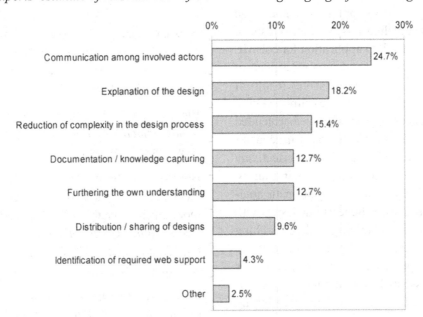

3. It is sometimes argued that strict and more formal visual notations are interesting and useful for computer-science people only. The participants unanimously voted against this proposition, even though they admitted that more formalized languages are often difficult to understand and use.

4. We were also interested in the experts' estimate of the use of visual modeling languages for instructional design. A number of relevant use cases were provided in the questionnaire, and participants' responses are highly supportive for coUML's focus: According to the experts, the top-three uses of visual modeling for learning design are "communication among involved actors" (24.7%), "explanation of the design" (18.2%), and "reduction of complexity in the design process" (15.4%). The full distribution of responses to this question is given in the histogram in Figure 45.

Even though the questionnaire was not directly related to coUML, the results show that there is considerable attention towards, and appreciation of, visual instructional design languages. Practitioners seem prepared and willing to use these languages and they are aware of potential support provided by these languages, e.g., for communication among involved actors, for explicating, sharing, and documenting learning designs, or for reducing the complexity in the design process. We hope that the current chapter does convey that these factors were also considered highly relevant in the development of coUML.

CONCLUSION

coUML is a simple, powerful visual modeling language for modeling instructional designs. Its notational power unfolds best in a blended course environment, when different modes of presence are aligned to achieve instructional objectives. It is based on UML, which is a standardized modeling language; we used UML's built-in extension mechanisms to define required modeling elements in addition to its basic set of structural and dynamic elements.

ID is an exceptionally diverse and complex discipline, making it an appropriate application area for visual modeling support. In this respect, the primary intended ID application for coUML is modeling of structural and dynamic aspects of blended course designs. We presented results of a small study among blended learning experts, which substantiates our presumption that blended learning designers and instructors are in need of a visual, conceptual toolkit to help them effectively create, analyze, and communicate their designs. We have experienced that the diagrammatic notation can help in sharing the learning design with colleagues and in organizing and researching courses. Also, the choice of proper abstractions, names, and the provision of multiple grain sizes have proved essential in communicating cooperative designs in general and in contributing to technology-enhanced learning elements in particular.

Future work on coUML will proceed in several major directions. First, we want to extend our efforts of modeling external courses from more subject domains and "teaching cultures" and include these in our pattern knowledge base (see http://elearn.pri.univie.ac.at/patterns). In this respect, readers are invited to provide feedback and share their own course designs and experiences. Second, we are working on an easy-to-use modeling tool for coUML users, easing the modeling process with computer tool support. Third, we plan to evaluate the use of the language for different cooperative processes outside of the instructional domain, such as professional community building, interdisciplinary curriculum development, and project management. Last but not least, through this chapter we want to promote the use of coUML among researchers and practitioners for feedback and further improvement.

REFERENCES

Alexander, C., Ishikawa, S., Silverstein, M., Jacobson, M., Fiksdahl-King, I., & Angel, S. (1977). *A pattern language—Towns, buildings, construction*. New York: Oxford University Press.

Bloom, B. S. (Ed.). (1956). *Taxonomy of educational objectives—Book 1: Cognitive domain*. New York: Longman.

Botturi, L., Derntl, M., Boot, E., & Figl, K. (2006). A classification framework for educational modeling languages. In *The Proceedings of IEEE International Conference on Advanced Learning Technologies (ICALT'06)*(pp. 1216-1220). Kerkrade, The Netherlands.

Derntl, M. (2005). *Patterns for person-centered e-learning*. Doctoral dissertation, University of Vienna, Vienna, Austria. Retrieved from http://elearn.pri.univie.ac.at/derntl/diss

Derntl, M., & Hummel, K. A. (2005). Modeling context-aware e-learning scenarios. In *The Proceedings of Third IEEE Conference on Pervasive Computing and Communication Workshops* (pp. 337-342). Kauai Island, Hawaii.

Derntl, M., & Motschnig-Pitrik, R. (2005). The role of structure, patterns, and people in blended learning. *The Internet and Higher Education, 8*(2), 111-130.

Eriksson, H.-E., & Penker, M. (1998). *UML Toolkit*. New York: John Wiley & Sons.

Garrison, D. R., & Kanuka, H. (2004). Blended learning: Uncovering its transformative potential in higher education. *The Internet and Higher Education, 7*(2), 95-105.

IMS Global. (2003). *IMS learning design specification*. Retrieved March 21, 2007, from http://www.imsglobal.org/learningdesign/index.html

Chapter X
poEML:
A Separation of Concerns Proposal to Instructional Design

Manuel Caeiro-Rodríguez
University of Vigo, Spain

ABSTRACT

This chapter introduces a new visual educational modeling language (EML) based on a separation-of-concerns approach, poEML: perspective-oriented EML. EMLs were proposed to support the modeling of educational units. These languages are related to ID, as they are intended to represent models of educational units. This chapter introduces the poEML separation of concerns and its graphic constructs. The main idea underlying poEML is to break down the modeling of educational units into separate parts that can be specified independently. poEML is mainly focused on supporting the computational execution of educational unit models. In addition, the separation of concerns allows us to approach the modeling of educational units in an incremental way, offering advantages in expressiveness, formality, adaptability and flexibility.

INTRODUCTION

As a design discipline, ID is devoted to produce effective **educational units** (e.g., a lesson, a course, a practice, a workshop). Botturi, Derntl, Boot and Figl (2006) show how **modeling languages** can contribute to ID by supporting the creation of visual models that facilitate the design, communication and execution of educational units. Specifically, some VIDLs are focused on supporting the creation of computational models of educational units that can be executed by customized LMSs. This is the main goal of the ID language described in this chapter, while other goals are secondary (e.g., to facilitate the design and the communication).

The achievement of a VIDL that allows us to create computational models of educational units is a complex endeavor. These are some of the problems involved:

- **Expressiveness:** One main problem is how the VIDL will support the creation of models representing the broad variety of static and behavioral issues involved in educational units. Depending on the learning goals, pedagogical approach (e.g., behaviorism, constructivism, social-collaborative) or learning context (e.g., face-to-face, blended, Web-based), teaching and training requires different resources and procedures. Here are some examples: in a traditional face-to-face course a teacher gives lectures and proposes tasks to learners; in a Web-based course a learner accesses a Web site to get documents and to perform tests; in a tennis lesson a player repeats the same movements several times under the supervision of an instructor; in a primary school, children play games to learn numbers and letters. There is a large variety of elements, resources, procedures, and behaviors present in educational units and a VIDL should allow us to express them in models.

- **Formality:** Formality is necessary to support the computational execution of the models in customized LMSs. To be executed, models need to include an appropriate level of detail, and need to be arranged in accordance with clear and unambiguous constructs. Therefore, the intended VIDL should allow us to create models with precision and consistency.

- **Adaptability** and **flexibility:** Another problem for VIDLs is that educational models are not fixed. Educational units rarely work perfectly in accordance with a predefined plan. Usually, educational plans have to choose between several alternative paths, or they have to be changed to solve unexpected situations. Therefore, a VIDL should allow us to create adaptable and flexible models of educational units.

The proposed VIDL tries to solve these problems by following a *separation-of-concerns* approach. Separation of concerns is an important principle in other design domains (e.g., architecture and software design). For example, in architecture, building models or plans are di-

vided into several parts. These include plans of the structure of the building, the layouts of floors, electrical installation, and plumbing installation. This separation of concerns facilitates the design task, as the designer's attention can be focused on one concern at a time. Similarly, the modeling of educational units can be approached from a separation-of-concerns approach as well. For example: the activity structure of educational units can be considered as one concern, and the order in which activities have to be performed as another. The proposed VIDL, developed with this separation-of-concerns principle, is called poEML: *perspective-oriented educational modeling language.*

The remainder of the chapter is organized as follows. The following section introduces the context of this proposal and its classification. The next section describes the main ideas of the language, together with the proposed separation of concerns. Then, the fourth section includes the description of the poEML elements and their graphical representations. This section only contains poEML elements that are most relevant to an ID point of view. Next the JPoEML graphical editor is introduced. In the sixth section, a simple course is modeled with poEML as a case study. The chapter ends with some conclusions.

BACKGROUND

The EML Context

poEML is introduced here as a VIDL, but it was developed as an EML: **educational modeling language** (Koper, 2001). EMLs have been proposed as modeling languages which "describe the content and process within a 'unit-of-learning' from a pedagogical perspective in order to support reuse and interoperability" (Rawlings et al., 2002). Several languages have been proposed as EMLs trying to satisfy this definition. IMS-LD (instructional management systems—learning design) (Koper *et al.*, 2003; Koper & Tattersall, 2005), issued by the IMS Global Consortium[1], is the principal attempt and the current *de-facto* EML standard. Since its publication, IMS-LD has become an important e-learning standard, and has promoted the development of active research and practitioner communities (see Chapter XV in this handbook). In any case, IMS-LD does not provide appropriate solutions to solve the problems identified in the introduction of this chapter (also described in Chapters XIII and XIV in this handbook). poEML is an attempt to develop a solution to some of these deficiencies.

Classification

This section introduces poEML in accordance with the classification framework proposed in Botturi, Derntl, Boot and Figl (2006) for ID languages. poEML features and classification is presented in Table 1.

THE SEPARATION OF CONCERNS

Separation-of-concerns is a long-standing idea that simply means that a large problem is easier to manage if it can be broken down into parts. It is an important design approach in other areas, such as software design, where it is used to facilitate the understanding, design and management of complex systems. Accordingly with the separation-of-concerns approach, programs are broken down into distinct parts that overlap in functionality as little as possible (Kazman, 2001). aspect-oriented programming (AOP) has further developed the separation-of-concerns approach to propose the concept of crosscutting concerns as concerns that cut across other concerns (Kiczales et al., 1997).

poEML follows the separation-of-concerns approach to support the modeling of educational units. Similarly to AOP, poEML identifies two kinds of concerns to break down educational unit models, namely: ***perspectives*** and ***aspects***. These two kinds of concerns can be represented in orthogonal axes (see Figure 1). On the one hand, the horizontal axis separates the elements involved in educational units in different *perspectives*. Static and behavioral elements are both taken into account in the perspectives. For example: the environments are considered in one perspective and the order between activities in another. On the other hand, the vertical axis separates models

Table 1. poEML features and classification

Classification of features of poEML	
Stratification	**Layered**, poEML offers different representations to describe entities of different types, namely: roles, activities, learning materials, etc.
Formalization	**Formal**, poEML defines a closed set of concepts and rules for composition of concepts.
Elaboration	poEML is mainly an **implementation** language as it is able to provide a high level of detail of elements and strategies involved in educational units.
Perspective	**Multiple**, as it provides different views on the same entities. For example, it provides structural, order and temporal diagrams related to different static and behavioral issues about the parts of educational units.
Notation system	poEML has both a **textual** (XML) and a **graphical** notation.
Classification of application	
Communication	poEML is **reflective** and **communicative**. It is **reflective** as it is intended to support structuring and conceiving solutions. It is **communicative** as the graphical representations can be used to share and interchange design solutions.
Creativity	poEML is both **generative** and **finalist**. It is **generative** in the sense that it can be used to create and refine design solutions. It is **finalist** as its purpose is to formalize the design models that can be processed by computational systems.

Figure 1. Separation of concerns in poEML through Perspectives and Aspects

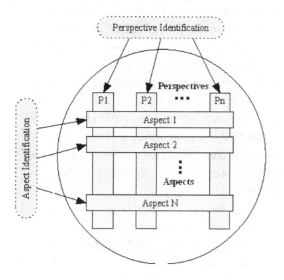

Perspectives

The **activity theory** is a meta-theory about activities and their constituent components (Engeström, 1987). Considering that any educational unit can be conceived as a set of hierarchical aggregated activities, the *expanded mediation model* provided by this theory provides an interesting framework to identify *perspectives* (see Figure 2). The core of this model is that any *activity* involves a *subject* playing a *role* acting on an *object* to achieve a certain *goal*. This connection is influenced by the *environment* and the *community* where the *activity* is performed. In other words, the *activity* depends on the *environment* and the *community*. The *environment* contains the tools and resources that can be used by the *subject* to act on the *object*. The *community* puts the emphasis in the social context where the *subject* operates, involving the influence of two new issues: *rules* and *division of labor*. The *rules* component highlights the fact that within a *community*, *subjects* are bound to rules and regulations that affect the way they interact in the *activity*, including also the interaction with the *environment* and its elements. The *division of labor* refers to the breaking down of

in accordance with different levels of control or *aspects*. Each *aspect* involves a certain level of control that can be used to determine changes in the structure or behavior of the elements in the perspectives. The basic level of control is *determined*, which does not allow any change in an educational unit model to be specified.

Figure 2. Proposed perspectives in accordance with the activity theory expanded mediation model

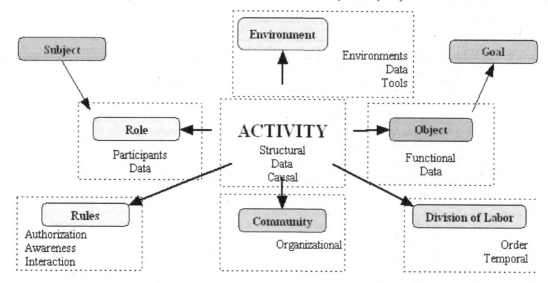

the goal into sub-goals and the distribution of responsibilities among the available *subjects*. As a result new subsidiary activities (*sub-activities*) are produced.

The *expanded mediation model* has guided the identification of 13 *perspectives*:

- **Structural:** The structural perspective is about the arrangement of the elements involved in educational units. The proposed structure is based on the activity concept. Educational units are conceived as a set of hierarchical activities grouping all the other elements: functional goals, actors, environments, sub-activities, and specifications. This structural perspective enables these elements to be grouped in an *activity hierarchical structure*. Each of the elements is further described in one of the following perspectives:

- **Functional:** This perspective is about the *functional goals* that have to be attained in an educational unit. Functional goals included in an activity specify the work that has to be performed by participants on it. For example, a functional goal can be "to produce a basic transistor circuit" or "to evaluate the learners." These functional goals are different from learning goals that refer to a desired knowledge, skill, or capability. This perspective involves the description of static and behavioral issues of functional goals. The static issues involve features and elements included in functional goals (e.g., input and output parameters). The behavioral issues involve relationships among functional goals (e.g., dependency and completion relationships). They can be used to create *functional flows* in educational units, indicating how goals included in an activity are related with goals included in its sub-activities.

- **Participants:** This perspective is about the participants involved in the educational unit.

Participants in the models are not specific persons. Instead, the desired participants are represented by **roles**. This perspective involves the description of the static and behavioral issues of participants. The static issues involve the description of the roles and the structure of groups included in each activity. The behavioral issues involve the *participants flow*, namely, how the participants performing a certain role in an activity have to be assigned to another role in a sub-activity.

- **Environments:** An environment is a place where the activity of an educational unit is performed. An environment is also made up of artifacts and tools that can be used by participants. For example, a lab environment is made up of several simulators as well as documentation about the simulators operation. This perspective involves the static description of the environments and the relationships among environments. It does not consider any behavior issues.

- **Data:** This perspective is about the data elements used in educational units. These data elements are included in the other elements: input and output parameters in functional goals; properties in roles; and artifacts in environments. This perspective involves the description of static and behavior issues of data elements. The static issues are about the features of data elements (e.g., type) and their structure. The behavior issues are about the transfer of data between data elements, namely, the *data flow*.

- **Tools:** The tool concept is used to represent the applications and services that can be used in an educational unit (e.g., simulators, editors, communication, and collaboration services). To facilitate the reuse of the educational unit models, tools are not fixed during design, but are described in an abstract way. During the run-time, tools provided by different vendors that satisfy such description can be used (this differentiation is similar to the distinction between roles and participants).

- **Organizations:** This refers to the organizational structure required to carry out an educational unit. This information may be used to constrain the behavior of other perspectives. For example, the assignment of a teacher to an evaluation activity may depend on his position in the organizational structure.

- **Order:** This perspective is about the sequence in which activities have to be performed. It indicates whether activities have to be performed in sequence or in parallel to set synchronization points among several activities performed in parallel, etc. In other domains this order perspective is also known as *control flow*.

- **Temporal:** Temporal constraints can be used to indicate when an activity must or can be initiated and when it must be finished. An example of temporal constraints would be to indicate that a lab practice must be initiated by 14:00 and that it has to be finished in 2 hours.

- **Authorization:** Authorization involves participants' rights to access the environments' elements, mainly access to the artifacts' and tools' functionalities. For example, a simulator may provide two different permissions: "expert" and "novice." Teachers may be assigned the "expert" permission while learners are assigned "novice."

- **Awareness:** Awareness refers to the processing of runtime information (events) and the notification of relevant situations. For example, in many educational units it is very important that teachers be aware of learners' actions. Nevertheless, as important as this is, it is not to overload the teacher with excessive information. Therefore, awareness involves giving the right participant the appropriate information and avoiding information overload. To accomplish this,

awareness should be focused, customized, and temporally constrained (Baker *et al.*, 2002).

- **Interaction:** This perspective is about the performance of automatic operations in tools. Many of the controls required to support collaboration among a group of participants involve the invocation of operations in collaborative tools at certain time points or as a result of events. This perspective involves the mechanisms required to support the invocation of operations.

- **Causal:** This causal perspective involves the use of competencies (Cooper & Ostyn, 2002), metadata (Duval, 2002), learning objectives, and pre-requisites to inform participants about why they should perform an educational unit.

This chapter is mainly focused on the ID features of this proposal. Some of the perspectives specifically exist to support collaboration in educational practices (e.g., *authorization*, *awareness* and *interaction*). As such, these perspectives may not be very important from an ID point of view and will not be discussed further in this chapter.

Aspects

In addition to the breaking down of static and behavioral issues in *perspectives*, the vertical axis distinguishes among different levels of control. They are introduced in order to support different kinds of control in educational unit models, from determined to decision-based. The *aspects* proposed in poEML are:

- **Determined:** This is the basic aspect. In accordance with this aspect, the structure and behavior of an educational unit is fixed in the model. During the run-time the educational unit is always carried out in the same way. A "determined" aspect does not introduce any element.

- **Data-based or conditioned:** This involves the use of conditions on data elements to control changes in the structure or behavior of educational unit elements. For example, the functional goals of a course may need to change from optional to mandatory depending on a data element of the learner profile.
- **Event-based:** Event-based aspects involve the use of events to control changes in the behavior of educational units. Events are used to signal situations that appear unexpectedly during the execution. For example, a lab activity has to be finished when a certain event is produced in a simulator.
- **Decision-based:** This involves the use of human decisions to control changes in the structure and behavior of educational units. Often, changes are not dependent on data or events, but on the judgment of responsible persons (one or several). For example, a teacher may decide the goals that should be optional or mandatory. This aspect is used to explicitly describe the human decisions that have to be taken during run-time.

poEML

This section introduces the poEML elements and graphical notations which are most relevant from an ID point of view. poEML is arranged in several packages reflecting the separation-of-concerns explained in the previous section. The modeling of each perspective and aspect is supported with the elements of a specific package. Therefore, the structural, functional, participants, environment, data, order, and temporal packages are described. For each package, a UML diagram showing its elements and relations is included. (See Chapter IX of this handbook for a good UML primer.) In addition, the graphical representation of such elements and relations is also presented. First, we will explain some general issues about the language.

General Issues

This section describes some general issues about the poEML elements and their features.

Common Features

All poEML elements have two common properties: a name and a description. The name is used as an identifier and a reference. The description is used to inform designers during design-time as well as participants during run-time about the purpose of the element. For example, for a functional goal:

- The *Name* identifies the functional goal in the educational unit model: "To design a microprocessor."
- A *Textual Description* informs participants about its purpose: "Design a microprocessor of eight bits that enables the performance…"

Abstract Elements

poEML includes several abstract elements. One of the most important is the *Choice Point* that belongs to the *Aspect* package. This element is an abstraction of a *Condition*, *Event*, or *Decision*. Conceptually it represents a point where a choice has to be performed during run-time. Obviously, this choice can be established using any of the elements considered in these aspects.

Graphical Conventions

poEML elements are represented using different geometric figures. In addition, it includes several kinds of relations (association, aggregation, specialization and dependence) that are represented using arrows. These arrows are depicted in accordance with UML conventions (see Chapter IX in this handbook). As there are many different kinds of dependencies, dependency arrows are annotated with a label that indicates the type of dependency.

Run-time Instances

poEML enables to specify the number of run-time instances that need to be created out of the elements defined. This feature is required in order to support the computational execution of educational unit models. For example, usually *Goals* have to be accomplished only once, but certain *Goals* have to be executed several times (e.g., "a teacher has to assess an examination as many times as individual learners have performed the exam"). In this situation, the functional goal is specified once, but it has to be performed repeatedly for each individual. poEML allows us indicate the number of run-time instances by the specification of a number. This number can be set during design-time or determined during run-time in accordance with the value of a *Choice Point*. In addition, it is also possible that the number of instances take the value zero. In this case the element will not exist during the run-time. This feature enables the adaptation and modification of models.

The Structural Package

The structural package is used to arrange and organize all the elements involved in educational unit models. To support such an arrangement, an activity-centered approach is followed, but instead of "activity," the term *Educational Scenario (ES)* is used. From a conceptual point of view, an *ES* represents a complete piece of instruction with a specific educational purpose. It can be used to represent educational unit models at different levels of aggregation, from simple lessons to complete curricula. From a practical point of view, any educational unit model involves a hierarchical structure of aggregated *ESs*. In other words, an educational unit is represented by an *ES* (named as *root-ES*) that is composed by other *ESs* (named

as *sub-ESs* or children *ESs*). These *sub-ESs* can also be made up of other *ESs*.

In addition, each *ES* involves a closed system of elements. The elements included in one ES can operate with elements included in the same ES, exclusively. The interactions with elements in other *ESs* have to be explicitly specified at certain perspectives as *functional flows*, *participant flows*, *data flows*, and *control flows*.

Elements Involved

Figure 3 illustrates the *ES* and its constituent elements. It represents an *ES* element involving an aggregated structure relating the elements considered in the 13 perspectives: (i) its own break down in *sub-ESs*; (ii) a *Goal* (or set of *Goals*) that need to be satisfied; (iii) a participant or set of participants (specified as *Roles*) that will work towards the goals achievement; (iv) one or several *Environments* where participants will work, composed by (v) *Data Elements* and (vi) *Tools* that represent applications and services; and optionally (vii) a particular *Organizational Structure* that situates participants in an organization scheme; (viii) *Order Specifications* to indicate the order in which the *sub-ESs* are intended to be performed; (ix) *Temporal Specifications* to indicate or constrain the moment at which each sub-*ES* has to be initiated and finished; (x) *Authorization Specifications* giving permissions to participants for the use of resources; (xi) *Awareness Specifications* indicating how events should be processed and notification submitted to participants; (xii) *Interaction Specifications* with constructs that permit the performance of automatic operations; and, (xiii) several *Records* containing descriptions of competencies, learning objectives and pre-requisites. Each one of these elements is modeled in a different package.

In addition to its constituent elements, an *ES* can involve the specification of multiple *instances*. Sometimes during execution several instances of the same *ES* must be created. For example, an

Figure 3. Main elements and relationships involved in the Educational Scenario element

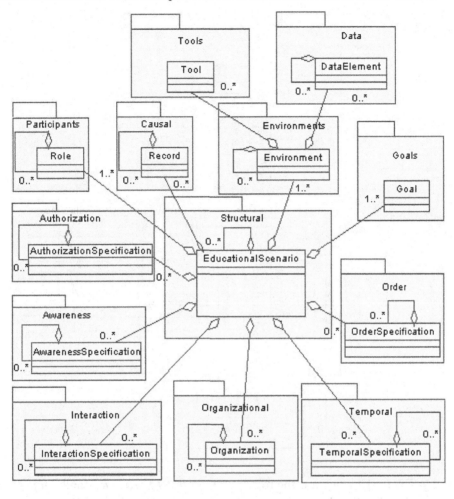

ES involving a pair of learners performing a lab practice has to be created for as many pairs of learners there are in the class, because the same lab practice has to be performed by each pair.

Graphical Representation

The elements of this package can be graphically represented as a set of hierarchical aggregated elements. At this time this representation is a hierarchical tree (see Figure 4). The root and the branches of the tree are *ESs*. The leaves of the tree are the other poEML elements that are represented by appropriate symbols. The root *ES* is represented with an icon different from the icon

Figure 4. Graphical representation of the elements of the Structural package

Figure 5. Main elements and relationships of the Goals package

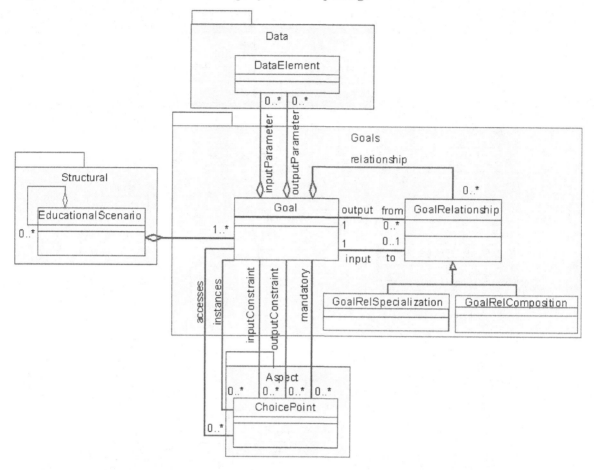

used for the other *ESs* to show that it is the root ES that represents the educational unit.

The Functional Package

The *Functional* package involves the modeling of *Goals* (functional goals). Every *ES* needs to include a *Goal* or set of *Goals* indicating what to do. It involves the modeling of the static and behavioral issues of functional goals.

Elements Involved

Figure 5 represents in an UML diagram the elements and relationships of this package.

The next items describe the elements of this package:

- *Input Parameters* and *Output Parameters* indicating the data elements that have to be provided to perform the *Goal,* and the data elements that must be produced as a result of the performance of the goal, respectively. For example: "Specifications of the problem," "The qualification obtained in an evaluation." These parameters are characterized in accordance with the *Data Element* of the *Data* package (see Figure 5).

- *Input Constraints* and *Output Constraints*. The *Input Constraints* enable control of when a functional goal can be attempted. For example: "The software tool that supports the design of microprocessors must be available," "The learner assigned to the corresponding *ES* has obtained a qualification greater than five in a previous questionnaire." Meanwhile, *Output Constraints* enable control of when a goal has been satisfied. For example: "The document containing the microprocessor design has been delivered." These constraints are specified using a *Choice Point* of the aspect package or they can reference to other functional goals.

- The *Mandatory or Optional* character of a *Goal*. Many times, educational units include certain parts that are not required. They are included as a complement to satisfy learners' curiosity or to get a better understanding. poEML recognizes this possibility and distinguishes between mandatory and optional goals. This aspect can be fixed during design-time or determined during run-time using a *Choice Point* of the aspect package.

- The *Instances* that have to be created of a *Goal*. In poEML, a *Goal* has to be performed as many times as instances are created from it. This construct permits us to indicate how many times a *Goal* has to be performed. The number of *Instances* of a *Goal* can be fixed to a value during design-time, be determined during run-time, or constrained in accordance with a *Choice Point*.

- The *Accesses* indication allows us to specify how many times a *Goal* can be accessed for performance. Some times *Goals* cannot be satisfied by an unlimited number of attempts, but have limits. For example: "A student airplane pilot has to learn to take off and land in less than a certain number of attempts." Similarly to the *Instances* indication, this value can be fixed during-design, determined during run-time or constrained.

- Relationships between *Goals*. Finally, poEML allows two different kinds of relationships to be indicated:
  - *Aggregation Relationships* are used to indicate that a *Goal* (G1) can be decomposed into several *sub-Goals* (G1, G2, ... GN). To satisfy G1 it is necessary to satisfy the N *sub-Goals*. This allows complex goals to be broken down into more simple ones. For example, a practice has as a goal "to develop a software application." This goal is broken down into the following sub-goals: "perform the analysis"; "design a solution"; "program the design"; and "perform tests."
  - *Specialization Relationships* are used to indicate that a *Goal* (G1) is detailed by several *sub-goals* (G2, G3, ... GN). To satisfy G1, some number of the N specialized *sub-goals* must be satisfied. This allows different paths to achieve the same purpose. For example, the goal "examine the learners" has the following possible specializations: "make a written examination;" "make an oral examination;" "make a portfolio examination;" etc.

Graphical Representation

Figure 6 shows the graphical representation of the elements of this package. Please note the following issues:

- *Goals* are represented with different colors depending on whether they are mandatory, optional or hidden. They include the name of the *ES* and the name of the *Goal*.
- The *Aggregation* and *Specialization* relationships connect *Goals* with other *Goals*.
- The *Mandatory or Optional* (MO), *Input* (I) and *Output* (O) dependencies connect *Goals* with *Choice Points*.
- The *Number of Instances* (NI) and *Number of Accesses* (NA) connect *Goals* with *Data Elements*.

Figure 6. Graphical representation of the elements of the Goals package

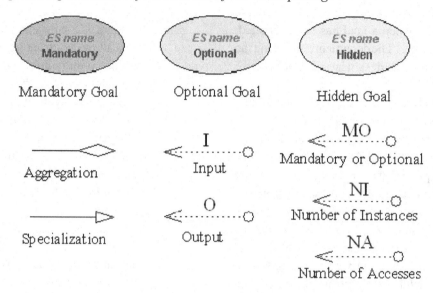

Dependencies with the Structural Perspective

The *Goals* specification has strong implications for the execution of the educational unit models. The *structural* package permits us to compose the structure of the educational unit through the aggregation of *ESs*. Meanwhile, the *Goals* package let us indicate what has to be done in the educational unit. This enables the design of "goal maps" where different paths through the structural model can be conceived.

The Participants Package

The *Participants* package involves the modeling of *Roles*. Every *ES* may include a *Role* or set of *Roles* representing the expected participants.

Notice that each *ES* has to define its own *Roles*. They can be the same or different from the *Roles* in its *Parent ES*. During the execution, participants will be transferred from the *Roles* in the *Parent ES* to the *Roles* in the *Sub-ESs* accordingly to a *participant flow* specification. This kind of specification facilitates the reuse of *ESs*.

Elements Involved

Figure 7 represents in a UML diagram the main elements and relationships of this package.

The next items describe the main elements of this package include the following:

- *Properties* involving *Data Elements* about the *Role*. The value of the *Properties* during the execution will correspond with the particular participant assigned to the *Role*. Some examples of properties associated with a *Role*: personal data as name, surname, address; previous knowledge, etc.
- *Role Aggregations* enabling the specification of *Composed Roles* made up by other *Roles* (*sub-Roles*). This feature allows the modeling of groups. For example a project group is made up by the following roles: one leader, three developers, one tester and one supervisor.
- The *Instances* that have to be created of each *Role*. During the execution each instance of a *Role* has to be performed by a different participant. In this way it is possible

Figure 7. Main elements and relationships of the Participants package

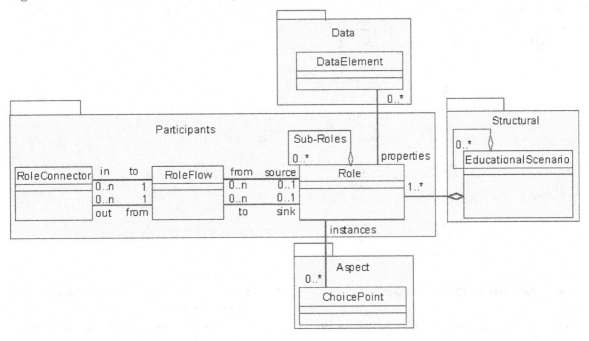

to indicate that a certain *ES* requires the participation of several persons in the same *Role*. For example: "A discussion *ES* needs to involve five learners."

- The *participant flow* recognizes that participants can change their *Role* between activities during the run-time. For example: "A participant performs as learner in a theoretical *ES* and as project leader in a practical *ES*." The *participant flow* can be modeled using two elements:
  - *Role Connectors.* These are operators that indicate how participants will be processed. Four types of connectors are supported: (i) *selection* connectors that permit us to take several participants from a larger set; (ii) *election* connectors that let us to take exactly one participant from a larger set; (iii) *relation* connectors that enable to constraint possible elections; and (iv) *assignment type* connectors distinguish between *forced assignment* and *voluntary assignment*.
  - *Role Flow* elements. These are simple arrows connecting *Roles* and *Role Connectors*.

Graphical Representation

Figure 8 shows the graphical representation of the elements of this package. Note the following issues:

- Three different kinds of *Roles* icons are provided: *Learner*, *Staff* and *Group*. They include the name of the *ES* where they are included and the name of the *Role*.
- The *Aggregation* association is used to model *Groups*.
- The *Parameter* (P) and *Number of Instances* (NI) dependencies are used to connect *Roles* with *Data Elements*.
- Each kind of *Role Connector* is represented with a different icon.
- The *Role Flow* dependency is used to connect *Roles* with *Role Connectors*.

Figure 8. Graphical representation of the elements of the Participants package

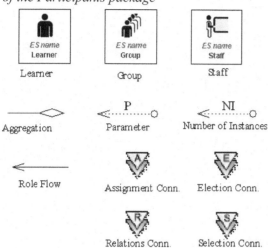

Figure 9. Main elements and relationships of the Environments package

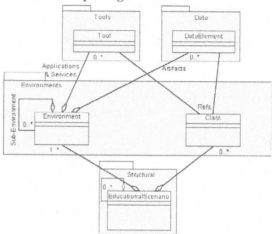

The Environments Package

The *Environments* package involves the modeling of *Environments*. Every *ES* may include an *Environment* or set of *Environments* containing the resources that can be used. *Environments* contain *Tools* and *Artifacts* specified with *Data Elements*. Two different kinds of *Environments* are considered: virtual and physical.

Elements Involved

Figure 9 represents in a UML diagram the elements of this package.

The next items describe the elements of this package:

- *Artifacts* contained in the *Environment*. These *Artifacts* are characterized using *Data Elements*. Some examples: "A document explaining a concept," "A variable indicating the grade obtained in a questionnaire."
- *Tools* contained in the *Environment*. These *Tools* are characterized in accordance with the *Tool* element of the *Tools* perspective. Some examples: "A simulator," "A text-editor," "A chat service."

- *Environment Aggregations* enabling the specification of *Composed Environments* made up by other *Environments* (*sub-Environments*). For example: "A laboratory room is made up by a working environment and a test environment."

- The *Class* element is used to support the classification of the resources included in the *Environments* of an *ES*. Many times, the resources of an environment need to be classified. For example: "Resources for expert learners and resources for novice learners." They are used in the specification of the *awareness*, *authorization*, and *interaction* perspectives.

- Finally, poEML considers that *Environments* will be characterized in an abstract way during design-time. Then, during runtime, a concrete environment containing the specified *Artifacts* and *Tools* will be provided. This is similar to the distinction between *Roles* and participants. Nevertheless, it is possible to specify the use of a concrete *Environment*. To do so, a *Reference* indication has to be specified to establish the concrete environment. In addition, this *Reference* can also be used to indicate that an *Environment* in an *ES* has to be the same that other *Environment* in other *ES*.

Graphical Representation

Figure 10 shows the graphical representation of the elements of this package. Please note the following issues:

- Special icons are used to represent *Physical*, *Virtual*, and *Class* elements. They include the name of the *ES* where they are included and the name of the element.
- A *Contains* (C) dependency is used to indicate which *Artifacts* and *Tools* are included in each *Environment*.
- A *Belongs* (B) dependency is used to relate resources with *Classes*.
- A *Reference* (R) dependency is used to indicate the reference from an *Environment* to other *Environment*.

The Data Package

The *Data* package supports the modeling of *Data Elements* and the transfer of data values between *Data Elements*. *Data Elements* may be included in *Goals*, *Roles* and *Environments* to feature parameters, properties and artifacts respectively.

Elements Involved

poEML proposes the elements depicted in Figure 11 to support the representation of data needs in educational unit models:

- The *Data Element* is the main component. For each *Data Element,* the following properties can be specified: name, description, type, and default value.
- The *External File* element allows one to specify data elements contained in a file external to the educational unit model. This element can be used to transfer information to or from the external context.
- The *Data Flow* element enables the indication of how data values flow between *Data Elements*, *External Files*, and *Data Connectors*.
- The *Data Connector* involves several alternatives to transfer values between data elements. Three different connectors are available:
  - The *Reference* connector shows that a *Data Element* has the same value as other one
  - The *Copy* connector shows that a *Data Element* takes the value of other *Data Element*. The *Copy* can be synchronous (if it is produced when the sink *Data Element* is created) or asynchronous

Figure 10. Graphical representation of the elements of the Environments package

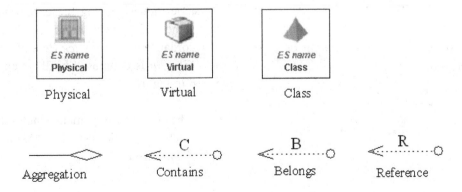

Figure 11. Main elements and relationships of the Data package

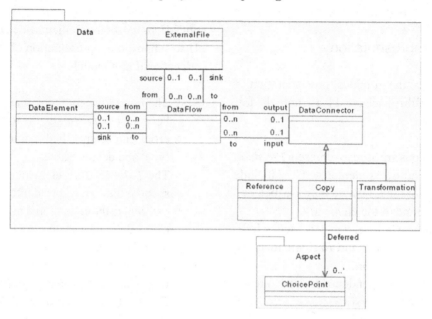

(if it is produced when a *Choice Point* is satisfied).

○ The *Transformation* involves the performance of operations using the data contained in *Data Elements*. Some operation types are: Boolean (e.g., AND, OR), mathematical (e.g., + , -, *), string processing (e.g., sub-string, delete).

Graphical Representation

Figure 12 shows the graphical representation of the basic elements in the *Data* package. The different *Data* types have particular graphical representations.

Figure 12. Graphical representation for the elements of the Data package

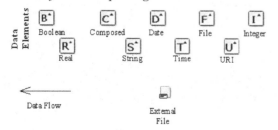

The Order Package

The *Order* package allows us to indicate the order in which the *sub-ESs* of an *ES* will be performed. It is not possible to establish order specifications among *sub-ESs* that belong to different parent *ESs*. This constraint is introduced to help facilitate the reusability of *ESs*.

Elements Involved

The indication of the *Order* among *sub-ESs* is maintained in *Order Specifications*. For an *ES*, several *Order Specifications* can be included in the same model. During the execution one or zero in the *Order Specifications* may be activated in accordance with a *Choice Point*. Each *Order Specification* is composed by the elements depicted in Figure 13:

- The *Order Flow* element enables the specification of links between *ESs* and *Order Connectors*.

- The *Order Connector* element is used to indicate different order operations. The provided connectors are:
  - **Sequence:** The Sequence specification describes a point where an *ES* can be initiated when the previous *ES* has finished.
  - **Unordered Sequence:** The Unordered Sequence specification describes a situation where several *ESs* can be initiated in sequence, but with no predefined order in which they must be performed. The order is decided during the execution.
  - **Parallel Split:** Parallel split specifies a point where several *ESs* can be initiated and performed in parallel.
  - **Loop:** Loop specifies a point where a return to an already finished or completed *ES* may be required.
  - **Merge:** Merge specifies a point where several *ESs* that were being performed in parallel converge. Each time one of the *ESs* finishes, a new instance of the next *ES* is created and initiated.
  - **Synchronization:** To specify a point where several *ESs* that were being performed in parallel converge, the synchronization specification is used. To initiate the next *ES,* all parallel *ESs* must finish. Using an association with a *Choice Point* it is possible to indicate that the synchronization has to be produced in a *Deferred* way, namely, when a condition, decision or event is satisfied.

Figure 13. Main elements and relationships of the Order package

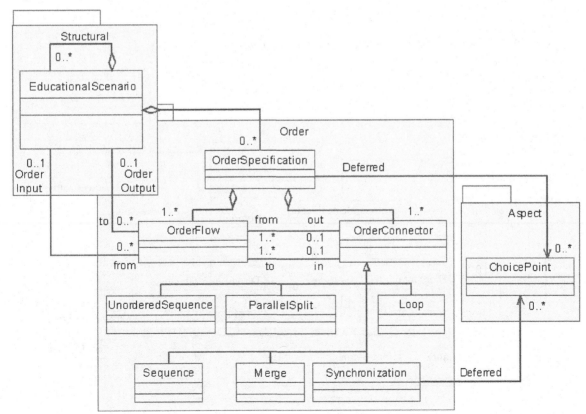

Figure 14. Graphical representation of the elements of the Process package

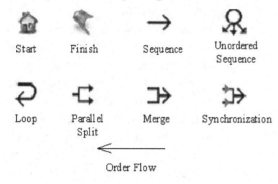

- Each *Order Connector* is represented by a different figure in accordance with its behavior.
- The *Order Flow* arrow is used to connect *ESs* with *Order Connectors*. Each *ES* and *Order Connector* has exactly one input *Order Flow* and one output *Order Flow*.

The Temporal Package

The *Temporal* package allows one to indicate and constrain the time at which an *ES* can/has to be initiated or finished.

During run-time, *Temporal Specifications* and *Order Specifications* may produce conflicting situations. For example: "Both the lab practice and the exam have to be performed in sequence. The exam has to be started at 16:00." To know what to do in these cases *Temporal Specifications* are assigned as a priority factor.

Graphical Representation

Figure 14 shows the graphic representation of the elements of this package. Note the following issues:

- Two special figures are used to indicate the start and the finish of the order execution.

Figure 15. Main elements and relationships of the Temporal package

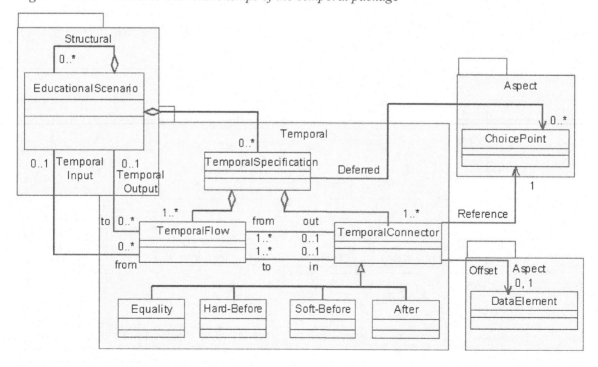

Elements Involved

Temporal indications and constraints are specified in *Temporal Specifications*. For an *ES,* several *Temporal Specifications* can be included in the same model. During the execution one or none of the *Temporal Specifications* may be activated in accordance with a *Choice Point*.

Each *Temporal Specification* is composed by elements depicted in Figure 15:

- The *Temporal Flow* element enables the specification of links between *ESs* and *Temporal Connectors*.
- The *Temporal Connector* element is used to indicate different temporal relations. It can be associated with a *Choice Point* or a *Data Element*. If it is associated with a *Data Element,* that element represents an absolute time (e.g., February 14th, 2007). In the other case, when a *Temporal Connector* is associated with a *Choice Point* it acts as a temporal reference (i.e., the time at which an event is produced). In this case an *Offset* can be included to indicate a delay to the relative time. These issues affect the four *Temporal Connectors*:
  - **Equality:** To specify that action A has to be performed just when another action B is produced. For example: "The exam has to be initiated just when the lab practice has been finished," "The course starts on September 19th."
  - **Hard-Before:** To specify that action A has to be performed before another action B is produced. If action B is produced and A has not yet been produced then action A is forced to be performed. For example: "The lab practice has to be finished *hard-before* the test activity is finished."
  - **Soft-Before:** To specify than action A can be performed before another action B is produced. If action B is produced

and A has not been produced yet then action A cannot be performed. For example: "An optional activity can be initiated *soft-before* the examination has been initiated."

  - **After:** To specify that an action A can be performed after action B is produced. For example: "The video session can be initiated after the debate has been initiated."

Graphical Representation

Figure 16 shows the graphic representation of the elements of this package. The dependencies are used in the following ways:

- The *Temporal Flow* connects an *ES Temporal Input* or *Temporal Output* with a *Temporal Connector*.
- A *Reference* (R) dependency is provided to link *Temporal Connectors* to *Choice Points* or *Data Elements* indicating relative or absolute temporal references, respectively.
- An *Offset* (O) dependency is provided to link *Temporal Connectors* to *Data Elements* to indicate an offset on the temporal specification.

THE JPoEML EDITOR

JPoEML is an authoring tool that enables the design of educational unit models in accordance

---

Figure 16. Graphical representation of the elements of the Temporal package

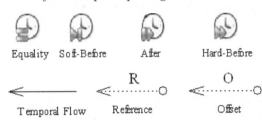

Equality   Soft-Before   After   Hard-Before

Temporal Flow   Reference   Offset

Figure 17. JPoEML editor graphical interface with an OrderSpecification in edition

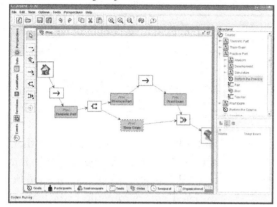

with the poEML structure and organization (see Figure 17). It is available at http://www.poeml. com. This application permits us to approach the design of educational units by focusing on each *perspective* and on each *aspect* each time. In this way, it is an appropriate tool to test the ID capabilities of the language.

The JPoEML graphical interface is separated in two main areas:

- The right side of the screen includes two panels to provide permanent information

about model elements. It is composed of two panels:

- ○ The top panel is used to represent the structure of the educational unit model. It shows the hierarchical tree structure of *ESs* and contained elements. This panel provides a permanent and global view of the educational unit model.

- ○ The bottom panel is an area where the properties (e.g., name, description, type) of the active element are displayed. Depending on the active element (e.g., *ES*, *Goal*, *Role*) different data fields are provided.

- The central portion of the screen is the more important part of the JPoEML editor. It permits the graphical representation of each perspective and aspect. At a given moment only one perspective or aspect can be represented. Perspectives and aspects are indicated at tabs in the bottom side and left side of this panel respectively. In addition, a contextual panel with tools for each perspective and aspect is available on the left side.

Figure 18. Graphical representation of the simulation course Goals perspective

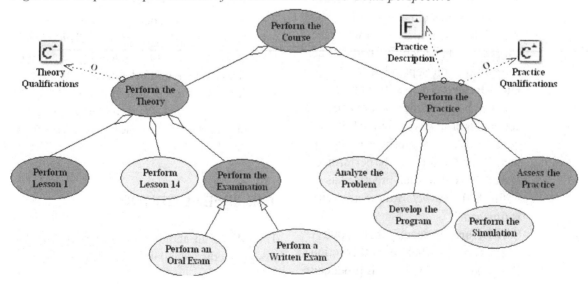

AN EXAMPLE

This section describes an example of an educational unit model. Another example can be found in chapter XVI of this handbook. This educational unit is made up by a theoretical part and a practical part with separated examinations.

poEML enables the incremental design of educational units. The following sections show the models for the functional, structural, participants, environments and order perspectives.

The Goals Model

The *Goals* perspective is an appropriate starting point to initiate the design. The idea is to specify the goals that indicate what participants have to do. The *Goals* specification may be done incrementally, first indicating the main *Goals* and then refining these *Goals* into more detail by specifying aggregated goals, specialized goals and other features.

Figure 18 depicts the graphical representation of the case study functional goals' model. This representation is incomplete as some goals may be further subdivided, and additional elements at each goal may be included. The "root" *Goal* is "Perform the Course." It breaks down into two *sub-Goals*: "Perform the Theory" and "Perform the Practice." The first one includes an *Output Parameter* (a *Composed Data Element*) and the second one includes an *Input Parameter* and an *Output Parameter*. These goals are further divided. Some of the *sub-Goals* are depicted in a light brown color indicating that they are optional. The "Perform the Examination" *sub-Goal* of the theory has two specializations: "Perform an Oral Exam" and "Perform a Written Exam." During execution, only one is required.

The Structural Model

The *Structural* perspective may also be used to initiate the design of educational unit models. In

Figure 19. Graphical representation of the simulation course Structural perspective

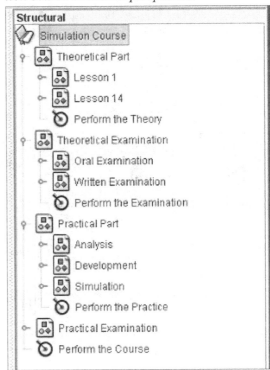

this case, it has been performed after the *Goals* were available. This is how the previous *Goals* are assigned to the *ESs*.

Figure 19 shows the example structure. The course breaks down into four main *ESs*: two for the theoretical and practical parts and two for the examinations. In addition, these main *ESs* also break down into other *sub-ESs*. At this design stage these *ESs* only include the *Goals*. *Roles, Environments* and the rest of elements will be added to each *ES* in accordance with the perspectives.

The Participants Model

Figure 20 shows the *Participants* model. The course *Roles* are represented in the top of the figure: a *Learner* and a *Teacher*. The *Learner* has two associations of type *Number Instances* with *Condition Elements*. They are included to indicate the minimum and maximum number of learners that may be involved. Similarly, the *Teacher* has an

Figure 20. Graphical representation of the simulation course Participants perspective

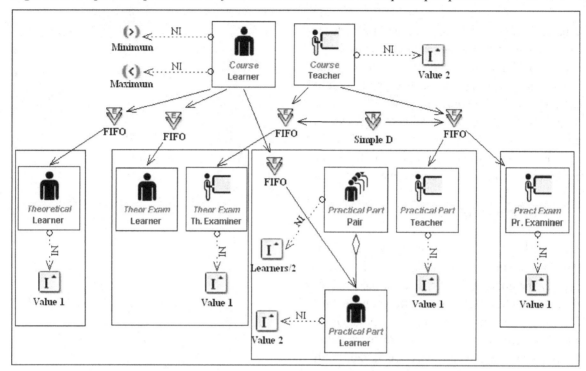

association of type *Number Instances* connected with an *Integer Data Element*, fixing the number required teachers (in this example two).

The *Roles* of other *ESs* also have associations of type *Number Instances*. Notice that the theoretical *ES* only includes a *Learner Role* with one instance. Obviously, all the learners have to perform the theoretical part of the course. To do it, the theoretical *ES* is assigned a number of instances equal to the eventual number of learners. In this way, each learner will work in a particular instance of the theoretical ES. The same is applied to the practical part *ES*, where two *Roles* are involved: a *Pair* of two *Learners* and a *Teacher*.

Notice that the *Pair* has an association *Number Instances* with an *Integer Data Element*. In the *Condition-based* aspect this element takes the value number of learners divided by 2 plus 1. This is the number of *Pairs* that have to be created.

The diagram also includes *Role Connectors* and *Role Flows* to indicate how participants are transferred from *Role* to *Role*. These connectors

are of type *Election* and *Relation*. The *Election* uses a "FIFO" (First-In-First-Out) algorithm establishing that learners are assigned in the order they are enrolled in the course. The *Selection* involves a "Difference" mode, establishing that the teacher assigned to the *Theoretical Exam* has to be different from the teacher assigned to the *Practical Part*.

The Environments Model

For this example, the instruction has been considered as a blended course where the theoretical part examination has to be performed face-to-face and the other parts are performed on the Web. Figure 21 shows the *Environments* for the main example *ESs*. In the "root" *ES* two *Environments* are specified: the "Course Env." contains a file with general information about the course and the "Teacher Environments" provides information for teachers. This environment should be visible and accessible for teachers (this can be specified with

Figure 21. Graphical representation of the simulation course Environments perspective

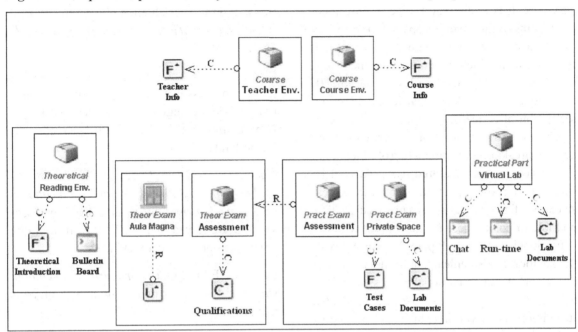

the elements of the *Authorization* package). The rest of the *ESs* includes particular environments containing different artifacts and tools. Notice that the theoretical exam *ES* includes two environments: a *Physical Environment* named as "Aula Magna," that is fixed using *Reference* association with *Data URI Element* to a particular room; and a *Virtual Environment* named as "Assessment" that contains a *Data Composed Element*. This last environment is also used in the practice examination *ES*. To do it, a *Virtual Environment* is specified in such *ES* and connected using a *Reference* to the previous one.

The Order Model

Figure 22 shows an *Order Specification* for the *ESs* under the "root" *ES*. It involves three types of *Order Connectors*: *Sequence*, *Parallel Split* and *Synchronization*. In accordance with this specification the course is initiated with the theoretical part *ES*. When it is complete, it is possible to initiate the practical part and to perform the theoretical exam. When the practical part is

Figure 22. Graphical representation of the simulation course Order perspective

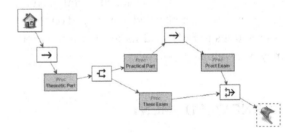

finished it is possible to perform the practical examination. The course ends when all the *ESs* are completed.

CONCLUSION

This chapter introduces poEML focusing on its ID capabilities. poEML has been proposed to contribute to the modeling of educational units in the context of EMLs. This language is oriented towards several goals: expressive power, formality, flexibility and adaptability. The eventual achievement of all these goals is not an easy task. It is likely that a large improvement process involving several steps will be required to improve the poEML language. Currently, it is not clear in which direction and which steps should be taken to improve EML and poEML is an attempt to explore a particular direction: separation-of-concerns.

Following a separation-of-concerns approach poEML breaks down the modeling of educational units into a set of separated parts that can be specified step-by-step. In this way, the expressiveness of the language is enhanced as it is possible to notate more issues and behaviors of educational units at each part. The formality of the solution is also enhanced, to make it easier to support the computational processing of the models by considering each part independently. In addition, models are adaptable, to make it possible to include several alternatives and consider their activation during run-time using *Choice Points*; and flexible, so that the modeling of a perspective/aspect can be changed affecting other perspectives in a controlled way. Based on these assumptions, poEML and its graphical notation may be a valuable tool for ID.

ACKNOWLEDGMENT

I want to thank *"Consellería de Innovación e Industria"* for its support to this work under grant *"E-BICS: E-learning—Bases de Integración e Coordinación sobre eStándares"* (PGIDIT-06PXIB322270PR).

REFERENCES

Baker, D., Georgakopoulos, D., Schuster, H., & Cichoki, A. (2002). Awareness provisioning in collaboration management. *International Journal of Cooperative Information Systems, 11*(1&2), 145-173.

Botturi, L. (2005). Visual languages for instructional design: An evaluation of the perception of E2ML. *Journal of Interactive Learning Research, 16*(4), 329-351.

Botturi, L., Derntl, M., Boot, E., & Figl, K. (2006). A classification framework for educational modeling languages in instructional design. *Proceedings of IEEE ICALT 2006*, Kerkrade, The Netherlands.

Cooper, A., & Ostyn, C. (Eds.). (2002). *IMS reusable definition of competency or educational objective—information model.* IMS Global Consortium. Retrieved March 27, 2007, from http://www.imsglobal.org/competencies

Duval, E. (Ed.). (2002). *Learning object metadata standard.* IEEE Learning Technology Standards Committee.

Engeström, Y. (1987). *Learning by expanding: An activity-theoretical approach to developmental research.* Orienta-Kosultit, Helsinki, Finland.

Kazman, R. (2001). Software Architecture. *Handbook of software engineering and knowledge engineering* (pp. 47-68). World Scientific Press.

Kiczales, G., Lamping, J., Mendhekar, A., Maeda, C., Lopes, J.-M., & Irwing, J. (1997). Aspect-Oriented Programming. *Proceedings of the European Conference on Object-Oriented Programming, Vol. 1241*, (pp. 220-242)

Koper, R. (2001). *Modeling units of study from a pedagogical perspective—The pedagogical metamodel behind EML.* Open University of The Netherlands.

Koper, R., Olivier, B., & Anderson, T. (2003). *IMS Learning design information model.* IMS Global Learning Consortium, Inc.

Koper, R., & Tattersall, C. (Eds.). (2005). *Learning design. A handbook on modelling and delivering networked education and training.* Springer Berlin Heidelberg.

Rawlings, A., Rosmalen, P. Van, Koper, R. Rodriguez-Artacho, M., & Lefrere, P. (2002). *Survey of educational modelling languages (EMLs)*. CEN/ISSS/WS/LT.

ENDNOTE

[1] The IMS Global Learning Consortium is a main e-learning standardization body involving main vendors of e-learning products, universities and educational institutions to promote the development and adoption of e-learning standards. Web site at http://www. imsglobal.org

Chapter XI
Performance Case Modeling

Ian Douglas
Florida State University, USA

ABSTRACT

This chapter introduces performance case modeling as a means of conducting a performance analysis. It argues that the design of any instruction focused on practical subjects should be preceded by understanding of the performance requirements for graduates of a course of instruction. This understanding is facilitated by the collaborative creation of diagrams that identify the different roles a performer takes and their associated goals, together with documentation of performance measures for the goals. The measures serve as a baseline for the evaluation of instructional effectiveness. Other approaches to visual languages in instructional design have been more focused on modeling the architecture of the instructional system rather than the performance environment in which its graduates will be expected to perform. The approach described is based on UML use cases and serves to focus thinking on the performance analysis that should occur prior to the design of instruction.

INTRODUCTION

The performance analysis stage of most instructional system design process models has long been seen as one of the most crucial stages (Harless, 1970). If designers do not sufficiently understand the problem they are unlikely to create an optimal solution. In addition to aiding the understanding of the problem, performance analysis is also focused on establishing performance measures and collecting initial data. It is not possible to determine the value of a solution, such as a new course of instruction, without having analysis data that would allow one to show improvement over a baseline level of performance (Deming, 1982). This is especially true if designers are aiming to achieve Kirkpatrick's level 3 (on the job application of acquired skills and knowledge) and level 4 (improved organizational outcomes as a result of the acquired skills and knowledge) (Kirkpatrick, 1998). Clark and Estes (2002) present a number of case studies illustrating that data-driven analysis leads to better solutions for performance improvement.

Some terms that are often used interchangeably in performance analysis are: needs assessment (Kaufman, 1988), needs analysis (Mager & Pipe, 1984), performance assessment (Robinson and Robinson, 1995), front-end analysis (FEA) (Harless, 1988), and training needs analysis (Rossett, 1998). In this chapter the term performance analysis is used as a general term for all of these types of analyses.

The majority of attempts to adapt visual languages for instructional design have been focused on designing the solution space (the nature of the instructional system). In this chapter we will consider an approach that is specifically focused on understanding the problem space (the performance requirements for the employers of the instructional system graduates). Understanding the desired performance is an important first step that should occur prior to developing instruction or any other means of improving human performance.

The specific approach is an adaptation of use case modeling, which is part of the unified modeling language (UML). UML is a systems modeling tool which, although developed primarily for computer systems modeling, is adaptable to the modeling of other types of systems. Despite its origins in software engineering, elements of it have been adapted for such diverse purposes as business process modeling (Marshall, 2000; Eriksson and Penker, 2000) and educational modeling (IMS, 2005). Different aspects and applications of UML relative to instructional design are described in a number of chapters in this book. In this chapter we will focus on one area of UML that has been relatively neglected.

UML is not a single language but rather a collection of diagramming techniques and specification languages that serve different purposes in systems analysis and design. It can be used both to model existing systems and to envisage models of new systems. The nine different diagramming techniques found in UML serve different purposes: describing what the static structure of a system is like (class, object, and component diagrams), describing how a system operates and information flows through the system (activity,

collaboration, sequence, and statechart diagrams), describing how a system is deployed (deployment diagram), and describing the functional requirements of the system (use case diagrams). A number of the chapters in this book describe the adaptation of elements of UML for instructional systems architecture design (e.g., Chapter IX). They primarily focus on the use of Structure and Flow diagrams. In this chapter the focus will be exclusively on use case diagrams.

Given that they are concerned with system inputs and outputs rather than the internal technical details, use cases are often seen as a crucial part of UML when used in software development. Use cases aim to establish what an efficient and effective system should achieve. They serve as the starting point and driving force behind all other analysis and design activities (Jacobson, 1992; Rosenberg & Scott, 1999).

This chapter explains the concept of use case modeling, shows how it can be adapted for performance analysis (performance case modeling), discusses software tools for repositories and reuse, and suggests guidelines for applying performance case modeling.

PERFORMANCE ANALYSIS

There are a number of approaches to performance analysis prescribed and studied in the literature (Rummler & Brache, 1995; Swanson, 1994; Wedman & Graham 1992; Schaffer, 2000).

The major tasks of performance analysis that they tend to share are the following process:

- Identify what people in particular roles are required to achieve.
- Identify gaps between exemplary (or expert) performers and typical performance or novice performers.
- Analyze causes for those gaps.
- Identify and select the solutions (e.g., required instruction) to close the gaps.

Modern approaches to performance analysis move beyond being tied to a single specific solution such as classroom instruction, and often include job support through electronic performance support systems (Raybould, 2000). Managers, supervisors, and executives may be inclined to believe that when performance problems exist it is the individual's knowledge or skills at fault; less frequently do they consider environmental factors. As a result, instruction in a traditional training setting is usually the solution they select. Optimal performance analysis identifies all factors contributing to performance by focusing on a performer and his or her work environment (Wedman & Graham, 1992).

There is evidence that the performance analysis stage of design is sometimes overlooked. Often the reason given for this is lack of time (Swanson, 1994). Rossett and Czech (1995) studied the practices of graduates of San Diego State University's Instructional Systems program and found that professionals are often unable to use their analysis skills because organizational leaders prefer a silver bullet approach to fixing problems. Ideally, performance analysis involves a partnering between the analysis team and stakeholders to define and achieve organizational goals, and it is during this process that some kind of visual modeling is likely to provide assistance in achieving a shared understanding. Performance analysis is used to describe what is happening, what ought to be happening, and what can be done to improve the current status of the organizational problem (Wedman and Graham, 1992).

USE CASE MODELING

Use cases (Schneider & Winters, 2001) are one of the main modeling approaches that were brought together into the initial version of UML. They were developed by Jacobson (1992) as an improvement over the situation of communicating software system requirements in a purely textual form.

Cockburn (1997) notes that despite the formal appearance of use case models, they are usually used informally. This is particularly so in the early stages of development.

There are two parts to creating use cases: diagramming and documentation. Diagram creation is done either on paper or a whiteboard, or using a diagram creating software tool. It is an iterative process and initial diagrams are often discarded. Figure 1 represents an initial use case diagram for a software system to support a travel booking system. The diagram elements are deliberately simple to allow sketching by people with little graphic design skill. The stick figure, referred to as an actor, represents an entity that is external to the system and interacts with it to obtain some service. This entity often represents human end-users, but it can also represent another computer system that exchanges data with the system being designed. The ellipses represent the actual use cases, which are the services provided by the system to the actors to enable them to achieve some goal.

Use case modeling is a useful informal tool for communicating with non-technical stakeholders during the domain analysis and requirements phase of a development project. Use case diagrams can also be used to brainstorm around possible functions of a new system, prior to more formal use cases being created to specify the actual functionality of a system to be built. UML diagrams are often used in an iterative development process,

Figure 1. Use case diagram for a flight booking system

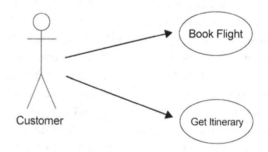

where you start at a high level and go through a process of review and further refinement. The diagrams become increasingly complex as the process continues.

Once the diagrams have become established and the key use cases are identified and named, the next stage is to document them. The documentation of use cases should be done after the informal modeling leads to a stable use case diagram. As with diagramming, this is also likely to go through an iterative process, starting with sketchy and informal narratives and progressing to more detailed formal documentation. For example, Brugge and Dutoit (2000) recommend the process of identifying informal scenarios of use. These take the form of stories about how the identified people would achieve some goal with the system being modeled. From a collection of these informal stories, a more formal representation of how a goal is achieved in the system is outlined in the use case documentation (see Table 1).

This is not necessarily a finished use case, as a stakeholder may find certain parts need to be clarified (e.g., how the customer selects the preferred trip). Once the use case is refined and in a stable state it becomes a useful resource for software engineers to identify which objects and components will be required for building the system (e.g., an interactive calendar). They would use the items highlighted in bold in the use case narrative as a starting point for UML object, class, and component diagrams which describe the structure of the system and the flow, and Interaction diagrams which show how data flows throughout the system. Many of the software tools that exist for creating UML diagrams allow the inter-relating of the different diagram types (see Figure 2).

It should be emphasized that Table 1 illustrates just one example of how a use case can be documented. Practitioners of use case modeling often use variants of this basic model. Cockburn (2001) suggests that different documentation models are appropriate depending on the purpose of the modeling. He identifies four basic functions that use case models can perform in an organization:

- Describe a business' work process (domain analysis)
- Focus discussion about new software features (establishing the possibilities)
- Create the functional requirements for a system (determining what will be built)
- Document the design of the system (creating a map for maintenance)

Table 1. Typical documentation for a use case

use case Name	Book Flight
Participating Actor	Initiated by Customer
Entry Condition	1. Customer has logged into the system and has identified a specific travel date and destination
Flow of Events	2. System presents flight **booking screen** to the customer 3. Customer fills in the form by entering **starting** and **ending point** in **entry fields,** selecting roundtrip or one way **button** and travel dates from **calendar object** 4. Customer presses the **go button** 5. System searches the **database** using the entered requirements 6. System presents the results to the user in **table** format 7. Customer selects preferred trip 8. System presents detailed information on **itinerary** 9. Customer selects **purchase** or **exit button**
Exit Condition	10. Customer selects **confirm booking** or selects exit
Special Requirements	**E-mail confirmation** is sent within one day of confirmation

Figure 2. Screenshot from a computer-aided software engineering tool that incorporates UML (Reprint Courtesy of International Business Machines Corporation copyright © International Business Machines Corporation)

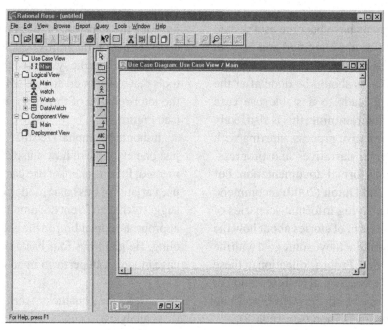

He also notes that the functions might vary depending on whether they are written by a small, close-knit group, or by a large, distributed group. In addition, use cases might be used by documentation and training specialists to identify training and documentation needs of the users. They can also be used as the basis for constructing system functionality and usability tests; with the completed system you should be able to get a test subject to play the role of the actor and, with representative input data, reach the exit condition of the use case. This should be done without encountering problems through failure of the system or poor usability (such as not easily being able to identify and use the appropriate controls).

The use case documentation is a resource for analysts and stakeholders, which captures a description of the functionality they wish to achieve in the system (why it is being built). It is also a documentation resource for designers and developers, allowing them to start the process of identifying and connecting the structural com-

ponents and information flows required within the systems they will design and build (how it should be built). In this sense, use cases drive all other modeling and development.

ADAPTING USE CASE MODELING FOR HUMAN PERFORMANCE

It follows that when adapting a similar modeling approach to UML for instruction, that an equivalent of use cases (to help determine why the system should be built) should be included. Those who have looked to UML to support non-software systems have tended to focus more on adapting the structural and flow diagram techniques (IMS, 2005). This modeling is focused on describing what will be built, how it is structured and how it works, rather than answering the important question of why the system should be built. That is, why will the system being built result in a better performance from the individuals that use it and the organizations that they participate in? This is as legitimate a question for a learning system as it is for a software system. Creating the equivalent to a use case would help determine the value, in terms of individual performance, that is to be obtained by the creation of a new learning system.

In order to adapt the use case modeling scheme to the task of modeling for learning and performance support systems, we need to re-conceptualize what is meant by the actor, the use case and the system. Actors can be re-characterized as Performance Roles and use cases can be re-characterized as performance cases (Douglas, 2003). Performance Cases are goals that a person attempts to achieve with his or her own skills and knowledge, using the available tools and support available. The system refers to the organizational system of which the individual's role is an integral part. The role does not reside outside the system as the actor does in software use case modeling.

The UML concept of a package is used to collect related performance cases into a meaningful unit and to illustrate the alignment of individual performance goals with organizational goals and processes. The performance cases within packages will usually represent high-level performance goals. A high level performance case can be refined into a more detailed model. For example, Figure 3 shows a package of administrative roles and goals. 'Office Manager' is an organizational role that corresponds to an identified job title within the organization. It includes the two operational roles identified in this diagram as 'New Employee Processor' and 'Travel Administrator.' An operational role is a role someone has to adopt as part of his or her job; a given job title is likely to encompass several operational roles. Operational roles in small companies may be primary roles in larger organizations. For example, a large organization may have a job title for travel administrator.

This diagram introduces the 'secondary role' to the interactions needed to achieve the performance goal. Identifying secondary roles is

Figure 3. Performance case for a company travel administrator

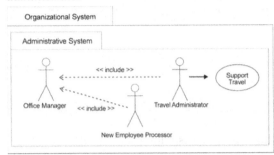

important because when looking at performance in an organization, people tend to focus on the knowledge and skills of the person occupying the primary role and often fail to consider those in the secondary roles. Failures in performance can be due to a lack of knowledge of the person in the secondary role, on whom performance is partially dependent, or poor communication between the two people occupying the roles.

Each of the use cases in Figure 4 is a high level Uses Case that can be refined to a lower level. Figure 5 represents an extended use case model for "Process Travel Request." In this model the person in the traveler role has to submit a travel authorization request (TAR) form, and this is processed by the travel administrator, who will check to see that the organization's travel rules are correctly applied. Already we are starting to identify knowledge needs, in that someone in the traveler role will need to know where to obtain the form, and how and when to fill it out. The travel administrator will have to know what organizational rules apply. In this particular case,

Figure 4. Travel processing performance case diagram

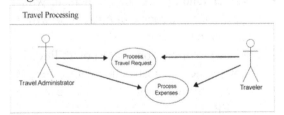

Figure 5. Extended performance case for a company travel administrator

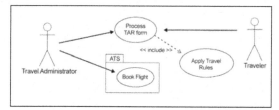

the travel administrator is responsible for actually booking the trip and you will note that the use case book flight is contained within a package. The package here is used to illustrate that the 'Book Flight' performance case is accomplished through a computer system (automated travel system or ATS).

While it is possible to adapt the notation of use case diagrams to learning and performance systems modeling, it is not so simple to apply the documentation schemes. As was noted earlier, practitioners of use case modeling in software engineering often use variants of the basic model presented in Table 1. Cockburn (2001) suggested that different documentation models are appropriate, depending on the purpose of the modeling. Certainly Table 1, which represents a basic task analysis, could be adapted to the needs of performance modeling. Any type of task analysis could be performed and documented in the performance case. Different documentation schemes would be appropriate, depending on the needs of the user and the role that performance case models can serve in an organization. This includes:

- Focusing discussion on the possibilities for improving performance through new instructional systems
- Understanding the environment in which graduates of a course of instruction will be expected to perform
- Focusing discussion on the possibilities for complementing instruction with other performance improving solutions, for example, an EPSS

- Creating the functional requirements for a proposed instructional system
- Creating the functional requirements for solutions that complement instruction (e.g., a quick reference sheet on the company travel rules)

In the above example, the examination of the travel processing would lead to an identification of the performance roles and goals of the various participants in this system. This would serve as a starting point to enable the identification and specification of performance aids and instruction, to help them achieve their individual goals and thus serve the higher-level goal of the organization (having an efficient travel process).

In software systems, use cases not only serve to identify requirements but also, once documented, allow developers to begin to determine the software objects required to build the system and how they will interact. performance cases can serve a similar role in regard to learning systems, which are beginning to utilize an object approach (Wiley, 2000). For example, if a course of instruction for travel administrators contained a set of learning objects (see Figure 6), some of which were of general relevance (e.g., an introduction to company travel rules). These objects could be adapted for the instruction of all the employees who are likely to find themselves in the traveler role in this performance model.

Figure 6. Performance case with documentation for a company travel administrator

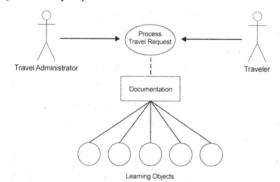

Performance case modeling would best be done in association with a methodology for performance analysis of the kind developed by scholars such as Gilbert (1996) and Robinson and Robinson (1995), and promoted by the International Society for Performance Improvement (ISPI). It should be seen as preceding instructional design and should not specifically presuppose the need for new instruction. Complementary (e.g., electronic performance support systems or EPSS) or alternative solutions (e.g., automating human tasks) should also be considered.

There are several approaches to performance analysis but they all tend to be in agreement on the need for the following:

- Take a systems view of problem solving
- Focus on results that should be achieved rather than tasks under taken
- Identify good measures of performance
- Identify gaps in performance and analyze their causes using evidence rather than opinion
- Consider a full range of potential interventions that can be applied to address the causes and close the gaps

For people trained in the application of a particular solution (instructional design or software design), there is a need to recognize a potential bias towards their method, which may not always be the most appropriate or sole answer to a particular problem. Inadequate performance from individuals in organizations may be due to a lack of skills and knowledge, but it may also be due to a dearth of good tools or of motivation. Any solution development should be preceded by a careful front-end analysis that looks at the intended goals of performance and the barriers to attaining them.

The following is some important performance-related information that could be included in the documentation of a performance analysis:

- A description of the desired performance result and linkage to desired organizational results
- The interaction of other performance roles
- The requisite knowledge and skills required by the performance roles
- Performance measures that identify standard and exemplary levels of performance

In addition, other information that may be linked to each performance case includes the following:

- Task analyses
- Cognitive models
- Detailed study of exemplary or expert performers

It is up to the community of analysts to decide the optimal documentation approaches to accompany performance diagramming and to work towards creating acceptable standards. The rest of this chapter will define and illustrate one approach that can be used to begin such a process.

PERFORMANCE CASE MODELING

Performance case modeling is a combination of the typical non-visual methods that performance analysts use, and an adaptation of the visual modeling method of the use case. Performance case modeling provides a visual method for identifying and analyzing performance requirements at the operational/individual performer level. Performance cases represent a performance goal within an organization or process that is the responsibility of one or more people. Performance goals are attained through the effort of people undertaking a performance role. Performance roles have individual responsibilities in relation to a performance case that can be achieved by anyone with the proper knowledge and skills.

Performance case models can provide a framework for examining optimal human performance in an organization and for selecting and specifying the appropriate instruction and performance support. Exemplary performers will provide analysts with a scenario, that is, specific information on how best to achieve the goals of the case. The performance cases documentation will be abstracted from several exemplary scenarios. The documentation for each performance case will provide the foundation for identifying the resources necessary to achieve performance support for those occupying the roles responsible for achieving the performance. The performance case documentation will also enable analysts, in collaboration with stakeholders, to determine the barriers to achieving optimal performance. These barriers help classify the performance problems by causes and potential solutions, which helps analysts develop recommendations to close performance gaps.

In the course of working with specialist performance analysis units in different parts of the U.S. military, Douglas et al. (2003, 2004) examined the methods used, data collected, and knowledge management practices. In the course of this work

Table 2. Elements of an analysis object

Data Element	Description	Example Data
Performance Goal	The desired achievement, result, or output that occurs at the individual level	Travel Administrator completes travel requests in a manner that is satisfactory for both the traveler and the organization
Primary Role	The individual performer who is the focus of the performance analysis process	Travel Administrator
Secondary Role	Other roles that interact with the primary role to achieve a performance goal	Traveler
Optimal Performance	Describes the desired performance at the individual level required to reach organizational goals	Process completed No errors in processing Organizational regulations are adhered to The traveler is satisfied Processed within three days
Gap Statement	The difference between desired performance and current performance	30% of travel transactions not meeting optimal performance goal
Indicators	Quantifiable criteria for a performance goal	Time to complete Errors requiring correction during processing Errors identified during auditing Traveler satisfaction survey
Cause	Statement of proposed root cause that is inhibiting optimal performance	The computer system has a difficult-to-use interface Travel requests received with little notice New staff not given enough time to adjust
Recommended Solution	Statement of a proposed instruction, or other intervention, that corrects the root cause	1. Recommend travel training be included in new employee orientation 2. Create computer system job aid 3. Request computer system usability improvements for next release 4. Create incentives for early submission of travel requests
Solution Links	Unique identifiers of any digital solutions that are reused or created subsequent to the analysis	Travel Training PowerPoint http://www.vpfa.fsu.edu/control/training/traveltraining.ppt
Metadata	Additional information provided that complies with established metadata standards	Author of object, date of creation, etc.

the concept of the performance analysis object was developed. An analysis object is a proposal for the standard digital capture of a unit of analysis (defined by a specific goal). It separates out the components of an analysis, rather than merging them all into a traditional analysis document. The analysis object distills knowledge into digital objects that can be stored in a searchable database. From the database they can be linked to elements in a diagram or any other digital objects relevant to a particular performance. Table 2 identifies the key elements of an analysis object, which form a potential standard documentation scheme for a performance case.

The key elements identify what performance is required, who is involved in attaining it, and how to measure it. The measurement indicators are particularly important not only in informing analysis and design, but also in serving as a template for subsequent evaluation efforts. That is, if a course of instruction is created based on the analysis of this performance, once someone graduates from the course you would expect to see an improvement in the identified performance measures in order for the instruction to be declared effective. The metadata requirement for the Analysis Object provides the background data on the object (e.g., what it is and who created it); the Dublin Core Metadata Initiative schema (Dublin Core Metadata Initiative, 2007) is a commonly accepted means of defining this metadata. Metadata is useful for assisting in the search for, and the reuse of, existing information resources.

Figure 7 illustrates a refinement of Figure 6 that demonstrates the interlinking of a performance case diagram, performance analysis objects, and digital solution objects. The performance analysis object will link to digital components and documents that relate to the solutions whether they are learning or non-learning. The solutions could be existing solutions stored in digital libraries and repositories, or solutions designed and developed subsequent to the analysis.

Figure 7. Performance case for a company travel administrator with interlinking of performance analysis objects and digital solution objects

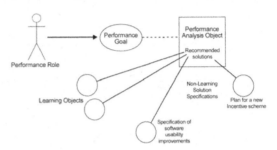

Figure 8 illustrates a performance case diagram from an actual analysis carried out by the Center for Army Lessons Learned, a specialist performance analysis unit in the U.S. army. It illustrates the stepwise nature of constructing such diagrams. The main performer in the system is the fire support officer, the person who is responsible for planning the supporting fire from aircraft and artillery. A performer in this role will have a number of high-level goals to achieve when supporting the planning of missions. Each one of these goals will have a number of more detailed sub-goals and the achievement of these goals will involve interaction with one or many (indicated by an asterisk) representatives of other performance roles. Indicating the interacting roles is crucial because any deficiency in performance may not just be due to lack of skills and knowledge of the FSO, it may be due to communication problems between people occupying the different roles. Thus in this example, analysts while looking at

Figure 8. Performance case package

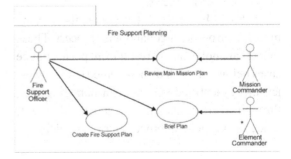

Figure 9. Refined performance case model for "Create Fire Support plan"

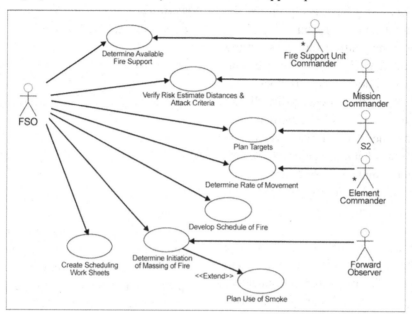

instructional requirements for a fire support officer, may in addition discover an instructional need for those who assist him.

Figure 9 represents a more detailed view of the performance goals that contribute to one of the high level goals of the FSO role in the mission planning process. The diagram allows for immediate identification of the roles, goals and interactions involved in creating a fire support plan. The next step would be to create detailed documentation for the problems identified in this process that may require the development of instruction, or some other means of supporting the performer. Table 3 demonstrates how one of these performance cases would be documented. The data would be derived from interviews, surveys, observations, discussions and reviews.

It should be stressed that the creation of the models is an on-going collaborative process. These models are not meant to result in all performance cases being refined and documented to the lowest level. The identified gaps in performance revealed through interactions with the stakeholders will guide the refinement process for the models.

Given that a great deal of effort is likely to be invested into an analysis process, it is important that the knowledge derived from this effort be archived and reused. If analysts need to reconsider problems or changes in the instruction of those involved in the various roles under consideration in the future, they will have this digital resource as a foundation to build on and modify, rather than having to redo all the analysis from scratch. It would therefore be useful for any large organization to store both completed diagrams and the related analysis objects in a digital repository. The metadata will be particularly important for this in that it will allow easy searching for relevant information in the repository.

There are a number of ways in which this documentation could be extended through the solution links and metadata relations. It has been noted that learning objects can be linked to the performance analysis object. In addition to relevant digital documents, archived interviews, and surveys, online discussions (informal analysis) can be linked into the analysis object. Another important resource that should be linked is any

Table 3. An analysis object for the FSO analysis

Data Element	Data
Primary Role	Fire Support Officer
Performance Goal	Verify risk estimate distances & attack criteria (i.e. the risks of landing on your own forces when using long range weapons)
Secondary Role	Mission Commander
Optimal Performance	Correctly identify risks for each weapon system used Develop a comprehensive knowledge of mission plans No errors in processing
Gap Statement	Only 60% of plans after execution meet satisfaction of mission commander
Indicators	Errors identified during peer review of plan No friendly fire incidents during execution of plan Mission commander satisfied with the plan
Cause	FSOs have difficulty finding and retaining knowledge about varying risks involved in the many different weapon systems they have to deal with Calculations difficult to accomplish in available time frame
Recommended Solution	Create job aid for quick look-up of risk data Integrate job-aid into training Create software application to assist in calculation
Solution Links	Fires integration: http://www.globalsecurity.org/military/library/policy/army/fm/3-90-2/appg.htm
Metadata (derived from Dublin Core)	Title: Verify Risk Estimate Distances & Attack criteria Analysis Object Creator: Ian Douglas Subject: Military, Mission Planning Description: Contains information on the analysis of fire support planning. Identifies the roles involved, problem causes, performance indicators, and recommended solutions for achieving an optimal level of performance. Publisher: Learning Systems Institute Date: 2006-08-06 Resource Type: Analysis Object Format: XML file Identifier: 02993109 Relation: Fire Support Analysis Report, Archive of threaded discussion on this object, Performance Case Diagram for the FSO Language: eng

subsequent evaluation study on solutions created, which will give an indication of how successful a given solution was at closing the performance gap identified in the analysis.

SOFTWARE TOOLS AND REPOSITORIES AND REUSE

Rather than using a written report at the end of a process of analysis as the main method of communicating knowledge, analysis knowledge can be collected, edited, and communicated on a continuous basis using the power of the Internet. A digital library can serve as a single point where analysis thinking, in the form of performance case diagrams and associated analysis objects, can be reviewed, commented on, and critiqued by others on a continuous basis. If a written report is still required, it can be generated from the data entered into the objects. Roles and goals provide a useful scheme for organizing this knowledge in a way that is useful to all stakeholders.

In the work of Douglas et al. (2003), prototypes for a Net-centric performance improvement (Net-PI) system that incorporates such digital object

Figure 10. Modeling performance in Net-PI

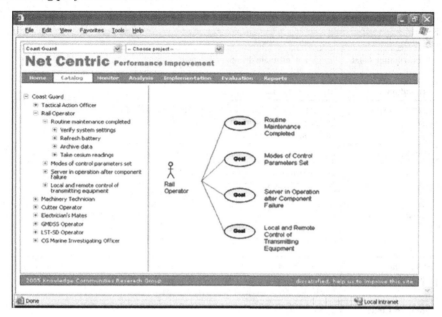

management systems are described (see Figure 10). The prototypes integrated the visual modeling scheme of performance cases, analysis objects, and a cataloguing system that contained records of previous roles and goals analyses. It also integrated a collaborative feature that allowed users to have threaded discussions on objects and diagrams under development. The latter is potentially important for maximizing the number of people that can review analyses and identify errors and misconceptions that would otherwise lead to faulty design and inferior performance support. The analysis is organized in the database according to roles (e.g., radio operator) and goals (e.g., establish communications), and a catalog feature that prevents the same role or goal from being analyzed and reported in two different geographic locations by two different analysts (which is easily the case without a centrally cataloged knowledge store). The analysis object also forms the basis for performance evaluation and performance support delivery. Thus, the basic model for organizing performance analysis knowledge is extended to delivery of performance support and tracking of individual and unit performance.

A standard system for modeling, together with a repository for analysis models and documentation, would mean that over time higher-level models would pre-exist to be reused in analysis. Comprehensive and evolving performance models for the whole organization would emerge. This would enable the analysis of problems of similar roles and performance goals to be reused both within and across organizations.

GUIDELINES FOR APPLYING PERFORMANCE CASE MODELING

The emphasis of this chapter is that performance case modeling is a potentially useful tool in the analysis that should precede the design of instruction, or any other form of human performance improvement. No matter what modeling tool is being used, it is important not to overemphasize the power of modeling languages. The success of modeling probably has more to do with the person doing it than with the tool itself. It is important to recognize the need to develop the skills of analysis and design rather than look to a specific tool to provide a magic solution. Bell (2005) has written an influential article called *UML Fever: Its Diagnosis and Recovery*. He was motivated to do so by the seemingly blind faith being placed in UML by some advocates in the software engineering community. The critique serves as a precautionary note for those seeking to develop and use modeling schemes in instructional systems design. Here are some of the symptoms of UML fever that are also applicable to modeling languages in general:

A UML-Centric Training Curriculum

Many organizations, noting the popularity of UML, have bought tools and training for UML without focusing on the more general skill gaps among their developers. Knowledge of UML diagrams does not substitute for knowledge and experience of analysis and design methods. Without the latter, UML diagrams will be of little use.

Design Brainstorming Degrades into UML Syntax Free-For-All

Bell notes that informal diagramming around a whiteboard is a common activity in the early stages of systems development. In this chapter we have noted that use case diagrams are particularly well suited to this. Their informal use in brainstorming can be disrupted when advocates of the more formal aspects of UML push to formalize the diagramming too early.

Absence of Stakeholder Input in Artifact Development

Whoever creates a diagram should be able to state not only its purpose but also who, other than themselves, will find value in it. Ideally it should serve as a means of shared communication between stakeholders and developers, and not just be an artifact demonstrating the creative skills of a single individual (see Chapter II).

A UML Model has Turned into the Product

The models are a means to an end, creating the most efficient and effective instruction or performance support; they are not the ends in themselves. There is the danger that if a lot of effort is put into diagram creation a project will be seen as having produced something of substance. Unless a diagram directly leads to system creation or improvement it has no substance. A diagram can even have a negative consequence if time that could be spent on building the system is instead spent on refining a diagram to perfection.

At no time should a design diagram be considered fixed and unalterable. It is also possible to initially draw diagrams only to help you understand the design (rather than document it) and then throw the diagrams away. In a sense, the process of creating the diagrams is more important than the diagrams themselves. Those who see design as a discrete process may be tempted to perfect all the diagrams before allowing any systems development to occur.

A set of guidelines for the use of modeling techniques include the following:

- Have a clear purpose for the diagram.
- Remember that the primary purpose of the diagram is communication—more than one person should be involved in its creation and as many people as possible should be involved in reviewing it.
- Do not feel you have to diagram everything.
- Do not feel you have to document everything you diagram.
- Focus your diagramming and documentation efforts on the most important things—i.e. do not create detailed, highly refined diagrams for areas where there are few performance problems.
- The effort involved in diagram creation should not substitute for system creation.

The diagram is useful only if it leads to a solution of proven effectiveness.

CONCLUSION

Use cases form a key role in UML modeling, as they are the starting point for requirements analysis, understandable by stakeholders and, through identifying objects and interactions within the documentation, an origin for the creation of other diagram types. This chapter has argued for a direct equivalent to use cases for those interested in developing modeling languages for instruction. Performance Cases as described in this chapter are intended to be used at the earliest point in the process to explore the problem, prior to selecting the appropriate solution.

Before planning instruction or any other solution aimed at improving human performance it is necessary to understand the performance environment in which individual performance takes place. It is also necessary to understand the metrics by which performance is evaluated. Performance Case modeling is a tool that can be used to facilitate this approach. It can focus instructional, and other solution designers, on what the solution is required to achieve and how it should be evaluated. It is aimed at understanding and overcoming identified causes for gaps in human performance.

REFERENCES

Bell, A. (2005). UML fever: Diagnosis and recovery. *ACM Queue, 3*(2), 48-57.

Brugge, B., & Dutoit, A.H. (2000). *Object-oriented software engineering: Conquering complex and changing systems.* Upper Saddle River, NJ: Prentice Hall.

Clark, R., & Estes, F. (2002). *Turning research into results: A guide to selecting the right performance solutions.* Atlanta, GA: CEP Press.

Cockburn. A. (1997). Structuring use cases with goals. *Journal of Object Oriented Programming, 10*(7), 35-40.

Cockburn, A. (2001). *Writing effective use cases.* Boston: Addison-Wesley.

Deming, W.E. (1982). *Quality, productivity, and competitive position.* Cambridge, MA: MIT, Centre for Advanced Engineering Study.

Douglas, I. (2003). Visualizing and sharing human performance analysis knowledge. *Seventh International Conference on Information Visualization* (IV 2003), (pp. 465-469).

Douglas, I., Butler, J., Nowicki, C., & Schaffer, S. (2003). Web-based collaborative analysis, reuse and sharing of human performance knowledge. *Proceedings of the Inter-service/Industry Training, Simulation and Education Conference (I/ITSEC),* (pp. 1023-1030).

Douglas, I., Wright, M., and Nowicki, C. (2004). Communicating performance knowledge among the services. *Proceedings of the Inter-service/Industry Training, Simulation and Education Conference (I/ITSEC).* 1630, (pp. 1-10).

Dublin Core Metadata Initiative (2007). Retrieved February 11, 2007 from http://dublincore.org/

Eriksson, H-E., and Penker, M. (2000). *Business modeling with UML: Business patterns at work.* New York: John Wiley & Sons.

Gilbert, T. (1996). *Human competence: Engineering worthy performance.* Washington, DC: International Society for Performance Improvement, Inc.

Harless, J.H. (1970). *An ounce of anlaysis is worth a pound of objectives.* Newnan, GA: Harless Performance Guild.

Harless, J.H. (1988). *Accomplishment-based curriculum development.* Newnan, GA: Harless Performance Guild.

IMS Global Learning Consortium (2005). Retrieved Febraury 19, 2007 from: http://www.imsglobal.org/learningdesign/

International Society for Performance Improvement. (2007). Retrieved February 15, 2007 from: http://www.ispi.org/

Jacobson, I. (1992). *Object-oriented software engineering: A use case driven approach.* Reading, MA: Addison-Wesley

Kaufman, R. (1988). Needs assessment: A menu. *Educational Technology Research and Development, 28*(7), 21-23.

Kirkpatrick, D.L (1998). *Evaluating training programs: The four levels.* San Francisco: Berrett-Koehler.

Mager, R.F., & Pipe, P. (1984). *Analyzing Performance Problems* (2nd ed.). Belmont, CA: Pitman Management Training.

Marshall, C. (2000). *Enterprise modeling with UML: Designing successful software through business analysis.* Reading, MA: Addison-Wesley.

Raybould, B. (2000). Performance support engineering: Building performance-centered Web-based systems, information systems, and knowledge management systems in the 21st century. *Performance Improvement, 39*(6), 32-39.

Robinson, D.G., & Robinson, J.C. (1995). *Performance consulting: Moving beyond training.* San Francisco: Berrett-Koehler Publishers.

Rosenberg, D., & Scott, K. (1999). *use case driven object modeling with UML: A practical approach.* Reading, MA: Addison-Wesley.

Rossett, A., & Czech, C. (1995). They really wanna, but….the aftermath of professional preparation in performance technology. *Performance Improvement Quarterly, 8*(4), 115-132.

Rossett, A. (1998). *First things fast: A handbook for performance analysi*s. San Francisco: Jossey-Bass.

Rummler, G., & Brache, A. (1995). *Improving performance: How to manage the white space on the organization chart* (2nd ed.). San Francisco: Jossey-Bass.

Schaffer, S.P. (2000). A review of organizational and human performance frameworks. *Performance Improvement Quarterly, 13*(3), 220-243.

Schneider, G., & Winters, J.P. (2001). *Applying uses cases: A practical guide* (2nd ed.). Boston: Addison Wesley Professional.

Swanson, R.A. (1994). *Analysis for improving performance: Tools for diagnosing organizations & documenting workplace expertise.* San Francisco: Berrett-Koehler.

Wedman, J.F., & Graham, S.W. (1992). *Performance improvement: Using the performance pyramid.* Columbia, MO: Training Program Analysis & Design.

Wiley, D. A. (2000). Connecting learning objects to instructional design theory: A definition, a metaphor, and a taxonomy. In D. A. Wiley (Ed.), *The instructional use of learning objects.* Bloomington, IN: Agency for Instructional Technology.

Chapter XII
LDL for Collaborative Activities

Christine Ferraris
Université de Savoie, France

Christian Martel
Pentila Corporation and Université de Savoie, France

Laurence Vignollet
Université de Savoie, France

ABSTRACT

LDL (learning design language) is an educational modeling language which was conceived to model collaborative activities. It has roots in social sciences, mainly linguistics, sociology and ethnomethodology. It proposes seven concepts that allow instructional designers to build the model of a collaborative learning activity. It has both a visual and a textual notation, the latter being computer-readable. This means that the produced models can be easily operationalized and executed in an existing virtual learning environment. This chapter introduces LDL, its concepts and the graphical notations associated with each of them. The methodology proposed to facilitate the modeling is also presented. Its use is illustrated by the example of the planet game, which was practically tested with other research teams as a benchmark/competition during the ICALT 2006 conference.

INTRODUCTION

Learning design language (LDL) is a language intended for use by instructional designers. It has been created to allow them to describe and specify learning activities on the Internet. Lots of activities may take place on the Internet—like a treasure hunt between groups of children, a training session to improve reading, a discussion between a teacher and students, an examination, etc. So, the focus is placed on collaborative activities, as the LDL authors are convinced that learning can no longer take place without considering and enhancing the interactions between the learners.

The ambition of the LDL authors is twofold: on the one hand, we want to provide instructional designers with simple means to build the formal description of whatever kind of learning activities (such as the ones previously mentioned, for example) and to combine them. On the other hand, we want the teachers to be able to transform easily these formal descriptions into effective online activities, without any intervention from computer science specialists. These activities will involve services and digital resources available on the teachers' school network and on the Internet.

We did not take into account the division of labor that usually occurs between the instructional designer and the teacher. On the contrary, we have considered that, in order to be exploited by an instructional designer, the language should allow the designer to describe activities as if she or he were a teacher and had to solve some of the problems encountered by teachers preparing lessons. Examples of these problems include determining the theme of the activity, gathering adequate documentation, defining some attainable learning objectives, evaluating the duration of the activity, proposing a division of the activity into sessions, indicating the way students will be arranged during learning sessions, defining individual work sequences and positioning them in the overall activity, defining the way and the means to measure the students' progress. They concern learning and pedagogy, of course, but also logistics, organization and evaluation.

This is an important preparatory task, which may be more or less precise, more or less detailed. It guarantees the teacher being able to conduct the activity once it has begun while keeping control of his or her objectives. Improvisation, on the other hand, is more risky. It is probably limited to the best teachers, in the same way that rally-style driving is restricted to the best drivers. It supposes a complete mastery of pedagogy.

After this preparatory phase, the teacher will be in charge of adapting the activity designed by the instructional designer. The teacher will consider the following:

- The students to be involved in the future activity, because the teacher knows their skills and their work practices,
- The personal objectives defined for each of these students,
- The technical context in which the teacher is operating.

Using LDL during the preparation phase leads the instructional designer to create a *scenario*. A scenario is a codified and formal description of a future activity. It can be considered as a specification of this activity. Designing a scenario to specify an activity consists in describing:

- Where the activity will take place,
- Who the participants in the activity will be,
- What the participants' interventions will be,
- How and when these interventions will be connected throughout the activity,
- The rules the participants will have to comply with,
- What the consequences of the participants' reactions, actions and points of view on the activity will be and how they will be able to express these points of view.

The distinction between a scenario and the activity modeled by this scenario is the same as the difference between a recipe and the future dish whose preparation is described by this recipe. If the ingredients used by the cook are actually the ones mentioned in the recipe, and if the way the dish is prepared is in conformity with the instructions in the recipe, then the tasting of the dish should go off well. In particular, if the codification proposed by LDL is respected, then a computer will be able to interpret a scenario. Thus the teacher will be able to operationalize it in a technical computer environment.

To support the description of a scenario, a graphical notation was defined. This enables the instructional designer or teacher to represent the scenarios produced more easily and comprehensibly. Once these representations have been produced, they are translated into a corresponding XML binding in conformity with the LDL syntax. (These bindings are not provided here as they are of no use in helping the reader understand the models or the notation.) They are the computer-readable representations of the scenarios. They are also a way of representing the scenarios in a normalized format suitable for exchanges and operationalization.

LDL does not describe the actual nature of the services and resources used by the learners and teachers during the ongoing activity. Neither does it describe the functionalities of these services. The transformation of a scenario, in which services and resources are described in an abstract way, into an actual online activity, in which actual services and resources are involved, is carried out during the operationalization phase. It is supported by learning design infrastructure (LDI), a global infrastructure which has been developed in relation with LDL to deal with both the operationalization and the execution of scenarios.

The authors of LDL think that teachers and instructional designers, who design activities for the teachers, should not have to concern themselves with the technical features of the computer tools they use. That is not their problem. They should be allowed to forget about it so that they can concentrate on the specification of the activities they intend to carry out with students. They have to suppose that the technical environment will be able to adapt to their needs. This is a strongly-held position of the LDL authors, which has had a huge impact in defining LDL and developing LDI. Indeed, LDI is in charge of seeking, finding, and building the technical environment best adapted to the teachers' needs.

What follows is a description of LDL. Before the description, the background of the language

will be presented. This will explain the origin of the language and will position it in the field of VIDLs. We will then categorize the language according to Botturi et al. (2006) classification. Next, a detailed description of LDL concepts will be given. For each of them, a definition will be provided together with some examples and the notation proposed to instructional designers to represent the concept in the activity modeling process. After that, the methodology defined to model learning activities with LDL will be described. The use of this methodology will then be exemplified in the planet game example. This example is a case study which was proposed as a modeling and implementing challenge during the last International Conference on Advanced Learning Technologies (ICALT) (Vignollet et al., 2006). It will be introduced just before describing how LDL was used to model it within the LDL methodology. Finally we will present the first results obtained, the strengths and the limitations of LDL and the future work.

THE ORIGIN AND BACKGROUND OF LDL

Modeling Collaborative Activities

The definition of LDL follows upon research we conducted in the domain of CSCW (computer support for collaborative work). Such research works asked the following questions: What are the essential properties of a groupware so that it effectively supports group activities while taking into account the social aspects of these activities? On which model should these tools be built?

The answer was to propose a model for group activities: the participation model (Martel, 1998; Ferraris et al., 2002). This model is grounded on properties that are inherent in the nature of collaborative activities. These properties were analyzed and revealed by research in social sciences. We have considered the following ones:

- Activities are *situated* in various contexts (social, cultural, technical, geographical, etc.) (see Suchman, 1987; Fitzpatrick et al., 1995; Garfinkel & Sacks, 1972). Thus it is necessary to consider both the *places* of the activity and the *roles* the participants will have in these places. Roles are relative to the location of participants: i.e., they are also situated (see Chapter XIII).

- Activities are *unforeseeable*. They are built gradually as they proceed (see the works on activity theory by Vygostky and Leontiev). So it is impossible to produce an *a priori* description of what an activity will be. Such a description can nevertheless be useful to support collaboration in CSCW tools but *if and only if* it can be revised *in situ,* according to what actually happens in the ongoing activity (Suchman, 1987).

- Collaborative activities suppose the existence of a *compromise* between the interests of the group and those of the individuals, between the dependencies that stem from relationships among individuals and their autonomy. Each individual must be able to negotiate her or his commitment to the activity (Martel, 1998). This was inspired by Goffman's theory (Goffman, 1981).

In addition, we were inspired by works in linguistics, mainly the dialogue models of the University of Geneva (Roulet et al., 1985) that attempt to explain the succession and the interweaving of conversational exchanges. Indeed, we have drawn a parallel between a teaching activity and a conversation. In a conversation, locutors speak to their interlocutors, who make an interpretation of what is said and may react in turn (Austin, 1955). Just like a conversation, we consider an activity as *a set of exchanges and interactions* between the users involved (the participants). As in a conversation, the exchanges are *structured* and *scaffolded* by rules. And as in a conversation, every exchange involves at least two participants: an *addresser* who acts and whose actions are aimed at an *addressee*.

A Socio-Constructivist View of Learning

Contemporary pedagogical movements attach great importance to socio-constructivism, a learning theory developed by Lev Vygotsky at the beginning of the 20th century (Vygotsky, 1934). This theory rests on the idea that knowledge acquisition is facilitated by the various social interactions a learner may have during her or his learning process.

This point of view seems to be shared with problem-based learning proponents such as Savery and Duffy (1996). These researchers also state that cooperation influences learning. Indeed, generally in their approach, learners, grouped in teams, are expected to collaborate, helped by their teacher, to explain phenomena underlying a problem.

Both theories thus state that learning activities are intrinsically cooperative: they are based on interactions which are richer and more complex than the traditional face-to-face exchanges between a teacher and her or his learners.

THE IMS-LD PROPOSAL

The main proposal in the domain of learning design languages is IMS-LD, which was a result of the work conducted at OUNL (Koper, 2002). It is based on a theatrical metaphor. Indeed, it considers a learning activity as being a succession of "acts" (in the theatrical meaning of that word) that leads to the realization of the "drama" which occurs between learners and teachers. Modeling such an activity is thus a matter of modeling the alternating or the sequencing of the exchanges that occur in the class.

The main contribution of this approach is to put forward this learning flow modeling, considering that the learning flow reflects the activity in an overall way. However, even though EML has been adopted by IMS, there remain barriers to its adoption. We mention in what follows the barriers which are particularly significant to our purposes. They led us to choose to develop a new LD language instead of using IMS-LD.

A Complex Language

The first barrier is the complexity of the IMS-LD language. Several researchers and end-users (teachers, instructional designers) share the point of view that IMS-LD is complicated, in particular because of its high number of concepts. Consequently, only someone who knows it well can handle it and capture its subtleties. For instance, it is very difficult to define the appropriate properties. Even if the associated best practices try to offer a method, it is still extremely difficult to use for instructional designers, and quite impossible for teachers to use (Le Pallec et al., 2006).

Indeed, as IMS-LD (EML in fact, its ancestor) has been designed to industrialize the creation of distance learning activities, it is not dedicated to teachers organizing learning activities in their classes. It operates as though the modeling phase has to be dealt with by an instructional designer who has a discussion with the teacher and who translates into IMS-LD the informal description of the learning activity the teacher has produced. However, once the modeling has been done, the teacher and the instructional designer have to discuss the formal model produced. This requires the teacher to be able at least to understand, even if she or he cannot produce, the model in a general way. If the language is too complex, this may not be possible

Difficulties in Modeling Collaborative Activities

Miao et al. (2005) have done an interesting and deep analysis of the capacity of IMS-LD for formalizing collaborative learning scenarios. They have pointed out five major difficulties, among which is the difficulty of modeling varied forms of social interactions. They show evidence that by using IMS-LD "it cannot be clearly modelled whether and how people collaborate" (see p.3 of Miao et al.'s paper).

As Hernandez-Leo et al. also noted this problem, they have proposed an extension of IMS-LD (see Chapter XX). But, as Harrer mentions in Chapter XIV, this extension at service level rather than at activity level cannot appropriately capture the characteristics of social interactions.

These difficulties were also reported by Caeiro (see Chapter X). They put forward that the theatrical metaphor is not suitable to model collaborative learning situations when they are not a succession of acts, in the theatrical sense. This led them to propose the poEML language.

No Concept Dedicated to the Activity Observation

All of the actors in the field of education are in agreement about the fact that an educational activity is characterized by its unpredictable nature. Le Pallec et al. (2006) claim that "a large part of scenario can only be defined during runtime" and "in learning science, models are driven by learning events to detect and to react upon" (Le Pallec et al., 2006, p. 2). In fact, teachers are usually able to give prescriptions of an activity, but they know that they will have to take into account the learners' reactions and what will happen during the activity to adapt it as it proceeds.

IMS-LD does not include a semantically-founded concept which could capture these reactions and the events coming from the ongoing activity. This is probably due to the theatrical metaphor which intrinsically does not take the reactions of the actors into account. Indeed, actors are supposed to play the part without deviating from the original text. So there is theoretically no need to consider these reactions and what is going on. Everything should go on according to what is written in the author's original text.

The IMS-LD "property" concept could be used to try to capture these reactions. However it has not been defined for that purpose but to be computational. That is probably why it is so difficult to use it to capture reactions and points of view of the participants. Moreover, it cannot be used to capture what is going on in the activity.

Learning Tools Confronted with Virtual Learning Environments

Learning tool designers were concerned very early on by the modeling, or, more exactly, the orchestration of these tools. They tried to describe and formalize the ways of interacting with them, taking into account the specificity of the learning activities they wanted to plan. This is true in all learning contexts: lifelong learning, school-based instruction, etc. This is for instance what Gueraud and her colleagues propose in FORMID (Gueraud et al., 2004), which implements learning activities that include the use of simulations in the electricity field.

However, the deployment of virtual learning environments (VLE) leads one to reconsider their proposals. Indeed, learning tools are now included in the VLE and can interact with other services (Durand & Martel, 2006). Then teachers or instructional designers populate the VLE with several resources, including instructions, learning tools, documents, case studies, etc. All these resources can be considered as small pieces of learning scenarios. Only the sequence which orders these elements is missing.

Towards the Creation of a New Language

In 2003, we were facing the following situation:

- We needed a language enabling one to describe collaborative learning activities and their learning flows,

- We wanted the language to take into account the unforeseeable nature of learning activities,
- We wanted the language to consider the situated and interactive nature of collaborative activities,
- We wanted the language to be computer-readable so that it would be possible to automate the construction of an adapted VLE and the delivery of learning activities via this VLE starting from the activities' description,
- The incipient IMS-LD standard language did not meet our requirements.

So we decided to define a new LD language, based on the participation model. As this model had been improved and validated—it had been used to specify and develop successfully one of the very first extant VLE in France, which has been used daily since 1999 at University of Savoie by more than 15,000 users (Martel et al., 2004)—the challenge sounded possible.

LDL was thus created in 2003 by Christian Martel, Laurence Vignollet and Christine Ferraris from "scenario Team" in collaboration with Pentila corporation (http://www.pentila.com/) and Jean-Pierre David and Anne Lejeune from LIG-METAH (Laboratoire d'Informatique de Grenoble—METAH Team). The related infrastructure LDI was specified by "scenario team" and Pentila corporation, and developed by Pentila corporation.

POSITIONING LDL TOWARDS BOTTURI ET AL.'S CLASSIFICATION

LDL can be considered as a *finalist communicative* language, in reference to the framework presented in Botturi et al. (2006). In the same paper, they have also defined a classification scheme for ID languages. According to this classification, LDL can be categorized as:

- **Stratification:** (layered) LDL proposes seven different concepts to describe the model of a learning activity. All these concepts are linked with each other in an information model (a meta-model).
- **Formalization:** (formal) LDL combines a graphical notation and a textual one. Indeed, the instructional designer is supposed to use the graphical notation to create a scenario. The resulting diagrams have then to be transformed in a corresponding LDL-XML binding, so that a computer will be able to make the scenario run on an existing VLE. The binding is of course formal as it is expressed in XML according to the LDL grammar. As the transformation is supposed to be carried out automatically in the future (this is not the case currently), the graphical notation requires precise syntactical rules.
- **Elaboration:** (Specification) The language has been primarily defined to build the specification of a learning activity. The specifications built have the particularity of being computer-understandable. They can be transformed automatically into machine-code in order to automate the delivery thanks to technology.
- **Notation:** (Both visual and textual) Initially, there was only a textual notation (an XML binding). We have added a graphical notation, assuming it would help teachers and instructional designers in building the scenarios. This still has to be validated.
- **Perspective:** (multiple) If we consider only the textual notation of LDL (i.e., the XML binding), the perspective is single. If we consider both the textual and visual notations, it is multiple. In fact, several views are required for some of the LDL concepts, for instance the *position* one (see Figure 13 and supplementary Table 1).

LDL: SEVEN CONCEPTS TO BUILD A SCENARIO

To build a scenario using LDL, the instructional designer has to analyze the activity to identify:

- « Who »: Who takes part in the activity?
- « Where »: Where does the activity take place?
- « What »: What is done during the activity?
- « How » and « When »: In which order do we play and under which constraints (when does it start and when does it stop)?

To those "classical" concepts. LDL adds two other, more original ones (Martel et al., 2006a):

- The « reactions » of the participants: What is the participant's evaluation of the difficulty of an activity? What is his or her point of view on a document? How does a participant view his or her place in the activity?
- The « rules of the game » of the activity: What is allowed? What is not? How could we take into account the participants' reactions to adapt the activity?

LDL concepts are detailed below. For each detail, we provide a definition of the concept together with its UML representation (which positions the concept relative to the others within the LDL meta model), some examples and the corresponding LDL graphical notation. This notation is intended for instructional designers. We have defined it in order to prevent instructional designers from having to use the XML notation. The objective is twofold: (1) to provide instructional designers with a graphical notation which is much easier to handle than XML and (2) to provide both teachers and instructional designers with a more user-friendly means of communication. The reader who is not familiar with UML will be able to find a good UML primer in Chapter IX of this handbook.

The Roles

The roles represent "classes of" participants who take part in the activity. In activities, participants have coherent interactions. A set of interactions reflects a "thematic" role.

Definition

The activity's participants are represented by the role concept (see Figure 1). A role is the set of interactions a participant can have with others taking part in the activity.

It is characterized by a name (the role's name), chosen by the instructional designer because of its relevance to the activity to be modeled.

Examples

Participants who write a course for their students, annotate their work and mark their examinations are teachers; participants who read the course, do the exercises and take the examination are the learners; participants who write an article for an online newspaper's readers are writers.

Figure 1. Role model (UML representation)

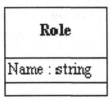

Figure 2. Role notation

Notation

The Figure 2 gives the graphical notation of the roles. This notation is taken from actors' notation in UML.

The Arenas

The arena is the place where the activity takes place: a service or a content. A forum, a search engine or a chat room are considered as service arenas. A course, an exercise, a photo album or a Web site are content arenas. This referencing to real space guides the modeling and delimits the interaction perimeter. Participants interact in these arenas through the interactions specified by their roles.

Definition

Places where activities take place are arenas. An arena refers to a service or digital content which supports the participant's activity. It is defined at least by a name and may contain other arenas (see Figure 3).

Examples

The library is an arena where participants can search for a book; the amphitheater is the place where the teacher gives a lecture: it is the lecture's arena. The usual arena used by participants for asynchronous online discussion is a forum.

Notation

The Figure 4 gives the graphical notation of the arena called "Forum to discuss the lecture."

The Interactions

The interactions represent what is done during the activity. They specify the exchanges the partici-

Figure 3. Arena model

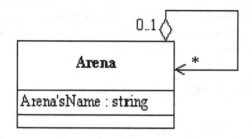

Figure 4. Notation of an arena

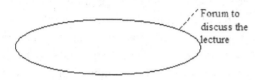

pants will have during the learning activity. They usually consist of verbal communication, document exchange and collaborative productions. They are situated: they occur in contents or via services. So they depend on the capacity of the places where they occur (for instance, a content can be read, a forum can offer communication functionalities, etc.)

Definition

Any exchanges which take place between the participants during the activity are called interactions.

In its simple form, an interaction is characterized by (see Figure 5):

- An identifier,
- The *action*, which describes what is done during the exchange,
- The roles of the participants involved in the exchange,
- The arena in which the interaction takes place.

An interaction always takes place between at least two participants, represented by their roles. The initiator is called the *addresser*, the one to whom the action is addressed is called the *addressee*. Addresser and addressee represent the respective places of the interaction's participants (here we have transposed the duality that exists in conversations between locutors and interlocutors). The association called "*involves*" which appears in Figure 5 between the "role" and "interaction" concepts thus needs to be divided into two more precise associations which consider these respective places: the ones appearing on Figure 6.

Furthermore, LDL allows the specification of start-up and stopping conditions of interactions, using *rules*. The rules are described further.

Examples

"The teacher provides a document to the learners," "the project leader sends an alert message to the members of her or his working group," "the learners answer a question given by the teacher" are just a few examples of interactions which can happen between an activity's participants.

Figure 5. Interaction model

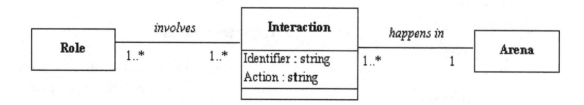

Figure 6. Addressers and addressees during an interaction

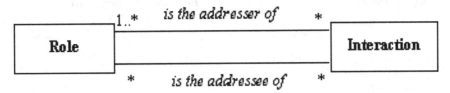

Students doing an exercise and sending it to their teacher are the addressers and the teacher is the addressee. Sometimes, the addresser and the addressee are identical and correspond to the same participant. It is for instance the case when a learner reads a document for her or his own information. It is also the case when a participant uses a search engine to find information.

Notation

Interaction notation consists of four constituents: its identifier, the action's name, the roles involved and the arena where it takes place. This is expressed by the notation presented in Figure 7 (R1 and R2 correspond to the name of the roles).

This notation has to be completed with the rules that express the start-up and stopping of the interaction. They are referenced by a diamond, which symbolizes a condition, as shown in Figure 8.

The Structures

How and when the interactions are connected throughout the activity is captured by the *structure* concept.

Definition

During the activity, interactions are played either sequentially or in parallel. In LDL, the *structures* describe these sequences.

A structure is characterized by (see Figure 9) a title, which identifies it in a unique way within a scenario, the list of the interactions, and the type which defines the interactions' organization. LDL distinguishes two types of structure, which correspond to two different manners of linking the interactions:

- A *sequence* structure means that the interactions will be executed one after the other, sequentially;

Figure 7. Notation of the interaction I

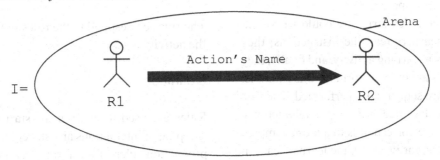

Figure 8. The interaction I_talk referencing its start-up and stopping rules.

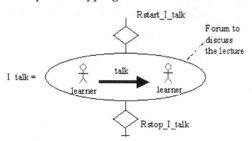

Figure 9. Structure model (types are represented using sub-class notation)

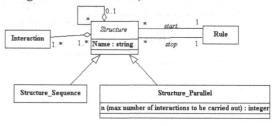

- A *parallel* structure means that all or some of the interactions will be executed in parallel. With this type of structure, the instructional designer could, if necessary, indicate the maximum number of interactions that the participant has to perform. By default, this number is equal to the total number of interactions which corresponds to the progress in parallel of all the interactions.

Like the interactions, the structures contain information on their conditions of start-up and stopping. These conditions are also expressed by rules. Finally, a structure can include other structures.

Examples

A *sequence* structure will allow one to express that an alert will be sent to tutors as soon as the teacher gives the specified document to learners. A *parallel* structure will make it possible to express that the learners must carry out three exercises, in any order, that they will have to choose from the list of the five proposed.

A more complex structure could be for example: the learners read the instructions, they can then play a learning activity, and finally, they have an assessment to perform. In this example, three steps are sequentially performed. The first one and the last one are simple interactions. The second one corresponds to a more complex activity where, for instance, the learners can, in parallel, read the lesson, discuss with their peers and do exercises.

Notation

The *sequence* structure is represented vertically and the *selection* structure horizontally. If the number of interactions to be performed is limited, this number is mentioned in brackets.

In Figure 10, we represent the main structure of the last example above: a sequential one which starts automatically and specifies that the reading interaction called I_ReadingOrders is followed by the learning structure called S_Learning, and closed by the assessment interaction called I_Assessment.

Figure 11 shows the "S_Learning" structure, a structure where three interactions can be played in parallel: the "read the lesson" interaction (I_ReadingLesson), "discussion" interaction (I_Discussing) and the "exercise" (I_Exercising) interaction.

The Rules

The rules correspond to the rules of the game of the activity.

Definition

Rules are used to express the start-up and the stopping of interactions and structures. They are production rules of the form: *If condition Then*

Figure 10. Sequential structure notation

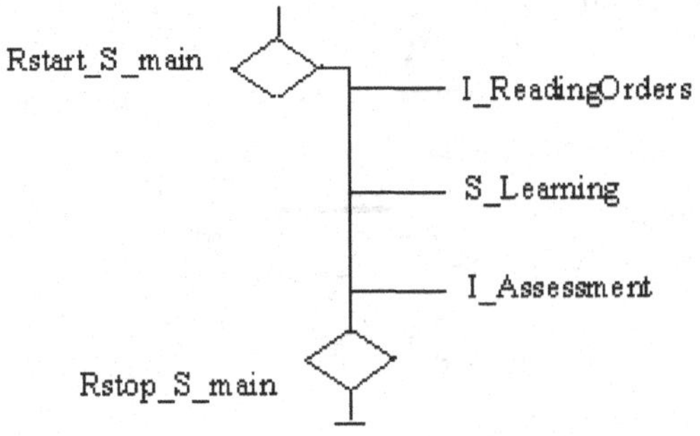

Rstart_S_main

I_ReadingOrders

S_Learning

I_Assessment

Rstop_S_main

action. The conditional part of a rule is a logical expression using the connectors OR, AND and NOT. The action can be the start-up or the stopping of a structure or an interaction.

Examples

Rules make it possible to express for example that a discussion can begin when all the learners have read the instructions and that it will stop when the teacher gives the signal.

Notation

A reference to the rules is added to the structure and interaction notations, as shown in Figures 8 and 10.

The Positions and the Observables

The conditions of the rules depend on the reactions of the participants. LDL includes a concept, that of *position*, which allows one to specify these reactions and thus to adapt the activity according to them. The value of a position is tested in the conditional part of a rule.

Definition

The position of a participant is the means of expressing the participant's reactions, perception and points of view on an ongoing activity. It is characterized by (see Figure 12):

- An identifier,
- A title, which expresses the semantics of the position,
- A value,
- A type: *declared* or *observed*,
- The role of the participant who takes the position,
- The arena on which the position is taken.

Two types of position exist, depending on how the value of the position is obtained. A *declared* position means that its value is given explicitly by the participant involved. The value of an *observed* position is assigned by the system which

Figure 11. The parallel structure called S_Learning

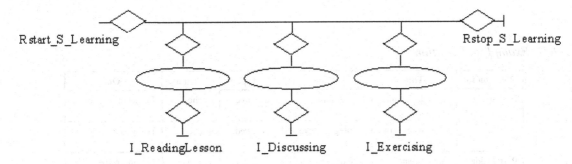

Rstart_S_Learning

Rstop_S_Learning

I_ReadingLesson

I_Discussing

I_Exercising

Figure 12. Position model with the links to other concepts

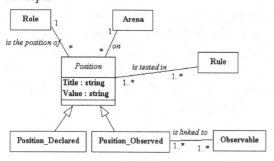

Figure 13. Interaction notation supplemented with positions

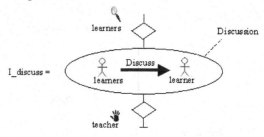

deduces it from observation data on the activity's progression. The instructional designer will have to define which aspects are to be observed. These aspects are called the *observables*.

Examples

A teacher can choose to interrupt a working session to allow learners to play games. This is a *declared* position taken *by* the participant having the "teacher" role *on* the "learning activity" arena. Its title may be "I stop the learning activity." Its value may be "true" or "false" and may vary as the activity proceeds. Another *declared* position allows the teacher to give a mark to the work of the learner. The presence or the absence of the students in the digital space shared by the group is an *observed* position. Table 1 shows the complete descriptions of these three positions.

Notation

Positions are represented by:

- A hand symbol for a *declared* position,
- A magnifying glass symbol for an *observed* position.

The role of the participant who takes the position is specified under the symbol.

In Figure 13, the discussion can begin when all the learners have read the instructions and it will stop when the teacher gives the signal.

When appearing on an interaction representation (such as in Figure 13), positions are not completely specified. Thus their definition has to be supplemented by fulfilling a table like the one presented in Table 1.

Table 1. Examples of position

Position Id	Title	Value	Type	Taken by	On
P_stop_act	I stop the learning activity	True or false	declared	teacher	The learning activity
P_vote	my evaluation of this work is	an integer between 0 and 20	declared	teacher	The learner work
P_is_inside	I am present	True or false	observed	learner	The group space

Please note that the rules are the means to personalize activities. For instance, a rule can be defined to propose complementary lessons to a learner who has declared that she or he is not able to do an exercise (her or his position to the arena "exercise").

The presentation of LDL and its concepts is now complete. The next three sections are devoted to the presentation of the methodology we have defined to help the instructional designer build a scenario with LDL. The methodology is of course subordinated to the LDL language. After this presentation, we will apply the methodology to an example.

THE METHODOLOGY

The proposed methodology distinguishes two steps clearly. Step 1 aims at building an informal scenario. Step 2 aims at formalizing this informal scenario.

Step 1: Building the Informal Scenario

Usually, a learning design begins with a more or less precise idea of a learning activity described in a narrative way. For instance, the teacher and the instructional designer could intend to propose an activity on the subject of planets and their organization in the solar system. In this example, the objective could be to enable the learners to discover that the differences between the distances of the planets from the sun can be explained by their properties. Another objective could be to allow the learners to acquire knowledge in the field of astronomy: the difference between a planet and a star, the notion of orbit, physical mass, etc.

To build a scenario, the instructional designer will first of all take into account the learning objectives of the teacher. Existing reference lists of skills will also be taken into account. Then the learning design consists in thinking about how the learners could individually or collectively use the resources during the activity. In other words, it is the construction and the description of interactional arrangements in which resources are used to facilitate effective learning. If possible, this learning has to be assessable.

Step 2: Formalizing the Informal Scenario

One only has to observe a group of learners working to become aware that the slightest educational activity is complex, and that its modeling could be quite difficult to carry out. In fact, a learning activity often conceals a myriad of interwoven activities, whose relationships are confused. Within this myriad of activities, we distinguish four types:

- The first type is obviously the *learning type*. Activities of this type are the heart of the learning. Learners manipulate the resources put at their disposal. They produce contents related to the learning objectives. They work individually or collaboratively.
- The second is the *observation type*. During activities of this type, the teacher observes the ongoing learning activity. The objective of this kind of activity is twofold. First, they are intended to help the teacher perform a formative assessment of the learning activity, for each participant. Second, they can allow the supervision and the regulation of the progression of the activity. Usually, teachers are the only participants in this kind of activity.
- The third is the *assessment type*. Any learning activity is preceded, associated with or followed by at least one assessment activity. This is the place and time to assess the knowledge of the learners. The place of the assessment activity in the overall learning flow depends on the kind of assessment desired by the designer (diagnostic, forma-

tive, summative, etc.) (Durand & Martel, 2006).

- Finally, we consider the *organizational type*. Activities of this kind are dedicated to organization problems. It is usually the time and place where the resources and tools are made accessible, and the orders are given to the learners. If needed, it is also the time and place where groups of learners are created. Finally, it is the time and place in which the other activities are started.

We regard these four kinds of activities as basic elements that constitute every learning activity to model. The overall learning activity results from the combination and the interrelations of these activities. Being activities *per se*, they can be modeled as independent scenarios. Building the formal scenario of a learning activity is thus no longer a matter of defining a unique scenario, which encapsulates everything. It becomes a matter of defining *at least four scenarios*, corresponding to the four different kinds of activities identified. As a consequence, it becomes a matter of describing the relationships between these scenarios. It is also a matter of describing each scenario in terms of the concepts proposed by LDL. Thus the current step of the methodology consists in: (1) identifying the activities and their relationships and (2) modeling each identified activity. These two phases are presented in the next two sections.

FORMALIZING THE INFORMAL SCENARIO (PART 1): IDENTIFYING THE ACTIVITIES AND THEIR RELATIONSHIPS

At this stage of the methodology, the instructional designer has to:

- Analyze the overall activity to identify the activities that constitute it and that cor-

respond to the four types of activities mentioned above: organization, learning, observation and assessment;
- Define the relationships between these activities.

Identification of the Activities

It is easier to begin with the identification of the learning activities, as most of the time the information provided in the informal scenario concerns learning. The identification of the observation activity is next, followed by the assessment activity. Then comes the identification of the organization scenario, as it may start the other activities. The description of what usually happens in these activities (see previous section) may help.

Identification of the Roles Involved

The "identification" phase has to be completed with a description of who is to be involved in each activity by identifying their *roles*. For each activity, the instructional designer identifies the main roles of the future participants. For instance, the teacher is the role of the observation activity. For each activity, she or he also has to define the *participation modes*.

Identification of the Participation Mode

"Participation mode" is the overall way participants will exchange and interact in an activity. It describes the kind of situation a teacher wants to carry out with his or her students. It allows *individual* participation in an activity to be distinguished from *collaborative* participation.

In individual participation, participants have individual activities and no relationship with each other. This is the case, for example, of an examination in which, by definition, learners have to work on their own. Figure 14 presents the notation proposed to describe individual participation.

Figure 14. Notation for individual participation in an activity

Figure 15. Notation for collective participation in an activity

On the other hand, in collective participation (see Figure 15), participants work and interact together. They are supposed to act in the activity as interdependent and engaged partners sharing a common goal. For example, teachers may ask students to work in a group of four to read texts about "instructional design," analyze them and produce a synthesis of their readings. In each group engaged in this activity, members work jointly. They will produce a unique synthesis.

In collaborative participation, we distinguish *frontal* situations from *open* ones. In frontal situations, participants have individual activities but no relationships with the other participants, except with the person having a particular role who oversees, stimulates, coordinates and controls. This person has a central position in the exchanges and in communication. This is the case for example of a course at university in a lecture hall: the teacher is in front of the students giving a lecture and the students are allowed to ask questions; to do that, they have to raise their hand to ask to speak. Figure 16 presents the notation proposed to describe such frontal situations.

In open situations (see Figure 17), participants can cooperate freely with their peers or with the teachers. It is the case for example of a panel session in which participants are invited to discuss and express freely their opinions and points of view.

Figure 16. Notation for a frontal situation

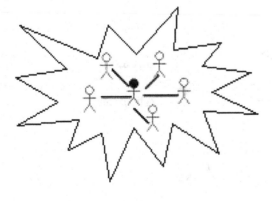

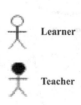

Learner

Teacher

Figure 17. Notation for an open situation

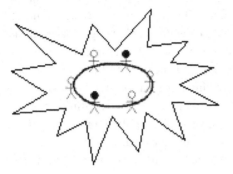

Definition of the Relationships Between the Activities

Once the instructional designer has identified the activities, the roles involved and the participation modes for each of them, these activities have to be positioned by the designer with respect to each other. This means that the designer has to:

- Define the learning flow; and,
- Define the objects the activities may share (arenas and positions).

In real educational practices, these various forms can be combined with each other to produce hybrid educational situations that can evolve over time. Figure 18 is an example of such a case. It combines individual participation for participants having a role (represented on Figure 18 with a black head) with open situation for participants having another role (represented on Figure 18 with a white head). It could be the case, for example, of a panel session with attendees. On the one hand, participants having the "attendee" role have an individual activity: they listen to the discussion and may take some personal notes. On the other side, participants having the "speaker" role are involved in an open situation: they are debating on a given subject.

These elements are presented in what follows, together with the notation proposed to represent them.

Defining the Learning Flow

The definition of the learning flow leads to both the building of the activity schedule (specification of the order according to which activities will have to be performed) and the definition of synchronization points between these activities. We have defined a notation to represent these two dimensions. For the schedule, the instructional designer may use the notation proposed in Figure 19 to represent activities which are connected

Figure 18. A hybrid situation.

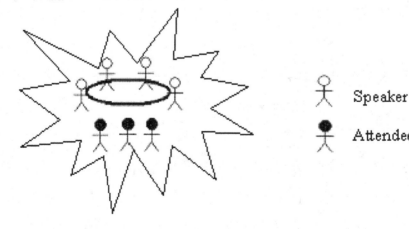

Figure 19. Activities performed sequentially

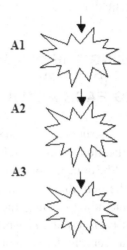

Figure 20. Activities performed in parallel

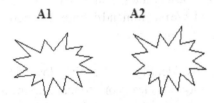

Figure 21. A1 and A2 start asynchronously

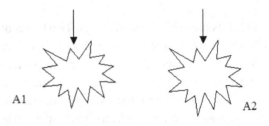

Figure 22. A1 and A2 start synchronously

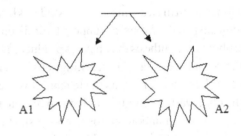

Figure 23. Synchronization between activities

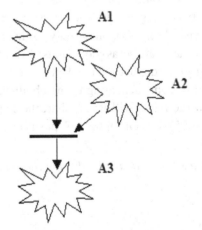

sequentially. The notation proposed in Figure 20 is for those activities which proceed in parallel.

The synchronization points allow the instructional designer to deal with the start-up and the stopping of activities. Two activities may start in an asynchronous way. If so, they will have different start-up conditions. This is represented by the notation proposed in Figure 21.

On the other hand, they may start simultaneously. This means that they share the same start-up rules. This is expressed by the notation presented in Figure 22.

Finally, the instructional designer may want to express synchronization at the end of activities. Figure 23 shows the notation proposed to express this in the case of three activities A1, A2 and A3: A3 cannot start until A1 and A2 are over.

Defining Shared Objects.

Activities may share some objects. Two kinds of objects can be shared: arenas and positions. Two activities may share an arena if their respective participants need to have interactions in the same arena. Let us consider the example mentioned previously (concerning collective participation) in which groups of students work on the production of a synthesis on instructional design theories. Imagine that in the learning activity, students have at their disposal a forum to support their discussion about the synthesis they have to produce. The observation activity and the learning activity will have to share this forum, as the teacher involved in the observation activity will have to be able to observe it. The notation proposed for the sharing of arenas is given in Figure 24, on the example of a shared forum.

In the same way, activities may share positions. For example, imagine that an assessment activity is going on. The teacher wants to propose an adapted remediation activity to the students whose marks are not as good (this is a learning type activity). To do that and to adapt the remediation to the students according to the obtained mark, the two activities will have to share the marks (see Figure 25). It is an "observed" position given by

Figure 24. Two activities sharing a forum

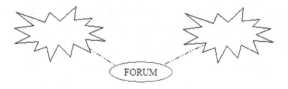

Figure 25. Notation for two activities sharing a position

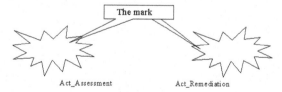

the teacher in the assessment activity. It will be used in the remediation one.

FORMALIZING THE INFORMAL SCENARIO (PART 2): MODELING EACH ACTIVITY

Until now, the instructional designer has focused on the identification of the activities and their relationships. She or he has built an overall view, positioning the activities with respect to each other. It is time now to change the focus and to go deeper into each activity. That means building a model, i.e. a scenario, for each of them.

An LDL scenario needs the definitions of the structures, interactions, roles, arenas, rules, positions and observables suitable to the activity to be modeled. We recommend defining these concepts in the following order:

- First, identify the learning flow of the activity. This leads one to make an inventory of the structures and the interactions they organize. At this stage, the instructional designer only needs to identify the interactions in a general way (only their names). This will give a first, overall view of the expected activity.
- Second, give a more precise specification of each interaction. That means identifying the roles and the arenas involved in each interaction.
- Third, complete the specification of the interactions and structures with the definition of their start-up and stopping conditions. This supposes modeling the corresponding rules.
- Fourth, define the positions. The conditional part of the rules tests the values of the positions. So, from the exhaustive list of rules, one can obtain an exhaustive list of positions to be defined.

- Last, define the observables. The instructional designer has to define for each "observed" position the associated observables.

The description of the methodology now is completed. With this approach, the instructional designer has all the material required to model a learning activity: a language, allowing a model of the targeted activity to be built, and a methodology for explaining how to handle the language and how to carry out the modeling process. The next section shows an example of how LDL and its associated methodology were used to create the model of the planet game case study.

APPLICATION OF THE METHODOLOGY TO AN EXAMPLE

We have chosen to show the use of LDL and the methodology with the planet game example. This example was proposed as a common case study to work on within the workshop entitled, *Comparing Educational Modeling Languages on a Case Study* (Vignollet et al., 2006) we organized during ICALT'2006. Each research team engaged as a competitor (they were 9) had to study a given real situation (the same for every team: the planet game), had to at least model this situation by using its own models and languages, and was asked to implement it as an activity running in a web learning environment.

The methodology recommends building the informal scenario first. Thus we begin by presenting the informal scenario of the planet game. Note that we will not provide the complete specification, as this would be too long. We will just show a part of it, which illustrates the approach satisfactorily. Additional information can be found in Martel et al. (2006b) or at http://ld.pentila.com.

Step 1 : The Planet Game Informal Scenario

The Context

The chosen activity is part of a real lifelong learning scenario in astronomy. The students have the same problem to solve. They are grouped into two teams. Each team has only a part of the knowledge and data required to solve the problem. So, they must collaborate.

The Proposed Activity

The activity objective is for learners to acquire knowledge in the field of astronomy. More precisely, they have to classify the planets with respect to their distance from the Sun (from the nearest to the most distant).

The strategy used by the teacher to reach these objectives is to propose a game for the learners. The latter are grouped into two teams (Team A and Team B). Resources and services will be available to help the learners in acquiring new knowledge, in exchanging with their team members, and in negotiating.

The Game Rules

Clues are distributed among teams. Team A knows some planets' properties, taken from an expert interview it has at its disposal. Its members can deduce the planets' order, but not the planets' names. Team B knows the planets' names and some properties taken from another expert interview. However, many properties are missing. Each team can use a chat room to enable its members to have discussions (about the problem to solve, the clues they have, etc). Each team also has at its disposal a shared whiteboard allowing its members to list the already discovered information.

The teams have to cooperate using a forum to negotiate the exchange of clues and information. The teacher has access to the forum, and can participate in the discussions. She or he can also add new clues to either of the expert interviews. When she or he decides, the exchanges are stopped. Then, each learner fills in a questionnaire about the planet classification. The winner is the first who gives the right associations (the planets in order from the sun). The activity finishes when a winner is nominated.

Step 2-Part 1: Identifying the Planet Game Activities and their Relationships

When analyzing the informal scenario above, we notice that the four kinds of activity mentioned in the methodology section (organization, learning, observation, assessment) actually exist in the planet game. For the learning activity, it is obvious. The informal scenario explicitly includes a lot of information about this activity. The learning objectives are listed, together with the way

Figure 26. Activities, roles and relations between activities are identified

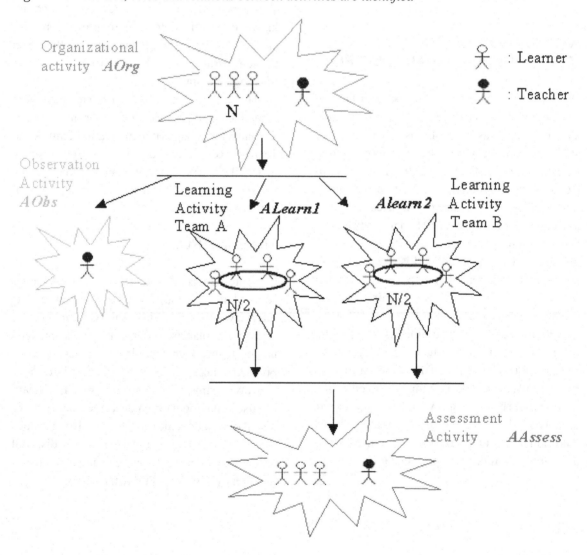

to reach these objectives (analysis of the clues, discussion in the chat room, negotiation with the other team, etc.). The aim is clearly for learners to acquire knowledge about the organization of the solar system.

The informal scenario also mentions the interventions of the teacher in relation with the learning activity. Indeed, the teacher has to observe the teams while the learning activity proceeds. She or he may observe the team members' exchanges, their productions, the way they use the clues, etc. This is an activity *per se*, during which the teacher may identify the difficulties encountered by the learners, may put new clues at their disposal, etc. This is the observation activity.

The assessment activity is also clearly mentioned. It consists in a summative assessment which occurs at the end of the learning period. It aims at checking the level and the solidity of their knowledge.

Finally, there are some elements which are related to organization which are possibly less explicit. The most evident one is to set up the two teams. To be carried out, the planet game requires this step. It also requires the teacher to prepare some instructions intended for learners, to put them at the learners' disposal, together with the useful resources (interviews, clues, shared whiteboard, chat room, etc.), to organize the course of the activities in time, etc.

These activities are represented graphically in Figure 26, together with the learning flow between them (the schedule and the synchronization points). Note that the learning activity appears twice, once for each team: they correspond to the same scenario.

The description of the relationships between activities has to be supplemented by the definition of the shared objects: arenas and position. The ALearn1 and ALearn2 learning activities share the forum which supports the negotiation of the exchange of clues. This arena is also shared with the AObs observation activity, as the teacher involved in the observation activity has to be able to at least observe what happens in it (see Figure 27).

Furthermore, the two learning activities and the observation one share the "end of the learning activities" position. This position is a decision of the teacher to be made explicitly in the AObs activity. Indeed, the teacher observes the two ongoing learning activities and chooses the time to stop them, when the learners have worked enough and have acquired enough clues and knowledge. Thus the AObs activity has to share this position with the two learning ones. As a consequence, these two activities will be aware of it and will be able to end. Note that it is also shared with the AAssess activity, as the end of ALearn1 and ALearn2 coincides with the beginning of AAssess.

Figure 27. ALearn1 and AObs activities share the "clue negotiation" forum

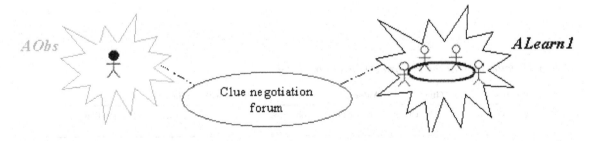

Figure 28. The main structure with the interactions

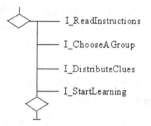

I_ReadInstructions

I_ChooseAGroup

I_DistributeClues

I_StartLearning

Step2-Part 2: Modeling Each Activity of the Planet Game

We have chosen to describe the organizational one (though only part of it). It is easy to imagine the design of the others, in the same way. The first step is the identification of the "Learning Flow," represented by the structures and the interactions.

The Structures and the Interactions

The main structure is a sequential one which combines four interactions:

- Read the instructions, called I_ReadInstructions
- Choose a group, I_ChooseAGroup
- Distribute clues, I_DistributedClues
- Start the learning activity, I_StartLearning.

This is noted as shown in Figure 28.

This identification leads to the determination of roles.

Table 2. The roles in AOrg and the associated interactions.

The Role	is involved in	as an addresser	as an addressee
Learner	I_ReadInstructions, I_ChooseAGroup I_DistributeClues I_StartLearning	Yes Yes	Yes Yes Yes Yes
Teacher	I_DistributeClues I_StartLearning	Yes Yes	

The Roles

Table 2 places the AOrg activity's roles in relation to the interactions that define them. It also provides the place of the role within the interaction: being an addresser or an addressee.

The Arenas

Now, the places where the activity takes place have to be identified. They can be more or less abstract. To find them, the instructional designer has to answer the following question: Where the interaction from role X to role Y takes place? What is the support of the interaction? In which space does the interaction take place?

In the example, the arenas are:

- I_ReadInstructions is done into the Instructions,
- I_ChooseAGroup is done in a questionnaire,
- I_DistributeClues is done in a group space,
- I_StartLearning is done in an activity.

Table 3. Specification of the P_Group-Chosen position

Position Id	Title	Value	type	shared with	taken by	on
P_Group-Chosen	I have chosen a group	True or false	observed	-	learner	The questionnaire

Rules

The distribution of clues can start when the learners have chosen their group. A rule has to be defined. Let us call this rule R_distrib_start. The conditional part of R_distrib_start checks the position of each learner. Its action part starts the distribution activity.

Positions

For each rule defined, there are related positions. The ones associated to R_distrib_start is a declared one. It is specified in Table 3.

Observables

The P_Group-Chosen position is an observed one. It is associated to an observable: the response provided by the learner in the questionnaire.

FIRST RESULTS AND CONCLUSION

As mentioned in Botturi et al. (2006), each design language was developed with a specific use framework in mind. For LDL, the use framework is the modeling of learning activities and the execution of the produced models (i.e., the scenarios) on existing VLE. As computer scientists, we have taken an engineering approach, moving toward the constant refinement of the language. We have made the deliberate choice of focusing on the expressiveness of the language and on the development of software tools enabling one to easily transform the models into actual activities running on VLE. Indeed, we think that it is of paramount importance that instructional designers and teachers are able "to see" what happens when a scenario is executed. So they can give some feedback. And this also enables learners to be involved in the evaluation process.

This has an important impact on the results we can present here. We provide results about the modeling capacity of the language and related to the experiments which were conducted with learners. But results related to the actual use of the language by instructional designers or teachers are still missing to date. This is commented on below.

Experiments Conducted

LDL's maturity can be evaluated by taking into consideration experiments already carried out: the three main ones are described here. They enabled us to improve the expressiveness of the language and to make the infrastructure more robust.

A Famous Scenario of the Internet: The Treasure Hunt

A first experiment took place which brought together 40 participants at a workshop held during the 2005 occurrence of the annual summer school of the French "Technology Enhanced Learning" research community (Lejeune et al., 2005). The chosen activity was an example of a treasure hunt. This type of activity is very widespread and numerous examples can be found on the Internet.

We used LDL to build the scenario and LDI and its associated player to operationalize, execute, play and follow the resulting activity. This experiment enabled us to validate the concepts of the model. It also allowed us to improve the robustness of the infrastructure, with 40 users playing simultaneously.

The Project "Shared Virtual Laboratory" (SVL) of the Kaleidoscope European Network of Excellence

The objective of this project was to provide researchers in ICT in Education with an integrated environment to collect and share experimental trails. This environment, developed by Pentila corporation, includes:

- Workspaces in which experiments can take place,
- The LDI infrastructure and the associated player,
- A trails repository.

TPELEC (French acronym for "practical work in the domain of electricity") was one of the experiments conducted to improve the developed environment. It concerns learning in the domain of electricity. The learning scenario's goal was on the one hand to destabilize the misconceptions and incorrect reasoning of learners, on the other hand to use the detected misconceptions for remediation, progression and building of new knowledge. To carry out the TPELEC experiment, LDL was used to create the scenario and its possible adaptations when misconceptions are detected. LDI was the operationalization, execution and observation infrastructure.

The TPELEC scenario was experimented with in classrooms in 2005-2006 (six experiments in three schools, with a total of 120 learners aged 14 to 16). As the teachers were involved in the experiments and could see the scenarios as they run, they gave some interesting feedback. In particular, they became aware of the modeling capacities of LDL. This stimulated their imagination and led them to produce new, richer scenarios. These scenarios will be formalized, operationalized and experimented within a new project that has been recently funded by the Kaleidoscope Network of Excellence. For a more in-depth description of the TPELEC experiment and its results, you can read the corresponding Kaleidoscope report (Kaleidoscope D7.8.1, 2006).

From a learning design point of view, the purpose of this work was to test the observation points: from their specification in LDL to their implantation and use in LDI.

The Planet Game

The previously presented planet game was tested by researchers during the ICALT 2006 conference. It allowed us to improve the capacity of the language to model different kinds of activities and led to the development of the methodology.

Qualities of LDL

We here want to highlight what constitutes, in our opinion, the main strengths of LDL. To do that, we will refer in particular to some of the "desired properties" proposed by Harrer in Chapter XIV. We also provide some limitations of the language.

A Theory-Based Language

LDL is activity-centered. It was conceived to model collaborative activities. It is grounded on social theories which explain what is inherent in these activities. It thus integrates concepts which enable to take these inherent features into account, mainly their unforeseeable, situated and interactional nature.

Simplicity

LDL comprises a small number of concepts, which facilitates its appropriation. This meets Harrer's "familiarity / intuitive intelligibility" desired property. One may object that "arena," "position" or even "interaction" are not that familiar to instructional designers or teachers. That is probably true. But the questions corresponding to the LDL concepts (who? where? what? how? etc.) should compensate for the relative unfamiliarity. And the number of questions should be small, as the number of concepts is. We are currently exploring ways of dealing with this problem through the development of an authoring online tool dedicated to instructional designers and teachers. In particular, we are considering the possibility of using metaphors to translate LDL concepts into corresponding concepts available in these metaphors. For example, in the "classroom" metaphor, the arenas could be the blackboard, the lesson, the poster, the video projector, the story book, etc., i.e. any resources or objects available in a classroom which are quite familiar to instructional designers and teachers. This should facilitate the use of LDL.

Expressiveness

The experiments conducted have improved LDL expressiveness. We were able to model different learning situations and activities of various kinds (learning, observation, assessment, organization). This is probably due to the neutrality of the underlying metaphor. Indeed conversation perfectly corresponds to activity and has the same inherent properties.

Support of Different Granularity

LDL also meets Harrer's "support of different granularity" desired property thanks to the activity-centered point of view and to the "arena" concept. Arenas are places where activities take place. An activity occurring in an arena can be described by means of a single interaction (for example, the interaction "to discuss about the lecture" taking place in a "forum" arena). But it could also be described by a more complex specification defining what may happen in the arena (for example in the forum, there may be a moderator; contributors may add new discussion subjects; a contributor may post something new; etc.). And this is a complete scenario (Martel &Vignollet, 2007). The grain of the activity to model has changed.

Future Works

LDL's expressiveness has been improved during the conducted experiments. Nevertheless we cannot claim that LDL can be used to model any kind of learning. And this is true for all design languages. To try to obtain evidence to support that claim, it is necessary to continue the improvement with a set of informal scenarios to model, which could be considered as a benchmark. We suggest dividing the effort of the building of this benchmark between LD language designers. The work currently done by the English Joint Information Systems Committee (JISC) on the evaluation of IMS-LD within the IMS Learning Design for Practitioners (LD4P) project could be the basis of this benchmark.

Furthermore, we have not yet considered the evaluation of the perception of LDL's usefulness and the associated methodology by end-users. This is a very difficult problem to deal with, as there are a lot of elements and variables to consider, which are tightly intertwined (Botturi, 2005). Some promising approaches have begun to clear it up, for examples chapters XVIII, XIX and XXI of this handbook and Botturi (2005). If we want to make such an evaluation, we need to make some experiments with practitioners (instructional designers and teachers), giving them the role of "scenario designer." If we wish to do that in the best conditions, we in fact have to provide an online authoring tool to support both the design process and the translation of the diagrams produced into LDL code. This tool has to be simple and intuitive enough to be used by end-users, as the learning activity management system (LAMS, Dalziel, 2003) authoring tool for instance. It has to support the graphical notation that we have proposed and the methodology. We have specified such a tool. It is currently under development and should be operational by summer 2007. This will allow us to start a validation phase, which will be supported by learning scientists, instructional designers and/or teachers.

ACKNOWLEDGMENT

We would like to thank the engineers of the Pentila Corporation for their work on the LDL project.

REFERENCES

Austin, J.N. (1955). *How to do things with words*. Oxford.

Botturi, L. (2005). Visual languages for instructional design: An evaluation of the perception of E²ML. *Journal of Interactive Learning Research*, *16*(4), 329-351.

Botturi, L., Derntl, M., Boot, E., & Figl, K. (2006). A classification framework for educational modeling languages in instructional design. In *The Proceedings of IEEE ICALT 2006* (pp. 1216-1220). Kerkrade, the Netherlands.

Dalziel, J. (2003). Implementing learning design: The learning activity management system (LAMS). In *The Proceedings of the ASCILITE 2003 conference, Adelaide, Australia*. Retrieved from http://www.melcoe.mq.edu.au/res.htm

Durand, G., & Martel, C. (2006). To scenarize the assessment of an educational activity. In *The Proceedings of ED'MEDIA 2006*. Orlando, Florida.

Ferraris, C., Brunier, P., & Martel, C. (2002). Constructing collaborative pedagogical situations in classrooms: A scenario and role based approach. In *The Proceedings of CSCL 2002* (pp. 290-299). Boulder, Colorado.

Fitzpatrick, G., Tolone, W. J., & Kaplan, S. M. (1995). Work, locales and distributed social worlds. In *The Proceedings of ECSCW'95* (pp. 1-16). Stockholm, Sweden.

Garfinkel, H., & Sacks, H. (1972). *Contributions in ethnomethodology*. Bloomington: Indiana University Press.

Goffman, E. (1981). *Forms of talk*. Philadelphia: University of Pennsylvania Press.

Guéraud, V., Adam, J.-M., Pernin, J.-P., Calvary, G., & David, J.-P. (2004). L'exploitation d'Objets Pédagogiques Interactifs à distance: le projet FORMID. *Revue STICEF*, *11*. Retrieved from http://www.sticef.org

IMS Global Learning Consortium. (2003). *IMS learning design information model*. Retrieved from http://www.imsglobal.org/learningdesign

JISC. (2007). *Web site of the joint information systems committee (UK)*. Retrieved from http://www.jisc.ac.uk/

Kaleidoscope (2006). *Demonstrator of an infrastructure for collect and exchange of experimental traces*. (SVL project deliverable, D7.8.1 [final, public]). Kaleidoscope network of excellence.

Koper, R. (2002). *Educational modeling language: Adding instructional design to existing specifications*. Retrieved from http://www.httc.de/nmb/images/Koper-v1.pdf

Lejeune, A., Martel, C., Choquet, C., El Kechai, H., & Pernin, J.P. (2005). Workshop «Manipulation des scénarios pédagogiques», Atelier 2, Troisième École thématique du CNRS sur les EIAH, Modèles, Architectures logicielles et normes pour le développement et l'intégration des EIAH. Autrans, France.

LAMS. (2006). *Learning activity management system*. Retrieved from http://www.lamsfoundation.org/

Le Pallec, X., de Moura Filho, C., Marvie, R., Nebut, M., & Tarby, J.-C. (2006). Supporting generic methodologies to assist IMS-LD modeling. In *The Proceedings of IEEE ICALT'2006* (pp. 923-927). Kerkrade, the Netherlands.

LD4P. (2007). *IMS learning design for practitioners (LD4P) project Web site*. Retrieved from. http://www.hope.ac.uk/ld4p/

Martel, C. (1998). *La modélisation des activités conjointes. Rôles, places et positions des participants.* (PhD Thesis, University of Savoie).

Martel, C., Ferraris, C., Caron, B., Carron, T., Chabert, G., Courtin, C., Gagnière, L., Marty, J.C., & Vignollet, L. (2004). A model for CSCL allowing tailorability: implementation in the electronic schoolbag groupware. In *The Proceedings of CRIWG'2004*, San Carlos, Costa Rica (LNCS 3198, pp. 322-338).

Martel, C., Vignollet, L., Ferraris, C., David, J.P., & Lejeune, A. (2006a). Modeling collaborative learning activities on e-learning platforms. In *The Proceedings of IEEE ICALT 2006* (pp. 707-709). Kerkrade, The Netherlands.

Martel, C., Vignollet, L., & Ferraris, C. (2006b). *Modeling the case study with LDL and implementing it with LDI.* Paper presented at IEEE ICALT 2006 (pp. 1149-1151). Kerkrade, The Netherlands.

Martel, C., & Vignollet, L. (2007). *Learning design language to specify services.* TENCompetence Open Workshop on Service Oriented Approaches and Lifelong Competence Development Infrastructures. Manchester, UK.

Miao, Y., Hoeksema, K., Hoppe, H. U., & Harrer, A. (2005). CSCL scripts: Modeling features and potential use. In *The Proceedings of CSCL'2005* (pp. 423-432). Taipei, Taiwan.

Roulet, E., Auchlin, A., Moeschler, J., Rubattel, C., & Schelling, M. (1985). *L'articulation du discours en français contemporain.* Berne: Peter Lang.

Savery, J., & Duffy, T. (1996). Problem based learning: An instructional model and its constructivist framework. In B. Wilson (Ed.). *Constructivist learning environments: Case studies in instructional design* (pp. 135-148). Englewood Cliffs, NJ: Educational Technology Publications.

Suchman, L. (1987). *Plans and situated actions: The problem of human-machine communication.* Cambridge University Press.

Vignollet, L., David, J.P., Ferraris, C., Martel, C., & Lejeune, A. (2006). Comparing educational modeling languages on a case study. In *The Proceedings of IEEE ICALT 2006* (pp. 1149-1151). Kerkrade, the Netherlands.

Vygotsky, L. (1934). *Thought and language.* Cambridge: MIT Press.

Chapter XIII
Visual Design of Coherent Technology–Enhanced Learning Systems:
A Few Lessons Learned from CPM Language

Thierry Nodenot
Université de Pau et des pays de l'Adour, France

Pierre Laforcade
Université du Maine, France

Xavier Le Pallec
Université de Lille, France

ABSTRACT

Visual instructional design languages currently provide notations for representing the intermediate and final results of a knowledge engineering process. As some languages particularly focus on the formal representation of a learning design that can be transformed into machine interpretable code (i.e., IML-LD players), others have been developed to support the creativity of designers while exploring their problem-spaces and solutions. This chapter introduces CPM (computer problem-based meta-model), a visual language for the instructional design of problem-based learning (PBL) situations. On the one hand, CPM sketches of a PBL situation can improve communication within multidisciplinary ID teams; on the other hand, CPM blueprints can describe the functional components that a technology-enhanced learning (TEL) system should offer to support such a PBL situation. We first present the aims and the fundamentals of CPM language. Then, we analyze CPM usability using a set of CPM diagrams produced in a case study in a 'real-world' setting.

INTRODUCTION

For several years, the IMS-LD specification (IMS, 2003b) has been the subject of converging theoretical and practical works from researchers and practitioners concerned with Learning Technologies.

The IMS-LD specification is now well documented (Hummel, Manderveld, Tattersall, & Koper, 2004; Koper et al., 2003; Koper & Olivier, 2004) and widely used for the semantic representation of learning designs. A *learning design* is defined as the description of the teaching-learning process that takes place in a unit of learning (Koper, 2006). The key principle in learning design is that it represents learning activities and support activities being performed by different persons (learners, teachers) in the context of a unit of learning. These activities can refer to different learning objects that are used/required by these activities at runtime (e.g., books, software programs, pictures); they can also refer to services (e.g., forums, chats, wikis) used to communicate and collaborate in the teaching-learning process.

Thus, IMS-LD is an educational modeling language that provides a representation of the components of a learning environment in a standardized XML schema that can be executed by compliant e-learning platforms. According to the classification framework defined in Botturi, Derntl, Boot, and Gigl, (2006), IMS-LD is an example of a finalist-communicative language: it is not intended to enable designers to produce intermediate models of the learning design being studied, nor to provide significant methodological support for designers to build a final representation complying with the IMS-LD specification.

Initially, designers had to use XML editors (like *XMLSpy*) to benefit from all IMS-LD expressive capabilities (levels A, B, C). *Reload*, a tree and form based authoring tool, was the first editor to significantly improve this situation. Chapter XV of this handbook provides an extensive presentation of currently available IMS-LD compliant tools (Tattersall, 2007):

- LD-editors like *Reload (Reload, 2005)*, *CopperAuthor (CopperAuthor, 2005), etc.*
- *Visual tools to support practitioners in the creation of IMS-LD compliant designs by means of using collaborative pattern-based templates (Hernández-Leo et al., 2006).*
- Authoring environments for IMS-LD designs like the *ASK Learning Designer Toolkit – ASK-LDT* (Sampson, Karampiperis, & Zervas, 2005).
- Runtime engines able to interpret a LD-scenario like *CopperCore* (Vogten & Martens, 2003).
- learning management systems able to interpret LD scenarios: *dotLRN (Santos, Boticario, & Barrera, 2005), LAMS (Dalziel, 2006), Moodle (Berggren et al., 2005), etc.*

However, standards like IMS-LD (2003) and IEEE LOM (2002) start from the principle that even though learning theories are not pedagogically neutral, neutral reference models and standards can still be designed: '*The aim is not to set up a prescriptive model but an integrative pedagogical meta-model which is neutral since it models what is common with any pedagogical model*' (Koper, 2001); this assumption promotes the concept of de-contextualized learning objects that can be specified once, and then reused to design learning scenarios relying on instructivist (acquisition metaphor) or constructivist (knowledge creation metaphor) principles.

This chapter proposes another way to address the design of learning scenarios. On the one hand, we consider that socio-constructivist learning scenarios must be designed in context. On the other hand, we think that even the final results of an instructional design (ID) process should clearly state the mapping between the contextualized activities specified by designers and the functionalities provided by a given learning management system (LMS).

In the first section, we present various on-going research work focusing on languages defined to help designers represent and share ideas about a learning scenario under study. Such languages are called 'generative-reflective languages' in (Botturi, Derntl et al., 2006). The second section introduces CPM (cooperative problem-based meta-model) language, a visual design-language focusing on the design of problem-based learning (PBL) situations; we present its syntax and semantics that rely on UML language. Then, we try to understand CPM usability from an analysis of a set of CPM diagrams produced in the framework of a real-world case study. This study illustrates CPM language expressivity; it also states that even though designing PBL situations with CPM notation remains a complex knowledge engineering activity, good practices can concretely improve designers' efficiency and confidence. Finally, the concluding section summarizes both CPM characteristics and proposals for improvement.

BACKGROUND

In this section, we only focus on current research work that could lead practitioners (teachers, educators, designers) to consider ID languages as adequate tools to explore their problem-spaces, not only to share ideas within a design team, but also to prepare the implementation of coherent technological enhanced learning systems.

Situated learning presupposes that meaning is both incorporated within the learning design as well as being prone to interpretation and shared understanding (Stahl, 2006): "*a blind spot of activity-centered models is their missing ability to describe the relation between the program (the learning design) and its context*" (Allert, 2004).

Thus, modeling coherent social systems for learning requires going beyond selecting and sequencing activities and resources, but also deciding and documenting for what purposes they are being used. This means that roles and activities are to be represented and assessed in context

(Derntl & Hummel, 2005). With this purpose in mind, Allert (2005) introduces the concept of second-order learning objects (SOLOs) which are resources that provide and reflect a strategy (generative strategy, learning strategy, problem solving strategy, or decision-making strategy). SOLOs provide means for structuring information or modeling certain aspects of the real world: they represent sets of interrelated concepts that can be used to describe the domain of concern. The use of different SOLOs will thus allow a designer to look at a system from different points of view (e.g., organizationally, structurally, and from social points of view).

Pawlowski (2002), Pawlowski and Bick (2006) introduce the didactical object model (DIN*)* which extends the aims of current educational modeling languages by introducing specifications for contexts, experiences and acceptance. The concept of reusability is, in this case, extended since it should be possible not only to share scenarios as technical specifications but also to exchange didactical expertise about such scenarios (from the knowledge of their context of use, of concrete experiences reported by the actors involved in its use).

Schneemayer (2002), Brusilovsky (2004), and Paramythis and Loidl-Reisinger (2004) extend the context notion to the environment context which clarifies the real characteristics of the LMS (or any other software) from which the learning situation is being exploited. This leads to an approach for the engineering of learning situations aiming to specify the learning situation together with the LMS which will later enable students to learn from this situation.

Works of Botturi (2003), Botturi, Cantoni, Lepori, and Tardini (2006) promote the adaptation of fast prototyping for the specific issues of e-learning project development with very particular stress on human-factor management (*i.e.,* the *eLab* model). They developed a visual design language called E²ML (cf Chapter VII of this handbook) to support fast prototyping to enable a developing interdisciplinary team to function (including educators and teachers). Outcomes of the language include better communication within the design team, availability of precise design documentation to evaluate designs and figure out agreed and more feasible solutions.

Despite having quite different objectives, the works that we have listed in this section (including those conducted in the framework of the IMS-LD initiative) share the fact that they address the complexity of ID. Developing future technology-enhanced learning (TEL) systems requires an interdisciplinary team with both pedagogical and technical skills: communication and minimal agreement on means and ends are conditions for success within such a team.

From the point of view of teachers and educators, ID languages can be communication catalysts (Botturi, Derntl et al., 2006) if these actors feel that the concepts of the language are in tune with the characteristics of the learning situation to be described and will enable them to explore, document and share their design decisions with others.

On the one hand, Allert (2005) states that teachers and educators need dedicated languages which reduce complexity by reflecting instruction (and the process of ID) according to specified criteria (p. 41): *i.e.,* formalization, compatibility and interoperability criteria (IMS, 2003b) are to be considered since most educators are now aware that the introduction of technologies in education has important consequences on any design process.

On the other hand, such instructional languages must not neglect didactics, which is the science of learning and teaching; even if in the domain of training (reproductive forms of learning), the learning design is often limited to the planning and sequencing of non-contextualized activities and resources. Pawlowski and Bick (2006) state that designing situated-learning requires languages that can precisely describe the context and the dynamics of the tutoring/learning activities and resources.

Our work on visual ID languages started just before Koper (2001) published his first results on the Educational Modeling Language (the precursor of the IMS-LD specification). From the very beginning, we intended to propose a visual design language that could be useful for both educators and developers of TEL systems. From the point of view of educators, the language requirements were:

1. To enable designers to represent learning-tutoring activities in context.
2. To reduce complexity by reflecting instruction (and the process of ID).

In the following sections, we shall first present the characteristics of the language; then we shall study the language usability from an analysis of its use on 'real-world' case studies.

CPM LANGUAGE

CPM stands for **c**ooperative **p**roblem-based learning **meta-model**. It is a visual design language that we developed at the LIUPPA Laboratory (Laboratoire Informatique de l'Université de Pau et des Pays de l'Adour, France) as a specialization of UML language. CPM language focuses on the design of problem-based learning (PBL) situations. We decided to work on such a dedicated language because we consider with Allert (2004) and Pawlowski and Bick (2006) that:

1. Pedagogical meta-models are not neutral
2. There is an important need for design languages that specifically address generative learning (learning in context, situated learning).

According to the ID classification scheme defined in Botturi, Derntl et al. (2006), it is a visual (notation level), layered (stratification level), semi-formal (formalization level) language promoting multiple perspectives (more than one view) upon the same entities. In the next paragraphs, we present the aims of the language and the information model captured by CPM language. Fundamentals of both its abstract syntax (the CPM meta-model) and its concrete syntax (the CPM profile) are then discussed. Finally, we briefly present three real-world case studies, which have enabled us to experiment on the usability of CPM language.

Aims of CPM Language

Even though learning by doing activities promoted by a PBL scenario may seem to be natural activities, PBL situations must be scripted. In the context of PBL, the support focuses on mentoring, motivating, creating simulated crises, showing how failures result from poor communication and lack of foresight, identifying and promoting areas in which teams and individuals have to make progress. Thus, PBL is different from traditional instructional methods which emphasize the content: This means the main focus is on the learner and genuine problems (Norman & Spohrer, 1996). Guided by tutors who take only a facilitator role, learners are engaged in active and meaningful cooperative learning. They collaborate with each other by using tools to represent problems, to generate solutions, to discuss different perspectives, to lead experiments and simulations, or to write reports, etc. The driving force is the problem given, the success is the solution of it, and apprenticeship is a condition for success. Thus, the object of any PBL activity is an ill-structured problem under study and the expected outcomes of a PBL activity are (Miao, 2000):

- Acquiring knowledge and skills which can be transferred to solve similar problems at individual level.
- Constructing shared knowledge and promoting mutual understanding at group level.

To address such objectives, our challenge was to explore UML modeling capabilities for the PBL domain and to adapt the semantics of this language, when required, using meta-modeling techniques.

UML is a standard controlled by the object management group (OMG) which is widely known as a design catalyst within teams of software developers Costagliola, De Lucia, Orefice, and Polese (2002), Ferruci, Tortora, and Vitello (2002). Readers needing a basic understanding of the UML language will find a useful introduction in chapter IX of this handbook.

UML language can be used as a sketch, blueprint or programming language (Fowler, 2005). In sketch usage, developers use UML to communicate some particular aspects of the system being studied. In the blueprint usage, the idea is to build a detailed design for a programmer to use in coding software. Blueprints may be used for all the details of a system or the designer may draw a blueprint for a particular area. In programming language usage, developers draw UML diagrams that are compiled directly into executable code, and UML becomes the source code.

Our studies demonstrated that UML is too general to correctly address PBL domain and interdisciplinary issues (Sallaberry, Nodenot, Marquesuzaà, Bessagnet, & Laforcade, 2002). Yet, UML activity diagrams are explicitly considered in (IMS, 2003a) as useful formalisms to capture requirements and build learning specifications. A UML-based language proved to supply more support to the interdisciplinary team of developers by means of well known (but debatable) UML features: standard notation, communication power, gateway between models and implementation platforms including software components and services.

Thus, we developed CPM, a specialization of UML language for PBL which we implemented by means of a profiling mechanism (OMG, 1999). This language addresses most of the design process, covering the different stages of conceptual and functional designing. This was a matter of differentiating two target audiences.

On the one hand, *educators and designers* use CPM language to draw models (similar to UML sketches) focusing initial requirements of a PBL situation including the PBL domain, situated roles of learners/teachers, learners skills, predicted obstacles which the educators want learners to overcome, goals and criteria for success within the PBL situation, resources available to learners, etc.

On the other hand, CPM language addresses *instructional engineers*. Their work involves designing a viable solution, in coordinating all the actors involved in the development team. Knowledge of UML is a prerequisite for such engineers who use CPM language to draw various models which capture different points of view or outlooks on the same PBL situation (pedagogical, structural, social, or operational). This set of models makes up the learning/tutoring scenario which can be planned (in terms of steps and learning/tutoring events) but cannot be totally predetermined at design time since PBL addresses generative learning (Allert, 2005). The blueprints they produce are expressed in terms of the concepts appearing in the sketches produced by educators, thus facilitating discussion and agreement.

CPM sketches and blueprints prepare the detailed design stage that involves mapping those agreed CPM models with platform-independent models (PIM), e.g., IMS-LD (Laforcade, 2004) or LMS abstractions (Renaux, Caron, & Le Pallec, 2005). Even though we implemented a toolset to generate Level A IMS-LD compliant models from our CPM models, abstractions of LMSs are our favourite platform-independent models. The idea consists in mapping conceptual design models with components representing abstract views of the services provided by an LMS: such a mapping leadsdesigners to use the CPM language in order to specialize and contextualize the services supplied by an LMS according to the specificities of the activities to be fulfilled.

The CPM Information Model

CPM relies on an information model depicted in Figure 1 (Nodenot, 2005). It is composed of three blocks:

Block 1 (gray area at the top) deals with the modeling of the situated roles played by the very actors involved in a PBL situation. *Roles* can be assigned to individuals or to groups of actors.

Figure 1. The CPM conceptual information model

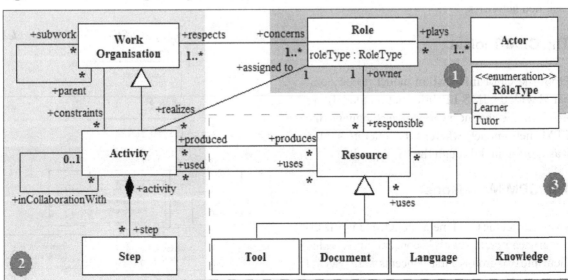

All roles do not imply the same knowledge and know-how; according to their learning goals and responsibilities, roles will often use specific *resources* to perform their learning/tutoring *activities.*

Block 2 (gray area at the left) deals with the *work organization* (rules that can constrain the way activities will be conducted by roles). This *work organization*, including collaborative work, can be decided by designers (learning scenario) or it can be in charge of the actors at runtime. When described at design stage, the organization rules may constrain the *activities* and *resources* at the learners'/tutors' disposal. *Activities* can be further detailed in terms of *steps,* enabling designers to elicit the way important learning/tutoring events should be taken into account when they are raised at runtime.

Block 3 (white area at the bottom right) deals with the *resources* used by actors. *Knowledge* can represent activity prerequisites/post requisites, information about what can be learned from available documents, etc. A *language* is useful to the extent it forces actors to use a fixed set of vocabulary when they try to reach agreements in collaborative activities or when they are asked to describe what they know, what they would like to know, etc. *Documents* and *tools* represent contextualized artifacts enabling actors to conduct assigned activities.

The CPM Toolset

From the CPM information model (to be compared with the IMS-LD Information model), we first built the abstract syntax of the language (the CPM meta-model) whereas its concrete syntax was represented through the CPM profile.

The CPM Meta-Model

To construct the CPM meta-model, an interdisciplinary team started with 35 concepts and divided them into two groups. First, concepts were selected

which related to the necessity for the educators to produce a PBL situation's conceptual design (using terminology from works by (Develay, 1993) and (Meirieu, 1994) and includes notions like *Learning Goal, Obstacle, Success Criterion*, etc.). Then, several concepts were identified which are useful to describe a) the learning scenario (its structure and its dynamics) or b) the tool-environment provided to actors to conduct their learning/teaching activities. These concepts are borrowed as often as possible from the IMS-LD terminology (*e.g., Activity, Activity-Structure, Role*, etc.). They are located in packages and sub-packages (see Figure 2): the *CPM_Foundation* (defined as a subset of UML 1.5) and the *CPM_Extensions* which adds the necessary concepts needed to describe PBL situations.

Among CPM extensions, cognitive concepts necessary to trace the learning/tutoring behaviors of the actors are included in the *PedagogicalPackage*. This package deals with information used to model the components of a PBLS: misconceptions of the learners, predicted obstacles that a teacher wants the learners to overcome, goals and success criteria of the PBLS, resources available to the learners, etc. The *StructuralPackage* includes concepts necessary to describe the PBL scenario and to break it down into simpler learning/tutor-

Figure 2. The packages of the CPM meta-model

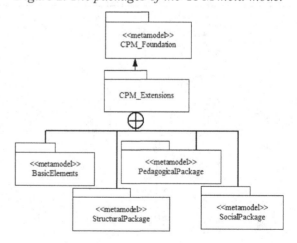

ing activities. Lastly, the *SocialPackage* deals includes all the concepts necessary to manage co-operative work including sharing of resources and of learning/tutoring activities.

There are interconnections between the concepts within these packages. Figure 3 presents two extracts: on the left, a *Structural Package* extract and on the right a *Social Package* extract. Grey concepts refer to elements from the *CPM_Foundation* package (see UML 1.5).

- *ActivityConcept* particularizes the UML concept of operation; it is a general concept to depict any hierarchy of activities.

- *Learning Phase* is used to sequence a learning scenario; its semantics are close to the *Act* IMS-LD Concept, except that an IMS-LD *Act* can only be broken down into one and only one sublevel. Since it specializes the *ActivityConcept*, the *LearningPhase* concept

can be used to describe a scenario with a hierarchy of acts including a hierarchy of scenes from which different roles will carry out particular activities.

- The *ActivityStructure* and *Activity* concepts are also specializations of *ActivityConcept*; they respectively represent a group of activities and a particular activity assigned to one role. Activity Structures can be of different types (i.e., the *structureKind* meta-attribute).

- The *CollaborativeActivity* concept also specializes the *ActivityConcept*; the meta-model states that such an activity is performed by one and only one role (a role can be assigned to a group of concrete actors). Cooperation is not explicit in our meta-model since we decided to describe cooperation by means of role sharing and resource sharing (i.e., the CPM conceptual information model presented in Figure 1).

Figure 3. Interconnections between the concepts of the CPM meta-model packages

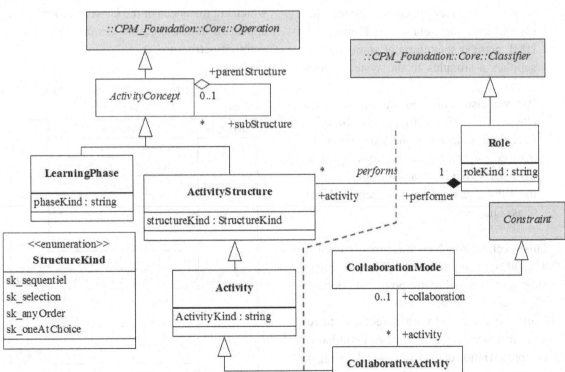

The CPM Profile

To enable designers to draw diagrams that are consistent with such a meta-model, we implemented the CPM profile. A profile uses the extension mechanisms of UML in a standardized way, for a particular purpose. It merely refines the standard semantics of UML by adding further constraints and interpretations that capture domain specific semantics and modeling patterns.

Like any UML profile, the CPM profile promotes *Stereotypes* which are defined for each specific meta-class of the UML meta-model. Thus, for each concept of the *CPM_Extensions* package, we defined a particular stereotype attached to a specific UML meta-class (the Base meta-class) which the CPM concept directly or indirectly particularizes. We also defined alternatives which are other UML meta-classes to enable designers to use a CPM concept in alternative UML diagrams than those suited to its Base meta-class. For example:

- A *Role* is a stereotype defined for the *Use-Cases::Actor* meta-class (i.e., Figure 5) (a UML actor is something or someone who supplies a stimulus to the system operations).
- But we also promoted alternative metaclasses (i.e., Figure 6): *ActivityGraphs::Partition* (to enable designers to use the CPM *Role* concept in UML activity-diagrams), Core::Classifier (to enable designers to use the CPM *LeaningPhase* concept in UML Class Diagrams).

This mechanism which was already used in OMG (2002a) means that *ActivityGraphs::Partition* and Core::Classifier are proxy notations of the *UseCases::Actor* meta-class.

Icons are associated with stereotypes to reduce the designers' cognitive load and to enhance visual appropriation of the CPM models. **Tagged values** are attached to the different stereotypes;

they represent meta-attributes (e.g., *phaseKind, structureKind, roleKind,* etc.) of the *CPM_Extensions* concepts.

We provided designers with an authoring environment supporting CPM language. This was developed alongside the *Objecteering/UML* CASE tool. This prototype allowed us to verify the coherence between the CPM profile entities (concrete syntax) and the CPM meta-model meta-types (abstract syntax). It also enabled us to store complete case studies (*e.g.,* the SMASH case study) as well as reusable design patterns in the objecteering shared repository. The current release of this CPM language is available within a module that can be integrated in and used with the free-of-charge-version of the *Objecteering/ UML Modeler.*

In the next sections, we shall denote a CPM stereotype with the <<>> symbol (e.g., the <<activity-structure>> stereotype. A UML metaclass will be highlighted in italics (e.g., the *ObjectFlowState* metaclass). For the purpose of the case studies that we shall be presenting here, model elements which are instances of the CPM stereotypes will appear in italics (*e.g.,* the *Testimonies analysis* <<activity-structure>>).

Figure 4. An extract of the stereotypes provided to designers by the CPM profile

Stereotype	Metaclass	Icon
Activity	Core::Operation	
	ActivityGraphs::ActionState	
	ActivityGraphs::SubactivityState	
	UseCases::UseCase	
	Core::Classifier	
Learning-Phase	Core::Operation	
	ActivityGraphs::ActionState	
	ActivityGraphs::SubactivityState	
	UseCases::UseCase	
	Core::Classifier	
Role	UseCases::Actor	
	ActivityGraphs::Partition	
	Core::Classifier	

REAL WORLD CASE STUDIES DESIGNED WITH THE CPM LANGUAGE

Chronologically, we started with the SMASH PBL situation that addresses 10 to 12 year- old pupils who must piece together eye-witness accounts to identify the causes of a bicycle accident. We set up an interdisciplinary team including two teachers, two CPM specialists, and two developers mastering the Moodle LMS. This team used CPM language to formalize the teaching/learning objectives, to imagine and to detail a cooperative learning scenario that could take advantage of available communication tools (chat, forum, etc.). The proposed scenario was then tested in real conditions during four half days within a classroom where groups of pupils assisted by their teacher had to cooperate according to the constraints of the specified learning/tutoring activities (using dedicated resources—see Figure 3). Dedicated tools (e.g., a dedicated e-whiteboard to help pupils share their understanding of the actors' spatial position when the accident occurred) were then developed to support learners activities; the scenario was then partly implemented for the Moodle LMS.

Proposed by Vignollet, David, Ferraris, Martel, and Lejeune (2006), the PLANET-GAME case study focused on the didactic transposition (see the initial requirements analysis in Figure 2; see also the account in Chapter XII) of a learning game about astronomy. Assisted by a primary teacher, we used CPM language to describe the conceptualization level that 12 year-old pupils can reach and, in the meantime, we selected different scientific properties of these planets: their distances from the sun, their day durations, their year durations, their compositions, their average temperatures, etc. This domain study led us to set more detailed learning/tutoring objectives from which we defined a learning scenario and tutoring strategies (Nodenot & Laforcade, 2006).

The GEODOC case study is an on-the-road project that leads us to formalize CPM scenarios putting the focus on learning/tutoring objectives dedicated to text comprehension as applied to geography. Learning activities which we formalized with CPM language include actual and inferential questions about what is being read (identification and localization of toponyms, topological identification, mapping-out of routes, *etc.*). This project investigates not only the specialization of LMS services according to formalized learning/teaching scenarios, but also the use of on-the-shelf computational applications in relation with the taught domain (*e.g., Postgis* and *GoogleEarth*).

In the next section, we briefly present the script of a learning scenario and we refer to the figures denoting the CPM diagrams produced in the course of the design of such a scenario. This will help us give concrete expression of the lessons learned from CPM language.

The *Act 2* of the SMASH PBLS: What is this Scenario About?

During *Act 2* (i.e., the IMS-LD terminology), learners (who were previously divided into different groups) have to analyze allocated testimonies. While some groups (that is, *Investigator role 1 to 3*) have access to a limited set, others can read the full set of testimonies (i.e., *Investigator role 4*). The scenario leads all groups (there are several concurrent groups playing *Investigator role 1 to 3* while a unique group of learners plays the *Investigator role 4*) to exchange information about what they learned/understood from the accounts of the testimonies (each group will produce a *belief graph*) and then to write a single *accident report* that all groups must finally acknowledge. The learning scenario is supervised by the *Session manager role* and by a tutor (i.e., *the PoliceChief role*) whose job is to help learners develop an exhaustive analysis of the available testimonies at their disposal.

From a pedagogical viewpoint, such scenario script encourages the groups of learners to confront their own ideas of road safety (knowledge, know-how, attitudes) with the safety rules promoted by road regulations (Highway Code).

In the subsequent text, the reader will find several figures produced with CPM language to specify the *Act 2* learning scenario. The model elements produced during the design process were all stored in the repository provided by the *Objecteering* UML Case tool (i.e., Figure 5) from the set of CPM diagrams produced by the ID Team in charge of the project. Each model element stored in the repository can be used in several diagrams: use-case diagrams, class-diagrams, activity diagrams, state-machines diagrams, etc. Among the different diagrams that were produced in the course of this project, the following were chosen for this chapter:

- Figure 6 and Figure 7 describe the roles taken by the actors and the coarse-grain activities they performed during *Act 2*.
- Figure 8 describes the resources that *Investigator role 1* can use and produce when performing their dedicated activities.
- Figure 9 details the sequencing of the different coarse-grain activities and the conditions that resources must fulfill to accept transitions from one activity to another.
- Figure 10 and Figure 11 detail the *Testimonies Analysis* <<activity-structure>>.

In the next section, we shall use these figures to elicit the lessons that we learned about CPM language usability. However, from the information given about *Act 2* in this subsection, we strongly encourage the reader to begin by analyzing the semantics conveyed by this set of interrelated CPM diagrams.

Lessons Learned from CPM Language

This section presents the lessons we learned about the usability of CPM language to edit/produce a learning scenario. From the three case studies summarized above, we drew two important lessons:

- Although CPM adopts the jargon that many pedagogues and educational designers already use, producing a set of coherent CPM models for a given case study is still a complex activity.
- Even though most pedagogues are not able to produce a set of CPM coherent models by themselves, both pedagogues and developers can contribute to and benefit from such design models.

Several observations led us to formalize these lessons. To give concrete expression to these observations, we shall rely on CPM models from the SMASH PBL; we shall particularly focus on the Act 2 learning scenario (the end of the previous section) leading learners to investigate the causes of a bicycle accident from a set of eye-witness testimonies:

Lesson U1: *Although CPM adopts the jargon that many pedagogues and educational designers already use, producing a set of coherent CPM models for a given case study is still a complex activity.*

During the conducted case studies, we noticed that designers encountered difficulties when seeking to organize efficiently the different kinds of model elements that they were eliciting at design time (see Lesson U1, Observation 1). From the analysis of encountered difficulties and observed solutions, we propose a structuring model, which proved useful to organize the different model elements under study within cohesive packages.

We also noticed (see Lesson U1: Observation 2) that without human assistance, most educational designers did not know which notation was the most appropriate to represent their design intents. Yet, when the same educational designers gained experience about both the UML notation and about the CPM meta-model, most could produce expressive yet simple CPM diagrams.

Finally, Lesson U1—Observation 3 shows that designers were sometimes frustrated because they were confusing CPM with a drawing tool: in particular, some did not clearly understand why the provided toolset (editors and wizards) considered some diagrams whose model elements did not conform with the CPM meta-model as erroneous.

Lesson U1, Observation 1: *Relevant model elements must be conveniently organized by designers within packages. CPM diagrams must also be attached to packages.*

Real world case studies that we specified with CPM language had in common that they could not be mastered by a single designer. All the modeling elements could not be represented in the same UML class diagram; learner, tutor roles, learning goals and success criteria had to be contextualized according to the steps of the learning process; both dynamics and structure of resources and activities had to be specified, etc. Relying on our experience in designing such case studies, we argue that in most cases, what is needed is an approach that structures the design of complex learning scenarios at different levels.

Packages are UML constructs which enable the grouping of model elements, making UML diagrams simpler and easier to understand. Packages themselves may be nested within others; they are depicted as file folders and may be Subsystems or Models. When we designed CPM language, we decided to provide designers with two stereotypes (see caption in Figure 5 which extends the *Package* metaclass: the *Learning Process* stereotype to

break down the learning process into subprocesses and the *Learning Package* stereotype to group other model elements. In the course of our case studies, we learned efficient ways to exploit these stereotypes for organizing model elements. For instance, Figure 5 describes the packages used in the SMASH PBLS:

This is a snapshot of the browser which enables a designer to edit the SMASH learning scenario. At root level, experience led us to create three learning packages whose model elements are exploited by the *Learning Process* package called the *SMASH Scenario Process*. At the bottom of the figure, worth noting is the *SMASH Scenario* denoted as an activity diagram used to generally describe how the different acts of the *SMASH Learning Process* are sequenced.

The model elements (and graphical views) of these four acts are then detailed within the *SMASH Scenario Process*.

In the snapshot of Figure 5, the details of the *Act 2 Process* were expanded. At this level, it will be observed that the package structure is the same as the one at root level: Act 2 shows a *Local Roles Package*, a *Local resources Package*, a *Local Learning Roles Package*, and an *Act 2 Scenes Package* which contains all the scenes within Act 2. This structuring promotes the contextualization of roles, learning goals, resources and learning activities. For example, the expanded *Act 2—Local Roles Package* shows different *Actor* stereotypes, which are model elements used during Act 2 to specialize the tutor role and the Learner role (i.e., the *Global Roles Package*).

It is worth noting that this approach is in tune with Derntl & Motschnig-Pitrik (2007), which encourages designers to elicit hierarchies of both learning goals and documents.

Lesson U1, Observation 2: *Among available CPM diagrams, designers must adequately choose those which can help them to produce some simple yet coherent perspectives of the relevant model elements.*

Figure 5. The SMASH PBLS browser

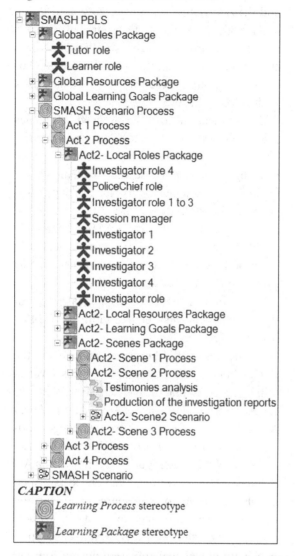

is a system that must be described in terms of learning roles, learning goals, resources made available to the learners, learning and tutoring interactions/activities, events used to regulate learners' activities, etc.

From previous works (Sallaberry et al., 2002) we predicted the new uses of UML diagrams that CPM language encourages. As stated in the section devoted to the presentation of the CPM profile (see Figure 4), a CPM stereotype such as the <<Role>> Stereotype can extend either the *Actor* metaclass (to represent it in use-case diagrams, or the *Partition* metaclass (to represent it in Activity diagrams) or the Classifier metaclass (to represent it in Class diagrams).

During the course of our experiments, we noticed that designers (educators and computer-scientists) encountered two types of difficulties when trying to map their design intentions with available notation (those provided by the different types of diagrams available). First, most designers were inclined to start from a visual notation (e.g., the notation for class diagrams) and then tried using this specific notation to represent all perspectives of the model being studied, even if such a notation was not convenient for all aspects of the model. Second, we noticed that designers had questions about the notation they would be advised to use, particularly at the beginning of a learning scenario design process.

The case studies we have conducted provide useful answers to these difficulties. Let us focus on the intention, "role models involved in a learning scenario." If we consider the CPM information model given in Figure 1, designers should address different perspectives for roles. What are these? How are they involved in the *Work Organization* that the learning scenario promotes? What are their responsibilities in the various (possibly collaborative) activities suggested to be performed in the scenario? What kind of resources do they exploit to carry out such activities? Applied to Act 2 of the SMASH PBLS, Figure 6 and the following are CPM diagrams which focus on the different perspectives listed above.

First, let us recall that UML is a language enabling designers to describe an abstraction of a system that focuses on interesting aspects (models) and ignores irrelevant details. A perspective (view) focuses on a subset of a model to make it understandable.

Choosing UML to describe learning scenarios requires rethinking current uses and to elicit new uses of UML diagrams for dealing with the complexity of learning scenarios. From an educational point of view, a learning scenario

Figure 6. A class diagram representing a hierarchy of SMASH actors

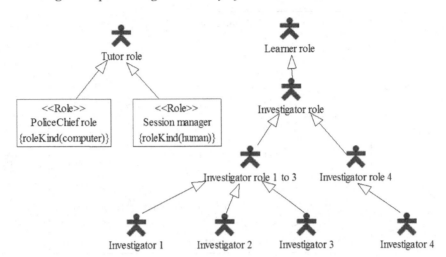

In Figure 6, SMASH roles specialize the *Class* metaclass. This class diagram shows that the *Learner* role and the *Tutor* role (from the *Global Roles* Package) were specialized to enable designers to denote all actors playing an important roles during Act 2. All roles are played by human beings except the *PoliceChief role (*we chose a detailed view of the *Tutor role* model element to make the *roleKind* tag-value visible). Figure 7 offers another perspective for these SMASH roles:

In this use-case diagram, roles specialize the *Actor* metaclass. This perspective focuses on the activities carried out by roles during Act 2. Each *role* either *performs* activities or *assists* other roles performing those activities. Like in IMS-LD, activities that can be broken down into simpler ones (*e.g., Testimonies analysis, Time and document management* or *Production of the investigation reports*) are depicted with the stereotype <<Activity-structure>>.

Figure 8 is another class diagram which designers sketched to focus on the resources used and produced by each role during Act2 (there is a dedicated class diagram for each leaf role that appears in Figure 6). Resources which are produced have the tag-value *output* while others have the tag-value *input*.

The different figures provided in this section clearly show that the different perspectives provided to describe the roles in Act 2 are complementary (all of them can be reached from the model elements browser presented in Figure 5). Other types of diagrams will be presented in Figure 10 (an Activity diagram) and in Figure 11 (a state-machine diagram) to respectively detail the *Testimonies analysis* model element and the belief graph model element that appeared in Figure 7 and Figure 8.

These figures also show that UML notations must be understood by designers to enable them to produce simple yet coherent perspectives of the learning scenario being studied. Table 1 provides a synthesis of the practices we noticed during our case studies. To build this table, we took into account only diagrams which appeared in the last version of the design produced for each of our case studies.

The reader may be surprised that we do not recommend the use of the object diagram for the definition of roles and of resources. In fact, experience led us to consider that concrete roles appear only when the scenario is deployed on a platform (LMS) and used by concrete (groups of) learners. It is only at deployment time that the *Investigator role 1* stereotype is instantiated

Figure 7. A use-case diagram representing the activities in which the different roles are involved

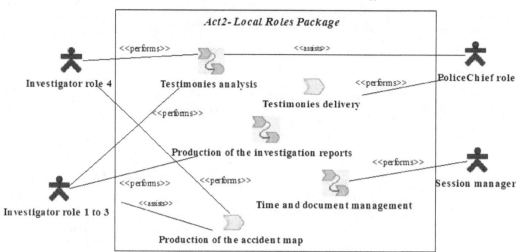

Figure 8. A class diagram describing the resources used and produced by the role Investigator 1

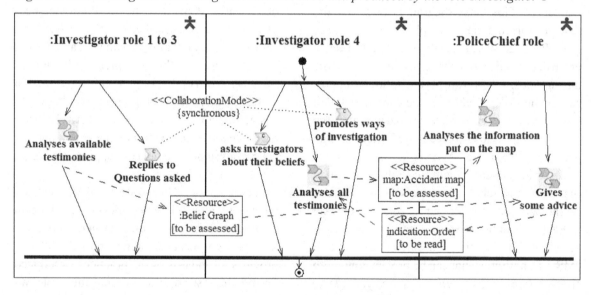

and played by concrete learners. And for similar reasons, the resources produced and used by *Investigator 1* are represented as classes (i.e., Figure 8) and not as objects.

Lesson U1, Observation 3: *To succeed in producing a perspective, designers must agree on both the UML notation and the CPM meta-model which both define the rules that the model elements in a CPM diagram must fulfill.*

During our experiments, designers were at first surprised (and a bit confused) that they were constrained by both the rules of UML notations and of the CPM meta-model. On the one hand rules from the UML notations, they could not add, for example, any information about the timeline in the class diagrams being sketched. On the other hand, the CPM meta-model forced them to respect, for example, the following rule: when the <<activity>> and the <<resource>> ste-

Table 1. Best practices for CPM diagrams

	Use
Activity Diagram	External analysis of the learning scenario
	Description of collaborative activities
	Internal analysis of activities and activity-structures
Use Case Diagram	Activity cut-out
	Role identification
Class Diagram	Learning goal description
	Role description
	Resource description
	External analysis of activities and activity-structures
	Description of the concepts from the domain model
State Machine Diagram	Description of the active classes (resources, roles, learning goals, activities)
Object Diagram	Instances from the domain model (concepts being studied, knowledge and know-how that learners must acquire)

reotypes both extend the *Classifier* metaclass (i.e., the class diagram in Figure 8), connection links between such stereotypes must be of type <<Relation>> (the tag-value can either be *input* or *output*). Most designers did not understand such CPM rules, because they did not realize that the same stereotype (e.g., the <<activity>> stereotype) could represent different metaclasses when used in different types of diagrams. For example, in Figure 7, the *Testimonies analysis* model element extends the *UseCase* metaclass while, in Figure 8, it extends the *Classifier* metaclass (i.e., Figure 4 for the available metaclasses of the CPM stereotypes).

The three types of observations presented in this section show that designers need time to gain the necessary experience required to relevantly exploit the CPM language. Our experience also showed that educators can understand the meaning of a set of CPM diagrams but that the (semi) formal nature of CPM language could hinder some educators' commitment in producing such visual designs. They ask for cognitive assistance during the design process: since CPM editors do not allow free drawing, designers require some feedback enabling them to do some opportunistic productions: to-do lists, checklists, wizards, etc.

The first cognitive tools developed were contextual menus that could infer the metaclass to be used from the knowledge of both the diagram type and the stereotype chosen by the designer. In the framework of our latest project (the GEODOC case study), we also provided designers (educators and computer-scientists) with the best-practices of CPM diagrams and with a set of sample CPM diagrams for each design intent listed in Table 1. Our first experimental results show that such a design team was more efficient (time and design quality) than another team that did not have such documents at their disposal.

But it is already clear that our toolset is still a research prototype that proved expressive capabilities but cannot be distributed to an interdisciplinary team without care and human guidance. Even though the current state of research presented in this section can provide substantial support in understanding PBL scenarios, in designing and documenting new scenarios, it is clear that our approach is specified by rather technically oriented computer science people and a lot of work is still necessary to transform educators into CPM autonomous designers.

Lesson U2: *Even though most pedagogues were not able to produce a set of CPM coherent models, both pedagogues and developers can contribute to and benefit from such design models.*

Through educational expressivity of CPM diagrams, Lesson 1 pinpointed some difficulties encountered by designers who used the CPM toolset. In this section, we present some methodological principles which can help an ID team control the design process complexity.

In the course of the conducted case studies, we first observed that, at any level of the learning scenario analysis (conceptual design, functional design), designers might produce simple yet expressive CPM diagrams (i.e., Lesson U2, Observation 1): it is a matter of focusing on one and only one perspective at a time.

We also noticed that a correct stratification of the learning scenario was important (i.e., Lesson U2, Observation 2) to ensure a smooth transition between the perspectives drawn during learning scenario conceptual design and those drawn to address the functional design of a TEL system that could manage such a learning scenario at runtime.

Both observations will lead us to elicit a design process in tune with CPM language characteristics.

Lesson U2, Observation 1: *Complexity of models can be mastered by designers using the following rule: Design only what is necessary for a given purpose and recognize overdesign.*

Our experience is that most pedagogues can concretely draw various CPM diagrams if they keep in mind that each diagram should focus on one perspective that remains simple and expressive. Consider the *Testimonies analysis* model element which appears in Figure 7 and in Figure 8. None of these perspectives provides information about the activity sequencing planned during *Act 2*. Adding such an information within Figure 7 is difficult since use-case diagrams are not suited to the description of activity sequencing: in general, UML specialists add OCL constraints (OMG, 2002b) to address such difficulty. Drawing another perspective focusing on such activity sequencing is much easier as stated in Figure 9:

In this figure, the reader will notice all activities and all activity-structures that already appeared in the *Act 2* use-case diagram presented in Figure 7: these model elements are grouped together according to the scene during which they are performed by these actors. The information flows between states as *ObjectFlowStates*: these represent some events that should be true either at the beginning (prerequisite) or at the end (post-requisite) of each scene. These different scenes (*e.g.,* the *Act 2- Scene 2 process*) are structuring model elements that can also be easily located in our SMASH Browser (i.e., Figure 5).

We consider that such a diagram can also illustrate what over-design means. At the conceptual design level where educators play the most important role, it would be useless to try to represent exception-handling in such a predicted learning scenario. At runtime, such a script can raise many exceptions (potentially meaningful for educators) that need to be managed (particularly those in relation with *the Time and document management* <<activity-structure>>). But adding exception handling in such a diagram would be likely to complicate the perspective and could mask the key ideas of the scenario, which were already spotted in Figure 9.

As a consequence, we consider that educators relying on CPM for conceptual design should strive for an 80% solution: at this stage, visual design should be used to represent the intermediate and then the final results of the design, thus providing means of communication between educators and computer scientists. All diagrams presented above are still intermediate results of design which helped educators clarifying and sharing their initial ideas.

Figure 9. An activity diagram describing the sequencing of the activities performed during Act 2

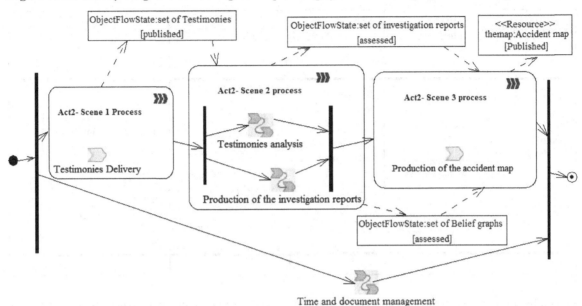

Time and document management

CPM activity diagrams are other important perspectives to consider because they are a (natural) bridge between the use-case diagrams (which are useful to represent educational roles, goals and activities) and the class-diagrams (that developers need to implement required functionality on a learning platform). During our experiments, such diagrams represented an interesting communication trade-off between our business logic experts (educators and interaction designers) and information technology experts (software designers, learning platform specialists, etc.).

For example, Figure 10 is an activity diagram that details the *Testimonies analysis* <<Activity-structure>>.

Three swimlanes are used to identify the specific activities performed by each role; these swimlanes are consistent with the roles assigned to the *Testimonies analysis* <<activity-structure>> in the use-case diagram presented in Figure 7. In Figure 10, we can notice that the *Testimonies analysis* <<activity-structure>> exposes four activity-structures (*e.g.,* the *Analysis available testimonies* <<activity-structure>>) that can be further detailed using a top-down approach, some

collaborative activities (e.g., *Replies to Questions asked* <<collaborative activity>>), some resources (e.g., *the Belief Graph* <<Resource>> to be assessed when it is updated by any real actor playing the <<role>> called *Investigator role 1 to 3*).

Figure 10 also denotes how designers can describe collaborative activities (i.e., activities with a *c* flag); in the scenario, *Investigator role 1 to 3* cannot initiate any synchronous conversation but this role can read information and answers questions asked by *Investigator role 4* (at implementation stage, and will lead developers to specialize a chat service according to these requirements).

An *ObjectFlowstate* denoting a <<Resource>> can be described with a UML State-machine diagram. For example, Figure 11 represents the lifecycle of the *Belief Graph* model element elicited in Figure 10.

The underlying semantics is the following: each time an investigator adds a belief in his belief graph (*e.g.,* a representation of the following belief: "the white car bumped into the back of the bicycle"), the state of the belief graph changes to "to be assessed" (since the *PoliceChief role* is

Figure 10. An activity diagram to represent the details of the Testimonies analysis activity-structure

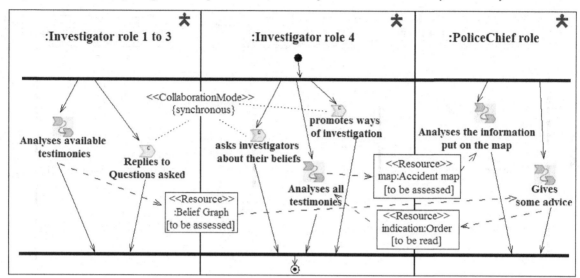

played by a machine—that is, the class diagram in Figure 6, such a decision will entail particular design concern about the assessment process elicitation).

We noticed that educators encountered various difficulties when seeking to draw some CPM activity diagrams by themselves. It is true that these diagrams are not simple to create but they allow complex system/interaction processing to be represented efficiently. In order to get round this obstacle, we advised educators to produce a use-case diagram (in our example, a use case-diagram detailing the *Testimonies analysis* <<<activity-structure>>) for identifying the activities of interest and their relationships; information technology designers used such sketches for discussion purposes with them; and together they produced the final 80% solution presented in Figure 10. Interestingly enough, once this deadlock was broken, educators were able to go further in the conceptual design process.

From this set of observations, we learned that when using CPM diagrams for modeling a learning/tutoring scenario, it is important to capture the requirements at a high level of abstraction. Whatever the diagram, the perspective must re-

main simple. Such an approach allows designers to emphasize important model elements while hiding low-level processing details. Indeed, such details may even obscure the model's true purpose, which is:

- To identify key activities and dependencies
- To promote exchanges and communication in the ID team.

This is particularly true when drawing activity diagrams. In our experiments, some of these proved to be potential deadlocks that frustrated most educators during the design process. Dedicated cognitive tools (wizards, to-do-lists, etc.) could probably give them more confidence; but we consider that the correct answer will rely on efficient communication in the ID team. With

Figure 11. A state-machine diagram to represent the lifecycle of the Belief Graph <<resource>>

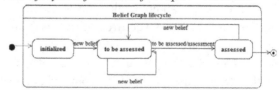

this in mind, sketches (even when they represent intermediate design results) can now play a central role in enhancing such communication.

Lesson U2, Observation 2: *CPM contributes to producing both stratified and multiple perspectives for a given learning scenario. This combination is a key-factor to enable a designer team to collaboratively determine the constraints under which a Technology-Enhanced Learning (TEL) system is to be designed.*

UML is a widely accepted language to describe software systems. With the different perspectives of a TEL system that CPM offers, our profile adopts the same fundamentals (UML notation, UML semantics which we specialized with the CPM meta-model semantics) to also describe the educational context:

- At conceptual level, the language addresses the need to manage educational requirements effectively.
- At functional level, the language addresses the need to describe the required functionality of a TEL System in tune with such educational requirements.

Whatever the design level (conceptual *vs.* functional), it is very important therefore to communicate design decisions (and understanding) in an unambiguous form to all partners involved in the ID Team (including educators, information technology specialists and platform of learning developers).

In the previous subsections, we showed that CPM enables designers to produce multiple perspectives for a learning scenario. These perspectives favor coherent, unambiguous (within the limit of the UML semantics) but intelligible design decisions. The conducted case studies have also demonstrated that to reach such a goal, these multiple perspectives of a learning scenario should be correctly stratified. During the GEODOC case

study, we noticed that, from the very beginning of the design process, some geographers were trying to map some educational goals with functionalities of the Geographical Information System viewer which they had been used to working with previously. Such design decisions were problematic because on the one side, educational goals had yet to be further detailed and on the other, such a detailed analysis failed because the designers were mixing conceptual and functional model elements.

The main gains of a correct stratification are modularity and design simplicity (i.e., Lesson U2-Observation 1 in the previous subsection). Modularity allows easier adaptability when changing requirements; it also allows clear separation of the domains of trust. By starting with the most fundamental educational factors (conceptual design) and designing them to be contextually appropriate, we were able in the course of the conducted case studies to build successive layers design and eventually reach functional design.

Figure 12 is an activity-diagram which exemplifies the frontier between conceptual and functional design. In this figure, some activities denote a <<CPL>> stereotype that represents a functionality offered by concrete software components. Such components may be those provided by most learning platforms (*e.g.,* a quiz component, a lecture component, a forum component, a whiteboard component, etc.) or they may be specialized components in relation with the domain to be taught (*e.g.,* a Geographical Information System viewer).

In Figure 13, the <<CPL>> stereotypes denote different functionalities that specialize a forum component: Depending on his role, a concrete actor will register differently; the teacher role has rights to add a topic in the forum while the learner role can write entries for the topic that is currently covered.

Both figures were produced in SMASH PBLs to denote the Reciprocal teaching pattern (Palincsar and Brown 1986). The term "reciprocal" describes the nature of the interactions each person has in response to the other(s). Teacher and student take turns assuming the role of a dialogue leader (see Figure 13); sequencing of the concrete activities performed by both roles is formalized by the dedicated swimlanes in Figure 12. The ID team chose this pattern because the designers wanted the students to improve their reading comprehension of the available SMASH testimonies; the designers also wanted them to learn to monitor their own learning and thinking. Thus, in SMASH PBLs, learners' peers are key actors in the reciprocal teaching pattern. These actors successively play the role of the teacher and the role of the student

when trying to understand texts or interviews. Figure 12 details how they move from one role to another and what the responsibilities of each role within the collaboration are. For each text (interview), the teacher role has to select one text. The specification states that the teacher role is the one that formulates statements about his reading and understanding but that the student role is the one that can ask questions and which, at the very end of the discussion, will formulate the agreed statements that can be inferred from the reading.

Detailing how such functionalities should be implemented in a specialized forum is outside

Figure 12. An activity diagram for the reciprocal teaching pattern

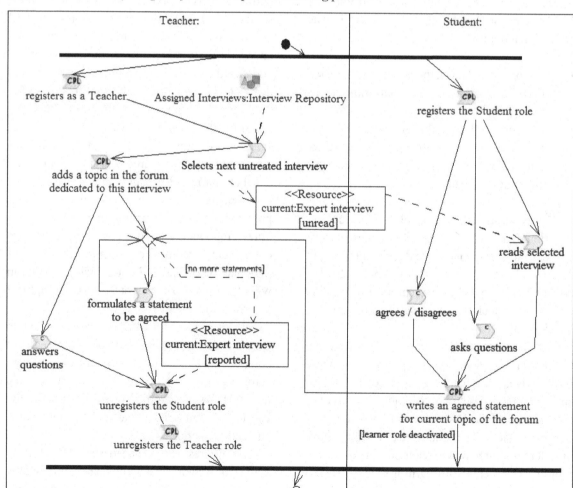

Figure 13. UML state-machine diagram describing both steps of the reciprocal teaching pattern

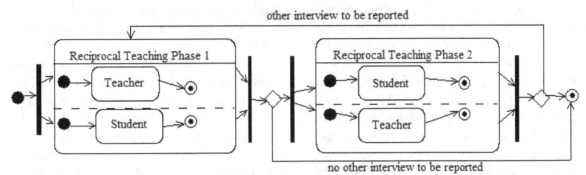

the scope of CPM. But the layered nature of CPM contributes to the smooth (top-down or bottom-up) transition between the different domains of trust.

Both lessons presented in this section lead us to the following conclusions: even though CPM was specified as a language and not as a design method, experience gained from our case studies enables us to promote a design process in tune with the characteristics of the CPM language. UML is a language; so is CPM. Current object-oriented methods focus on the specification of the static structure of software objects. A noticeable deficiency of these methods is that they do not provide any help on how requirements are refined, how class diagrams can be derived from scenarios, how to specify the active/dynamic parts of a system, or how such a specification may be transformed into an implementation.

During conceptual design, the analysis of the different case studies that we have conducted promotes the idea of bridging the gap between educational needs elicitation (including requirements elicitation, requirements refinement using a combination of use-case diagrams, of activity diagrams, of class diagrams and state-machine diagrams), and the more formal specification of class diagrams which are required to prepare the implementation of a TEL System (Nodenot, Marquesuzaà, Laforcade, & Sallaberry, 2004). The way we used CPM language is as follows. The specification process starts from the definition

of use-cases. Each use-case diagram is refined either by other use-case diagrams or by one ore more activity diagrams (representing teaching/learning scenarios). All model elements used in these diagrams are not unrelated parts; they are attributes, messages, etc. which are finally declared in the class diagrams. The behavior of each class is represented by a set of scenarios (activity diagrams/state machine diagrams) covering the events declared in the specification part of the class.

CONCLUSION AND PERSPECTIVES

CPM is a visual, layered, semi-formal, multiple perspectives language dedicated to the description of collaborative learning scenarios with special emphasis on problem-based learning (PBL). By means of the layering mechanism, designers may more easily tackle a complex situation using this graphical and conceptual feature: they start with a coarse-grained description to grasp the global situation and can then decompose each element to get a complete and detailed description (Lesson U2 Observation 1). Next, with the multiple perspectives mechanism, the designers may focus on the sequencing of activities, the behavior of a particular activity, role responsibilities, *etc.* A complex situation may be described through a set of simple and clear views (Lesson U1—Observation 2). Equally, the combination of these two mechanisms promotes collaboration within a team of designers (Lesson U2—Observation 2). Finally, as CPM is dedicated to a specific type of learning situations, it allows the designer using it to be more likely to be able to describe such situations more quickly than with more general educational languages like IMS-LD. According to model-driven approaches like OMG-MDA (OMG, 2003), these specialized (but limited) languages offer conceptual frameworks for preliminary analysis of learning situations before transforming the resulting models into more operational languages.

Lessons presented in this chapter also reveal some possible ways to improve CPM.

Improvements of CPM

Computer Support for Design Processes

Modeling learning situations is not an easy or usual task for practitioners. Among the several reasons that account for this, we might mention the two most obvious ones. First, practitioners seek to adapt their courses to learners *in situ,* as events occur/happen (opportunistic approach) and they tend to prefer to think in terms of content and coarse-grained activities. Second, in educational sciences, models are driven by learning events to detect and to react upon, rather than by a mere sequence of activities which are more typical within the computer world (i.e., workflow sub-domain). So practitioners are not used to getting involved in highly structured course modeling in their everyday routine. Because we are aware of this, we have already proposed guidelines related to CPM through 'best-practices' (Lesson U1-Observation 2) and a design process (Lesson U2-Observation 3) in order to help practitioners. Kent (2002) already pointed out the problem of 'how to define a model'. He defines it as a main hindrance for the emerging model driven en-gineering trend. While he generally highlights work about macro-processes ('the order in which models are produced and how they are coordinated'), Kent affirms the need for the MDE community to work on micro-processes, that is to say 'guidelines for producing a particular model'. We consider therefore that we need to improve *CPM micro-processes.* A related perspective must be to provide a computer support for our guidelines. First, such a support will make the application of guidelines easier (and accelerates it). Next, it limits the occurrence of errors caused by the misinterpretation of guidelines. Finally assisting the definition of a model allows designers to learn guidelines in a better way than by only reading the related document.

We have already worked on the computer support for a method dedicated to IMS-LD (Le Pallec, Moura, Marvie, Nebut, & Tarby, 2006). We intend to transpose this previous work to CPM.

Templates

Starting from scratch is another barrier to practitioners when defining models. The *Objecteering* repository provides a way of reusing existing and approved fragments of CPM models (i.e., Figure 12). UML templates address this issue much better. A UML template is a set of parameters to be applied to model elements before use. Such models have the advantage of clearly rendering explicit both the fixed part and the changing part of a model. Equally, defining a template is driven by reusability and modularity which is not the case when defining new model elements duplicated with copy/cut/paste. The application field of a template is consequently broader. However, using this mechanism, particularly when defining a template, is not an easy task, especially for a non-UML specialist. Even if *Objecteering* may provide a UML template mechanism, future work will likely involve embedding it into a more user-friendly interface.

Model Transformations

The different CPM perspectives are not entirely bound together. The attribute *Testimonies analysis* of *Investigator role 4* (i.e., Figure 10) is not automatically but manually 'deduced' from the link *performs* between *Investigator role 4* and *Testimonies analysis* (i.e., Figure 7). If the link *performs* is removed, the previous attribute will not be automatically removed. Not to impose constraints about the ubiquity of model elements can provide much freedom, and hence flexibility while defining models, especially for practitioners. But in addition to being a source of mistakes, it does not render explicit the repercussion of each action which the designer is performing. To address these two problems, we might consider, for example, developing dynamic transformations between all perspectives so that each action from a perspective should induce logic repercussion on other perspectives. These transformations would be proposed to designers through clickable operations.

Towards Other Conceptual Frameworks

UML and its profile mechanism offers a framework which may prove quickly efficient. First it provides several types of diagrams which enable many aspects to be described. Second, several design processes have emerged from the UML community over the last decade. They describe best-practices related to navigation between previous types of diagrams. Nevertheless, there are some weaknesses. First, defining new modeling concepts with a UML profile requires using (through inheritance) existing UML metaclasses like *Class* or *Actor*. UML profile designers do not necessarily need all inherited attributes or methods. They have to block access to these undesirable properties both in conceptual and graphical ways to respect the semantic of the language

they are designing (this can be achieved through OCL constraints or through *J* code (Objecteering, 2006) in case *Objecteering* is used). It is a complex and tedious process if we consider the definition of graphical languages for complex, condensed and non-software engineering meta-models (like IMS-LD). In addition, an efficient profile (that is to say, with conceptual and graphical filtered accesses) generally works only with the UML tool used to define it.

Lastly, for the time being, it is difficult to provide practitioners with a totally free UML-based model editor given that UML efficient tools are still expensive. Moreover using a UML profile means requiring the use of a whole software engineering oriented environment which may constitute a handicap for practitioners.

It is therefore important to explore alternatives like OMG-MOF (OMG, 2007) or Eclipse/EMF (EMF, 2007) environments. Based on a meta-modeling approach, they present some advantages. For example, defining a language starts with defining a meta-model (abstract syntax) which is not created from existing concepts but from scratch. So, there is no need to filter access to model elements because of undesirable inherited features. Another useful functionality of EMF is that creating a meta-model may be done simply by analyzing an XML schema or a DTD. Additionally, there are currently powerful graphical tools like TopCaseD (Farail et al., 2006) and the forthcoming GMF (GMF, 2007) which both allow defining an efficient graphical syntax for a language (concrete syntax). There are of course other facilities which are not as efficient in the UML community, like model transformation engines (GMT for Eclipse (GMT, 2007), YATL for MOF-based models (Patrascoiu, 2004)) and code generation engines like JET (JET, 2007).

But we believe it is still very important to see beyond technology and to maintain a global awareness of how organizational, social and technical issues are impinging on the usability of VIDL.

REFERENCES

Allert, H. (2004). Coherent social systems for learning: An approach for contextualized and community-centred metadata. *Journal of Interactive Media in Education, 2.*

Allert, H. (2005). *Modeling coherent social systems for learning.* (Thesis dissertation, Hannover University, Germany).

Berggren, A., Burgos, D., Fontana, J. M., Hinkelman, D., Hung, V., Hursh, A., et al. (2005). Practical and pedagogical issues for teacher adoption of IMS learning design standards in Moodle LMS. *Journal of Interactive Media.*

Botturi, L. (2003). *E²ML: Educational environment modeling language.* (PhD dissertation, University of Lugano, Italy).

Botturi, L., Cantoni, L., Lepori, B., & Tardini, S. (2006). *Fast prototyping as a communication catalyst for e-Learning design: Making the transition to e-Learning: strategies and issues.* Hershey, PA: IGI Global.

Botturi, L., Derntl, M., Boot, E., & Gigl, K. (2006). *A classification framework for educational modeling languages in instructional design.* Paper presented at the 6ᵗʰ IEEE International Conference on Advanced Learning Technologies (ICALT 2006), Kerkrade, The Netherlands.

Brusilovsky, P. (2004). *KnowledgeTree: A distributed architecture for adaptive e-learning.* Paper presented at the 13ᵗʰ International World Wide Web Conference on Alternate Track Papers, New York.

CopperAuthor. (2005). *CopperAuthor learning design editor.* Retrieved October 27, 2005 from http://sourceforge.net/projects/copperauthor/

Costagliola, G., De Lucia, A., Orefice, S., & Polese, G. (2002). A classification framework for the design of visual languages. *Journal of Visual Languages and Computing, 13*, 573-600.

Dalziel, J. R. (2006). *Lessons from LAMS for IMS learning design.* Paper presented at the 6ᵗʰ IEEE International Conference on Advanced Learning Technologies (ICALT 2006), Kerkrade, The Netherlands.

Derntl, M., & Hummel, K. (2005). *Modeling context-aware e-Learning scenarios.* Paper presented at the 3ʳᵈ International Conference on Pervasive Computing and Communications Workshops, Kauai Island, HI.

Derntl, M., & Motschnig-Pitrik, R. (2008). coUML: A visual modeling language for cooperative environments. In L. Botturi & T. Stubbs (Eds.), *Handbook of visual languages in instructional design; Theories and practice* (pp. 154-182). Hershey, PA: IGI Global.

Develay, M. (Ed.). (1993). *De l'apprentissage à l'enseignement*: Collection Pédagogies, ESF Edition.

EMF. (2007). *Eclipse Modeling Framework Project.* Retrieved February 2007, from http://www.eclipse.org/modeling/

Farail, P., Gaufillet, P., Canals, A., Le Camus, C., Sciamma, D., Michel, P., et al. (2006). *The TOPCASED project: A toolkit in open source for critical aeronautic systEms design.* Paper presented at the Eclipse Technology eXchange workshop (eTX) at ECOOP 2006, Nantes, France.

Ferruci, F., Tortora, G., & Vitello, G. (2002). *Exploiting visual languages in software engineering*: Handbook of Software Engineering and Knowledge Engineering. Singapore: World Scientific Publishing Company.

Fowler, M. (2005). *UML Distilled: Third Edition.* Addison-Wesley.

GMF. (2007). *GMF Project.* Retrieved February 2007, from http://www.eclipse.org/gmf/

GMT. (2007). *GMT Project.* Retrieved February 2007, from http://www.eclipse.org/gmt/

Hernández-Leo, D., Villasclaras-Fernández, E. D., Asensio-Pérez, J. I., Dimitriadis, Y., Jorrín-Abellán, I. M., Ruiz-Requies, I., et al. (2006). COLLAGE: A collaborative learning design editor based on patterns. *Educational Technology & Society, 9*(1), 58-71.

Hummel, H., Manderveld, J., Tattersall, C., & Koper, R. (2004). Educational modeling language and learning design: New opportunities for instructional reusability and personalized learning. *International Journal of Learning Technology, 1*(1), 111-126.

IMS. (2003a). *IMS learning design best practice and implementation guide.* IMS Global Learning Consortium.

IMS. (2003b). *IMS learning design information model.* IMS Global Learning Consortium.

JET. (2007). *JET Project.* Retrieved February 2007, from http://www.eclipse.org/emft/projects/jet/

Kent, S. (2002). *Model driven engineering.* Paper presented at the Third International Conference on Integrated Formal Method, IFM 2002, Turku, Finland.

Koper, R. (2001). *Modeling units of study from a pedagogical perspective: The pedagogical meta-model behind EML.* Educational Expertise Technology Centre, Open University of The Netherlands.

Koper, R. (2006). Current research in learning design. *Educational Technology & Society, 9*(1), 13-22.

Koper, R., Giesbers, K., Van Rosmalen, P., Tattersall, C., Sloep, P. B., Van Bruggen, J., et al. (Eds.). (2003). *A design model for lifelong learning networks.*

Koper, R., & Olivier, B. (2004). Representing the learning design of units of learning. *Educational Technology and Society, 7*(3), 97-111.

Laforcade, P. (2004). *Méta-modélisation UML pour la mise en oeuvre de situations problèmes coopératives.* Doctorat en informatique de l'Université de Pau et des Pays de l'Adour (France).

Le Pallec, X., Moura, O., Marvie, R., Nebut, M., & Tarby, J.-C. (2006). *Supporting generic methodologies to assist IMS-LD modelling.* Paper presented at the 6th IEEE International Conference on Advanced Learning Technologies (ICALT 2006), Kerkrade, The Netherlands.

Meirieu, P. (Ed.). (1994). *Apprendre... Oui mais comment?.* ESF Edition.

Miao, Y. (2000). *Design and implementation of a collaborative virtual problem-based learning environment.* (Thesis, University of Darmstadt, Germany).

Nodenot, T. (2005). *Contribution à l'Ingénierie dirigée par les modèles en EIAH : le cas des situations-problèmes coopératives.* Habilitation à diriger les recherches en Informatique de l'Université de Pau et des Pays de l'Adour (France).

Nodenot, T., & Laforcade, P. (2006). A game about planets: Elements for a didactical transposition described with the CPM language. Paper presented at the *6th IEEE International Conference on Advanced Learning Technologies (ICALT 2006).* Kerkrade, The Netherlands.

Nodenot, T., Marquesuzaà, C., Laforcade, P., & Sallaberry, C. (2004, May 17-22). *Model based engineering of learnings Situations for adaptive Web-based educational systems.* Paper presented at the ACM Thirteenth International World Wide Web Conference (IW3C2 Conference), New-York.

Norman, D. A., & Spohrer, H. G. (1996). Learner-centered education. *Communication of the ACM, 39*(4).

Objecteering. (2006). *Objecteering J Language User Guide.* Retrieved February 2007, from http://www.objecteering.com/doc/j_language/toc.htm

OMG. (1999). *White Paper on the Profile Mechanism*: Object Management Group Analysis and Design Task Force.

OMG. (2002a). *The Software Process Engineering Management Meta-model (SPEM)* (Technical Report formal/2002-11-14).

OMG. (2002b, Août 2002). *UML 2.0 Superstructure Specification*, from http://www.omg.org/docs/ptc/03-08-02.pdf

OMG. (2003). *MDA Guide Version 1.0.1*, from http://www.omg.org/docs/omg/03-06-01.pdf

OMG. (2007). *Meta-Object Facility (MOF) Specification*. Retrieved February 2007, from http://www.omg.org/mof/

Paramythis, A., & Loidl-Reisinger, S. (2004). Adaptive learning environments and e-Learning standards. *Electronic Journal of e-Learning, 2*(2).

Patrascoiu, O. (2004). *YATL:Yet another transformation language*. Paper presented at the 1st European MDA Workshop, University of Twente, The Netherlands.

Pawlowski, J. (2002). *Reusable models of pedagogical concepts: A framework for pedagogical and content design*. Paper presented at the International Conference ED-MEDIA 2002, Denver, CO.

Pawlowski, J., & Bick, M. (2006). Managing and re-using didactical expertise: The didactical object model. *Educational Technology and Society, 9*(1), 84-96.

Reload. (2005). *Reusable eLearning object authoring & delivery project*. Retrieved October 27, 2005 from http://www.reload.ac.uk/

Renaux, E., Caron, P.-A., & Le Pallec, X. (2005). *Learning management system component-based design: A model driven approach*. Paper presented at the Montreal Conference on e-Technologies (Mcetech), Montréal, Canada.

Sallaberry, C., Nodenot, T., Marquesuzaà, C., Bessagnet, M.-N., & Laforcade, P. (2002). *Information modelling within a Net-Learning Environment*. Paper presented at the 12th Conference on Information Modelling and Knowledge Bases, Krippen, Swiss Saxony, Germany.

Sampson, D., Karampiperis, P., & Zervas, P. (2005). ASK-LDT: A Web-based learning scenarios authoring environment based on IMS learning design. *International Journal on Advanced Technology for Learning (ATL), 2*(4), 207-215.

Santos, O. C., Boticario, J. G., & Barrera, C. (2005). *aLFanet: An adaptive and standard-based learning environment built upon dotLRN and other open source developments*. Paper presented at the 2005 dotLRN conference, Madrid, Spain.

Schneemayer, G. (2002). *Contextual Web services for teaching*. Ludwig Maximilians Universität, München, Germany.

Stahl, G. (2006). *Group cognition: Computer support for building collaborative knowledge*. Cambridge, MA: MIT Press.

Tattersall, C., Sodhi, T., Burgos, D., & Koper, R. (2007). Using the IMS Learning Design notation for the modelling and delivery of education. In L. Botturi & T. Stubbs (Eds.), *Handbook of visual languages for instructional design: Theories and practices* (pp. 299-315). Hershey, PA: IGI Global.

Vignollet, L., David, J.-P., Ferraris, C., Martel, C., & Lejeune, A. (2006). Comparing educational modeling languages on a case study. *Workshop in conjunction with the 6th IEEE International Conference on Advanced Learning Technologies (ICALT 2006)*. Kerkrade, The Netherlands.

Vogten, H., & Martens, H. (2003). *CopperCore—The IMS learning designeEngine*, retrieved October 27, 2005 from http://www.coppercore.org

Chapter XIV
Visual Modeling of Collaborative Learning Processes:
Uses, Desired Properties, and Approaches

Andreas Harrer
University of Duisburg—Essen, Germany

H. Ulrich Hoppe
University of Duisburg—Essen, Germany

ABSTRACT

The modeling of learning processes and its use in computer-supported learning scenarios attracted attention in a wide variety of research fields in the last years, e.g., in Web-based education, computer supported collaboration scripts, and intelligent tutoring systems (ITS). Most of the discussion is either focused on the conceptual level of instructional design for exchange between designers or on the automated execution of predefined designs and learning scripts. In this chapter we will elaborate on the whole spectrum of different uses that visual learning models provide for teachers, learners, and researchers. Based on our discussions in an international research project on computer-supported collaboration scripts we identify desired properties for such modeling languages especially considering the needs of the practitioners. Finally we propose MoCoLADe (model for collaborative learning activity design), an exemplary approach of a visual language for collaborative learning processes that was designed according to the presented principles.

INTRODUCTION

The modeling of learning processes attracted attention in a wide variety of research fields in the last years, e.g., in Web-based education, computer supported collaboration scripts, and intelligent tutoring systems (ITS). While in former times, especially in ITS, proprietary notations or hard-coded process models were used, the adoption of EML into the IMS/LD standard (IMS Learning Design Specification, 2003 and Chapter XV of this handbook) contributed to re-usability of specified learning processes. Yet it also brought up intensive discussion about expressiveness (Hernandez et al., 2004), notational aspects (Miao et al., 2005) and the intelligibility for the practitioner (Dalziel, 2006), i.e., teachers and researchers with non-technical background. This book discusses a wide spectrum of facets of instructional design, from foundational issues of graphical languages to concrete language proposals. Most of the approaches make specific assumptions about the user groups and their goals: from our survey of existing approaches we identified mainly either a "pure design" perspective, i.e.,, having a language as a means of expression towards other experts and practitioners, or a "system oriented" perspective that aims at automatable execution of formalized learning.

In the following sections we will describe a broader spectrum of the different uses that explicit learning models provide for teachers, learners, and researchers, and will refer to possible solutions and means for how systems can support these uses.

Based on our research in a European project on computer-supported scripting of collaborative activities, we identify desired properties for such modeling languages especially considering the needs of the practitioners. These considerations resulted in an exemplary approach that was designed according to the presented principles. The resulting VIDL called MoCoLADe (model for collaborative learning activity design) and

its implementation as an authoring tool for ID is described briefly at the end of the chapter.

APPLICATION CONTEXTS OF ID LANGUAGES

The specification of learning processes using an instructional design language may have a broad variety of purposes for both the designer and also the system. Some educational designers use it as a note-taking tool for lesson planning, some for discussion with colleagues and some expect these models to be executed automatically within a customized computer-based learning environment. With this in mind, we want to explore and elaborate on the different motivations designers might have and potential functionalities a run-time system may provide based on a given learning process specification.

In Botturi, Derntl, Boot & Figl (2006) the space of exploration is spanned by the dimensions of *communication* and *creativity*: The communication dimension ranges from *reflective*, i.e., mainly used for personal consideration, to *communicative*, i.e., the exchange with other persons. The creativity dimension ranges from *generative*, i.e., meant for production and refinement, to *finalist*, i.e., the fixed description of a design for formal use.

In our exploration we will use the degree of *"informedness"* on the part of the computer system necessary to provide supportive functionality as an important aspect: we see a continuum from complete "uninformedness" of the system and exclusive interpretation on the user's side up to quite high requirements of interpreting/understanding the learning processes within the system. We will begin our discussion with the user perspective and then proceed with the usage of formalized process models for ID-facilitated computer-supported learning.

Potential Uses for ID Languages from a User Perspective

Because instructional design languages are used in the first place by educational practitioners and researchers to codify and make explicit their pedagogical intentions, the different types of usage that a designer can apply with visual languages are an obvious choice to explore the potential of instructional design languages and resulting artifacts. In the following paragraphs we will elaborate on our initial ideas in (Miao, Hoeksema, Hoppe, & Harrer, 2005) and discuss several types of usage of instructional processes and how computer-based support can facilitate its creation, representation, and re-use.

Visual Languages as Communication Artifacts

This usage of instructional design is oriented towards the communication between designers or different stakeholders in a pedagogical context (such as researchers and teachers). This usage of an instructional design as a communication artifact is frequently done using ad-hoc notations, scribbled diagrams, and other informal notations, such as the one in Figure 1, that shows an artifact created in a recent workshop where the participating students designed their own cooperative learning scripts in an ad-hoc notation inspired by several computer science techniques (e.g., UML, state machines, or flowcharts).

Figure 1. Visual instructional design as an artifact of communication

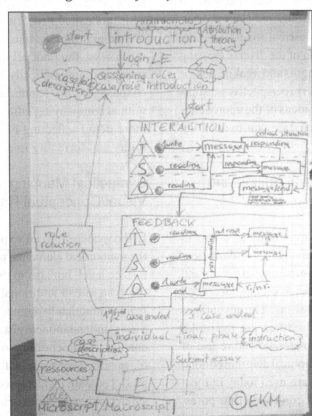

Nevertheless the use of a standardized notation system helps all participants in the communication to interpret the design according to common principles and meaning. For example, in computer science UML diagrams are used to a high degree as documents for quick communication between system designers because of the widely standardized use and interpretation of UML as a *lingua franca* for system modeling. Another example is the AUTC (Australian Universities Teaching Committee) Visual Learning Design Sequence described by Agostinho et al. in Chapter XIX. Currently such an agreement for one dedicated language for instructional design has not been reached as can also be seen in the scope and variety of language proposals in section II of this handbook. Regardless of the notational exactness or informality used for the communication between practitioners, the intentional use here is exclusively targeted towards human users, not toward notational representations that can be interpreted by formal systems and computers.

This handbook will contribute to establishing conceptual understanding of the diverse existing approaches and their strengths and weaknesses for the readers, in the longer term perspective presumably also to integrate the ideas of the approaches into unified notations that ease communication between humans.

Computer-Based Visual Editing and Re-Use

Computer systems can support human actors in the creation of visual artifacts in a wide variety of domains, such as technical construction and architecture with CAD systems (computer aided design) or electronic publishing. The advantages of using computer-based editors are manifold, especially with respect to storage and re-use of artifacts at a later time. Graphical diagram editors, e.g., for UML diagrams, are used today in most development projects for documentation purposes. It is obvious that visual languages for instructional

Figure 2. Computer-supported visual editing of instructional design

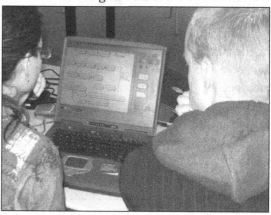

design can and should be accompanied by visual editing tools to support the designer in creating, archiving, and re-using her or his design documents. Figure 2 shows an example of a visual editing tool that has been used by some of the students in our recent seminar for PhD students. This tool called *FreeStyler* allows for mixed use of formal flowchart-like notations and handwritten marks, thus not all of the elements can be processed automatically by the editor. In other chapters of this handbook different languages with accompanying editors will be described in more detail reflecting different degrees of flexibility and formality in editing.

Syntactical Mapping to a Visual/Conceptual Representation

If the system has an explicit representation of the syntactical elements, not only on the user interface level, but also in the internal data model, the system can additionally provide a mapping from syntactically defined learning processes to a user-understandable visual representation. This enables interoperability in terms of the exchange of learning process specifications that have been produced with different tools given a compatible syntax (either the same, or transformable via a syntactic mapping, or a conceptual meta-model).

With a well-defined syntax available in the system, tools can support the learning designers in producing syntactically correct models (with techniques like highlighting of syntax errors) an important prerequisite for further processing of the model. This is especially valid for the approaches that use ontologies for the definition of language constructs and relations, such as MOT+ (see Chapter VIII) and poEML (see Chapter X).

Examples of editors supporting the creation of syntactically correct designs are the Reload Editor for IMS learning design documents and the visual editor for the E²ML language (Botturi, 2003 and Chapter VII).

Modeling with Various Perspectives

Rich, expressive modeling techniques usually bring along the problem that models get excessively complex and hard to overview. Therefore either reduction of the complexity (by applying projections of specific elements or filtering techniques) or the separation into different perspectives (like the different diagram types in UML) is a typical way to cope with the complexity. This issue has also been raised in Botturi, Derntl, Boot, & Figl (2006) in that their classification schema of languages has *single* or *multiple perspectives*. For learning processes typically the following aspects are relevant and thus candidates for special perspectives (Miao, Hoeksema, Hoppe, & Harrer, 2005):

- **Procedural/temporal perspective:** Naturally the sequence and timing, i.e., the process-oriented aspects of the whole learning process should be represented explicitly. Visual notations, such as workflow diagrams, activity diagrams, or phase models are obvious representations for this perspective.

- **Artifacts perspective:** Artifacts given as resources, used as temporary results, and the final outcomes of learning activities constitute an important aspect of learning processes. Especially the change of artifacts over time (version history) is information to be considered by all participants of a learning process.

- **Roles perspective:** For organization of specific tasks in group processes, the various roles needed for the tasks are essential information both for designer and for learners. With a suitable perspective the designer keeps the overview about the work organization and the learners can reduce their uncertainty (Mäkitalo, Weinberger, Häkkinen, Järvelä, & Fischer, 2005) about their role, i.e., the function that is expected from them, in the learning process.

- **Individual/group perspective:** To get an impression of the workload of one specific member or one subgroup within a group process a perspective stressing these individual aspects is valuable information for the designer to keep balance between the participants of the process. For the participants this perspective can give orientation about their progress and a "ToDo list" as a scaffold for their activities.

The multi-perspective representation of the learning design requires that the system explicitly has information about which elements belong to which perspective(s), especially when relations between perspectives should be highlighted. Therefore an additional level of information, i.e., the assignment of syntactical elements to the different perspectives should be present to support the users properly. Otherwise the modeling in different perspectives is possible, but interpreted exclusively on the human side, i.e., without any syntactical or semantic support while editing. The recent poEML proposal (Caeiro, Anido, & Llamas, 2006 and Chapter X) is an approach for representing instructional designs according to several distinct and interrelated perspectives, such as social, organizational, and temporal. LDL, the learning design language (see Chapter XII) similarly provides multiple perspectives to make the ID easier to handle than in one integrated representation.

Model-Based Predictions

An explicit representation of the model can be used to give advice or comments to the designer of the learning process with respect to her or his design: e.g.,, dependencies or constraints between elements can be highlighted, such as necessity of sequential phases or synchronizing the flow after a split into cooperative sub-processes.

If the designer specified temporal constraints (minimum or maximum time) for elements of the process, techniques from operations research, such as optimization in network flows or critical path analysis can be applied. With this kind of support the designer can find weak spots in the design, such as an inappropriately long waiting time for the participants in one sub-process when synchronizing with another subgroup whose

activities take much more time. Scheduling algorithms may then propose a different sequencing for the revision of the design.

Figure 3 shows an example of a model-based prediction for the group formation process of a learning design. The designer used a list of participants, such as the list with all pupils in a school class, and checked the validity of his intended group formation on this list. A supporting tool as in the figure can assign pupils according to the chosen group formation strategy and shows the result of this assignment: in the case above the strategy fails to produce the intended group sizes with the given pupils, because one of the groups is missing a member to be fully operational. This is reflected to the designer with a status message "Not OK" and the highlighting of the incorrectly formed group visible on the right.

Up to this point, we can call the computer support described so far as syntactic, without considering higher level properties of the learning flow, such as executability or structural aspects on the semantic level. In the following paragraphs we

Figure 3. Model-based prediction of a visual model

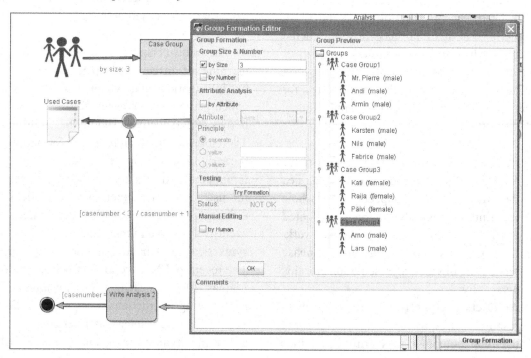

will shed some light on these kinds of advanced support mechanisms.

Simulation of Visual Models

A simulated execution of the specified learning process can give the designer more profound feedback on "what works and what does not." Imagine the benefit of doing a "simulation run" with information about sequence, time requirements, and produced artifacts before applying the whole design to a real experiment. The plausibility of the design can be checked much easier than just based on the static structure of the model. This clearly requires an "operational semantics" of the learning process modeling language to provide execution runs of the specified learning process. It should be possible to explore such a simulation interactively and stepwise. For more thorough testing of the processes' feasibility, a "'batch mode'" or even exhaustive simulation with different inputs may be desirable. Deadlocks

in the process specification (e.g., when subgroups are waiting for each other's input) can be detected before having the bitter experience in practical use. An example for such a deadlock resulting from interactive simulation can be found in Figure 4: All the groups in the simulation run cannot proceed to their next steps of the learning process, because all the transitions (the "move" buttons in the graphical interface) are currently disabled. This failure in the simulation resulted from the number of initial available resources being too small to satisfy the number of learning groups in this scenario.

The degree of detail for simulation is highly variable, from a rather general level, such as interactively giving a specific ordering of activities such as in our tool from the figure above, to simulation of the users' interfaces which would be equivalent to a full-fledged execution engine for the process and thus to the expected functionality of a *player* for the instructional design (i.e., the Webplayer for IMS LD).

Figure 4. Interactive simulation of a visual model: Deadlock situation

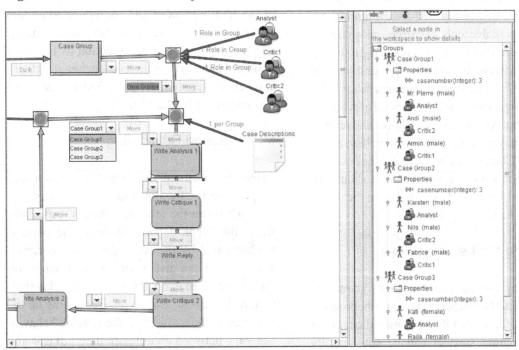

Potential Uses for ID Languages from a System Perspective

While the simulation of learning processes already required some operational semantics of the models to be present within the system, the initiative of an interactive simulation remains with the designer. After finalizing the instructional design (Botturi, Derntl, Boot & Figl, 2006) to be used in practice, computer systems have ample potential to assist the practitioner to implement the design in real learning situations. Depending on the richness of the model and the capabilities of the interpreting components, different levels of support result:

- Static configuration of learning environments
- Monitoring the learning flow
- Model-based scaffolding

Static Configuration of Learning Environments

The first, weakest, approach to operationalizing the learning process for the target user "at run time" is the configuration of the learning environment with available tools, resources, communication structure and so on. If this configuration is done once without dynamic addition and removal of elements, we call this *static configuration*. This gives the target users the full potential of available elements, but without the constraints and restrictions that may have already been specified by the designer. "Compiling and instantiating" such an environment from the specification should be the minimal functionality of a system meant for "playing" the learning design.

Monitoring the Learning Flow

Enriched by computable conditions (how and when to end activities, how to measure the progress state of artifacts, etc.) the operational character of the computer support can be substantially enhanced. Given this additional information, monitoring the learning flow and managing the constraints specified by the designer is possible. The computer support takes the form of a fully operational execution of the process. This level has been achieved for IMS-LD players since the implementation of Level B, which uses properties and conditions to dynamically handle the process flow at runtime. Monitoring functionality could be used in two ways: On the one hand the information can be used internally to adapt the process according to the exact specification. On the other hand the monitored information can be visualized to participants of the learning process to give them information on what they have done and produced. This additional feedback can be used to promote reflection about the process or about the participants' own behavior, such stimulating meta-cognitive activities. Yet, just thinking of the execution of a predefined learning process is not enough: Modern interactive learning environments allow the learners to structure their learning process very flexibly. Here, the recognition problem is known to be very hard. On the other hand, striving for monitoring features in the environment should not induce additional restrictions on the learner, such as explaining and tagging each and every action as has been done formerly with sentence opener interfaces and self-explanation prompts, just so that it can be understood by the system.

Model-Based Scaffolding

At the "informed end" of the spectrum of computer support we see the potential use of the system for scaffolding the learning process, especially when the "typical path" through the process is abandoned by the participants. An enriched specification can give advice to the learners on "what and when to do," "how they can play their assigned role best" and so on. Depending on the strictness of the scaffolding, the system's behavior can vary between an unrestraining advisor and

Figure 5. Model-based scaffolding in learning environments

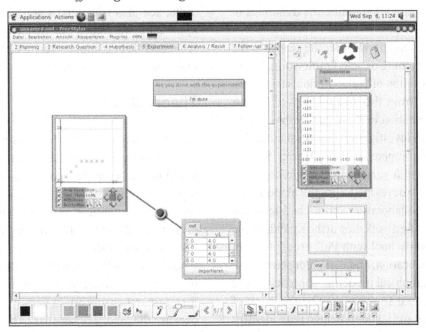

an intervening tutor. For this functionality, existing approaches both from the area of "intelligent tutoring systems" and from "interaction scripts" as discussed in cognitive and social psychology can be considered.

Figure 5 shows a screenshot from a learning scenario that is scaffolded using an explicit description in IMS-LD format. The inquiry learning process defined here consists of specific phases of the learning process, tools and resources that are associated to the phases and adaptive feedback elements that structure each learning phase by creating situations of student self-reflection (such as the reflection prompt in the top middle of the figure). The architecture supporting this scenario uses the freely available IMS/LD engine Coppercore and our own collaborative application FreeStyler in a loosely coupled way described in more detail in Harrer, Malzahn and Roth (2006).

In the following sections we will present our steps towards supporting some of these usage types and refer back to this set of usage types to highlight the potential of our achieved results in each.

IDENTIFYING DESIRED PROPERTIES OF A LANGUAGE FOR INSTRUCTIONAL DESIGN

The European Research Team CoSSICLE (computer-supported scripting of interaction in collaborative learning environments) within the Kaleidoscope Network of Excellence is a research initiative that investigates in methods and practical experiments for applying computer-based scripts to collaborative learning scenarios. Our main work area in this project is the formal modeling of collaboration scripts and their mapping to an operational level that can be executed by suitable scripting engines. The project work resulted first in a conceptual framework report (Cossicle Framework, 2005) on specification of collaboration scripts in textual form, which we will call the CoSSICLE framework in the following. One of its distinctive features from previous approaches to describe CSCL scripts is the division of script constituents into the *components* (participants, groups, roles, resources, and actions), and the *mechanisms* (sequencing, group formation, component distribution) that define the dynamics of collaboration scripts.

For further reading we refer the reader to the original document (Cossicle Framework, 2005). The formal notation of collaboration scripts that we developed from this document will be our focus of presentation in these paragraphs.

Based on an investigation in several modeling techniques of computer science (Harrer & Malzahn, 2006) and a participatory approach with practitioners we developed a graphical modeling language for collaboration scripts and learning processes. During a workshop of the Kaleidoscope virtual doctoral school with PhD students from psychology, education, and computer science we tested a first graphical modeling approach based on the conceptual framework. The feedback of the researchers and students helped us to identify the desired properties for a modeling language for collaboration scripts and learning processes. The main properties elicited are:

- Familiarity/intuitive intelligibility
- Theory basis
- Graphical representation
- Hierarchical structures / support of different granularity
- Precise operational semantics

These properties, first published in Harrer and Malzahn (2006) are presented more thoroughly in the next subsections.

Familiarity / Intuitive Intelligibility

The language used for formalization has to refer to the concepts the practitioner is familiar with or has to be understandable intuitively. This is especially important to enable non-computer scientists to use this formal language for describing learning process models (see also Hernandez et al., 2005). While our initial designs of a VIDL for collaborative process models was based on ideas

following state charts in UML (Harrer & Malzahn, 2006, see also Chapter IX for a similar design approach), we found out that for practitioners from outside of computer science, the familiarity criterion was not fulfilled properly.

Theory-Basis

This property might be very desirable for a researcher or evaluator of learning processes. If the notation used considers concepts that are rooted in an established theory, a mapping from the researcher's intentions to the modeling language is not needed, potentially avoiding distortions or losses in the transformation. This property is potentially conflicting with the familiarity/intuitive intelligibility property, depending on the user: for a researcher this might very well fit together, because the theory is familiar to him or her; but, for the practitioner at school, an intuitive understanding and theory-basis might be inhibiting one another, requiring training in the theory before practical use.

Graphical Representation

Since completely textual representations tend to not allow the user an overview about the model, the use of a graphical notation for learning process models—at least for some aspects of the model—might raise the usability of the notation. Besides the introductory chapters motivating VIDL in section I of this handbook, this has been confirmed to be well-accepted in a seminar of the Kaleidoscope Virtual Doctoral School[1] organized by the CoSSICLE partners; graphical notations were introduced to the doctoral students and have been used by them in practical sessions to express the scripts they were interested in for their research work. Figure 1 shows one of the graphical artifacts produced during the workshop and Figure 2 shows participants working on a graphical model using our FreeStyler application.

The results and the feedback received during this workshop were supporting our assumption that graphical notations can be taken up intuitively and convey the meaning of the modeler quite succinctly. This was especially encouraging because most of the Ph.D. students did not have a background in computer science and thus were quite unfamiliar with the notational elements presented to them.

Hierarchical Structures / Support of Different Granularity

CSCL scripts and learning process models are defined on a wide range of granularity, from coarse-grained pedagogical scripts (Dillenbourg, 2002) that define whole learning processes to fine-grained scripts (Kollar, Fischer, & Slotta, 2005), that scaffold the learners, when specific skills are lacking, such as how to construct argumentative sequences properly (Leitao, 2000). A modeling language has to enable the modeling of scripts at different levels of granularity; we consider the hierarchical combination as well as composition of separate components as required properties for such a language.

An example of this can be seen in the following figures that represent different granularities of scripts for argumentation.

Figure 6 shows the process sequence of the ArgueGraph script (Dillenbourg, 2002), while Figure 7 shows a detailed script prescribing the construction of arguments (Weinberger, Stegmann, & Fischer, 2005). The latter script could refine the coarse-grained one, if the students do not have the appropriate argumentation skills. This is symbolized by a miniature version of the fine-grained script visible in the argumentation phase of the ArgueGraph (see Figure 6 in phase "Pair Questionnaire").

Preliminary work on this aspect has been described in Miao, Hoeksema, Hoppe and Harrer (2005) and Harrer and Malzahn (2006) where we proposed the state chart formalism (Harel

Figure 6. Macro level description—the Argue Graph (cf. Dillenbourg, 2000)

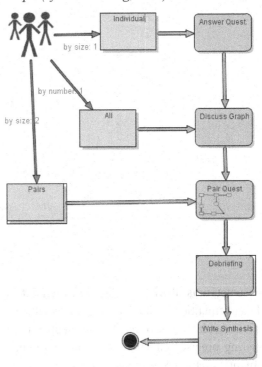

& Namaad, 1996) to model learning processes hierarchically, thus bridging the gap between different granularities of instructional designs. Another rationale for this approach has been that the formalism is close to the internal representation of an IMS-LD engine and its execution model as a state machine (Vogten, Koper, Martens, & Tattersall, 2005) and thus very compatible with our approach of integrating the external LD engine Coppercore into our collaborative learning scenarios for the process regulation (Harrer, Malzahn, Hoeksema, & Hoppe, 2005).

Precise Operational Semantics

For the use in computer-based learning support systems, the formal description of the process model defined by an unambiguous syntax has to be mapped to an operational level, i.e., each language construct and the combination of language

Figure 7. Micro level description: An argumentation script

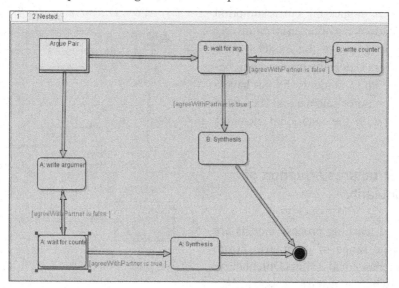

constructs must also have well-defined semantics. These semantics have to be defined exactly for the chosen language or have to be mapped to an existing precise semantics, e.g., the state chart semantics (Harel & Namaad, 1996).

This inductive and participatory elicitation of requirements that we conducted for the specific needs of the CoSSICLE project, is complemented and supported in this volume by dedicated chapters that elaborate on the theory of visual languages (see chapters in section I of this handbook, such as III, V, and VI).

The wide acceptance of LAMS (learning activity management system) with teachers is very probably caused by the intuitive character of the specification when compared to formal text-based notations, such as IMS-LD at its specification level. This can be attributed to the properties of familiarity/intuitive intelligibility and the graphical character of modeling the processes. Yet the expressiveness of this approach is constrained by the available built-in tools. IMS-LD, when used with all finesse, such as conditions, properties, and notifications, is a very versatile notation for learning processes, but is currently hard to handle by users that are not adept in the specifi-

cation. A challenge for modeling languages for learning processes will be the balancing of the identified properties, ideally with a high degree in most dimensions; but more usually the language will enable designers to address priority needs, making compromises on other properties. In the last section of this chapter we will describe our progress towards a visual language built upon these considerations.

DESIGNING A LANGUAGE FOR MODELING OF COLLABORATIVE LEARNING PROCESSES

Starting from the conceptualization of collaboration scripts that was conducted in the CoSSICLE project and our experiences with visual languages (Hoppe et al., 2000), we designed MoCoLADe (model for collaborative learning activity design), the visual language for learning process models and collaboration scripts. This VIDL addresses the issues raised in the previous sections explicitly and tries to find an appropriate balance between expressiveness and usefulness for practitioners.

Based on the desired properties we identified, we chose the CoSSICLE conceptualization (CoSSICLE Framework, 2005) that defines the concepts relevant for modeling collaboration scripts as the main constituents of the modeling language. The visual language designed uses a systematic mapping of CoSSICLE components (participants, groups, roles, resources, and actions) to graphical nodes and of the mechanisms (sequencing, group formation, component distribution) to edges linking between nodes. These elements of the VIDL are shown on the right side of Figure 8 and the most relevant relations between components are shown in the workspace on the left side.

For the researchers associated with the project this fulfils both the *familiarity* and the *theory-basis* properties; for teachers defining their school scenarios this will be tested practically in the future with our associated communities of practitioners.

Since we have a strong interest in supporting both students and teachers also during the concrete learning episodes, our notation was built with *operational aspects* in mind: the graphical models can be simulated interactively by the teacher in advance (see Figure 3 and Figure 4) and can be compiled to IMS-LD descriptions and content packages to be used with other learning platforms, such as the Web player for IMS-LD.

To facilitate both incremental refinement of models and the re-use of model parts we allow *hierarchical composition* of learning activities and (sub-)scripts of different granularity (see Figure 6 and Figure 7).

In the design and tool implementation of this visual language we also had in mind to support a broad scope of potential uses of instructional designs, as elaborated in the earlier section. The tool that was developed as a visual language plugin for our FreeStyler application (all the screenshots produced for Figures 3 to 9 have been taken directly from the FreeStyler and the plugin) currently supports:

- **Visual models as communication artifacts:** The graphical language has been realized as a plugin to our collaborative application FreeStyler; thus it is possible to use the collaborative mode for synchronous co-design or the repository-based communication through the artifact (Wichmann, Kuhn, & Hoppe, 2006) to exchange ideas and designs between experts and practitioners.

Figure 8. Graphical elements of the VLID

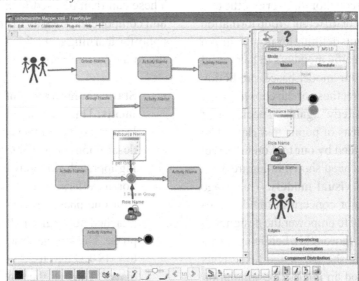

- **Computer-based visual editing and re-use:** with its clearly defined notational elements the supported visual editor supports the creation, storage and later re-use and modification of graphical models.
- **Syntactical mapping to a visual/conceptual representation:** The internal mapping to the conceptual model of CoSSICLE is supported by the tool; even more important for widespread use is the semantic mapping and export functionality to IMS/LD documents, that can be used with other LD tools, such as editors and runtime engines.
- **Modeling with various perspectives:** This usage is currently supported partially by enabling the designer to reduce complexity of a visual model by hierarchical structures and incremental refinement. The usefulness of specific perspectives, e.g., by projections on the whole model or dedicated views on the phase structure, will be discussed with our partners in the CoSSICLE project and integrated if necessary.
- **Model-based predictions:** The support of the designer in validating the model is specifically realized in our tool as a prediction about the correctness of group formations. Since the set up of groups is an essential factor for most collaboration scripts, the tool offers a variety of different group formation strategies (such as defining group size, group numbers or specific members to be present in a group). Our model-based prediction checks the correctness of the chosen group formation strategy against specific test data, such as lists of pupils in a class. The feedback provided by our tool on incorrect formations has been shown in Figure 3.
- **Simulation of visual models:** This usage has been a major concern in the development of our tool to empower the designer to test his design thoroughly before applying it in practice in the lab or the field. Thus we implemented an interactive simulation mode, where the designer can trace the paths

of collaboration groups through the visual model. In each activity the designer can check which groups are present there, which roles the members currently have and which resources they can use. Details of such a simulation run can be seen in Figure 9 in the right tab. Using token semantics (similar to Petri nets) the simulation offers the allowed steps through the learning process for each group (the group being represented as a token with information about associated roles and resources). In analogy to IMS-LD, properties and conditional branches can be defined to vary the learning process according to the situational context. The evaluation of the conditions is also done by the simulation mode and constrains the possible options of groups through the process by activating / deactivating specific transitions.

Because we did not conceptualize our visual editing tool as a full-fledged integrated engine for the specified models, we chose an indirect way of supporting the practical application of learning processes in computer-supported scenarios. Besides our specific representation according to the CoSSICLE framework, we support the export of graphical models into IMS-LD documents. These can then be used with existing platforms and components, such as LD players to formally apply the learning scenarios. Our support according to the system perspective is as follows:

- **Static configuration of learning environments:** This is the simplest form of tailoring learning environments according to formal descriptions of available tools. In our modeling approach, this non-sequenced configuration and offering of tools would be represented as a one-phase process with all resources attached to a group before entering this phase. This simple structure can be exported to IMS-LD and used with a corresponding player. Thus all the tools/resources will be available for the whole learning activity.

- **Monitoring the learning flow:** This level of support is reached by using properties and conditional variations of the learning process according to the property values. By our mappings to IMS-LD it is possible to let learners and teachers trace the current state of the activity using an IMS-LD player. This can facilitate the orientation and self-reflection of the actors in the learning process.
- **Model-based scaffolding:** In this usage the conditional variations are used to adapt the learning flow and the available resources, roles, and tools according to the situational context. For example, it is possible to fade the level of support to the learners, when they reach advanced levels of expertise represented in properties. This approach has been realized in our work described in (Harrer, Malzahn, & Roth, 2006) where we use explicit process models with conditions in the IMS-LD format to give incremental and adaptive process guidance to the learners.

This relatively broad coverage of the different types of use of instructional designs that we achieved in our approaches lets us believe that—given an appropriate notation system—the seamless transition within this continuum is feasible, enabling designers in the creative phase, the exploration/validation phase, as well in practical use in computer-based scenarios. This would allow for incremental design and refinement starting out with coarse structures and ending with specific and operational descriptions.

The issue of versatile *elaboration* of visual models has also been raised in Botturi, Derntl, Boot, and Figl (2006) where this dimension was proposed in order to differentiate the detail level of ID languages. According to this classification framework our visual language can be categorized as:

- **Stratification = layered:** The language uses different entities for roles, groups, resources, dynamics etc. according to the CoSICLE framework.
- **Formalization = formal:** The language has syntactical rules for creating correct instructional designs and also provides operational semantics for the simulation functionality.
- **Elaboration = all levels:** The language supports a spectrum from initial ideas of rough process structures (conceptual level) up to very detailed learning process models with direct mapping to executable IMS-LD (implementation level). There are still some constraints on the implementation level, e.g., Not every graphical model, especially with cyclic phase, structures can be mapped directly to implementations, because of limitations of the mapping to LD.
- **Perspective = multiple:** Different projections on a full model can be realized easily and are currently under discussion with our project partners. The hierarchical modeling of activities provides a means to have differently granular perspectives.
- **Notation = visual:** Our language was designed as a graphical representation of the CoSICLE framework that stresses the intuitive nature of graphical 2-dimensional phase structures and associations of components to activities.

This modeling language has been used to model some standard collaboration scripts in the literature, such as the Social Script (Weinberger, Fischer, & Mandl, 2004) in Figure 9 and will be put to the test practically in the scope of the CoSICLE project. Additionally, we currently plan practical studies involving adaptive scripts and fading of scaffolds to the learners (Wichmann & Harrer, 2007) using our model-based scaffolding approach (Harrer, Malzahn, & Roth, 2006) with IMS-LD.

Figure 9. Visual model of the social script (cf. Weinberger et al., 2004)

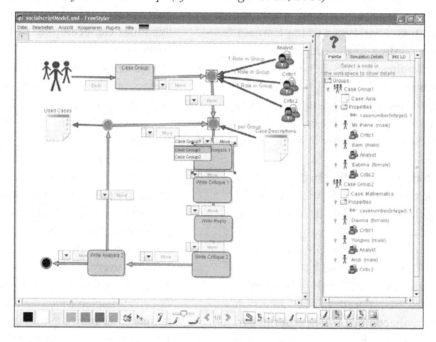

REFERENCES

Botturi, L. (2003). E²ml: Educational environment modeling language. In *Proceedings of Edmedia 2003* (Vol. 1, p. 304-311). Honolulu, HI.

Botturi, L., Derntl, M., Boot, E., & Figl, K. (2006). A classification framework for educational modeling languages in instructional design. In Kinshuk, R. Koper, P. Kommers, P. Kirschner, D. Sampson, & W. Didderen (Eds.), *Advanced learning technologies (ICALT 2006)*. Los Alamitos, CA: IEEE Computer Society.

Caeiro Rodriguez, M., Anido-Rifon, L., & Llamas Nistal, M. (2006). A proposal of separation of concerns in EMLs and its relation with LD. In Kinshuk, R. Koper, P. Kommers, P. Kirschner, D. Sampson, & W. Didderen (Eds.), *Advanced learning technologies (ICALT 2006)* (pp. 76-80). Los Alamitos, CA: IEEE Computer Society.

CoSSICLE Framework (2005). Framework for the specification of collaboration scripts (Tech. Rep.). Kaleidoscope European Network of Excellence. Retrived from http://www.iwm-kmrc. de/CoSICLE/resources/D29-02-01-F.pdf

Dalziel, J. (2006). Lessons from LAMS for IMS learning design. In Kinshuk, R. Koper, P. Kommers, P. Kirschner, D. Sampson, & W. Didderen (Eds.), *Advanced learning technologies (ICALT 2006)* (pp. 1101-1102). Los Alamitos, CA: IEEE Computer Society.

Dillenbourg, P. (2002). Overscripting CSCL: The risks of blending collaborative learning with instructional design. In P. A. Kirschner (Ed.), *Three worlds of CSCL. Can we support CSCL?* (pp. 61-91). Open Universiteit Nederland.

Harel, D., & Naamad, A. (1996). The statemate semantics of statecharts. *ACM Transactions on Software Engineering and Methodology, 5*(4).

Harrer, A., & Malzahn, N. (2006). Bridging the gap—towards a graphical modelling language for learning designs and collaboration scripts of various granularities. In Kinshuk, R. Koper, P. Kommers, P. Kirschner, D. Sampson, & W. Didderen (Eds.), *Advanced learning technologies icalt 2006* (pp. 296-300). Los Alamitos, CA: IEEE Computer Society.

Harrer, A., Malzahn, N., Hoeksema, K., & Hoppe, U. (2005). Learning design engines as remote control to learning support environments. *Journal of Interactive Media in Education, Special Issue on Advances in Learning Design.*

Harrer, A., Malzahn, N., & Roth, B. (2006). The remote control approach—how to apply scaffolds to existing collaborative learning environments. In Y. Dimitriadis, I. Zigurs, & E. Gomez-Sanchez (Eds.), *Groupware: design, implementation, and use The Proceedings of CRIWG 2006* (LNCS 4154, pp. 118-131). Berlin: Springer.

Hernandez Leo, D., Asensio Perez, J., & Dimitriadis, Y. (2004). IMS learning design support for the formalization of collaborative learning patterns. In Kinshuk et al. (Eds.), *Proceedings of IEEE international conference on advanced learning technologies ICALT 2004* (pp. 350-354). Los Alamitos, CA.: IEEE Computer Society.

Hernandez Leo, D., Asensio Perez, J., Dimitriadis, Y., Bote Lorenzo, M., Jorrin Abelln, I., & Villasclaras Fernandez, E. (2005, October). Reusing IMS-LD formalized best practices in collaborative learning structuring. *Advanced Technology for Learning (extended version of the WBE05 paper), 2*(4), 223-232.

Hoppe, H. U., Gaßner, K. G., Mühlenbrock, M., & Tewissen, F. (2000). Distributed visual language environments for cooperation and learning: Applications and intelligent support. *The Journal of Group Decision and Negotiation, 9,* 205-220.

IMS Learning Design Specification (2003). IMS Learning design best practice and implementa-tion. Retrieved October 8, 2007 from http://www.imsglobal.org/learningdesign/ldv1p0/imsld_bestv1p0.html

Kollar, I., Fischer, F., & Slotta, J. (2005). Internal and external collaboration scripts in Web-based science learning at schools. In T. Koschmann, D. Suthers, & T.-W. Chan (Eds.), *Computer-supported collaborative learning 2005* (pp. 331-340). Mahwah, NJ: Lawrence Earlbaum Associates.

Leitao, S. (2000). The potential of argument in knowledge building. *Human Development, 43,* 332-360.

Mäkitalo, K., Weinberger, A., Häkkinen, P., Järvelä, S., & Fischer, F. (2005). Epistemic cooperation scripts in online learning environments: Fostering learning by reducing uncertainty in discourse? *Computers in Human Behavior, 21*(4), 603-622.

Miao, Y., Hoeksema, K., Hoppe, U., & Harrer, A. (2005). CSCL scripts: Modelling features and potential use. In T. Koschmann, D. Suthers, & T.-W. Chan (Eds.), *Computer-supported collaborative learning 2005* (p. 423-432). Mahwah, NJ: Lawrence Earlbaum Associates.

Vogten, H., Koper, R., Martens, H., & Tattersall, C. (2005). An architecture for learning design engines. In R. Koper & C. Tattersall (Eds.), *Learning design—modelling and implementing network-based education & training.* Berlin: Springer.

Weinberger, A., Fischer, F., & Mandl, H. (2004). Knowledge convergence in computer-mediated learning environments. Effects of collaboration scripts. Paper presented at *Annual Meeting of the American Educational Research Association.* San Diego.

Weinberger, A., Stegmann, K., & Fischer, F. (2005). Computer-supported collaborative learning in higher education: Scripts for argumentative knowledge construction in distributed groups. In

T. Koschmann, D. Suthers, & T.-W. Chan (Eds.), *Computer-supported collaborative learning 2005* (pp. 717-726). Mahwah, NJ: Lawrence Earlbaum Associates.

Wichmann, A., & Harrer, A. (2007). Adaption of explanation-based inquiry scripts using IMS/LD. in *The Proceedings of the 12th Biennial Conference for Research on Learning and Instruction (EARLI 2007)*. Budapest, Hungary.

Wichmann, A., Kuhn, M., & Hoppe, U. (2006). Communication through the artefact by means of synchronous co-construction. In *Proceedings of the 7th international conference on learning sciences, ICLS 2006* (pp. 825-831). Bloomington, Indiana: International Society of the Learning Sciences.

ENDNOTE

[1]   Workshop Web site at URL http://www. iwmkmrc.de/CoSICLE/workshop/2005/ workshop_about.html

Chapter XV
Using the IMS Learning Design Notation for the Modeling and Delivery of Education

Colin Tattersall
The Open University of the Netherlands, The Netherlands

Tim Sodhi
The Open University of the Netherlands, The Netherlands

Daniel Burgos
The Open University of the Netherlands, The Netherlands

Rob Koper
The Open University of the Netherlands, The Netherlands

ABSTRACT

IMS learning design (IMS-LD) is a notation system for learning and instruction. It supports the description of learning processes using a set of standardized concepts, including roles, activities, acts, objectives and prerequisites. With the availability of such a notation, descriptions of learning processes can be shared, critiqued, modified, rated, compared and evaluated. Moreover, the machine-interpretable nature of the notation means that designs can be executed by software to support the dynamic orchestration of multi-learner, multi-role learning processes. This chapter introduces IMS-LD and describes experience with its use, supported by the first generation of tooling. We then combine these experiences with observations on the tools in the light of new developments in e-learning in order to derive a set of requirements for IMS-LD enabled visual design environments.

INTRODUCTION

In a recent paper, Merrill (2006) highlights that training is often created by designers-by-assignment without the use of a systematic process, and that instructional products are often designed without sufficient consideration of the applicable instructional design theory. Other research indicates that even when designers are aware of theories, there appears to be a difference between their practice and instructional design models (Eseryel, Schuver-van Blanken, & Spector, 2001; Kenny, Zhang, Schwier, & Campbell, 2005; Kirschner, Carr, Van Merriënboer, & Sloep, 2002). Part of this problem is the absence of a tradition of the use of notations (Gibbons & Brewer, 2005; Tattersall et al., 2005; Waters & Gibbons, 2004). In order to address this issue, several initiatives have been pursued to derive a modeling language for education (Koper & Manderveld, 2004; Rodríguez-Artacho & Verdejo Maíllo, 2004; Süß & Freitag, 2002). The results of these initiatives, notations for describing educational processes, have been input to standardization processes (Rawlings, Van Rosmalen, Koper, Rodríguez-Artacho, & Lefrere, 2002) and, in 2003, an open technical specification known as IMS learning design (IMS-LD, 2003), was approved by a consortium of universities, system vendors, providers and other e-learning stakeholders.

In Waters and Gibbons' (2004) terms, IMS-LD can be positioned as a notation system. The notation is characterized in Botturi, Derntl, Boot, and Figl (2006) as a layered, formal, textual specification offering a single perspective. This chapter describes the IMS-LD notation system and reviews experience with its use. We then identify a number of requirements for IMS-LD-aware design environments with broad utility, a high degree of usability and support for interoperability.

IMS LEARNING DESIGN: A NOTATION SYSTEM FOR EDUCATION

IMS-LD focuses on the creation of a formal description of educational processes known as a unit of learning (UoL). In practice, UoLs define the set of learning activities, for example courses, assessments, workshops or seminars in a specific pedagogical setting and can serve various functions depending on the learning objective and design (Burgos & Griffiths, 2005; Koper, 2005). A wide variety of pedagogical approaches can be represented by IMS-LD, such as problem-based learning, competence-based learning and game-based learning. Prior to turning to the details of the specification, it is helpful to review the requirements the specification was written to meet:

1. **Completeness:** Describe the teaching-learning process in a UoL, including references to the digital and non-digital learning objects and services needed during the process.
2. **Pedagogical flexibility:** Describe different kinds of pedagogies without prescribing any specific pedagogical approach.
3. **Personalization:** Describe personalization aspects within a learning design, so that the content and activities within a UoL can be adapted based on the preferences, portfolio, educational needs, and situational circumstances of users. In addition, the control over the adaptation process must be given, as desired, to the student, a staff member, the computer, and/or the designer.
4. **Formalization:** Describe a learning design in the context of a UoL in a formal way, so that automatic processing is possible.
5. **Reproducibility:** Describe the learning design abstracted in such a way that repeated execution in different settings with different persons is possible.
6. **Interoperability:** Support interoperability of learning designs.

7. **Compatibility:** Use available standards and specifications where possible.

8. **Reusability:** Identify, isolate, de-contextualize and exchange useful learning artifacts, and to re-use these in other contexts.

The specification meets these requirements by defining a modeling language. The specification defines the various concepts in the IMS-LD language in an information model—descriptive text together with diagrams of the relationships between the concepts expressed in the unified modeling language (UML) (ISO, 2005; see also Chapter IX in this handbook). Advice and explanation on putting the language to use is included in the *Best Practice and Implementation Guide*, and a representation is given as an XML Binding—whereby the learning design and the concepts specified, are represented in machine interpretable XML documents.

The specification prescribes a standardized, flexible language for representing learning scenarios for multiple or individual learners, able to be executed by software responsible for coordinating learners, teachers, learning resources and activities as the learning process progresses. The specification reflects a general model which underlies many different behaviorist, cognitive, and (social) constructivist approaches to learning and instruction: People act in different roles in a teaching-learning process. In these roles, they work towards certain outcomes by performing learning and/or support activities within an environment, consisting of learning objects and services to be used during the performance of the activities. A learning object is defined by the IEEE LTSC (2000) as, "any entity, digital or non-digital, that can be used, reused or referenced to during technology-supported learning." The approach separates learning objects and services from the educational method used in the UoL. Put succinctly, IMS-LD allows designers to specify who should do what, when and with which support facilities in order to reach learning objectives.

Which concepts, then, does the specification prescribe? Central to the modeling language are the *activities* to be carried out by learners and staff (or other *roles* involved in the learning process). An activity is associated with learning objectives, prerequisites, a description and an *environment*. Environments include the material, tools and facilities needed by learners and staff in order to carry out their activities, and include learning objects (such as documents, explanatory videos, and animations) and learning services (such as forums and chat facilities). These core components (roles, activities and environments) are orchestrated in a *method*. Methods use the metaphor of a theatrical play to describe the temporal flow of events, whereby sequential acts are described, with the play ending with the completion of the last act. The transition from one act to another serves as a synchronization point for the multiple participants, ensuring that they can all start the next act at the same time.

In addition to the basic language constructs, referred to as level A, the specification provides additional concepts to cater for more sophisticated process descriptions. IMS-LD levels B and C (Koper & Burgos, 2005) allow the expression of conditions, so that designers may describe circumstances under which specified actions should follow. For example, a designer may wish to arrange for the learning process to accommodate different paths through learning activities depending on the results of a self-assessment by learners, or given learners' preferred approach to learning. Additional constructs allow information to be stored during a learning process and used subsequently to influence the flow of events. In this way, designers can arrange for peer review of documents, whereby one learner's contribution is rated and critiqued by peers before being returned to the original author for reflection. The ability to notify roles that an event has happened or that intervention is required is also afforded by the IMS-LD modeling language.

The language constructs offered by IMS-LD allow a wide range of educational processes to be modeled in a standardized way (Van Es & Koper, 2006). Use of the language provides the basis to rejuvenate e-learning systems, increasing the 'richness' of learning activities. New, more effective, efficient and attractive learning models can be specified (e.g., active learning, problem based learning) giving specific attention to support of the teaching/learning process to decrease workload (particularly that of teachers). Furthermore, the advantages of a standard notation can be realized: reflection, communication, sharing, reuse, research, similarity studies and evaluation.

These benefits are, however, predicated on more factors than those addressed by the open technical specification itself. Just as the HTML specification (W3C, 1999) describes the constructs offered by the HTML language without specifying the nature of the software which interprets it, the IMS-LD specification does not address how to record or create the notation, how to adapt or edit it, how to aggregate several uses of the notation and other factors involved when putting IMS-LD to use.

IMS-LD DESIGN PROCESS AND TOOLS

As noted in the abstract, e-learning production processes (Koper, 2003) have sub-processes in which units of learning (UoL) are developed and stored, populated with specific learners and teaching staff, and, to continue the theatrical analogy, performed, or 'run.' Since UoLs do not relate to specific individual learners and teaching staff, they can be created once and delivered many times (Tattersall et al., 2005).

The IMS-LD specification prescribes the form and structure of UoLs so that software applications may be created for their interpretation. As noted above, XML is used as the machine interpretable language in which UoLs must be described to be IMS-LD compliant. A fragment of the XML representation of a UoL is shown in Figure 1.

The software which interprets this XML notation is referred to as an IMS-LD engine (Martens & Vogten, 2005; Vogten, Koper, Martens, & Tattersall, 2005), a software service used by an IMS-LD player (McAndrew, Nadolski, & Little, 2005), the interface with which learners and staff

Figure 1. A fragment of the XML representation of a UoL

```
<imsld:play identifier="P-1" isvisible="true">
    <imsld:title>A unit of learning on the European Constitution</imsld:title>
    <imsld:act identifier="A-1">
        <imsld:title>Views on the European Constitution</imsld:title>
        <imsld:role-part identifier="RP-Learner-1">
            <imsld:title>Learner RP</imsld:title>
            <imsld:role-ref ref="Learner"/>
            <imsld:activity-structure-ref ref="AS-first-step"/>
        </imsld:role-part>
        <imsld:role-part identifier="RP-Facilitator-1">
            <imsld:title>Facilitator RP</imsld:title>
            <imsld:role-ref ref="Facilitator"/>
            <imsld:support-activity-ref ref="SA-first-step"/>
        </imsld:role-part>
        <imsld:complete-act>
            <imsld:when-role-part-completed ref="RP-Facilitator-1"/>
        </imsld:complete-act>
    </imsld:act>
    <imsld:complete-play>
        <imsld:when-last-act-completed/>
    </imsld:complete-play>
</imsld:play>
```

Figure 2. An IMS-LD player interpreting a UoL

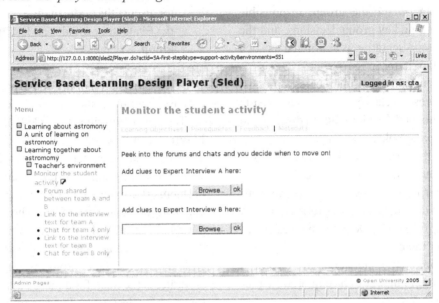

interact. The engine makes the appropriate activities and environments available to people playing the various roles, through the player, coordinating and synchronizing the dynamics of a learning process as multiple learners work through a learning process. The distinction between engine and player allows a variety of approaches to the look and feel of interaction in learning processes (different players) to be supported by a single orchestration service (engine).

Figure 2 shows a member of staff interacting with an IMS-LD player.

The player shown in Figure 2 is a Web server-based application. Once the user has surfed to the appropriate Web address and been authenticated, learning or support activities are made available. Note that what is seen by a particular user (learner or staff member), is a personalized, specific set of activities and associated environments according to the design recorded in the IMS-LD notation and the current state-of-play of the learning process. The content of the Web page is generated from the ongoing processing of the notation by the engine. Drop-down boxes, forms and buttons are all derived from concepts in the language. Whether

and when the learner is presented with a given activity depends on the conditions specified by the designer of the learning process.

So, along which processes and using, which tools do designers create UoLs? The IMS-LD *Best Practice and Implementation Guide* offers a suggestion for a three-step approach to the creation of UoLs. Individuals or teams involved in the design of e-learning start with a narrative description of the proposed learning process. unified modeling language activity diagrams are used to make the flow of events within and between roles explicit, before a final phase in which the XML-based UoL is created. Sloep, Hummel and Manderveld (2005) offer a related procedure for UoL design, and Janssen and Hermans (2005) provide experience with the approach in a distance learning context.

Applying such an approach to designing within a problem-based learning context, a narrative description would be:

- The coordinator for the course makes a problem description available to the group.
- Each of the students in the group reads the problem, as does the facilitator.

- The students decide on a chairperson, the spokesperson for the group, responsible for recording key group decisions, and the chosen representative is appointed as such by the facilitator.
- The group then communicates amongst themselves to clarify the problem, using each other and the facilitator to discuss and clarify terminology and any open issues, eventually arriving at their own succinct statement of the problem at hand.
- The chairperson states this problem description in a document and the group continues by identifying possible solutions or explanations for the problem.
- These possible explanations are clustered into a small number to be explored further by the students.
- The explanations to be pursued are listed in a document.
- The group then identifies the learning goals of the problem and individuals embark on the required research.
- Eventually, the group meet up to discuss their findings, again assisted by the facilitator.
- The chairperson summarizes the findings in a document.

- Subsequently, an Evaluator and the Facilitator discuss the performance of the group and the Evaluator provides an Evaluation of the group.

A transformation of the above narrative to an activity diagram is shown in Figure 3.

Turning to tooling, the XML illustrated in Figure 1 can be created with text-based editors such as Windows Notepad. This is, of course, a time-consuming and error-prone activity. Syntax problems (for example, missing angled brackets and string quotes), the need for authors to maintain a mental list of XML element names and long "create-test-debug" cycles reminiscent of the early days of computer programming languages, all indicate the need for a more supportive environment for designers. The use of XML editors alleviates the difficulties to only a small degree. Template-based approaches such as that described by Janssen and Hermans (2005) either require the development of significant tooling skills by learning designers or a team-based approach which includes notational specialists.

A number of initiatives have been carried out to create a higher degree of support for the creation of UoLs. Reload (Milligan, Beauvoir, & Sharples,

Figure 3. A partial activity diagram for problem-based learning

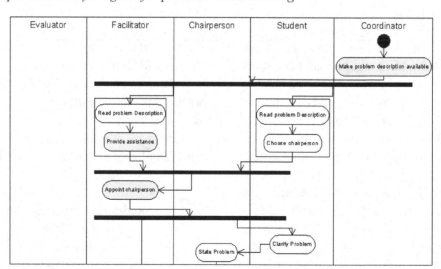

Figure 4. The Reload editor

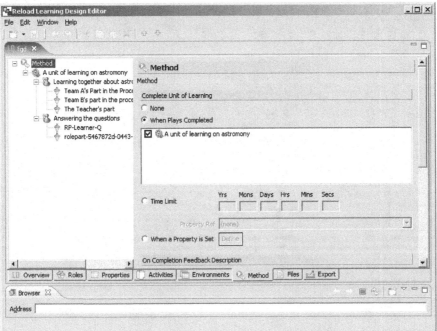

2005) is a tree and form-based editor which has seen significant use in the IMS-LD community. Figure 4 shows the editor in use.

Reload takes the learning designer away from the intricacies of the XML binding, organizing the user interface around core IMS-LD concepts (the tabs for overview, roles, properties and so on) using forms to gather data through particular controls (check boxes, drop down lists etc). Designers' work can be checked for completeness with respect to the requirements on a UoL, and can be exported as a UoL content package. Once in this format, the UoL can be uploaded to an IMS-LD player environment and tested.

Experience with using Reload (Barrett Baxendale, 2005) highlights a steep learning curve and a need to resort to combinations of editors (e.g.,, Reload plus Notepad) to cope with IMS-LD level B. Fundamentally, since Reload was written as reference implementation of an IMS-LD editor, everything which is possible to be encoded in IMS-LD notation (whether using Reload or another IMS-LD editor) must be able to be imported, adapted and exported. This leads the tool to be close to the specification (Griffiths, Blat, Garcia, Vogten, & Kwong, 2005), requiring the user to be familiar with the notation. A variation on this style of support can be seen in the CoSMoS editor (Miao, 2005), shown in Figure 5, and in CopperAuthor (Van der Vegt & Koper, 2006), shown in Figure 6.

Yu, Zhang and Chen (2006) highlight the need to support those who may have little or no knowledge of the IMS-LD notation yet are involved in the design of e-learning, giving teachers as an example target group. The authors cite MOT+ (De la Teja, Lundgren-Cayrol, & Paquette, 2005; see also Chapter 2.3) and ASK-LDT (Sampson, Karampiperis, & Zervas, 2005) as more appropriate for this user group. Figures 7 and 8 show the graphical approaches used by MOT+ and ASK-LDT.

Although certainly offering a more protective environment in which designers can work, caution is needed before concluding that use of graphical interfaces will remove barriers to UoL production.

Figure 5. The CoSMoS editor

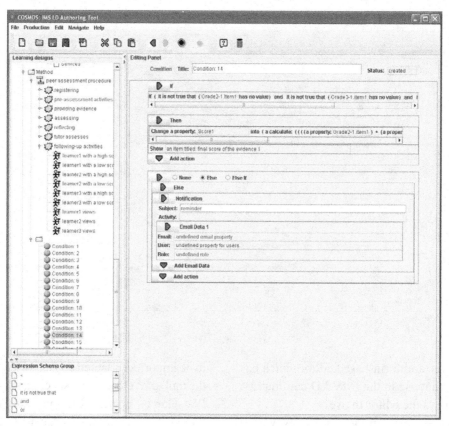

Figure 6. CopperAuthor

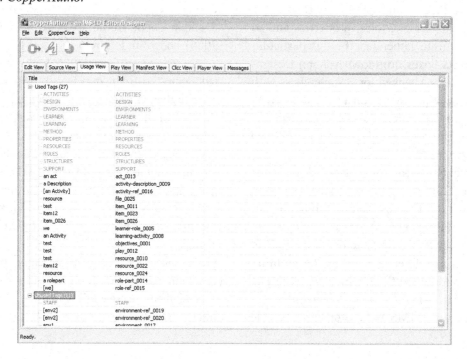

Figure 7. The MOT+ environment

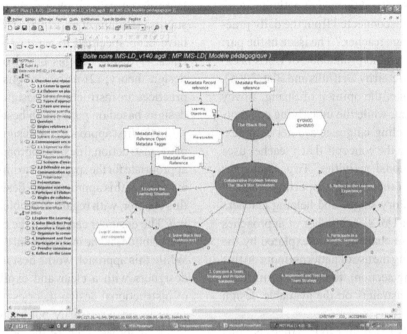

Figure 8. The ASK-LDT environment

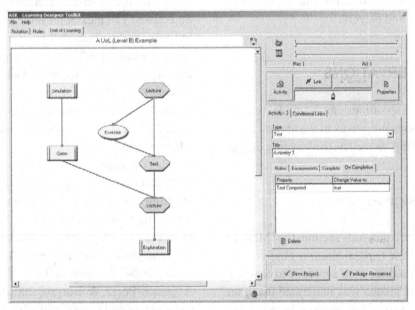

Spang, Bovey and Dunand (2006) highlight that modeling a complex sequence of activities with MOT+ is "too disconnected from the daily practice of the average teacher." The issue of the part played by teachers' in production of UoLs is explored in some detail by Griffiths and Blat (2005). The authors share the opinion of Spang, Bovey and Dunand that, while the underlying concepts of the LD modeling language are not complex, they differ from the concepts that a teacher uses to plan educational activities. Two challenges are identified in the article: supporting teachers during preparatory stages and helping teachers author and edit UoLs. A number of approaches to meeting these challenges are explored by the authors including the use of patterns (more on this in the following section), templates, primitives, and placing constraints on the available design options.

Putting IMS-LD to use today, then, is done along multi-step UoL production processes supported by a number of different editing environments, engines and players.

SOME OBSERVATIONS

A number of observations can be made, reflecting on the various initiatives in the area of IMS-LD-aware tooling, as well as the learning design process.

IMS-LD Design Process

As mentioned in a previous section, the IMS-LD *Best Practice and Implementation* guide offers suggestions for a three-step approach to creation of UoLs. The approach was illustrated using an example from the world of problem-based learning. The question, "How does a designer create quality and effective UoLs using design rules that can be used to capture knowledge and assist in developing the best suited learning design?" bodes further study. A learning design rule describes the learning method that can be applied to a specific learning situation with a certain probability of success (Brouns et al., 2005). Three approaches have been specified to capture learning design rules: (1) using designs based on instructional design theory; (2) using designs based on best practices in instructional design; and (3) using designs based on patterns in best practices.

In the first approach, the designer is cognizant of the instructional design approach that would be appropriate for the specified learning objective. An example of this approach was described earlier in this chapter, with regard to problem-based learning. The designer can create the course based on prescriptions in the instructional design approach. While this approach works best for instructional designers with a clear and explicit knowledge of instructional design theories and models, the same is not necessarily put center-stage in the second approach, where the designer looks for comparable successful example UoLs, and can customize the same based on the current learning objectives. The idea of reusable learning design, led to a study conducted by Bennett, Lockyer, and Agostinho (2004), which demonstrated the efficacy of adapting successful learning designs, to suit various learning contexts, in the creation of quality courses. The authors' approach in a visual context is comprehensively covered in Chapter XIX.

There is at present, substantial interest in the application of pedagogical design patterns to learning design. Here, the designer searches for course patterns which represent "best practice" in terms of both pedagogy and use of information and communication technologies (Bennett et al., 2004; Hernández-Leo, Harrer, Dodero, Asension-Pérez, & Burgos, 2006). Patterns can then be chained together like building blocks to create a new course. Pedagogical patterns capture effective learning designs, allowing newcomers and non-experts in education to learn from more experienced developers, providing solutions that can be applied in many learning scenarios, functioning as a communication medium and means and enhance knowledge management and knowledge transfer (Alexander, 1979; Bergin, Eckstein, Manns, Sharp, & Voelter, 2005; Brouns et al., 2005; Hernández Leo, Asensio Pérez, & Dimitriadis, 2004; McAndrew, Goodyear, & Dalziel, 2005). It has been argued that the point of patterns is not to support immediate reuse, but rather to support creativity, supporting the practitioner engagement rather than relieving practitioners of pedagogic responsibility. This view finds resonance with Olivier (2004), who expressed that the ability to share and modify learning designs will enable the building of better practice for e-learning. The Collage system (Hernández-Leo et al., 2006, see also Chapter XX) builds upon this approach to model collaborative learning in IMS-LD.

IMS-LD Tool Support

The first generation of IMS-LD-aware tool supports only part of the design process. The early stages, in which ideas are sketched, initial narratives developed and storyboards worked out, tend to fall outside the tools' scope. Similarly, the tools tend to offer partial support for the development of UoLs, relying on separate tools for the creation of textual and graphical content, assessments, simulations etc. The design process using IMS-LD today, involves writing down a design as described in the best practice guide, and involving building use cases, representing activities through UML diagrams (suggested, but not compulsory) and then codifying the design in XML—which is at best time consuming (Es & Koper, 2006; McAndrew & Goodyear, 2004). Only the last stage of this is apparent in the current range of software tools. While pragmatic in terms of reusing existing tools and other initiatives, this approach tends to lead to a rather fragmented design experience and limited practitioner engagement. Once created, these components must be integrated into an orchestrated learning process described by the

learning design of a UoL. Moreover, the issue is not only one of linking to passive resources on the Web, but integrating and orchestrating active components into a learning process (e.g.,,, posts to a blog, new entries in a wiki). What happens in an assessment, or in a simulation, should be able to be used to influence the rest of the learning flow.

Most of the first generation tools discussed, are geared towards the IMS-LD community, and serve more as reference implementations of the specification (e.g., Reload, CoSMoS, etc.). An author working with these tools needs to possess detailed knowledge of the elements of IMS-LD and their function in order to create a UoL. The next generation of IMS-LD tools endeavor to hide the specification from the end-user, allowing the user to realize the learning design process without necessarily being exposed to the underlying complexity (Burgos & Koper, 2005). The endeavor in the IMS-LD community currently is on developing tools that, being standards compliant in their outputs, are not standards oriented in the interface they present to the end-user (Griffiths & Blat, 2005).

Although most of the tools have seen evaluation, these have often been small-scale studies, not investigating the practitioner acceptance and usage of the tools. A body of evidence on how designers use today's tools is still being accumulated. But who are the users of these tools? Some tools explicitly address technically-savvy users who are interested in using the tools to learn more about the specification rather than for use in educational production processes (e.g.,,, Reload). Others state the target group as being teachers. This group is, however, extremely diverse and may rely on very different production processes and need a variety of tools. Teachers in primary education have different approaches to e-learning than those in vocational education, which differ again from those in higher education. Even within a particular type of education, different approaches are seen, such as the faculty-driven model and design-team driven model in higher education, described in (Rungtusanatham, Ellram, Siferd & Salik, 2004). While the use of the word teacher suggests a traditional academic setting, e-learning is heavily applied in corporate training and human resource development environments (Dagada & Jakovljevic, 2004; Trombley & Lee, 2002). Designers in these environments may well require different support environments. Moreover, the group "designers of e-learning" is broadening as those outside traditional educational and training contexts use networking technologies to help others learn. This help takes the form both of suggestions or recommendations of how to *approach* the attainment of a particular competence, as well as the full "recreational design" of learning processes (such as designs for learning languages, sports, musical instruments, project management, plumbing, architecture and so on).

Part of the challenge when designing e-learning (whether by schooled instructional designers, designers-by-assignment or recreational designers) revolves around how to take advantage of theoretical insights and best practices. Merrill and Wilson argue for embedding principles of effective and efficient learning design so that tools "provide intellectual leverage to designers who may not know the required instructional design theory" (Merrill & Wilson, 2006). Although such principles can be encoded in IMS-LD, exposing designers to the raw notation does not give the required leverage. In this context, Waters and Gibbons (2004) refer to the intuitive versus non-intuitive dimension of notation systems, and the trade-off which needs to be stuck between human and computer use of a notation.

Could IMS-LD, then, be married to a standardized graphical notation which would appeal to the intuition of designers, allowing them to express the learning design in concepts familiar to their design practices? Which could then be mapped to IMS-LD concepts? This abstraction is analogous to creation of HTML pages in WYSIWYG HTML editing tools like Microsoft FrontPage,

Adobe Dreamweaver, etc. Here the user may have limited to no knowledge of HTML code, but can create rich Web pages quickly. This should not, however, be interpreted as a mere representation of IMS-LD constructs in a graphical interface. These concepts or representations used can be aggregations of activities and roles which are then mapped to IMS-LD constructs (Es & Koper, 2006; Griffiths et al., 2005). Mappings could then be defined between the graphical notation and IMS-LD allowing translations between the two, and visual design environments could be created to support the notation. The comparison to WYSIWYG HTML editors, it should be noted, is not rigorous because different WYSIWYG HTML editors do share common vocabulary and concepts like pages, fonts, tables, etc.—a common notion that is, however, missing in today's implementations of IMS-LD editors and design environments.

It seems however, that faced with a large diversity of users, a single intuitive visual notation may not suffice. Experience with UML (Arlow, Emmerich, & Quinn, 1999) suggests its models are no panacea for the many and varied stakeholders involved in system development. We note, however, that diversity of graphical notations, as is the situation today with ASK-LDT and MOT+, makes the interoperability situation more complex—today's tools all export IMS-LD able to be interpreted by compliant engines, yet round-tripping between the tools is not possible. Supporting variety in visual notations while preserving interoperability is a key research topic for the next generation of visual design environments.

CONCLUSION: REQUIREMENTS FOR A NEW GENERATION OF INTEROPERABLE E-LEARNING DESIGN ENVIRONMENTS

With these observations in mind, we list with a series of requirements that form the basis for our ongoing research in the area of visual design environments for IMS-LD:

- There is a need for end-to-end support of design processes from idea formation through to complete UoL (see Botturi, 2006 for results in this area).

- IMS-LD design environments should support holistic e-learning design, incorporating formative assessment, simulations, multimedia content and other parts of an e-learning experience. This is not merely a question of linking to objects or services on the Web, but requires designers to be in a position to specify which information should be passed to, and taken back from, learners' interactions with content and services.

- E-learning designers should be shielded from the intricacies of notational bindings. Wizards, templates, alternatives metaphors and techniques from the world of visual design environments, can all help in meeting this need. Moreover, research in end user development (Sutcliffe & Mehanddjiev, 2004) offers a number of pointers to address this problem. A closer involvement of groups of designers in the development of environments (rather than solely in their evaluation) would seem appropriate.

- Design environments should accommodate a high degree of variation in designers' knowledge and experience with pedagogies, both traditional and those focused on e-learning. Although some groups of designers may require extensive handholding, Hoogveld (2003) notes that teachers do not like prescriptive methods. Having the flexibility for designers to experiment with, tune and indeed, create templates, patterns and primitives might help strike the correct balance between too restrictive an environment and an unsupportive one.

- Finally, we emphasize the need for design environments to be created to be interoper-

able. Without the capability to both import and export standardized notations such as IMS-LD, tools users become shackled to a particular design tool, fragmenting the community and creating competition where cooperation would offer more benefits.

Creating environments to meet these needs will help reach the goals of sharing, critiquing, modifying, executing, rating, comparing and evaluating learning designs across the broad spectrum of e-learning designers and teachers.

REFERENCES

Alexander, C. (1979). *The timeless way of building.* New York: Oxford University Press.

Arlow, J., Emmerich, W., & Quinn, J. (1999). Literate modeling capturing business knowledge with the UML. In *Proceedings of The First International Workshop on the Unified Modeling Language, UML'98—Beyond the Notation.* Mulhouse, France.

Barrett Baxendale, M. (2005). E-learning technical framework and tools—Demonstrator Projects: SLeD Integration Demonstrator Final Report. Retrieved October 11th, 2006, from http://www. hope.ac.uk/slide/documents/slide_final.doc

Bennett, S., Lockyer, L., & Agostinho, S. (2004). *Investigation how learning designs can be used as a framework to incorporate learning objects.* Paper presented at the 21st ASCILITE Conference, Perth, Australia.

Bergin, J., Eckstein, J., Manns, M., Sharp, H., & Voelter, M. (2005). Pedagogical Patterns. Retrieved December 13, 2006, from http://www. pedagogicalpatterns.org

Botturi, L. (2006). E²ML. A visual language for the design of instruction. *Educational Technologies Research & Development, 54*(3), 265-293.

Botturi, L., Derntl, M., Boot, E., & Figl, K. (2006). A classification framework for educational modeling languages in instructional design. In Kinshuk, R. Koper, P. Kommers, P. Kirschner, D. G. Sampson & E. Kerkrade, Netherlands. (Eds.), *Proceedings of the Sixth International Conference on Advanced Learning Technologies (ICALT2006)*. Los Alamitos, CA: IEEE.

Brouns, F., Koper, R., Manderveld, J., Bruggen, J. v., Sloep, P., Rosmalen, P. v., et al. (2005). A first exploration of inductive analysis approach for detecting learning design patterns. *Journal of Interactive Media in Education, Advances in Learning Design Special Issue.*

Burgos, D., & Griffiths, D. (2005). *The UNFOLD project. Understanding and using learning design.* Heerlen: Open University of The Netherlands.

Burgos, D., & Koper, R. (2005). Virtual communities, research groups and projects on IMS learning design. State of the art, key factors and forthcoming challenges. *E-Journal of Educational Research, Assessment and Evaluation, 11*(2).

Dagada, R., & Jakovljevic, M. (2004). 'Where have all the trainers gone?' E-learning strategies and tools in the corporate training environment. In *Proceedings of the 2004 Annual Research Conference of the South African Institute Of Computer Scientists and Information Technologists on IT Research in Developing Countries.* Stellenbosch, Western Cape, South Africa ACM.

De la Teja, I., Lundgren-Cayrol, K., & Paquette, G. (2005). Transposing MISA learning scenarios into IMS units of learning. *Journal of Interactive Media in Education, Advances in Learning Design Special Issue, 2005/14.*

Es, R. v., & Koper, R. (2006). Testing the pedagogical expressiveness of IMS-LD. *Education Technology & Society, 9*(1), 229-249.

Eseryel, D., Schuver-van Blanken, M., & Spector, J. M. (2001). Current practice in designing training for complex skills: Implications for design and evaluation of ADAPT-IT. In C. Montgomerie & J. Vitelli (Eds.), *Proceedings of ED-MEDIA 2001: World Conference on Educational Multimedia, Hypermedia, & Telecommunications* (pp. 474-479). Tampere, Finland Association for Advancement of Computing in Education.

Gibbons, A. S., & Brewer, E. K. (2005). Elementary principles of design languages and design notation systems for instructional design. In J. M. Spector, C. Ohrazda, A. Van Schaak & D. A. Wiley (Eds.), *Innovations in Instructional Technology: Essays in honor of M. David Merrill* (pp. 111-130). Mahwah, NJ: Lawrence Erlbaum Associates.

Griffiths, D., & Blat, J. (2005). The role of teachers in editing and authoring units of learning using IMS Learning Design. *Advanced Technology for Learning,* (4).

Griffiths, D., Blat, J., Garcia, R., Vogten, H., & Kwong, K. (2005). Learning fesign tools. In R. Koper & C. Tattersall (Eds.), *Learning design: A Handbook on modeling and delivering networked education and training* (pp. 109-136). Berlin-Heidelberg: Springer Verlag.

Hernández-Leo, D., Harrer, A., Dodero, J. M., Asension-Pérez, J. I., & Burgos, D. (2006). *Creating by reusing learning design solutions.* Paper presented at the Proceedings of the 8th Simposo Internacional de Informática Educativa. León, Spain: IEEE Technical Committee on Learning Technology.

Hernández-Leo, D., Villasclaras-Fernández, E. D., Asensio-Pérez, J. I., Dimitriadis, Y., Jorrín-Abellán, I. M., Ruiz-Requies, I., et al. (2006). COLLAGE: A collaborative learning design editor based on patterns. *Educational Technology & Society, 9*(1), 58-71.

Hernández Leo, D., Asensio Pérez, J. I., & Dimitriadis, Y. A. (2004, 30 August-1 September, 2004). *IMS Learning Design Support for the Formaliza-*

tion of Collaborative Learning Patterns. Paper presented at the IEEE International Conference on Advanced Learning Technologies (ICALT'04). Joensuu, Finland.

Hoogveld, A. W. M. (2003). *The teacher as designer of competency-based education.* Heerlen: Open Universiteit Nederland.

IMS-LD. (2003). *IMS learning design specification.* Retrieved February 27, 2004, from http://www.imsglobal.org/learningdesign/index.cfm

ISO. (2005). *ISO/IEC 19501:2005 Information technology—Open Distributed Processing—Unified Modeling Language (UML) Version 1.4.2* Geneva, Switzerland International Organization for Standardization.

Janssen, J., & Hermans, H. (2005). How to integrate learning design into existing practice. In R. Koper & C. Tattersall (Eds.), *Learning design: A handbook on modeling and delivering networked education and training* (pp. 253-266). Berlin-Heidelberg: Springer Verlag.

Kenny, R. F., Zhang, Z., Schwier, R. A., & Campbell, K. (2005). A review of what instructional designers do: Questions answered and questions not asked. *Canadian Journal of Learning and Technology, 31*(1).

Kirschner, P., Carr, C., Van Merriënboer, J. J. G., & Sloep, P. (2002). How expert designers design. *Performance Improvement Quarterly, 15*(4), 86-104.

Koper, R. (2003). Learning technologies: an integrated domain model. In W. Jochems, J. Van Merrienboer & R. Koper (Eds.), *Integrated eLearning* (pp. 64-79). London: RoutledgeFalmer.

Koper, R. (2005). *Modeling lifelong learning networks.* Paper presented at the IPSI Conference. Retrieved from http://hdl.handle.net/1820/331

Koper, R., & Burgos, D. (2005). Developing advanced units of learning using IMS Learning Design level B. *The International Journal on Advanced Technology for Learning, 2*(4), 252-259.

Koper, R., & Manderveld, J. M. (2004). Educational modeling language: Modeling reusable, interoperable, rich and personalised units of learning. *The British Journal of Educational Technology, 35*(5), 537-551.

Martens, H., & Vogten, H. (2005). A reference implementation of a learning design engine. In R. Koper & C. Tattersall (Eds.), *Learning design: A handbook on modeling and delivering networked education and training* (pp. 91-108). Berlin-Heidelberg: Springer Verlag.

McAndrew, P., & Goodyear, P. (2004). *Representing practitioner experiences through learning design and patterns.* Retrieved from http://www.jisc.ac.uk/uploaded_documents/practioner-patterns-v2.doc

McAndrew, P., Goodyear, P., & Dalziel, J. (2005). Patterns, designs and activities: Unifying descriptions of learning structures. Retrieved December 13, 2006 from http://kn.open.ac.uk/public/document.cfm?docid=5295

McAndrew, P., Nadolski, R., & Little, A. (2005). Developing an approach for learning design players. *Journal of Interactive Media in Education Advances in Learning Design Special Issue, 2005/14.*

Merrill, M. D., & Wilson, B. (2006). The future of instructional design (Point/Counterpoint). In R. Reiser & J. V. Dempsey (Eds.), *Trends and Issues in Instructional Design and Technology,* Second Edition (pp. 335-351). NJ, USA: Prentice Hall.

Miao, Y. (2005). CoSMoS: Facilitating learning designers to author units of learning using IMS-LD, In C. K. Looi, D. H. Jonassen & I. Mitsuru (Eds.), *Proceedings of the International Conference on Computers in Education* (pp. 275-282). Singapore: IOS Press.

Milligan, C. D., Beauvoir, P., & Sharples, P. (2005). The reload learning design tools. *Journal of Interactive Media in Education, Advances in Learning Design Special Issue, 2005/14.*

Olivier, B. (2004). *UNFOLD: Discussion of learning design, state of play.* Retrieved December 13, 2006 from https://www.unfold-project. net:8082/UNFOLD/about_folder/events/online/ billjuly04/

Rawlings, A., Van Rosmalen, P., Koper, R., Rodrí-guez-Artacho, M., & Lefrere, P. (2002). *CEN/ISSS WS/LT Learning Technologies Workshop: Survey of Educational Modeling Languages (EMLs).*

Rodríguez-Artacho, M., & Verdejo Maíllo, M. F. (2004). Modeling educational content: The cognitive approach of the PALO language. *Educational Technology & Society, 7*(3), 124-137.

Rungtusanatham, M., Ellram, L. M., Siferd, S. P., & Salik, S. (2004). Toward a typology of business education in the Internet age. *Decision Sciences The Journal of Innovative Education, 2*(2), 101-120.

Sampson, D. G., Karampiperis, P., & Zervas, P. (2005). ASK-LDT: A Web-based learning scenarios authoring environment based on IMS learning design. *Advanced Technology for Learning 2005*(4).

Sloep, P., Hummel, H., & Manderveld, J. M. (2005). Basic design procedures for e-learning courses. In R. Koper & C. Tattersall (Eds.), *Learning design: A Handbook on modeling and delivering networked education and training* (pp. 139-160). Berlin-Heidelberg: Springer Verlag.

Spang Bovey, N., & Dunand, N. (2006). Seamless production of interoperable e-Learning units: Stakes and pitfalls. In R. Koper & K. Stefanov (Eds.), *Proceedings of the Workshop on Learning Networks for Lifelong Competence Development,* Sofia, Bulgaria: INCOMA Ltd.

Süß, C., & Freitag, B. (2002). *LMML—The learning material markup language framework.* Paper presented at the International Workshop: Interactive Computer Aided Learning, Villach, Austria,.

Sutcliffe, A., & Mehanddjiev, N. (2004). Special issue: End-user development - tools that empower users to create their own software solutions. *Communications of the ACM, 47*(9).

Tattersall, C., Vogten, H., Brouns, F., Koper, R., van Rosmalen, P., Sloep, P., et al. (2005). How to create flexible runtime delivery of distance learning courses. *Educational Technology & Society, 8*(3), 226-236.

Trombley, B. K., & Lee, D. (2002). Web-based learning in corporations: Who is using it and why, who is not and why not? *Journal of Educational Media, 27*(3), 137-146.

Van der Vegt, W., & Koper, R. (2006). *Copper Author 1.6.* Retrieved October 11, 2006, from www.copperauthor.org

Van Es, R., & Koper, R. (2006). Testing the pedagogical expressiveness of IMS-LD. *Educational Technology & Society, 9*(1), 229-249.

Vogten, H., Koper, R., Martens, H., & Tattersall, C. (2005). An architecture for learning design engines. In R. Koper & C. Tattersall (Eds.), *Learning design: A handbook on modeling and delivering networked education and training* (pp. 75-90). Berlin-Heidelberg: Springer Verlag.

W3C. (1999). HTML 4.01 Specification, W3C Recommendation. Retrieved October 11th, 2006, from http://www.w3.org/TR/html401/

Waters, S. H., & Gibbons, A. S. (2004). Design languages, notation systems and instrictional technology: A case study. *Education Technology Research & Development, 52*(2), 57-63.

Yu, D., Zhang, W., & Chen, X. (2006). New generation of e-learning technologies. In *Proceedings of the First International Multi-Symposiums on Computer and Computational Sciences (IMSCCS'06)* (Vol. 2, pp. 455-459).

Chapter XVI
Comparing Visual Instructional Design Languages:
A Case Study

Luca Botturi
University of Lugano, Switzerland

Daniel Burgos
The Open University of the Netherlands, The Netherlands

Manuel Caeiro-Rodríguez
University of Vigo, Spain

Michael Derntl
University of Vienna, Austria

Rob Koper
The Open University of the Netherlands, The Netherlands

Patrick Parrish
The COMET® Program/University Corporation for Atmospheric Research, USA

Tim Sodhi
The Open University of the Netherlands, The Netherlands

Colin Tattersall
The Open University of the Netherlands, The Netherlands

ABSTRACT

This handbook testifies that research on VIDL is lively, and has produced a number of interesting design languages and tools. This chapter wants to support readers in understanding the similarities and differences of some of the VIDL presented in the previous chapters, not in theory, but applying them to a specific instructional design case.

INTRODUCTION

The sequence of Chapters in Section II of this handbook is the evidence that research in the field of VIDL is lively, and that interested readers have only to choose a language among many in order to apply some of the ideas presented in her/his own professional context. However, how to choose a language is not self-evident. Chapter XVIII will provide a structured framework for this—but with this chapter we already want to provide a first space for comparing some of the proposed VIDL.

The chapter is built around an instructional design case study, which is presented in the next section. The case study was submitted to all authors of chapters in part II of this handbook. Some of them took time to model it with their VIDL, and we collected here the results, which are presented in the following sections. In particular, the focus is on how each single design language contributes to the design, in what stages it intervenes, and what benefits it brings.

The languages represented here are narrative-based design (Patrick Parrish, Chapter VI in this handbook), E^{2}ML (Luca Botturi, Chapter VII), coUML (Michael Derntl, Chapter IX), POEML (Manuel Caeiro-Rodríguez, Chapter X), and IMS Learning Design (Daniel Burgos, Tim Sodhi, Colin Tattersall and Rob Koper, Chapter XV). The differences in style among the sections of the chapter are a natural consequence; as such, this is also a good example of international collaboration.

Throughout the chapter, comments are kept to a minimum, as the main purpose is illustrative: to let the readers see the languages at work, in order to foster reflection and to provide elements for selection and discussion.

THE CASE STUDY

Setting

The case study describes a 16-hour course in a blended learning environment. The topic of the course is *Introduction to Instructional Design*, and it follows a case-based and project-based teaching strategy.

The client, who asked for the course, is the director of a non-profit organization. The target is a group of 15 people, employed in a network of non-profit organizations that organize vocational training programs for dropout students at the age of 14-19. They are all social workers, and want to improve their skills in the design of instructional activities in order to better cope with their daily job.

The course is held by a single instructor, who can count on the help of a tutor for uploading materials online and for monitoring online discussions.

Learning Goals

After the instruction, the course participants will be able to:

1. Plan and manage an instructional design process in their professional environment
2. Define the main roles and task involved in instructional design
3. Foresee the critical points in instructional design projects
4. Given a design task, effectively apply specific design techniques, namely
    a. Conducting a complete instructional analysis
    b. Properly define learning goals
    c. Define an instructional strategy
    d. Design a sound evaluation plan

Instructional Strategy

The course must take into account its short duration and at the same time its ambitious learning goals. The main instructional idea is to develop concepts inductively through case studies, and then develop new skills by developing a project.

Before the course starts, the instructor worked with the client and identified four real ongoing projects with the organization, which will be used as group projects during the course.

Course Structure

This 16-hour course is articulated into five sessions: the first and the last are face-to-face, while the three in between are online. For all sessions is available a LMS which collects all course materials and supports online communication. In the following is presented the rough course schedule.

Session 1: Face to Face Introduction (Saturday Afternoon, 3h)

1. Introduction to the course (learning goals, schedule, evaluation), presentation of participants (45')
2. Discussion of some basic concepts, such as "instruction," "training," "education," and "design". The instructor does this by presenting three case studies through slides and stimulating the discussion among the participants (1h).
3. Introduction of the main phases of the AD-DIE model (with slides, 45')
4. Division into four groups of four people each, assignment of a project to each group (30'). There is a one-page project assignment for each group, plus some general written project guidelines.

All the materials used for this face-to-face session are collected in the LMS.

Session 2: Instructional Analysis (from Monday to Friday, 3h over 1 week)

1. **Reading:** For this session, the students connect to the LMS, and download a reading that introduces the main elements to be considered in an instructional analysis. After that, they view a Flash presentation of a case study. If they have questions, they can post them to a discussion forum.
2. **Group work:** After completing the readings, the participants can work in their group forum (supervised by the instructor). Their goal is developing a sound instructional analysis plan. The instructor provides feedback during the work.
3. **Submission:** On Friday at 5:00 PM, all groups should submit a document presenting their instructional analysis plan.
4. **Feedback:** By Monday, the instructor reviews the plans and provides both group-specific feedback and general feedback (valid for all groups).

Session 3: Learning Goals (from Monday to Friday, 3h over 1 week)

1. Reading. For this session, the students connect to the LMS, and download two readings
    a. A reading that introduces the idea of learning goals
    b. A reading presenting Anderson and Krathwohl's learning goals classification table
    After that, they view a Flash presentation that presents the learning goals for the case study they already saw in session 2.
3. Group work. After completing the readings, the participants can work in their group forum (supervised by the instructor). Their goal is defining the four main learning goals for their project and classifying them on Anderson & Krathwohl's table. The instructor provides feedback during the work.

4. Submission. On Friday at 5:00 PM, all groups should submit a document presenting their work.
5. Feedback. By Monday, the instructor reviews the plans and provides both group-specific feedback and general feedback (valid for all groups).

Session 4: Instructional Strategy (from Monday to Friday, 3h over 1 week)

1. **Reading:** For this session, the students connect to the LMS, and download Merrill's paper about 5-stars instruction.
2. **Flash Presentation:** After reading, they view a Flash presentation that presents five case studies, focusing on the different instructional strategies used in each of them.
3. **Group work:** After completing the readings, the participants can work in their group forum (supervised by the instructor). Their goal is developing and instructional strategy. The instructor provides feedback during the work.
4. **Submission:** On Friday at 5:00 PM, all groups should submit a document presenting their work.
5. **Feedback:** By Monday, the instructor reviews the plans and provides both group-specific feedback and general feedback (valid for all groups).

Session 5: Face to Face (4h)

1. Short introduction to the session, and wrap-up of the work so far (15')
2. Group presentation of each project's work (1h)
3. Presentation of the key issues in evaluation (with slides, 45' h)
4. Group work: develop an evaluation plan (1h)
5. Short group presentations (30')
6. Conclusion and course evaluation (30')

Evaluation

Formative evaluation is done on the basis of the project work. It has no certification value, but the instructor uses it for writing a report about the course for the client.

The overall quality of the course is assessed with a standard paper-based survey provided by the participants' home organization.

Tools

The course exploits a LMS, where all the learning materials are collected (slides, readings in PDF format, Flash animations with case studies), and which also hosts the main discussion forum and group discussion forums.

Notice that the access to group discussion forums are restricted to group members, to the tutor, and the instructor.

NARRATIVE-BASED APPROACH

ID is always an iterative process, requiring successive levels of detail and revision as the design begins to take shape. The use of a narrative diagram for design deliberations might best begin very early in the design phase of a project, much earlier than the stage at which the case study stands as presented at the start of this chapter. But it can also be introduced at any stage in the design process to help evaluate the design for possible revisions or for adding the necessary detail to flesh it out further.

This example will demonstrate the latter application, how a narrative diagram can be brought into the design phase to evaluate the current status and to help add further details. Perhaps I am a consulting ID being brought late in the project, or perhaps I am a new instructor asked to teach a course that has already been delivered, and I am working from a course plan passed to me from the previous instructor. At any rate, I am assuming the logistics are set, and the basic structure of the five sessions is required. My task is to find ways to make sure the course experience will be engaging and effective for students, and so I will be examining its inherent aesthetic and narrative qualities and searching for ways to increase these.

In beginning to consider the qualities of the course, I see many positive aspects already in place that will contribute to creating an aesthetic learning experience. The course has generative goals, with a challenging project and natural conclusion that will unify the experience. All course sessions and the content they offer are included to lead toward this conclusion, which should help students experience a closing consummation more easily than they might without the project focus. The symmetrical structure, with opening and closing face-to-face sessions providing bookends for the three week-long online learning sessions, offers a nice pattern to work with as well, because the bookend sessions offer a grounding experience, a natural "call to adventure" and return to the starting point that may encourage students to reflect upon what has occurred between them, and how they have changed during the course.

Because I will be looking for opportunities to create a three-act "plot" structure, with a well-formed opening and conclusion and clear "plot points" to help stimulate engagement, this structure is already supportive. But I want to

lay it out visually and see what details will be needed to ensure that a good plot structure can be achieved. For example, I want to make sure that early engagement is stimulated and urged to rise, and to make certain that the action of the course rises steadily as well, with limited opportunities for waning engagement. In other words, one of my design goals will be to create a situation in which a student becomes inextricably involved in the course and whole-heartedly committed to see it through. A higher level goal will be to make the experience as meaningful as possible, so I need to look for additional ways to have the ideas and events build upon one another and come to a conclusion that unifies and heightens the course experience. Figure 1 illustrates the ideal plot structure for the experience—my goal, before considering how actual events will map to it.

I begin by laying out the temporal axis of narrative diagram, deciding how the five-part structure of course structure can be imposed onto the three-act structure of the narrative. Which elements will fall into each of the three acts? I decide that the breaks between acts and positions for the plot points will not always be the obvious beginnings or endings of the sessions as defined, but will instead be key points of instructor/student interactions. These are the places where the experience can be enriched and redirected by the instructor, or where deeper reflection on the part of students will create significant growth

Figure 1. The narrative goal of the course experience

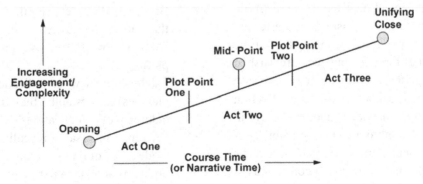

Figure 2. A first iteration, determining the three-act structure of the course

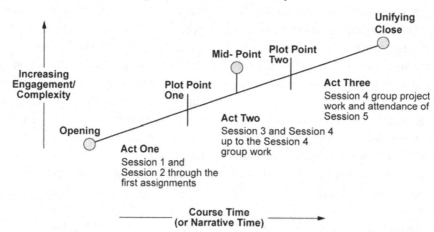

opportunities and shifts in their own subjective experience. Figure 2 shows my first iteration in laying out the course plot.

Looking at Figure 2, you can see that I have designated Act One as including the entire first two sessions. Even though Session 1 is critical to establishing the course direction, Act One includes Session 2 because the pattern of the course is not set until the first assignments are undertaken. Similarly, Act Three is not merely Session 5, but also the group project work from Session 4 immediately preceding it, because the height of the final session is most likely the presentation of the group projects completed in Session 4. As it turns out, this breakout makes the acts similar in duration, but this was not necessarily my goal.

But at this point I am not entirely convinced that this structure and the student group work to complete the project will be sufficient to create the rising engagement depicted in the diagram. The course could just as easily be experienced as four plodding project phases that, due to time constraints and for convenience, are rushed through and patterned directly from the case studies provided, without sufficient reflection to create growing knowledge and investment in the outcomes. I want to avoid the possibility of falling engagement at the end of each session as students merely check off another completed as-

signment, and I begin thinking about how badly the engagement curve might look without attention paid to continuity and rising action. Figure 3 reflects what I am trying to avoid. In addition to the falling engagement at points within the course, this figure also depicts a less than fully engaging Session 1 and a closing Session 5 that includes diminishing energy.

The opening session should create initial engagement by establishing tension or a problematic situation, as well as the promise of resolution. The closing session should sustain or even amplify the engagement by bringing the entire enterprise to a consummation that unifies all the activities that came before. Along the way, the plot points and mid-point should both reinvigorate engagement and stimulate reflection by doing one or more of the following:

- Bringing to light new, significant knowledge that causes the learner to see the situation from a new perspective (enriching the plot)
- Establishing new complications or complexities that reestablish the opening tension (adding plot complications)
- Creating a reversal by revealing a fallacy or inadequacy of previous thinking about the problems at hand (a peripeteia)

Figure 3. The engagement curve to avoid in this case

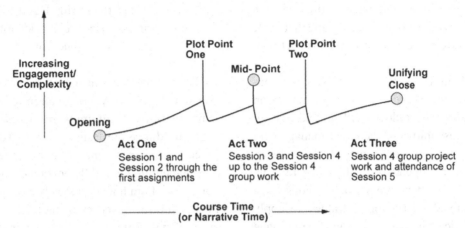

Bringing a phase to completion, but also revealing new problems that existed, but were not yet apparent in the previous phases (moving the plot forward)

Based on these desired features, I identify several possibilities for the design enhancements I would like to achieve.

• In the opening session, I will use an activity that gets students talking about their roles as designers of instruction, even if they had not thought much about that role before. This will help establish the problematic situation the course is meant to address, their novice status as IDs, and may help personalize the course, generating goals students will embrace throughout.

• In the opening session, I will choose cases that are related to the kinds of projects this group may be involved with on the job, and ask learners to discern distinctions in the cases. I will choose cases that demonstrate differing levels of complexity in regards to the instructional situation, the learning goals, and the instructional strategy applied. I will also consider including a case that can be classified as a failure to give urgency to the projects and to allow later reflection about the reasons for the failure.

• In the opening session, I will avoid excessive "exposition" and, rather than a lecture about the ADDIE model, use Socratic Method to allow learners to discover the logic of the model. This will create ownership of the method that may carry through the course.

• I will have the project groups submit all assignments in a place where all other students have access. This not only creates a pool of additional examples, but increases the urgency of project decisions.

• Plot Point One will be the feedback provided by the instructor for the first group assignment to do an instructional analysis. The instructor should be supportive, but find ways to challenge the groups to look more deeply into the instructional situation. The instructor should set an expectation that the additional assignments should be based on this deeper instructional analysis plan. Because it is unlikely that students can actually perform the instructional analysis, they will need to be asked to generate a set of expected, or possible, analysis data (as an author might generate a backstory).

• The mid-point will be a similar feedback provided for the second group assignment. The instructor should find ways to make students think more deeply about the learning goals and objectives, for example, making sure they have adequately addressed both cognitive and affective goals, and that these goals are well connected to the instructional analysis.

- Plot Point Two will be an instructor intervention on the weekend prior to the final group assignment. Students will be told that (a) a representative of the client management will attend the final course session to listen to and comment on final project reports, and (b) student groups must choose one additional instructional strategy to apply to the learning goals, and write a one-page description of how this strategy will address them, suggesting strengths and weaknesses over the primary strategy receiving a fuller treatment.

- The closing session, especially with a client representative in attendance, provides natural closure and intensity. But in addition, the instructor should, as much as possible, point out where the groups did or did not make strong connections to their previous steps in the project.

- In the closing session, I will create a sense of ceremony after the final tasks to highlight the journey of discovery and identity growth that students have gone through.

The end result of this narrative analysis of the course is Figure 4. Although an infinite number of final narrative diagrams were possible, this one seems to address the design goals I laid out for the process. It assumes a small amount of diminishing engagement in the middle portion of the course, but overall I am hoping a steady rise in engagement can be achieved by using this design. The costs of performing the narrative analysis and creating the diagrams have been on the order of a few hours additional design time, especially if the diagrams were simply sketched on paper or a white board. However, these hours may have been spread over several days to allow reflection time. If desired, the final diagram might be formalized to document this aspect of the design for others in perhaps one additional hour or less. The benefits of using this process are that it may stimulate the designer or design team to pay closer attention to learner engagement and to create a more highly integrated instructional design.

Figure 4. The final design of the course narrative

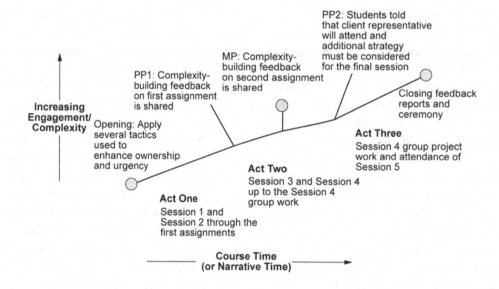

Course Time
(or Narrative Time)

E²ML

E²ML is a visual language designed to enhance communication among the people involved in an instructional design project. As such, in order to understand where it could actually make a difference, it is important to understand who is trying to communicate with whom.

At the early stage of design, right after the first meeting with the client or the instructional requirements analysis, the instructional designer can rely on E²ML to structure her or his design ideas, as a sort of inner language. This is likely to happen through the development of pencil and paper informal diagrams, such as the ones presented in Chapter VII. E²ML in this case is a sort of jargon that the designer can use, exactly as the skilled student has her own symbolic way of taking notes.

At a later stage, such as the one presented in the case study statement, the designer can exploit E²ML for conveying her or his design ideas to the client and to other team members, in this case, to the tutor. In this case, diagrams will be more clearly and carefully designed. In this scenario, the design might think of developing a first diagram—a *dependencies diagram*—to describe the main division of the five sessions: two face-to-face and three online, as in Figure 5.

The five blocks represent the five sessions. Arrows indicate the sequence of products (project deliverables) produced during the three online sessions, while round-ended arrows indicate that the three online sessions require having attended the first one in order to be properly executed. Already at this point the diagram provides a synthetic view of the core idea of the course in terms of structure. The following step would be the progressive refinement of the dependencies diagram into a detailed map which includes all the single activities (*actions*) foreseen in the course, as represented in Figure 6.

At a glance the diagram shows that the three online sessions have the same outline, and that group work is foreseen in all sessions except the first one. Also, Session 5 appears very crowded, indicating an extreme subdivision of time: that might actually be a concern for the designer, who might want to reduce the workload in that session. Notice that the FEEDBACK action could be more detailed, as it contains both collective feedback, addressed to all groups (as indicated) and group specific feedback. Why is this not represented? The whole goal of E²ML is being clear to those using it, and therefore there is no "right" level of detail, as long as the diagrams clearly convey the design team ideas effectively for the purpose they are intended.

At this time the designer might take the dependencies diagram and turn them into an activity flow diagram, which takes into account the temporal sequence of activities in the calendar.

Figure 5. Simple dependencies diagram

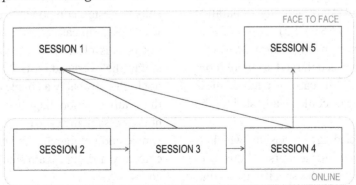

Figure 6. Detailed dependencies diagram

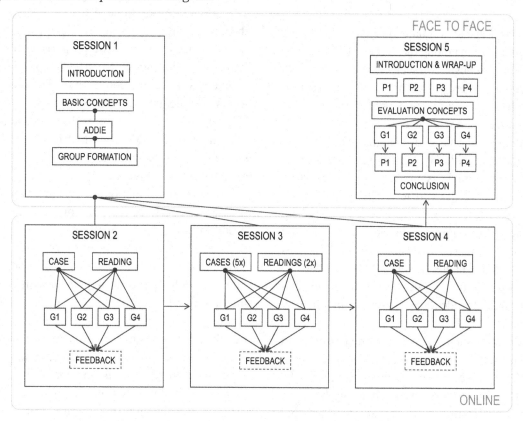

The result would appear as in Figure 7, and could serve as course outline for (a) communicating with the client; (b) collaborating with the tutor; and (c) presenting the course to the students.

Notice that some ambiguities are here cleared: e.g.,, actions G1 to G4 are actually in parallel, while P1 to P5 (in SESSION 5) are sequenced (presentations happen one at a time!). The time-frame for SESSION 5 is enlarged, as more room is needed. Of course, in case of need of more precision, the timescale could be adjusted for the whole course.

The next step of diagram design, which is probably not necessary for a course of this size, is detailing each action with a specific action dia-gram, clearly indicating prerequisites, outcomes, input and output, learning goals, method, etc. Figure 8 provides an illustrative example.

After the course, these diagrams can be used to more systematically trace back evaluation re-sults to design components, and address course weaknesses in case of redesign.

As it is clear from the diagrams presented so far, the overhead costs for producing them is not high—probably a couple of hours, excluding the detailed action diagrams which are probably not necessary in this case. Basically, E^{2}ML is a simple and flexible design language that can ac-company a design team's activity throughout a course lifecycle.

Figure 7. Activity flow

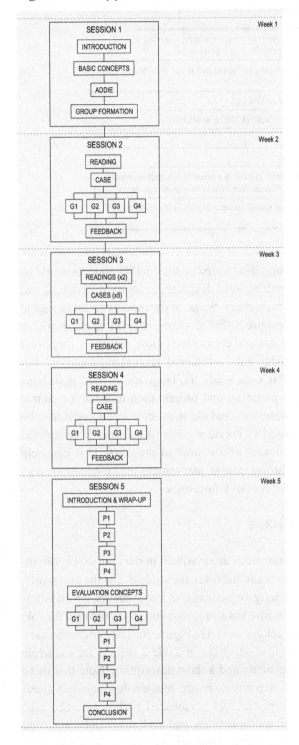

Figure 8. Illustrative example of action diagram

SESSION 4: CASE	
Students (individual)	LEARNING
General idea of ID project process (ADDIE) Concept of „instructional strategy"	Examples of instructional strategies in concrete settings
-	-
-	-
View a Flash presentation that presents 5 case studies, focusing on the different instructional strategies used in each of them.	
Online	
Flash presentation	

coUML

To approach the case study with coUML, we first provide a tabular overview of the course information provided in the verbal case study description, so to say the course's "fact sheet." To do so, we identify the following course description parameters proposed by coUML as relevant: Course name, summary, structure, presence mode, online support, participants, teaching staff, instructional strategy, coUML models. Additional parameters are not (yet) needed to describe the case-study course. The content for these descriptive parameters is extracted from relevant information in the verbal case study description. The primary intent here is adding more structure to the existing course description. Note that the course's fact sheet is not only useful to instructors and designers—it can as well be used to provide relevant course-related information to the prospective participants.

This tabular fact sheet is complemented by the course's *course package model* (CPM; see Figure 9). It shows that the coUML course model[1], represented by the "Introduction to Instructional Design" package, comprises the following sub-packages detailing the course design:

Table 1. Tabular course information ("fact sheet")

"Introduction to Instructional Design"	
Summary	16 hours course in a blended learning environment aiming to improve instructional design skills of social workers
Structure	Held in five sessions; two face-to-face at begin and end, three online sessions in-between
Presence mode	Blended face-to-face and online
Online support	A learning management system (LMS) is available
Participants	15 social workers
Teaching staff	One instructor, one tutor
Instructional strategy	Case and project-based learning using a blended learning approach; "integrated" instruction through lecture and hands-on experience
coUML models	Course structure, learning goals, documents, detailed course activities

- Roles
- Learning goals
- Documents
- Course structure model (CSM)
- Course activity model (CAM)

As defined in the coUML specification, each of these packages may contain an arbitrary number of diagrams detailing the respective course information. The following sections present each package in detail. Note that the presentation of the course activities was moved to the back as the other packages provide relevant input (e.g.,, documents, goals, structure, etc.) for this package.

Generally, coUML can be used in any stage of the course design and development process where visual models and structured descriptions of the current and planned design are useful to the design team. The contents of the CPM show that

the main "users" of the coUML models would be instructional designers/analysts, instructors, and researchers. Some of the models could be useful resources for students as well (e.g.,, learning goals and course activities), maybe in simplified form with additional textual information. For this case study the language is used mainly as a planning and presentation tool for the course designers and the instructor, but it could also be used to create models of an already completed course, or a course in progress. This can help during course assessment and evaluation, e.g., for research purposes.

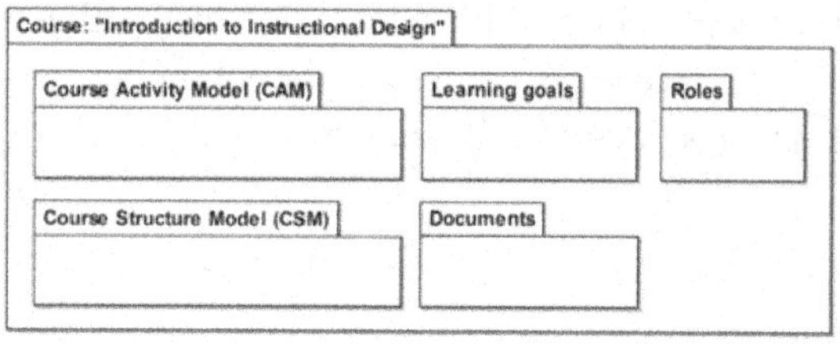

Roles

Four roles are involved in the course, i.e. the instructor, the tutor, the student, and the group role. Each group consists of four students, which is represented as an aggregation relationship in the role package model in Figure 10. The complementary role description in Table 2 depicts for each role its name and a short description. Note that there is a many-to-many relationship between these roles and real persons, as each person can take on multiple roles, and each role can be assumed by more than one person. The roles are later used with other coUML modeling artifacts, such as course activities, showing a role's responsibilities

Figure 9. Course Package Model (CPM) for the "Introduction to Instructional Design" course

Figure 10. Roles participating in the course

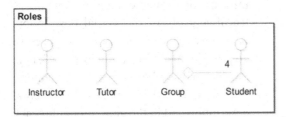

Table 2. Role descriptions

Role	Description
Instructor	Responsible for organization and conduct of the course
Tutor	Helps the instructor with certain tasks, e.g., facilitating student groups, collecting documents, seeing through online activity, etc.
Student	Takes part in the course by participating in the course's activities to achieve the course's learning goals
Group	Group of four students working together on project assignments

and tasks throughout the course, and documents, showing providers and consumers.

We observe that one of the primary uses of coUML is visualizing and documenting instructional designs for communication among involved actors, as well as for implementation and archiving. For instance, one useful communication aspect of these models would be that each relevant item or entity is *represented*, receives an explicit *name*, and is usually put into *relation* with other entities. Note that, as the course design can be modeled at different levels of detail and abstraction, it can also be used to model instructional design patterns.

Learning Goals

The goal model of the course as depicted in Figure 11 was derived straightforwardly from the verbal description provided in the case study. The only aspect worth being mentioned is the goal hierarchy of learning goal 4, i.e. "Application of specific design techniques." The verbal description does

not explicitly define the relationship between this goal and its sub-goals (a, b, c, and d). We assume that an *aggregation* of these goals is the most appropriate conceptual representation, meaning that goal 4 is an "abstract" goal, which can be fully achieved only through achieving each one of its sub-goals.

It is important to realize that the coUML goal models are not intended to align a course's learning goals on any standard scale or taxonomy. For instance, coUML does not require adding the information whether a goal is located on the cognitive or personal level, even though this would be possible. The main purpose is "getting a handle" on learning goals that would otherwise be hidden in various text paragraphs. That is, we want to visualize, and, if needed, prioritize the learning goals.

Figure 11. Model of the course's learning goals

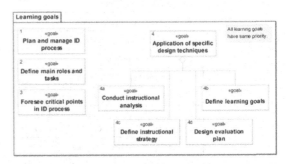

Table 3. Learning goal descriptions

ID	Description
1	Plan and manage an instructional design process in their professional environment
2	Define the main roles and task involved in instructional design
3	Foresee the critical points in instructional design projects
4	Given a design task, effectively apply specific design techniques
4a	Conducting a complete instructional analysis
4b	Properly define learning goals
4c	Define an instructional strategy
4d	Design a sound evaluation plan

Note that two of the features of coUML goal modeling are not fully in use here:

1. The verbal definitions make no statement on learning goal priorities. Thus, the "learning goals" package is simply attached with a note carrying the information stating that "all learning goals have same priority."
2. coUML would suggest—in addition to the goal model—a tabular overview with more detailed information on each of the learning goals. However, there is no further detailed information available regarding any of the learning goals in the verbal description. Nonetheless, for demonstration purposes we do provide this information in Table 3; note that the goal number in the leftmost column refers to the number indicated in the verbal description and in the goals model for each goal, respectively.

Table 4. Course document list

ID	Name	Type	Provider	Deadline
1	Three case studies of basic concepts	Slides	Instructor	Session 1
2	ADDIE model	Slides	Instructor	Session 1
3	Project assignments (4)	Text	Instructor	Session 1
4	Project guidelines	Text	Instructor	Session 1
5	Instructional analysis	Text	Instructor	Session 2
6	Case-study presentation	Flash	Instructor	Session 2
7	Instructional analysis plans	Text	Groups	Session 2, Friday 5pm
8	Group feedback on #7	Text	Instructor	Session 2, Monday
9	General feedback on #7	Text	Instructor	Session 2, Monday
10	Idea of learning goals (for reading)	Text	Instructor	Session 3
11	Learning goal classification by Anderson & Krathwohl (for reading)	Text	Instructor	Session 3
12	Case-study learning goals	Flash	Instructor	Session 3
13	Definition and classification of four main learning goals	Text	Groups	Session 3, Friday 5pm
14	Group feedback on #13	Text	Instructor	Session 3, Monday
15	General feedback on #13	Text	Instructor	Session 3, Monday
16	Merrill's paper on 5-stars instruction	Paper	Instructor	Session 4
17	Five case studies on instructional strategies	Flash	Instructor	Session 4
18	Instructional strategy	Text	Groups	Session 4, Friday 5pm
19	Group feedback on #18	Text	Instructor	Session 4, Monday
20	General feedback on #18	Text	Instructor	Session 4, Monday
21	Project presentations	Slides	Groups	Session 5
22	Key issues in evaluation	Slides	Instructor	Session 5
23	Evaluation plan	Text	Groups	Session 5
24	Quality assessment survey	Paper	Instructor	Session 5
25	Course report	Report	Instructor	(End)

Figure 12. Course document model

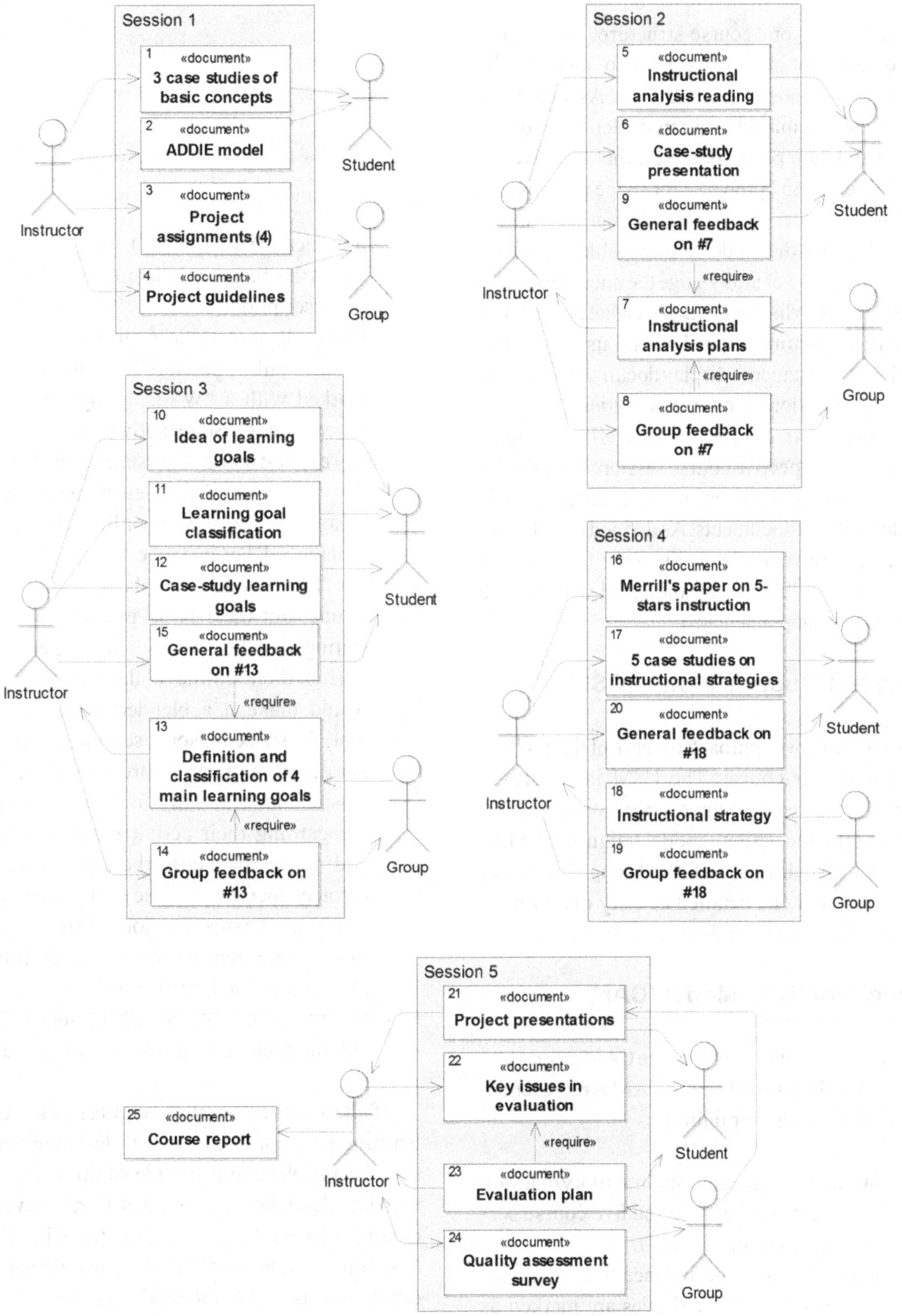

Documents

From the part on "course structure" in the case study description we are able to identify the documents modeled in Figure 12. As suggested by coUML, Table 4 lists in more detail the documents and their properties. Note that we leave out the "description" property for space reasons and because the document names appear descriptive enough. With the model and the table it is easily possible to answer at any stage the question, "Who must provide which document at what time?" Any identified document can later be used in other models, for instance to display document provision and consumption by course activities.

Grouping is used to arrange all documents used in the respective course session. This should make the diagram easier to read, even though it is loaded with 25 documents. As defined by coUML, the roles are represented by actor figures, and the document "flows" are indicated with dashed arrows (i.e., dependencies).

Course Structure Model (CSM)

In this section we approach the core of the coUML models of our course. The CSM in Figure 13 shows that the whole course model consists of one main aggregate activity model (aligning the five sessions; visually emphasized through light-grey fill color), and one detailed activity diagram for *each* of the sessions 1-5.

Course Activity Model (CAM)

From the CSM it is clear that the CAM comprises six models. In this section the CAM is represented by the following four figures:

- Figure 14 presents the main activity diagram of the course, aligning the five course sessions in consecutive order.
- Figure 15 shows the first face-to-face session of the course. All activities are marked as

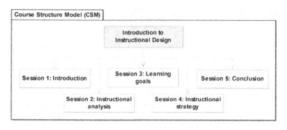

Figure 13. The course structure model (CSM)

presence activities ("P"). Table 5 complements the diagram with more detailed activity descriptions.

- Figure 16 and Table 6 present session 2, the first online session. Most activities are marked with a "W" standing for a Web-based activity. Some activities do not carry any explicit mode of presence, which means that it is not completely determined by which means (face-to-face or online) the activity is achieved. For instance, the groups can do the "Develop analysis plans" activity fully online, but there is no explicit constraint stating that they cannot meet personally during their online collaboration (which would make it a blended activity). Note that, for space reasons, session 3 and 4 are not depicted in any figure. However, these sessions are basically identical to session 2 regarding their activities, arrangement, and objectives—only the actual outcome (project document) of the group work is different, i.e. the specification of learning goals in session 3 and the instructional strategy plan in session 4, respectively.
- Figure 17 and Table 7 finally present the concluding face-to-face session of the course.

If the course planning requires connecting learning goals or documents to learning activities, the modeler could provide additional models which include these aspects at arbitrary levels of detail. For example, each single activity in a CAM diagram could be detailed in a separate activity diagram. It is within the modelers' responsibili-

Figure 14. Main activity diagram of the course activity model (CAM)

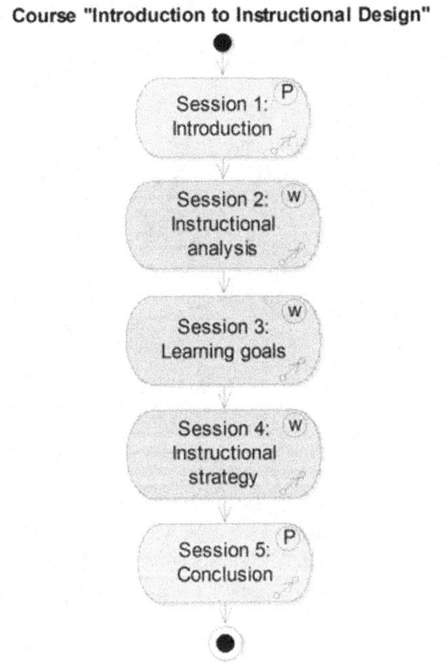

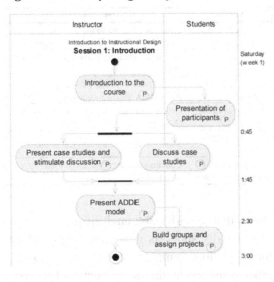

Figure 15. Activity diagram of session 1

Table 5. Activity descriptions for session 1

Activity	Description
Introduction to the course	Introduction to learning goals, schedule, evaluation (45 minutes, including presentation of participants)
Presentation of participants	The participants introduce themselves to each other.
Present case studies and stimulate discussion	Discussion of some basic concepts, such as "instruction," "training," "education," and "design." The instructor does this by presenting three case studies through slides and stimulating the discussion among the participants. (1 hour)
Discuss case studies	Students are stimulated to participate in the discussion.
Present ADDIE model	Introduction of the main phases of the ADDIE model (with slides, 45 minutes)
Build groups and assign projects	Division into four groups of four people each, assignment of a project to each group (30 minutes) There is a one-page project assignment for each group, plus some general written project guidelines.

Figure 16. Activity diagram of session 2

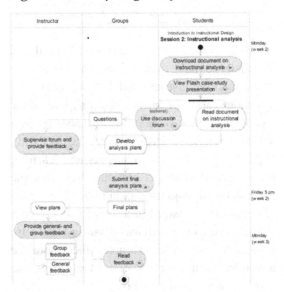

Table 6. Activity descriptions for session 2

Activity	Description
Download document on instructional analysis	For this session, the students connect to the LMS, and download a reading that introduces the main elements to be considered in an instructional analysis.
View Flash case study presentation	Participants view a Flash presentation of a case study.
Read document on instructional analysis	–
Use discussion forum	If participants have questions regarding the reading, they can post them to a discussion forum. After completing the readings, the participants can work in their group forum (supervised by the instructor).
Develop analysis plans	Their goal is developing a sound instructional analysis plan.
Supervise forum and provide feedback	The instructor supervises the discussion forum and provides feedback during the project work.
Submit final analysis plans	Submission: On Friday at 5:00 PM, all groups should submit a document presenting their instructional analysis plan
View plans	By Monday, the instructor reviews the plans and provides both group-specific feedback and general feedback (valid for all groups).
Provide general and group feedback	
Read feedback	Students and groups may read the feedback provided by the instructor

ties to keep the diagrams at levels of detail and simplicity to make them useful to and usable by partners in the instructional design process. As a demonstration of further detail supported by coUML, we pick session 2 to be modeled in a separate activity diagram (Figure 18) including explicit links to more documents and learning goals defined in earlier sections. Note that the more detailed diagram should rather be seen as a complement, instead of a replacement, of the model of session 2 with less detail in Figure 16. This makes sense, for example, when there are misunderstandings or lack of clarity among people involved with the design task.

Figure 18 shows a part of the activity diagram of session 2, with additional documents modeled as input to the first two online activities. It also

Figure 17. Activity diagram of session 5

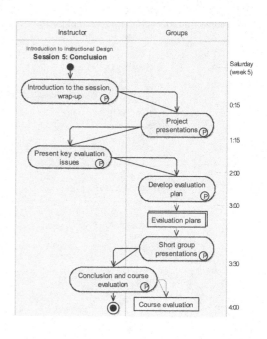

Table 7. Activity descriptions for session 5

Activity	Description
Introduction to the session, wrap-up	Short introduction to the session, and wrap-up of the work so far (15 minutes)
Project presentations	Group presentation of each project's work (1 hour)
Present key evaluation issues	Presentation of the key issues in evaluation (with slides, 45 minutes)
Develop evaluation plan	Group work: develop an evaluation plan (1 hour)
Short group presentations	Short group presentations (30 minutes)
Conclusion and course evaluation	Conclusion and course evaluation (30 minutes)

shows that the "Develop analysis plan" activity substantially supports goals number 3 and 4a; these are foreseeing critical points in the ID process and conducting an instructional analysis, respectively. If required, similar refinements could be achieved in other activity diagrams as well.

As a final note, we see that it costs a substantial amount of time and consideration to create the course models and to describe all relevant course details. However, this additional effort produces

Figure 18. More detailed activity model of parts of session 2

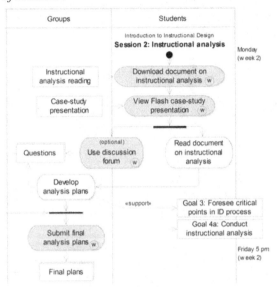

a number of potential benefits, which are related to the fact that all relevant course aspects—such as learning goals, documents used and created, roles involved, structure and activities of the course—are *explicitly* available in a *standard* notation system, and complemented by verbal descriptions. Probably the main benefit is that coUML makes explicit what would otherwise be only implicitly available in the designers' and instructors' minds.

poEML

As a modeling language poEML is mainly intended to produce computable models of educational units. Nevertheless, its visual notation may be useful for ID. The modeling of this case study using some of the main poEML perspectives tries to demonstrate this second capability. In particular, the example includes the specification of the following models: structural, goal, participant, order and temporal.

The Structural Model

poEML structural model is concerned with the organization of the elements involved in the educational unit model. This organization is based on the ES element. Each ES may be composed by a set of goals, roles, environments, order specifications, temporal specifications and other ESs. If an ES does not contain any role or environment it uses the roles and environments specified in its parent ES. Some elements may include an indicator of the number of instances to create during runtime. This feature is indicated through a number or expression included within parenthetical marks.

Figure 19 shows the structural representation of this model in the tree-view form. The main ES includes one goal and three roles (it is required that the student role is performed by more than 14 people). Then, it includes six ESs: one for each of the five sessions and an additional one for the *Tutor* activities. Regarding the rest of the model, it is worthy to notice that the number of instances of some elements depends on the number of instances of other elements. For example, the number of instances of the *Reading* ES in session 2 has to be the same that the number of instances of *Student* role.

The Goal Model

We have identified high-level goals for each session and sub-goals for each activity. In some cases, these sub-goals are further composed by new sub-goals. In addition, some goals have input (I) and output (O) parameters that represent the artifacts that are provided to perform the goal and the artifacts produced in the goal performance, respectively. The value taken by these artifacts and the transfer of value among artifacts have to be expressed in the data model. The goal model of this case study is made up by goals aggregations exclusively. Therefore the graphical representation is not depicted, but Table 8 gathers the description and parameters of the identified goals.

Figure 19. Visual representation of the structural model

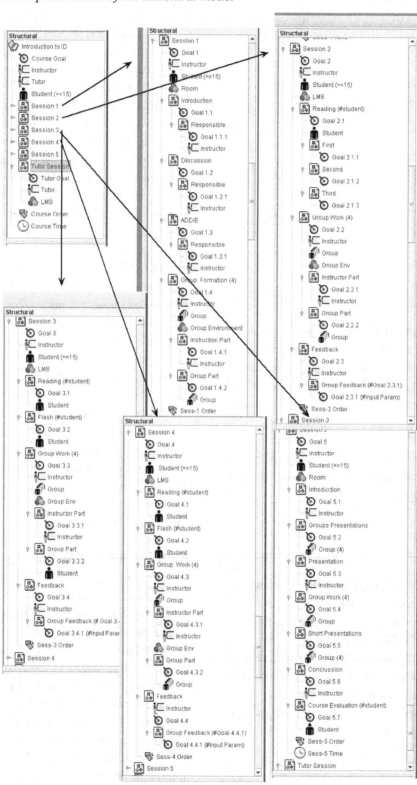

The Participant Model

The participant perspective enables us to specify detailed information about the roles required in each ES and the transfer of participants between roles at different ESs. Figure 20 shows a part of the case study participant model demonstrating both capabilities. In relation with the first capability, the model indicates the number of instances required for the Student role and the members of the Group role. In relation with the second capability, the example shows how the roles from the *Course* ES are transferred to the roles of the *Session 1* and *Session 2* sub-ESs, and from them to roles of further sub-ESs. Specifically, the participants of the *Student* role in ES *Session 1* must be assigned

to the *Group* members in the *Group Formation* ES following a FIFO *Election* mechanism (namely: the participants are assigned in the order in which they were enrolled in the course). Similarly, the participants of the *Student* role in ES *Session 2* must be assigned to the *Group* members in ES *Group Work*. In addition, the *Relation* connector of type "Composed Equality" is introduced to indicate that the members of each group have to be the same participants.

The Order Model

Each ES can include order specifications to indicate the order in which its sub-ESs have to be performed. In this case study the main ESs

Table 8. Goals description from the goals mode

Goal name	Goal description	Parameters
Course Goal	**To perform the course "Introduction to Instructional Design"**	
Goal 1	To perform the Introduction to the course	
Goal 1.1	To introduce the course and the participants involved	
Goal 1.1.1	To introduce the course, to ask the participants to introduce themselves.	
Goal 1.2	To discuss some basic concepts such as "instruction," "training," etc.	
Goal 1.2.1	To introduce the three case studies through slides, to stimulate the discussion among the participants.	I: Slides
Goal 1.3	To view the main phases of the ADDIE model	
Goal 1.3.1	To introduce the main phases of the ADDIE model	I: Slides
Goal 1.4	To view project assignment and guidelines, there are four instances of this goal, each one with a different project.	I: Project + guidelines
Goal 1.4.1	To support the group work	
Goal 1.4.2	To read the project assignment and analyze it	
Goal 2	To get an appropriate knowledge about Instructional Analysis	
Goal 2.1	To get some foundations about Instructional Analysis	
Goal 2.1.1	To connect to the LMS, download a reading and read it	
Goal 2.1.2	To view a flash presentation of a case study	I: Flash
Goal 2.1.3	To post your questions and concerns to the discussion forum	
Goal 2.2	To develop a sound instructional analysis plan for project	
Goal 2.2.1	To supervise the group activities providing feedback	
Goal 2.2.2	To work in the group forum trying to develop the instructional analysis plan	O: Plan
Goal 2.3	To review the plans and provide global feedback	O: Feedback
Goal 2.3.1	To review the plan of a group and provide feedback	I: Plan; O: Feedback

Continued on following page

Table 8. continued

Goal 3	To get a basic knowledge about learning goals	
Goal 3.1	To connect to the LMS, to download the two readings and to read them	
Goal 3.2	To view the Flash presentation	I: Flash
Goal 3.3	To work in the project group defining the four main learning goals for the project and classifying them on Anderson & Krathwohl's table	
Goal 3.3.1	To supervise the group activities in the group forum providing feedback	
Goal 3.3.2	To work in the group forum trying to attain the group task	O: report
Goal 3.4	To review the plans and provide global feedback	O: Feedback
Goal 3.4.1	To review the plan of a group and provide feedback	I: Report; O: Feedback
Goal 4	To get a basic knowledge about instructional strategy	
Goal 4.1	To connect to the LMS, to download Merrill's paper about 5-stars instruction	
Goal 4.2	To view the flash presentation about five case studies showing different instructional strategies	I: Flash
Goal 4.3	To work in the project group developing an instructional strategy	
Goal 4.3.1	To supervise the group activities in the group forum providing feedback	
Goal 4.3.2	To work in the group forum trying to attain the group task	O: Strategy
Goal 4.4	To review the plans and provide global feedback	O: Feedback
Goal 4.4.1	To review the plan of a group and provide feedback	I: Strategy; O: Feedback
Goal 5	To conclude the course	
Goal 5.1	To introduce the session	
Goal 5.2	To present each project's group	
Goal 5.3	To present the key issues in evaluation	
Goal 5.4	To develop an evaluation plan	O: Plan
Goal 5.5.	To present the group plans	
Goal 5.6	To close the course	
Goal 5.7	To fill in the course evaluation	I: Evaluation O: Data
Tutor Goal	To upload materials online and to monitor discussions	

(Sessions 1 to 5) do not require an order specification as they require the specification of temporal constraints. Nevertheless, each of the five sessions do require the modeling of order specifications: Figure 21 shows the order specifications of the ESs corresponding to sessions 1 to 3:

- **Session 1** follows a sequential ordering of sub-ESs. The particular case is the *Group Formation* ES that requires the creation of four instances. The split and merge operators are used to indicate these four instances can be performed in parallel.

- **Session 2** includes two sub-ESs with multiple instances. The *Reading* ES produces as many instances as the number of *Students* and the *Group Work* requires creating four instances. This order specification begins with a split operator to allow the performance of the *Reading* instances in parallel. The Sub-ESs contained in the *Reading* ES have to be performed in sequence as is specified in the corresponding order specification. Next, the *Session 2* order specification contains a merge operator and a split operator

Figure 20. Visual representation of some parts of the participant model

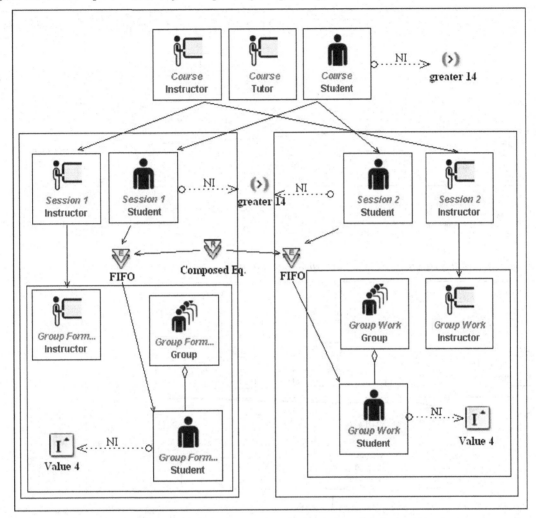

to allow the four *Group Work* instances to be performed in parallel. In this way each *Student* can begin the *Group Work* as soon as she ends the *Reading* is finished. Finally, there is the *Feedback* ES. This ES contains a sub-ES involving four instances to be performed in parallel. The *synchronization* operator forces all the instances to be finished before continuing.

• **Session 3** order specification shows how the two first Sub-ESs require the creation of several instances. They are connected using a *sequence* operator to indicate that each pair of instances assigned to the same

Student is performed in parallel with the other ones.

The Temporal Model

Each ES can include temporal specifications to indicate when to initiate and finish each one of its sub-ESs. In the case study it is considered that the course begins on Saturday February 25th and ends on March 19th. *Sessions* 2, 3 and 4 take from Monday to Sunday, because their last ES is the *Feedback* that has to be performed by Monday. Figure 22 shows the temporal models included in the *Course*, *Session 1* and *Session 2* ESs. All the

Figure 21. Visual representation of some parts of the order model

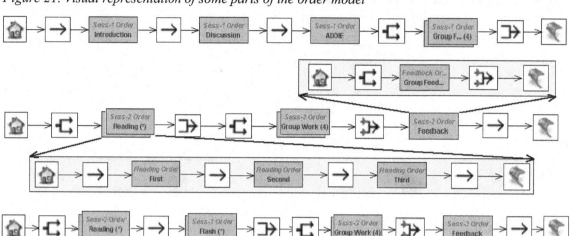

Figure 22. Visual representation of some parts of the temporal model

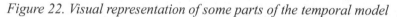

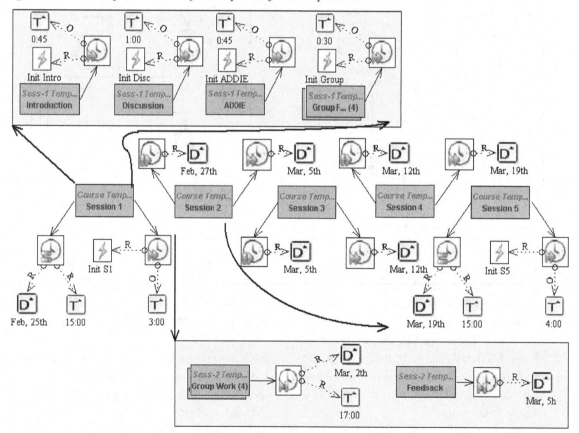

temporal operators are used in the example. The duration of ESs is controlled by considering an offset (O) in relation to the init of the ES. Such init is signaled by an appropriate event taken from the *event-based* aspect.

IMS LEARNING DESIGN

IMS learning design is designed to model learning flows. Although it is mainly focused on online learning, blended and face-to-face learning can also be modeled. In the proposed case study "Introduction to Instructional Design" there are two face-to-face parts (1 and 5) and three online parts (2, 3 and 4). Sessions 1 and 5 need to be modeled in the general learning flow. We suggest to incorporate a summary and a briefing of every face-to-face session to the general flow, in order to keep a centralized backup of every activity. If this connection is not done, the essence of blended-learning will be gone and we will have two isolated types of learning, instead of the so looked blended approach, with an actual learning flow between both. Then, we have two types of activities.

Figure 23. Definition of the activity tree

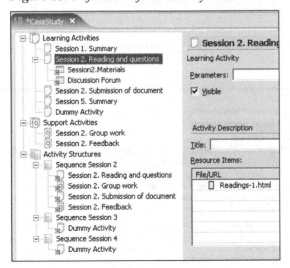

Modeling

Further on we describe the authoring process with a stress on the key modeling issues. Due to the length paper constraints, and since this book is focused on visual editing tools, and not in players, we only provide some specific basic coding and a few related screenshots on this authoring process. We have used Reload LD Editor and XML Spy for the development of IMS-LD Levels A and B. First, we define every single Learning-Activity, Support-Activity and Activity-Structure

Activity Type 1: Face-to-Face Task

What happens outside of the online system is not modeled with IMS-LD. However, it could and should be reported to keep a common track and a consistent learning experience.

To make such a reporting action we can use either of two elements:

1. **Properties set up with global elements:** IMS-LD Level B provides properties and global elements, among other elements. Properties are taken as variables to store values. There are several types of properties: local, global, personal and role. A variable must be defined and initialized. For instance, the property Report-1 type-string is defined and initialized to the value "Write your summary report." (See Figure 24)

   In a second step, this property can be set and viewed using global elements from an external XML file linked to the imsmanifest. xml file:

```
<set-property ref= "Report-1" property-of= "sup-
ported-person"/>
```

```
<view-property ref= "Report-1" property-of=
"supported-person"/>
```

2. **Type-file property to upload a file:** In a similar way, a type-file property can be defined, allowing for a later upload of an external document

```
<global-property identifier= "Report-1">
    <title>Feedback from first session</title>
    <datatype datatype= "file"/>
</global-property>
```

Activity Type 2: Collaborative Online Work

Sessions 2, 3 and 4 follow the same pattern:

1. Reading, with two actions: reading a paper and feeding a discussion forum. There is a role per group of four participants and a service (conference). As there are four groups, there are four roles, so far. The forum has to be connected from the Environment in a Support-Activity or it can directly linked from the Activity-Description of a Support-Activity (see

point 4 further on). Readings can be stored in an environment. (See Figure 25)

2. **Group work in a forum with supervision of an instructor:** We find a second role (Instructor) and a collaborative service (the same forum)

```
<imsld:roles>
    <imsld:staff identifier= "Instructor">
        <imsld:title>Instructor</imsld:title>
    </imsld:staff>
</imsld:roles>
```

3. **Submission of a common document out of the group work:** Someone from the group, maybe the instructor himself, uploads a document to a type-file role-property. This means that every group has their own property

```
<role-property identifier= "Document-1">
    <title>Document from session 2</title>
    <datatype datatype= "file"/>
</role-property>
```

Figure 24. Definition of properties

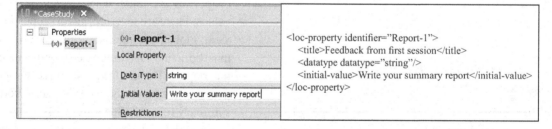

Figure 25. Definition of roles

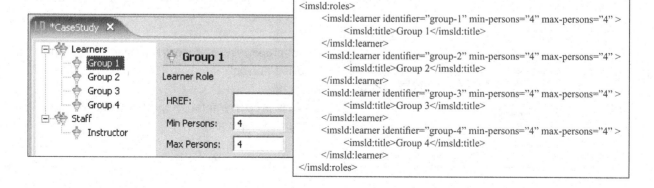

Figure 26. Definition of the conference service

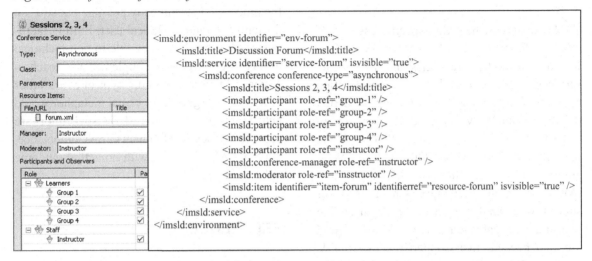

4. **Feedback:** The instructor provides back two types of feedback: group-based and general. We find two different properties (role-property for the group, and global-property for everyone). This review can be done using a monitoring service in an Environment (like in the forum afore described) and-or the use of global elements in a Support-Activity. (See Figure 27)

Learning Flow: Integration of Activities

As it is stated currently, the learning flow is sequence-based and the integration of every ac-

tivity does not need more than a Level A use of the IMS-LD structures. In concrete, a nested set of Acts, Activity-Structures, Learning-Activities and Support-Activities is enough to model the course: every session is an Act, every task is a Learning-Activity or a Support-Activity, bundled around an Activity-Structure. However, we should pay attention to the relation between role-parts inside the same act, since the several activities are in parallel but not every role has always something to do. Furthermore, they have to be run in turn. This definition of the Method specifies who does what and when. (See Figure 28.)

Figure 27. Integration of the monitoring service in the support-activity

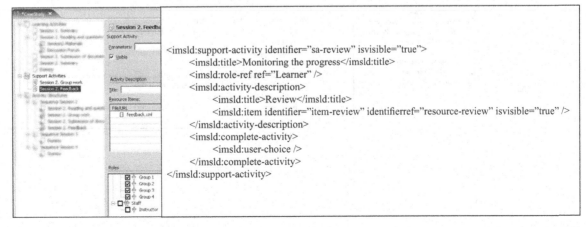

CONCLUSION

We have showed how this specific case study can be fully modeled with IMS-LD. IMS-LD is intended to model pedagogies and not specific services. Services are taken into consideration along the full learning flow although the actual delivery is made by any external provider. In order to model such a case an IMS-LD editing tool (Bolton, 2004; Miao, 2005; Van der Vegt, 2005) or a general purpose XML based tool (Altova, 2006) are needed (see Chapter XIII for some further analysis). In addition, an engine and a player capable to run the Unit of Learning are also needed, like CopperCore (Vogten & Martens, 2005), .LRN or Sled (OUUK, 2005). But tools need still a low level knowledge of the specification to come across with this type of

results, involving Level B elements. Therefore, the modeling is technically possible but still too difficult for a non-technical user. Editing facilities need to be more accesible to non-technical users in order to develop, implement and reach an easier and further use of this type of case studies in reality. A higher level visual metaphor would help. In this direction, some LD visual editors are currently under development (TENCompetence, 2005; UCM, 2006) but with no actual outcome to be used yet.

REFERENCES

Altova. (2006). *XML spy editor*. Retrieved Dec 18, 2006 from http://www.altova.com

Bolton. (2004). *Reload project*. Retrieved April 16, 2006, from www.reload.ac.uk

Figure 28. Definition of the method: Who does what and when

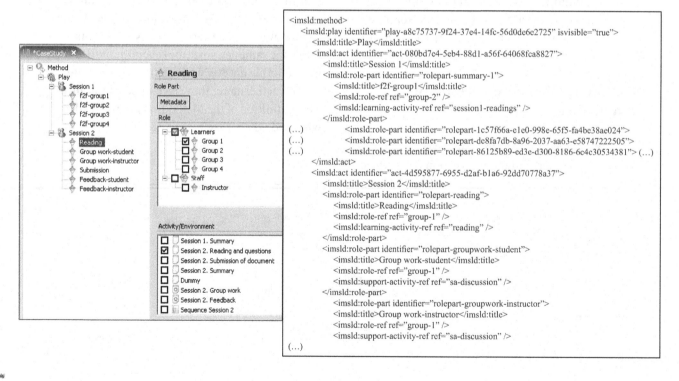

Miao, Y. (2005). *Cosmos LD Editor.*

OUUK. (2005). *Sled player.* Retrieved April 13, 2006, from http://sled.open.ac.uk

TENCompetence. (2005). *TENCompetence project.* Retrieved July 31, 2006, from www.tencompetence.org

UCM. (2006). *Complutense university. <e-Ucm> research group.* Retrieved December 18, 2006, from www.e-ucm.es

Van der Vegt, W. (2005). *CopperAuthor.* Retrieved April 13, 2006, from www.copperauthor.org

Vogten, H., & Martens, H. (2005). *CopperCore 3.0.* Retrieved April 13, 2006. from www.coppercore.org

ENDNOTE

[1] Regarding tool support, to create a course's coUML models, the only "tools" really required are pencil and paper. Electronic versions can be created with simple drawing tools or with any office application, as it makes use of basic drawing shapes only. There is currently no freely available editor for coUML models.

Section III
Research Studies

Chapter XVII
The Pervasiveness of Design Drawing in ID[1]

S. Todd Stubbs
Brigham Young University, USA

Andrew S. Gibbons
Brigham Young University, USA

ABSTRACT

This chapter is a survey of the literature of ID to look at the breadth and usage of design drawings in this discipline to better understand the emerging use of VIDLs to improve designs. To conduct this research, we sampled several ID textbooks, ID journals, software, and case studies looking for examples of design drawing. Design drawings found were then categorized using Gibbons' (2003) seven ID layers as a taxonomy to understand the drawings' purposes. We did not find the same pervasiveness or level of self-awareness as found in other design fields. Examples of design drawings were found, but were somewhat rare. Furthermore, we discovered that those examples we found tended to document only two of Gibbons' seven layers, indicating narrow application. We believe this gap represents a serious shortcoming in ID, indicating a lack of tradition, skill, and standards for visual representations of design except in limited ways. At present, design drawing is a rare but growing phenomenon in ID, which, when fully understood and implemented, can only benefit the practice of ID.

INTRODUCTION

This chapter applies a layered concept of instructional design (ID) architecture described by Gibbons and Rogers (in press) to a taxonomy of design drawings described by Stubbs (2006) to produce a refined category system for describing the use of drawing and sketching in ID. The value of doing so is dramatized by Stubbs, who compares the use of design drawing in ID to its use in other design fields, detecting a large disparity. If Stubbs' analysis is correct, then designers in other fields have a much richer tradition of the use of drawing in design and a literature that shows a much higher level of self-awareness in the use of drawings during design than most instructional designers would expect.

Design drawing might be considered the primitive of visual instructional design languages (VIDLs). In this chapter we hope to understand where we are with this basic form of VIDL to better understand where we are going.

Though instructional designers excel in the use of drawings of many kinds in their *produced* designs, it would appear that they lag behind other design fields in exploiting the value of drawings and sketches while *designing*.

This deficit has important consequences for the economics, quality, and quantity of instructional designs. Whereas other design fields have begun to capitalize on the power of computers as a design tool, instructional designers seem to be more at the mercy of the tools and design interfaces created for use by others who have more vibrant economies, such as Web and software design. Early attempts to create tools to express designs in the instructional designer's vernaculars appear to have been swallowed up in the success of other design fields, notably the Web and Web development tools (Fairweather & Gibbons, 2000). Only recently has interest in the authoring of learning objects revitalized interest in design interfaces that emphasize ID structures, a trend that we hope will persist and broaden.

The value of the computer to design lies in its ability to take part in routine and mundane decision-making. Successes in computer-aided design have come largely from the ability to describe a design problem (or some portion of a design problem) in terms that can be translated into computer languages. For instance, the design of an architectural column can be translated into sub-problems for the design of the capital, the shaft, and the column base (Mitchell, 1990). If only the shaft sub-problem could be expressed in computer terms, then that portion of the design could be given computer support, and the remaining sub-problems would depend entirely on human decision-making. By the same reasoning, if only portions (sub-problems of sub-problems) of the design of each of the capital, shaft, and column base could be expressed in such terms, then the design of each of these would require human effort and decision-making, supplemented by some degree of computer assistance. This is the principle today of popular development systems for Web and software design. The involvement of the computer—which is capable of making numerous routine decisions very rapidly and dealing with representation issues at the same time—creates an economic lever. More quantity at higher quality can be produced more rapidly—cheaper, better, faster. And as languages for problem description and solution improve and become more nuanced, the quality and sophistication of the designs improves. This is exactly what has happened to the design of computer chips over the past thirty-five years. Chips designs today are created to human specifications with human decision-making concentrating mainly on high-level design issues. As a result the economics of computer chip design have changed so that a return to hand-drawn circuit design would be an expensive luxury.

This chapter addresses how ID problems can be described in terms of design languages (some portion of which may be translatable into computer languages). It begins by describing research by Stubbs (2006) on the use of design drawing by instructional designers. Stubbs conducted a review of ID literature, and categorized the drawings he found there according to the layers described by Gibbons and Rogers. Stubbs discovered the disparity we have already mentioned between the level of interest in design drawing in ID and other fields of of design (see chapter III). He found that, though in the field of design studies there is strong interest in design drawing, there is not a corresponding interest and self-awareness of the use of drawing in the literature of ID.

According to Stubbs:

The general design studies literature has both theoretical and empirical studies on the subject of design drawing. In this literature, design drawing is considered an important, even vital part of design thinking. It is thought of as a design language, which comes in a variety of distinguishable forms, and accompanies and contributes to the design process as it progresses through various stages of development. Studies in this literature show how the intentional ambiguity of design drawing provides space to the designer for creativity and innovation, invoking a kind of dialogue between the designer and the design, which is deemed essential to the design process.... By contrast, the literature of ID has nothing like this level of consideration for design drawing. Instead, the few available articles in the literature of ID touching on design drawing are about proposed notation systems. Evidence of design drawing in the practice of ID as seen in the literature finds that, when it does appear, it is most often concentrated in two aspects of ID identified with Gibbons' content and strategy layers.... To say that there were no examples of design drawing in ID would be hyperbole. However, considering how little was found and how narrowly focused it was, it prompts the question, "What might ID be missing by its lack of attention to this language, so valued in other fields of design?"(p. 85–86. See also chapter III).

Stubbs notes McKim's (1980) observation "that designers with versatility and skill in graphic languages have an advantage, which may apply to instructional designers as well" (p. 134). McKim postulates that "not only [will designers]...find more complete expression for their thinking but also [they will be able to] re-center their thinking by moving from one graphic language to another" (p. 134). On this basis, Stubbs proposes that design drawing in ID "deserves a thorough examination" and presents the typology of design drawings, described below, that distinguishes six types of drawing that commonly appear in the literature of the field. Only one of these six types is considered design drawing.

Next, the chapter uses the layered ID architecture proposed by Gibbons and Rogers (in press) to categorize design drawings by function. This architecture draws on concepts from many design fields, showing that designs in those fields have a layered architecture that decomposes design problems in functional terms. Baldwin and Clark (2000) describe how this principle of decomposition lies at the economic center of the modern computer industry, making possible design modularity. Gibbons and Rogers demonstrate that layering applies to instructional designs as well, with the benefit that the problem thus described can be solved in terms of existing design languages, most of which are derived from instructional theory or proven design practice.

EVIDENCES OF DESIGN DRAWING IN ID

The experience of many instructional designers strongly suggests that design drawing is a part of ID. However, this chapter will show that ID does not appear to have the same tradition for design drawing, especially during the early phases of design, as is found in other design fields. For this review, evidence of design drawing in ID was sought in several sources: a sampling of ID textbooks, journals, software, and case studies were examined. The ID literature for research about design drawing in ID was also searched. With some notable exceptions, very little was found.

To facilitate the study of design graphics, a typology was created to identify the types of graphics found in ID literature. This section describes this typology as a means to categorize graphics of interest to this study. Gibbons' instructional design layers are then used to provide further sub-categorization of one of the types of graphics found in the literature.

A Typology of Images

A variety of types of illustrations can be found in the literature of ID. Some are design graphics, but many are not. This typology of images has been devised to aid in distinguishing those that are from those that are not. A sampling of the literature of ID was scanned for graphics, and then those graphics found were categorized into one of five types based on their apparent intent:

1. **Design graphics:** Design graphics illustrate some aspect of the design of a specific piece of instruction for the purpose of planning or building that instruction.
2. **Content graphics:** Content graphics are part of the instruction delivered to learners that aid or support learning.
3. **Reporting graphics:** These graphics are used to illustrate or report the outcomes of research.
4. **Illustrations of ID models:** Graphics of this sort are illustrations that represent processes of design or construction of instruction. Diagrams of the popular ADDIE or ISD processes fall into this category.
5. **Instructional models & learning models:** These graphics include illustrations of the components of instructional theories or learning theories and the relationships among them. They are sometimes not differentiated from ID models (type 4).

The principal difference among these types is intent; the surface form may not be the discriminator. For example, it is possible to imagine a graphic, whose intent is unclear without the accompanying explanation. The mere existence of a diagram with circles and boxes connected with lines would not be enough to determine a graphic's purpose.

Let's examine each of these different types of graphics found in the research literature.

Figure 1 is an example of a type 1 graphic. It is clearly related to some specific piece of instruction, charting the flow of procedures for training a specific piece of content. It may have been created to help a programmer or developer understand what was supposed to happen in this instruction.

Notice the specific content in the graphic in Figure 1. Type 1 graphics have information, either in the diagram or in the accompanying context, that ties them directly and clearly to the design of a specific piece of instruction. They may refer to specific content, as does Figure 1. They illustrate the structural elements, flow, process, information chunking, or some other aspect of the specific instructional design. To determine if a graphic is of type 1, ask, "Was this graphic representation created to assist in the creation of specific instruction?"

Type 2 illustrations are distinguished from type 1 by being part of the content of the instruction, rather than part of the design. That is, they are presented to the learner. Figure 2 was part of the content of experimental instruction trying to determine the difference in value between using mimetic icons versus standard square icons in a content graphic.

Computer screen shots of finished computer assisted instruction (CAI) are common illustrations in the sources reviewed. These screen shots should be considered type 2. To decide if something is type 2, ask, "Was this graphic representation part of what was presented to learners during instruction?"

Figure 1. An example of a type 1 graphic from ETR&D (Kalyuga & Sweller, 2005) (Copyright © 2005, The Association for Educational Communications and Technology [AECT]. Used with permission.)

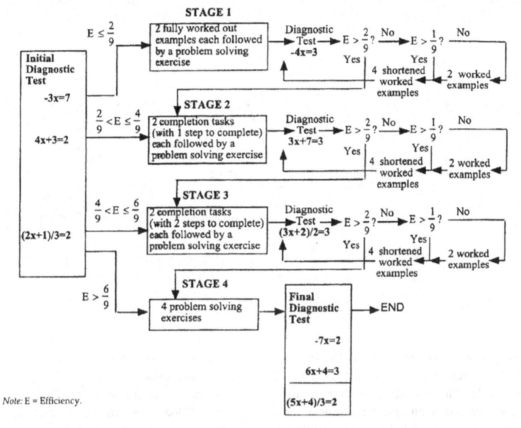

Figure 2. An example of two type 2 graphics from ETR&D (Griffin & Robinson, 2005) (Copyright © 2005, The Association for Educational Communications and Technology [AECT]. Used with permission.)

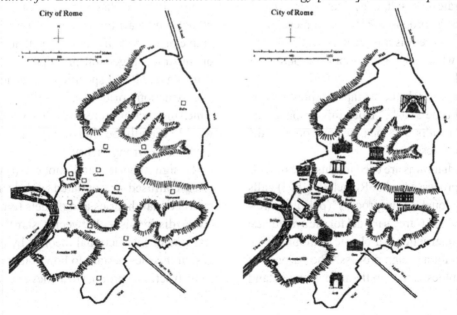

Figure 3. An example of a type 3 graphic from ETR&D (Liu & Bera, 2005) (Copyright © 2005, The Association for Educational Communications and Technology [AECT] Used with permission.)

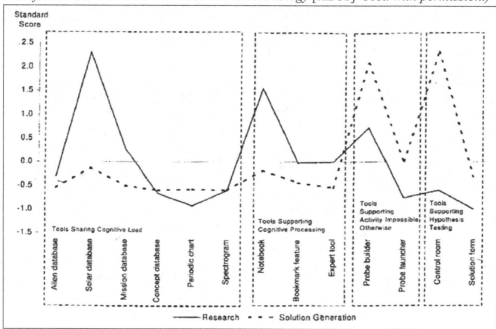

Type 3 graphics are used to illustrate the outcomes of research. They are often employed to help make statistical results more transparent to the reader. Bar graphs, pie charts, line graphs, etc., are common, though they are not limited to these. They are distinguished from type 1 because they illustrate the results of evaluation or research rather than the proposed design of a piece of instruction. Figure 3 is a typical example of type 3 graphic which supports a report on outcomes of research.

To determine whether a graphic representation belongs to type 3, ask, "Does this graphic help report the results data or other outcome of the evaluation or research?"

Type 4 diagrams are used to illustrate models of design processes, what Reigeluth (1993) calls an "instructional-design process" (p. 13). Figure 4 shows Dick and Carey's model for the systematic design of instruction—a classic example of an illustration for a design process. The purpose of type 4 graphics is to help the reader understand a design process model, i.e., how to design or create instruction.

To clarify whether a diagram belongs to type 4, ask, "Does this graphic illustrate a design process or theory about how instruction ought to be designed?"

Finally, type 5 diagrams illustrate instructional models and learning models. Figure 5 is an example of a type 5 diagram. Note that it describes or illustrates a general principle of teaching or learning and is not specific to a particular piece of instruction nor does it describe a process by which instruction is created. This type of diagram would normally be illustrating an instructional theory or learning theory.

Design theories and models (type 4) are often confused or conflated with learning and instructional theories and models (type 5). May (2006) distinguishes between design theories and learning or instructional theories by noting that design theories pertain to how someone designs an instructional product to achieve certain objec-

Figure 4. From Dick, Carey, and Carey, The systematic design of education, 5ᵗʰ ed. (Published by Allyn and Bacon, Boston, MA. Copyright 1985 by Pearson Education. Reprinted by permission of the publisher.)

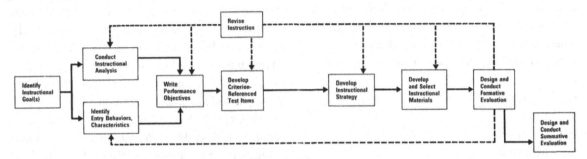

Figure 5. An example of a type 5 graphic from ETR&D (Copyright © 2005, The Association for Educational Communications and Technology [AECT] Used with permission.)

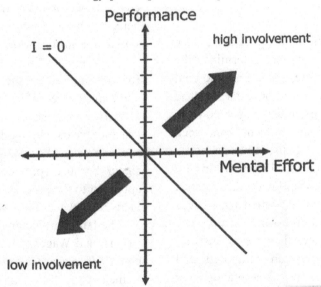

tives, whereas learning theories pertain to how someone receives, processes, and remembers information. Though similar in some respects to type 4, design process model diagrams, type 5 diagrams can be distinguished from the others by asking, "Does this graphic illustrate a theory of learning or a theory of instruction?"

While this typology covers the majority of illustrations one might expect in research about instructional design, other kinds of images occasionally occur. For example, a photograph of the principal of a school where an intervention took place, is probably not easily placed into any of the types proposed.

Extending the Typology of Type 1 Design Graphics with ID Layers

Once graphics have been established as type 1, design graphics, is possible to extend the typology to identify and distinguish them from each other. This sub-level of categorization provides the ability to see how widely design drawings are used throughout the design process.

This sub-categorization is accomplished by adapting a concept put forth by Gibbons (2003) called instructional design layers. Gibbons has observed that instructional design often takes place as the design of several interrelated layers. Design of each layer can be considered separately from the other layers, providing an important modularization to the design effort. The design of each layer is expressed in design languages, and these languages define the scope of designers' thinking. Gibbons' instructional design layers are:

- Content
- Strategy
- Control
- Message
- Representation
- Media-logic
- Data management

At the content layer, the designer defines the units of content segmentation, determines the method of content capture, and defines the kind of content elements that will be gathered. The design problem in the strategy layer consists of several interrelated sub-problems concerned with structures of time, goals, sequence, activity, physical setting, and social relationships are decided. The design problem within the control layer is the means of communication of messages from the learner to the source of the learning. The message layer determines the types of instructional messages, how they are composed, and how they are generated. The representation layer is the selection of media types, the selection of media, its generation, and the rules governing its structure and display. The design problem within the media-logic layer involves the description of execution structures that enact the representation and interactions. The design problem at the data management layer is to plan the capture, storage, analysis, aggregation, interpretation, and reporting of data produced during instruction.

To determine the pervasiveness of design drawing in ID, this typology and its extension of type 1 graphics by ID layers has been applied to a number of sources to discover and analyze examples of design drawing in ID. These sources are discussed below.

ID LITERATURE SAMPLING

A sampling of common texts in the field of ID was searched for images. Images found were then filtered through the typology above to identify examples of design drawings, type 1, in the texts. The texts included in this review are common, well-known textbooks about instructional design. Included in this review are the following textbooks: *The Systematic Design of Instruction* (Dick & Carey, 1990), *Principles of Instructional Design* (Gagné, Briggs, & Wager, 1992), and the two volumes of *Classic Writings on Instructional Technology* (Ely & Plomp, 1996). An argument could be made to bring in other texts not included here, but these are an adequate representative sample for our purposes.

The original edition of Dick and Carey's book from the late 1970s is the source of the first "Dick and Carey model" of instructional design known to nearly every instructional design student of the last thirty years. This model is particularly helpful to inexperienced or beginning instructional designers because it provides a complete systematic approach to the process of instructional design. (This review uses the 1990 edition of the text.)

The familiar blue and violet book by Gagné, Briggs, and Wager (1992) can be found on the bookshelf of nearly every instructional designer trained in the 1990s. Its presence on the bookshelves of colleagues often means that it was purchased as a class textbook, but it was kept for its ongoing value as a reference. This textbook provides a rational basis for much of the practice in instructional design, based in cognitive psychology and information processing theory.

The two-volume set from Ely and Plomp (1996) is a collection of classic literature in the field of ID. As such, it has value for both its historical reach, and the breadth of coverage. These volumes of classic articles reveal some of the roots of the field of instructional technology in audio/visual production and distribution, about which many of the papers are concerned.

For the purpose of this review, three respected ID journals were also scanned for graphics. Graphics found were categorized by the types above to discover any type 1, design graphics. The journals surveyed included: *Educational Technology Research and Development* (ETR&D), *Interactive Learning Environments* (ILE) and the *Journal of Educational Technology Systems* (JETS). It was felt that this combination of journals gave a sufficiently broad cross section of the field to effectively represent graphic communication in ID research literature.

ETR&D is a bi-monthly research publication of the Association for Educational Communications and Technology (AECT). It contains sections on both research and development, as well as book reviews, international reviews, and research abstracts. AECT has a historical connection to schools and libraries (especially audio/visual departments) and has good relationships with the faculty and students from universities that have degrees in instructional technology. AECT is an international organization, but its roots are American, and the majority of its members are from the United States. Articles in ETR&D tend to reflect this orientation. For this study we looked at all the graphics in volume 52 (2004), one full year.

ILE is an international journal published in Europe about the impact of technologies (the Internet, groupware, multimedia, etc.) on education, training, and life-long learning. The journal includes articles that cover both tools and organizational support required for authoring and implementing courseware. ILE is published three times a year; one publication contains two volumes. we reviewed volume 12, numbers 1 and 2 (a single publication), volume 13, numbers 1 and 2 (also a single publication), and volume 13, number 3. This covers roughly a year and one third.

JETS is published by Society for Applied Learning Technology (SALT). This quarterly journal deals with systems in which technology and education interface with special emphasis given to the use of computers as a component of education systems. Members of SALT tend to come from the ranks of government and military, industry, and education, in that order. JETS reflects this priority in the types of articles it contains. For purposes of this study volume 33 (2004-5), covering one year, was reviewed.

Instructional design software was also considered. Since the early days of multiple slide projectors driven by cues on a sound track, multimedia has been explored as an instructional medium. Since the computerization of these tools, there have been graphic user interfaces among instructional multimedia authoring tools. PCV3 from Control Data and forms of visual PILOT (a computer-assisted instruction language; the acronym stands for programmed instruction, learning, or teaching) are examples of these. Of all these systems, Authorware enjoyed a unique position by being popular as a general-purpose multimedia authoring system as well as an instructional design solution, in spite of the fact that it was expressly developed to serve the needs of ID. Though they are very popular with instructional designers, Macromedia Director and Flash, are not reviewed for this study because they are general-purpose multimedia authoring tools, though they are used extensively in the production of instructional materials.

Authorware was selected for discussion in this section because it is by far the most popular ID-specific tool and it uses a graphic user interface that mimics traditional flowcharting familiar to instructional designers and others.

It may be argued that ID textbooks and journals would not be a fruitful source of ID graphics because they are mostly concerned with general theory and broad explanations. If that were true, then one particular kind of study would be more apt to provide evidence of design drawing in instructional design: case studies.

Indications that cases may be a fruitful source of examples of design drawing in ID can be found in a popular set of competencies for instructional designers called "Competencies and Skills for Instructional Designers" (Analysis & Technology, 1995) of this list of competencies suggests that instructional designers be competent in the ability to:

- Develop flowcharts to identify learning events at the frame specific level using standardized symbology
- Develop storyboards using a template appropriate to the needs of the project

Case studies may be found in journal articles, dissertations, and books. For purposes of this study, one book of ID case studies, plus five additional case studies were reviewed.

The book of ID case studies reviewed is *The ID Casebook: Case Studies in Instructional Design* (Ertmer & Quinn, 2003) which is a compilation of 36 instructional design cases for use as practice by beginning instructional designers. Five additional case studies, four dissertations and one research article, were also reviewed. Most of the additional case studies were found by searching Doctoral research in educational technology (2005) as well as Digital Dissertations (University Microfilms) and ISI Web of Science (Institute for Scientific Information), searching for the term "case study" in the title of instructional design articles and dissertations. Case studies were considered that seemed to cover the instructional design of materials, rather than other cases (such as those about educational programs or processes), as it was thought that these would be the most productive sources of design drawing. The article is by Gastfriend, Gowan, and Lane (2001) and the dissertations include Ludwig-Hardman (2003), Hall (2004), and Twitchell (2001). Another dissertation, May (2006), was recommended by a colleague.

Although drawing as a method of design has been discussed in general literature of design studies since the 1960s and before (Jones, 1970), it has only recently become the object of study in ID. Initially, the search for ID literature about design drawing was frustrating—particularly with automated search tools. Any attempt to combine terms like "drawing," "graphic," or "representation" with "instructional design" or "instructional technology" invariably resulted in research titles that had to do with the use of visual media in designed materials (type 2), not for their design and development (type 1). However, by careful screening, a few studies were identified that seemed relevant. These are: some articles authored by Gilbert Paquette and others (Paquette, 1996; Paquette, Aubin, & Crevier, 1994; Paquette, de la Teja, Lundgren-Cayrol, Léonard, & Ruelland, 2002; Paquette, Léonard, Lundgren-Cayrol, Mihaila, & Gareau, 2006; that design language is presented here in Chapter 2.3) about proposed graphic notation systems for ID; and, an article by Figl and Derntl (2006) which discuss visual instructional design languages (VIDL). One of the VIDLs discussed in Figl and Derntl is Botturi's E^2ML. we will also discuss Botturi's (2003) dissertation on E^2ML in detail.

Results of ID Literature Review

Textbooks

For this literature review, three textbooks, Dick and Carey (1990), Gagné, Briggs, and Wager (1992), and Ely and Plomp (1996) were reviewed. All the graphics and illustrations in these textbooks were classified according to the typology discussed earlier into one of five types (or miscellaneous if they did not seem to fit any of the categories). This classification is presented in Table 1.

In two of the books, design drawings predominate, taking 42% in Dick and Carey (1990) and 62% in Gagné, Briggs, and Wager (1992). In Ely and Plomp (1996), design process model diagrams—type 4—lead, but with only 33% of the total. The difference in dominance of type 1 in the first two books versus type 4 in the last book can be explained by the differences in the purposes for which the books were written. The textbooks by Dick and Carey, and by Gagné, Briggs, and Wager are both intended as textbooks for the beginning designer. As such, they provide basic instructional design process information for guiding the novice instructional designer in her beginning work. This explains the prevalence of instructional design examples represented by these design drawings. Ely and Plomp, on the other hand, is a collection of miscellaneous papers from various sources brought together because of their seminal value to the field of ID. Because many of these papers propose instructional design models, the prevalence of type 4 model graphics should not surprise us.

The beginning of each chapter of Dick and Carey starts with a duplicate of the diagram of their model, with that chapter's step highlighted. Because the same diagram is repeated each time to aid in navigating the book, these model graphics were only counted once. Also, Dick and Carey contains a relatively large number of graphics categorized as "miscellaneous." Most of these miscellaneous graphics are depictions of proposed elements of their notation system for skills analysis. As such, they do not fit neatly into any of the categories.

The preponderance of design drawings or graphics in both Gagné, Briggs, and Wager, and in Dick and Carey was unexpected. Closer inspection of these graphics reveals that nearly all of these type 1 design graphics occur in the first third of both books, and all of them are examples of skills analyses. Each book sets forth a slightly different notation system for illustrating the results of skills analysis.

Viewing the skills analysis drawings through Gibbons' (2003) instructional design layers, discussed earlier we found that all the type 1, design graphics, in Dick and Carey, and in Gagné, Briggs, and Wager, fall within the content layer. As such, they are an important use of design drawing in their own right, but represent only a small fraction of the potential uses of design drawing in ID.

In summary, examples of design graphics in these textbooks are common, but limited to only one of Gibbon's seven layers of instructional design: content. If design drawing itself were considered an important aspect of instructional design work by these authors, we would have expected to examples illustrating other of Gibbons' design layers represented in this sample literature. Interestingly, content or skills analysis is often used as the starting point for instructional design, so the use of graphic as an aid to the start of instruction is noted.

Journals

For this literature review, three ID journals were reviewed. They are *Interactive Learning Environments* (*ILE*), *Educational Technology Research and Development* (*ETR&D*), and the *Journal of Educational Technology Systems* (*JETS*). All the graphics and illustrations in selected issues were classified according to the typology discussed earlier into one of five types. This classification is presented in Table 2.

The three journal titles that were sampled for this study show some variation from the results of the textbooks.

Table 1. Types of graphics found in three ID textbooks

	Type 1 Design	Type 2 Content	Type 3 Report	Type 4 Process	Type 5 Instr'l	Misc
Dick & Carey	28	2	6	6	9	15
Gagné, Briggs & Wager	16	4	1	4	1	0
Ely & Plomp	2	7	4	12	4	7

In these journals, many articles demonstrated or discussed specific instructional design projects. As a result, type 2 graphics (screen shots from instructional computer programs and other illustrations of content) predominated: in *ILE* 56%, in *ETR&D*, 31%, and in *JETS*, 48%.

In *ETR&D*, the balance between research and development articles is reflected in the balance between type 2, content graphics (31%), and type 3, report graphics (29%). *JETS* is similarly balanced between type 2 and type 3.

Type 1 graphics, while not the least common, are always in the minority. In *ETR&D* they were the smallest category, 2%; they are the third smallest category in both *ILE* at 14% and, in *JETS*, at 9%.

In summary, even more dramatically than in the textbooks analyzed, these numbers indicate the relatively light value placed on type 1, design graphics, in the journal literature of ID. Instead, we find a preponderance of type 2, content graphics, often, captured computer screens or graphics, used to illustrate reports about specific products.

Software

Authorware is the ID multimedia authoring software reviewed in this study. The original Authorware, called Course of Action, was created by programmer and instructional designer Michael Allen who had been working on Control Data's PLATO courseware. It was his intent to build a system that would require little or no programming to produce instructional courseware. (Wikipedia: Authorware)

To build a presentation in Authorware, the designer drags pre-defined behavior icons from a palette of behaviors onto a design window. Once in the design window, a behavior's specific attributes can be set. The behavior icons in the design window are connected into a visual flowchart called a flowline, which determines the sequence in which the behaviors are executed. Figure 6 shows several design windows with flowlines in them. Also note the palette of behaviors on the left side of the figure. Behaviors include display, motion, erase, navigation, interaction, calculation, movie, and others. The available behaviors have changed over the life of the product. When an Authorware presentation is executed, the behaviors play out their actions on the presentation window (not shown).

It is surprising that Authorware is one of the few ID products that uses a visual approach to design. The dragging of behaviors to the design window and connecting them into a *flowline* is a good example of a visual metaphor. Authorware's iconic, visual interface allows designers and authors to work more efficiently. The visual metaphor excels at providing the author the ability to see the flow of media-logic and to catch logical errors in thinking.

However, much of Authorware's functionality is not accessed visually, but by means of dialog boxes for specifying the attributes of behaviors and in other non-graphic ways, including a complete scripting language inside the application. Viewed through Gibbons' layers of ID we find that the flowline—the most graphic aspect of Authorware—is limited to Gibbons' strategy layer and

Table 2. Types of graphics found in three ID journals

	Type 1 Design	Type 2 Content	Type 3 Report	Type 4 Process	Type 5 Instr'l	Misc
ILE	11	46	7	14	3	0
ETR&D	1	13	12	8	4	4
JETS	5	30	26	2	0	0

Figure 6. Authorware presentation's behavior palette (far left) and several flowlines

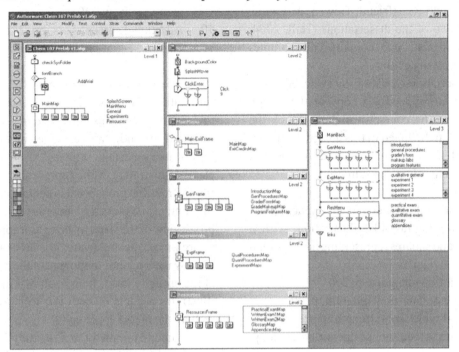

media logic layer because it allows the designer to define the sequence of instructional events, and it directly affects the logic of execution. Visual means are also provided for composing the screen presented to users (the representation layer) but each screen must be composed separately—there is no way to compose families of screens through the visual interface (though it might be scripted in the scripting language). There are also ways to add control elements to the screen (addressing the control layer), but, except for their placement on the screen, the manipulation of these screen controls is not performed through the visual interface. Authorware does have some built-in student tracking capability (supporting the data management layer), but more than basic functions of this capability require scripting. Authorware has no provision for the content layer, or for the message layer to be addressed by the designer.

Case Studies

Of the six sources for case studies reviewed, only two illustrated significant examples of design drawing. In the other four, there was little or no evidence of type 1 design graphics (though several of them did have examples of types 4 and 5—graphics supporting instructional design process models and instructional or learning models).

The first source of ID case studies examined was Ertmer and Quinn's *The ID Casebook: Case Studies in Instructional Design* (2003). Ertmer and Quinn contains only one illustration of type 1, shown in Figure 7. It is the results of a skills inventory for flight attendants. Like the design graphics found in the textbooks, it addresses Gibbons' content layer.

Of the five additional case studies chosen, the research article (Gastfriend, Gowen, & Layne, 2001) and two of the dissertations (Hall, 2004; Ludwig-Hardman, 2003) contained no examples of design drawing at all.

The dissertation-case study by Twitchell (2001) contains in an appendix a copy of the design document for the courseware about which the case is written. Included in this design document are several instances of design drawings and representations. Here is a sampling:

1. A structural perspective: component parts (a venn-diagram-like illustration, with a circle and squares representing instructional components), p. 199.
2. A data-flow diagram, p. 200.
3. A logic & data-flow diagram, p. 202.
4. Several tables containing important data.
5. A rough screen shot of the initial screen, p. 214.
6. Several other rough (wire-frame?) screen shots, pp. 10, 11.
7. A flowchart of instructional logic for a drill, p. 234.
8. The instructional flow of the program, p. 237. (see Figure 8)
9. A screen shot (more refined than previous screen shots, but still not final) + pull-down menu items, p. 240.
10. Additional screen shots, pp. 242, 244, 245, 247, and 249.

These figures comprise a fairly broad representation Gibbons' ID layers. For example, the rough screen shots (items *e, f, i,* and *j*) are intended to guide the developer in the production of user-interface screens. As such they are clearly illustrative of the representation layer in the abstract, but probably also contain elements of the content and message layers as well. Item *a* is a broad view of the strategy layer as it applies to the entire piece of courseware; *g* is an example of a narrow view of one component of the courseware at the strategy layer. Item *h*, shown in Figure 8, illustrates aspects of both the strategy layer as well as the media-logic layer.

Another example of a case study is a dissertation by May (2006) which analyzed the use of Gibbons' (2003) model-centered instructional design theory by a team of instructional designers tasked to design an instructional simulation. May carefully transcribed design sessions, and analyzed photographs of the rough design sketches drawn on the white board during design sessions. One of these photographs is shown in Figure 9. Many of the features of design drawing, are apparent in May's study.

May's study was unique among the case studies that we encountered in the depth to which he analyzed the design process. Parallels between the general field of design and ID became clear in May because of his careful and thorough reconstruction of events and words. May's study is a wonderful window on the ID process in general and model-centered instructional design in detail.

To summarize, only two of the case studies reviewed gave insight in the role of design drawing in ID. The fact that we found so few speaks to the point that design drawing is not commonly discussed in ID at it is in the general design literature.

Figure 7. Simplified job map for level 1 flight attendants (Ertmer & Quinn, 2003, p. 68). Reprinted by permission of Pearson Education, Inc., Upper Saddle River, NJ)

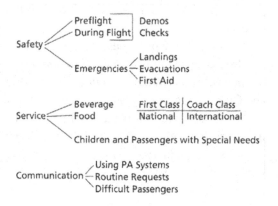

Figure 8. Program instructional flow from Twitchell (2001)

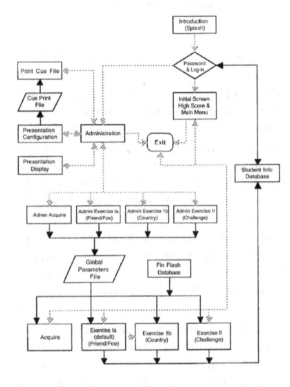

ID Literature about Design Graphics: VIDLs

Our search uncovered three important sources of research on the topic of design drawing in ID. They are an article by Figl and Derntl (2006), a dissertation by Botturi (2003), and the research of Paquette, et al. (Paquette, 1996; Paquette, Aubin, & Crevier, 1994; Paquette, Léonard, Lundgren-Cayrol, Mihaila, & Gareau, 2006). These three sources are reviewed below. They are part of an increased interest in visual ID Languages (VIDLs) (Boot, 2005; Schatz, 2003; Seo & Gibbons, 2003; Waters & Gibbons, 2004).

One example of this increased interest is the report of Figl and Derntl (2006), comparing the value of three VIDLs for the design of blended learning courses. What all these VIDLs have in common is their connection to the concept of learning objects and the SCORM (sharable courseware object reference model) standard. The three VIDLs compared are E²ML (educational environment modeling language), PCeL (Person-centered e-learning), and EduWeaver.

E²ML, a VIDL by Botturi (2003) is a semi-formal modeling notation for creating and documenting instructional designs. Its notation is

Figure 9. Example design drawings from May (2006)

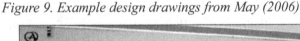

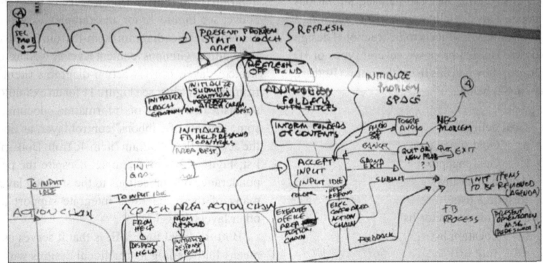

similar to the unified modeling language (UML) used in object-oriented computer programming, substituting learning objects for computer-code objects. PCeL is founded on the person-centered philosophy of Carl Rogers (1983) but related to Alexander's (1979) concept of architectural pattern languages. PCeL includes a library of instructional patterns, modeled in UML activity diagrams, which serve as templates for the creation of instructional instantiations. EduWeaver is a Web-based courseware design tool that uses a modeling framework for grouping and sequencing learning objects into cohesive lessons, modules, and courses into its own visual format.

Of these three, Botturi's E^{2}ML can notate the widest variety of instructional constructs (see also Chapter VII). Botturi (2003) describes the intent of E^{2}ML as a kind of blueprint for instructional designs, allowing all stakeholders in an instructional design effort the ability to agree on details of design. His goals for E^{2}ML are to provide a notation system that will visually support design and development, document a design, and support evaluation.

While Chapter VII of this handbook presents a more lightweight version of E^{2}ML, its original presentation, in 2003, proposes a wider set of interrelated diagrams. One of the principal strengths of E^{2}ML is indeed the many varied types of diagrams that can be used for various purposes. This flexibility comes from adapting a majority of UML's views to instructional design purposes. Botturi proposes several types of ID diagrams, shown in this list of diagrams (Botturi, 2003, p. 82) below:

1. Goal definitions
   a. Goal statement
   b. Goal mapping
2. Action diagrams
3. Resource lists
   a. Role and actor list
   b. Location list
   c. Tool list

4. Overview diagrams
   a. Course breakdown statement
   b. Dependencies diagram
   c. Activity flow

Figures 10, 11 and 12 are examples of a few of these types of diagrams. Figure 10 is an example of a goal map (item 1b on Botturi's list, above), showing dependencies among instructional goals. It was produced following the specifications of the QUAIL model, a sub-model of the original E^{2}ML specification. The symbols on the diagram labeled "G1," "G2," etc., represent different goals, Figure 11 is an example of an action or activity diagram (item 2 from Botturi's list). Note the goals which this instructional action is supposed to address, listed along the right side. Figure 12 is an activity flow diagram (item 4c on the list above), "A1," "A2," etc., are the identifiers for specific activities and the diagram shows their order of occurrence. All of the various types of representation in E^{2}ML are related to design, and fall under type 1.

While E^{2}ML's many types of diagrams give it broad coverage, nearly every diagram can be related to Gibbons' strategy layer in one way or another. However, most diagrams also contain elements for multiple layers and integrate those layers together. For example, the goal mapping diagram (item 1b from Botturi's list of diagrams above; see Figure 10 for an example) as well as his dependencies diagram (item 4b from Botturi's list) address Gibbons' content layer as well as the strategy layer. E^{2}ML's action diagrams (item 2 from Botturi's list; see Figure 11 for an example), sophisticated tables of information, document some aspects of Gibbons' control layer, as does the activity flow diagram (item 4c from Botturi's list; Figure 12 is an example). Despite the preponderance of connections to the strategy layer, many of these diagrams integrate support for other layers as well.

Botturi's goal for E^{2}ML is that it serves as a means for detailing instructional designs with a high level of specificity like the finished blue-prints in architecture, or the detailed orthographic projection drawings in engineering. E^{2}ML is being used to provide unified curricula among schools in Switzerland with different languages and cultures. Its high level of specificity allows it to do this. E^{2}ML portrays the final, detailed outcome of design thinking, not the process by which it occurred, much like the design document examples found in Twitchell's (2001) case study discussed above. E^{2}ML diagrams provide a level of detail that supports collaboration as well as detailing, documenting, and communicating a fully developed instructional design (as a language of design).

Paquette (1996; see also Chapter 8) created a graphic notation system, with supporting software, called MOT (an acronym for the French term Modélisation d'Ojets Typés). MOT includes symbols (see Figure 13) for abstract knowledge classes (concepts, procedures, and principles), as well corresponding individual facts (examples, traces, and statements). Similarly, lines (arrows) connecting the symbols also come in a number of types. MOT's abstract knowledge classes correspond to object-oriented programming *classes* and individual facts correspond to the *instantiations* of the classes.

Because MOT can be used for both abstract classes as well as specific instantiations, it is able to describe both models (types 4 or 5) and instances

Figure 10. An example of an E^{2}ML goal mapping diagram showing dependencies (Botturi, 2003, p. 94)

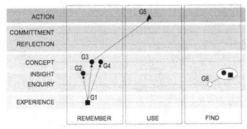

Figure 11. An E^{2}ML action diagram (Botturi, 2003, p. 98)

Website analysis		WA
Students (all, assigned groups), Tutor		LEARNING
Master the W2000 hypemedia design model	Increased mastery in W2000; critical analysis of a Web site (distinguish good design from errors)	G3 G4
Browsing the Web; Using MS PowerPoint + MS Word	-	G5 G6
The Web site to be analyzed	Analysis report (10 pages max., diagrams in PowerPoint)	
(Group) Visit the assigned Website, reconstruct its content and navigational structure. Represent it with W2000. According with the Web site requirements, identify design inconsistencies and potential usability problems. Write a report according to the guidelines (Tutor – available in defined timespans during the week) provide support and guidance at intermediate states of the analysis. DURATION: 8 hours in the 4th course week		
[anywhere] | PC129		
W2000 specification, course syllabus		

Figure 12. An example of an E^{2}ML activity flow diagram, (Botturi, 2003, p. 103)

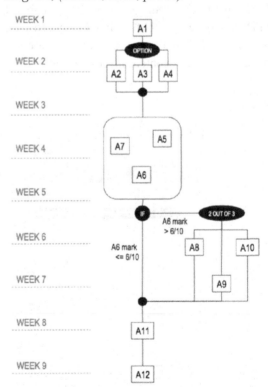

Figure 13. The integrated vocabulary of the MOT representation (Paquette, Léonard, Lundgren-Cayrol, Mihaila, & Gareau, 2006)

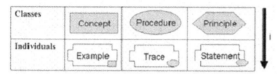

of instruction (type 1). Figure 14 shows an example of a generic cognitive skill model ("Simulate a process") on the left, and an activity structure based on this general skill ("Choose a multimedia production process") on the right. Figure 14 does not show a third level of specificity with specific instantiations of the classes in the general skill diagram, using the second set of symbols. The level of specificity it adds to the common hierarchical flowcharts of skills analyses, such as those found in Dick and Carey (1990), and in Gagné, Briggs, & Wager (1992) make it a good augmentation to these diagrams of content layer material.

Examples of MOT from Paquette's writing most often document Gibbons' content layer (for example, knowledge analyses), and strategy layer (for example, instructional activities). With MOT's primitives, this notation system can be applied to virtually any general notation task that uses containers and arrows, such as Laseau's (1986) bubble diagrams and networks. Because of its basic structure, MOT might be used to illustrate other layers of design if those layers can be illustrated abstractly.

MOT's basic approach also makes it flexible enough to serve the various stages of design. As noted, Paquette and his colleagues have created software for creating MOT diagrams, but virtually any diagramming software that allows custom symbols (such as Visio or Omnigraffle) would be capable of implementing MOT. In addition, MOT's symbol set and concept are simple enough that they could be the basis of hand-drawn design drawings.

Figure 14. A MOT diagram showing both a meta-knowledge representation and a learning scenario (Paquette, Léonard, Lundgren-Cayrol, Mihaila, & Gareau, 2006)

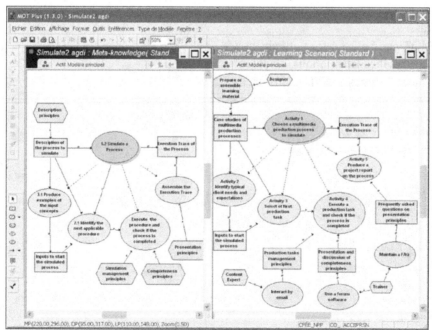

SUMMARY OF DESIGN DRAWING IN ID

Our purpose in this chapter has been to understand the usage and breadth of design drawings in ID. These visual representations of instructional design are closely related to VIDLs. In other design fields, the use of graphics, sketches, or drawings in design is highly developed widely studied (see, for example, Robbins' (1998) book *Why Architects Draw*.)

We began with a review of ID literature to see if we could observe a similar tradition in ID. To conduct this review, we sampled several ID textbooks, ID journals, software, and case studies looking for examples of design drawing. We learned to distinguish design graphics from four other types of design drawings typically found in the literature (content graphics, reporting graphics, illustrations of ID models, and instructional and learning models). With design graphics identified, we categorized them using Gibbons' (2003) seven ID layers as a kind of taxonomy to understand the purposes for which these design drawings were created. These layers are: content, strategy, control, message representation, media-logic, and data management.

We did not find the same pervasiveness or level of self-awareness as found in other design fields. Examples of design drawings were found, but were somewhat rare. Furthermore, we discovered that those examples we found tended to document only two of Gibbons' seven layers: content and strategy (with some exceptions) indicating narrow application. We believe this gap represents a serious shortcoming in ID, indicating a lack of tradition, skill, and standards for visual representations of design except in limited ways.

It is widely held that a common visual language for conveying design ideas has facilitated progress in many other fields of design. The lack of such as medium in ID may be a roadblock to improving the practice of ID. This book represents a possible groundswell of interest in the subject of visual design languages for ID. At present, design drawing is a rare but growing phenomenon in ID, which, when fully understood and implemented, can only benefit the practice of ID.

REFERENCES

Alexander, C. (1979). *The timeless way of building.* New York: Oxford University Press.

Analysis & Technology, I. (1995). Competencies and skills for instructional designers. Retrieved May 2006 from http://www.coedu.usf.edu/it/resources/competency.cfm

Boot, E. W. (2005). *Building-block solutions for developing instructional software.* Unpublished Dissertation, Open Universiteit, Nederland.

Botturi, L. (2003). *E²ML: Educational environment modeling langauge.* Unpublished Dissertation, Switzerland, Lugano.

Caffarella, E. P. (2005, January). *Doctoral research in educational technology: A directory of dissertations, 1977–2004.* Retrieved October 2005, 2006, from http://cortland.edu/education/dissdir/displai4.htm

Dick, W., & Carey, L. (1990). *The systematic design of instruction* (3rd ed.). Glenview, IL: Scott, Foresman/Little, Brown Higher Education.

Ely, D. P., & Plomp, T. (1996). *Classic writings on instructional technology.* Englewood, CA: Libraries Unlimited.

Ertmer, P. A., & Quinn, J. (2003). *The ID casebook: Case studies in instructional design* (2nd ed.). Upper Saddle River, NJ: Merrill.

Fairweather, P., & Gibbons, A. S. (2000). Distributed learning: Two steps forward, one back? One forward, two back? *IEEE Concurrency, 8*(2), 8-9.

Figl, K., & Derntl, M. (2006, June 26–30). *A comparison of visual instructional design languages for blended learning.* Paper presented at the World Conference on Educational Multimedia, Hypermedia, & Telecommunications, Orlando FL.

Gagné, R. M., Briggs, L. J., & Wager, W. W. (1992). *Principles of instructional design* (4th ed.). Fort Worth: Harcourt Brace Jovanovich College Publishers.

Gastfriend, H. H., Gowen, S. A., & Layne, B. H. (2001, November 8–12, 2001). *Tranforming a lecture-based course to an internet-based course: a case study.* Paper presented at the National convention of the Association for Educational Communications and Technology, Atlanta GA.

Gibbons, A. S. (2003). What and how do designers design? A theory of design structure. *TechTrends, 47*(5), 22-27.

Griffin, M. M., & Robinson, D. H. (2005). Does spacial or visual information in maps facilitate text recall? Reconsidering conjoint retention hypothesis. *Educational Technology Research and Development, 53*(1), 23-36.

Hall, H. M. (2004). *An examination of instructional design from theory to practice: A collective case study.* Unpublished Dissertation, University of New Mexico, Albuquerque NM.

Institute for Scientific Information. (2005). *ISI web of science.* from http://isiknowledge.com/wos

Kalyuga, S., & Sweller, J. (2005). Rapid dynamic assessement of expertise to improve the efficiency of adaptive e-learning. *Educational Technology Research and Development, 53*(3), 83-93.

Laseau, P. (1986). *Graphic problem solving for architects and designers* (2nd ed.). New York: Van Nostrand Reinhold.

Liu, M., & Bera, S. (2005). An analysis of cognitive tool use patterns in a hypermedia learning environment. *Educational Technology Research and Development, 53*(1), 5-21.

Ludwig-Hardman, S. (2003). *Case study: Instructional design strategies that contribute to the development of online learning community.* Unpublished Dissertation, University of Colorado at Denver, Denver CO.

May, W. E. (2006). *An analysis of the usability of Model-Centered Instructional Design theory and implication for the design of training: A case study.* Unpublished Dissertation, University of Idaho, Moscow ID.

McKim, R. H. (1980). *Thinking visually : A strategy manual for problem solving.* Belmont, CA: Lifetime Learning Publications.

Mitchell, W. J. (1990). *The logic of architecture : Design, computation, and cognition.* Cambridge, MA: MIT Press.

Paquette, G. (1996). La modélisation par objets typés. *L LICEF.*

Paquette, G., Aubin, C., & Crevier, F. (1994). An intelligent support system for course design. *Educational Technology, 31*(9), 50-57.

Paquette, G., de la Teja, I., Lundgren-Cayrol, K., Léonard, M., & Ruelland, D. (2002). La modélisation cognitive, un outil de conception des processus et des méthodes d'un campus virtuel. *Revue de l'ACED.*

Paquette, G., Léonard, M., Lundgren-Cayrol, K., Mihaila, S., & Gareau, D. (2006). Learning design based on graphical knowledge-modeling. *Educational Technology & Society, 9*(1), 97-112.

Rogers, C. R. (1983). *Freedom to learn for the 80's.* Columbus, OH: C.E. Merrill Pub. Co.

Schatz, S. (2003). A matter of design: A proposal to encourage the evolution of design in instructional design. *Performance Improvement Quarterly, 16*(4).

Seo, K. K., & Gibbons, A. S. (2003). Design languages: A powerful medium for communicating designs. *Educational Technology, 43*(6).

Stubbs, S. T. (2006). *Design drawing in instructional design and Brigham Young University's Center for Instructional Design: A case study.* Unpublished Dissertation, Brigham Young University, Provo, Utah.

Twitchell, D. (2001). *A rapid prototyping model for the design and development of instructional systems in practice:A case study.* Unpublished Dissertation, Utah State University, Logan UT.

University Microfilms. (2007). ProQuest digital dissertations. Retrieved from http://wwwlib.umi.com/dissertations

Waters, S. H., & Gibbons, A. S. (2004). Design languages, notation systems, and instructional technology: A case study. *Educational and Training Technology International, 52*(2), 57-68.

ENDNOTE

[1] This chapter was adapted from parts of Stubbs (2006, unpublished dissertation)

Chapter XVIII
Lost in Translation:
Improving the Transition Between Design and Production of Instructional Software

Eddy Boot
TNO Human Factors, The Netherlands

Jon Nelson
Utah State University, USA

Daniela De Faveri
Università della Svizzera Italiana, Switzerland

ABSTRACT

Developing modern instructional software has become very complex. As a result, the communication between instructional designers and other stakeholders in the development process is becoming increasingly important. However, due to differences in background, focus, and tools among ISD stakeholders instructional designers lack the means to provide reasonably unequivocal design documentation for these stakeholders. These differences in stakeholders create a context where the design documents produced are not sufficiently related to the specific needs of the stakeholders, in terms of meaningful organization and differentiation of level of detail. This problem is complicated by the lack of shared design languages. These problems prevent precise expression of design information. The 3D-model is introduced to support instructional designers to stratify, elaborate, and formalize design documents, even if design languages are hardly shared between designers and other stakeholders. Two validation studies show that the 3D-model contributes to a better information transition between instructional designers and software producers—one of the stakeholders in the development process.

INTRODUCTION

Currently, the educational field is characterized by many innovations: mobile learning, next-generation e-learning systems that retrieve information from business processes, or case-based learning in virtual environments. These innovations, and others, provide the flexibility to enable the integration of working and learning, with time and place independent learning, and adaptive learning, personalized for individual learners (Rosenberg, 2000). These innovations illustrate how organizational, technological, and pedagogical aspects of instructional software can change rapidly. Also affected by these innovations is the way instructional software is developed. The combination of organizational considerations (e.g., "What are the new roles of teachers using instructional software?"), pedagogical considerations (e.g., "How can authentic learning tasks be implemented in the instructional software?"), and technological considerations (e.g., "Which media mix is optimal?") makes the development process highly complex (Jochems, van Merrienboer, & Koper, 2003). Consequently, a structured approach to design, production, and implementation of instructional software is required.

One area in the instructional software development process that appears to be negatively affected by this increased complexity is the transition of information from the design phase to subsequent phases, or, from an instructional designer to the other stakeholders in the process (Boot, van Merriënboer & Theunissen, submitted). A bottleneck is created in that the intentions of the instructional design, described in training blueprints and storyboards, are not communicated clearly enough to other stakeholders of the development process. For example, instructional design information may be insufficiently represented in the specifications created by software producers. As a result, time-consuming reviews and frequent discussions between instructional designers and software producers are often required to reach correct technical specifications that are fully in line with the blueprint and storyboard. This suboptimal transition process is further undermined by the fact that many software producers are not specialized in instructional software, and therefore inexperienced in specifying and creating instructional software programs. When reviews and discussions are impossible, due, for example, to legal reasons, the production process often results in an unsatisfactory outcome: flawed instructional software that requires correction afterwards ("design by debugging"). This example focused on the most obvious stakeholders, as designers traditionally interact mostly with producers. Of course, modern, complex development processes require that a large number of other stakeholders are also sufficiently informed.

In this chapter, we discuss the transition problem between design and other development phases, and identify three major causes for this problem. To overcome these three problems, we introduce the 3D-model as an aid to stratify, elaborate, and formalize design documents, even if design languages are hardly shared between designers and stakeholders. Finally, we present an empirical validation of the 3D-model and discuss the implications of the use of that model.

THE TRANSITION BETWEEN DESIGN AND PRODUCTION

Most instructional software is developed using some variation of the instructional systems development (ISD) model, which often is an instantiation of the generic, five-step ADDIE model: analysis, design, development, implementation, and evaluation model (Dick & Carey, 1996). Every phase in the ISD model identifies specific types of activities and outcomes for which any number of different specialists (e.g., subject matter experts, instructional designers, or software producers) are responsible.

In contrast to ISD models, instructional design (ID) models are a subset of ISD models and encompass only the first two steps of ISD, namely analysis and design (van Merriënboer, 1997). This distinction is useful because it helps to highlight a logical grouping of activities. In general, instructional designers are the specialists responsible for the activities that occur during these two phases (van Merriënboer, 1994).

By the end of the instructional design, the designer usually has some sort of description or documentation of his design (e.g., a training blueprint or a storyboard) that is ready to be delivered to the next phase to be used by the specialists responsible. This is central to the task of the instructional designer, or, as McDonald states in Chapter II (p. 19): "It may not be overstating the point to say that the business of instructional design cannot be separated from communication." The next phase is the development phase and the responsible specialists may include software programmers, audio and/or video producers, graphic designers, or other multimedia specialists.

Regardless of the form the design documentation takes, there is an expectation that it will be able to effectively communicate the intentions of the instructional designer. This is an important assumption as producers will make specifications for their products based upon this design and subsequently create the instructional software (see Figure 1 for a process description of the several

transitions that take place). Although producers are an important target group, the design documents are also used to communicate the instructional design to other stakeholders who are responsible for the following steps in the ISD process (i.e., implementation and evaluation) or validating the previous ISD steps (i.e., analysis and design).

The transition process from design to production and other ISD phases is not without problems. Many instructional designers lack the necessary means to provide design documentation that ensures a reasonably unequivocal representation of the design to the other ISD stakeholders. As can be seen in Table 1, the concerns of different ISD stakeholders are related to a variety of organizational, pedagogical, and technical issues. Consequently, there is an expectation placed upon the instructional designer to produce a design document that will answer the need for different kinds of information. However, in most situations, instructional designers will have a different background than most of the other stakeholders (e.g., educational vs. management) and use different tools (e.g., analysis and design tools vs. technical production tools), and are therefore unaware or unable to provide the right information to the right stakeholder. As McDonald (Chapter II) puts it:

"Designers do need to act with integrity and communicate in ways that maintain the essential qualities of their message. But they also need to remember that they are not designing only for

Figure 1. Transition process of instructional design information

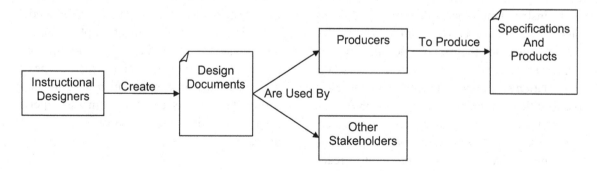

Table 1. Concerns of different stakeholders in the ISD process

Kind of stakeholders	Types of Stakeholder Activities	Examples of Concerns
Project Leader	Manage the whole ISD process	Optimal transfer of information and product during the ISD process
Subject Matter Experts	Validate the domain content	Impact on work floor
Instructors	Validate the didactical model	Impact of instructional design on their teaching (e.g., classroom based, coaching in practice)
Managers	Approve the instructional design	Impact of instructional design on their organization (e.g., financial, roles, infrastructure)
Producers	Translate instructional design into technical specifications (often conduct their own type of analysis and design)	Impact of instructional design on production process (e.g., selection of tools and media, programming, interfacing, usability)
Implementers	Use the instructional design as guidelines	Impact of instructional design on infrastructure, roles, school management, etc.
Learners	Participate in usability studies, interface design studies, and other formative evaluation activities.	Personal preferences and impact of instructional design on their learning processes
Evaluators	Use the objectives set in the instructional design as evaluation criteria	Impact of instructional design on assessment process

themselves, and so have an obligation to make sure they present ideas in ways that communicate clearly to others outside of design communities" (p.28). Yet, it is quite unfeasible that instructional designers are able to "collect" all the needs of the other ISD stakeholders, for it is quite difficult to speak in a design language that is not mastered by others. Nonetheless, *"instructional designers should be careful not to confuse meaning with mechanics so that when necessary they can separate the two and express their meaning in other ways"* (McDonald, Chapter II, p. 24).

The next section discusses three problems with conventional design documentation, which are the result of the differences between instructional designers and other ISD stakeholders.

THREE PROBLEMS IN THE TRANSITION PROCESS

Highly Integrated Design Documents

The first problem relates to the meaningful organization of the design documentation, more precisely, its highly integrated character. In conventional design documents, there is often little to differentiate the organizational, technical, and pedagogical aspects of the documents. As a result, if a particular aspect of the design changes, it is difficult and time-consuming to trace the resulting consequences throughout the design. For instance, if a stakeholder such as a manager decides that instruction by synchronous communication (e.g., using Webcams or instant messaging) is not feasible due to relative high costs or security issues, all aspects in the instructional design related to the possibilities of synchronous communication must be traced and modified. This one change could affect organizational aspects such as different infrastructure, technical aspects such as different e-learning systems, and pedagogical aspects such as different learning tasks, which are all connected to each other

Inconsistent Level of Detail in Design Documents

The second problem relates to the level of detail of the design documentation. The level of detail in conventional design documents varies depending on the capabilities of the designer. For example, more capable designers will typically add more detail to instructional issues but not to technical issues. However, the level of detail should also depend on the needs of the receiver of the information, that is, a particular stakeholder. For instance, for designers to communicate among themselves, the application of delayed cognitive feedback following a particular learning task, a rather conceptual description will suffice. The designers will readily understand each other. But for a producer or an implementer, much more detailed descriptions of timing, content, and presentation of feedback are needed to be able to specify, produce, and implement it as intended by the designer.

The result from the two problems described above is that design documents are not related to the specific needs of particular stakeholders, in terms of meaningful organization and differentiation in level of detail.

Lack of Design Languages for Design Documents

The third problem may deserve more attention, for the lack of design languages that are shared between designers and other ID stakeholders is actually more serious than the previous concerns, because unless an agreed-upon design language is established, it may be difficult also to define an optimal organization and detail level of design documents. In domains other than the instructional design field (e.g., architecture, music, movies), visual design languages are able to capture and describe the design in design documents (e.g., building blueprints, music-books, storyboards) with such a level of detail that they will be interpreted reasonably unequivocally by other stakeholders (e.g., contractors, musicians, directors). Gibbons & Brewer (2005) state that we may speculate that some of the differences in composer excellence are the result of a more expressive set of (personal) design language terms or a better set of (personal) rules for synthesizing expressions from the terms. In the field of Instructional Design, visual design languages are mostly used to explore design spaces and solutions, for they provide common, explicit notation systems for describing an instructional design in design documents (Gibbons, Nelson, & Richards, 2000; Waters & Gibbons, 2004). A notation system is an embedded element of a visual design language and captures abstract ideas to create transferable designs (Gibbons & Brewer, 2005). Examples are the blueprints symbols of an architect or the musical notation system for composers.

In instructional design, visual design languages require such notation systems to convey their message by means of symbolic, graphical, textual or other conventions. An example of a graphical modeling language, not bound to the field of instructional design, is the unified modeling language (UML; Booch, 1994; see also Chapter 11). The notation system of UML (i.e., diagrams) enables different stakeholders to describe and understand a particular software design.

Among the most recent attempts to introduce design languages in the field of instructional software development is IMS learning design (IMS-LD; Koper & Tattersall, 2005; see also Chapter

XV). Yet, the IMS-LD language is meant to promote the design of de-contextualized learning objects (Chapter XIII), needed for instructional strategies "that engage the learners in authentic tasks that are relevant to their personal needs and goals" (Reigeluth, 2005, p. 212). Hence, the cooperative problem-based learning meta-model (CPM; Nodenot et al., 2003, Chapter XIII) was introduced to design contextualized learning scenarios, particularly problem-based ones. Other design languages are at stake too. Think for instance of the recently proposed educational environment modeling language (E^2ML; Botturi, 2006; see also Chapter VII), which allows its users to represent the components of an instructional environment through a visual notation system. Another example is the typified objects visual modeling language MOT and its extentions, whose purpose is to help designers to visualize activity sequences, actors and tools (Chapter VIII) of the instruction to be designed. The classification scheme of Botturi, Derntl, Boot, and Figl (2006) shows that each of these design languages has a set of identifiable features and may be used for various purposes (e.g., creative purposes versus final documentation). However, for the most part, each design language is created for a particular target group, and therefore seldom shared among different stakeholders in the ISD process. For instance, the more precise the design language is, the more technical its notation system is likely to be, making the language too difficult for non-technical stakeholders.

Ideally, the design should be transferred from the instructional designer (or design team) to the software producer and other stakeholders only once, and be completely understood. In this way, there is either no further information exchange necessary, or stakeholders can formulate clear and concrete questions about, for instance, details of the task domain. Thus, in the case of outsourcing, an ideal design document should allow the production company to make an exact estimation of costs and time (before the contract is signed), and ensure a product that is fully compatible with the original design (after the contract is signed).

In the next section, a decision model for instructional designers is introduced to provide support in improving design documents for better communication of their designs, taking into account the three problems described above.

THE 3D-MODEL FOR SUPPORTING INSTRUCTIONAL DESIGNERS

A good solution to overcome the transition problem should focus on supporting instructional designers to provide stakeholders with exactly the design-related information they need. This chapter focuses on supporting instructional designers rather than software producers or other stakeholders; this choice was not without reason, because the designers are pre-eminently responsible for the didactic quality of the final instructional products (defined as the extent to which desired learning outcomes are attained in an efficient manner). This didactic quality is of utmost importance, because technical quality (defined as the extent to which the software takes care of the input, information processing, and output as intended, and the responsibility of the producers) alone is a necessary but insufficient condition to fuel the desired learning processes and reach intended learning outcomes.

As described in the previous sections, the three problems regarding the transition of the instructional design are related to the affect upon the various stakeholders due to (a) the integrated character of instructional design documents, (b) the lack of differentiation in level of detail, and (c) lack of instructional design languages and matching notation systems. As a result, design documents may be difficult to interpret for three reasons: (a) different instructional and technical structures are often not meaningfully organized; (b) different levels of detail are inconsistently applied, and (c) different expressions are used in a non-standardized manner, as designers and producers have hardly any shared design languages to their proposal.

The 3D-model (developing design documents) was developed to support designers in creating better design documents. The three components of the model include (a) stratification, (b) elaboration, and (c) formalization.

Stratification

To overcome the highly integrated nature of design documents and to create more meaningful organization, Gibbons' model of design layers (Gibbons, 2003; see also Chapter XVII) is used to stratify the instructional software design into seven, interrelated layers: content, strategy, control, message, representation, media logic, and data management. Each layer is typified by the designer's selection of design languages pertaining to the solution of different instructional design sub problems. Collectively, the functional designs at each layer together make up the total design. Stratification helps to determine the relations between the functionally different instructional and technical structures that are relevant for a particular stakeholder, while at the same time staying cognizant of the need for integration of those structures within the complete design.

Elaboration

To overcome the inconsistent level of detail and to create more differentiation between the information offer to stakeholders, the three perspectives of Fowler (2004) are used for the *elaboration* of the instructional software design: (a) A conceptual perspective, with more or less superficial and descriptive information; (b) a specification perspective, with more or less comprehensive and detailed information, and (c) an implementation perspective, with more or less technical and highly-detailed information. Elaboration helps to determine the required level of detail used

in the design documentation, depending on the capabilities of the designer and the needs of a particular stakeholder.

Formalization

To overcome the lack of instructional design languages and matching notation systems and to promote more unequivocal understanding of the design, designers may achieve *formalization* of their design by making their selection between informal and formal design languages explicit. They should strive for combinations of formal languages, as these languages provide the most precise and concrete designs descriptions. However, depending on their capabilities and the needs of a particular stakeholder, they can also apply combinations of informal languages as well. Formalization is not necessarily a requirement, nor is it always desirable because, as stated above, not many complete formal instructional design languages are available yet. Formalization helps to determine the required various levels of standardization used in the design documentation.

As Figure 2 shows, the 3D-model uses stratification, elaboration and formalization as its three dimensions. Designers, with or without producers, may first analyze their design situation in order

Figure 2. The 3D-model for developing design documents in its full configuration

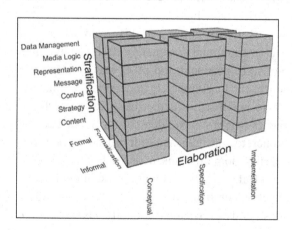

Figure 3. Two possible configurations of the 3D-model

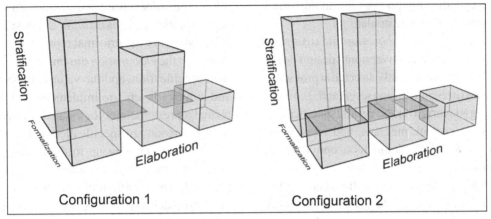

to determine the optimal configuration of the 3D-model (e.g., What kind of designers are involved? Who are the stakeholders to be addressed? What kind of design languages are shared with those stakeholders? Which design tools are available?), and then use this configuration to stratify, elaborate, and formalize their design documents. For instance, they can determine which design layers to address along the stratification dimension, and which combination of level of detail (elaboration dimension) and notation system (formalization) will be used for that layer. Figure 3 shows two possible resulting configurations of the 3D-model.

For stakeholders, on the other hand, the particular configuration of the 3D-model provides insight in the underlying structure and content of the design documentation they were given, even when the design languages used are not standardized or completely shared.

VALIDATION OF THE 3D-MODEL

In order to evaluate the 3D-model, an empirical study was set up (Boot, Nelson, van Merriënboer, Gibbons submitted), which was replicated in a second study. Both studies will be described here briefly. The studies focused on the communication of the instructional design to one important kind of stakeholders, software producers.

Participants

Study 1. Sixteen master and PhD students from an American University's Computer Science Department participated in this study, acting as producers of instructional software. They were randomly assigned to either the conventional instructional design documents group (n = 8) or the improved instructional design documents (based upon the 3D-model, see below) group (n = 8).

Study 2. Thirteen bachelor students from a Swiss university's Computer Science Faculty participated in the same role as in the first study. They were randomly assigned to either the conventional documents group (n = 6) or the improved documents group (n = 7).

Both groups had considerable experience in specifying and programming software. Table 2 presents the experience of the participants with typical producer tasks such as object-oriented modeling and programming. There were no significant differences with regard to this experience between the conventional and improved conditions within both studies.

Materials

The conventional and improved design documents covered an identical topic (an instructional software application for learning to drive a car) and had identical functionality (providing input for the technical specification process for an advanced educational car-driving simulation).

With respect to the *elaboration* and *stratification* dimensions of the conventional design document, the document is mostly directed at providing much detail (implementation level) at the content and strategy layers, average detail (specification level) on the control, message, and representation layers, and little detail (conceptual level) at the media logic and data management layers. Considering the *formalization* dimension in the 3D-model, the conventional design document is based upon informal representations only, such as text and sketches. This configuration reflects the traditional approach towards design documents (see for instance Driscoll, 1998; Kruse & Keil, 2000; Van Merriënboer, Clark, & de Croock, 2002), and is presented as Configuration 1 in Figure 3. Figure 4 presents an example page of the conventional design document.

The improved design document is based upon both informal representations and formal representations (*formalization* dimension in the 3D-model). For the informal representations, the values on the *elaboration* dimension are conceptual, specification, and the values on the content and strategy layers are implementation. For the formal representations, the values on the *elaboration* dimension are specification and conceptual for the layers content up to data management. For these formal representations, UML diagrams are used. This configuration reflects the use of the 3D-model to stimulate and support designers to stratify, elaborate, and formalize design documents more than they usually do, and is presented as Configuration 2 in Figure 3. For instance, Figure 5 presents an example page of the improved design document, showing such a formal representation of a media logic structure, from a specification perspective.

Figure 4. Example page of conventional design document

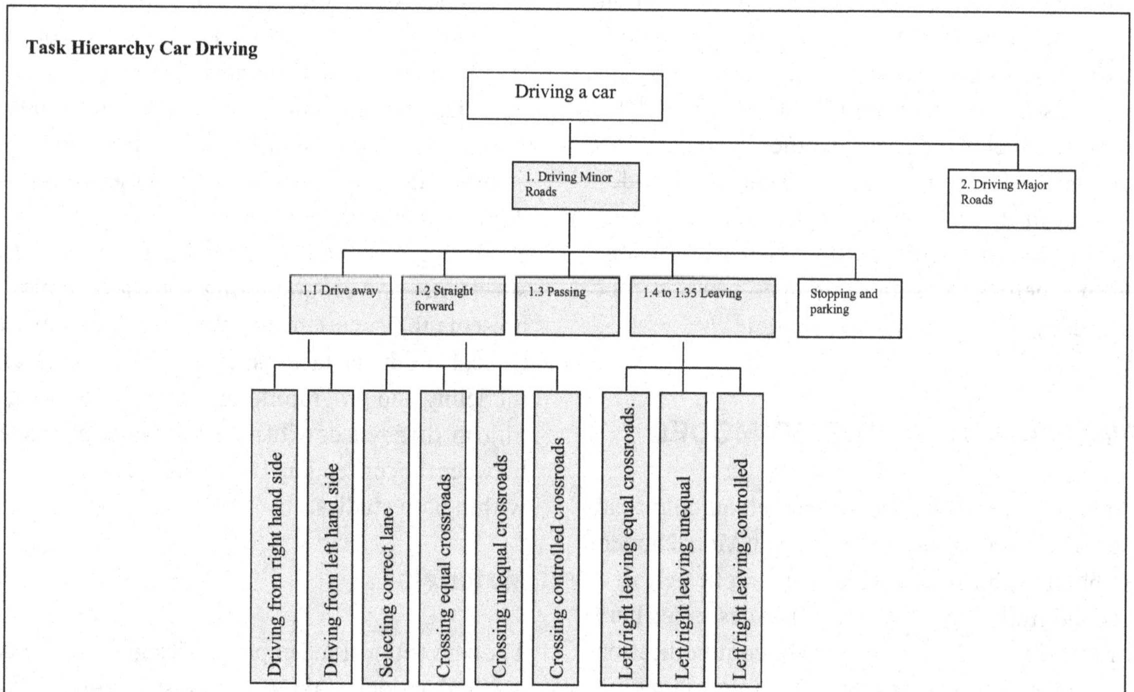

Table 2. Means and standard deviations of proficiency with programming languages and ratings on experience with object-oriented software development

	Study 1				Study 2			
	Conventional design documents group (n = 8)		Improved design documents group (n = 8)		Conventional design documents group (n = 6)		Improved design documents group (n = 7)	
	M	SD	M	SD	M	SD	M	SD
Number of familiar OOP languages	2.37	0.92	1.87	0.99	4.00	1.41	4.29	1.60
Object-Oriented Programming [a]	7.13	0.99	6.63	1.99	7.17	0.75	7.29	1.11
Object-Oriented Modeling [a]	6.75	0.88	6.37	1.41	6.67	1.03	6.00	1.41
Unified Modeling Language [a]	5.75	2.52	5.25	2.31	5.33	1.51	5.29	0.95

[a] Rated on a 9-point scale (1 = "very, very low"; 9 = "very, very high").

Figure 5. Example page of improved design document

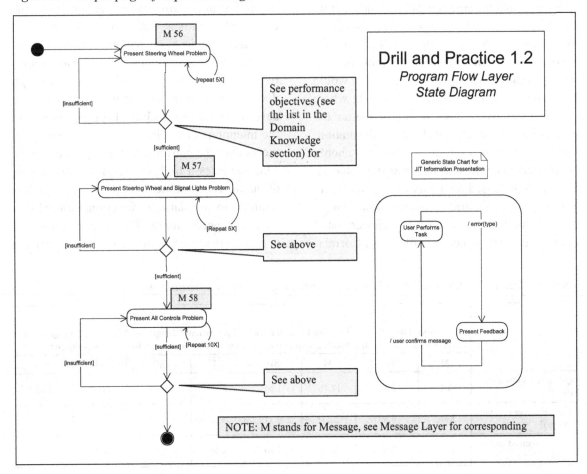

Measurements

Specification questionnaire. The ability to translate the design document into technical specifications, defined as the agreement between technical specifications and the intentions of the instructional design documents, was measured by the specification questionnaire. It consisted of 25 open questions, each question on one printed page with sufficient space to note down the answer. There was no time limit for answering the questionnaire, but the experimenter measured the time on task for each question unobtrusively. Each question addressed a particular aspect of translating the design document into technical specifications. For instance, the participants had to distill from the design document how many databases should be used in the instructional software; what the consequences would be from changing text-based messages into audio-based messages (the so-called "ripple effect"); how a particular program flow should be implemented; what it meant if just-in-time information would be applied in a particular learning task; where the producer would need a subject matter expert to provide additional domain information; which instructional design components should be implemented as reusable learning objects, and so forth. Based on a checklist with correct answers (as determined by instructional designers and production experts), two reviewers rated items as correct or incorrect (the Intra Correla-

tion Coefficient, ICC, is .94, which is very good, Fleiss, 1981).

Cognitive load questionnaire. This questionnaire measured the perceived cognitive load for each question in the specification questionnaire, defined as part of the costs of the translation process. It used the standard 9-point rating scale developed by Paas (1992; see also Paas, Tuovinen, Tabbers, & van Gerven, 2003). The rating scale was included at the bottom of each page of the specification questionnaire, and ranged from 1 = "very, very low perceived load" to 9 = "very, very high perceived load." The ICC for the questionnaire is .89, which is good.

Results

The use of the 3D-model for generating instructional design documentation, as applied in the enhanced document set, showed a significant increase in efficiency of creating technical specifications while requiring the same time and cognitive load. Table 3 shows that the improved design documents indeed resulted in higher scores for the agreement between technical specifications and the intentions of the instructional design documents than the conventional design documents. This indicates a higher level of understanding of the instructional design documents, which is required to translate the functional model into technical specifications. The results with regard to time were mixed. In Study 1, working with the

Table 3. Means and standard deviations for measures of the communication process

	Study 1				Study 2			
	Conventional design documents group (n = 8)		Improved design documents group (n = 8)		Conventional design documents group (n = 6)		Improved design documents group (n = 7)	
	M	SD	M	SD	M	SD	M	SD
Quality of production (0 – 25)	12.25[a]	2.35	17.18[a]	1.94	8.33[c]	2.34	12.57[c]	1.62
Mean time per question (mins.)[b]	3.46[b]	0.89	2.75[b]	0.71	3.36	0.41	3.25	0.39
Mean perceived cognitive load per question	4.43	0.42	4.06	1.10	4.54	1.23	4.35	0.75

[a] $t = 4.58, p < .001$ [b] $t = 1.77, p < .05$ [c] $t = 3.85, p < .001$

improved design documents required less time, but in Study 2 there was no significant difference. In both studies, there were no significant differences in perceived cognitive load when comparing the same question on the conventional and the improved design documents.

CONCLUSION

This study investigated the transition problem between design and other development phases and identified three major causes for this problem. It also introduced a means to improve the efficiency of the translation process between the design phase and the production phase. The results of two studies show that the application of a structured, three-dimensional approach by designers helps producers come to an understanding of the design that is more in agreement with the intentions of the instructional designer. Developing design documents while supported by the 3D-model results in a higher efficiency of the translation process, reflecting better results with the same time and cognitive load input. Further study should demonstrate if design documents based upon the 3D-model also promote a better transition process to other ISD stakeholders, as listed in Table 1.

The use of the 3D-model by ISD stakeholders has several implications, among others, for training/education, support tools, and the further development of design languages.

First, with respect to training/education, this study suggests that instructional designers need to become proficient in at least three new activities. Besides being knowledgeable and skilled in traditional instructional design activities such as domain and task analysis, strategy selection, and media selection (see Richey, Fields, & Foxon, 2001), our results indicate that they should be able to (a) stratify instructional design documents to describe aspects associated with design as well as the concerns of different ISD stakeholders (see Table 1), (b) decide for each layer how much

detail is required for unequivocal understanding of the design by these stakeholders, and (c) represent—where possible—their designs in formal design languages. Second, with respect to support tools, this study suggests new generation tools should be used. An example of such a support tool is ADAPT-IT (De Croock, Paas, Schlanbusch, & van Merriënboer, 2002), which supports the creation of design documents in a structured manner. If analyzed based upon the dimensions of the 3D-model, then ADAPT-IT helps designers to create design documents that are both formal and informal, are elaborated at the conceptual and specification level, and describe the content and strategy layers. Future research may either investigate the contribution of support tools such as ADAPT-IT to the creation of design documents, or use the 3D-model to develop new tools that take the stratification, elaboration, and formalization dimensions into account.

Second, with respect to further development of design languages, this study suggests that more instructional design languages are necessary to provide formal representations of instructional designs in order to sufficiently balance formal and informal representations according to the formalization dimension. Although the number of visual instructional design languages is rising, it is yet to be demonstrated which impact this has on the development process. For instance, it is likely it will promote a better transition process in terms of shared understanding, but as the application of such rich languages can be quite complex, will it also save time? And will less-skilled developers be able to deal with this (additional) complexity, or does it require more proficient developers, therefore potentially limiting the wide acceptance of such design languages in the developer community?

Ultimately, the proposed research efforts should result in improved design languages and design documents, so less of the designers' intentions are "lost in translation," preventing the specification and production of sub-optimal products.

REFERENCES

Booch, G. (1994). *Object-oriented analysis and design with applications*. Redwood City, CA: Benjamin/Cummings.

Boot, E., Nelson, J., van Merriënboer, J. J. G., & Gibbons, A. S. (in press). *Stratification, elaboration, and formalization of design documents: Effects on the production of instructional materials*.

Boot, E., van Merriënboer, J.J.G., & Theunissen, N.C.M. (in press). *Improving the development of instructional software: Three building-block solutions to interrelate design and production*.

Botturi, L. (2006). E²ML. A visual language for the design of instruction. *Educational Technology Research & Development, 54*(3), 265-293.

Botturi, L., Derntl, M., Boot, E., & Figl, K. (2006, July 5-7). A classification framework for educational modeling languages in instructional design. *Proceedings of 6th IEEE International Conference on Advanced Learning Technologies (ICALT2006)* (pp. 1216-1220). Kerkrade, The Netherlands.

De Croock, M. B. M., Paas, F., Schlanbusch, H., & van Merriënboer, J. J. G. (2002). ADAPTit: Tools for training design and evaluation. *Educational Technology, Research and Development, 50*(4), 47-58.

Dick, W., & Carey, L. (1996). *The systematic design of instruction* (4th ed.). New York: Harper Collins.

Fowler, M. (2003). *UML distilled: A brief guide to the standard object modeling language*. Boston: Addison-Wesley.

Gibbons, A. S. (2003). What and how do designers design? A theory of design structure. *Tech Trends, 47*(5), 22-27.

Gibbons, A. S., & Brewer, E. K. (2005). Elementary principles of design languages and design notation systems for instructional design. In J. M. Spector, C. Ohrazda, A. Van Schaack & D. Wiley (Eds.), *Innovations to instructional technology: Essays in honor of M. David Merrill* (pp. 111-129). Mahwah, NJ: Lawrence Erlbaum Associates.

Gibbons, A. S., Nelson, J., & Richards, R. (2001). The nature and origin of instructional objects. In D. A. Wiley (Ed.), *The instructional use of learning objects* (pp. 25-58). Bloomington, IN: Association for Educational Communications and Technology.

Jochems, W., van Merriënboer, J. J. G., & Koper, R. (Eds.). (2003). *Integrated e-learning: Implications for pedagogy, technology, and organization*. London, UK: RoutledgeFalmer.

Koper, R., & Tattersall, C. (Eds.). (2005). *Learning design: A handbook on modelling and delivering networked education and training*. Berlin, Germany: SpringerVerlag.

Paas, F. (1992). Training strategies for attaining transfer of problem-solving skill in statistics: A cognitive-load approach. *Journal of Educational Psychology, 84*, 429-434.

Paas, F., Tuovinen, J., Tabbers, H., & van Gerven, P. W. M. (2003). Cognitive load measurement as a means to advance cognitive load theory. *Educational Psychologist, 38,* 63-71.

Reigeluth, C. M. (2005). New instructional theories and strategies for a knowledge-based society. In J.M. Spector, C. Ohrazda, A. Van Schaack, & D.A. Wiley (Eds.). *Innovations in instructional technology: Essays in honor of M. David Merrill*. Mahwah, NJ: Lawrence Erlbaum Associates.

Richey, R. C., Fields, D. C., & Foxon, M. (Eds.). (2001). *Instructional design competencies: The standards* (3rd ed.). Syracuse, NY: ERIC Clearinghouse on Information and Technology.

Rosenberg, M. J. (2000). *E-learning, strategies for delivering knowledge in the digital age.* New York: McGraw-Hill.

Van Merriënboer, J. J. G. (1997). *Training complex cognitive skills: A four-component instructional design model for technical training.* Englewood Cliffs, NJ: Educational Technology Publications.

Waters, S. H., & Gibbons, A. S. (2004). Design languages, notation systems, and instructional technology: A case study. *Educational Technology, Research and Development, 52*(2), 57-68.

Chapter XIX
A Visual Learning Design Representation to Facilitate Dissemination and Reuse of Innovative Pedagogical Strategies in University Teaching

Shirley Agostinho
University of Wollongong, Australia

Barry Harper
University of Wollongong, Australia

Ron Oliver
Edith Cowan University, Australia

John Hedberg
Macquarie University, Australia

Sandra Wills
University of Wollongong, Australia

ABSTRACT

This chapter describes a visual learning design representation devised in an Australian funded project that focused on identifying and describing innovative educational practices employing the use of information and communication technologies (ICT). Referred to as the learning designs project (www. learningdesigns.uow.edu.au), the aim was to produce generic learning design resources and tools to help academics in higher education implement innovative ICT-based learning designs in their own teaching contexts. The chapter describes the learning designs project, details how and why the graphical learning design representation was created and provides an example to illustrate the visual formalism. How the authors have built on this work since the completion of the project is also discussed. The purpose of this chapter is to explain how this visual representation works so as to inform teachers and educational researchers of its potential to serve as a common language to describe learning designs.

INTRODUCTION

In 2000, the Australian Universities Teaching Committee (AUTC) (now referred to as the Carrick Institute for Learning and Teaching in Higher Education) funded a two-year project titled: Information and Communication Technologies and Their Role in Flexible Learning. The aim of the project was to encourage the sharing and uptake of high quality learning designs supported by information and communication technologies (ICT). The project brief was to produce generic/reusable learning design resources to assist teachers in higher education to create high quality, flexible learning experiences for students. The process undertaken to achieve this involved:

- Developing an evaluation instrument to characterize high quality learning designs;
- Identifying high quality learning designs used in higher education;
- Selecting those suitable to be redeveloped in the form of reusable software, templates, and/or generic guidelines;
- Developing these reusable resources; and,
- Making them accessible from a central Web site.

A learning design refers to a description of a learning experience in terms of the activities a teacher devises for students, and how students interact with the teacher and amongst themselves when undertaking the activities. The focus for this project was to identify learning designs that represented "good practice" in the implementation of ICT in terms of providing flexible learning opportunities for students, that is, breaking the hegemony of on-campus face-to-face delivery, and promoting high quality learning experiences. High quality learning experiences were considered in general terms as experiences that encourage students to seek understanding rather than memorizing content and encourage the development of lifelong learning skills.

The need for the project stemmed from the main issue evident in practice and in the literature, namely that the uptake of the use of high quality ICT-based learning designs in higher education has been slow. Attributing factors include: low levels of dissemination of ICT-based learning projects beyond the originating institution (Alexander & McKenzie, 1998), lack of ICT-based learning examples to model (Dijkstra, Collis, & Eseryel, 1999; Tsichritzis, 1999), and barriers to change current practice such as lack of time, support, and training (Collis, 1998). Thus, the significance of the project was that teachers in higher education could benefit from sharing innovative and pedagogically sound ideas, particularly in a climate where there is increasing demand to offer flexible learning opportunities to students (Nicoll, 1998) yet at an institutional level there is pressure to operate at greater efficiency (Cunningham, 1998).

This was a large-scale project that involved an international academic community of approximately 140 people who contributed in various capacities. The project team comprised four team leaders, a four-member research team, an international review panel of 18 and a steering committee of four. There were over 50 designers that submitted ICT-based learning designs for review, and an evaluation team of 60+ that reviewed these learning designs, plus a number of development teams that produced the reusable learning design resources. A project manager orchestrated all project activities. The main artifact produced from the project is the learning designs project Web site (www.learningdesigns.uow.edu.au), which has been heralded as one of the most extensive Web-based teaching resources available in higher education (Hicks, 2004). The site includes five generic learning design guides, four generic learning design software tools and over thirty contextualized learning design exemplars. Also provided are project publications and information about how the project was undertaken.

In a review of AUTC funded projects, Hicks stated that the learning designs project Web site "provides a detailed, highly structured presentation of masses of information of considerable value to the sector. The 'exemplars' provided are grounded in the experiences of 'coal-face' academics and are searchable by discipline, and ICTs used, as well as by 'focus choices'. The novel representation of learning designs allows a helpful and concrete elaboration of each exemplar, assisting adoption or adaptation by potential users" (Hicks, 2004, p. v). Hicks, thus, suggests that the learning design representation developed by the project is a useful construct for the target audience, that is higher education academics. It is this "novel representation of learning designs" (Hicks, 2004) that is the focus of this chapter. The next section explains how the project team defined a "high quality learning design" in specific terms. This then leads into the discussion that explains how the visual learning design representation was devised.

DEFINING A HIGH QUALITY LEARNING DESIGN

Two pivotal aspects of the project involved determining how to describe a learning design and determining how to identify a high quality learning design.

Describing a Learning Design

The team needed to define a learning design in terms of the common elements or components it comprised, so that different learning designs could be described in a consistent manner using a documentation format. This was crucial to the project in order to review, compare and contrast different learning designs in the process of identifying those suitable for redevelopment in a more generic/abstract form.

The work of Ron Oliver and Jan Herrington informed the project's definition and composition of a learning design (Oliver, 1999; Oliver & Herrington, 2000; Oliver & Herrington, 2001).

While teachers can design and develop a myriad of learning experiences for their students, within ICT-mediated learning environments Oliver and Herrington propose there are three key elements that comprise a learning design:

1. The **tasks** or activities learners are required to undertake;
2. The content **resources** provided to help learners complete the tasks; and,
3. The **support** mechanisms provided to assist learners to engage with the tasks and resources.

Their learning design model is illustrated in Figure 1.

The project team sought a range of learning design exemplars predominantly from the Australian higher education teaching community. These exemplars represented a diversity of disciplines, learning outcomes, use of ICT, and they were perceived or empirically evaluated to contribute to high quality learning experiences. (For a detailed explanation of how learning designs were identified for review by the project refer to AUTC Project: Information and Communication Technologies and their Role in Flexible Learning: Final Report, 2002).

A learning design submission form was developed, based on the Oliver and Herrington learning design model, to solicit detailed information about each of the learning design exemplars that had been sought. The learning design submission form (accessible from the project Web site) was e-mailed to each of the learning design exemplar designers and they were asked to provide details about their learning designs in terms of the following:

1. General information about the learning design exemplar such as its title, designer(s) names and contact details, discipline focus, target audience, cohort size catered for, and level of granularity of the learning design, (e.g., implemented as a lesson of a 1-3 hour

Figure 1. The key elements of a learning design (Adapted from Oliver and Herrington, 2001)

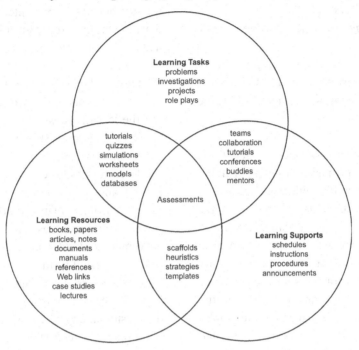

duration, over a series of lessons, entire length of a course, etc.).

2. A textual description of the learning design based on the Oliver and Herrington key elements of a learning design, that is, the tasks, resources, and supports, as well as the intended learning outcomes.

3. Contextual information about the implementation of the learning design, such as how ICT is used, how learners are assessed, what prerequisite knowledge is required by the learners, etc.

4. Information about evaluative research findings of the learning design implementation and access to the learning design exemplar itself, such as access to a CD, course Web site, reading materials, etc.

This activity enabled the collection of a rich set of data for each learning design exemplar. The challenge then faced by the team was to identify learning design exemplars considered as having the potential of fostering high quality learning, and of those, which could be redeveloped in a more generic form.

Determining What Constitutes a "High Quality Learning Design"

Two experts in the field of learning in higher education, David Boud and Michael Prosser, were commissioned to advise the project team about what constitutes high quality learning in higher education. Through a number of project workshops, which included the research team and members of the review panel, high quality learning designs were defined as those that met the following criteria:

1. They *engaged* learners by considering their prior knowledge and building on their expectations.

2. They *acknowledged the learning context* by considering how the learning experience

is positioned with the broader program of study for learners.

3. They *challenged* learners through active participation.

4. They encouraged learners to *practice* or apply their learning through articulating and demonstrating their understanding to themselves and peers.

These four principles (Boud & Prosser, 2002) formed the basis of an evaluation instrument that was used to identify high quality learning designs. (The instrument is referred to as the evaluation and redevelopment framework and is accessible from the project Web site.) The project evaluation team applied this instrument by firstly reviewing the submission form for each learning design exemplar and then annotating and rating how well each of the four principles was implemented within each learning design exemplar. The evaluation team was also asked to make a judgement on the suitability of redeveloping the learning design exemplars in a more generic form and provided recommendations on the aspects or features of the learning design exemplars that could be redeveloped. (See Agostinho, Oliver, Harper, Hedberg and Wills, 2002 for more information about the evaluation instrument and how the learning designs were reviewed.)

This activity enabled the project team to cull the original set of learning design exemplars to a smaller set that represented high quality learning design exemplars and those also considered suitable for redevelopment in a more generic form, as determined by the expert review team via the evaluation instrument developed within the project.

DEVISING A LEARNING DESIGN VISUAL REPRESENTATION

To further inform the project team's choice on which learning design exemplars to select for

redevelopment, that not only represented high quality but also represented different types of learning designs, the team engaged in an analysis activity to classify and categorize the exemplars according to common themes, namely pedagogical strategies. The team was guided by work of Ip & Naidu (2001) and Jonassen (2000) in categorizing the learning design exemplars according to similar pedagogical strategies. The analysis was based on a grounded approach by examining all the learning design exemplars collected by the project and categorizing each learning design exemplar in terms of its overall pedagogical focus. It was from this intense analysis activity that an idea emerged about representing learning designs in a more visual form.

As "clusters" of pedagogical strategies were formed, the team then examined whether similarities existed amongst the learning design exemplars within each cluster in terms of the tasks, resources, and supports. An idea emerged that each of these clusters, referred to as generic learning designs, could be illustrated visually by using the Oliver and Herrington (2001) model. Each element of a learning design was assigned a symbol: rectangles for tasks, triangles for resources and circles for supports, and the learning design was illustrated in the form of a temporal sequence to show the chronology of tasks, resources, and supports a teacher has designed for learners to engage with over a period of time.

Figure 2. Example of the initial learning design visual sequence (Oliver et al., 2002)

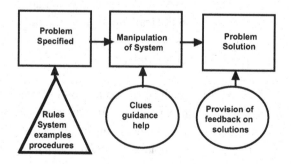

Figure 3. The learning design visual sequence for the teaching and learning in multimedia learning design (Herrington & Oliver, 2002)

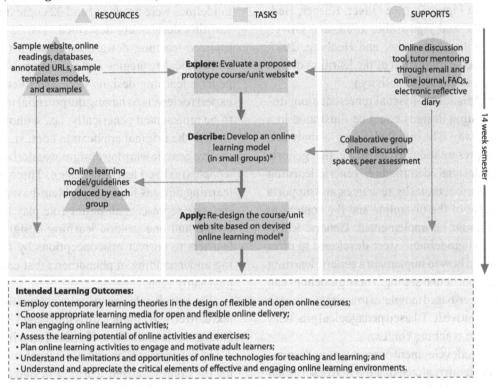

Figure 4. The learning design visual sequence for the generic learning design: Explore, describe apply (Oliver & Herrington, 2002)

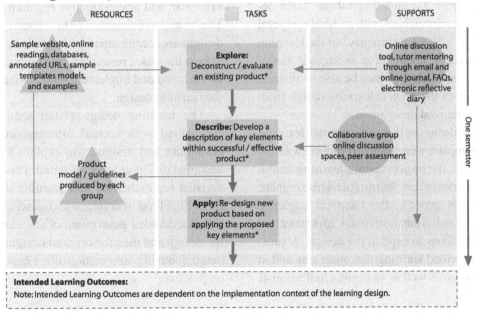

The initial temporal sequences produced were represented horizontally as shown in the example provided in Figure 2. (See Oliver, Harper, Hedberg, Wills, and Agostinho, 2002, and Oliver, Harper, Wills, Agostinho, and Hedberg, 2007, for a detailed explanation of the learning design categorization analysis activity.)

Using this form of visual representation, different learning designs could be illustrated in a consistent way. The initial idea was to apply this visual representation to illustrate the generic learning designs identified. A generic learning design describes the tasks, resources, and supports irrespective of the discipline and the context in which it could be implemented. Generic learning design "guidelines" were developed to offer guidance on how to implement a generic learning design in a particular setting. These guidelines can serve as paper-based templates to assist teachers to reuse innovative ICT-based pedagogical practices in their own teaching context.

As this redevelopment process was underway, the project team realized that the rich description collected for each learning design exemplar was valuable for inclusion regardless of the exemplar's suitability for redevelopment in a more generic form. The project team felt that these "thick descriptions" accompanied with a visual temporal sequence as a "visual summary" of the learning design exemplar could serve as implicit guidelines. That is, academics may be able to abstract for themselves the generic learning design from the contextualized description.

Thus, all designers that had submitted learning design exemplars were asked to produce (with assistance from the project team) a learning design visual sequence of their learning design exemplar. Through this process, the temporal sequence layout changed from horizontal to vertical to allow more room to explain the design. A summary of intended learning outcomes was added to the diagram as well as an explicit indication of time required for implementation of the learning design. As a result, five generic learning designs guidelines were produced and 32 contextualized learning designs are described. The 32 contextualized learning designs represent a range of pedagogical strategies and disciplines. The five generic learning designs were identified by the expert reviewers as having the potential to be able to be represented generically, i.e., without reference to the original application context. Each of the five generic learning designs was derived from a contextualized learning design. Three generic learning designs focus on problem-based activities, one represents an online role play learning design and one generic learning design assists learners to correct misconceptions by facilitating understanding of phenomena that cannot be physically seen.

The learning design visual sequence for a contextualized learning design is illustrated in Figure 3. Its generic counterpart is illustrated in Figure 4. On the project Web site, the visual sequences for the contextualized learning designs are accompanied with textual information that explains in detail the tasks, resources and supports, that the implementation context of the learning design exemplar, and any evaluative research findings. The visual sequences for the generic learning designs are accompanied with detailed guidelines of how the tasks, resources, and supports should be designed and implementation advice to reuse the learning design.

The learning design visual sequence accompanied with textual information enables academics and designers to explore a learning design at different levels of detail. For example, a visual representation of a learning design offers a high level overview, a text description then offers a detailed description of the elements of the design and then the original designers' comments about implementation offers expert advice on practice.

HOW TO CONSTRUCT A LEARNING DESIGN VISUAL SEQUENCE

The learning design visual sequence illustrates the chronology of tasks, resources, and supports that a teacher has designed for a learner or cohort of learners to engage in over a period of time. It represents a visual summary of a learning design from the perspective of the teacher. A summary of the intended learning outcomes and an indication of the level of granularity (in terms of the time required to implement the learning design) completes the visual sequence.

The tasks form the focus of the diagram. As seen in Figures 3 and 4, tasks are represented by a series of rectangles, which are positioned in the center and arranged vertically. Within each rectangle there is a brief textual description of what learners are required to do or produce. Each task's description can be prefixed by a thematic word that summarises the aim of the task, for example, explore, predict, reflect, etc. Assessable tasks are distinguished with an asterisk (*). To represent different tasks that may be available for learners and that are to be completed concurrently, the visual sequence would include task rectangles drawn in parallel for that section of the sequence. An example is illustrated in Figure 5.

Tasks are diagrammatically accompanied with resources and supports. Resources are represented by triangles and positioned to the left of the diagram. They indicate the content material provided to help learners work through a task. The learning supports are represented by circles and are positioned to the right of the diagram. Supports refer to the strategies a teacher implements to help learners engage with and complete each task.

Each resource triangle includes a brief textual description of the kind of resource provided, for example, readings, URL links, pro formas, etc. The textual description can include multiple resources (as highlighted in the first resource triangle in Figures 3 and 4). An arrow from a resource

symbol (triangle) to a task symbol (rectangle) indicates those resources provided to the learner to help them complete the task. An arrow drawn from a task symbol to a resource symbol indicates that a resource is produced as an artifact from completion of the task (which may be used as a resource for learners to use in subsequent tasks). Refer to the second task illustrated in Figures 3 and 4 for an example.

Each support circle also includes brief text to describe the kind of support provided. Examples of supports include: feedback from the teacher, such as instructions on how to undertake a task, posting regular announcements in an online course to keep learners informed and on track, task assessment; online asynchronous/synchronous class discussions; group work; peer assessment, etc. As per resources, the textual description within each support circle can refer to multiple supports (as seen in the support circles in Figures 3 and 4). An arrow from a circle (support) to a rectangle (task) indicates the support strategies implemented to assist learners to complete the tasks.

Resources and supports can be specific to one task or they may be available for the entire duration of the learning experience. When learning resources or supports are limited to particular tasks, their availability is represented graphically with a horizontal arrow to the specific task for which they are available (see the first task as illustrated in Figures 3 and 4 for an example). If learning resources and/or supports are available for multiple tasks, then the resource triangle

Figure 5. Depicting concurrent tasks in a learning design visual sequence

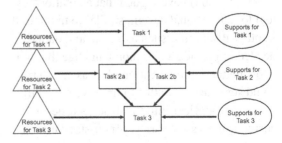

and/or support circle is drawn once (where it is firstly introduced to the students) and a vertical arrow indicates the resource and/or support is also provided for subsequent tasks. See the first resource triangle and support circle in Figures 3 and 4 for an example.

DISCUSSION

The learning design visual sequence was devised as a "means to an end" because developing a mechanism to document and communicate learning designs in a consistent way was part of the research process towards the ultimate goal of producing generic learning design resources. The focus of the project was to produce generic learning designs, to encourage the reuse of innovative ICT-based learning designs. In order to select suitable learning designs worthy of redevelopment in a more generic form the team had to devise a way of describing learning designs in a consistent format so that the learning design exemplars could be reviewed in terms of their potential to foster high quality learning and categorized in some way. These needs led to the development of the graphical learning design representation, described above, which provides a visual summary of a learning design accompanied with detailed textual description.

In hindsight, this research process has produced an "end in itself" as the learning design visual sequence is a form of communication, like a language. This is a significant outcome as there is currently no common language or notation system to describe learning designs. Waters and Gibbons (2004) have argued that a notation system for educational design, similar to that found in other disciplines such as music and dance, is needed to provide a common language that will allow better communication of ideas and in turn could serve as a stimulus to improve the quality of teaching and learning. "Instructional designers currently use a great variety of non-standard nota-

tion conventions to communicate their designs: flowcharts, storyboard forms, scripts, diagrams, sketches, and text descriptions. But there is little overlap and few standard practices among conventions… Further research into design structure, design languages, and design notation systems will better equip designers to create powerful, more precise designs" (pp. 66-68).

Work is being conducted in this area as there are several emerging learning design representations (Botturi, Derntl, Boot, & Figl, 2006; McAndrew, Goodyear, & Dalziel, 2006; Pedagogy Case Study Templates, 2006; Richards and Knight, 2005). Examples include: the technical specification IMS-LD (http://www.imsglobal.org/learningdesign/index.html; see also Chapter 15); design patterns (Goodyear, 2005; http://www.pedagogicalpatterns.org/); learning activity management system (http://www.lamsinternational.com/); E²ML (Chapter VII) and templates that can be used to describe online learning designs (Pedagogy Case Study Templates, 2006). These representations are documented in different forms and thus serve different purposes. For example, some representations are specifically designed for human interpretation such as textual descriptions and visual diagrams, whereas others are tailored more for technical interoperability and thus represented in the form of computer readable languages (e.g., IMS-LD). A system such as LAMS is able to serve both purposes as a teacher can design and run learning activities online using a visual flow chart type interface. However, all these representations define a "learning design" in their own particular way, thus there is no one encompassing standard documentation form of representing learning designs.

The graphical aspect of the learning design visual sequence is considered by Botturi Derntl, Boot, and Figl (2006) as having the potential to be a useful instructional design language. A classification framework for proposed instructional design (ID) languages highlights how the learning design visual sequence (LDVS) is positioned against other

Table 1. Classification framework that positions the ldvs against other emerging instructional design languages (Botturi et al., 2006)

Comparison Characteristics:	Classification of LDVS	Comments
Stratification: Whether a language offers a layered perspective (describing entities of different types as different representations) or a flat perspective (describing all entities in a single representation)	Flat	A single representation used to visually illustrate the chronological sequence of tasks, resources, supports designed for a learning experience.
Perspective: Whether the same entities can be viewed in single or multiple perspectives	Single	
Formalization: Whether the design is described using a formal language that follows a stringent set of rules or an informal language that provides general guidelines but is open to interpretation.	Informal	The way tasks, resources, and supports are described is open to interpretation.
Elaboration: The level of detail of a design: conceptual (overview); specification (comprehensive description); implementation (highest level of detail).	Specification	The LDVS provides a visual summary of a learning design and is accompanied with a detailed textual description that elaborates how the tasks, resources, and supports are designed and implemented.
Notation: Whether the notation system is primarily visual or non-visual	Visual	A learning design is graphically represented as comprising three main elements: tasks (represented as rectangles), resources (depicted as triangles), and supports (illustrated by circles). Intended learning outcomes and an indication of time required to implement the learning design completes the visual diagram.
Application: How the language can be used to communicate a design and generate design solutions.	Communication axis: communicative Creativity axis: Finalist	The LDVS was used to communicate learning designs to the higher education academic teaching community. The LDVS was used to depict a final design solution that has been implemented.

emerging visual ID languages. The comparison characteristics are outlined in Table 1.

Botturi, Derntl, Boot, and Figl (2006) conclude that further research is required to examine how such ID languages can be applied in practice. This chapter has explained how one emerging visual ID language has been developed and applied within a particular project.

The perceived usefulness of the visual learning design representation discussed in this chapter is its relative simplicity in construction and flexibility in describing tasks, resources, and supports. The time sequence explicates the chronology of tasks thus facilitating the overall learning design to be more easily understood. These are perceptions held by the project team. Further research is required to validate these claims and also examine whether this visual representation is being used beyond the project in which it was devised.

Some research has been conducted to investigate how the generic learning designs developed

have been reused and how reuse can occur (see Bennett, Agostinho, & Lockyer, 2005; Bennett, Lockyer, & Agostinho, 2004). There has also been research work focused on embedding the learning designs and their visual representations in tools to support instructors (see Bennett, Agostinho, Lockyer, & Harper, 2006; Harper, Agostinho, Bennett, Lukasiak, & Lockyer, 2005). This research is being extended through a national competitive grant to incorporate learning designs into design support tools (Bennett, 2005). This research study involves working with a learning management system industry partner and in collaboration with Rob Koper and his team at the Open University of The Netherlands (OUNL) to develop an understanding of synergies between the learning design construct described in this chapter and the IMS-LD standard for representing learning designs.

A research grant, obtained by the first author, investigated how the learning design graphical representation is being used and interpreted, what is its perceived usefulness and limitations and what refinements are required to improve the representation. The study involved recruiting 11 participants that have used the Learning Design Visual Sequence in the capacity of either interpreting learning designs documented in the Learning Design project Web site and/or using the graphical formalism to document their own learning designs that they have implemented in their work context. Preliminary findings indicate there is evidence that the graphical learning design representation is being used by some academic staff to document teaching ideas and its visual characteristic is viewed as one of its main strengths (Agostinho, 2006).

Other projects being undertaken by the researchers which is extending the work of the learning designs project includes the development of online repositories showing models of best practice in ICT-facilitated learning and teaching. A project underway in the local context is seeking examples of best practice in the communications area in order to develop an online resource for teachers to facilitate the sharing and reuse of learning activities. The project is exploring strategies for presenting learning designs describing the models of best practice in ways that attract and engage mainstream teachers.

The last named author uses learning design visual sequences in design work and workshops with university teachers. A guide to developing simple role plays in the Vista Learning Management System has been written which uses a learning design visual sequence to describe at a glance what is involved in this form of online collaborative learning. Other Vista guides for the other learning designs are almost complete.

Wills has also received a large national competitive grant to facilitate the uptake of one of the generic learning designs devised in the Learning Designs project, that is: online role play (see http://www.carrickinstitute.edu.au/carrick/go/op/edit/pid/17 for a summary about Project EnRoLE).

There are a number of facilitation strategies utilized in Project EnRoLE, such as university-based clusters of new and existing role play designers building into state networks to facilitate cross-disciplinary and cross-institutional partnerships. However, one of the strategies underpinning the project at the national level is documentation of each role play learning design in a national repository for peer review. This part of the project builds on the work of the Learning Designs project, which documented six contextualized role play designs, by aiming to document one hundred role play learning designs in the next two years. (The growth of online role-play to date has been tracked from 1990 to 2005 and published in Wills & McDougall, 2006.)

McAndrew, Goodyear & Dalziel (2006) have suggested that it is now an appropriate time for reflection on current representational forms to determine how sharing can be best facilitated amongst teachers and designers. The visual learning design representation developed by the learning designs project has the potential to be a promising contribution to this dialogue.

CONCLUSION

This chapter has explained how a graphical formalism, referred to as a learning design visual sequence, was developed to illustrate a learning design as comprising three main elements: tasks, resources, and supports. Each element of a learning design is assigned a symbol: rectangles for tasks, triangles for resources and circles for supports, and the learning design sequence shows the chronology of tasks, resources, and supports a teacher has designed for learners to engage with over a period of time. This graphical representation is accompanied by detailed textual information that explains the learning design, including the theoretical basis, research evidence for the approach, and details the particular context in which it has been implemented.

The Learning Designs project has highlighted the challenge in describing learning designs and the need for further work. It is hoped that the work conducted in creating a graphical formalism will contribute to the call for a learning design "language" and help move forward the mission of improving the quality of learning in higher education institutions by enabling teachers to share innovative ICT-based pedagogical strategies.

ACKNOWLEDGMENT

The authors would like to acknowledge that this publication was made possible through participation in the 2000-2002 Australian Universities Teaching Committee project titled: "Information and Communication Technologies and Their Role in Flexible Learning" (http://www.learningdesigns.uow.edu.au) funded through the Higher Education Innovation Programme (HEIP) via the Commonwealth Department of Education, Science and Training. Consortium: Project Team—Professor Barry Harper (University of Wollongong), Professor Ron Oliver (Edith Cowan University), Professor John Hedberg (formerly from University of Wollongong), Professor Sandra Wills (University of Wollongong); Research Team—Dr. Jan Herrington (University of Wollongong), Dr. Garry Hoban (University of Wollongong), Dr. Lori Lockyer (University of Wollongong), Associate Professor Catherine McLoughlin (Australian Catholic University); Project Manager—Dr. Shirley Agostinho (University of Wollongong).

REFERENCES

Agostinho, S. (2006, December). The use of a visual learning design representation to document and communicate teaching ideas. In L. Markauskaite, P. Goodyear, & P. Reimann (Eds.), *The Proceedings of the 23rd Annual Conference of the Astralasian Society for Computers in Learning in Tertiary Education: Who's Learning? Whose Technology?* (pp. 3-7). Sydney: Sydney University Press.

Agostinho, S, Oliver, R., Harper, B., Hedberg, H., & Wills, S. (2002). A tool to evaluate the potential for an ICT-based learning design to foster "high-quality learning". In A. Williamson, C. Gunn, A. Young, & T. Clear (Eds.), *The Proceedings of the 19th Annual Conference of the Australasian Society for Computers in Learning in Tertiary Education* (pp. 29-38). Auckland, New Zealand. UNITEC Institute of Technology.

Alexander, S., & McKenzie, J. (1998). *An evaluation of information technology projects for university learning.* CAUT, Canberra: Australian Government Publishing Service.

AUTC Project (2002). Information and communication technologies and their role in flexible learning final report. Retrieved September 1, 2006, from http://www.autc.gov.au/projects/completed/comp_projects_ICT_flex_learning.htm

Bennett, S. J. (2005). Online support for collaborative authentic activities. In C. Howard, J. Boettcher, L. Justice, K. Schenk, P. Rogers, & G. Berg (Eds.), *Encyclopedia of distance learning* Vol I-IV (pp. 1412-1416). Hershey, PA: Idea Group Reference.

Bennett, S., Agostinho, S., & Lockyer, L. (2005, July 4-6). Reusable learning designs in university education. In *The Proceedings of the IASTED International Conference on Education and Technology (ICET 2005)* (pp. 102-106). Calgary, Alberta, Canada.

Bennett, S., Agostinho, S., Lockyer, L., & Harper, B. (2006). Supporting university teachers create pedagogically sound learning environments using learning designs and learning objects. *IADIS International Journal on WWW/Internet, 4*(1), 16-26. Retrieved July 10, 2006, from http://www.iadis.org/ijwi/

Bennett, S., Lockyer, L. & Agostinho, S. (2004, December 5-8). Investigating how learning designs can be used as a framework to incorporate learning objects. In R. Atkinson, C. McBeath, D. Jonas-Dwyer, & R. Phillips (Eds.), *The Proceedings of the 21st ASCILITE Conference* (pp. 116-122). Perth, Australia. Retrieved from http://www.ascilite.org.au/conferences/perth04/procs/bennett.html

Botturi, L., Derntl, M., Boot, E., & Figl, K. (2006). A classification framework for educational modeling languages in instructional design. In *The Proceedings of IEEE ICALT 2006* (pp. 1216-1220). Kerkrade, The Netherlands.

Boud, D. & Prosser, M. (2002). Appraising new technologies for learning: A framework for development. *Educational Media International, 39*(3-4), 237-245.

Collis, B. (1998). Implementing innovative teaching across the faculty via the WWW. In S. McNeil, J. Price, S. Boger-Mehall, B. Robin, & J. Willis. (Eds.), *The Proceedings of SITE '98, Society for Information Technology and Teacher Education, 9th International Conference* (pp. 1328-1335). Washington, DC: Association for the Advancement of Computing in Education.

Cunningham, S. (1998). Technology and delivery: Assessing the impact of new media on "borderless" education. *Australian Universities' Review, 41*(1), 10-13.

Dijkstra, S., Collis, B., & Eseryel, D. (1999). Instructional design for tele-learning. *Journal of Computing in Higher Education, 10*(2), 3-18.

Goodyear, P. (2005). Educational design and networked learning: Patterns, pattern languages and design practice. *Australian Journal of Educational Technology, 21*(1), 82-101.

Harper, B., Agostinho, S., Bennett, S., Lukasiak, J., & Lockyer, L. (2005). Constructing high quality learning environments using learning designs and learning objects. In P. Goodyear, D. G. Sampson, D. J.-T. Y.Kinshuk, T. Okamoto, R. Hartley, & N.-S. Chen (Eds.), *The Proceedings of the 5th IEEE International Conference on Advanced Learning Technologies (ICALT 2005)* (pp. 266-270). Kaohsiung, Taiwan. IEEE Computer Society.

Herrington, J. & Oliver, R. (2002). *Description of online teaching and learning (Edith Cowan University Online Unit IMM4141 in Graduate Certificate in Online Learning).* Retrieved September 19, 2006, from http://www.learningdesigns.uow.edu.au/exemplars/info/LD20/index.html

Hicks, O. (2004). *Composite report on projects funded through the Australian universities teaching committee 2000-2003.* Retrieved September 1, 2006, from http://www.autc.gov.au/projects/completed/comp_projects_proj_funded_autc_2000-2003.htm

Ip, A., & Naidu, S. (2001). Experienced-based pedagogical designs for e-learning. *Educational Technology: The Magazine for Managers of Change in Education, 41*(5),53-58.

Jonassen, D., H. (2000). Toward a design theory of problem solving. *Educational Technology Research and Development, 48*(4), 63-85.

McAndrew, P., Goodyear, P., & Dalziel, J. (2006). Patterns, designs and activities: Unifying descriptions of learning structures. *International Journal of Learning Technology, 2*(2/3), 216-242.

Nicoll, K. (1998). "Fixing" the "Facts": Flexible learning as policy invention. *Higher Education Research and Development, 17*(3), 291-304.

Oliver, R. (1999). Exploring strategies for online teaching and learning. *Distance Education, 20*(2), 240-254.

Oliver, R., & Herrington, J. (2000). Using situated learning as a design strategy for Web-based learning. In B. Abbey (Ed.), *Instructional and cognitive impacts of Web-based education* (pp. 178-191). Hershey PA: Idea Group Publishing.

Oliver, R., & Herrington, J. (2001). *Teaching and learning online: A beginner's guide to e-learning and e-teaching in higher education.* Edith Cowan University: Western Australia.

Oliver, R. & Herrington, J. (2002). *Explore, describe, apply: A problem focused learning design.* Retrieved September 19, 2006, from http://www. learningdesigns.uow.edu.au/guides/info/G4/index.htm

Oliver, R., Harper, B., Hedberg, J., Wills, S., & Agostinho, S. (2002). Formalizing the description of learning designs. In A. Goody, J. Herrington, & M. Northcote (Eds.), *Quality conversations: Research and development in higher education,* (Volume 25, pp. 496-504). Jamison, ACT: HERDSA.

Oliver, R., Harper, B., Wills, S. Agostinho, S. & Hedberg, J. (2007). Describing ICT-based learning designs that promote quality learning outcomes. In H. Beetham & R. Sharpe (Eds.), *Rethinking pedagogy for the digital age: Designing and delivering e-learning* (pp. 64-80). Routledge.

Pedagogy case study templates. (2006). Retrieved September 19, 2006, from http://www.jisc.ac.uk/whatwedo/programmes/elearning_pedagogy/elp_templates.aspx

Richards, G., & Knight, C. (2005, 26 January). *UNFOLD Learning design and representations of instructional intent.* Retrieved April 5, 2005, from http://www.unfold-project.net:8085/UNFOLD/about_folder/events/online/griff/paper/

Waters, S. H., & Gibbons, A. S. (2004). Design languages, notation systems, and instructional technology: A case study. *Educational Technology, Research and Development, 52*(2), 57-68.

Wills, S. & McDougall, A. (2006, December). Facilitating uptake of online role play: Learning objects versus learning designs. In *The Proceedings of the 23rd Annual Conference of the Australasian Society for Computers in Learning in Tertiary Education* (pp. 889-892). Sydney: Sydney University Press.

Tsichritzis, D. (1999). Reengineering the university. *Communications of the ACM, 42*(6), 93-100.

Chapter XX
Diagrams of Learning Flow Patterns' Solutions as Visual Representations of Refinable IMS Learning Design Templates

Davinia Hernández-Leo
University of Valladolid, Spain

Eloy D. Villasclaras-Fernández
University of Valladolid, Spain

Juan I. Asensio-Pérez
University of Valladolid, Spain

Yannis Dimitriadis
University of Valladolid, Spain

ABSTRACT

This chapter introduces the use of diagrammatic representations of learning flow patterns as a means of visualizing refinable IMS learning design (IMS-LD) templates. It argues that the incorporation of pattern-based IMS-LD templates in authoring tools, which graphically guide users to create their own learning designs, offers a solution to the problem of IMS-LD constructs not being familiar to educators because of its technical nature and text-based notation. Furthermore, this solution facilitates the reuse of good practices formulated as patterns, permitting a design process that promotes potentially effective results. This issue is especially important in collaborative learning designs, in which elicitations of desired social interactions are planned beforehand. Based on these ideas, the chapter also presents Collage, an IMS-LD editor which provides templates based on collaborative learning flow patterns (CLFPs), and includes an example drawn from a real scenario that shows the feasibility and usefulness of the approach.

INTRODUCTION

Learning technology standards and specifications are used increasingly to support the professional activity of instructional designers (Rodríguez-Estévez, Caeiro-Rodríguez, & Santos-Gago, 2003). Significantly, the recent IMS Learning Design (IMS-LD) specification (IMS, 2003) highlights the use of computers to facilitate the teaching-learning processes instead of for delivering educational content (Burgos & Griffiths, 2005). That is to say, IMS-LD provides a machine-readable notation (XML language) to formalize learning scenarios that can be automatically interpreted by compliant players or learning management systems (LMS) (Koper & Tattersall, 2005). These formalized scenarios or units of learning (UoLs) are abstract representations of any individual or group-based learning situation (a course, a lesson, etc.). The main benefits of using a specification like IMS-LD are twofold. First, teachers, instructors and trainers can specify the behavior and functionality of a computer-supported learning system by providing a UoL (Bote-Lorenzo et al., 2004). And, second, because UoLs are interoperable and reusable, they can be executed in various compliant systems and in various settings with different participants (Tattersall et al., 2005).

However, as pointed out in Chapter XV, IMS-LD is a notation system that is layered, formal, textual and of a single perspective (Waters & Gibbons, 2004; Botturi, Derntl, Boot, & Figl, 2006). Due to its textual and formal nature, IMS-LD does not look familiar (i.e., cannot be understood intuitively) by the majority of educators, as argued by Harrer and Malzah (2006) and in Chapter XIV of this handbook. For this reason IMS-LD is not really practical as a teacher-friendly design and authoring approach for UoLs, nor is it useful as a means of communication in participatory design teams involving different stakeholders (Griffiths & Blat, 2005). To overcome these drawbacks, visual design languages and tools are envisaged as a solution for the reflective communication and creative generation of designs (see Chapter XXI).

This chapter focuses on the design of IMS-LD-formalized collaborative learning scenarios (or *scripts*) (Hernández-Leo, Asensio-Pérez, & Dimitriadis, 2005). Collaborative learning is a relevant educational approach, whose learning benefits are positively recognized by practitioners (Johnson & Johnson, 1999). This approach highlights the importance of social interaction and active learning processes. Computer-supported collaborative learning (CSCL) is the domain that studies the use of computers and networks as mediation technologies to support collaborative learning (Dillenbourg, 1999). It is worth noticing that the context dependency and social variables involved in CSCL make this domain particularly complex. This fact motivates the agreement of many authors on that CSCL settings need more flexibility (or less rigidity) than traditional, individual instructional sequences (Karagiorgi & Symeou, 2005; Dillenbourg, 2002; Oliver, Harper, Hedberg, Wills, & Agostinho, 2002). On the other hand, it is generally accepted that unplanned collaboration does not necessarily lead to learning outcomes (NISE, 1997; Dillenbourg, 2002). Efficient collaborative learning greatly depends on the effort employed at design time (Goodyear, 2005). Particularly required are systematic approaches to designing CSCL that focus on the elicitations of well-known effective desired interactions (Strijbos, Martens, & Jochems, 2004).

Considering the difficulties of finding an appropriate trade-off between coercion and free collaboration, re-inventing and designing collaborative UoLs for each specific learning situation is costly. A solution to this problem is unraveling content, tools, specific learning tasks, etc., from the structure (the learning flow) of the "CSCL script" (hereafter referenced as *scripts*) so that this structure can be applied and reused in different settings, in a similar spirit to the approach presented in the previous Chapter XIX. The effort involved in developing separated generic structures of scripts is justified if these learning flows have been extensively tested and applied in a broad range of different situations. Examples of deeply evaluated collaborative learning flows are the well-known jigsaw (Aronson & Patnoe, 1997), simulation or role-play and think-pair-share strategies (NISE, 1997). Therefore, scripts exhibiting these commonly used structures (good or best practices) represent potentially effective scripts.

This chapter is based on our proposal (Hernández-Leo et al., 2005) related to the formulation of these generalized learning flows as patterns (Alexander et al., 1977), so that they are written in structured formats (including a diagrammatic representation of the solution) that make them easier to understand, (re)use, classify, etc. The resulting patterns, what we call CLFPs (collaborative learning flow patterns), offer a conceptual common ground among instructional designers and technology developers and a way of communicating collaborative learning expertise. In particular, this chapter provides an answer to the question: how can these types of patterns be integrated into instructional design practice? The pedagogical patterns collected in repositories are not broadly or satisfactorily (re)used (PPP, 2000; E-LEN, 2004). Our approach relies on the incorporation of patterns in authoring tools that graphically guide users to creatively obtain their own collaborative IMS-LD compliant designs (Hernández-Leo et al., 2006). From a pedagogical angle (Strijbos et al., 2004), this assistance aims at reducing the complexity of the learning design process, as well as at guaranteeing potential effective results, since the guidance is based on the reuse of best practices in collaborative learning. To incorporate the patterns in authoring tools, we make use of refinable templates, i.e. partly completed re-usable designs (Hernández-Leo, Harrer, Dodero, Asensio-Pérez, & Burgos, 2006). With the aim of reducing the complexity from the technical angle (Griffiths et al., 2005),

we use a specific graphical notation intended to be more intuitive: the diagrams of the patterns' solutions. Remarkably, we have developed an IMS-LD compliant editor called *Collage*, whose implemented design process incorporates combinable CLFPs as IMS-LD templates (Hernández-Leo et al., 2006). This tool employs the CLFPs' diagrams as the visual representation of the templates.

The structure of the chapter is as follows. The next section is devoted to introducing the idea of pattern-based design. It focuses on CLFPs, as a type of patterns for designing scripts, and discusses the role of patterns when they are integrated in authoring tools. Then, we face the implementation of CLFPs as IMS-LD templates and their visual incorporation in the *Collage* authoring tool for the production of scripts (collaborative UoLs). Then follows an example that illustrates the creation of a script based on a combination of tree CLFPs. The chapter ends with a discussion and some concluding remarks.

PATTERN-BASED DESIGN

The word "pattern" has been used for centuries (e.g., patterns for dressmaking Holkeboer, 1987). However, it is broadly accepted that the idea of "pattern-based design" comes originally from architecture (Alexander et al., 1977), and has been also successfully used in software engineering (Gamma, Helm, Johnson, & Vlissides, 1995). Recently other domain specific patterns have been proposed, including (technology-supported) education (Derntl & Botturi, 2006). On page X of Alexander et al. (1977) Alexander defines a pattern as follows:

Each pattern describes a problem that occurs over and over again in our environment, and then describes the core of the solution to that problem, in such a way that you can use this solution a million times over, without ever doing it the same way twice.

Therefore, patterns provide a structure for integrating the analysis and solution that can be found to a problem, in a way that is sensitive to context. They offer guidance, but require embellishment. Alexander introduces 253 patterns in the architecture domain. He presents patterns for everything from designing independent regions, to cities, buildings and even single rooms. By connecting these patterns with common forces and other relations he transforms this collection of patterns into a pattern language, which provides a consistent way of creating a comfortable environment for people to live in. Apart from being a vehicle of creativity and communication in which structured ideas of good practices can be discussed, shared and modified, Alexander (1999) points out three essential features of a pattern language: a moral preoccupation (the ability to improve an environment), an aim of creating (morphological) coherence, and generativeness (e.g., the power to create morally sound and coherent objects).

For clarity purposes and in order to present each pattern connected to other patterns, Alexander uses the same general format for each pattern (Alexander et al., 1977; E-LEN, 2004). The relations with other patterns are indicated in the introductory paragraph, setting the context of the pattern, and the final paragraph, explaining how it can be embellished or completed. The essence of the problem and the solution are highlighted in bold type. The solution is also shown in form of a diagram, with labels to indicate its main components. This diagram is key to promoting a good understanding of the solution.

On the other hand, design patterns in software engineering are formulated using a different format, and tackle different types of problems. They describe how to solve particular problems that come up in software development. Gamma (Gamma et al., 1995) defines design patterns as, "descriptions of communicating objects and classes that are customized to solve a general problem in a particular context" (p. 3).

Nevertheless, these patterns also target the provision of a common vocabulary, a common base of understanding regarding what is important in the area (programming vs. architecture) and a large corpus of solutions that makes users (developers vs. architects) more effective. With the same goal of collecting best practices, proven solutions and lessons learned, there are several initiatives that aim at applying the patterns approach to the educational domain, especially to technology-enhanced learning. Hernández-Leo, Villasclaras-Fernández, Asensio-Pérez, Dimitriadis, and Retalis (2006) expose a unifying view of some proposals for patterns in e-learning. It differentiates "patterns for analysis," which deal with analyzing the usage of e-learning systems in order to improve them, from "patterns for design," which are devoted to the design of e-learning systems (Retalis, Georgiakakis, & Dimitriadis, 2006) and pedagogical scenarios (PPP, 2000). Within the CSCL domain, there are also efforts that try to take advantage of the idea of pattern-based design. Currently, the TELL project represents the main initiative of collecting design patterns for teachers and educational CSCL (system) designers (TELL, 2005). Some of these patterns are devoted to the design of scripts, which is the focus of the following subsection.

CSCL Scripting Patterns: Collaborative Learning Flow Patterns

A "CSCL scripting pattern" (hereafter *scripting pattern*) describes a common problem and its corresponding broadly-accepted solution which can be used repeatedly in the design of collaboration scripts that are suitable of being formalized using a computer-interpretable notation. In other words, the final goal is that the resulting pattern-based scripts can be interpreted by an LMS. The main users of scripting patterns are practitioners and instructional designers, who construct collaborative learning plans. Scripting patterns can be formulated from general design ideas or structures based on any best/good practice when designing scripts to their reusable specialization. These practices can be grouped at different levels of granularity: set of activities that are organized in CL flows (coarser granularity level), the single activities themselves (actions within activities),

The authoring tool and the example that we present in the next sections of this chapter make use of the scripting patterns at the coarser granularity level, we focus the next paragraph on this type of patterns: collaborative learning flow patterns, or CLFPs (Hernández-Leo et al., 2005). As we advanced in the introduction,

Table 1. Pyramid CLFP (short version)

TITLE	**Pyramid** Collaborative Learning Flow Pattern
CONTEXT	This pattern gives the collaborative learning flow for a context in which several participants face the collaborative resolution of the same problem
	***
PROBLEM	**If groups of students face resolution of a complex problem/task, usually without a concrete solution, whose resolution implies the achievement of gradual consensus among all the participants, an adequate collaborative learning flow may be planned.**
FORCES	The flow of collaborative learning activities to be followed in order to solve a complex task, whose resolution implies the achievement of gradual consensus, should promote the following educational benefits:
	• To promote the feeling that team members need each other to succeed (positive interdependence)
	• To foster discussion in order to construct students' knowledge
	The risk involved in structuring collaboration so that a gradual consensus is achieved is medium. That is, the experience needed in collaborative learning needed is not too high.
SOLUTION	**Each participant studies the problem and proposes a solution. Groups (usually pairs) of participants compare and discuss their proposals and, finally, propose a new shared solution. Those groups join in larger groups in order to generate new agreed proposal. At the end, all the participants must propose a final and agreed solution.**
DIAGRAM	
	***
RATIONALE	The Jigsaw (or Snowball) structure has been extensively tested and applied in a broad range of different settings and on which there are abundance of research (see, for instance, the references pointed out in the additional information section).
EXAMPLE	Collaborative proposal of a computing system for a client with particular requirements where each participant contributes with a proposal that is compared with other contribution and consequently refined. More information available at http://gsic.tel.uva.es/collage.
ADDITIONAL INFORMATION	(Davis, 2002; Gibbs, 1995)

Table 2. Jigsaw CLFP (short version)

TITLE	**Jigsaw** Collaborative Learning Flow Pattern
CONTEXT	This pattern gives the collaborative learning flow for a context in which several small groups are facing the study of a lot of information for the resolution of the same problem.
	***
PROBLEM	**If groups of students face resolution of a complex problem/task that can be easily divided into sections or independent sub-problems, an adequate collaborative learning flow may be planned.**
FORCES	The flow of collaborative learning activities to be followed in order to solve a complex divisible task should promote the following educational benefits: • To promote the feeling that team members need each other to succeed (positive interdependence) • To foster discussion in order to construct students' knowledge • To ensure that students must contribute their fare share (individual accountability) However, the solution for structuring collaboration in order to tackle this problem may be complex and probably more appropriate for collaborative learning experienced teachers and learners.
SOLUTION	**Each participant (individual or initial group) in a group ("Jigsaw Group") studies or works around a particular sub-problem. The participants of different groups that study the same problem meet in an "Expert Group" for exchanging ideas. These temporary focus groups become experts in the section of the problem given to them. At last, participants of each "Jigsaw group" meet to contribute with its "expertise" in order to solve the whole problem.**
DIAGRAM	
	***
RATIONALE	The Jigsaw structure, first introduced by Aronson et al. (Aronson & Patnoe, 1997), derives from practice (didacticism used in the practice) rather than from general learning theories (Johnson & Johnson, 1999), i.e. it represents a method that has been extensively tested and applied in a broad range of different settings and on which there are abundance of research (see, for instance, the references pointed out in the additional information section).
EXAMPLE	Collaborative understanding of a paper where each subsection (excluding the summary and introduction) is assigned to each member or every "Jigsaw Group." More information available at http://gsic.tel.uva.es/collage.
ADDITIONAL INFORMATION	(Aronson & Patnoe, 1997; Clarke, 1994; Johnson & Johnson, 1999)

and the resources (materials and tools) that support the single activities. Besides, there are some aspects (such as roles or common collaborative mechanisms, namely group formation, roles/resources distribution, floor control, awareness) that can be related to some of the patterns at any of the aforementioned granularity levels. In this way, patterns at the different levels are complementary and need each other for completeness, so they can be related forming a hierarchical structure as discussed in Hernández-Leo et al. (2006).

Table 3. Think-Pair-Share CLFP (short version)

TITLE	**Think-Pair-Share** Collaborative Learning Flow Pattern
CONTEXT	This pattern gives the collaborative learning flow for a context in which students are paired to solve a challenging or open-ended question.
	***
PROBLEM	**If groups of students face resolution of a challenging or open-ended question.**
FORCES	The flow of collaborative learning activities to be followed in order to solve a challenging or open-ended question: • To promote the feeling that team members need each other to succeed (positive interdependence). • To foster discussion in order to construct students' knowledge. • To focus students' attention on a particular topic. • To give a chance to formulate answers by retrieving information from long-term memory. The solution for structuring collaboration in order to tackle this problem may be ideally suited for individuals who are new to collaborative learning.
SOLUTION	**Each participant has time to think about the question. They pair and discuss their ideas about the question. Then, they comment or take a classroom "vote."**
DIAGRAM	
	***
RATIONALE	Students are much more willing to respond after they have had a chance to discuss their ideas with a classmate because if the answer is wrong, the embarrassment is shared. Also, the responses received are often more intellectually concise since students have had a chance to reflect on their ideas with one another. See also the references pointed out in the additional information section).
EXAMPLE	Thinking, paring and sharing best ways to save energy. More information available at http://gsic.tel.uva.es/collage.
ADDITIONAL INFORMATION	(NISE, 1997; Millis & Cottell, 1998)

CLFPs capture the essence of broadly accepted well-known techniques for structuring the flow of activities involved in collaborative learning scenarios. These good practices pre-structure collaboration at a macro-level (Dillenbourg & Tchounikine, 2006) in such a way that they promote productive interactions, so that the potential effectiveness of the educational situation is enhanced. Tables 1, 2 and 3 show short versions of three CLFPs (complete versions of pyramid and jigsaw CLFPs are available in TELL, 2005), which are represented according to a structure based on the use of natural language. The format is similar to Alexander's form, including also the diagrammatic representation of the solution.

It is not realistic to consider that collaborative learning scenarios are always structured as indicated by a unique CLFP. Like Alexandrian patterns, CLFPs can be used collectively in order to define richer collaborative learning flows. CLFPs can be *combined*: a particular phase of a CLFP can be structured according to another CLFP (that can be eventually the same). Or, they can be *concatenated*: some phases of a learning design are structured according to one CLFP and other (separated but consecutive) phases of the learning design are structured using another CLFP (that can be eventually the same).

Similarly to the patterns for architecture or software engineering, the main advantages of CLFPs (and scripting patterns in general) are that they provide a conceptual common ground and a way of communicating, in this case, collaborative learning expertise of best practices to others, eventually novice practitioners. Instead of trying to create their own scripts from scratch, practitioners can use these patterns as a starting point. Consequently, the potential effectiveness of the scripts is enhanced, as is the design processes in terms of complexity and time demands. At this point, the following question arises: How can scripting patterns be effectively integrated into design processes? Since the patterns collected in repositories are not broadly and satisfactorily reused, our approach relies on the incorporation of patterns in authoring tools. An authoring tool based on patterns can guide educators to obtain effective scripts for their specific collaborative learning situations. In other words, the selection of a CLFP as the basis for the desired script would guarantee, to a great extent, the achievement of a set of objectives as dictated by previous experiences from which the CLFP emerged.

Therefore, the following question arises: How should the patterns be implemented in authoring tools? In other words, what is the role of patterns in authoring tools?

The Role of Patterns: Assistant vs. Template

As mentioned above, incorporating patterns in authoring tools potentially facilitates their reuse and the design of experience-founded scripts. The incorporation of patterns in authoring tools can be accomplished in two (complementary) ways so that the patterns act as assistants or as templates:

- **Pattern-based assistant:** A context-aware advising mechanism based on the knowledge formulated in the patterns. It is possible to imagine this type of assistant similar to, for example, the animated Microsoft Office Assistant that becomes visible whenever the system detects the user could benefit from its advice.
- **Pattern-based template:** A ready-made skeleton based on the knowledge formulated in a pattern that can be refined to create finished designs. This idea may remind readers, for example, of Web page templates (e.g., for Adobe Dreamweaver or Microsoft Front Page) that enable the easy production of Web pages by separating their presentation from the content.

The traditional dressmaking patterns are very close to this idea of template while more abstract rules, such as what types of buttons should be employed for a certain type of costume, are more related to the idea of assistant. Depending on the nature of the different types of scripting patterns they can be implemented as assistant or as templates. In the case of the patterns at the collaborative learning flow level, when the degree of specialization of the pattern is such that its solution offers a learning flow (e.g., the CLFPs of Table 1, 2 and 3), this pattern is suitable of being provided as a template. On the contrary, if the pattern offers abstract advice, for example, to enrich the learning flow (see *Enriching the learning process* pattern of TELL, 2005), it may be implemented as an assistant. A similar analysis is applicable to the patterns at the activity level. On the other hand, there are already some proposals of the use of pattern-based templates for the creation of learning objects (Jones, 2004). Also at the resource level, patterns concerning educational tools may be offered as assistant that can act as a mediator between tool searchers and the teacher or instructional designer (Vega-Gorgojo et al., 2006).

The implementation of pattern-based assistant in authoring tools is outside the scope of this chapter. However, the next section faces the implementation of CLFPs whose solutions are flows of activity types as templates. Similar ideas could be adopted for the patterns at the activity level that provide ways of organizing single activities.

IMPLEMENTING CLFPs AS IMS-LD TEMPLATES

The approach of providing CLFPs as templates of scripts can be accomplished with any educational modeling language that enables the computational representation of the scripts. With this purpose, we use IMS-LD specification since it is currently

accepted as the de facto standard for formalizing teaching-learning processes, such as the learning flows suggested in the CLFPs.

IMS-LD for Computationally Representing CLFP-Based Scripts

IMS-LD was realized by the IMS Global Consortium in 2003 (IMS, 2003). Chapter XV describes the IMS-LD notation in detail and reviews experience with its use. A *learning design* (LD) is a description of a *method* enabling learners to attain particular *objectives* by performing learning *activities* in a certain order in the context of a learning *environment*. The environment consists of the appropriate *learning objects* and *services* to be used during the performance of the activities. A method contains the *play*, which is modeled according to a theatrical play with *acts* and *role-parts*. Since the specification provides a standard language for formally expressing learning situations based on different pedagogical theories (Koper & Tattersall, 2005), the reuse and interoperability of LDs in different systems is facilitated. A unit of learning (UoL) is a content package including an LD and a set of physical resources, or their location. It is an abstract representation of any learning event (a course, a lesson, etc.).

Although certain limitations have been observed, describing collaborative learning scenarios using IMS-LD is feasible (Hernández-Leo et al., 2005). The main features of the specification that should be considered when describing group-based characteristics are the following. First, groups can be formed with IMS-LD by binding multiple individuals to the same (instance of a) role or by associating multiple roles to activities that provide a shared environment that mediates collaboration. Since roles can be nested (Hernández-Leo et al., 2005), indicating that a role is divided into sub-roles, it is possible to specify groups composed of other (smaller) groups or different roles. Second, IMS-LD enables activities to be specified in coordinated collaborative learning flows in the *method* using mainly the *act* and the *activity structure* elements as well as *conditions*. Moreover, the *play* and the *monitoring service* are also helpful when coordinating activities. Nevertheless, the teacher (or instructional designer) does not need to be familiar with the technical IMS-LD constructs if high-level editors, such as the authoring tool presented in next section, are provided.

Collage, a CLFP-Based IMS-LD Editor of CSCL Scripts

Collage (Hernández-Leo et al., 2006) is a high-level IMS-LD authoring tool specially created to allow teachers to create their own collaborative UoLs (scripts) for collaborative learning by reusing CLFPs as templates. The scripts produced are IMS-LD (level A) compliant. Therefore, they can be interpreted by any IMS-LD player (Bote-Lorenzo et al., 2004; Tattersall et al., 2005), so that the participants of the educational design (learners and teachers) are automatically guided through the sequence of activities planned in the learning flow. Participants are also provided with the required resources in each activity.

With this tool, the user can create a UoL by specifying a set of objectives and prerequisites, the resources and tools that will be available, and the learning flow, i.e., the sequence of activities that the participants will perform and the roles that they will play. In fact, the edition of the collaborative learning flows by means of visual representations is Collage's key feature. This edition is accomplished through the selection and configuration of whichever graphical CLFP-based IMS-LD templates is best suited for a particular scenario. The learning activities specified by the templates can then be set up with a description and a set of resources and supporting tools. An activity may also be structured according to another CLFP. Thus, a single script may be composed by several CLFPs organized hierarchically as mentioned in a previous section.

The resulting learning flow (suggested by a single CLFP or a combination of several CLFPs) is presented in an intuitive way to help the user keep in mind a global view of the design, and to facilitate their comprehension and authoring. This presentation consists in two views. First, a global view of the LD structure is shown as a tree graph. When LD embraces several CLFPs, each pattern constitutes a node. Users can browse through the different sections that compose the LD by clicking on the nodes. The second view allows the user to zoom in to a particular section of the activity flow. This detailed view, is a graphical representation of the CLFP-based template to which the selected section belongs. This graphical representation corresponds to the diagram of the pattern's solution so that the good practice offered by the CLFP is easily recognized and understood. In addition, it is worth mentioning that the implementation of the CLFP-based templates in Collage has been done so that their visual representations are highly interactive and including pattern-specific functions (e.g., selection of levels in a Pyramid CLFP-based template).

Thanks to these graphical representations, Collage reduces the complexity of the design process of potentially-effective collaborative UoLs. Given that we can create quite complex collaborative designs, in which several roles participate through a number of phases, it is useful to clearly represent each of these elements. While the resulting IMS-LD document contains just a series of textual-notated *acts* with different activities, the graphical representation provided by Collage helps understanding the significance of each phase within the whole LD. This is possibly due to the CLFP-based design process, which takes advantage of previous knowledge that the practitioners may have (or may acquire) about the reusable good practices depicted in the patterns. At the same time, the use of these visualizations hides some difficult to understand IMS-LD elements in such a way that the user does not need to know about their existence and function.

These benefits reflect a trade-off between constrained design options, and good reuse and particularization of CLFPs and an easy edition of collaborative LDs. These characteristics are not considered in more generic approaches, such as RELOAD LD editor (University of Bolton, 2004; Milligan, Beauvoir, & Sharples, 2005) and CopperAuthor (van der Vegt, 2005), which are close to the technical source of the specification and use text-based notation, or MOT+ (de la Teja, Lundgren-Cayro, & Paquette, 2005; see also Chapter VIII) and ASK-LDT (Sampson, Karampiperis, & Zervas, 2005), which use graphical notations but do not incorporate abstractions easier to understand by teachers. The main features of Collage are illustrated in the following example drawn from a real case study.

AN EXAMPLE BASED ON A COMBINATION OF THREE CLFPs

This example illustrates how to use Collage for the CLFPs-based design of a script that belongs to an undergraduate engineering course on "Operation, Administration and Maintenance of Communication Networks." The course is part of the 5th year (out of five) of the "Telecommunications Engineering" curriculum at the University of Valladolid, Spain.

The teacher (also playing the role of an instructional designer) wants his 12 students to collaboratively read a long, technical paper on a particular subject related to the course contents. The teacher, by setting this scenario, aims at achieving several learning objectives that include: improving the knowledge of the paper's contents, using scientific and technical literature, and being able to synthesize what has been read. Also, the teacher expects that the collaborative nature of the setting helps the students to achieve other objectives not directly related to the course contents such as promoting positive

interdependence among group members, fostering discussion, and individually accountability (each participant should be responsible for his/her contribution to the group work).

For fulfilling the above objectives, the teacher wants to design a *blended* collaborative learning setting spanning two two-hour face-to-face synchronous sessions at the lab; and a virtual (or distant) asynchronous collaborative session in between. For both types of sessions, several supporting telematic tools are available: document viewers and editors, a Web-based shared document repository, a Web-based questionnaire tool, and a chat tool.

Taking into account the context and the number of students as well as the time restrictions, the teacher has to face the complex task of designing a set of sequenced collaborative learning activities, eventually supported by the available tools, which effectively guide the students towards the achievement of the desired learning objectives. As it was mentioned throughout the chapter, this task becomes even more complex if the resulting learning design needs to be formalized using IMD LD so that it can be interpreted by a LMS. How might the Collage authoring tool, as well as the underlying CLFP-based design process it enforces, help the teacher?

The first step when using Collage (Hernández-Leo et al., 2006) consists of selecting the set of CLFPs that, according to the desired learning objectives and the type of learning task to be faced by the students (in this case, reading a technical paper), which might be more suitable for structuring the flow of learning activities. Although this first step avoids having the teacher/instructional designer start the design process from scratch, it is not a straightforward step: Not all CLFPs are suitable for all types of learning tasks and objectives, and a bad selection might result in unsuccessful design.

Taking into account the description of Table 1, the pyramid CLFP promotes positive interdependence and fosters discussion with the final goal of achieving gradual consensus on the resolution of a task without a concrete solution. Within the context of this example, the teacher might opt for requesting the students to read the same paper and reach a final consensus, following the structuring of the pyramid, on the eight most important ideas of the paper and two questions they would like to be solved. In this way the teacher does not simply limit the learning task to reading the paper, he is proposing a collaborative way of solving a problem (without a concrete solution) that might help to achieve further learning objectives, according to the experience from which the good practice collected in the CLFP has been drawn.

But the pyramid CLFP by its own does not seem to provide all the confidence in achieving all the desired learning objectives. In this sense, and according to the descriptions of Table 2, the jigsaw CLFP promotes individual accountability when a general problem is divided into sub-problems to be faced by collaborating small groups. How could the teacher combine the potential advantages of the jigsaw CLFP with those of the pyramid CLFP? And, how could this CLFP be applied to the particular task that has been proposed above? (i.e., reading the paper and agreeing in a set of ideas and questions). One potential solution would be to consider that at the first level of the pyramid ("Each participant studies the problem and proposes a solution..." in Table 1) instead of individual students, groups of them propose a solution after having worked together according to the jigsaw CLFP. For applying this pattern, the general problem (reading the paper) is divided into sub-problems (each member of the group reads just one part of the paper). Then "experts" of the different groups exchange ideas (those students that have read the same part of the paper) in order to contribute to the resolution of the general problem within their groups (again, agreeing in a set of ideas and questions). Using the jigsaw CLFP in this case reduces the workload (each student just reads one part of the paper) without precluding the overall understanding of the paper

contents (thanks to the "expertise" provided by other group members).

According to the pyramid CLFP solution, the final expected learning activity (last level of the pyramid) implies that all the students discuss and agree on a final proposal of ideas and questions on the paper. For structuring and fostering this final discussion, the think-pair-share CLFP may also be useful (see Table 3). In this case, each participant of the CLFP would be a group of students (not an individual). The first phase of the think-pair-share (Think) would not be needed as each participating group has its own proposal on ideas and questions about the paper (derived from the previous Pyramid activities). The Pair phase might be carried out by means of a speaker from each group that explains each proposal. Finally, the Share phase (overall discussion) might be mediated by the teacher.

Therefore, the first teacher's decision might result in structuring the learning design according to the Pyramid CLFP but using the Jigsaw CLFP for the first level and the think-pair-share CLFP for the last one. As we detailed in the previous section, the Collage tool incorporates the diagrams of the CLFPs (see Table 1, 2, and 3) as a graphical notation that facilitates users' (teacher/instructional designers) selection and combination. Figure 1 illustrates how this graphical notation is used for the proposed example.

After selecting and combining CLFPs, the next step in the Collage CLFP-based design process implies refining those CLFPs (implemented as IMS-LD templates) so as to obtain the final UoL. This step includes design activities such as describing the learning activities (e.g., reading a part of the paper, discussing questions/ideas, etc.), providing information about roles (including groups), establishing group-size limits, and determining and configuring the resources needed to support each activities. Table 4 summarizes a potential result of this refining step for the number of students of the example (12), the available tools, and the time frame.

Figure 1. Planning the learning flow: Combining Pyramid, Jigsaw and Think-Pair-Share CLFPs in form of IMS-LD templates using a graphical notation in which the visual representation of each template corresponds to the diagram of its related pattern's solution

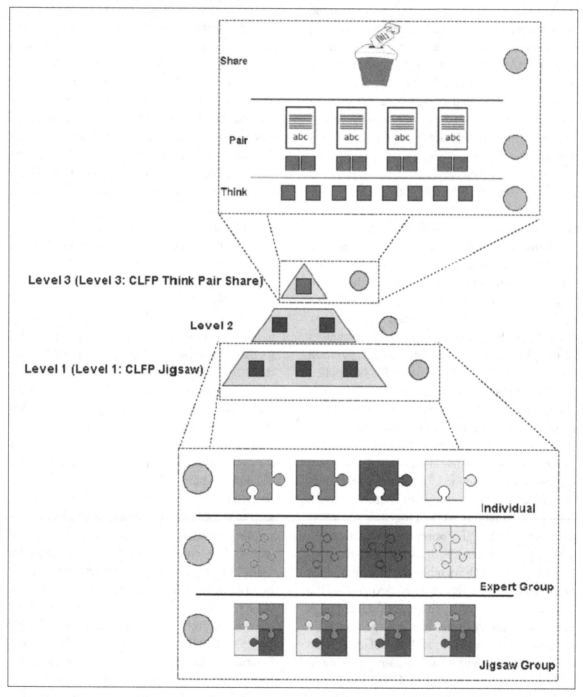

The described refining step is graphically supported by the Collage tool. Figure 2 shows how the teacher provides details on the "pair" phase of the TPS CLFP that structures the activities at the level 3 of the pyramid CLFP. (The complete UoL is available at http://gsic.tel.uva.es/collage.)

DISCUSSION

Our proposal of our using the diagrams of learning flow patterns' solutions as visual representations of refinable IMS learning design templates adds intuitiveness (as characterized by Waters et al., 2004) and familiarity (as described in Chapter XIV) to the IMS-LD notation system. This intuitive intelligibility results from the visual similarity to the mental images and ideas that the potential users have or build regarding the patterns. On the other hand, this approach represents a pragmatic solution grounded in practice to apply moderate constructivism assumptions compatible with ID practices and with the support of technology tools, as demanded in (Karagiorgi et al., 2005).

There are currently only six patterns incorporated in Collage. However, since they can be creatively combined in order to create new richer learning flows, it offers some degree of flexibility. As categorized in Botturi et al. (2006), Collage provides generative patterns which can

Table 4. Refining the template resulting of the combination of CLFPs towards the ready-to-run Unit of Learning (students' activities)

	Learning Flow Phase	Group characteristics	Task and supporting resources	
Pyramid level 1	**individual phase of Jigsaw**	Each "jigsaw group" has at least three people and no more than four. (original plan: four jigsaw groups of three members.)	Read the introduction and one of the three sections of the paper. (The classmates in your "jigsaw group" read the other sections.)	**First face-to-face session**
	"expert" phase of Jigsaw	Each "expert group" has at least one member of each "jigsaw group." (There are three different possible expertises, i.e. three sections of the paper. Original plan: three "expert" groups with four students.)	Discuss (using a chat) your part of the paper with the classmates that have read the same part in order to understand it well.	
	"jigsaw" phase of Jigsaw	(See Pyramid level 1: individual phase of Jigsaw)	Explain to the rest of the members of your "jigsaw group" your part of the paper. The group has to agree on which are the 10 main ideas of the whole paper and 2 questions. Use the available tool for questionnaires.	
Pyramid level 2		Each group of the second Pyramid level comprises from six to eight students. (original plan: two groups in this level of the pyramid.)	Read other groups' results of the previous phase at home. Their results are available in a shared repository. Critically comment their answers.	**Distant session**
			Discuss with another "jigsaw group" and jointly agree on the 8 main ideas of the paper and 2 questions.	**Second face-to-face session**
Pyramid level 3	**"think" phase of TPS**	In this pyramid level there is only one group: the whole class works according to a common TPS structure.	Not visible (there is no task in this phase)	
	"pair" phase of TPS	In this application of TPS CLFP, each member of the pair group is each group of the second level of the pyramid.	A spokesperson of each group exposes their conclusions to the other group.	
	"share" phase of TPS	The whole class (see Pyramid level 3: "think" phase of TPS).	The teacher mediates a discussion aiming at reaching consensus.	

Figure 2. Graphical refinement of the template resulting of the combination of CLFPs using Collage authoring tool

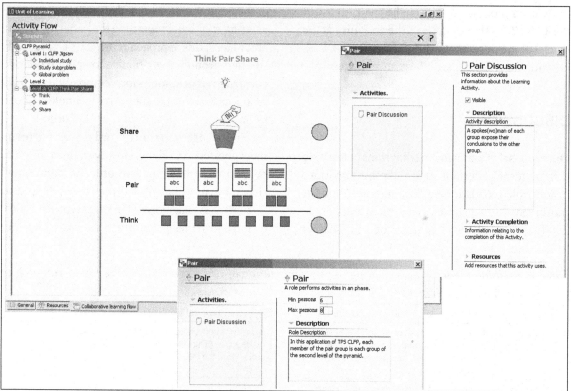

then communicate with a more finalist language (IMS-LD) using the graphical representations of the patterns' solutions. However, one of the limitations of Collage is that the addition of new templates based on other patterns is laborious: each template has its own representation and includes pattern-specific functions. To overcome these drawbacks, it would be interesting to study the possibility of using visual languages for instructional design, such as E²ML (Botturi, 2006; see also Chapter VII) or the others VIDLs presented in Section II of this handbook, to graphically represent patterns' solutions. This may not only facilitate the addition of new patterns (using the same graphical notation) to Collage, but it may also afford more flexible editing possibilities of the learning flow (e.g.,, using drag-and-drop elements of the visual language that can be added or removed from the templates).

CONCLUSION

With the aim of integrating technology in education, instructional designers and teachers can use learning technology standards, such as IMS-LD. However, these standards and specifications provide technical-oriented, text-based notation systems that do not offer visual representation of instructional activities and do not enforce design processes that support the creation of pedagogically sound designs. This chapter has offered an approach that provides good practices formulated as patterns and visualized through graphical diagrams within authoring tools. These tools support users in the creation of IMS-LD compliant designs (UoLs) by means of reusable pattern-based templates. The three different ideas linked in this approach are:

- **The use of patterns for the design of experienced-founded learning scenarios:** Our particular focus is on CSCL scripts, i.e., collaborative learning scenarios that can be interpreted by LMSs. That is the reason why we describe the different types of patterns that can be used in the design of scripts, and analyze in more detail the CLFPs, which suggest flows of learning activity types. In addition, we argue that some patterns can act as assistants (advising mechanisms) while others are more suitable as refinable templates (partially completed designs).

- **The incorporation of pattern-based templates in authoring tools using visualizations inspired by the patterns' solutions:** Collage authoring tool represents an example of a pattern-based editor that facilitates teachers (and instructional designers) in the creation of scripts based on combinations of CLFPs. The pattern-based design process implemented in Collage relies on the use of a visual notation in which the graphical representation of each learning flow template corresponds to the diagram of the related CLFP. Apart from the reuse of good practices that facilitate planning elicitations of desired social interactions, the Collage design process reduces the technical complexity associated with creating computer-interpretable collaboration scripts.

- **The production of CSCL scripts compliant with IMS-LD:** IMS-LD specification can be used to computationally represent CLFPs-based templates. In fact, the scripts produced by Collage are IMS-LD (level A) compliant.

These ideas have been thoroughly illustrated with an example drawn from a real course, which shows the feasibility and usefulness of the whole approach. We are currently carrying out several case studies with teachers, who use Collage creating pattern-based scripts, and students, who experience these scripts. The conclusions of these case studies will provide further insights about the possibilities of the approach presented in this chapter. Future work includes the study of using visual languages to represent patterns' solutions (and thus pattern-based templates). This work envisages a potential chance to face the challenges of easily adding new patterns to Collage and providing more flexible refinement possibilities in the authoring.

ACKNOWLEDGMENT

The authors wish to thank the rest of the members of the GSIC/EMIC group at the University of Valladolid, Spain. Special thanks to Iván M. Jorrín-Abellán, Bartolomé Rubia-Avi and Inés Ruiz-Requies. This work has been partially funded by the Spanish Ministry of Education and Science project TSI2005-08225-C07-04, the Autonomous Government of Castilla and León project VA009A05 and the Kaleidoscope Network of Excellence FP6-2002-IST-507838.

REFERENCES

Alexander, C. (1999). The origins of pattern theory: The future of the theory and the generation of a living world. *IEEE Software, 16*(5), 71-82.

Alexander, C., Ishikawa, S., Silverstein, M., Jacobson, M., Fiksdahl-King, I., & Angel, S. (1977). *A pattern language: Towns, buildings, construction.* New York: Oxford University Press.

Aronson, E., & Patnoe, S. (1997). *The jigsaw classroom: Building cooperation in the classroom.* (2nd ed.). New York: Addison-Wesley Educational Publishers Inc.

Bote-Lorenzo, M.L., Hernández-Leo, D., Dimitriadis, Y., Asensio-Pérez, J.I., Gómez-Sánchez, E., Vega-Gorgojo, G., & Vaquero-González, L.M. (2004). Towards reusability and tailorability in collaborative learning systems using IMS-LD and Grid Services. *Advanced Technology for Learning, 1*(3), 129-138.

Botturi, L. (2006). E²ML: A visual language for the design of instruction. *Educational Technology Research and Development, 54*(3), 265-293.

Botturi, L., Derntl, M., Boot, E., & Figl, K. (2006). A classification framework for educational modeling languages in instructional design. In Kinshuk, R. Koper, P. Kommers, P. Kirschner, D. G. Sampson, & W. Didderen (Eds.), *Proceedings of the 6ᵗʰ IEEE International Conference on Advanced Learning Technologies* (pp. 1216-1220). Kerkrade, The Netherlands: IEEE Computer Society.

Burgos, D., & Griffiths, D. (Eds.). (2005). *The UNFOLD project. Understanding and using Learning Design.* Heerlen, The Netherlands: Open University of The Netherlands.

Clarke, J. (1994). Pieces of the puzzle: The jigsaw method. In S. Sharan (Ed.), *Handbook of cooperative learning methods* (pp. 34-50). Westport CT: Greenwood Press.

Davis, W.A. (2002). A comparison of pyramids versus brainstorming in a problem based learning environment. In *Focusing on the student: Proceedings of 11ᵗʰ Annual Teaching Learning Forum.* Perth: Edith Cowan University.

de la Teja, I., Lundgren-Cayro, K., & Paquette, G. (2005). Transposing MISA learning scenarios into IMS units of learning. *Journal of Interactive Media in Education,* (13). Retrieved from http://www-jime.open.ac.uk/2005/13/

Derntl, M., & Botturi, L. (2006). Essential use cases for pedagogical patterns. *Computer Science Education, special issue on Pedagogic Patterns, 16*(2), 137-156.

Dillenbourg, P. (2002). Over-scripting CSCL: The risks of blending collaborative learning with instructional design. In P. A. Kirschner (Ed.), *Inaugural Address, Three Worlds of CSCL. Can We Support CSCL?* (pp. 61-91). Heerlen: Open Universiteit Nederland.

Dillenbourg, P., & Tchounikine, P. (2006). Flexibility in macro-scripts for CSCL. *Journal of Computer Assisted Learning, 23*(1), 1-13.

Dillenbourg, P. (Ed.). (1999). *Collaborative learning: Cognitive and computational approaches.* Oxford, UK: Elsevier Science.

E-LEN (2004). *E-LEN project website.* Retrieved February 2007 from http://www2.tisip.no/E-LEN/

Gamma, E., Helm, R., Johnson, R., & Vlissides, J. (1995). *Design patterns, elements of reusable object-orientedsSoftware.* Boston: Addison-Wesley.

Gibbs, G. (1995). *Teaching more students 3: Discussion with more students.* Headington, Oxford: The Oxford Centre for Staff Development.

Goodyear, P. (2005). Educational design and networked learning: Patterns, pattern languages and design practice. *Australasian Journal of Educational Technology, 21*(1), 82-101.

Griffiths, D., & Blat, J. (2005). The role of teachers in editing and authoring units of learning using IMS Learning Design. *Advanced Technology for Learning, 2*(4), 243-251.

Harrer, A., & Malzah, N. (2006). Bridging the gap, towards a graphical modeling language for learning designs and collaboration scripts of various granularities. *Proceedings of the 6ᵗʰ IEEE International Conference on Advanced Learning Technologies* (pp. 296-300). Kerkrade, The Netherlands: IEEE Computer Society.

Hernández-Leo, D., Asensio-Pérez, J.I., & Dimitriadis, Y. (2005). Computational representation of collaborative learning flow patterns using IMS learning design. *Educational Technology & Society, 8*(3), 75-89.

Hernández-Leo, D., Asensio-Pérez, J.I., Dimitriadis, Y., Bote-Lorenzo, M.L., Jorrín-Abellán, I.M., & Villasclaras-Fernández, E.D. (2005). Reusing IMS-LD formalized best practices in collaborative learning structuring. *Advanced Technology for Learning, 2*(4), 223-232.

Hernández-Leo, D., Harrer, A., Dodero, J.M., Asensio-Pérez, J.I., & Burgos, D. (2006). Creating by reusing learning design solutions. *Proceedings of the 8th International Symposium on Computers in Education* (pp. 417-424). León, Spain: University of León.

Hernández-Leo, D., Villasclaras-Fernández, E.D., Asensio-Pérez, J.I., Dimitriadis, Y., & Retalis, S. (2006). CSCL scripting patterns: Hierarchical relationships and applicability. *Proceedings of 6th IEEE International Conference on Advanced Learning Technologies.* Kerkrade, The Netherlands: IEEE Computer Society.

Hernández-Leo, D., Villasclaras-Fernández, E.D., Jorrín-Abellán, I.M., Asensio-Pérez, J.I., Dimitriadis, Y., Ruiz-Requies, I., & Rubia-Avi, B. (2006). COLLAGE, a collaborative learning design editor based on patterns. *Educational Technology and Society, 9*(1), 58-71.

Holkeboer, K. (1987). *Patterns for theatrical costumes: garments, trims, and accessories from ancient Egypt to 1915.* New York: Prentice-Hall.

IMS (2003). *IMS Learning Design specification.* Retrieved February 2007 from http://www.ims-global.org/learningdesign/

Johnson, D.W., & Johnson, R.T. (1999). *Learning together and alone: Cooperative, competitive and individualistic learning* (5th ed.). Needham Heights, MA: Allyn and Bacon.

Jones, R. (2004). Designing adaptable learning resources with learning objects patterns. *Journal of Digital Information, 6*(1), Article No. 305. Available at http://jodi.ecs.soton.ac.uk/Articles/v06/i01/Jones/

Karagiorgi, Y., & Symeou, L. (2005). Translating constructivism into instructional design: Potential and limitations. *Educational Technology & Society, 8*(1), 17-27.

Koper, R., & Tattersall, C. (Eds.). (2005). *Learning Design, a handbook on modeling and delivering networked education and training.* Heidelberg: Springer-Verlag.

Milligan, C.D., Beauvoir, P., & Sharples, P. (2005). The reload learning design tools. *Journal of Interactive Media in Education,* (7). Available at http://jime.open.ac.uk/2005/06/

Millis, B.J., & Cottell, P.G. (1998). *Cooperative learning for higher education faculty.* Phoenix, AZ: The Oryx Press.

NISE (97). *Doing CL: CL Structures.* Retrieved February 2007 from http://www.wcer.wisc.edu/archive/cl1/CL/

Oliver, R., Harper, B., Hedberg, J., Wills, S., & Agostinho, S. (2002). Formalizing the description of learning designs. In A. Goody, J. Herrington, & M. Northcote (Eds.), *Quality conversations: research and development in higher education* (pp. 496-504). Jamison, ACT: HERDSA.

PPP (2000). *The pedagogical patterns project Web site.* Retrieved February 2007 from http://www.pedagogicalpatterns.org/

Retalis, S., Georgiakakis, P., & Dimitriadis, Y. (2006). Eliciting design patterns for e-learning systems. *Computer Science Education, special issue on Pedagogic Patterns, 16*(2), 105-118.

Rodríguez-Estévez, J., Caeiro-Rodríguez, M., & Santos-Gago, J.M. (2003). Standarization in computer-based learning. *Upgrade (European Journal for the Informatics Professional), special issue on e-Learning: Boarderless education, 4*(5), 8-15.

Sampson, D.G., Karampiperis, P., & Zervas, P. (2005). ASK-LDT: A Web-based learning scenarios authoring environment based on IMS earning esign. *Advanced Technology for Learning, 2*(4), 207-215.

Strijbos, J.W., Martens, R.L., & Jochems, W.M.G. (2004). Designing for interaction: Six steps to designing computer-supported group-based learning. *Computers & Education, 42*(4), 403-424.

Tattersall, C., Vogten, H., Brouns, F., Koper, R., van Rosmalen, P., Sloep, P., & van Bruggen, J. (2005). How to create flexible runtime delivery of distance learning courses. *Educational Technology and Society, 8*(3), 226-236.

TELL (2005). *Design patterns for teachers and educational (system) designers.* TELL project deliverable. Retrieved from http://cosy.ted.unipi.gr/TELL/media/TELL_pattern_book.pdf

University of Bolton (2004). *Reload project website*. Retrieved February 2007 from http://www.reload.ac.uk/

van der Vegt, W. (2005). *CopperAuthor project website*. Retrieved February 2007 from http://www.copperauthor.org/

Vega-Gorgojo, G., Bote-Lorenzo, M.L., Gómez-Sánchez, E., Asensio-Pérez, J.I., Dimitriadis, Y., & Jorrín-Abellán, I.M. (2006). Ontoolcole: An ontology for the semantic search of CSCL services. In Y. Dimitriadis, I. Zigurs, & E. Gómez-Sánchez (Eds), *Proceedings of 12th International Workshop, LNCS 4154* (pp. 310-325). Heidelberg: Springer-Verlag.

Waters, S.H., & Gibbons, A.S. (2004). Design languages, notation systems and instructional technology: A case study. *Educational Technology Research and Development, 52*(2), 57-68.

Chapter XXI
Designing for Change:
Visual Design Tools to Support Process Change in Education

John Casey
UHI Millennium Institute, Scotland

Kevin Brosnan
University of Stirling, Scotland

Wolfgang Greller
University of Klagenfurt, Austria

Alan Masson
University of Ulster, Northern Ireland

Áine MacNeill
University of Ulster, Northern Ireland

Colette Murphy
University of Ulster, Northern Ireland

ABSTRACT

This chapter looks at the possible uses of visual forms of instructional design (ID) languages as possible 'change agents' for design practice in the public post-secondary education sector. A lot of work is being done in the technical realm of the standardization and interoperability for educational modeling languages (EMLs), but this is largely restricted to existing ID specialists that use 'dialects' of ID languages and schemes. This is important work but it does not address the vast majority of educators working in the post-secondary public educational sector whose design work is highly individualized and deeply embedded in rich institutional contexts. The challenge for visual ID languages and EMLs in general is how they can move beyond their current specialist niche applications to be useful to mainstream educators. In this chapter we argue that this development needs to happen along two related dimensions: (i) changes in the organization of the educational workplace and related training—what might be termed 'push factors;' and, (ii) the use of tools such as visual ID languages to support that change process at individual and group levels—what might be termed 'pull' factors. We shall be concentrating on this second dimension. Specifically, in this chapter we shall be looking at ideas for how we might apply visual ID languages as a support mechanism in helping educators externalize and share their design models and ideas in order to develop them into semi-formal abstractions that might be developed to feed into the use of EMLs. To ground these ideas, we shall be looking at the experiences of those who have tried these types of approaches in practice. Finally we discuss the effect this type of perspective might have on the future development of visual ID languages and related tools.

OVERVIEW[1]

An important characteristic of this chapter is that, as a starting point, we do not regard teachers as fully formed instructional designers, we think it is better to regard them as novice learners in this field and explore how we might help them by the use of visual ID tools. We provide our rationale for this approach in section 3. The IMS learning design best practice guide and much of the current work in the area has, by necessity, tended to assume that the teachers can produce a formal narrative of their design that can then be converted into the various abstract representations the language and tools provide. Our experiences suggest that in the mainstream the journey from individualized and isolated design activities, that characterizes the majority of current practice, to a semi-formal expression that can be shared and elaborated upon is the first crucial step that we need to concentrate our activities upon. The need to direct support to this 'preparatory' stage of design was recognized during the discussions of the

European Commission funded UNFOLD project that brought teachers and IMS learning design developers together (Griffiths & Blat, 2005).

Figure 1, illustrates the relationship between current practice and possible sources of information that can be utilized to produce semi-formal expressions of instructional design that can act as a 'halfway house' to a fully formalized narrative.

Thus the visual design languages and tools we are concerned with in this chapter are predominantly in the top left quadrant of the Use classification scheme diagram devised by Botturi et al. (2006) for visual design languages, see Figure 2. Namely, we are concerned with reflective communication and creative generation of designs for individuals and groups. But, as it will become clearer as we progress it may well be possible to use such languages for communication of 'final' designs—depending on what the community of users sees as a 'final' design.

This consideration of the purpose of use of visual design languages also leads to a central theme that we develop in this chapter: to enable

Figure 1. Moving from current 'embedded' design practice towards more formal expressions

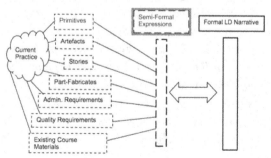

Figure 2. Usage classification of visual ID languages (Botturi , Derntl, Boot, & Figl, 2006)

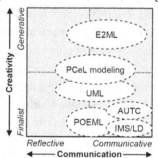

the process of change in an academic community. An important point that we argue here is that in respect to instructional design activity in academia (i.e. creation, articulation and sharing) there is currently no effective design community. For us it is vitally important to provide a means of communication to describe this design activity. As Botturi, Derntl, Boot, and Figl. (2006, pp. 1217) put it:

The combination of design language and notation system is a central concept in the definition of a design team or community, as a shared language is the medium for the creation of shared culture. From a practical point of view, a language is fundamental for a community to share their practices and to engage in reflective thinking.

Once the academics start to communicate ideas about design only then does it become possible to change practice.

But much of the discourse to date in this field has been aimed at the ID community and has tended to project their organizational and conceptual models onto the mainstream. As in many other areas of e-learning these types of assumption are way-off from the reality. Greller (2005) brings us down to earth with a bump when he informs us that there are hardly any ID professionals in the mainstream, and that therefore the 'understandability' of languages is crucial. This is why we are taking the approach we mentioned above in this chapter.

In section 4 we briefly describe the current state of play as regards to existing work on IMS learning design and tooling to support design creation and instantiation. We also summarize some relevant existing approaches to visual ID languages and tools.

To ground our discussions in realistic contexts, in sections 5, 6 and 7 we report on the experiences of three different projects that have sought to enable the sharing of instructional designs in a number of different ways using visual language

approaches. We feel that the results of these case studies give weight to our earlier observations and conclusions about current design practice and provide some useful guidance for future development.

Finally in section 8 we bring together our discussions and experiences to develop a set of suggestions and guidelines for future development in this area that include a generic architecture for a visual design *environment* that might be capable of supporting individual and group activities.

Taking a Systems Perspective

As Carol Twigg (2005) has observed, e-learning has tended to remain as a 'bolt-on' to existing institutional structures and processes and is therefore unable to realize its full potential. Many researchers and practitioners are coming to the conclusion that the real challenge to successfully implementing e-learning is in changing the structures and cultures of our institutions so that they can effectively use e-learning and flexible learning (Collis & Moonen, 2004; van der Klink & Jochems, 2004). This entails taking a systematic approach to the problem of incorporating technology usefully into our educational institutions; such an approach is relatively new in mainstream education but by necessity has long been the norm in specialized open learning and vocational training providers. In an influential book entitled *Integrated E-Learning: Implications for pedagogy, technology and organization,* (Jochems, van Merriënboer, & Koper, 2004) the authors make the case for regarding the introduction of e-learning as not merely an addition to the existing system of instruction but as something that requires a fundamental redesign of the educational system. They envisage that this redesign has to address the pedagogical, organizational and technological aspects in order to solve the educational problem of providing high quality education, to a greater number of students from more diverse backgrounds, in more flexible ways with limited resources. To help in this task of redesigning the educational system (at, say, an institutional level) the authors advocate the deliberate use of use of e-learning tools as a catalyst for changes to the system:

In order to bridge the gap between the different disciplines, tools and concepts should be available that can serve as mediators on the conceptual level in analysis and design, as well as actual implementation. So-called learning technologies play a critical role in this bridging function. They can be considered as a means of formalising pedagogical and organizational thinking in such a way that it can be implemented in a technical solution. (Jochems, van Merriënboer, & Koper, 2004, p.7)

It is exactly this wider role for VIDL and tools that we envisage in this chapter as a means of supporting change in pedagogic design practice in the mainstream.

WHY PROCESS CHANGE?

Drivers for Change

Generally, across the industrialized and developing world, the demand for post-secondary education is rising and public sector educational providers are expected to deal with larger number of students, from more diverse backgrounds, in more flexible ways, with little extra increase in resources. Even campus-based students are beginning to be treated in some respects as distance learners (Ask & Haugen, 1995). In this situation, ever-greater expectations are being placed on the use of technology to support teaching at university level and in the vocational and community sectors, implicitly, to increase the efficiency of the process. To this end, large amounts of money are being spent by governments to improve the IT infrastructure and student facilities in these institutions.

The lifelong learning agenda is another driver for greater access to education and training as the needs of workers and citizens in the modern 'knowledge economy' require more flexible, timely and personalized support. The link between education provision and economic prosperity is being increasingly recognized by governments and policy developers, the EU Lisbon agenda being a classic example. It is also recognized that the existing educational system has to change to meet these new challenges. The European Open and Distance Learning Liaison committee nicely summarize the situation as follows:

The Lisbon Agenda has been adapted in 2005 to act as an updated focus for European policy development. The adapted agenda calls for a strong and fundamental effort to equip the European citizens at all levels with the right knowledge, skills, and attitudes, and society at large with a full understanding why this is needed. The present education and training systems are not completely equipped to face this challenge through conventional learning methods. A substantial amount of learning innovation will be required for which the knowledge base is only fragmentary now. (http://www.odl-liaison. org/pages.php?PN=policy-paper_2006)

The specialist open and distance learning providers certainly do put a great deal of emphasis and value on their learning materials which are designed to carry part of the pedagogic load, the courses they support are also intensively designed. But most mainstream educational institutions do not have the design and pedagogic skills base to engage in this market. Fernandez-Young et al. (2006) described their experience of making learning objects for the UK eU (The UK e-University—which collapsed in 2004 with debts of £100million) as a very difficult exercise which they were only partly successful in, the notion of de-contextualization and granularity being a wholly alien concept to them. Ultimately, they state that they were not convinced of the merits of the approach either. This is not surprising as the existing academic workforce simply do not have these types of instructional design skills. To clarify: academics do not need or acquire these skills because they teach in a face-to-face mode; their teaching is literally 'embedded' in the bricks and mortar of the institution (Koper, 2003); to use a medical analogy they are the overworked 'general practitioners' of teaching—combining a host of other duties and responsibilities. In contrast the profession of instructional design for distance learning is relatively narrow, but deeper, and to continue the medical analogy they are more like consultant specialists.

Individual and Group Learning for Teachers

Individuals at different levels in an organization find it difficult to conceive of the 'bigger picture' due to the local detail of their own situations and working cultures. To overcome this obstacle, modern systems theory seems to offer some help. It provides some useful analytical tools for identifying and understanding the dynamic relations between the factors we are discussing in this chapter. Senge and Sterman (1994) develop this theme in the context of *organizational learning*—a concept that is growing in interest, and it is worth briefly looking at some of their recommendations. They propose a three-stage process for developing a better understanding of how an organization actually works by the people within it:

1. **Mapping mental models:** Explicating and structuring assumptions via systems models;

2. **Challenging mental models:** Revealing inconsistencies in assumptions;

3. **Improving mental models:** Continually extending and testing mental models.

They make the important point that flaws in the understanding of how an organization works cannot be corrected until they are made explicit, which is the purpose of the modeling exercise. There is no reason to think that such an exercise could not be applied to higher education. The three-stage process of mapping, challenging and improving mental models proposed by Senge and Sterman (1994) seems equally applicable to the task of improving the individual instructional design skills of teachers.

The particular staff learning need we are interested in here is instructional design for e-learning. The heart of the problem is that teaching staff generally do not share and reuse learning resources and learning activities, instead they concentrate on preparing 'their' content to deliver to 'their' students (Koper, 2003). The teaching activity that is carried out is deeply embedded in an institutional context and therefore difficult to share and abstract. In this pedagogic environment lecturers feel most at ease developing content and delivering it to their students. Conceptualizing learning activities for their students is not a particularly common activity (Koper, 2003), and sharing these conceptions with colleagues is even rarer. As Allison Littlejohn (2003) observes: "Designing for reuse means designing with multiple users in mind and this is a new experience for most teachers in all sectors of education."

A seminar of the JISC (Joint Information Services Committee)X4L programme in January 2004 building on earlier discussions in the e-learning community suggested that what was needed were a number of initiatives and support tools to help teachers bridge the gap between traditional embedded pedagogy and the more abstract representations required by IMS learning design (Beetham, 2004). One of the conclusions of the X4L seminar was: "That many teachers do not possess a vocabulary for articulating and sharing their pedagogic strategies and designs with others, particularly beyond their cognate discipline areas" (p. 11).

Technologies such as VLEs, learning objects and learning design all strongly imply working as a team to design, develop and deliver courses—the importance of this should not be underestimated. Working as a team, sharing learning resources and discussing approaches to teaching are currently comparatively rare in higher education in the UK.

The most important building block in our proposals for the development of academics is for them to work in teams that do not just include academics but also media designers, learning technologists, and educational design specialists such as instructional designers. This division of labor is necessary for efficiency (Laurillard, 1994) but from our point of view this is where the real usefulness of technologies such as learning objects and IMS learning designs becomes clear. They become what Wenger calls 'boundary objects.' Chapter 3 describes a similar role for the use of design drawings by architects and others that support communication between different stakeholders and gradually moves towards more formal representations. This simple idea has some important ramifications about the uses of these technologies:

1. They act as a form of collective memory for a particular community that can be accessed and reused by that community in the future.
2. They support the construction of, and sharing of enough meaning between different groups (subject academics, tutors, administrators, instructional designers, media designers, etc.) to allow them to understand their place in the educational system they are working in.

Working as a team to design, develop and deliver courses, sharing their learning materials and conceptions about the teaching and learning are the basis for potentially powerful staff and institutional development processes. The ability of learning objects and IMS learning designs to support this process can be exploited. Properly conceived and planned this process may also play a role in building and strengthening scholarly communities. Hernandez-Leo et al. (2005; see also Chapter 20) recommend this approach to support the design of online collaborative learning activities pointing out that this is a requirement of participatory design (PD) approaches (Muller & Kuhn, 1993) to the design of social systems.

EXISTING WORK ON IMS LEARNING DESIGN AND USES OF VIDL

Currently there is a lot of research work going on that aims to support teachers to articulate their designs and activities in ways that can then be further developed into formal IMS learning designs. All this work is valuable, but we need to also recognize the rougher and more tentative conceptions of pedagogy that practitioners really use: we would call these 'primitives' and 'artifacts,' terms introduced by John Casey into the UNFOLD (http://www.unfold-project.net:8085/UNFOLD) project discussions (Griffiths & Blat, 2005). These in turn can become the building blocks of more elaborated and structured representations that are still 'fuzzy,' that lie midway between actual embedded practice and the formalized narrative required to initiate a IMS learning design. The IMS learning design best practice guide describes the starting point of creating a design as an analysis phase that results in a structured narrative. As Griffiths and Blat (2005) point out no structure or methodology is recommended in the IMS best practice guide to support this activity.

This leads us to suggest the useful notion of a 'learning design continuum' as shown in Figure 3.

In this chapter we are particularly interested in the ability of visual instructional design languages to support the process of individuals and groups being able to move their design practice to

Figure 3. A proposed IMS learning design continuum

Primitives/Artifacts......................Semi-Structured.........................Formal

a midway position on this continuum—to produce a semi-formal narrative.

Some tools are highly specialized and powerful instantiations of existing ID models such as the MOT+LD (Chapter VIII; de la Teja et al., 2005). This is aimed at existing instructional designer specialists who are able to work within the 'doctrine' and vocabulary of the accompanying ID model. Although an admirable piece of work, the tool interface and vocabulary and concepts are still far too complex and abstract for mainstream teachers—which to be fair it is surely not aimed at. Naturally, many developers think the solution is to get the interface right; the ASK-LDT tool from the University of Piraeus and of course the LAMS tool from Australia are both good moves in this direction, but the price they pay is a decrease in power and expressiveness—in order to be easy to use the complexity has to be reduced, sometimes drastically. We think that the long-term reality though, is that the teachers and their workplaces will have to

change in order take full advantage of EMLs etc. The whole basis for the use of EMLs, ID methods and reusable learning objects is predicated on a division of labor approach (Friesen, 2004), which has not been discussed, to any great degree in the literature to date.

We think the stage before creating a formal learning design narrative is important to address and requires a combination of some staff development and training and some simple conceptual and methodological tools, intuitive design aids and ideally some 'just in time learning' aids; all of which should be as low-tech as possible. The existing tools are moving in the right direction but there is much more to do to address where teachers are in reality, not where the developer community thinks they ought to be.

This is the area we think is currently neglected: understanding current design practice and context and exploring ways to move it from its current embedded, individual, isolated and non-transferable practice to a state where it may

Figure 4. The learning design continuum

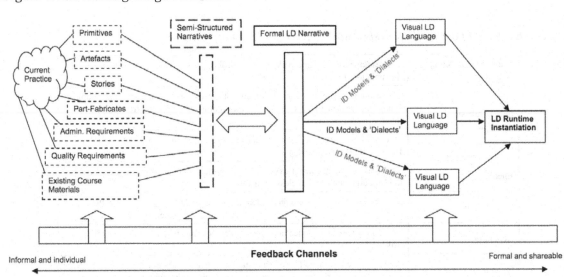

be abstracted and understood, in the first instance by the author as an aid to self-reflection (Botturi et al., 2006) and then shared by others. In this we think simple approaches that are informed by mainstream reality will be most effective. At the moment the IMS learning design specification and its attendant communities are useful insofar as they clearly identify the far end of a learning design continuum. Having said that, we think this is valuable as it provides a fixed point of reference to relate our discussion to at our end of the continuum. The diagram below would illustrate our overall view of the continuum.

CASE STUDY: UNIVERSITY OF STIRLING, SCOTLAND

Background: Choosing an ID Framework

The Learning to Learn project (L2L) received funding under the JISC Exchange for Learning programme (X4L) for the period September 2002 to July 2005.

The aim of the project was to focus on learner activity and pedagogic outcomes related to the sharing of learning-objects and learning designs.

Table 1. Shuell's learning functions

Shuell's Learning Functions		
Define Learning Expectations	Encoding	Feedback
Motivation	Comparison	Monitoring
Prior Knowledge Activation	Hypothesis Generation	Evaluation
Attention	Repetition	Combination, Integration, Synthesis (CIS)

The subjects of the study were learning-support tutors in post-secondary education. The L2L project adopted an ID design framework provided by Tom Shuell (1992) a prominent educational psychologist that placed teachers' conceptions about the learner's cognitive activity at the center of the design process. The Shuell ID framework was intended to be used as means of helping them express their pedagogic designs for a particular learning-object in a structured and shareable way that could then be incorporated as part of the metadata associated with each learning-object.

In summary the Shuell ID framework argues that for any learning episode to be effective a set of twelve 'learning functions' must be activated: it is essentially a taxonomy of cognitive learning activities. It is based, as all taxonomies are, on a set of ontological agreements or statements (tacit

Table 2. Example of a Shuell analysis associated with a learning-object

Knowledge Building Activities	The resource uses a framework based on different categories of weak arguments as the main tool for learning.
Combination, Integration, Synthesis	The resource identifies the main elements of an argument – students must be able to synthesize these elements to be able to differentiate an argument from a non-argument.
Attention	Directs student attention towards weak arguments by using particular examples from the film 12 Angry Men
Encoding	The weak argument categories provide a way for students to think about different kinds of arguments and to classify them.
Comparison	In assessing each video clip the student is encouraged to think about how the clip compares to an argument they have experienced directly themselves.
Repetition	There are a number of video clips used; each clip must be analyzed in a similar way.
Hypothesis Generation	Students are encouraged to reach a tentative conclusion about a video clip and then test this more rigorously through asynchronous discussion with their colleagues.

or formal) about the meaning of each taxonomic element. In the Shuell framework it is believed that a learning function can be activated by any one of three agents, a learner, a resource or a teacher.

A list of the 12 functions is provided in Table 1.

The learning-support tutors' explicit and structured pedagogic ideas were gathered by interview and form completion and then incorporated into the learning-object metadata and became known as the 'Shuell analysis' within the L2L project. An example of part of a Shuell analysis for one of the L2L learning objects is provided below in Table 2. This particular learning object focused on the study skill of critical thinking and argument analysis.

The Shuell analysis was viewed as a possible way of enhancing the reusability (exchangeability) of learning objects deposited in a repository as well as trying to provide a design framework for the original tutor and future users. Adopting the Shuell framework as part of the pedagogic design process was a significant part of the ongoing work of the project.

Expressing the Designs in Metadata

In retrospect this was an ambitious objective. The difficulties of creating effective metadata are now well known. As Rehak and Mason (2003) state "[t]here is no ultimate or perfect metadata description of any LO [learning object]. Each LO will have multiple overlapping partial descriptions, created by different communities depending on their needs or for different uses of the LO" (p.28). In addition, as Allert et al. (2002) state: " [The IEEE] LOM [learning object metadata] does not support metadata about instructional models and instructional theory, even though authors are implicitly or explicitly using specific instructional theories, and LOM does not support information about the use of learning-objects in learning processes, which are a central concern in instructional design" (p.16).

On the whole the results from the evaluations reveal that expressing pedagogic ideas in this mode was both difficult and alien to the tutors involved and it offered little benefit as a means of sharing pedagogic ideas. Despite this, there was also evidence of greater self-reflection and the development of a shared language amongst the participant group, which we see as a positive indicator for using this kind of activity in the future to support process change.

Responding to the Designer's Reactions

The reaction of the tutor-designers confirms the impression that they do not abstract, describe and share their pedagogic design on a routine basis, nor do they have a common vocabulary for doing so. We needed to find a way to help the tutors engage with the Shuell framework that was more meaningful and relevant to them. After some discussion and experimentation, we mapped the framework onto the very old, simple and intuitive teaching model that might be summarized as: 'prepare-teach-review.' We reproduce this mapping in Table 3.

We also produced a graphical representation of this revised Shuell framework (shown in Figure 5).

The visual mapping was useful as a visualization tool for the project workers and, we felt,

Table 3. Shuell's functions mapped to the prepare-teach-review, model

Preparation Activities	Teaching /Knowledge Construction Activities	Review Activities
Motivation	Attention	Feedback
Defining Learning Expectations	Encoding	Monitoring
Prior Knowledge Activation	Comparison	Evaluation
	Repetition	Feedback
	Hypothesis Generation	Monitoring
	Combination, Integration, Synthesis	Evaluation

Figure 5. Prepare-teach-review mapped onto Shuell's framework

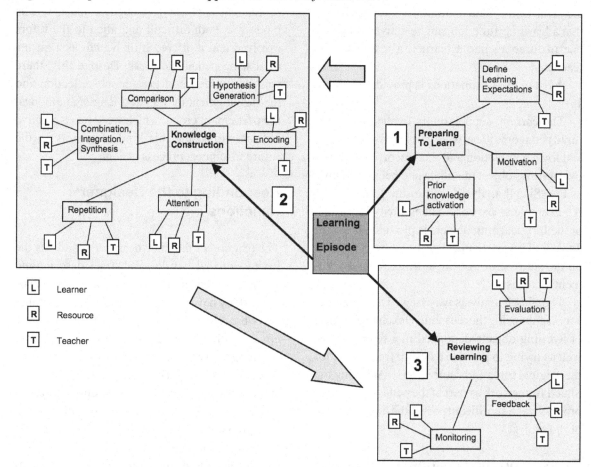

could be adapted into a design aid for group use and for media designers, but would still need the intervention of a specialist. At the time we speculated about creating simple interactive versions that could be used to link to text documents that could populate the 'nodes' of the framework. From this we also produced a revised form to help capture tutor-designers conceptions that seemed easier for them to use.

In evaluating the usefulness of trying to use the learning object metadata as a means of sharing pedagogic ideas, the replies received from the tutors involved in the project reflected the challenges involved. The completion of the metadata record (including the L2L Shuell analysis) is an example of trying to impose a method for creating a formal expression of a form of knowledge (practice

knowledge), which may not easily translate to this particular formalism. As Kimble et al. (2001) note, this kind of 'soft-knowledge' is difficult to articulate. The situation for the L2L tutors was particularly difficult because so much of what an effective learning-support tutor does relies on a sensitivity to the feelings and dispositions of their students, a kind of knowledge that can be very difficult to express in words let alone the formalism required by the L2L project.

Significantly, none of the completed tutor evaluation questionnaires mentioned the Shuell analysis stored in the metadata as part of their process of deciding whether or not to download a learning object from the repository. It seems they 'scanned' the descriptive textual data in the metadata.

Conclusions: The Need for Authenticity

The empirical evidence within this research was elicited through three main processes: documentary analysis, an interview survey and participant observation in an attempt to achieve validity through methodological triangulation. The analysis of this evidence highlights the considerable challenges faced by teaching staff in attempting to develop and share learning objects and learning designs as part of their ongoing teaching practice. However, the analysis also provides some insight into the possibility of using the exchange as a means of knowledge sharing supporting professional development and collaboration.

In conclusion, we emphasize the need to pay significant attention to the (contextually specific) social practices within which the use of learning objects and learning designs are enmeshed. By explicating the details of such practices (rather than adopting a narrow, technical focus on the attributes of the learning objects themselves) it is envisaged that the efficacy of using these resources may be improved.

The key problem that must be overcome is to make tools and methods available to the users that they can relate to, contextualize and find relevant and useful. A way we have sought to describe how such an approach may be successful is that the vocabulary, the tools and methods etc., must be 'authentic' to the teachers working realities. Such an authentic approach must, however, be subject to a certain creative tension between helping to articulate current practice and changing it—often quite radically. We shall return to this theme in the final section of this chapter to illuminate possible visual design support mechanisms for the future.

CASE STUDY: UNIVERSITY OF KLAGENFURT, AUSTRIA

Background: Cultural Change Towards E-Pedagogy

At present, the majority of learning experiences relating to online course elements or blended learning courses restrict themselves to "digital bookshelves," i.e., lecture notes for download, pushing copy and printing costs from the institution onto students. The pedagogic value of such use of learning technology is highly limited and thus prevents further take-up or demand for learning technology by both staff and students. This usage pattern does not do justice to the ability and potential of available learning technology and creates a widening gap between non-educational uses of information technology (e.g., online socializing, online transactions, self management, etc.) and e-learning.

The vision at Klagenfurt University, therefore, is to enhance pedagogic use of learning technologies and the institutional learning management system, particularly a shift from the mere consumption of static content towards online activity. Lecturers are expected to conceptually take the step from "what do I provide" to "how should my students use what I provide." The philosophy of working towards this goal is to instigate a change in mindset—that the provision of university teaching is a changing and developing profession.

Two projects have been initiated to provide a jumping off board for these developments on an institutional level: (a) a production guide to online learning, a kind of didactic toolbox; and, (b) a collection of best practice teaching strategy designs.

Educational Reality and Cultural Change

Our case study has followed these two projects and reveals a shift in our focus to a concentration on supplying a more holistic design environment that can support the work of academic staff. This approach takes into account the reality of the authoring environment and skills of tutors. We found that practically all machine-readable design languages, such as IMS-LD or EML are at the abstract remote end of the continuum of learning design expressions. The use of visual design languages for modeling educational activities is still a rather complex and specialist skill that is beyond the reach of most members of staff, but we think has the longer-term potential to bringing it closer to home. This resembles other layered linguistic approaches such as the Creative Commons (http://creativecommons.org/) legal licensing model which consists of three comparable usage levels: 1: human readable code; 2: lawyer (expert) readable code; and 3: machine readable code.

Observational evidence suggested that lecturing staff are faced with two main subconscious challenges when confronted with the implementation of e-learning design into their teaching practice: (1) The unreflected and deeply embedded routine activities of their teaching; and, (2) the transfer of current off-line practice into virtual space—the latter being a consequence of the former.

While issue 2 may be seen as the first and quite important step for newcomers to cross the e-learning threshold, issue 1 strongly indicates that at grass-root level teaching "design just happens," i.e., is often ad-hoc and instantaneously developing via classroom dynamics. It is generally our aim to move beyond this type of design as well as away from solely content-based delivery towards more advanced forms of interaction and collaboration.

Educational Workspace

Virtual learning environments (VLEs) have done a great deal in helping staff take the first steps toward online learning and teaching. However, although these platforms are usually well equipped with various tools that can be used to support online and collaborative learning effectively, e.g., wikis, discussion boards, chat, etc., these tools can also be ignored or misused.

As mentioned above, tutors often cannot see beyond their routine and context, and there are perhaps too few drivers to stimulate reflection. In our opinion, therefore, many members of staff need support in taking the next step and visualizing new opportunities, reviewing their methodology, overcoming fears and generally getting creative in their teaching. This is where, in our opinion, visual modeling approaches could be a useful tool for professional development of lecturing staff.

Project Motivation: Sharing Designs

Despite the many advantages of VLEs, among which we want to mention explicitly the security and privacy of the individual learning space, this also is a disadvantage when it comes to sharing and learning from others. During extensive talks with staff at our institution, it emerged that what would be needed is viewing and learning from other people's practice in order to get inspired in one's own delivery.

A look at various courses brought to light the most common methodologies in use. Apart from the common use as digital bookshelf for downloads, the other striking feature was the pedagogic absence of what might be called "connected tools." There was evidence that lecturers tried to use most of the tools available through the VLE platform, but in many cases the uses did not share a common learning objective, and instead were sitting side-by-side, without semantic and/or pedagogic connection—evidence of a fragmented approach and awareness.

The proposition was that in order to help staff meaningfully connect tools together in teaching strategies or units of learning (UoLs), visual languages might play a positive role in illustrating the connections between the activities and eventually perhaps even allow entire course maps to be transferred between users and disciplines. We think these more abstract ID visualizations would need to have the ability of attaching a description of the tools and resources used to achieve the outcomes, basically an annotation system. Of course, the means of connection should also follow expression of current pedagogic thinking as well as good delivery and support practice.

Pedagogic Strategies and Notational Challenges

The above aspects of online delivery and demand for inspirational strategies prompted us to initiate a project to address these issues. We were looking for an integrated and pedagogically sound way of capturing, describing, modeling, and presenting back delivery strategies with the aim of being able to analyze, store and share them among members of staff. To achieve this we started a project to create a best practice collection of teaching strategy patterns.

The project is experimenting with the practical implications of capturing and describing learning sequences. These will not be full course modules, but rather pattern style sequences or pedagogic primitives and artifacts. The aim is to sift through existing practice and handpick a representative selection of more complex designs that are deemed good educational practice and potentially transferable.

The main phase looks at the following aspects:

1. Capturing: visualization of IMS-LDs
2. Categorizing
3. Describing/Evaluating
4. Storing/Retrieving

In the first phase, that has been completed recently, we aimed to define the conceptual framework conditions of capturing and visualizing instructional designs and patterns. This was followed with selected courses being modeled as a pilot.

While the purpose of the project was reasonably clear, the way forward was not. Questions that raised their heads immediately were:

- What represents pedagogic and didactic quality?
- Which instructional design language should we use?
- How can we articulate what happens in class?
- What is an appropriate level of abstraction and complexity?
- What pedagogic model(s) are used?

Quality

The first issue was whether we would aim to capture and model what represents quality in delivery. However, it proved rather impossible to decide what pedagogic quality in this context actually means or even whether it bears any significance in ID notations (Wenning et al., 2006, p. 8ff). Even if marked as pedagogically sound, a captured educational pattern could still be misused by applying it to the wrong context. We therefore decided to provide user-centred freedom of interpretation and trial and error opportunities instead of prefabricated quality approval. This was generally supported by the fact that ID languages are quality neutral and do not capture quality notations, but rather confine themselves to illustrating sequences of events (see Botturi, Derntl, Boot, and Figl, 2006). We did, however, envisage inter-subjective feedback and the use of recommender technology to be integrated later on a meta-level, much in the way that personal ratings are used in shopping portals such as *e-bay* or for shared learning designs in the LAMS community (http://www.lamscommunity. org/lamscentral/).

Language

The choice of ID language was dominated by the available products and the competency to use them. Among the plethora of VIDLs and emerging tools, a Web-based in-house product called EduWeaver was used for modeling the pilot. This application has its own visual notation system not connected to the available IMS specs and more oriented towards RLOs (reusable learning objects), which proved rather useful since most courses are content heavy. It does provide the option of exporting to IMS content packages but in its present version it lacks roles. Despite being

Figure 6. Modeling sequences with EduWeaver: Screenshot from EduWeaver Manual (J. Bajnai, 2005, 27)

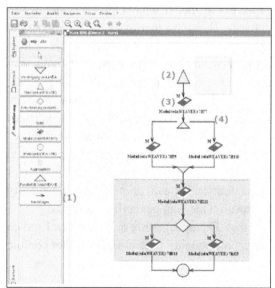

teacher-centered, for simple object sequencing it was an interesting experience to model course activities with it and allowed parallel pathways in the delivery structure.

One question regarding the usefulness of educational design tools is: "Who's talking?" EduWeaver being teacher-centred allowed only modeling the teacher activities. Thus it is used as a personal planning tool. An alternative approach that we applied simultaneously was to introduce student-centered design approaches via the 8LEM (Verpoorten, Poumay & Leclercq, 2005) model from LabSET at the University of Liege. 8LEM (= 8 Learning Events Model) is a user-friendly way of identifying types of learner engagement. 8LEM provides a series of learner/teacher events or interactions; we used the learner side of the model to complement our use of EduWeaver.

For categorization purposes we again follow the 8LEM model, as we believe that through its accessible and easily intelligible semantics it provides a perfect learner-centered design-aid as well as a browsing and searching framework. This is based on the heuristic assumption that lecturers (should) ask themselves: "What do I want my students to do?" Thus, this can provide a low threshold entry to searching for inspiration for one's teaching methodology. Categorizing IMS-LD primitives and artifacts has to emphasize the main criteria of any pattern in question—in this case student activities.

Another challenge was to articulate the intentions connected to a particular teaching sequence and modeling the process. Interviews with the designers/authors showed the deficiency in common vocabulary to express what was otherwise a well thought out educational pattern. The actual modeling work proved a useful tool for reflective analysis of the chosen delivery strategy. However, the presentation varied widely from lecturer to lecturer as some went more into detail than others or used different expression methods. This is in line with the experiences of the OUNL in Holland (Janssen & Hermans, 2005, p.255).

Conclusions: The Linguistics of Design

Beyond the specific ID modeling agents, it was an interesting finding of the project that the teaching delivery tool (VLE) mixed with 'human code' determined the shared vocabulary. A comparable analogy among motorists would be the code in use by truck drivers being different to that of Formula 1 drivers. Though they both perform closely related activities, the technology determines the vocabulary. This led to the conclusion that while there may be a limited number of baseline notations such as IMS-LD XML structures, there are an infinite number of possible user-facing modeling agents, ranging from the very simple to the very complex and detailed. The challenge is to find the right 'human code,' vocabularies and concepts that teaching staff can relate to, allowing human interactions with designs, both in creating and communicating.

Thus the VLE itself, although not a specific instructional design platform, provides a common vocabulary and iconography for people to share activities. Not only is the design articulated to students in that it tells them what steps to take within the VLE, and how to interact, it also is a useful communication base for academic users of a particular system, and sometimes between systems. Thus, the sharing of designs and strategies can reduce itself to a tools-based approach for a particular learning goal, e.g., MCQ test construction.

When taking a bird's-eye-view on the workflow patterns of lecturers, it emerged that many of the current instructional design tools would be something that sits outside the habitual usage patterns of day-to-day online and off-line tuition. Highly abstract in notation, requiring alternative vocabulary, taxonomies, and training for translating it into a design map. Thus their likelihood of adoption is likely to resemble that of artificial languages such as Esperanto or the earlier Volapük, which despite being created as a deliberately simple-to-use code, never really came to more than a manifestation in a particular academic community. This differs from the lingua franca evidence where a real language (usually of strong economic impact) despite all its disadvantages becomes a de facto standard for a region or a community.

Translating this perspective into the world of learning design leaves us with a desire to take a closer look at what is already in use, such as 'VLE-talk', 'human code' and popular tools such as concept maps, mind maps and other ad-hoc representations to find ways and methods to visualize those expressions. As Stubbs and Gibbons (Chapter 3) point out, the role of rough design sketches is an established part of many design professions but rather underdeveloped in the field of instructional design. Current design languages sit at the far end of the spectrum between real and abstract, between actual and wishful, between expressive and rigid. Our perspective would provide a way to identify the mid-way point we are aiming to reach for our semi-formal expressions and which lecturers are able to generate and share.

CASE STUDY: UNIVERSITY OF ULSTER, NORTHERN IRELAND

Background: Developing a Reference Model to Capture and Share Learning Designs

The University of Ulster hosts the "Centre For The Utilization Of Institutional E-Learning Services To Enhance The Learning Experience." It is part of a network of Centres of Excellence in Teaching and Learning (CETL) Initiative across the UK.

The aim of the center is to "promote, facilitate and reward the adoption of a learner centred reflective practice approach to the development of teaching and learning, in particular with respect to the use of e-learning technologies." A key aim of the center was to seek to develop a reference model for excellent and effective practice that could be used to promote and evaluate practice. The strategy of the center is to extend and develop existing teaching practice and e-learning rubrics in order to capture them and codify them to provide a simple reference framework for practitioners.

However, the challenge of describing and disseminating effective practice was soon recognized to be a more critical factor in the promotion and facilitation of changes in academic practice. With this in mind, the center focused on the potential use of learning design models to establish an effective means of describing and disseminating good practice, in the development of online learning activities, in an easily understandable manner.

The need to describe and disseminate effective practice has become increasingly important and there are many emerging trends and technologies to capture, record and disseminate current practice.

Existing approaches to describe teaching and learning activities tend to focus on the practical acts and supporting resources rather than the processes and tend to lack a detailed 'human context.' There are many pedagogic and instructional models and theories that can describe activities in some detail but they suffer from a doctrinaire approach, which while useful and necessary in specific educational work contexts—such as open learning and vocational training—suffer from considerable semantic and syntactic restrictions when applied to the mainstream. The Stirling case study in this chapter would be a classic example of this phenomenon.

Requirements

The specific requirements of this initiative are to establish, pilot and disseminate findings on a simple and consistent recording procedure to capture current teaching and learning processes and practices. The main aim of the procedure is to demonstrate how all activities can be mapped onto a series of widely understandable set of

teaching and learning events, where the tutors' and students' activities and roles are clearly defined at each stage. The strength of the method proposed below is its transparency, use of plain English and its potential for breaking down complex learning activities into a generic, re-usable format so that good practice can be disseminated, reused and evaluated easily. The method has added value, in that it promotes self and peer reflection of teaching and learning practices and communicates teaching and learning practices to in a way that can support evaluation.

Approach: Adopting the 8LEM Model

The introduction of the IMS learning design specification has given great encouragement to those who would like to share their learning design practices to provide a meaningful dissemination of practice, especially as this opens the way to sharing learning designs and their respective models with the potential to be re-used by others. Inspired by this development the aim of this current project is to better describe the overall process of teaching and learning in a more effective and shareable manner. The need for a "learner focus" required any modeling approach to have a dual perspective (learner and tutor) to best capture the distinct activities of the two stakeholders and their interactions.

The project examined several emerging approaches in development and identified the 8 learn-

Figure 7. The 8LEM model

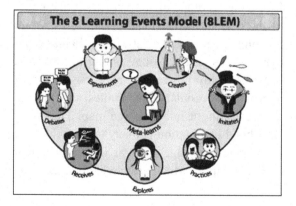

ing events model (8LEM) developed by LabSET of the University of Liège, Belgium, as a viable foundation for this work. This model focuses on processes in teaching and learning rather than on actual content being taught, so it had the potential to be mapped to IMS learning design. It proposes a 'palette' of eight specific ways (learning events) of learning/teaching that the teacher or learning designer can use to describe any point in the development and analysis of learning activities, as shown below in Figure 7.

The model does not specify a particular order to these learning events; it simply provides a choice of learning/teaching processes, which can be used in mapping or creating learning scenarios. The model connects the interdependent learner's demand and the teacher's supply, providing a social interaction perspective to each learning activity and event. The advantage of this model is that it allows learning activities to be mapped onto a series of widely understandable set of learning events so that the tutors' and students' experiences and roles can be clearly defined at each stage. It results in a simple, easy to understand method of describing key activities in plain English—a key requirement.

The eight main learning events are:

1. **Receives:** (Traditional didactic transmission of information: lecture/ content delivery/recommended reading)
2. **Debates:** (Learning through social interactions, collaborative, challenging discussions e.g., f2f debates, online discussions)
3. **Experiments:** (Learner manipulating the environment to test personal hypotheses e.g. lab work, workshops, computer simulations, problem solving)
4. **Creates:** (Creating something new, producing work e.g., essays, projects etc.)
5. **Explores:** (Personal exploration by learner, e.g., literature reviews, Internet searches, information handling)
6. **Practices:** (Application of theory and its assessment, to include tutor feedback, e.g., exam, quiz, exercises, work based learning, etc.)
7. **Imitates:** (Learning from observation and imitation, e.g., where the tutor models techniques, modeling/simulation, practicals, walk through tutorials, role plays)
8. **Meta-learns:** (self reflection.)

Adding More Detail to the 8LEM Model

This initiative aimed to further explore these learning events in terms of the student and tutor activities in more detail. To achieve this, a decision was made to employ a simple reflection tool to allow users to develop this area. The outputs of the learning designs project at the University of Wollongong (see Chapter XIX) produced a list of aproximately 30 generic verbs that provide a common sense set of terms to describe teaching and learning that teachers are comfortable with; these were kindly supplied by Sue Bennett through the final meeting of the EU UNFOLD project in Berlin, 2005. These 30 verbs were chosen to extend each 8LEM event to clearly define potential tutor and student "activities." These succeed in providing a further simple yet powerful aid to describing practice by allocating appropriate verbs to each role within each individual 8LEM event, the verbs are shown in Table 4.

A prototype process was established to trial the model with academic practitioners, this involved a face-to-face meeting with a structured introduction and was facilitated using simple flash cards that help to record detailed information for each learning activity in the 8LEM model. A process and sequence of structured questions were used as prompts. To provide an initial reference point for the modeling, users were asked to provide a lesson plan/outline of the activity to be described. This helped the interviewers to be more prepared and more aware of the context of the learning

Table 4. Learning activity verbs from the University of Wollongong

University of Wollongong Learning Activity Verbs		
Access	Discuss	Present
Analyze	Explain	Question
Apply	Explore	React/Respond
Assess	Evaluate	Refine
Construct/Produce/Create	Interpret	Reflect
Critique	Justify	Report
Debate	Observe	Represent
Decide	Perform	Research
Describe	Practice	Resolve
Design	Predict	Review

activity and provided a useful reference resource during the modeling process.

Overview of the Developed Hybrid Teaching and Learning Model

1. **Basic structure is the 8LEM model:** Provides a high level breakdown of the practice in question with distinct teacher and learner perspectives.
2. **Addition of the Wollongong Learning Verbs:** Provides a detailed description of interactions and activities for each role within each 8LEM event. To provide additional support for the modeler, relevant subsets of the 30 learning verbs are suggested for each role in an 8LEM learning event, these lists provide teachers with a supportive framework to best describe their own and their learners' activities.

To facilitate the modeling process, a series of simple two-sided flash cards were produced, each representing an 8LEM event on one side and the 8LEM event with relevant teacher/learner verbs on the other. A number of visual aids were incorporated into these flash cards to provide reinforcement of the 8LEM interaction type and the distinct learner and teacher roles. One of the visual cues utilized was a random pair of background facial images to stress the distinct teacher and learner roles. Users introduced to these cards stressed strong (and often differing) views on the types of faces used to represent learners and teachers. This feedback clearly demonstrated the effectiveness of these additional visual cues but also that they could act as a distractor as well as a reinforcer. A second set of flash cards using more heavily watermarked images of androgynous faces were tested with the initial sample group and found not to induce any negative feedback.

Figure 8. Front and back of the 8LEM + verbs flash cards

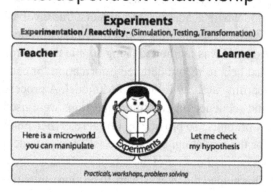 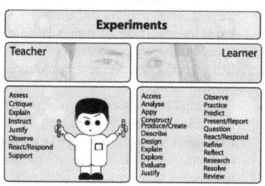

Table 5. Ulster template form for review and reflection completed

Tutor objectives	Tutor Role	Learning Event	Student Role	Student Objective	Environment	Resources
Students are presented with a case study (via VLE)	Describes	RECEIVES	Question		VLE	Printed matter: case study, lecture notes, reading, URLs via WebCT
	Presents		Review			
	Explains		Interpret			
	Instructs					
Students are split into groups and are asked to discuss and analyze the case study for 1 week	Critique	EXPLORES	Analyze			
	Evaluate		Interpret			
	React/Respond		Describe			
	Review		Explore			
	Explain		Evaluate			
			Explain			
			Justify			
			Create			
			Question			
			Present			
Each individual group discuss their case study and report their findings back to the whole group	Review	DEBATES	Present			
	Summarize		Describe			
	Observe		Interpret			
	Evaluate		Present			
			Reflect			
Exam on case studies	Assess	Practices	Produce/Create			
	Evaluate		Interpret			
	Reinforce		Reflect			
Tutor objectives	Tutor Role	Learning Event	Student Role	Student Objective	Environment	Resources
	Explore	META-LEARN Ongoing throughout linked with experiential learning	Reflect (on practice)	Self reflect, self assessment, hypothesize, experiential learning.		
	Question		Hypothesize			
	Summarize					

The Modeling Process

To date, the project team have used a facilitation approach carried out in an informal setting such as a coffee bar. Following a brief overview to the modeling process and the 8LEM events, staff were provided with a set of flash cards. Using a lesson plan as a reference point, the teacher was encouraged to select appropriate 8LEM event cards and place them on the table. Once an overall sequence of events had been described, the member of staff was then encouraged to turn over the flash cards one by one and to pick the verbs that most closely describe their own activities with the 8LEM event and also that of their learners. In cases where more than one verb per role were selected, the member of staff was encouraged to consider if these activities form an asynchronous sequence within the event or an overall synchronous interaction, providing a useful granular interaction sequence within an 8LEM learning event.

At the end of this process, the facilitator transcribes the model onto a template form for review and reflection (see Table 5).

The following notes accompany this completed form:

Theme: *Communication and experiential learning and element of assessment.*

Students receive case studies of two conditions per week over 8 weeks in a Web-enhanced module with an exam based on these at the end of the semester; they are expected to explore and discuss these with members of their group and then feed-back on the case study to the entire group.

After analyzing the learning activity the academic concerned is considering changes and may consider doing the practice bit and assessing throughout, perhaps including a rubric to mark contribution to the discussions and feedback to the entire group, rather than an assessment at the end of the course.

The academic found the process very useful in breaking down this learning activity and thought that it would be useful to apply at the design stage of learning activities.

Conclusions: Results of the Pilot Modeling Activities

A pilot group of staff from the University of Ulster worked with CETL staff to describe a practice from their own teaching experience. These staff were selected from a range of academic disciplines and provided a diverse group in terms of age and gender. Each staff member successfully created a model of their practice that they felt accurately described their own activities and the interactions they believed they had with their learners. All found the selection of 8LEM activities to break the modeled practice into a sequence of distinct interactions simple and informative.

Staff reported that they found the use of the narrative verbs to be very helpful, with some indicating that achieving precision in the choice of the correct verb forced them to reflect on their actual experiences rather than their intentions. The informal nature of the flash cards promoted experimentation with the sequencing and description of the learning process, indicating ongoing questioning and reflection by the participant.

At the end of the initial pilot phase, the CETL team believe that this hybrid model is simple to use and can provide significant insight into the human aspects of teaching and learning activities in a clear and widely understandable way.

Potential Benefits

1. Powerful tool for recording practice and processes in learning activities
2. Provides a rich reflective opportunity for practitioners to review their learning activities and their design and their interrelations with students
3. Widely understood, plain-English terminology

4. Could be used to help design and refine lesson plans and learning outcomes

5. Could form the basis for a conversational evaluation of practice through the comparison of learner and teacher perspective models

6. Provides simple checklists and complementary teaching/learning plans to assist in the adoption of the modeled practice

7. Provides the basis for a learning design transcription 'nexus' between face-to-face and online and vice versa

Possible Extension of the Hybrid Model to Encompass Formal IMS Learning Design Schemas

In order to provide a fuller context to the activity and to permit reusable frameworks of the activity to be generated for use in VLEs and other learning management-like systems, the potential to add additional context information to construct a formal (IMS based) IMS-LD narrative of the activity has been investigated. This can be achieved by revisiting the developed 8LEM/Verb model and appending the following data to each of the 8LEM events for both the tutor and learner perspectives:

*   Objectives (outcomes) for each LEM / interaction
*   Resources used (if any) in support of this activity
*   Environment (tools, locations etc.) used to facilitate the activity/resource access

Prospects for Automation

The project team feels that it is very important that this analysis starts with face-to-face interaction, precisely because these academics work in such an isolated way. Automation would increase rather than decrease this isolation, if building a community is the priority—to enable

meaningful communication and the developing of skills—then face-to-face is the way to go. As one trainer/facilitator said: "You need to see the whites of their eyes!" However, once a certain level of understanding and trust is built up, it might be possible to automate this process to a degree by providing online forms and templates to fill in. However, the best technical support mechanism may just be a simple access to a shared collection of learning designs using this rubric. Arranging face-to-face meetings at the start and end of a semester to develop and check designs is a highly beneficial activity that would be likely to be needed to support any 'automation' functions.

A PROSPECTUS FOR FUTURE DEVELOPMENT OF VISUAL ID ENVIRONMENTS

Analysis and Requirements

Analysis

Given the observations, arguments and case studies we have developed so far we think that, for our purposes, it makes much more sense to think in terms of what kind of support environments teachers might need to articulate and share their semi-formal designs. The discipline of ergonomics (the study of work) has much to say about how we should go about creating such work-support environments (Singleton, 1989).

In e-learning, teaching and learning is dependent on technology—although this says nothing about what drives what. As the technology develops, more complex services are applied. However, no simple technology disappeared from this step-stone environment (see the illustration). Higher levels simply use more components. In the context of visual languages, a useful analogy may be the linguistic relationships of speech: no words without sounds, no sentences without words, no paragraph without sentences, no speech without

Figure 9. A stepping stone picture of e-learning, from Wolfgang Greller

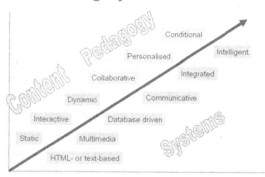

paragraphs, and no speech without sounds, without words, without sentences! One leading to the other to transport more and more meaning. Our ideas for a support environment are informed by this linguistic analogy, where communication may be supported at both the 'primitive' and formal end of the learning design continuum, and move between.

Educational design has always existed. It may be implicit, vague and based on self-directed learning by lecturers operating largely outside formal educational theory and disciplines. But the accuracy of expression required by the technology, where one symbol e.g., "<" in the wrong place can cause a catastrophic break-down, is a powerful force for change from an implicit environment to an analytic explicit environment. This dialectic between the implicit and formal in e-learning is still in the process of resolution; this chapter, indeed, many chapters in this book, being examples.

We should remind ourselves of the target users of such environments and their organizational contexts. Most HE teachers are pedagogically untrained and have rather modest information technology (IT) skills (word processing, e-mail and Web browsing being the IT skill set). This provides a realistic baseline. To this we can add our earlier comments about the sharing of learning materials and designs being unusual (other

than very small scale), the lack of a common pedagogic vocabulary and no widespread tradition of team teaching and ownership of courses. Organizationally, it would be fair to say these teachers are just as concerned with issues of administration, quality control and assessment, as with pedagogy, and any environment that could alleviate these burdens would have considerable interest. The possibility of using such data to aid design activities in order to reduce the bureaucratic quality inspection duties and keep courses inline with their original design and marketing details would be useful.

Requirements

Instructional Design Activities

In the light of the analysis and the rest of the chapter we might sum up our primary requirement as: communication before everything. In other words, the main priority is to assist the teachers to use the environment for the following types of activity. The key words are in italics and are taken as classification of uses suggested by Botturi, Derntl, Boot, and Figl (2006):

- Create and *Generate* their designs by exploring the design 'space', refine designs and examine alternatives;
- *Reflective* communication with themselves about their designs—useful in the first conceptual stages before they collaborate with others;
- *Communicative* activities with others about the design for groupwork and may involve different views;
- The development of *Finalist* version to 'freeze' a final version for sharing and elaboration into a more formal version.

We have adapted that usage classification diagram to apply to our domain. These activities place our initial projected activities for teachers

Figure 10. Semi-formal design activities mapped to Botturi, Derntl, Boot, and Figl. (2006) use classification

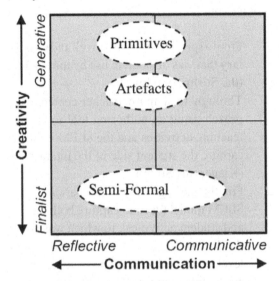

and their colleagues in the top left hand of Botturi, Derntl, Boot, and Figl (2006) suggested classification scheme for the possible applications of visual design languages (see Figure 9; adapted form Botturi et al., 2006). As Botturi, Derntl, Boot, and Figl (2006) point out, these classifications can cover a range as indicated in the figure. In our context as the artifacts and primitives are generated and reflected upon, they then move towards becoming incorporated into a semi-formal expression of design. This means the environment needs to be able to also support a move to the bottom right hand quadrant of the diagram. There may be a number of semi-formal designs required to represent a course or unit of learning.

Data Management Support

The needs of this community are both simple and difficult:

- Individuals will need their own personal space and be able to easily annotate their designs.

- Groups will also need a similar space to share their designs and add annotations about their work.

- Finally, a 'formal' institutional space where designs can be 'signed-off' and stored long-term will be needed.

- The ability to access student management information in different ways would be very useful for course design and evaluation. For example, to be able to project student exit points and numbers, reasons and assessment results, etc., on a curriculum map could be a useful diagnostic tool for redesign.

- Similarly the ability to access course description information easily and map on to visual designs would be useful to help courses 'drifting' away from the original marketing descriptions given to students (a problem in the UK).

Outline Architecture for an Instructional Design Support Environment

In many ways, so far, this description is very similar to the Xerox Parc IDE (instructional design environment) support system of the late 1980s which was a repository of hypertext documents that could be linked as the designers saw fit, to support customized workflows and different design models (Goodyear, 1997). The IDE model included 'decision' design cards and 'rationale' links with the decisions being made according to a set of design components. We can see a similarity to the Ulster case study here. The IDE software provides the means to supply a repository of designs and components that can be annotated for future users—especially useful for trainee designers and knowledge capture exercises. The other attractive aspect of IDE is that it is not linked to any ID model and is intended to support an iterative 'spiral' style development model, which would be very attractive to our target audience. Again, there are clear parallels here with the comments Stubbs and Gibbons (Chapter III) make about the role of design drawings in the wider design field.

To be clear, we are not proposing to use IDE, but we would like these kinds of services. What we see is a system that would allow people to customize it at different levels for different design styles and workflows, this would provide for 'localization.' Something like a modern digital repository system like Fedora and the associated annotation and groupware tools like Project Pad would provide a powerful infrastructure, but would Microsoft Sharepoint (the latest version of which incorporates blogs and wikis), and even a system composed of a simple database, word templates and a shared directory would be good enough used with e-mail. The point here is not to get hung up on the technical aspects to what is primarily a human and organizational problem.

CONCLUSION

We have introduced the idea that teachers in the post-secondary public education sector are novice instructional designers and are likely to find creating formal design narratives difficult. We make the case for aiming to create semi-formal design statements by teachers as an intermediary point before continuing to create more formalized and abstracted narrative that can be converted into an EML, if required. We have argued that this problem is best solved by adopting a systems approach. We go on to describe some of the drivers for change and the difficulties teachers experience in the instructional design field when using technology and the potential benefits of adopting semi-formal methods that incorporate visual approaches. We briefly look at existing work in the learning design field and provide a useful 'learning design continuum' to help the reader situate our discussion within. Following this, to illustrate our points, we provide three different case studies of

efforts to capture and share instructional designs that included visual components. These three (independent) case studies show an interesting progression:

1. From a specialist ID framework and vocabulary that was difficult to use by the teachers (the Stirling Study).
2. Through to a more teacher-centered approach using an authoring tool to capture teaching activities and the 8LEM model to capture the student side of the interactions (Klagenfurt Study).
3. Finally ending with combination of the 8LEM model (used to capture both teacher and student activities), to which was added the Wollongong verbs to provide a good level of granular descriptive detail in an acceptable manner (Ulster Study).

The Ulster approach looks very promising and we can see clear precursors to this in the other two studies—despite their happening independently. Ulster is also fortunate in having greater resources to devote to this and it is notable that they have decided on a strongly human-facilitated approach.

We have then continued to discuss the likely characteristics of future design support environments and made suggestions for their future development in the light of our discussions and case studies.

Finally, we think we have made the case for taking informal and semi-formal approaches to instructional design seriously. There are serious limitations in the current approaches to creating instructional designs advocated by the communities involved with educational and cognitive theory, and the IT developer communities. We have situated this discussion in the context of wider changes in the academic community including staff development, changing roles and institutional reorganization.

REFERENCES

Ask, B. & Haugen, H. (1995). The Norwegian JITOL experience and NITOL as a national extension. In R. Lewis (Ed.), *Journal of Computer Assisted Learning, 11*(4), 203-209.

Bajnai, J. (2005). *EduWeaver Benutzerhandbuch [EduWeaver Manual]*. Retrieved 24 Sept. 2006 from http://www.eduweaver.net/

Beetham, H. 2004. *Review of developing e-learning models for the JISC practitioner communities version 2.1*. Retrieved from http://www.jisc.ac.uk/elearning_pedagogy.html

Botturi, L., Derntl, M., Boot, E., & Figl, K. (2006). A classification framework for educational modeling languages in instructional design. In the *Proceedings of IEEE ICALT 2006* (pp. 1216-1220). Kerkrade, the Netherlands.

Carey, T., Swallow, J., & Oldfield, W. (2002). Educational rationale metadata for learning objects. *Canadian Journal of Learning and Technology, 28*(3).

Collis, B., & Moonen, J. (2004). *Flexible learning in a digital world* (2nd ed.). London: Routledge & Falmer.

de la Teja, I., Lundgren-Cayrol, K., & Paquette, G. (2005). Transposing MISA learning scenarios into IMS units of learning. *Journal of Interactive Media in Education*. Retrieved from http://jime.open.ac.uk/2005/13/

Fernandez-Young, A., Ennew, C., Owen, N., & Dehaan, C. (2006). *Developing material for online management education—A UK eUniversity Experience*. Oxford, Brookes University: Business, Management, Accountancy and Finance Subject Centre.

Friesen, N. (2004). Three objections to learning objects and e-Learning standards. In R. McGreal (Ed.), *Online education using learning objects*. (pp. 59-70). London: Routledge.

Greller, W. (2005, September 22-23). Planning the implementation of IMS learning design. In R. Koper, C. Tattersall, & D. Burgos, (Eds.), *Proceedings of the UNFOLD-PROLEARN Joint Workshop*, Valkenburg, The Netherlands.

Griffiths, D. Blat, J. (2005, October). The role of teachers in editing and authoring units of learning using IMS learning design. *The International Journal on Advanced Technology for Learning, 2*(4).

Goodyear, P. (1997). Instructional design environments: Methods and tools for the design of complex instructional systems. In S. Dijkstra, N. Seel, F. Schott & R. Tennyson (Eds.), *Instructional design: International perspectives* (pp. 83-111). Mahwah NJ: Lawrence Erlbaum Associates.

Hernández-Leo, D., Villasclaras-Fernández, E. D., Asensio-Pérez, J. I., Dimitriadis, Y., Jorrín-Abellán, I. M., Ruiz-Requies, I., & Rubia-Avi, B. (2006). COLLAGE: A collaborative Learning Design editor based on patterns. *Educational Technology & Society, 9*(1), 58-71.

Janssen J., & Hermans H. (2005). How to integrate learning design into existing practice. In R. Koper & C. Tattersal (Eds.), *Learning design—A handbook on modeling and delivering networked education and training* (pp. 253-267). New York: Springer.

Jochems, W., van Merriënboer, J., & Koper, R. (2004). *Integrated e-learning: Implications for pedagogy, technology and organization*. Routledge & Falmer.

Kimble, C., Hildreth, P., & Wright, P. (2001). Communities of practice: Going virtual. *In Knowledge management and business model innovation* (pp. 220-234). Hershey, USA: Idea Group Publishing.

Laurillard, D. (1994). *Rethinking university teaching*. London: Routledge.

Littlejohn, A (2003). An incremental approach to staff development in the reuse of learning resources. In A. Littlejohn (Ed.), *Reusing online resources: A sustainable approach to e-learning.* London: Kogan Page.

Koper, R. (2003). Combining reusable learning resources and services with pedagogical purposeful units of learning. In A. Littlejohn (Ed), *Reusing online resources: A sustainable approach to e-learning.* London: Kogan Page.

Merriënboer, Bastiaens, & Hoogveld (2004). *Instructional design for integrated e-learning.*

Muller, M., & Kuhn, S. (1993). Participatory design. *Communications of the ACM, 36*(4), 25-28.

Parlett, M., & Hamilton, D. (1977). Evaluation as illumination: A new approach to the study of innovatory programmes. In D. Hamilton (Ed.), *Beyond the numbers game* (pp. 6-22). London: Macmillan.

Pollock, N., & Cornford, J. (2000). Theory and practice of the virtual university: Report on UK universities use of new technologies. *In ARIADNE issue 24.* http://www.ariadne.ac.uk/issue24/virtual-universities/

Rehak, D., Mason, R. (2003). Keeping the learning in learning objects. In A. Littlejohn (Ed.), *Reusing online resources: a sustainable approach to e-learning.* London: Kogan Page.

Senge, P., & Sterman, J. (1994). Systems thinking and organizational learning: Acting locally and thinking globally in the organization of the future. In J. Morecroft & J. Sterman (Eds.), *Modeling for learning organizations.* Portland, Oregon: Productivity Press.

Shuell, T. (1992). Designing instructional computing systems for meaningful learning. In P. Winne & M. Jones (Eds.), *Adaptive learning environments: Foundations and frontiers.* New York: Springer Verlag.

Twigg, C. (2005). *Keynote summary: Improving learning and reducing costs—New models for online learning.* Retrieved from http://www.alt.ac.uk/altc2005/keynotes.html#carol

van der Klink, M., & Jochems, W. (2004), Management and organization of integrated e-learning. In W. Jochems, J. van Merriënboer, & R. Koper (Eds.), *Integrated e-learning: Implications for pedagogy, technology and organization.* London: Routledge & Falmer.

Verpoorten, D., Poumay, M., & Leclercq, D. (2005, December 14-16). The 8 learning events model (8LEM): A pedagogic conceptual framework for the design of dedicated (and generic?) scenarios. In Kinshuk & Sampson (Eds.), *Proceedings of the IADIS International Conference on Cognition and Exploratory Learning in Digital Age* (pp. 503-508).

Wenning, N., Frankl, G., Bischof, E., & Schiestl, P. (2006). *E-education Designs—Lehrstrategien—Mikrodidaktische Muster* [e-Educations Designs, Teaching Strategies, and Micro-Didactic Patterns]; working paper

Wenger, E. (1998). *Communities of practice.* Cambridge, MA: Cambridge University Press.

ENDNOTE

[1] **A note on terminology:** In this chapter, we use pedagogy interchangeably with teaching and when we use the term pedagogic design it equates to instructional design.

Compilation of References

Agostinho, S, Oliver, R., Harper, B., Hedberg, H., & Wills, S. (2002). A tool to evaluate the potential for an ICT-based learning design to foster "high-quality learning". In A. Williamson, C. Gunn, A. Young, & T. Clear (Eds.), *The Proceedings of the 19th Annual Conference of the Australasian Society for Computers in Learning in Tertiary Education* (pp. 29-38). Auckland, New Zealand. UNITEC Institute of Technology.

Agostinho, S. (2006, December). The use of a visual learning design representation to document and communicate teaching ideas. In L. Markauskaite, P. Goodyear, & P. Reimann (Eds.), *The Proceedings of the 23rd Annual Conference of the Astralasian Society for Computers in Learning in Tertiary Education: Who's Learning? Whose Technology?* (pp. 3-7). Sydney: Sydney University Press.

Alexander, C. (1979). *The timeless way of building.* New York: Oxford University Press.

Alexander, C. (1999). The origins of pattern theory: The future of the theory and the generation of a living world. *IEEE Software, 16*(5), 71-82.

Alexander, C., Ishikawa, S., Silverstein, M., Jacobson, M., Fiksdahl-King, I., & Angel, S. (1977). *A pattern language—Towns, buildings, construction.* New York: Oxford University Press.

Alexander, S., & McKenzie, J. (1998). *An evaluation of information technology projects for university learning.* CAUT, Canberra: Australian Government Publishing Service.

Allert, H. (2004). Coherent social systems for learning: An approach for contextualized and community-centred metadata. *Journal of Interactive Media in Education, 2.*

Allert, H. (2005). *Modeling coherent social systems for learning.* (Thesis dissertation, Hannover University, Germany).

Altova. (2006). *XML spy editor.* Retrieved Dec 18, 2006 from http://www.altova.com

Amorim R., Lama, M., & Sanchez, E. (2006). Using Ontologies to model and execute IMS Learning Design Documents. In *The 6th IEE International Conference on Advanced Learning Technologies (ICALT-06)* (pp.115-116). Kerkrade: The Netherlands.

Analysis & Technology, I. (1995). Competencies and skills for instructional designers. Retrieved May 2006 from http://www.coedu.usf.edu/it/resources/competency.cfm

Anderson, L. W., & Krathwohl, D. R. (2001). *A taxonomy for learning, teaching and assessing. A revision of Bloom's taxonomy of educational objectives.* New York: Addison Wesley Longman.

Andersson, J.R. Corbett, A.T., Koeudinger, K.R., & Pelletier, R. (1995). Cognitive tutors: Lessons learned. *The Journal of Learning Sciences, 4*(2), 167-207.

Appelbaum, S. H., & Steed, A. J. (2005). The critical success factors in the client-consulting relationship. *The Journal of Management Development, 24*(1), 68-93.

Archer, B. (1992). As complex as ABC. In P. Roberts, B. Archer, & K. Baynes (Eds.), *Modelling: The language of design.* Loughborough University of Technology, Department of Design and Technology.

Archer, B., & Roberts, P. (1992). Design and technological awareness in education. In P. Roberts, B. Archer, & K. Baynes (Eds.), *Modelling : The language of design.* Loughborough University of Technology, Department of Design and Technology.

Aristotle. (1984). Poetics. In J. Barnes (Tran.), *The complete works of Aristotle* (Vol. 2, pp. 2316-2340). Princeton, NJ: Princeton University Press.

Arlow, J., Emmerich, W., & Quinn, J. (1999). Literate modeling capturing business knowledge with the UML. In *Proceedings of The First International Workshop on the Unified Modeling Language, UML'98—Beyond the Notation.* Mulhouse, France.

Arnheim, R. (1995). Sketching and the psychology of design. In V. Margolin & R. Buchanan (Eds.), *The idea of design* (pp. xxii, 285 p.). Cambridge, MA: MIT Press.

Aronson, E., & Patnoe, S. (1997). *The jigsaw classroom: Building cooperation in the classroom.* (2nd ed.). New York: Addison-Wesley Educational Publishers Inc.

Ask, B. & Haugen, H. (1995). The Norwegian JITOL experience and NITOL as a national extension. In R. Lewis (Ed.), *Journal of Computer Assisted Learning, 11*(4), 203-209.

Aspillagae, M. (1991). Screen design: A location of information and its effects on learning. *Journal of Computer Based Instruction, 18*(3), 89-92.

Austin, J.N. (1955). *How to do things with words.* Oxford.

Ausubel, D.P. (1968). *Educational Psychology; A cognitive view.* New York: Rhinehart & Winston.

AUTC Project (2002). Information and communication technologies and their role in flexible learning final report. Retrieved September 1, 2006, from http://www.autc.gov.au/projects/completed/comp_projects_ICT_flex_learning.htm

Baader, F., Calvanese, D., McGuinness, D., Nardi, D., & Patel-Schneider, P. (Eds.). (2003). *The description logic handbook.* Cambridge University Press.

Bajnai, J. (2005). *EduWeaver Benutzerhandbuch [EduWeaver Manual].* Retrieved 24 Sept. 2006 from http://www.eduweaver.net/

Baker, D., Georgakopoulos, D., Schuster, H., & Cichoki, A. (2002). Awareness provisioning in collaboration management. *International Journal of Cooperative Information Systems, 11*(1&2), 145-173.

Baker, M. (1992). *In other words: A coursebook on translation.* New York: Routledge.

Banks, J. & Banks, C. (Eds.). (2003). *Handbook of research on multicultural education.* San Francisco: Jossey-Bass Publishers.

Barrett Baxendale, M. (2005). E-learning technical framework and tools—Demonstrator Projects: SLeD Integration Demonstrator Final Report. Retrieved October 11th, 2006, from http://www.hope.ac.uk/slide/documents/slide_final.doc

Bates, T. W. (1999). *Managing technological change.* San Francisco: Jossey-Bass.

Baynes, K. (1992). The role of modelling in the industrial revolution. In P. Roberts, B. Archer, & K. Baynes (Eds.), *Modelling: The language of design.* Loughborough University of Technology, Department of Design and Technology.

Beetham, H. 2004. *Review of developing e-learning models for the JISC practitioner communities version 2.1.* Retrieved from http://www.jisc.ac.uk/elearning_pedagogy.html

Belch, G. E., & Belch, M. A. (1995). *Introduction to advertising and promotion: An integrated marketing communications perspective* (3rd ed.). Chicago: Irwin.

Belfer, K., & Botturi, L. (2003). Pedagogical patterns for online learning. *Proceedings of the World Conference on E-Learning in Corporate, Government, Healthcare and Higher Education ELEARN*, Phoenix, Arizona, (pp.881-884).

Belfer, K., & Botturi, L. (2004). *Online learning design with pedagogical patterns.* Paper presented at the SALT Orlando Conference 2004, Orlando, Florida, USA.

Bell, A. (2005). UML fever: Diagnosis and recovery. *ACM Queue, 3*(2), 48-57.

Bell, R. T. (1991). *Translation and translating: Theory and practice.* New York: Longman, Inc.

Bennett, S. J. (2005). Online support for collaborative authentic activities. In C. Howard, J. Boettcher, L. Justice, K. Schenk, P. Rogers, & G. Berg (Eds.), *Encyclopedia of distance learning* Vol I-IV (pp. 1412-1416). Hershey, PA: Idea Group Reference.

Bennett, S., Agostinho, S., & Lockyer, L. (2005, July 4-6). Reusable learning designs in university education. In *The Proceedings of the IASTED International Conference on Education and Technology (ICET 2005)* (pp. 102-106). Calgary, Alberta, Canada.

Bennett, S., Agostinho, S., Lockyer, L., & Harper, B. (2006). Supporting university teachers create pedagogically sound learning environments using learning designs and learning objects. *IADIS International Journal on WWW/Internet, 4*(1), 16-26. Retrieved July 10, 2006, from http://www.iadis.org/ijwi/

Bennett, S., Lockyer, L. & Agostinho, S. (2004, December 5-8). Investigating how learning designs can be used as a framework to incorporate learning objects. In R. Atkinson, C. McBeath, D. Jonas-Dwyer, & R. Phillips (Eds.), *The Proceedings of the 21ˢᵗ ASCILITE Conference* (pp. 116-122). Perth, Australia. Retrieved from http://www.ascilite.org.au/conferences/perth04/procs/bennett.html

Berggren, A., Burgos, D., Fontana, J. M., Hinkelman, D., Hung, V., Hursh, A., et al. (2005). Practical and pedagogical issues for teacher adoption of IMS learning design standards in Moodle LMS. *Journal of Interactive Media.*

Bergin, J., Eckstein, J., Manns, M., Sharp, H., & Voelter, M. (2005). Pedagogical Patterns. Retrieved December 13, 2006, from http://www.pedagogicalpatterns.org

Berleant, A. (1991). *Art and engagement.* Philadelphia: Temple University Press.

Birkerts, S. (1994). *The Gutenberg elegies: The fate of reading in an electronic age.* New York: Ballentine.

Bloom, B. S. (Ed.). (1956). *Taxonomy of educational objectives—Book 1: Cognitive domain.* New York: Longman.

Bolchini, D., & Paolini, P. (2006). Interactive dialogue model: A design technique for multichannel applications. *IEEE Transactions on Moltumedia, 8*(3), 529-542.

Bolton. (2004). *Reload project.* Retrieved April 16, 2006, from www.reload.ac.uk

Booch, G. (1994). *Object-oriented analysis and design with applications.* Redwood City, CA: Benjamin/Cummings.

Booch., G., Jacobson, J. & Rumbaugh, I. (1999). *The unified modeling language user guide.* Addison-Wesley.

Boot, E. W. (2005). *Building-block solutions for developing instructional software.* Unpublished Dissertation, Open Universiteit, Nederland.

Boot, E., Nelson, J., van Merriënboer, J. J. G., & Gibbons, A. S. (in press). *Stratification, elaboration, and formalization of design documents: Effects on the production of instructional materials.*

Boot, E., van Merriënboer, J.J.G., & Theunissen, N.C.M. (in press). *Improving the development of instructional software: Three building-block solutions to interrelate design and production.*

Bote-Lorenzo, M.L., Hernández-Leo, D., Dimitriadis, Y., Asensio-Pérez, J.I., Gómez-Sánchez, E., Vega-Gorgojo, G., & Vaquero-González, L.M. (2004). Towards reusability and tailorability in collaborative learning systems using IMS-LD and Grid Services. *Advanced Technology for Learning, 1*(3), 129-138.

Botturi, L. (2003). *E²ML: Educational Environments Modeling Language.* Unpublished doctoral dissertation. Lugano, Switzerland: University of Lugano. Retrieved online on January 15ᵗʰ, 2007 from http://www.rero.ch

Botturi, L. (2004). Visualizing learning goals with the quail model. *Australasian Journal of Educational Technologies—AJET, 20*(2), 248-273.

Botturi, L. (2005). Visual languages for instructional design: An evaluation of the perception of E²ML. *Journal of Interactive Learning Research, 16*(4), 329-351

Botturi, L. (2006). Design models as emergent features: An empirical study in communication and shared mental models in instructional design. *Canadian Journal of Learning Technologies, 31*(2), 119-148.

Botturi, L. (2006). E²ML. A visual language for the design of instruction. *Educational Technologies Research & Development, 54*(3), 265-293.

Botturi, L. (2008). E²ML: A tool for sketching instructional designs. In L. Botturi & S. T. Stubbs (Eds.), *Handbook of visual languages for instructional design: Theories and practice* (pp. 111-131). Hershey, PA: IGI Global, Inc.

Botturi, L., Cantoni, L., Lepori, B., & Tardini, S. (2006). *Fast prototyping as a communication catalyst for e-Learning design: Making the transition to e-Learning: strategies and issues.* Hershey, PA: IGI Global.

Botturi, L., Derntl, M., Boot, E., & Figl, K. (2006) A classification framework for educational modeling languages in instructional design. In *The 6ᵗʰ IEEE International Conference on Advanced Learning Technologies (ICALT-06)* (pp. 1216-1220). Kerkrade: The Netherlands.

Boud, D. & Prosser, M. (2002). Appraising new technologies for learning: A framework for development. *Educational Media International, 39*(3-4), 237-245.

Brouns, F., Koper, R., Manderveld, J., Bruggen, J. v., Sloep, P., Rosmalen, P. v., et al. (2005). A first exploration of inductive analysis approach for detecting learning design patterns. *Journal of Interactive Media in Education, Advances in Learning Design Special Issue.*

Brown, D. (2003). *The Da Vinci code.* New York: Random House.

Brown, J.S., & Duguid, P. (2002). *The social life of information.* Boston: Harvard Business School Press.

Brugge, B., & Dutoit, A.H. (2000). *Object-oriented software engineering: Conquering complex and changing systems.* Upper Saddle River, NJ: Prentice Hall.

Bruner, J. (1973). *Beyond the information given.* New York: Norton.

Bruner, J. (1990). *Acts of meaning.* Cambridge: Harvard University Press.

Bruner, J. (2002). *Making stories: Law, literature, and life.* New York: Farrar, Straus, and Giroux.

Brunner, J. (2003). The narrative construction of reality. In M. Mateas & P. Sengers (Eds.), *Narrative intelligence* (pp. vii, 340). Amsterdam: John Benjamins Publishing.

Brusilovsky, P. (2004). *KnowledgeTree: A distributed architecture for adaptive e-learning.* Paper presented at the 13ᵗʰ International World Wide Web Conference on Alternate Track Papers, New York.

Bucciarelli, L. L. (1994). *Designing engineers.* Cambridge, MA: MIT Press.

Burgos, D., & Griffiths, D. (Eds.). (2005). *The UNFOLD project. Understanding and using Learning Design.* Heerlen, The Netherlands: Open University of The Netherlands.

Burgos, D., & Koper, R. (2005). Virtual communities, research groups and projects on IMS learning design. State of the art, key factors and forthcoming challenges. *E-Journal of Educational Research, Assessment and Evaluation, 11*(2).

Caeiro Rodriguez, M., Anido-Rifon, L., & Llamas Nistal, M. (2006). A proposal of separation of concerns in EMLs and its relation with LD. In Kinshuk, R. Koper, P. Kommers, P. Kirschner, D. Sampson, & W. Didderen (Eds.), *Advanced learning technologies (ICALT 2006)* (pp. 76-80). Los Alamitos, CA: IEEE Computer Society.

Caffarella, E. P. (2005, January). *Doctoral research in educational technology: A directory of dissertations, 1977–2004.* Retrieved October 2005, 2006, from http://cortland.edu/education/dissdir/displai4.htm

Campbell, J. (1968). *The hero with a thousand faces* (2ⁿᵈ ed.). Princeton, NJ: Princeton University Press.

Carey, B. (2006, April 26). Analyze these. *New York Times.* Retrieved 05.06.06 from http://www.nyam.org/news/2657.html

Carey, T., Swallow, J., & Oldfield, W. (2002). Educational rationale metadata for learning objects. *Canadian Journal of Learning and Technology, 28*(3).

Chen, A., Mashhadi, A., Ang, D., & Harkrider, N. (1999). Cultural issues in the design of technology-enhanced learning systems. *British Journal of Educational Technology, 30*(3), 217-230.

Chen, P.P.S (1976).The entity-relationship model —Toward a unified view of data. *ACM Transactions on Database Systems I, 1*(1), 9-36.

Cheng, Y. C. (2002). *New paradigm of borderless education: Challenges, strategies, and implications for effective education through localization and internationalization.* Paper presented at the International conference on learning & teaching: Challenge of learning and teaching in a Brave New World: Issues and opportunities in borderless education, Hatyai, Thailand.

Chesterman, A. (2004). Beyond the particular. In A. Mauranen & P. Kujamäki (Eds.), *Translation universals: Do they exist?* (pp. 33-49). Philadelphia: John Benjamins Publishing Company.

Chu, G., & Reeves, T. C. (2000). *The relationship between cultural differences among American and Chinese university students and the design of personal pages on the World Wide Web.* New Orleans, LA: Paper presented at the annual meeting of the American Educational Research Association.

Clark, R., & Estes, F. (2002). *Turning research into results: A guide to selecting the right performance solutions.* Atlanta, GA: CEP Press.

Clarke, J. (1994). Pieces of the puzzle: The jigsaw method. In S. Sharan (Ed.), *Handbook of cooperative learning methods* (pp. 34-50). Westport CT: Greenwood Press.

Cockburn, A. (1997). Structuring use cases with goals. *Journal of Object Oriented Programming, 10*(7), 35-40.

Cockburn, A. (2001). *Writing effective use cases.* Boston: Addison-Wesley.

Collins, A., & Stevens, A. L. (1983). A cognitive theory of inquiry teaching. In C. M. Reigeluth (Ed.), *Instructional-design theories and models: An overview of their current status* (pp. 247-278). Hillsdale, NJ: Lawrence Erlbaum Associates.

Collis, B. (1998). Implementing innovative teaching across the faculty via the WWW. In S. McNeil, J. Price, S. Boger-Mehall, B. Robin, & J. Willis. (Eds.), *The Proceedings of SITE '98, Society for Information Technology and Teacher Education, 9th International Conference* (pp. 1328-1335). Washington, DC: Association for the Advancement of Computing in Education.

Collis, B., & Moonen, J. (2004). *Flexible learning in a digital world* (2nd ed.). London: Routledge & Falmer.

Condon, J. C., & Yousef, F. S. (1975). *An introduction to intercultural communication.* Indianapolis, IN: Bobbs-Merrill Educational Publishing.

Cooper, A., & Ostyn, C. (Eds.). (2002). *IMS reusable definition of competency or educational objective—information model.* IMS Global Consortium. Retrieved March 27, 2007, from http://www.imsglobal.org/competencies

CopperAuthor. (2005). *CopperAuthor learning design editor.* Retrieved October 27, 2005 from http://sourceforge.net/projects/copperauthor/

Correal. D., & Marino O. (2006). *Software requirements specification document for general purpose function's editor* (Technical Report V0.4), Montréal, Canada: Télé-université LICEF Research Centre, Montreal.

CoSSICLE Framework (2005). Framework for the specification of collaboration scripts (Tech. Rep.). Kaleidoscope European Network of Excellence. Retrived from http://www.iwm-kmrc.de/CoSICLE/resources/D29-02-01-F.pdf

Costagliola, G., De Lucia, A., Orefice, S., & Polese, G. (2002). A classification framework for the design of visual languages. *Journal of Visual Languages and Computing, 13*, 573-600.

Cross, N. (2001). Design cognition: Results from protocol and other empirical studies of design activity. In C. M. Eastman, W. M. McCracken, & W. C. Newstetter (Eds.), *Design knowing and learning: cognition in design education* (pp. 79-103). Amsterdam: Elsevier.

Cunningham, S. (1998). Technology and delivery: Assessing the impact of new media on "borderless" education. *Australian Universities' Review, 41*(1), 10-13.

D'Andrade, R. (1990). Some propositions about the relations between culture and human cognition. In J. W. Stigler, R. A. Shweder, & G. Herdt (Eds.), *Cultural psychology: Essays on comparative human development* (pp. 65-129). New York, NY: Cambridge University Press.

Dagada, R., & Jakovljevic, M. (2004). 'Where have all the trainers gone?' E-learning strategies and tools in the corporate training environment. In *Proceedings of the 2004 Annual Research Conference of the South African Institute Of Computer Scientists and Information Technologists on IT Research in Developing Countries.* Stellenbosch, Western Cape, South Africa ACM.

Dalziel, J. (2003). Implementing learning design: The learning activity management system (LAMS). In *The Proceedings of the ASCILITE 2003 conference, Adelaide, Australia.* Retrieved from http://www.melcoe.mq.edu.au/res.htm

Dalziel, J. (2005). LAMS: *Learning activity management system 2.0.* Retrieved January 22, 2007, from http://wiki.oamsfoundation.org/display/lams/Home

Dalziel, J. (2006). Lessons from LAMS for IMS learning design. In Kinshuk, R. Koper, P. Kommers, P. Kirschner, D. Sampson, & W. Didderen (Eds.), *Advanced learning technologies (ICALT 2006)* (pp. 1101-1102). Los Alamitos, CA: IEEE Computer Society.

Dansereau D.F. (1978). The development of a learning strategies curriculum. In H. F. O'Neil Jr. (Ed.), *Learning strategies.* New York: Academic Press.

Dansereau, D.F., & Holley, C.D. (1982). Development and evaluation of a text mapping strategy. In A. Flammer & W. Kintsch (Eds.), *Discourse processing.* The Netherlands: North Holland.

Davis, M. P. (1997). *Successful advertising: Key alternative approaches.* London: Cassell.

Davis, W.A. (2002). A comparison of pyramids versus brainstorming in a problem based learning environment. In *Focusing on the student: Proceedings of 11th Annual Teaching Learning Forum.* Perth: Edith Cowan University.

De Croock, M. B. M., Paas, F., Schlanbusch, H., & van Merriënboer, J. J. G. (2002). ADAPTit: Tools for training design and evaluation. *Educational Technology, Research and Development, 50*(4), 47-58.

de la Teja, I., Lundgren-Cayro, K., & Paquette, G. (2005). Transposing MISA learning scenarios into IMS units of learning. *Journal of Interactive Media in Education,* (13). Retrieved from http://www-jime.open.ac.uk/2005/13/

De Vries, F. (n.d.). EML 1.0. Retrieved on October 4, 2006 from http://dspace.learningnetworks.org/handle/1820/81

Deming, W.E. (1982). *Quality, productivity, and competitive position.* Cambridge, MA: MIT, Centre for Advanced Engineering Study.

Derntl, M. (2005). *Patterns for person-centered e-learning.* Doctoral dissertation, University of Vienna, Vienna, Austria. Retrieved from http://elearn.pri.univie.ac.at/derntl/diss

Derntl, M., & Botturi, L. (2006). Essential use cases for pedagogical patterns. *Computer Science Education, special issue on Pedagogic Patterns, 16*(2), 137-156.

Derntl, M., & Hummel, K. A. (2005). Modeling context-aware e-learning scenarios. In *The Proceedings of Third IEEE Conference on Pervasive Computing and Communication Workshops* (pp. 337-342). Kauai Island, Hawaii.

Derntl, M., & Motschnig-Pitrik, R. (2005). The role of structure, patterns, and people in blended learning. *The Internet and Higher Education, 8*(2), 111-130.

Derntl, M., & Motschnig-Pitrik, R. (2008). coUML: A visual modeling language for cooperative environments. In L. Botturi & T. Stubbs (Eds.), *Handbook of visual languages in instructional design; Theories and practice* (pp. 154-182). Hershey, PA: IGI Global.

Develay, M. (Ed.). (1993). *De l'apprentissage à l'enseignement*: Collection Pédagogies, ESF Edition.

Dewey, J. (1934/1989). *Art as experience* (Vol. 10). Carbondale: Southern Illinois University Press.

Dick, W., & Carey, L. (1996). *The systematic design of instruction* (4th ed.). New York: Harper Collins.

Dijkstra, S., Collis, B., & Eseryel, D. (1999). Instructional design for tele-learning. *Journal of Computing in Higher Education, 10*(2), 3-18.

Dillenbourg, P. (2002). Overscripting CSCL: The risks of blending collaborative learning with instructional design. In P. A. Kirschner (Ed.), *Three worlds of CSCL. Can we support CSCL?* (pp. 61-91). Open Universiteit Nederland.

Dillenbourg, P. (Ed.). (1999). *Collaborative learning: Cognitive and computational approaches.* Oxford, UK: Elsevier Science.

Dillenbourg, P., & Tchounikine, P. (2006). Flexibility in macro-scripts for CSCL. *Journal of Computer Assisted Learning, 23*(1), 1-13.

Dorst, K., & Cross, N. (1996). Creativity in the design process: Co-evolution of problem—solution. *Studies, 17*(4), 341-361.

Douglas, I. (2003). Visualizing and sharing human performance analysis knowledge. *Seventh International Conference on Information Visualization* (IV 2003), (pp. 465-469).

Douglas, I. (2006). Issues in software engineering of relevance to instructional design. *Tech Trends, 50*(5), 28-35.

Douglas, I., Butler, J., Nowicki, C., & Schaffer, S. (2003). Web-based collaborative analysis, reuse and sharing of human performance knowledge. *Proceedings of the Inter-service/Industry Training, Simulation and Education Conference (I/ITSEC),* (pp. 1023-1030).

Douglas, I., Wright, M., and Nowicki, C. (2004). Communicating performance knowledge among the services. *Proceedings of the Inter-service/Industry Training, Simulation and Education Conference (I/ITSEC).* 1630, (pp. 1-10).

Drucker, P.F. (1994). *Knowledge work and knowledge society: The social transformations of this century.* [transcript of a lecture]. Retrieved August 11, 2006 from http://www.ksg.harvard.edu/ifactory/ksgpress/www/ksg_news/transcripts/drucklec.htm

Drucker, P.F. (1999, April). Beyond the information revolution. *The Atlantic Monthly, 284*(4) p.47-57.

Dublin Core Metadata Initiative (2007). Retrieved February 11, 2007 from http://dublincore.org/

Durand, G., & Martel, C. (2006). To scenarize the assessment of an educational activity. In *The Proceedings of ED'MEDIA 2006.* Orlando, Florida.

Duval, E. (Ed.). (2002). *Learning object metadata standard.* IEEE Learning Technology Standards Committee.

Eastman, C. M. (1969). Cognitive processes and ill-defined problems: A case study from design. *In The Proceedings of the First Joint International Conference on IA,* Washington, DC, pp. 669-690.

Edumundson, A. (2007). The Cultural Adaptation Process (CAP) Model: Designing e-learning for another culture. In A. Edumundson (Ed.), *Globalized e-learning cultural challenges* (pp. 267-290). Hershey, PA: Information Science Publishing.

Eisner, E. W. (1998). *The enlightened eye: Qualitative inquiry and the enhancement of educational practice* (2nd ed.). Upper Saddle River, NJ: Merrill.

E-LEN (2004). *E-LEN project website.* Retrieved February 2007 from http://www2.tisip.no/E-LEN/

Ely, D. P., & Plomp, T. (1996). *Classic writings on instructional technology.* Englewood, CA: Libraries Unlimited.

EMF. (2007). *Eclipse Modeling Framework Project*. Retrieved February 2007, from http://www.eclipse. org/modeling/

Engeström, Y. (1987). *Learning by expanding: An activity-theoretical approach to developmental research*. Orienta-Kosultit, Helsinki, Finland.

Eriksson, H.-E., & Penker, M. (1998). *UML Toolkit*. New York: John Wiley & Sons.

Eriksson, H-E., and Penker, M. (2000). *Business modeling with UML: Business patterns at work*. New York: John Wiley & Sons.

Ertmer, P. A., & Quinn, J. (2003). *The ID casebook: Case studies in instructional design* (2nd ed.). Upper Saddle River, NJ: Merrill.

Es, R. V., & Koper, R. (2006). Testing the pedagogical expressiveness of IMS-LD. *Education Technology & Society, 9*(1), 229-249.

Eseryel, D., Schuver-van Blanken, M., & Spector, J. M. (2001). Current practice in designing training for complex skills: Implications for design and evaluation of ADAPT-IT. In C. Montgomerie & J. Vitelli (Eds.), *Proceedings of ED-MEDIA 2001: World Conference on Educational Multimedia, Hypermedia, & Telecommunications* (pp. 474-479). Tampere , Finland Association for Advancement of Computing in Education.

Fairweather, P., & Gibbons, A. S. (2000). Distributed learning: Two steps forward, one back? One forward, two back? *IEEE Concurency, 8*(2), 8-9.

Farail, P., Gaufillet, P., Canals, A., Le Camus, C., Sciamma, D., Michel, P., et al. (2006). *The TOPCASED project: A toolkit in open source for critical aeronautic systEms design*. Paper presented at the Eclipse Technology eXchange workshop (eTX) at ECOOP 2006, Nantes, France.

Fernandez-Young, A., Ennew, C., Owen, N., & Dehaan, C. (2006). *Developing material for online management education—A UK eUniversity Experience*. Oxford, Brookes University: Business, Management, Accountancy and Finance Subject Centre.

Ferraris, C., Brunier, P., & Martel, C. (2002). Constructing collaborative pedagogical situations in classrooms: A scenario and role based approach. In *The Proceedings of CSCL 2002* (pp. 290-299). Boulder, Colorado.

Ferruci, F., Tortora, G., & Vitello, G. (2002). *Exploiting visual languages in software engineering*: Handbook of Software Engineering and Knowledge Engineering. Singapore: World Scientific Publishing Company.

Figl, K., & Derntl, M. (2006, June 26–30). *A comparison of visual instructional design languages for blended learning*. Paper presented at the World Conference on Educational Multimedia, Hypermedia, & Telecommunications, Orlando FL.

Fitzpatrick, G., Tolone, W. J., & Kaplan, S. M. (1995). Work, locales and distributed social worlds. In *The Proceedings of ECSCW'95* (pp. 1-16). Stockholm, Sweden.

Foucault, B. E., Russell, R. S., & Bell, G. (2004, April 24-29). *Techniques for research and designing global products in an unstable world: A case study*. Paper presented at the Computer Human Interaction, Vienna, Austria.

Fowler, M. (2001, June 29). *Put your process on a diet*. Retrieved April 1, 2007, from http://www.ddj.com/dept/ architect/184414675

Fowler, M. (2003). *UML distilled: A brief guide to the standard object modeling language*. Boston: Addison-Wesley.

Franklin, B. (1749). *Proposals relating to the education of youth in Pensilvania*, B. Franklin, Printer, Philadelphia. Retrieved online 7/29/06 from http://www.archives. upenn.edu/primdocs/1749proposals.html

Fraser, I. & Henmi, R., (1994). *Envisioning architecture: An analysis of drawing*. New York: Van Nostrant-Reinhold.

Friesen, N. (2004). Three objections to learning objects and e-Learning standards. In R. McGreal (Ed.), *Online education using learning objects*. (pp. 59-70). London: Routledge.

Gagné, R. M., Briggs, L. J., & Wager, W. W. (1992). *Principles of instructional design* (4th ed.). Fort Worth: Harcourt Brace Jovanovich College Publishers.

Gamma, E., Helm, R., Johnson, R., & Vlissides, J. (1995). *Design patterns, elements of reusable object-orientedsSoftware.* Boston: Addison-Wesley.

Gardner, H. (2000). *Intelligence reframed: Multiple Intelligences for the 21st Century.* New York: Basic Books.

Garfinkel, H., & Sacks, H. (1972). *Contributions in ethno-methodology.* Bloomington: Indiana University Press.

Garrison, D. R., & Kanuka, H. (2004). Blended learning: Uncovering its transformative potential in higher education. *The Internet and Higher Education, 7*(2), 95-105.

Gastfriend, H. H., Gowen, S. A., & Layne, B. H. (2001, November 8–12, 2001). *Tranforming a lecture-based course to an internet-based course: a case study.* Paper presented at the National convention of the Association for Educational Communications and Technology, Atlanta GA.

Gay, G. (2000). *Culturally responsive teaching.* New York: Teachers College Press.

Gedenryd, H. (1998). *How designers work—Making sense of authentic cognitive activities.* Unpublished Dissertation, Lund University, Lund, UK.

Geertz, C. (1973). *The interpretation of cultures.* New York: Basic Books.

Gibbons, A. S. (2003). What and how designers design? A theory of design structure. *TechTrends, 47*(5), 22-27.

Gibbons, A. S., & Brewer, E. K. (2005). Elementary principles of design languages and design notation systems for instructional design. In J. M. Spector, C. Ohrazda, A. VanSchaack, & D. A. Wiley (Eds.), *Innovations in instructional technology* (pp. 111-129). Mahwah, NJ: Lawrence Erlbaum Associates.

Gibbons, A. S., & Rogers, P. C. (2006). *Coming at design from a different angle: Functional design.* Brigham Young University.

Gibbons, A. S., Nelson, J., & Richards, R. (2001). The nature and origin of instructional objects. In D. A. Wiley (Ed.), *The instructional use of learning objects* (pp. 25-58). Bloomington, IN: Association for Educational Communications and Technology.

Gibbs, G. (1995). *Teaching more students 3: Discussion with more students.* Headington, Oxford: The Oxford Centre for Staff Development.

Gibson, J.J. (1979). *The ecological approach to visual perception.* Hillsdale, NJ: Lawrence Earlbaum.

Gilbert, T. (1996). *Human competence: Engineering worthy performance.* Washington, DC: International Society for Performance Improvement, Inc.

Gladwell, M. (2005, March 25). The social life of paper. *The New Yorker.* Retrieved 5/7/06 from http://www.gladwell.com/pdf/paper.pdf

GMF. (2007). *GMF Project.* Retrieved February 2007, from http://www.eclipse.org/gmf/

GMT. (2007). *GMT Project.* Retrieved February 2007, from http://www.eclipse.org/gmt/

Goel, V. (1995). *Sketches of thought.* Cambridge, MA: MIT Press.

Goffman, E. (1981). *Forms of talk.* Philadelphia: University of Pennsylvania Press.

Goldschmidt, G. (1991). The dialectics of sketching. *Creativity Research Journal, 4*(2), 123-143.

Goldschmidt, G. (1999). *The backtalk of self-generated sketches.* retrieved online from http://www.arch.usyd.edu.au/kcdc/books/VR99/Gold.html June 7, 2005.

Goodyear, P. (1997). Instructional design environments: Methods and tools for the design of complex instructional systems. In S. Dijkstra, N. Seel, F. Schott & R. Tennyson (Eds.), *Instructional design: International perspectives* (pp. 83-111). Mahwah NJ: Lawrence Erlbaum Associates.

Goodyear, P. (2005). Educational design and networked learning: Patterns, pattern languages and design practice. *Australian Journal of Educational Technology, 21*(1), 82-101.

Gray, A., & McGuigan, J. (1997). Introduction. In A. Gray & J. McGuigan (Eds.), *Studying culture: An introductory reader* (pp. xi-xv). New York: Arnold, A member of the Hodder Headline Group.

Greer, M. (1991). Organizing and managing the instructional design process. In L.J. Briggs, K.L. Gustafson, & M.H. Tillman (Eds.), *Instructional design: Principles and applications* (2nd ed., pp. 315-343). Englewood Cliffs, NJ: Educational Technology.

Greller, W. (2005, September 22-23). Planning the implementation of IMS learning design. In R. Koper, C. Tattersall, & D. Burgos, (Eds.), *Proceedings of the UNFOLD-PROLEARN Joint Workshop*, Valkenburg, The Netherlands.

Griffin, M. M., & Robinson, D. H. (2005). Does spacial or visual information in maps facilitate text recall? Reconsidering conjoint retention hypothesis. *Educational Technology Research and Development, 53*(1), 23-36.

Griffiths, D., & Blat, J. (2005). The role of teachers in editing and authoring units of learning using IMS Learning Design. *Advanced Technology for Learning, 2*(4), 243-251.

Griffiths, D., Blat, J., Garcia, R., Vogten, H., & Kwong, K. (2005). Learning fesign tools. In R. Koper & C. Tattersall (Eds.), *Learning design: A Handbook on modeling and delivering networked education and training* (pp. 109-136). Berlin-Heidelberg: Springer Verlag.

Guéraud, V., Adam, J.-M., Pernin, J.-P., Calvary, G., & David, J.-P. (2004). L'exploitation d'Objets Pédagogiques Interactifs à distance: le projet FORMID. *Revue STICEF, 11*. Retrieved from http://www.sticef.org

Gustafson, K. L., & Branch, R. M. (2002). *Survey of instructional development models.* Syracuse, NY: ERIC Clearinghouse On Information & Technology.

Hall, E. T. (1966). *The hidden dimension.* Garden City, NY: Doubleday.

Hall, E. T. (1976). *Beyond culture.* New York: Double Day.

Hall, E. T. (1983). *The dance of life: The other dimension of time.* Garden City, NY: Anchor Press/Doubleday.

Hall, H. M. (2004). *An examination of instructional design from theory to practice: A collective case study.* Unpublished Dissertation, University of New Mexico, Albuquerque NM.

Hall, P., & Hudson, R. (1997). *Software without frontiers: A multi-platform, multi-cultural, multi-nation approach.* New York: John Wiley & Sons, Ltd.

Hall, S. (1996). Cultural studies and its theoretical legacies. In D. Morley & K.-H. Chen (Eds.), *Critical dialogues in cultural studies* (pp. 262-275). London: Routledge.

Hall, S. (1997). Minimal selves. In A. Gray & J. McGuigan (Eds.), *Studying culture.* London: Arnold, a member of the Hodder Headline Group.

Hanks, K., & Belliston, L. (1977). *Draw: A visual approach to thinking, learning, and communicating.* Los Altos, CA: W. Kaufmann.

Hansen, Y. (1999). Visualization for thinking, planning, and problem solving. *Information Design*, 193-220.

Harel, D., & Naamad, A. (1996). The statemate semantics of statecharts. *ACM Transactions on Software Engineering and Methodology, 5*(4).

Harless, J.H. (1970). *An ounce of anlaysis is worth a pound of objectives.* Newnan, GA: Harless Performance Guild.

Harless, J.H. (1988). *Accomplishment-based curriculum development.* Newnan, GA: Harless Performance Guild.

Harper, B., Agostinho, S., Bennett, S., Lukasiak, J., & Lockyer, L. (2005). Constructing high quality learning environments using learning designs and learning objects. In P. Goodyear, D. G. Sampson, D. J.-T. Y.Kinshuk, T. Okamoto, R. Hartley, & N.-S. Chen (Eds.), *The Proceedings of the 5th IEEE International Conference on Advanced Learning Technologies (ICALT 2005)* (pp. 266-270). Kaohsiung, Taiwan. IEEE Computer Society.

Harrer, A., & Malzahn, N. (2006). Bridging the gap—towards a graphical modelling language for learning designs and collaboration scripts of various granularities. In Kinshuk, R. Koper, P. Kommers, P. Kirschner, D. Sampson, & W. Didderen (Eds.), *Advanced learning technologies icalt 2006* (pp. 296-300). Los Alamitos, CA: IEEE Computer Society.

Harrer, A., Malzahn, N., & Roth, B. (2006). The remote control approach—how to apply scaffolds to existing collaborative learning environments. In Y. Dimitriadis, I. Zigurs, & E. Gomez-Sanchez (Eds.), *Groupware: design, implementation, and use The Proceedings of CRIWG 2006* (LNCS 4154, pp. 118-131). Berlin: Springer.

Harrer, A., Malzahn, N., Hoeksema, K., & Hoppe, U. (2005). Learning design engines as remote control to learning support environments. *Journal of Interactive Media in Education, Special Issue on Advances in Learning Design.*

Hart, J. (1999). *The art of the storyboard: Storyboarding for film, TV, and animation.* Boston: Focal Press.

Henderson, K. (1998). The role of material objects in the design process: A comparison of two design cultures and how they contend with automation. *Science, Technology, & Human Values, 23*(2), 139-174.

Henderson, L. (1996). Instructional design of interactive multimedia: A cultural critique. *Education Technology Research and Development, 44*(4), 85-104.

Henderson, L. (2007). Theorizing a multiple cultures instructional design model for e-learning and e-teaching. In A. Edmundson (Ed.), *Globalized e-learning cultural challenges* (pp. 130-153). Hershey, PA: Information Science Publishing.

Hernandez Leo, D., Asensio Perez, J., & Dimitriadis, Y. (2004). IMS learning design support for the formalization of collaborative learning patterns. In Kinshuk et al. (Eds.), *Proceedings of IEEE international conference on advanced learning technologies ICALT 2004* (pp. 350-354). Los Alamitos, CA.: IEEE Computer Society.

Hernández-Leo, D., Asensio-Pérez, J.I., & Dimitriadis, Y. (2005). Computational representation of collabora-

tive learning flow patterns using IMS learning design. *Educational Technology & Society, 8*(3), 75-89.

Hernández-Leo, D., Asensio-Pérez, J.I., Dimitriadis, Y., Bote-Lorenzo, M.L., Jorrín-Abellán, I.M., & Villasclaras-Fernández, E.D. (2005). Reusing IMS-LD formalized best practices in collaborative learning structuring. *Advanced Technology for Learning, 2*(4), 223-232.

Hernández-Leo, D., Harrer, A., Dodero, J.M., Asensio-Pérez, J.I., & Burgos, D. (2006). Creating by reusing learning design solutions. *Proceedings of the 8th International Symposium on Computers in Education* (pp. 417-424). León, Spain: University of León.

Hernández-Leo, D., Villasclaras-Fernández, E. D., Asensio-Pérez, J. I., Dimitriadis, Y., Jorrín-Abellán, I. M., Ruiz-Requies, I., et al. (2006). COLLAGE: A collaborative learning design editor based on patterns. *Educational Technology & Society, 9*(1), 58-71.

Hernández-Leo, D., Villasclaras-Fernández, E.D., Asensio-Pérez, J.I., Dimitriadis, Y., & Retalis, S. (2006). CSCL scripting patterns: Hierarchical relationships and applicability. *Proceedings of 6th IEEE International Conference on Advanced Learning Technologies.* Kerkrade, The Netherlands: IEEE Computer Society.

Herrington, J. & Oliver, R. (2002). *Description of online teaching and learning (Edith Cowan University Online Unit IMM4141 in Graduate Certificate in Online Learning).* Retrieved September 19, 2006, from http://www.learningdesigns.uow.edu.au/exemplars/info/LD20/index.html

Hicks, O. (2004). *Composite report on projects funded through the Australian universities teaching committee 2000-2003.* Retrieved September 1, 2006, from http://www.autc.gov.au/projects/completed/comp_projects_proj_funded_autc_2000-2003.htm

Hofstede, G. (1980). *Cultures consequences: International differences in work related values.* Beverly Hills, CA: Sage Publications.

Hofstede, G. (1991). *Cultures and organizations: Software of the mind.* London: McGraw Hill Book Company.

Hokanson, B. (2001). Digital image creation and analysis as a means to examine learning and cognition. In M. Beynon, C. Nehaniv, & K. Dautenhahn (Eds.), *Proceedings of the 4th International Conference on Cognitive Technology*. Berlin: Springer.

Hokanson, B., & Hooper, S. (2000). Computers as cognitive media: Examining the potential of computers in education. *Computers in Human Behavior, 16*, 537-552.

Holkeboer, K. (1987). *Patterns for theatrical costumes: garments, trims, and accessories from ancient Egypt to 1915*. New York: Prentice-Hall.

Holoyak, K.J. (1991). Symbolic connectionism: Toward third generation-theories of expertise. In K.A. Ericsson & J. Smith (Eds.), *Toward a general theory of expertise: Prospects and limits*. New York: Cambridge University Press.

Hoogveld, A. W. M. (2003). *The teacher as designer of competency-based education*. Heerlen:Open Universiteit Nederland.

Hoppe, H. U., Gaßner, K. G., Mühlenbrock, M., & Tewissen, F. (2000). Distributed visual language environments for cooperation and learning: Applications and intelligent support. *The Journal of Group Decision and Negotiation, 9*, 205-220.

Horton, W. (2005). Graphics: The not quite universal language. In N. Aykin (Ed.), *Usability and internationalization of Information Technology* (pp. 157-188). Mahwah, NJ: Lawrence Erlbaum & Associates Publishers.

Hughes, R. (1991). *The shock of the new*. New York: Knopf.

Hummel, H., Manderveld, J., Tattersall, C., & Koper, R. (2004). Educational modeling language and learning design: New opportunities for instructional reusability and personalized learning. *International Journal of Learning Technology, 1*(1), 111-126.

IDLD (2006). *Implementation and deployment of the learning design specification portal*. Retrieved from http://www.idld.org

IMS (2003). *IMS Learning Design specification*. Retrieved February 2007 from http://www.imsglobal.org/learningdesign/

IMS Learning Design Specification (2003). *IMS Learning design best practice and implementation*. Retrieved October 8, 2007 from http://www.imsglobal.org/learningdesign/ldv1p0/imsld_bestv1p0.html

IMS. (2003). *IMS learning design best practice and implementation guide*. IMS Global Learning Consortium.

IMS. (2003). *IMS learning design information model*. IMS Global Learning Consortium.

Inhelder, B., & Piaget, J. (1958). *The growth of logical thinking from childhood to adolescence*. New York: Basic Books.

Innis, H. (1951). *The bias of communication*. Toronto: University of Toronto Press.

Institute for Scientific Information. (2005). *ISI web of science*. from http://isiknowledge.com/wos

International Board of Standards for Training Performance and Instruction. (2006). *Instructional design competencies*. Retrieved October 18, 2006, from http://www.ibstpi.org/Competencies/instruct_design_competencies_2000.htm

International Society for Performance Improvement. (2007). Retrieved February 15, 2007 from: http://www.ispi.org/

Ip, A., & Naidu, S. (2001). Experienced-based pedagogical designs for e-learning. *Educational Technology: The Magazine for Managers of Change in Education, 41*(5),53-58.

Ishiguro, K. (2005). *Never let me go*. New York: Vintage Books.

ISO. (2005). *ISO/IEC 19501:2005 Information technology—Open Distributed Processing—Unified Modeling Language (UML) Version 1.4.2* Geneva, Switzerland International Organization for Standardization.

Jackendoff, R. (1996). *The architecture of the language faculty*. Cambridge, MA: MIT Press.

Jackson, P. W. (1998). *John Dewey and the lessons of art*. New Haven: Yale University Press.

Jacobson, I. (1992). *Object-oriented software engineering: A use case driven approach*. Reading, MA: Addison-Wesley

Janssen, J., & Hermans, H. (2005). How to integrate learning design into existing practice. In R. Koper & C. Tattersall (Eds.), *Learning design: A handbook on modeling and delivering networked education and training* (pp. 253-266). Berlin-Heidelberg: Springer Verlag.

Javidan, M., & House, R. J. (2001). Cultural acumen for the global manager: Lessons from Project GLOBE. *Organizational Dynamics, 29*(4), 289-305.

JET. (2007). *JET Project*. Retrieved February 2007, from http://www.eclipse.org/emft/projects/jet/

JISC. (2007). *Web site of the joint information systems committee (UK)*. Retrieved from http://www.jisc.ac.uk/

Jochems, W., van Merriënboer, J., & Koper, R. (2004). *Integrated e-learning: Implications for pedagogy, technology and organization*. Routledge & Falmer.

Johnson, D.W., & Johnson, R.T. (1999). *Learning together and alone: Cooperative, competitive and individualistic learning* (5th ed.). Needham Heights, MA: Allyn and Bacon.

Johnson, P. (1994). *The theory of architecture: Concepts, themes, and practices*. New York: Van Nostrand Reinhold.

Jonassen D.H., Beissner K., & Yacci M. (1993). *Structural knowledge—Techniques for representing, conveying and acquiring structural knowledge*. NJ: Laurence Earlbaum Associates.

Jonassen, D. H. (1996). Learning with technology: Using computers as cognitive tools. In D.H. Jonassen (Ed.), *The handbook of research for educational communication and technology* (pp. 112-142). New York: Macmillan.

Jonassen, D. H. (2004). *Learning to solve problems: An instructional design guide*. San Francisco: Pfeiffer.

Jonassen, D. H. (2006). A constructivist's perspective on functional contextualism. *Educational Technology: Research and Development, 54*(1), 43-47.

Jonassen, D. H. (Ed.). (1996). *Handbook of research for educational communications and technology*. New York: Macmillian Library Reference USA.

Jonassen, D. H. (Ed.). (2004). *Handbook of research on educational communications and technology*. Mahwah, NJ: Lawrence Erlbaum Associates, Inc.

Jonassen, D., H. (2000). Toward a design theory of problem solving. *Educational Technology Research and Development, 48*(4), 63-85.

Jones, R. (2004). Designing adaptable learning resources with learning objects patterns. *Journal of Digital Information, 6*(1), Article No. 305. Available at http://jodi.ecs.soton.ac.uk/Articles/v06/i01/Jones/

Kaleidoscope (2006). *Demonstrator of an infrastructure for collect and exchange of experimental traces*. (SVL project deliverable, D7.8.1 [final, public]). Kaleidoscope network of excellence.

Kalyuga, S., & Sweller, J. (2005). Rapid dynamic assessement of expertise to improve the efficiency of adaptive e-learning. *Educational Technology Research and Development, 53*(3), 83-93.

Kao, J. (1997). *Innovation: Breakthrough thinking at 3M, Dupont, GE, Pfizer and Rubbermaid*. New York: Collins.

Karagiorgi, Y., & Symeou, L. (2005). Translating constructivism into instructional design: Potential and limitations. *Educational Technology & Society, 8*(1), 17-27.

Kaufman, R. (1988). Needs assessment: A menu. *Educational Technology Research and Development, 28*(7), 21-23.

Kays, E. J. (2003). *Architecture and instructional design: A conceptual model for e-learning*. Unpublished Dissertation, Capella University.

Kazman, R. (2001). Software Architecture. *Handbook of software engineering and knowledge engineering* (pp. 47-68). World Scientific Press.

Kelley, D., & Hartfield, B. (1996). The designer's stance. In T. Winograd (Ed.), *Bringing design to software* (pp. 151-164). New York: ACM Press.

Kenny, R. F., Zhang, Z., Schwier, R. A., & Campbell, K. (2005). A review of what instructional designers do: Questions answered and questions not asked. *Canadian Journal of Learning and Technology, 31*(1).

Kent, S. (2002). *Model driven engineering.* Paper presented at the Third International Conference on Integrated Formal Method, IFM 2002, Turku, Finland.

Keppell, M. (2001). Optimizing instructional designer-subject matter expert communications in the design and development of multimedia projects. *Journal of Interactive Learning Research, 12*(2/3), 205-223.

Keppell, M. (2004). *Legitimate participation? Instructional designer-subject matter expert interactions in communities of practice.* Paper presented at the World Conference on Educational Multimedia, Hypermedia, and Telecommunications.

Kersten, G. E., Matwin, S., Noronha, S. J., & Kersten, M. A. (2000). *The software for cultures and the cultures in software.* Paper presented at the European Conference on Information System ECI2000, Vienna, Austria.

Kiczales, G., Lamping, J., Mendhekar, A., Maeda, C., Lopes, J.-M., & Irwing, J. (1997). Aspect-Oriented Programming. *Proceedings of the European Conference on Object-Oriented Programming, Vol. 1241,* (pp. 220-242)

Kimble, C., Hildreth, P., & Wright, P. (2001). Communities of practice: Going virtual. *In Knowledge management and business model innovation* (pp. 220-234). Hershey, USA: Idea Group Publishing.

Kirkpatrick, D.L (1998). *Evaluating training programs: The four levels.* San Francisco: Berrett-Koehler.

Kirschner, P., Carr, C., Van Merriënboer, J. J. G., & Sloep, P. (2002). How expert designers design. *Performance Improvement Quarterly, 15*(4), 86-104.

Kirschner, P., Strijbos, J., Kreijns, K., & Beers, P. J. (2004). Designing electronic collaborative learning environments. *Educational Technology Research and Development, 52*(3), 47-66.

Kivett, H. A. (1998). Free-hand sketching: A lost art? *Art, Architecture and Design, 12*(1).

Kollar, I., Fischer, F., & Slotta, J. (2005). Internal and external collaboration scripts in Web-based science learning at schools. In T. Koschmann, D. Suthers, & T.-W. Chan (Eds.), *Computer-supported collaborative learning 2005* (pp. 331-340). Mahwah, NJ: Lawrence Earlbaum Associates.

Kolodner, J. L., & Guzdial, M. (2000). Theory and practice of case-based learning aids. In D. H. Jonassen & S. M. Land (Eds.), *Theoretical foundations of learning environments* (pp. 215-242). Mahwah, NJ: Lawrence Erlbaum Associates.

Koper, R. (2001). *Modeling units of study from a pedagogical perspective: The pedagogical meta-model behind EML.* Educational Expertise Technology Centre, Open University of The Netherlands.

Koper, R. (2002). *Educational modeling language: Adding instructional design to existing specifications.* Retrieved from http://www.httc.de/nmb/images/Koper-v1.pdf

Koper, R. (2003). Combining reusable learning resources and services with pedagogical purposeful units of learning. In A. Littlejohn (Ed), *Reusing online resources: A sustainable approach to e-learning.* London: Kogan Page.

Koper, R. (2003). Learning technologies: an integrated domain model. In W. Jochems, J. Van Merrienboer & R. Koper (Eds.), *Integrated eLearning* (pp. 64-79). London: RoutledgeFalmer.

Koper, R. (2005). *Modeling lifelong learning networks.* Paper presented at the IPSI Conference. Retrieved from http://hdl.handle.net/1820/331

Koper, R. (2006). Current research in learning design. *Educational Technology & Society, 9*(1), 13-22.

Koper, R., & Burgos, D. (2005). Developing advanced units of learning using IMS Learning Design level B.

The International Journal on Advanced Technology for Learning, 2(4), 252-259.

Koper, R., & Manderveld, J. M. (2004). Educational modeling language: Modeling reusable, interoperable, rich and personalised units of learning. *The British Journal of Educational Technology, 35*(5), 537-551.

Koper, R., & Olivier, B. (2004). Representing the learning design of units of learning. *Educational Technology and Society, 7*(3), 97-111.

Koper, R., & Tattersall, C. (Eds.). (2005). *Learning Design, a handbook on modeling and delivering networked education and training*. Heidelberg: Springer-Verlag.

Koper, R., Giesbers, K., Van Rosmalen, P., Tattersall, C., Sloep, P. B., Van Bruggen, J., et al. (Eds.). (2003). *A design model for lifelong learning networks*.

Koper, R., Olivier, B., & Anderson, T. (2003). *IMS Learning design information model*. IMS Global Learning Consortium, Inc.

Kress, G., & VanLeeuwen, T. (2006). *Reading images: The grammar of visual design* (2nd ed.). London: Routledge.

Kroeber, A. L., & Kluckhohn, C. (1966). *Culture: A critical review of concepts and definitions*. New York: Vintage Books.

Kujamäki, P. (2004). What happens to "Unique items" In learners' translations? "Theories" And "Concepts" As a challenge for novices' views on "Good translation". In A. Mauranen & P. Kujamäki (Eds.), *Translation universals: Do they exist?* (pp. 187-204). Philadelphia: John Benjamins Publishing Company.

Laforcade, P. (2004). *Méta-modélisation UML pour la mise en oeuvre de situations problèmes coopératives*. Doctorat en informatique de l'Université de Pau et des Pays de l'Adour (France).

LAMS. (2006). *Learning activity management system*. Retrieved from http://www.lamsfoundation.org/

Laseau, P. (1975). *Graphic problem solving for architects & builders*. Boston: Cahners Books.

Laseau, P. (1986). *Graphic problem solving for architects and designers* (2nd ed.). New York: Van Nostrand Reinhold.

Laseau, P. (1989). *Graphic thinking for architects and designers* (2nd ed.). New York: Van Nostrand Reinhold.

Laurel, B. (1993). *Computers as theatre*. Reading, MA: Addison-Wesley.

Laurillard, D. (1994). *Rethinking university teaching*. London: Routledge.

Lavie, T., & Tractinsky, N. (2004). Assessing dimensions of perceived visual aesthetics of web sites. *International Journal of Human-Computer Studies, 60*, 269-298.

Lawson, B. (1997). *How designers think: The design process demystified* (3rd ed.). Amsterdam: Architectural Press.

Lawson, B. (2000). *How designers think: The design process demystified*. Oxford: Elsevier/Architectural.

LD4P. (2007). *IMS learning design for practitioners (LD4P) project Web site*. Retrieved from http://www.hope.ac.uk/ld4p/

Le Pallec, X., de Moura Filho, C., Marvie, R., Nebut, M., & Tarby, J.-C. (2006). Supporting generic methodologies to assist IMS-LD modeling. In *The Proceedings of IEEE ICALT'2006* (pp. 923-927). Kerkrade, the Netherlands.

Lee, C. D. (2003). Toward a framework for culturally responsive design in multimedia computer environments: Cultural modeling as a case. *Mind, Culture and Activity, 10*(1), 42-61.

Lee, M., & Johnson, C. (1999). *Principles of advertising: A global perspective*. Binghamton, NY: The Haworth Press.

Leitao, S. (2000). The potential of argument in knowledge building. *Human Development, 43*, 332-360.

Lejeune, A., Martel, C., Choquet, C., El Kechai, H., & Pernin, J.P. (2005). Workshop «Manipulation des scénarios pédagogiques», Atelier 2, Troisième École thématique du CNRS sur les EIAH, Modèles, Architectures logicielles et normes pour le développement et l'intégration des EIAH. Autrans, France.

Liker, J.K., & Meier, D. (2006). *The Toyota way fieldbook: A practical guide for implementing Toyota's 4Ps*. New York: McGraw-Hill.

Littlejohn, A (2003). An incremental approach to staff development in the reuse of learning resources. In A. Littlejohn (Ed.), *Reusing online resources: A sustainable approach to e-learning*. London: Kogan Page.

Liu, M., & Bera, S. (2005). An analysis of cognitive tool use patterns in a hypermedia learning environment. *Educational Technology Research and Development, 53*(1), 5-21.

Lockard, W. K. (1977). *Drawing as a means to architecture*. Tucson, AZ: Pepper Pub.

Ludwig-Hardman, S. (2003). *Case study: Instructional design strategies that contribute to the development of online learning community*. Unpublished Dissertation, University of Colorado at Denver, Denver CO.

Mager, R.F., & Pipe, P. (1984). *Analyzing Performance Problems* (2nd ed.). Belmont, CA: Pitman Management Training.

Magnan, F., & Paquette, G. (2006). TELOS: An ontology driven e-learning OS. In S. Weibelzahl & A. Cristea (Eds.), *Proceedings of the Fourth International Conference on Adaptive Hypermedia and Adaptive Web-Based Systems 2006* (pp. 131-139). Dublin, Ireland: National College of Ireland.

Mäkitalo, K., Weinberger, A., Häkkinen, P., Järvelä, S., & Fischer, F. (2005). Epistemic copperation scripts in online learning environments: Fostering learning by reducing uncertainty in discourse? *Computers in Human Behavior, 21*(4), 603-622.

Maple, R. J. (1994). "Well, you're the CE... I'm the ID..." Describing your role—and selling your worth—to content experts. *Performance & Instruction, 33*(8), 36-40.

Marino, O., Casallas, R., Villalobos, J., Correal, D. & Contamines, J. (2006). Bridging the gap between e-learning modeling and delivery through the transformation of

learnflows into workflows. In S. Pierre (Ed.) *E-Learning networked environments and architectures: A knowledge processing perspective*. Springer-Verlag.

Marshall, C. (2000). *Enterprise modeling with UML: Designing successful software through business analysis*. Reading, MA: Addison-Wesley.

Martel, C. (1998). *La modélisation des activités conjointes. Rôles, places et positions des participants*. (PhD Thesis, University of Savoie).

Martel, C., & Vignollet, L. (2007). *Learning design language to specify services*. TENCompetence Open Workshop on Service Oriented Approaches and Lifelong Competence Development Infrastructures. Manchester, UK.

Martel, C., Ferraris, C., Caron, B., Carron, T., Chabert, G., Courtin, C., Gagnière, L., Marty, J.C., & Vignollet, L. (2004). A model for CSCL allowing tailorability: implementation in the electronic schoolbag groupware. In *The Proceedings of CRIWG'2004*, San Carlos, Costa Rica (LNCS 3198, pp. 322-338).

Martel, C., Vignollet, L., & Ferraris, C. (2006). *Modeling the case study with LDL and implementing it with LDI*. Paper presented at IEEE ICALT 2006 (pp. 1149-1151). Kerkrade, The Netherlands.

Martel, C., Vignollet, L., Ferraris, C., David, J.P., & Lejeune, A. (2006). Modeling collaborative learning activities on e-learning platforms. In *The Proceedings of IEEE ICALT 2006* (pp. 707-709). Kerkrade, The Netherlands.

Martens, H., & Vogten, H. (2005). A reference implementation of a learning design engine. In R. Koper & C. Tattersall (Eds.), *Learning design: A handbook on modeling and delivering networked education and training* (pp. 91-108). Berlin-Heidelberg: Springer Verlag.

Massironi, M. (2002). *The psychology of graphic image: Seeing, drawing, communicating*. Mahwah, NJ: L. Erlbaum.

Massoud, M. M. F. (1988). *Translate to communicate: A guide for translators*. Elgin, IL: David C. Cook Foundation.

May, W. E. (2006). *An analysis of the usability of Model-Centered Instructional Design theory and implication for the design of training: A case study.* Unpublished Dissertation, University of Idaho, Moscow ID.

Mbangwana, P. (1990). Cross cultural communication and miscommunication through connotation usage in translation: The case of two African classics in translation. *Journal of Multilingual and Multicultural Development, 11*(4), 319-335.

McAndrew, P., & Goodyear, P. (2004). *Representing practitioner experiences through learning design and patterns.* Retrieved from http://www.jisc.ac.uk/uploaded_documents/practioner-patterns-v2.doc

McAndrew, P., Goodyear, P., & Dalziel, J. (2006). Patterns, designs and activities: Unifying descriptions of learning structures. *International Journal of Learning Technology, 2*(2/3), 216-242.

McAndrew, P., Nadolski, R., & Little, A. (2005). Developing an approach for learning design players. *Journal of Interactive Media in Education Advances in Learning Design Special Issue, 2005/14.*

McCloud, S. (1993). *Understanding comics.* Northampton, MA: Kitchen Sink Press.

McEwen, I. (2004). *Vitruvius: Writing the body of architecture.* Cambridge: MIT Press.

McKim, R. H. (1980). *Thinking visually : A strategy manual for problem solving.* Belmont, CA: Lifetime Learning Publications.

Meirieu, P. (Ed.). (1994). *Apprendre... Oui mais comment?.* ESF Edition.

Merriënboer, Bastiaens, & Hoogveld (2004). *Instructional design for integrated e-learning.*

Merrill, M. D., & Wilson, B. (2006). The future of instructional design (Point/Counterpoint). In R. Reiser & J. V. Dempsey (Eds.), *Trends and Issues in Instructional Design and Technology,* Second Edition (pp. 335-351). NJ, USA: Prentice Hall.

Merrill, M.D. (1983). Component display theory. In C.M. Reigeluth (Ed.), *Instructional-Design Theories and Models: An Overview of Their Current Status* (vol. 1, pp. 279-333). Hillsdale, NJ: Lawrence Erlbaum Associates.

Merrill, M.D. (1994). *Principles of instructional Design.* Englewood Cliffs, NJ: Educational Technology Publications.

Meyrowitz, J. (1998). Multiple media literacies, *Journal of communication, 48*(1), 96-108.

Miao, Y. (2000). *Design and implementation of a collaborative virtual problem-based learning environment.* (Thesis, University of Darmstadt, Germany).

Miao, Y. (2005). *Cosmos LD Editor.*

Miao, Y. (2005). CoSMoS: Facilitating learning designers to author units of learning using IMS-LD, In C. K. Looi, D. H. Jonassen & I. Mitsuru (Eds.), *Proceedings of the International Conference on Computers in Education* (pp. 275-282). Singapore: IOS Press.

Miao, Y., Hoeksema, K., Hoppe, H. U., & Harrer, A. (2005). CSCL scripts: Modeling features and potential use. In *The Proceedings of CSCL'2005* (pp. 423-432). Taipei, Taiwan.

Miles, G. D. (1983). Evaluating four years of ID experience. *Journal of Instructional Development, 6*(2), 9-14.

Milligan, C.D., Beauvoir, P., & Sharples, P. (2005). The reload learning design tools. *Journal of Interactive Media in Education,* (7). Available at http://jime.open.ac.uk/2005/06/

Millis, B.J., & Cottell, P.G. (1998). *Cooperative learning for higher education faculty.* Phoenix, AZ: The Oryx Press.

Minski, M. (1975). A framework for representing knowledge. In P. H. Winston (Ed.), *The psychology of computer vision.* New York: McGraw-Hill.

Mitchell, W. J. (1990). *The logic of architecture : Design, computation, and cognition.* Cambridge, MA: MIT Press.

Moore, K. (2000). Between the lines: The role of drawing in design. *Environments by Design.*

Motschnig-Pitrik, R., & Derntl, M. (2005). Can the web improve the effectiveness of person-centered learning?: Case study in web engineering and beyond. *IASIS International Journal of WWW/Internet, 2*(1), 49-62.

Muller, M., & Kuhn, S. (1993). Participatory design. *Communications of the ACM, 36*(4), 25-28.

Murphy, D. (1992). Is instructional design truly a design activity? *Educational and Training Technology International, 29*(4), 279-282.

Negroponte, N. (1995). *Being digital.* New York: Knopf.

Nelson, H. G., & Stolterman, E. (2003). *The design way.* Englewood Cliffs, NJ: Educational Technology Publications.

Newell, A., & Simon, H. A. (1972). *Human problem solving.* Englewood Cliffs, NJ: Prentice-Hall.

Newmark, P. (2003). No global communication without translation. In G. Anderman & M. Rogers (Eds.), *Translation today: Trends and perspectives* (pp. 55-67). Tonawanda, NY: Ultilingual Matters Ltd.

Nicoll, K. (1998). "Fixing" the "Facts": Flexible learning as policy invention. *Higher Education Research and Development, 17*(3), 291-304.

NISE (97). *Doing CL: CL Structures.* Retrieved February 2007 from http://www.wcer.wisc.edu/archive/cl1/CL/

Nodenot, T. (2005). *Contribution à l'Ingénierie dirigée par les modèles en EIAH : le cas des situations-problèmes coopératives.* Habilitation à diriger les recherches en Informatique de l'Université de Pau et des Pays de l'Adour (France).

Nodenot, T., & Laforcade, P. (2006). A game about planets: Elements for a didactical transposition described with the CPM language. Paper presented at the *6ᵗʰ IEEE International Conference on Advanced Learning Technologies (ICALT 2006).* Kerkrade, The Netherlands.

Nodenot, T., Marquesuzaà, C., Laforcade, P., & Sallaberry, C. (2004, May 17-22). *Model based engineering of learnings Situations for adaptive Web-based educational systems.* Paper presented at the ACM Thirteenth International World Wide Web Conference (IW3C2 Conference), New-York.

Norman, D. (2004). *Emotional design: Why we love (or hate) everyday things.* New York: Basic Books.

Norman, D. A., & Spohrer, H. G. (1996). Learner-centered education. *Communication of the ACM, 39*(4).

Novak, J. D. (1993). How do we learn our lesson? Taking students through the process. *The Science Teacher, 60*(3), 50-55.

O'Keefe, D. J. (2006). Persuasion. In O. Hargie (Ed.), *The handbook of communication skills* (6th ed.). New York: Routledge.

O'Regan, K. (2003). Emotion and e-learning. *Journal of Asynchronous Learning Networks, 7*(3), 78-92.

Objecteering. (2006). *Objecteering J Language User Guide.* Retrieved February 2007, from http://www.objecteering.com/doc/j_language/toc.htm

Oliver, R. (1999). Exploring strategies for on-line teaching and learning. *Distance Education, 20*(2), 240-254.

Oliver, R., & Herrington, J. (2000). Using situated learning as a design strategy for Web-based learning. In B. Abbey (Ed.), *Instructional and cognitive impacts of Web-based education* (pp. 178-191). Hershey PA: Idea Group Publishing.

Oliver, R., & Herrington, J. (2001). *Teaching and learning online: A beginner's guide to e-learning and e-teaching in higher education.* Edith Cowan University: Western Australia.

Oliver, R., & Herrington, J. (2002). *Explore, describe, apply: A problem focused learning design.* Retrieved September 19, 2006, from http://www.learningdesigns.uow.edu.au/guides/info/G4/index.htm

Oliver, R., Harper, B., Hedberg, J., Wills, S., & Agostinho, S. (2002). Formalizing the description of learning designs. In A. Goody, J. Herrington, & M. Northcote (Eds.), *Quality conversations: Research and development in higher education*, (Volume 25, pp. 496-504). Jamison, ACT: HERDSA.

Oliver, R., Harper, B., Wills, S. Agostinho, S. & Hedberg, J. (2007). Describing ICT-based learning designs that promote quality learning outcomes. In H. Beetham & R. Sharpe (Eds.), *Rethinking pedagogy for the digital age: Designing and delivering e-learning* (pp. 64-80). Routledge.

Olivier, B. (2004). *UNFOLD: Discussion of learning design, state of play*. Retrieved December 13, 2006 from https://www.unfold-project.net:8082/UNFOLD/about_folder/events/online/billjuly04/

OMG (2006). *Business process modeling notation (BPMM)*. Retrieved on July 24, 2006, from http://www.bpmn.org/

OMG. (1999). *White Paper on the Profile Mechanism*: Object Management Group Analysis and Design Task Force.

OMG. (2002). *The Software Process Engineering Management Meta-model (SPEM)* (Technical Report formal/2002-11-14).

OMG. (2002). *UML 2.0 Superstructure Specification*, from http://www.omg.org/docs/ptc/03-08-02.pdf

OMG. (2003). *MDA Guide Version 1.0.1*, from http://www.omg.org/docs/omg/03-06-01.pdf

OMG. (2007). *Meta-Object Facility (MOF) Specification*. Retrieved February 2007, from http://www.omg.org/mof/

Orwell, G. (1948). *1984*. Retrieved April 9, 2006 from http://www.online-literature.com/orwell/1984/1/

Osguthorpe, R. T. (2006). *Learning that grows*. Paper presented at the Fourth International Conference on Multimedia and Information and Cummunication Technologies in Education (MICTE), Seville, Spain.

Osguthorpe, R. T., Osguthorpe, R. D., Jacob, W. J., & Davies, R. (2003). The moral dimensions of instructional design. *Educational Technology, 43*(2), 19-23.

OUUK. (2005). *Sled player*. Retrieved April 13, 2006, from http://sled.open.ac.uk

Paas, F. (1992). Training strategies for attaining transfer of problem-solving skill in statistics: A cognitive-load approach. *Journal of Educational Psychology, 84*, 429-434.

Paas, F., Tuovinen, J., Tabbers, H., & van Gerven, P. W. M. (2003). Cognitive load measurement as a means to advance cognitive load theory. *Educational Psychologist, 38*, 63-71.

Paquette G., Marino, O., De la Teja, I., Lundgren-Cayrol, K., Léonard, M., & Contamines (2005). Implementation and deployment of the IMS learning design specification. *Canadian Journal of Learning Technologies* (CJLT), *31*(2). Retrieved from http://www.cjlt.ca/

Paquette, G. (1996). La modélisation par objets typés: une méthode de représentation pour les systèmes d'apprentissage et d'aide à la tâche. *Sciences et techniques éducatives, (4)*, 9-42

Paquette, G. (1999). Meta-knowledge Representation for learning scenarios engineering. In S. Lajoie & M. Vivet (Eds.), *Proceedings of AI-Ed'99 in AI and Education—Open learning environments*. IOS.

Paquette, G. (2001). Designing virtual learning centers. In H. Adelsberger, B. Collis, & J. Pawlowski (Eds.), *Handbook on information technologies for education & training* (pp. 249-272). Springer-Verlag.

Paquette, G. (2002). *Modélisation des connaissances et des compétences, un langage graphique pour concevoir et apprendre*. Québec, Canada: Presses de l'Université du Québec.

Paquette, G. (2002). TeleLearning systems engineering—Towards a new ISD model. *Journal of Structural Learning, 14*, 1-35.

Paquette, G. (2004). *Instructional engineering for network-based learning*. Pfeiffer/Wiley Publishing Co.

Paquette, G., & Léonard, M. (2006). The educational modeling of a collaborative game using MOT+LD. In *Proceedings of the 6th IEEE International Conference on Advanced Learning Technologies* (pp.115-116). Kerkrade, The Netherlands.

Paquette, G., & Marino, O. (2005). Learning objects, collaborative learning designs and knowledge representation. *Technology, Instruction, Cognition and Learning, 3*, 85-108.

Paquette, G., & Rogozan, D. (2006). *Primitives de représentation OWL-DL—Correspondance avec le langage graphique MOT+OWL et le langage des prédicats du premier ordre*. TELOS documentation. Montreal, Québec: LICEF Research Center.

Paquette, G., & Rosca, I. (2004). *An ontology-based referencing of actors, operations and resources in elearning systems*. SW-EL/2004 Workshop. The Netherlands: Eindhoven.

Paquette, G., Aubin, C., & Crevier, F. (1994). An intelligent support system for course design. *Educational Technology, 31*(9), 50-57.

Paquette, G., Crevier F. & Aubin, C. (1994). ID knowledge in a course design workbench. *Educational Technology, 34*(9), 50-57.

Paquette, G., De la Teja, I., Léonard, M., Lundgren-Cayrol, K., & Marino, O. (2005). How to use an instructional engineering method and a modelling tool. In R. Koper & C. Tattersall (Eds.). *Learning design—A handbook on modeling and delivering networked education and training* (pp. 161-184). Springer-Verlag.

Paquette, G., de la Teja, I., Lundgren-Cayrol, K., Léonard, M., & Ruelland, D. (2002). La modélisation cognitive, un outil de conception des processus et des méthodes d'un campus virtuel. *Revue de l'ACED*.

Paquette, G., Léonard, M., Lundgren-Cayrol, K., Mihaila, S., & Gareau, D. (2006). Learning design based on graphical knowledge-modeling. *Educational Technology & Society, 9*(1), 97-112.

Paquette, G., Rosca, I., Mihaila, S., & Masmoudi, A. (2007). TELOS, a service-oriented framework to support learning and knowledge management. In S. Pierre (Ed). *E-Learning networked environments and architectures: A knowledge processing perspective*. Springer-Verlag

Paquette, G., Marino, O., De la Teja, I., Léonard, M., & Lundgren-Cayrol, K., (2005). Delivery of learning design: the Explor@ system's case. In R. Koper & C. Tattersall (Eds.). *Learning Design—A handbook on modelling and delivering networked education and training* (pp. 311-326). Springer Verlag.

Paramythis, A., & Loidl-Reisinger, S. (2004). Adaptive learning environments and e-Learning standards. *Electronic Journal of e-Learning, 2*(2).

Paris, S., Lipson, M.Y., & Wixson, K.K. (1983). Becoming a strategic reader. *Contemporary Educational Psychology, 8*, 293-311.

Parizotto-Ribeiro, R., & Hammond, N. (2004). What is aesthetics anyway? Investigating the use of design principles. *Proceedings of the NordCHI 2004 Workshop*, Finland, (pp. 37-40).

Parlett, M., & Hamilton, D. (1977). Evaluation as illumination: A new approach to the study of innovatory programmes. In D. Hamilton (Ed.), *Beyond the numbers game* (pp. 6-22). London: Macmillan.

Parrish, P. E. (2004). *Investigating the aesthetic decisions of teachers and instructional designers*. Paper presented at the Annual Meeting of the American Educational Research Association, San Diego, CA. Retrieved from http://www.comet.ucar.edu/~pparrish/

Parrish, P. E. (2005). Embracing the aesthetics of instructional design. *Educational Technology, 45*(2), 16-25.

Parrish, P. E. (2006). Design as storytelling. *TechTrends, 50*(4), 72-82.

Parrish, P. E. (2006). *Learning as aesthetic experience: John Dewey's integration of art, inquiry, and education*. Unpublished manuscript. Retrieved from http://www.comet.ucar.edu/~pparrish

Parrish, P. E. (in press). Aesthetic principles for instructional design. *Educational Technology Research & Development*.

Patrascoiu, O. (2004). *YATL:Yet another transformation language*. Paper presented at the 1ˢᵗ European MDA Workshop, University of Twente, The Netherlands.

Pawlowski, J. (2002). *Reusable models of pedagogical concepts: A framework for pedagogical and content design*. Paper presented at the International Conference ED-MEDIA 2002, Denver, CO.

Pawlowski, J., & Bick, M. (2006). Managing and re-using didactical expertise: The didactical object model. *Educational Technology and Society, 9*(1), 84-96.

Pedagogy case study templates. (2006). Retrieved September 19, 2006, from http://www.jisc.ac.uk/whatwedo/programmes/elearning_pedagogy/elp_templates.aspx

Polkinghorne, D. E. (1988). *Narrative knowing and the human sciences*. Albany, NY: State University of New York Press.

Pollock, N., & Cornford, J. (2000). Theory and practice of the virtual university: Report on UK universities use of new technologies. *In ARIADNE issue 24*. http://www.ariadne.ac.uk/issue24/virtual-universities/

Powell, G. C. (March/April 1997). Understanding the language of diversity. *Educational Technology, 37*(2), 15-18.

PPP (2000). *The pedagogical patterns project Web site*. Retrieved February 2007 from http://www.pedagogicalpatterns.org/

Press, M., & Cooper, R. (2003). *The design experience: The role of design and designers in the twenty-first century*. Burlington, VT: Ashgate.

PROTÉGÉ, (2006). *Protégé Homepage*. Retrieved July 24, 2006 from http://protege.stanford.edu/

Quinn, N. (1987). Convergent evidence for a cultural model of American marriage. In D. Holland & N. Quinn (Eds.), *Cultural models in language & thought* (pp. 173-192). New York: Cambridge University Press.

Rawlings, A., Rosmalen, P. Van, Koper, R. Rodriguez-Artacho, M., & Lefrere, P. (2002). *Survey of educational modelling languages (EMLs)*. CEN/ISSS/WS/LT.

Rawlings, A., Van Rosmalen, P., Koper, R., Rodríguez-Artacho, M., & Lefrere, P. (2002). *CEN/ISSS WS/LT Learning Technologies Workshop: Survey of Educational Modeling Languages (EMLs)*.

Ray, R. J. (1994). *The weekend novelist*. New York: Dell Publishing.

Raybould, B. (2000). Performance support engineering: Building performance-centered Web-based systems, information systems, and knowledge management systems in the 21st century. *Performance Improvement, 39*(6), 32-39.

Rehak, D., Mason, R. (2003). Keeping the learning in learning objects. In A. Littlejohn (Ed.), *Reusing online resources: a sustainable approach to e-learning*. London: Kogan Page.

Reigeluth, C. M. (2005). New instructional theories and strategies for a knowledge-based society. In J.M. Spector, C. Ohrazda, A. Van Schaack, & D.A. Wiley (Eds.). *Innovations in instructional technology: Essays in honor of M. David Merrill*. Mahwah, NJ: Lawrence Erlbaum Associates.

Reigeluth, C. M. (Ed.). (1983). *Instructional-design theories and models: An overview of their current status*. Hillsdale, NJ: Lawrence Erlbaum Associates, Publishers.

Reiser, R. (2001). A history of instructional design and technology: Part I: A history of instructional media. *Educational Technology Research and Development, 49*(1), 53-64.

Reitman, W. R. (1965). *Cognition and thought; An information-processing approach*. New York: Wiley.

RELOAD (2005).*RELOAD homepage editor and player*. Retrieved July 24, 2006, from http://www.reload.ac.uk/

Renaux, E., Caron, P.-A., & Le Pallec, X. (2005). *Learning management system component-based design: A model driven approach*. Paper presented at the Montreal Conference on e-Technologies (Mcetech), Montréal, Canada.

Retalis, S., Georgiakakis, P., & Dimitriadis, Y. (2006). Eliciting design patterns for e-learning systems. *Computer Science Education, special issue on Pedagogic Patterns, 16*(2), 105-118.

Rheinfrank, J., & Evenson, S. (1996). Design languages. In T. Winograd (Ed.), *Bringing design to software* (pp. 63-80). New York: ACM Press.

Richards, G., & Knight, C. (2005, 26 January). *UNFOLD Learning design and representations of instructional intent*. Retrieved April 5, 2005, from http://www.unfold-project.net:8085/UNFOLD/about_folder/events/online/griff/paper/

Richey, R. C., Fields, D. C., & Foxon, M. (Eds.). (2001). *Instructional design competencies: The standards* (3rd ed.). Syracuse, NY: ERIC Clearinghouse on Information and Technology.

Rittel, H., & Webber, M. M. V. (1973). Dilemmas in a general theory of planning. *Policy Sciences, 4*(2), 155-169.

Robbins, E., & Cullinan, E. (1994). *Why architects draw*. Cambridge, MA: MIT Press.

Robinson, D.G., & Robinson, J.C. (1995). *Performance consulting: Moving beyond training*. San Francisco: Berrett-Koehler Publishers.

Rodríguez-Artacho, M., & Verdejo Maíllo, M. F. (2004). Modeling educational content: The cognitive approach of the PALO language. *Educational Technology & Society, 7*(3), 124-137.

Rodríguez-Estévez, J., Caeiro-Rodríguez, M., & Santos-Gago, J.M. (2003). Standarization in computer-based learning. *Upgrade (European Journal for the Informatics Professional), special issue on e-Learning: Boarderless education, 4*(5), 8-15.

Rogers, C. R. (1983). *Freedom to learn for the 80's*. Columbus, OH: C.E. Merrill Pub. Co.

Rogers, E. (1995). *Diffusion of innovations* (4th ed.). New York: The Free Press.

Roman, K., & Maas, J. (1976). *How to advertise*. New York: St. Martin's Press.

Romiszowski, A. J. (1981). *Designing instructional systems*. New York: Kogan Page.

Rosca, I. (2005). *TELOS conceptual architecture*. (LORNET Technical Report: 0.5.).Canada: LICEF Research Centre, Télé-université.

Rose, G. (2001). *Visual methodologies: An introduction to the interpretation of visual materials*. Thousand Oaks, CA: SAGE Publications.

Rosenberg, D., & Scott, K. (1999). *use case driven object modeling with UML: A practical approach*. Reading, MA: Addison-Wesley.

Rosenberg, M. J. (2000). *E-learning, strategies for delivering knowledge in the digital age*. New York: McGraw-Hill.

Rossett, A. (1998). *First things fast: A handbook for performance analysis*. San Francisco: Jossey-Bass.

Rossett, A., & Czech, C. (1995). They really wanna, but…. the aftermath of professional preparation in performance technology. *Performance Improvement Quarterly, 8*(4), 115-132.

Roulet, E., Auchlin, A., Moeschler, J., Rubattel, C., & Schelling, M. (1985). *L'articulation du discours en français contemporain*. Berne: Peter Lang.

Rowland, G. H. (1993). Designing and instructional design *Educational Technology Research and Development, 41*(1), 79-91.

Rowling, J.K. (1998). *Harry Potter and the Sorcerer's Stone*. London: Scholastic.

Rumbaugh, J., Blaha, M., Premerlani, W., Eddy, F., & Lorensen, W. (1991). *Object-oriented modelling and design*. USA: Prentice Hall.

Rummler, G., & Brache, A. (1995). *Improving performance: How to manage the white space on the organization chart* (2nd ed.). San Francisco: Jossey-Bass.

Rungtusanatham, M., Ellram, L. M., Siferd, S. P., & Salik, S. (2004). Toward a typology of business education in the Internet age. *Decision Sciences The Journal of Innovative Education, 2*(2), 101-120.

Saddler, H. J. (2001). Understanding design representations. *Interactions, 8*(4), 17-24.

Sallaberry, C., Nodenot, T., Marquesuzaà, C., Bessagnet, M.-N., & Laforcade, P. (2002). *Information modelling within a Net-Learning Environment.* Paper presented at the 12th Conference on Information Modelling and Knowledge Bases, Krippen, Swiss Saxony, Germany.

Sampson, D., Karampiperis, P., & Zervas, P. (2005). ASK-LDT: A Web-based learning scenarios authoring environment based on IMS learning design. *International Journal on Advanced Technology for Learning (ATL), 2*(4), 207-215.

Sandage, C. H., Fryburger, V., & Rotzoll, K. (1983). *Advertising theory and practice* (11th ed.). Homewood, IL: Richard D. Irwin, Inc.

Sandoval, W. & Bell, P. (2004) Design-based research methods for studying learning in context: Introduction. *Educational Psychologist, 39*(4), 199-201.

Santos, O. C., Boticario, J. G., & Barrera, C. (2005). *aLFanet: An adaptive and standard-based learning environment built upon dotLRN and other open source developments.* Paper presented at the 2005 dotLRN conference, Madrid, Spain.

Savery, J., & Duffy, T. (1996). Problem based learning: An instructional model and its constructivist framework. In B. Wilson (Ed.). *Constructivist learning environments: Case studies in instructional design* (pp. 135-148). Englewood Cliffs, NJ: Educational Technology Publications.

Scandura, J.M. (1973). *Structural learning I: Theory and research.* New York: Gordon & Breach Science Publishers.

Schaffer, S.P. (2000). A review of organizational and human performance frameworks. *Performance Improvement Quarterly, 13*(3), 220-243.

Schama, S. (2006). *The power of art.* Great Britain: BBC Books.

Schank, R. C., Berman, T. R., & Macpherson, K. A. (1999). Learning by doing. In C. M. Reigeluth (Ed.), *Instructional-design theories and models: A new paradigm of instructional theory* (Vol. II, pp. 161-181). Mahwah, NJ: Lawrence Erlbaum Associates.

Schank, R., & Abelson, R. (1977). *Scripts, plans, goals, and understanding: An inquiry into human knowledge structures.* Hillsdale, NJ: Lawrence Erlbaum Associates.

Schatz, S. (2003). A matter of design: A proposal to encourage the evolution of design in instructional design. *Performance Improvement Quarterly, 16*(4).

Scheel, N. P., & Branch, R. C. (August 1993). The role of conversation and culture in the systematic design of instruction. *Educational Technology, 33*, 7-18.

Schneemayer, G. (2002). *Contextual Web services for teaching.* Ludwig Maximilians Universität, München, Germany.

Schneider, G., & Winters, J.P. (2001). *Applying uses cases: A practical guide* (2nd ed.). Boston: Addison Wesley Professional.

Schön, D. A. (1987). *Educating the reflective practitioner: Toward a new design for teaching and learning in the professions* (1st ed.). San Francisco: Jossey-Bass.

Schreiber, G., Wielinga, B., & Breuker, J. (1993). *KADS—A principled approach to knowledge-based system development.* San Diego, USA: Academic Press.

Schwier, R. A., Campbell, K., & Kenny, R. (2004). Instructional designer's observations about identity, communities of practice and change agency. *Australasian Journal of Educational Technology, 20*(4), 69-100.

Sellen, A. & Harper, R. (1997). Paper as an analytic resource for the design of new technologies. In *the Proceedings of CHI '97.* Atlanta: ACM-SIGCHI.

Sellen, A., & Harper, R. (2003). *The myth of the paperless office.* Cambridge: MIT Press.

Senge, P., & Sterman, J. (1994). Systems thinking and organizational learning: Acting locally and thinking globally in the organization of the future. In J. Morecroft & J. Sterman (Eds.), *Modeling for learning organizations.* Portland, Oregon: Productivity Press.

Seo, K. K., & Gibbons, A. S. (2003). Design languages: A powerful medium for communicating designs. *Educational Technology, 43*(6).

Shreve, G. M. (1999). *Translation at the millennium: Prospects for the evolution of a profession.* Paper presented at the 30th Anniversary Conference of the Monterey Institute for International Studies, Monterey, CA.

Shuell, T. (1992). Designing instructional computing systems for meaningful learning. In P. Winne & M. Jones (Eds.), *Adaptive learning environments: Foundations and frontiers.* New York: Springer Verlag.

Simon, H. A. (1996). *The sciences of the artificial* (3rd ed.). Cambridge, MA: MIT Press.

Sloep, P., Hummel, H., & Manderveld, J. M. (2005). Basic design procedures for e-learning courses. In R. Koper & C. Tattersall (Eds.), *Learning design: A Handbook on modeling and delivering networked education and training* (pp. 139-160). Berlin-Heidelberg: Springer Verlag.

Sobek, D. & Jimmerson, C. (2004). A3 Reports: Tool for process improvement. In *The Proceedings of the 2004 Industrial Engineering Research Conference,* Houston, TX.

Solomon, R. (2003). *The art of client service.* Chicago: Dearborn Trade Publishing.

Sowa, J. F. (1984). *Conceptual structures, information processing in mind and machine.* Addison-Wesley Publishing Co.

Spang Bovey, N., & Dunand, N. (2006). Seamless production of interoperable e-Learning units: Stakes and pitfalls. In R. Koper & K. Stefanov (Eds.), *Proceedings of the Workshop on Learning Networks for Lifelong Competence Development,* Sofia, Bulgaria: INCOMA Ltd.

Stahl, G. (2006). *Group cognition: Computer support for building collaborative knowledge.* Cambridge, MA: MIT Press.

Strijbos, J.W., Martens, R.L., & Jochems, W.M.G. (2004). Designing for interaction: Six steps to designing computer-supported group-based learning. *Computers & Education, 42*(4), 403-424.

Stubbs, S. T. (2006). *Design drawing in instructional design and Brigham Young University's Center for Instructional Design: A case study.* Unpublished Dissertation, Brigham Young University, Provo, Utah.

Stubbs, S. T., & Gibbons, A. S. (2008). The power of design drawing in other design fields. In L. Botturi & S. T. Stubbs (Eds.), *Handbook of visual languages for instructional design: Theories and practice* (pp. 33-51). Hershey, PA: IGI Global, Inc.

Subramony, D. P. (July/August 2004). Instructional technologists' inattention to issues of cultural diversity among learners. *Educational Technology,* 19-24.

Suchman, L. (1987). *Plans and situated actions: The problem of human-machine communication.* Cambridge University Press.

Süß, C., & Freitag, B. (2002). *LMML—The learning material markup language framework.* Paper presented at the International Workshop: Interactive Computer Aided Learning, Villach, Austria,.

Sutcliffe, A., & Mehanddjiev, N. (2004). Special issue: End-user development - tools that empower users to create their own software solutions. *Communications of the ACM, 47*(9).

Swanson, R.A. (1994). *Analysis for improving performance: Tools for diagnosing organizations & documenting workplace expertise.* San Francisco: Berrett-Koehler.

Szabo, M. (2002). Competencies for educators. In H .H. Adelsberger, B. Collis, & J. M. Pawlowsky (Eds.), *Handbook on information technologies for education and training* (pp. 381-397). Berlin, Germany: Springer.

Tang, H. H., & Gero, J. S. (2001). Sketches as affordances of meanings in the design process. *Visual and Spatial Reasoning in Design II, Key Centre of Design Computing and Cognition,* University of Sydney, Sydney, (pp. 271-282).

Tattersall, C., Sodhi, T., Burgos, D., & Koper, R. (2007). Using the IMS Learning Design notation for the modelling and delivery of education. In L. Botturi & T. Stubbs (Eds.), *Handbook of visual languages for instructional design: Theories and practices* (pp. 299-315). Hershey, PA: IGI Global.

Tattersall, C., Vogten, H., Brouns, F., Koper, R., van Rosmalen, P., Sloep, P., & van Bruggen, J. (2005). How to create flexible runtime delivery of distance learning courses. *Educational Technology and Society, 8*(3), 226-236.

Taylor, D. (1992). *Global software: Developing applications for the international market.* New York, NY: Springer.

TELL (2005). *Design patterns for teachers and educational (system) designers.* TELL project deliverable. Retrieved from http://cosy.ted.unipi.gr/TELL/media/TELL_pattern_book.pdf

TENCompetence. (2005). *TENCompetence project.* Retrieved July 31, 2006, from www.tencompetence.org

Tennyson, R. D., & Schott, F. (1997). Instructional design theory, research, and models. In R. D. Tennyson, F. Schott, N. M. Seel, & S. Dijkstra (Eds.), *Instructional design international perspectives* (Vol. 1, pp. 1-16). Mahwah: Lawrence Erlbaum Associates, Publishers.

Tennyson, R., & Rasch, M. (1988). Linking cognitive learning theory to instructional prescriptions. *Instructional Science, 17*, 369-385.

Tessmer, M. & Wedman, J. (1995). Context-sensitive instructional design models: A response to design research, studies and criticism. *Performance Improvement Quarterly, 8*(3) 38-54.

The COMET® Program (2006). *Using the AFWA WRF mesoscale model.* Retrieved from http://meted.ucar.edu/nwp/afwa_wrf/index.htm

The COMET® Program (2002). Hurricane Strike! Retrieved from http://meted.ucar.edu/hurrican/strike/index.htm

Thomas, F., & Johnston, O. (1981). *Disney animation: The illusion of life.* New York: Abbeville Press.

Thomas, M., Mitchell, M., & Joseph, R. (2002). The third dimension of ADDIE: A cultural experience. *Tech Trends, 46*(2), 40-45.

Tractinsky, N. (2004). Toward the study of aesthetics in information technology. *Proceedings from the 25th International Conference on Information Systems,* USA, (pp. 11-20).

Triandis, H. C. (1989). The self and social behavior in differing cultural contexts. *Psychological review, 96*(3), 506-520.

Triandis, H. C. (1995). *Individualism and collectivism.* Boulder, CO: Westview Press.

Triandis, H. C., & Gelfand, M. J. (1998). Converging measurement of horizontal and vertical individualism and collectivism. *Journal of Personality and Social Psychology, 74*(1), 118-128.

Trombley, B. K., & Lee, D. (2002). Web-based learning in corporations: Who is using it and why, who is not and why not? *Journal of Educational Media, 27*(3), 137-146.

Trompenaars, F., & Hampden-Turner, C. (1998). *Riding the waves of culture.* New York: McGraw-Hill Companies, Inc.

Tsichritzis, D. (1999). Reengineering the university. *Communications of the ACM, 42*(6), 93-100.

Tufte, E. (2003). *The cognitive style of PowerPoint.* Cheshire, CT: Graphics Press.

Tversky, B. (2002). *What do sketches say about thinking?* (AAAI Technical Report SS-02-08). Stanford University.

Twigg, C. (2005). *Keynote summary: Improving learning and reducing costs—New models for online learning.* Retrieved from http://www.alt.ac.uk/altc2005/keynotes.html#carol

Twitchell, D. (2001). *A rapid prototyping model for the design and development of instructional systems in practice: A case study.* Unpublished Dissertation, Utah State University, Logan UT.

UCM. (2006). *Complutense university. <e-Ucm> research group.* Retrieved December 18, 2006, from www.e-ucm.es

Ullman, D. G., Wood, S., & Craig, D. L. (1990). The importance of drawing in the mechanical design process. *Computers & Graphics, 14*(2), 263-274.

University Microfilms. (2007). ProQuest digital dissertations. Retrieved from http://wwwlib.umi.com/dissertations

University of Bolton (2004). *Reload project website.* Retrieved February 2007 from http://www.reload.ac.uk/

van der Klink, M., & Jochems, W. (2004), Management and organization of integrated e-learning. In W. Jochems, J. van Merriënboer, & R. Koper (Eds.), *Integrated e-learning: Implications for pedagogy, technology and organization.* London: Routledge & Falmer.

Van der Vegt, W., & Koper, R. (2006). *Copper Author 1.6.* Retrieved October 11, 2006, from www.copperauthor.org

Van Es, R., & Koper, R. (2006). Testing the pedagogical expressiveness of IMS-LD. *Educational Technology & Society, 9*(1), 229-249.

Van Merriënboer, J. J. G. (1997). *Training complex cognitive skills: A four-component instructional design model for technical training.* Englewood Cliffs, NJ: Educational Technology Publications.

Van Patten, J. (1989). What is instructional design? In K. A. Johnson & L. J. Foa (Eds.), *Instructional design: New alternatives for effective education and training* (pp. 16-31). New York: National University Continuing Education Association.

Vega-Gorgojo, G., Bote-Lorenzo, M.L., Gómez-Sánchez, E., Asensio-Pérez, J.I., Dimitriadis, Y., & Jorrín-Abellán, I.M. (2006). Ontoolcole: An ontology for the semantic search of CSCL services. In Y. Dimitriadis, I. Zigurs, & E. Gómez-Sánchez (Eds), *Proceedings of 12th International Workshop, LNCS 4154* (pp. 310-325). Heidelberg: Springer-Verlag.

Verpoorten, D., Poumay, M., & Leclercq, D. (2005, December 14-16). The 8 learning events model (8LEM): A pedagogic conceptual framework for the design of dedicated (and generic?) scenarios. In Kinshuk & Sampson (Eds.), *Proceedings of the IADIS International Conference on Cognition and Exploratory Learning in Digital Age* (pp. 503-508).

Verstijnen, I. M., Hennessey, J. M., van Leeuwen, C., Hamel, R., & Goldschmidt, G. (1998). Sketching and creative discovery. *Design Studies, 19*(4).

Vignollet, L., David, J.P., Ferraris, C., Martel, C., & Lejeune, A. (2006). Comparing educational modeling languages on a case study. In *The Proceedings of IEEE ICALT 2006* (pp. 1149-1151).Kerkrade, the Netherlands.

Visscher-Voerman, I., & Gustafson, K. L. (2004). Paradigms in the theory and practice of education and training design. *Educational Technology Research & Development, 52*(2), 69-89.

Vogten, H., & Martens, H. (2003). *CopperCore—The IMS learning designeEngine,* retrieved October 27, 2005 from http://www.coppercore.org

Vogten, H., & Martens, H. (2005). *CopperCore 3.0.* Retrieved April 13, 2006. from www.coppercore.org

Vogten, H., Koper, R., Martens, H., & Tattersall, C. (2005). An architecture for learning design engines. In R. Koper & C. Tattersall (Eds.), *Learning design: A handbook on modeling and delivering networked education and training* (pp. 75-90). Berlin-Heidelberg: Springer Verlag.

Von Bertalanffy, L. (1965). On the definition of the symbol. In J. R. Royce (Ed.), *Psychology and the symbol* (pp. 26-72). New York: Random House.

Vygotsky, L. (1934). *Thought and language.* Cambridge: MIT Press.

Vygotsky, L. S., & Kozulin, A. (1986). *Thought and language.* Cambridge, MA: MIT Press.

W3C (2004). *OWL overview document.* Retrieved February 10, 2004, from http://www.w3.org/TR/2004/REC-owl-features-20040210/

W3C. (1999). HTML 4.01 Specification, W3C Recommendation. Retrieved October 11th, 2006, from http://www.w3.org/TR/html401/

Walker, J. (Producer) (2005). *The Incredibles* (DVD). Buena Vista Home Entertainment.

Waters, S., & Gibbons, A. (2004). Design languages: Notation systems and instructional technology: A case study. *Educational Technology Research and Development, 52*(2), 57-68.

Wedman, J.F., & Graham, S.W. (1992). *Performance improvement: Using the performance pyramid.* Columbia, MO: Training Program Analysis & Design.

Weinberger, A., Fischer, F., & Mandl, H. (2004). Knowledge convergence in computer-mediated learning environments. Effects of collaboration scripts. Paper presented at *Annual Meeting of the American Educational Research Association.* San Diego.

Weinberger, A., Stegmann, K., & Fischer, F. (2005). Computer-supported collaborative learning in higher education: Scripts for argumentative knowledge construction in distributed groups. In T. Koschmann, D. Suthers, & T.-W. Chan (Eds.), *Computer-supported collaborative learning 2005* (pp. 717-726). Mahwah, NJ: Lawrence Earlbaum Associates.

Wenger, E. (1998). *Communities of practice.* Cambridge, MA: Cambridge University Press.

Wenning, N., Frankl, G., Bischof, E., & Schiestl, P. (2006). *E-education Designs—Lehrstrategien—Mikrodidaktische Muster* [e-Educations Designs, Teaching Strategies, and Micro-Didactic Patterns]; working paper

West, C. K., Farmer, J. A., & Wolff, P. M. (1991). *Instructional design: Implications from cognitive science.* Englewood Cliffs, NJ: Prentice Hall.

Wichmann, A., & Harrer, A. (2007). Adaption of explanation-based inquiry scripts using IMS/LD. in *The Proceedings of the 12th Biennial Conference for Research on Learning and Instruction (EARLI 2007).* Budapest, Hungary.

Wichmann, A., Kuhn, M., & Hoppe, U. (2006). Communication through the artefact by means of synchronous co-construction. In *Proceedings of the 7th international conference on learning sciences, ICLS 2006* (pp. 825-831). Bloomington, Indiana: International Society of the Learning Sciences.

Wiley, D. A. (2000). Connecting learning objects to instructional design theory: A definition, a metaphor, and a taxonomy. In D. A. Wiley (Ed.), *The instructional use of learning objects.* Bloomington, IN: Agency for Instructional Technology.

Williams, R. (1958). Culture is ordinary. In N. McKenzie (Ed.), *Convictions* (pp. 74-92). London: MacGibbon and Kee.

Williams-Green, J., Holmes, G., & Sherman, T. (1997-1998). Culture as a decision variable for designing computer software. *Journal of Educational Technology, 26*(1), 3-18.

Wills, S. & McDougall, A. (2006, December). Facilitating uptake of online role play: Learning objects versus learning designs. In *The Proceedings of the 23rd Annual Conference of the Australasian Society for Computers in Learning in Tertiary Education* (pp. 889-892). Sydney: Sydney University Press.

Wilson, B. (2005). Broadening our foundation for instructional design: Four pillars of practice. *Educational Technology, 45*(2), 10-15.

Wilson, B. G. (2005). Broadening our foundation for instructional design: Four pillars of practice. *Educational Technology, 45*(2), 10-16.

Winograd, T. (1996). Introduction. In T. Winograd (Ed.), *Bringing design to software* (pp. xiii-xxv). New York: ACM Press.

Young, P. A. (2001). Roads to travel: A historical look at The Freedman's Torchlight—An African American contribution to 19th century instructional technologies. *Journal of Black Studies, 31*(5), 671-698.

Young, P. A. (2008). Exploring culture in the design of new technologies of literacy. In J. Coiro, M. Knobel, C. Lankshear & D. J. Leu (Eds.), *Handbook of research on new literacies*. London: Routledge.

Young, P. A. (in press). The culture based model: constructing a model of culture. *Education, Technology & Society Journal*.

Young, P.A. (1999). *Roads To Travel: A historical look at African American contributions to instructional technology*. Unpublished Dissertation, University of California Berkeley, Berkeley, CA.

Young, P.A. (in press). Integrating culture in the design of ICTs. *British Journal of Educational Technology*.

Yu, D., Zhang, W., & Chen, X. (2006). New generation of e-learning technologies. In *Proceedings of the First International Multi-Symposiums on Computer and Computational Sciences (IMSCCS'06)* (Vol. 2, pp. 455-459).

Zimring, C., & Craig, D. L. (2001). Defining design between domains: An argument for design research á la carte. In C. M. Eastman, W. M. McCracken, & W. C. Newstetter (Eds.), *Design knowing and learning: Cognition in design education* (pp. 79-103). Amsterdam: Elsevier.

About the Contributors

Luca Botturi holds a master's degree in communication and technologies and a PhD in communication and instructional design from the University of Lugano, where he currently works. He has worked as an instructional designer and researcher in Switzerland, Italy, Austria, Canada and Spain. He is founder and project manager of Seed, a non-profit organization supporting training and educational projects in international cooperation.

Todd Stubbs is an instructional architect with Brigham Young University's Center for Instructional Design. Dr. Stubbs has had a long interest applying technology to learning in both K-12 and higher education. At one time or another during his career, Dr. Stubbs has taught kindergarten through graduate school. He has written on the potential effectiveness of electronic distance education systems, on computer operating systems, and on Web design. His current research interests include instructional design processes, including the representations of designs in loose design drawings as well as more formal visual instructional design languages.

***

Shirley Agostinho was the project manager for the Australian federally funded project: *Information and Communication Technologies and Their Role in Flexible Learning*. She is a lecturer in the Faculty of Education at the University of Wollongong with an active research interest in learning designs. She is a co-editor of the *Handbook of Research on Learning Design and Learning Objects: Issues, Applications and Technologies*, which will be published by IGI Global in early 2008.

Juan I. Asensio-Perez received the MS and the PhD degrees in telecommunications engineering from the University of Valladolid, Spain (1995 and 2000, respectively). He is currently an associate professor at the Department of Signal Theory, Communications and Telematics Engineering, University of Valladolid. His research interests include distributed systems and, particularly, distributed CSCL applications and integrated systems and network management.

Eddy Boot is a researcher at TNO Human Factors, and is involved in R&D projects concerning the application of information and communication technology (ICT) to improve learning processes. He holds a PhD in instructional technology and specializes in complex learning and competency-based learning by means of advanced learning technology. Much of his research is related with the integration of work and learning and ubiquitous learning.

Kevin Brosnan works as a lecturer and researcher in the Institute of Education at the University of Stirling, Scotland. Kevin was project manager of the JISC funded Learning to Learn project that examined teachers' uses and reactions to learning objects and learning designs. He is particularly interested in examining the implications of new ICT systems and artifacts for the social organization of teaching and learning and in particular the implications for staff development.

Daniel Burgos joined The Open University of The Netherlands (2004) after working fourteen years as a teacher, multimedia developer and academic manager in Europe and South America, also with his own company. As an assistant professor, he is mainly focused on IMS learning design, adaptive e-learning, educational e-games and learning networks and he is involved in the research projects Unfold, Learning Network for Learning Design, ProLearn and TenCompetence.

Manuel Caciro-Rodríguez received the telecommunication engineering (1999) degree from the University of Vigo, Spain. Currently, he is an associate teacher at the Telematics Engineering Department of the University of Vigo where he teaches computer architecture and software engineering. His main research interests are in the field of communication and information technologies applied to education.

John Casey is currently working as the learning materials manager at the UHI Millennium Institute, Scotland. An important part of John's work is examining ways to develop the pedagogic design (learning design) capacities in the UHI academic community. John has had a long-standing interest in cognitive psychology, the design of learning materials and learning activities. Through his involvement in the design of online and distance courses, John has become increasingly interested in the cultural, economic and political aspects of e-learning and their implications for organizational change in the education system.

Daniela De Faveri graduated from the University of Lugano, Switzerland (2006). She holds a master's degree in communication sciences with a major in education and training. In her final thesis she focused on the instructional designer-software producer-communication issue, by discussing through an empirical study the utility of using visuals to improve design documents and thus the communicative quality of the instructional design process as such.

Michael Derntl is a researcher and lecturer at the Research Lab for Educational Technologies at the University of Vienna, where he is also serving as vice-head. From 2001 to 2005 he was research assistant and doctoral candidate at the Research Lab for Educational Technologies. His doctoral research and his thesis were on patterns for blended learning. He is currently employed as postdoctoral researcher in the "Technology-Enhanced Learning" project. His current research interests include technology enhanced learning, design patterns, conceptual modeling, and social aspects of information technology.

Yannis A. Dimitriadis received the BS degree from the National Technical University of Athens, Greece (1981), the MS degree from the University of Virginia, Charlottesville (1983), and the PhD degree from the University of Valladolid, Spain (1992), all in telecommunications engineering. He is currently an associate professor at the University of Valladolid and director since 1994 of the multidisciplinary group GSIC/EMIC focusing on technology for learning and more specifically on CSCL.

Ian Douglas is an associate program director at the Learning Systems Institute (LSI) and associate professor in the College of Information at Florida State University. He has a multidisciplinary background, with degrees in psychology and computer science. Dr. Douglas leads LSI's Knowledge Communities' Research Group (www.lpg.fsu.edu/KCRG/), which has conducted a number of multimillion dollar research projects for the U.S. military. His research interests are knowledge management, organizational learning and learning technology.

Christine Ferraris is a researcher and a lecturer in computer science at the University of Savoie since 1992. She studied computer science at the University of Nancy and received her doctorate in computer science from the University of Nancy (1992). Her research topics are computer support for collaborative learning (CSCL) and learning design since 1999. Until 2003, she contributed to the *cartable électronique* (electronic schoolbag) project (development of a collaborative virtual learning environment). She currently works on LDL, considering the adaptation feature of scenarios.

Andy Gibbons is the department chair in the Instructional Psychology and Technology Department at Brigham Young University. Dr. Gibbons has worked both in industry (18 years) and higher education (for over 10 years). He has created innovative systems for low-cost development of simulations and has published on the use of simulation problems combined with modularized instructional techniques. Dr. Gibbons' current research interests focus on the architecture of the technology-based instructional product. He has published a design theory of model-centered instruction, proposed a general layering theory of instructional designs, and is currently studying the use of design languages in relation to design layers as a means of creating instructional systems that are adaptive, generative, and scalable.

Wolfgang Greller is the head of e-Learning at the Alpen-Adria University, Austria. Previously to this post he worked at the UHI Millennium Institute, Scotland as the head of e-learning. Originally trained as a historical linguist, Wolfgang has gravitated towards applying technology in the field of education. Through his most recent roles Wolfgang has developed a strong interest in the areas of cultural and organizational change associated with e-learning.

Barry Harper is the dean of education at the University of Wollongong. He has published widely on the use of educational technology in leaning, and currently he is a collaborator in a number of national competitive grants projects. His areas of research interest include cognitive strategies and instructional processes in education and training and the use of learning designs in the instructional process.

Andreas Harrer is a research assistant at the Department of Computer Science at the University of Duisburg-Essen. He holds a degree and PhD title both from Technische Universität München. His main research interests are the support of collaborative learning utilizing intelligent analysis, feedback mechanisms, and learning process modeling. He is the leader of the subproject artificial intelligence in education and member of computer-supported scripting of collaborative learning within the EU network of excellence, "Kaleidoscope".

John G. Hedberg is Millennium Innovations chair in ICT and education and director of the Macquarie ICT Innovations Centre at Macquarie University. He has wide experience in the design of open and distance learning programs, and is known for the constructivist learning environments he has designed.

He has been professor of learning sciences and technologies at Nanyang Technological University, where he directed several research projects exploring the role of technologies in engaging students in mathematics, science, history and geography classrooms. Dr Hedberg is the author of work on navigation, cognition and multimodality, and design and evaluation in interactive multimedia.

Davinia Hernández-Leo received the MS degree in telecommunications engineering from the University of Valladolid, Spain (2003). She is currently an assistant professor at the Department of Signal Theory, Communications and Telematics Engineering, University of Valladolid. Her current research focuses on the technological support to the design of computer-supported collaborative learning situations using learning technology specifications and patterns. She is co-recipient of the 2006-2007 Kaleidoscope European Award for Excellence in the Field of CSCL Technology.

Brad Hokanson is an associate professor in the College of Design at the University of Minnesota. While most of his classes are in the area of graphic design and multimedia, he also teaches critical thinking and creative problem solving. He received his PhD in instructional technology and his research focuses on the use of technology to aid cognition. He is also a registered architect in the State of Minnesota with a number of award winning projects, although no longer in active practice. Argentine Tango is one of his passions.

H. Ulrich Hoppe holds a full professorship for cooperative and learning support systems at the University of Duisburg-Essen, Germany. He founded the research group *Collide* (Collaborative Learning in Intelligent Distributed Environments) that aims at developing distributed, intelligently supported environments for collaborative learning. He has been program co-chair of the international conferences *AI in Education* and *CSCL*. He is a member of the steering group of the European Network of Excellence "Kaleidoscope".

Simon Hooper is an associate professor in the learning technologies program at the University of Minnesota. He received his PhD from Penn State University (1989). His research has shifted over time from studying how technology can be used to deliver education to his present interest in how technology can support teaching and learning. He studies the software design process, interface and usability design, and wants to understand how to translate emerging technological affordances into new forms of experience. In his spare time he likes to play squash and run.

Rob Koper holds a master's degree in educational psychology and a doctor's degree in educational technology. He was director of a company for teacher training, before he became the head of ICT application development (e-learning infrastructures and educational software development) at the OUNL. Since 1998 he is a full professor of educational technology, specifically in e-learning technologies. He was program manager for the development of educational modeling languages.

Pierre Laforcade received a PhD in computer science from the UPPA University at Pau (France) (2004). He is currently an associate professor at the Laval University Institute of Technology and a researcher fellow at the Computer Science Laboratory of Le Mans (LIUM). His research interests include instructional design, model-driven-engineering, and visual educational modeling languages.

Xavier Le Pallec is an associate professor in computer science at the University of Lille 1 (France). He obtained his PhD from the same university in the field of meta-groupware and meta-modeling (2002). He is interested into application of model driven engineering to construct learning environment on LMS. He is responsible for a distance learning master in computer science (called e-Services).

Michel Léonard is a research professional at the LICEF research centre of Télé-université and a researcher and the research chair in instructional and cognitive engineering. Since 1994, he has participated in the development and validation of methods of instructional engineering, knowledge and competences modeling techniques, modeling tools, learning design tools, preparation and diffusion of training within projects of development or transfer of knowledge and competences.

Karin Lundgren-Cayrol has a PhD in educational technology and specializes in online collaborative learning, educational modeling techniques, learning object repository development, interoperability standard implementation and media. For the past 12 years, at LICEF, she has been involved in educational, corporate and governmental applications. She has participated in various Canadian and European initiatives to implement international interoperability standards, such as CanCore, Normétic, Canada's e-Learning Quality Guidelines, and UNFOLD. She has authored and co-authored numerous book chapters, articles, research reports and conferences on e-Learning issues.

Aine MacNeill is an e-learning development officer in the University of Ulster Institute of Lifelong Learning. Aine has been involved in developing innovative approaches to helping academic teaching staff articulate their pedagogic strategies.

Christian Martel is the research manager of Pentila Corporation since 2004. He works on topics related to learning design and technology enhanced learning. He was the inventor of learning design language with Laurence Vignollet and Christine Ferraris. He studied linguistics at the University of Lyon. He received his doctorate in computer science from the University of Savoie (1998), with a thesis on computer supported collaborative work (CSCW). He collaborated with Laurence Vignollet and Christine Ferraris and founded the electronic schoolbag framework.

Alan Masson is the assistant director of the Institute of Lifelong Learning at the University of Ulster. His current duties include the design, co-ordination and management of e-learning related systems such as the institutional deployment of and the integration of a VLE and library services and systems. In addition to these duties, he supports a number of central departments and initiatives to leverage online instructional and communication tools to their advantage.

Jason McDonald is an instructional design consultant who has been involved in education and training for ten years. His research centers on principles to help educators remain focused on the essential characteristics of well-designed learning environments, as well as to help them focus on the questions and problems of most worth. Apart from his work and research, Jason enjoys history, classic films, and enjoying a good time.

Charles Miller is a lecturer and education specialist in the learning technologies program at the University of Minnesota. His research explores the design of technologies to transform the instructional experience, moving beyond the surface-level activities of creating face-to-face affordances and diagnosing efficiency obstacles in traditional instructional design. Specifically, he has focused his research, design, and development efforts on positioning aesthetics at the core of instructional design, integrated with pedagogy, utility, and usability. He has developed and instructed undergraduate and graduate courses on educational multimedia development, new media design and integration, information visualization, database engineering, and traditional graphic design.

Renate Motschnig is professor of computer science at the University of Vienna and heads the research lab for Educational Technologies at the Faculty of Computer Science. Her research goals center in the discovery of principles and the development of methods and techniques to improve the development, effectiveness, and the quality of socio-technical systems. Her current research interests include conceptual modeling, humanistic education, process models, group and team processes, technology enhanced learning, motivation, development of meta-cognitive competence, cognitions and emotions in learning, the person centered approach, communication and new media. Most recently, Ms. Motschnig has focused on exploring the potentials of the person-centered approach in the fields of knowledge—learning—management.

Colette Murphy is a staff development officer in the University of Ulster Staff Development Unit, which has been given a strategic role in developing the uptake of e-learning related skills amongst academic teaching staff. Colette has a strong interest in developing the pedagogic design skills amongst academic.

Jon Nelson is currently a graduate student at Utah State University and is working toward the completion of his PhD in instructional technology. His areas of interest include design languages, grounded theory, and the interaction between instructional designers and software developers during the instructional development process.

Thierry Nodenot is a former primary school teacher who received the PhD degree from Toulouse University (France) (1992) and the Research Supervisor degree from Pau University (France) (2005), both in computer science. He is currently an associate professor at the Institute of Technology of Bayonne (France) and does his research at the LIUPPA laboratory. His research interests include visual languages for instructional design, knowledge engineering for TEL systems, model driven engineering techniques and tools applied to the design of TEL systems.

Ron Oliver is professor of interactive multimedia at Edith Cowan University in Perth, Western Australia, where he teaches in the School of Communications and Contemporary Arts, and he is the associate dean (teaching and learning) in the Faculty of Education and Arts. Within the University, he is chair of the academic board, a member of the ECU Council, a member of the University Curriculum Teaching and Learning Committee, the University Research and Higher Degrees Committee and the Vice Chancellor's Planning and Management Group. He is also active on many sub-committees and working parties. He is a member of various editorial boards including the *British Journal of Educational Technology, Journal of Educational Media and Hypermedia, Distance Education, Journal of*

Interactive Learning Research, Australian Journal of Educational Technology, Australian Educational Computing, and *ALT-J.*

Gilbert Paquette has a PhD in artificial intelligence and education and is a director of research at the Center for Interuniversity Research on Telelearning Applications, (CIRTA-LICEF) he founded in 1992. He holds a Canada research chair in instructional and cognitive engineering. He acts as the scientific director of the LORNET Canadian research network. Recent publications include three books on technology-based learning. He participates in the scientific committee for six journals, three in France, one in the U.S. and two in Canada, and in different international initiatives such as the World Technology Network, the Globe international consortium and the scientific committee of the European network TENCompetence.

Patrick Parrish is a production manager with the COMET® Program, providing instructional design management supporting the creation of education and training for operational meteorologists in government, military, and private positions. Patrick holds an MA in instructional technology and is currently completing doctoral studies at the University of Colorado at Denver. His interests include design process, technology innovation, and the aesthetic nature of teaching and learning.

Tim Sodhi is a PhD researcher at the Open University of The Netherlands. His research interests include visual learning design environments for IMSLD, support for practitioners in the design of instruction, learning design patterns, etc. He obtained his master's degree in software systems engineering and is actively involved in the EU TENCompetence project. His current research is focused on the TENCompetence project.

Colin Tattersall studied computational science and has a PhD from the Computer Based Learning Unit at Leeds University. He subsequently moved to The Netherlands to work in both the telecommunications and software industries. In mid-2002 he joined The Open University of The Netherlands as an educational technologist where his responsibilities cover work related to innovation in learning technology standardisation (IMS Learning Design, IMS Question and Test Interoperability, IMS Content Packaging, Scorm, etc.) and e-learning projects (UNFOLD, ROMA, etc.).

Laurence Vignollet is a researcher and a lecturer at the University of Savoie in computer science. She holds a doctorate from the University of Savoie, in computer science (1991). Since 2003, her research field is learning design of collaborative learning activities. She contributes to the definition of LDL to formalize learning designs and on the specification of the associated computational means to operationalize and execute them. From 1999 to 2003, she actively participated in the specifications and development of a collaborative learning management system called *le cartable électronique* (the electronic schoolbag).

Eloy D. Villasclaras-Fernández received the MS degree in telecommunications engineering from the University of Valladolid, Spain (2005). He is currently a research assistant at the Department of Signal Theory, Communications and Telematics Engineering, University of Valladolid. His research focuses on the technological support to the design of the assessment embedded in computer-supported collaborative learning settings.

Sandra Wills has authored over 200 publications and educational products and attracted $12 million in grants, both over the span of 30 years. Elected Fellow of Australian Computer Society (1991) and Fellow of Australian Council for Computers in Education (2002), she has also received an International Federation for Information Processing Silver Core Award (1995), Education Innovation Award (1990) and Australian Computer Society Lecturer of the Year Award (1980).

Patricia A. Young is an assistant professor in literacy education at the University of Maryland, Baltimore County. Her current research involves the implementation of the culture based model as a design construct and mapping the model to a variety of interdisciplinary uses. Her other research examines the history of instructional design and technologies made by and for African-Americans.

Index

Symbols

8 learning events model (8LEM) 426, 428–430, 432–433, 436, 438, 464

A

activity theory 188
ADISA 134, 154. *See also* MISA 4.0
aesthetic experience 91–95, 99, 106–108. *See also* narrative
aesthetic experience, designing for 95–101
aesthetics 3, 5–7, 9, 12–13, 17, 91–95, 99–100, 104–108, 453
aesthetics, definition 5–7
analyis, design, development, implementation, evaluation (ADDIE) process, analysis 159
analyis, design, development, implementation, evaluation (ADDIE) process, design 159–160
analyis, design, development, implementation, evaluation (ADDIE) process, development 160
analyis, design, development, implementation, evaluation (ADDIE) process, evaluation 160
analyis, design, development, implementation, evaluation (ADDIE) process, implementation 160
analyis, design, development, implementation, evaluation (ADDIE) process model 52, 56, 69, 159–160, 317, 321, 328, 331, 335, 367, 463

analysis objects 219–221
Aristotle's Incline 96. *See also* narratives, diagramming of
ASK-LDT 305, 307–308, 310, 314
ASK-LDT tool 419
aspect-oriented programming (AOP) 187

B

blended learning 155–157, 165, 173, 179, 181–184

C

client communication 19, 28
collaborative activities 226, 228–229, 231, 250
collaborative learning 394–404, 409–411
collaborative learning flow patterns (CLFPs) 394, 396, 398, 401–409, 410, 449
communication artifacts 283, 293. *See* graphical models
complications 96–100. *See also* narratives, diagramming of; *See* rising action
computer-supported collaborative learning (CSCL) 395, 397, 403, 409–412
computer-supported collaborative learning (CSCL), script 281, 289, 291, 296–297, 395, 445
computer aided design (CAD) systems 284–285
computer problem-based meta-model (CPM) 254–280
conceptual modeling 160, 164
conclusion. *See* consummation
consummation 94, 100, 104. *See* narratives, dia-

gramming of

content graphics 348, 356, 363

cooperative learning designs 155

cooperative learning environments 155, 182

cooperative UML(coUML) 112, 155–184, 325–333

cooperative UML(coUML), CAM 330–333

cooperative UML(coUML), CSM 330

cooperative UML(coUML), modeling artifacts 157–158. *See* course activity model (CAM); *See* course package model (CPM); *See* course structure model (CSM); *See* documents; *See* goals; *See* roles

course activity model (CAM) 157–158. *See* cooperative UML(coUML), modeling artifacts

course package model (CPM) 158, 371. *See* cooperative UML(coUML), modeling artifacts

course package model (CPM), diagrams 254, 256, 263–267, 269–270, 272

course structure model (CSM) 158. *See* cooperative UML(coUML), modeling artifacts

cultural adaptation process (CAP) 56

cultural remnants 59

culture, as design construct 52–75

culture, definition 54–55

culture, models of 55–56

culture based circumference 58

culture based model (CBM) 52–53, 57, 59–61, 63–64, 66

culture based model (CBM), areas. *See* inquiry, development, team, assessments, brainstorming, learners, elements and training (ID-TABLET)

culture neutrality 58

culture sensitivity 56, 62

culture specificity 58

D

denouement 96–99. *See also* narratives, diagramming of

design documents 366–378

design drawing 33–40, 37–41, 42, 47–48, 345–348, 352, 354–355, 357–358, 363. *See also* design languages

design drawing, characteristics of 37–41

design drawing, forms of 41–46

design drawing, stages of 38–41

designer-client communications 19

design graphics 348, 351–352, 355–356, 357, 363

design languages 18–19, 23–24, 26–28, 30, 33, 38, 366–367, 370–373, 377–378

design languages, translation 23–30. *See also* design languages; *See also* translation

design layers 372–373

design patterns 156

design stories 95–96

design studies 33, 35, 48

developing design documents (3D) model 366–367, 371–374, 376–377

didactical object model (DIN) 256, 280, 459

documents 158. *See* cooperative UML(coUML), modeling artifacts

drawing 33–40, 42, 44, 46–48, 50, 76, 78, 81–89, 454. *See also* sketching

drawing, reasons 83–86

E

educational environment modeling language (E²ML) 112–132, 256, 278, 285, 323–324, 354, 359–361, 363, 371, 378, 408, 410. *See* lightweight aspects; *See* visual aspects

educational environment modeling language (E²ML), action diagrams 120–125, 127–128, 131

educational environment modeling language (E²ML), activity flow 115–116, 118, 126–129

educational environment modeling language (E²ML), dependencies diagram 115, 118–120, 125–129. *See also* educational environment modeling language (E²ML), overview diagrams

educational environment modeling language (E²ML), design team 114–115, 128

educational environment modeling language (E²ML), features 115

educational environment modeling language (E²ML), in practice 115–116

educational environment modeling language (E²ML), overview diagrams 116, 120, 125, 127–129, 130

educational modeling languages (EMLs) 185–187, 208, 255–256, 278, 280, 413–414, 419, 424, 436–437

educational unit models, aspects 187–188, 190–191, 204

educational unit models, perspectives 187–190, 192, 198, 205, 208

educational units 185–187, 189–191, 195, 204, 205, 207–208

electronic performance support systems (EPSS) 212, 216–217

ending. *See* consummation

engagement curves 100–106

engagement curves, plotting of 101–105

expanded mediation model 189–190

F

finalist communicative language. *See* learning design language (LDL)

finalist communicative languages 112, 231. *See also* visual instructional design languages (VIDLs)

firmitas. *See* Vitruvian values, firmness

Freytag's triangle 98–99. *See also* narratives, diagramming of

front-end analysis (FEA) 211

G

Gibbons' model of design layers 372

goals 158. *See* cooperative UML(coUML), modeling artifacts

graphical models 290, 293–295. *See* communication artifacts

graphic language 138–139, 145, 150–151. *See also* visual languages

H

Hofstede's dimensions of culture 55

I

inquiry, development, team, assessments, brainstorming, learners, elements and training (ID-TABLET) 58, 60, 66

inquiry, development, team, assessments, brainstorming, learners, elements and training (ID-TABLET), assessments area 62–63

inquiry, development, team, assessments, brainstorming, learners, elements and training (ID-TABLET), brainstorming area 63

inquiry, development, team, assessments, brainstorming, learners, elements and training (ID-TABLET), development area 61–62

inquiry, development, team, assessments, brainstorming, learners, elements and training (ID-TABLET), elements area 64–65

inquiry, development, team, assessments, brainstorming, learners, elements and training (ID-TABLET), inquiry area 61

inquiry, development, team, assessments, brainstorming, learners, elements and training (ID-TABLET), learners area 63–64

inquiry, development, team, assessments, brainstorming, learners, elements and training (ID-TABLET), team area 62

inquiry, development, team, assessments, brainstorming, learners, elements and training (ID-TABLET), training area 65–66

instructional architect 1, 5, 7–15

instructional artist 1–3, 5, 7–16

instructional design (ID) 33–35, 38, 48, 52–55, 58, 60, 66, 76–78, 82–83, 86–88, 91–96, 100, 103, 105, 107–108, 112, 113, 114, 127, 128, 129, 131, 132, 158–159, 162, 168, 169–171, 177, 180, 183–184, 185–187, 190–191, 204, 207–208, 254–258, 264, 270, 272, 274, 278–279, 280, 345–365, 367–373, 376–379, 381, 388, 392, 413–415, 417–421, 425–427, 433, 435–438, 442, 448, 463

instructional design (ID), aesthetic qualities of 92–95. *See also* aethetics

instructional design (ID), and globalization 52, 56, 66–68

instructional design (ID), content layer 352, 355, 357, 360, 362

instructional design (ID), diagramming of 99–101. *See also* narratives, diagramming of

instructional design (ID), languages 413–415, 425

instructional design (ID), layers 345, 347–348, 351, 355–358, 360, 362. *See also* taxonomy; *See also* typology

instructional design (ID), narrative based approach 318–322

instructional design (ID), strategy layer 352, 356–357, 360, 362

instructional design (ID) languages 187

instructional design (ID) process 114

instructional design environment (IDE) 435–436

instructional designers 91–92, 94–95, 99–100, 104–105, 108, 402–404, 458

instructional design languages. *See* design languages

instructional engineer 1, 5, 7–14

instructional engineering 133, 134, 145

instructional management systems-learning design (IMS-LD) 112, 114–115, 186–187, 229–231, 251–252, 255, 257, 259–261, 263, 267, 276–277, 279, 299–314, 339–341, 370–371, 388–389, 394–396, 402–403, 405–411, 414–415, 417–418, 420, 424, 426–429, 433, 437, 448

instructional management systems-learning design (IMS-LD), Collage editor 394, 396, 403–405, 407–409

instructional management systems-learning design (IMS-LD), design process 308–309

instructional management systems-learning design (IMS-LD), tools 302–308, 309–310

instructional manufacturer 1, 5, 8–14
instructional models 348, 350
instructional software 366–368, 370, 372–373, 376, 378, 441
instructional systems development (ISD) model 366–369, 371, 377
intelligent tutoring systems (ITSs) 281, 282, 289
interaction 233–238, 244, 248, 250–251

J

job aid 218, 221. *See* electronic performance support systems (EPSS)
JPoEML authoring tool 186, 203–204. *See* perspective-oriented EML(poEML)

K

knowledge modeling 133–134, 136
knowledge work 77, 79–81, 87
knowledge work, definition 77–78

L

learner engagement 91–92, 94–97, 99–107
learning activity management system (LAMS) tool 388, 419, 426
learning design infrastructure (LDI) 228, 231, 249–250, 253, 454
learning design language (LDL) 112, 226–253. *See* visual instructional design languages (VIDLs)
learning design language (LDL), arenas 233
learning design language (LDL), catagorization of 232
learning design language (LDL), interactions 233–235
learning design language (LDL), observables 237–239
learning design language (LDL), positions 237–239
learning design language (LDL), roles 233
learning design language (LDL), rules 236–237
learning design language (LDL), structures 235–236
learning design language (LDL) activities 226–253
learning design language (LDL) scenarios 227–228, 230–232, 235, 239–240, 244–247, 249–252
learning design language (LDL) scenarios, construction methodology 226, 228, 239–240, 245–246, 250–251
learning designs (LDs) 133–135, 140–142, 146–147, 150–152, 299–303, 305, 308–314, 394–396, 402–411, 414–415, 417–420, 424, 427–429, 433–434, 436–437
learning designs (LDs), "high quality" 383–393
learning designs (LDs), description 382–383
learning designs (LDs), graphical interfaces 305, 310
learning designs (LDs), graphical notations 300, 310–311
learning designs (LDs), resources 380–393
learning designs (LDs), visual sequence (LDVS) 384–388, 390
learning designs (LDs) continuum 418–420, 434, 436
learning flow 229–230, 239, 242, 244, 247, 394–396, 398–400, 402–403, 406–409, 410, 449
learning management systems (LMSs) 112, 185–186, 255–256, 259–260, 263, 267, 278, 317–318, 326, 332, 335–336, 395, 397, 404, 441
learning models 348, 350, 357, 363. *See also* instructional models
learning objectives 227, 239, 246
learning object metadata (LOM) 421–422
learning objects (LOs) 136, 143, 216, 220, 225, 416, 418, 421, 423, 426, 437, 438, 443, 446, 459, 465
learning objects (LOs), reusable 419, 426
Learning to Learn project (L2L) 420–422
learning units 135–136, 148
lightweight aspects 112, 114, 116, 128. *See* educational environment modeling language (E²ML)

M

Marcus Vitruvius Pollio 7. *See also* Vitruvius
MISA 4.0 134–135, 134–136, 140, 141–142, 147, 154
MISA 4.0, delivery models 133–136
MISA 4.0, documentation elements (DEs) 134–136
MISA 4.0, instructional model 136
MISA 4.0, knowledge model 135–136, 141, 145
MISA 4.0, learning resource models 136
MISA 4.0, problem solving approach 134–136
model-based predictions 286, 294
model for collaborative learning activity design (MoCoLADe) 281–282, 292
modeling 226, 228–231, 233, 239–240, 244–245, 249–253
modeling languages 136–137, 141, 145, 148–149, 156, 173, 182–184, 185–186
modélisation d'ojets typés (MOT) 361–362, 371

modélisation d'ojets typés (MOT) modeling language 136–137, 148

modélisation d'ojets typés (MOT) visual modeling language 138–140

modélisation d'ojets typés (MOT+) 133–134, 136–137, 140–142, 140–143, 148, 151, 285, 305, 307–308, 310. *See* visual instructional design languages (VIDLs)

modélisation d'ojets typés (MOT+), graphic editor 140

modélisation d'ojets typés (MOT+)LD 133–134, 142–144, 148, 151, 153, 419, 458. *See also* learning design (LD)

modélisation d'ojets typés (MOT+)OWL 133–134, 145–148, 151, 153, 458. *See also* ontology web language (OWL)

modélisation d'ojets typés (MOT+) visual modeling editor 136

models 33–36, 36–37, 39, 49, 451. *See also* design drawing

monitoring 288

multiple cultures model (MCM) 56

N

narratives 91, 94–99, 101–107

narratives, diagramming of 96–99. *See also* complications; *See also* consummation; *See also* denouement; *See also* plot points; *See also* rising action

needs analysis 211

needs assessment 210

Net-centric performance improvement (Net-PI) system 221–222

notation systems 19, 29–32, 77, 82, 370–372, 378–379. *See also* design languages

O

object modelling technique (OMT) 137

ontology web language (OWL) 134

operationalization 228, 250

operational semantics 287–288, 290–291, 295

organizational learning 417, 438, 461

original text 20, 28. *See also* translation, source text

P

paper 78–82

paper, affordances of 80

paperless office 78–79, 89, 461

pattern-based design 396–402

pedagogical model 140

performance analysis 210–212, 217–219, 222, 224–225, 445

performance analysis object 219, 220. *See* learning object (LO)

performance assessment 211

performance case 210–211, 215–219, 221–222, 224

performance case diagram 215, 219

performance case modeling 210–225

performance goals 217

performance roles 216–217, 219

perspective-oriented EML(poEML) 112, 185–209, 230, 285, 333–339. *See* JPoEML authoring tool

perspective-oriented EML(poEML), adaptability 185–186, 207

perspective-oriented EML(poEML), data package 199–200

perspective-oriented EML(poEML), expressiveness 185, 208

perspective-oriented EML(poEML), flexibility 185–186, 207

perspective-oriented EML(poEML), formality 185–186, 207–208

perspective-oriented EML(poEML), functional package 194–196

perspective-oriented EML(poEML), general issues 191–192

perspective-oriented EML(poEML), order package 200–202

perspective-oriented EML(poEML), participants package 196–197

perspective-oriented EML(poEML), structural package 192–194

perspective-oriented EML(poEML), temporal package 202–205

plot points 96–98, 104. *See* narratives, diagramming of

prerequisite competencies 135–136

problem-based learning (PBL) situations 254, 256–261, 263–264, 269, 275, 279, 455

Project EnRoLE 390

R

reflective design tools 114

Reload editor 305, 309

reporting graphics 348, 363

representation language 137, 150

rising action 96–97, 99, 106. *See* narratives, diagramming of

RLOs 426

roles 158. *See* cooperative UML(coUML), modeling artifacts

S

scaffolding 288–289, 295
second-order learning objects (SOLOs) 256
separation-of-concerns approach 185–188, 191, 208
sketches 112, 130
sketching 34–37, 39–40, 44–45, 46, 46–48, 48–49, 84
SMASH PBL situation 262–266, 270, 273–274
socio-constructivism 229
software, Adobe Authorware 353–354, 356–358
software, Adobe Director 353
specification 227–228, 232, 234, 242, 244–245, 248, 250–251
static configuration 288, 294
stories 95–103. *See also* narratives

T

target competencies 135–136, 147
target competency 134
taxonomy 345–346, 363. *See also* typology
training needs analysis 211
translation 18–32
translation, principles 20
translation, source text 20–23, 27, 30
translation, target language 20–23, 25, 29–30
turning points. *See* plot points
typology 347–348, 351–352, 354–355. *See also* taxonomy

U

unified modeling language (UML) 137, 155, 157, 160–163, 166–167, 181–184, 210–215, 223–225, 256–266, 267–269, 271–272, 275, 276–279, 301, 303, 309–311, 313, 360, 370, 374, 378, 446, 450
unified modeling language (UML), activity diagrams 162–163
unified modeling language (UML), static structure diagram 160–162

units of learning (UoLs) 142, 147, 300–303, 305, 305–306, 311–314, 395–396, 402–403, 405, 407, 408–409, 425, 437–438
use case 211–217, 223, 225, 451
use case modeling 212–214, 214–217
user scenarios. *See* design stories
utilitas. *See* Vitruvian values, commodity

V

venustas. *See* Vitruvian values, delight
virtual learning environments (VLEs) 226, 231–232, 249, 418, 424, 427, 431, 433
visual aspects 112–114, 116, 124, 127–128, 130–131. *See* educational environment modeling language (E²ML)
visual design languages. *See* design languages
visual editing tools 284, 294
visual instructional design languages (VIDLs) 33–34, 48, 52–53, 60–63, 64–66, 112–132, 133–154, 155–184, 185–209, 226–253, 254–280, 282–283, 290–291, 292–293, 293–294, 315–344, 345–346, 354, 359–360, 363, 408, 416, 418. *See also* design languages; *See* cooperative UML(coUML); *See* E²ML; *See* instructional management systems-learning design (IMS-LD); *See* learning design language (LDL); *See* perspective-oriented EML(poEML)
visual instructional design languages (VIDLs), case study 315–344
visual languages 52–53, 56, 57, 60, 67, 77, 133–134, 142, 151, 210–211
visual modeling 155–156, 182–184
visual thinking 84
Vitruvian values 2, 5
Vitruvian values, balance of 7–11
Vitruvian values, commodity 1–2, 4–5, 7–10, 15
Vitruvian values, delight 1–2, 4–5, 7–8, 10, 12, 14, 15
Vitruvian values, firmness 1–2, 4–5, 7–10, 15
Vitruvius 5, 7, 17, 455